# SCO COMPANION

## THE ESSENTIAL GUIDE FOR USERS AND SYSTEM ADMINISTRATORS

## James Mohr

For book and bookstore information

http://www.prenhall.com

Prentice Hall PTR
Upper Saddle River, New Jersey 07458

**Library of Congress Cataloging-in-Publication Data**

Mohr, James
    SCO Companion : the essential guide for users and system
administrators / James Mohr.
        p.    cm.
    Includes index.
    ISBN 0–13–451683–4
    1. Operating Systems (Computers)   2. UNIX (Computer file)   3. SCO
software.   I. Title.
QA76.063M62   1997
005.4'469—dc20
                                                    96-18098
                                                        CIP


Acquisitions editor: Mark L. Taub
Cover designer: DeFranco Design
Cover design director: Jerry Votta
Manufacturing manager: Alexis R. Heydt
Compositor/Production services: Pine Tree Composition, Inc.

© 1996 by James Mohr
Published by Prentice Hall PTR
Prentice-Hall, Inc.
A Simon & Schuster Company
Upper Saddle River, New Jersey 07458

The publisher offers discounts on this book when ordered in
bulk quantities. For more information contact:

Corporate Sales Department
Prentice Hall PTR
One Lake Street
Upper Saddle River, New Jersey 07458

Phone: 800–382–3419
Fax: 201–236–7141
email: corpsales@prenhall.com

Printed in the United States of America
10   9   8   7   6   5   4   3   2


ISBN: 1-13-451683-4


Prentice-Hall International (UK) Limited, *London*
Prentice-Hall of Australia Pty. Limited, *Sydney*
Prentice-Hall Canada, Inc., *Toronto*
Prentice-Hall Hispanoamericana, S.A., *Mexico*
Prentice-Hall of India Private Limited, *New Delhi*
Prentice-Hall of Japan, Inc., *Tokyo*
Simon & Schuster Asia Pte. Ltd., *Singapore*
Editora Prentice-Hall do Brasil, Ltda., *Rio de Janeiro*

Because writing a book like this has two sides, technical and production, I wish to dedicate this book to two sets of people.

**To my family: Anja, Daniel, and David:**

Thank you for your extreme patience and understanding and for allowing me to fulfill this dream.

**To the folks who served in SCO Support, past and present:**

I wish to thank you not only for the technical support you gave me during the course of this project, but for the friendship I have enjoyed for the past five years. You will always be in my heart.

# Contents

# Acknowledgements

There were so many people that helped with this book. Many helped with the technical side, while others supported me in the dream I had. I felt it necessary to either just say thanks to everyone at once or to list all their names. Since I am grateful to everyone who helped, I decided it was necessary to thank everyone personally. I hope I didn't leave anyone out. If I did, please accept my apologies. I appreciated the support everyone gave.

I would first like to thank my parents-in-law, Gerd and Renate Hofmann. Aside from giving me the most wonderful woman in the world, they did a tremendous amount of work on my house. I wish to thank them for understanding how important this book was to me.

Thanks to my editor at Prentice Hall, Mark Taub. His calm e-mail voice was much appreciated during all those times I was stressing out about getting this thing done "on time."

Thanks to Lothar Schultheiß for the nice art work he provided for me.

Special thanks to Paul Hurford of SCO who gave me ideas for what to include and how to approach this project. I feel that this book is much better organized because of him. I would also like to thank him for the caring ear he lent me while I was in SCO Support.

Special thanks also go to David Howell. David was my last supervisor at SCO and was the kind of leader who when he gave you a "chewing out," you felt better than after most people praised you. Sir, it was an honor and a privilege to have served with you.

Special thanks to Yasmin Kureshi for getting me what I needed to make this project a success and serving as a focal point at SCO.

A lot of thanks go to John Gray, Penny Portillo, Doug Tozier, and Doreen Lozano who gave me my original interview at SCO. I am sincerely grateful for the chance I had to prove myself.

Thanks to my reviewers Craig Dale, Tillman Dickson, Christopher Durham, Steve Gardiner, John Richards, and Mike Shallop. You guys did a great job and definitely made the book even better. I owe you all a big one!

Thanks to Ralf Schwämlein for doing a lot of the electrical work on my house, which freed me to spend more time working on the book.

Thanks to my brother, August Mohr, who gave me my first shot at publishing my work. Also thanks for being the best brother a person could have.

During the course of this project, there were many people from many different companies that helped me with materials, as well as provided technical and emotional support. I wish to thank:

Don Abel, Karen Adams, Alex Alvarez, Jane Appleyard, Tillmann Basien, George Basset, Yadira Benitez, Dave Berger, Carrie Berger, David Blinn, Brian Bok, Steve Bordwell, Val Brand, Marianne Brokaw, Adalid Bruno, Rob Buck, Ann Burrell, Dave Butler, James Butsch, Paul Buzby, Isiah Carew, Sabrina Castandeda, Rafael Castillo, Dorothy Cheek, Tracy Clark, Dennis Cline, Pam Cole, Alan Colmenares, Ann Colvin, Bill Cope, Despina Coutsoukos, Sandy Crisel, Charlie Cronon, Ellie Cutler, Dave D'Arcey, Valorie Dallas, David Dang, Janine Darling, Allie Davidson, Patty Davis, Scott Deardorff, Cathy Downes, Don Draper, Jennifer Drozen, John Dubois, Melinda Dunkle, Karen Edwards, Tejas Edwards, Ramin Elahi, Eileen Engle, John Esak, Tomas Escobar, Jonathan Fesmire, Bill Fischer, Noelle Fontaine, Greg Forrest, Albert Fu, Jeff Gallagher, Andreas Geißler, Joel Goldberger, Anne Gondreau, Leigh Anne Gould, Rick Graziani, Daniel Gutierrez, Steve Gzesh, Jeff Halvorsen, Alton (Chip) Handley, Pam Hassel, Elena Hawkins, Henry Heikkinen, Karen Hershberger, Wendy Hess, Jim Hill, Melissa Hoeg, Ned Hogan, Wyliam Holder, Evan Hunt, Craig Hunt, Jeff Hyman, Ricky Jacobson, Jeff Jenkins, Dion Johnson, Michael Johnson, Gail Johnston, James Jones, Dan Jung, Hamid Karimi, Jay Kensinger, Tisha Kindred, Gene Kindred, Kathy Kindred, Lea Kivi, Peter Körner, Beth Konesky, Tracy Larrabee, Sheryl Lee, Bill Leikam, Glenda Leuning, Dianne Lewis, Pat Lin, Wang Hwa Lin, Alex Lopez, Alice Lu, Bela Lubkin, Lesley MacDonald, Tom Madison, Sanjay Manchanda, Mark Mason, Sinnika Masri, Cherrie McCoy, Kaite McGrew, Jennifer McMullin, Dave Meeks, Janett Merrell, Kim Merriman, Marita-Elena Michaell, Henry Miller, Aaron Miller, Christine Montross, Bob Morrey, Stephen Moss, Krystal Moss, Peter Mui, Kamal Mostafa, Joseph Nagy, Bob (Nate) Nathanson, Zoliyan Nazaari, Phil Newman, Tammy Noren, Mike O'Baugh, Greg

Oetting, Tracie Okamura, Ken Onwuteaka, Adam Paul, Tony Pelton, Max Perez, Greg Peters, Nathan Petersen, Mark Poteet, Jule Potter, Rhonda Powers, Kenton Rahn, Ganesh Rajappan, Grace Rathe, Malcolm Rieke, Mark Robb, Rachel Rosencrantz, Pete Rumsey, Bill Rusch, Kathy Sammons, Jim Schnitter, Donna Senko, Shannon Shaffer, Andrew Sharpe, Bill Shaw, Chris Shelton, Karen Shipe, Sheri Shipe, Scott Simmons, Susannah Skyer, Mark Slater, Pete Sole, Bruce Steinberg, Nancy Stewart, Galen Sullivan, Lorie Summers, Candance Sutherland, Steven Thompson, Carter Thompson, Bob Tinsman, Julie Tokunaga, Shawna Tracy, Loc Tran, Rich Trivett, Jack Velte, Juliana Vidich, Debbie Vorndran, Kerrie Wallach, Manfred Warmuth, Brian Watrous, Crystal Weathers, Melissa Williams, Liz Williams, Orion Wilson, Bill Wolverton, Don Wright, Karl Young, David Zimmerman, Stuart Zimny, W. Paul Zola.

Special thanks go out to the SysOps and staff of the SCOFORUM on CompuServe: Tim Ruckle, Jean-Pierre Radley, Bob Stockler, Tom Parsons, David Van Allen, and Mark Woolfson. You guys do a great job of keeping things flowing, as well as doing a terrific job of getting answers to people's questions.

I would also like to thank the many people who have posted both questions and answers on CompuServe SCOFORUM. The answers gave me new insight into the SCO products and the questions provided me with tips on things I should include. So, thanks to:

Michael Adams, Al Alexander, Russell Allen, John Anderson, Jay Aymond, Kent Bailey, Tim Barhorst, Denis Baron, Bernard Barton, Nitin Barve, Bryan Batten, David Beecher, John Bilyj, Greg Bino, Geoff Bleau, Linda Bonanno, Hu Bonar, Jerome Boulon, Greg Bourassa, Philip Bowry, Al Bracco, Steven Brand, Ben Brandon, Mark Brennan, Michael Brodie, James Buckley, Jim Burrill, Andy Burton, Bill Campbell, Carlos Canas, Pete Carino, Sergio Carnero, Malcolm Carter, Glenn Casteran, Chris Cermak, Bashar Chalabi, Eric Chauvin, Ray Chien, Graham Cluley, Richard Colety, David Cook, Merrill Cook, Don Cooper, David Corey, Rafel Coyle, Matt Cummings, Tom Dao, Adrian Davis, Kent Davis, Dave Dickerson, Robert Diersing, Randy Dietz, Michel Donais, Doyle Dreiling, Bill Drescher, Randall Duckworth, Lon Ellis, Dennis Ellul, Robert Engels, Tom Everson, Clay Fast, Steve Fatula, Ed Faunce, Alan Fenstermacher, Willhelmina Fitzger, Ken Fox, Hal Fuquay, John Gaskell, Juergen Geltinge, Guy Germonpre, Gary Gibson, Greg Giedd, Denis Gilbert, Scott Gillespie, Gale Gorman, Tony Green, Brian Greer, Cheryl Gross, Georges Guinchard, Kevin Guyll, Dean Guzman, Matt Hagadorn, Frank Hajek, Shel Hall, Dave Hammond, Linda Hapner,  Earl Hartman, Marla Hartson, Ed Hatton, Tom Hauer, Brian Heaton, Kelly Hendrickson, Jean Hendrickx, Dan Henry, Neal Henzle, W. J. Heritage, Russell Hermanso, Pablo Hernandez, Ernesto Hernández, Ron Herrmann, Alan Hilton, Han Holl, Thomas

Hool, Curt Imanse, Bud Izen, James Jackson, Leroy Janda, Scott Johnson, Nathan Kahn, Derek Kamp, Robert Kerr, Randy Kersey, Brett Kinney, Steven Klos, Andy Knight, Kevin Knight, Keith Lamb, Roy Lamberton, Dan Lapp, Jean-Paul Le Bricqu, Shawn Leard, Lucky Leavell, Charles Lei, Joel Levine, Jack Levy, David Lines, Nancy Lorenz, Vincent Lowe, Jeffrey Manning, Martin Marris, Colin Marshall, Pam Marshall, Brian Martin, David Martin, David Martino, Jackson McCann, Michael McConaghy, Bill McEachran, Scott McEvoy, Alonzo McFarling, James McLane, Col McLaughlin, Rene Menschel, Mike Merriman, Ricardo Michell, Edmond Momartin, Mario Moran, Matt Mrowicki, Matthias Mueller, Steve Musacchia, Tom Napier, Tom Nedbal, Sam Nelson, Guillermo Nevado, J. Eric Nicholson, Long Nguyen, Michael Norton, Joe Novitski, Jose Nuñez, Mike O'Connor, Terry O'Keefe, Hans Obermueller, Rory Orkin, Ian Parsons, Mervyn Passmore, Dimitri Patakidis, Lee Penn, Orlando Perez, George Petrilak, Randy Phillips, Bart Pichal, Richard Pitts, Tom Podnar, Charlie Ponder, Dwight Potvin, Ron Pruse, Jordi Puente, Theo Purmer, Ian Rabbitt, Stephen Ranson, David Reeves, Robert Repko, David Rider, Wolfgang Riedmann, Laurence Roberts, Douglas Robinson, Joel Robinson, David Rogers, Jeff Rosen, Trevor Rowley, John Rucker, Tom Ruess, Sergio Ruiz, Charlie Russel, Gordon Rustvold, Keith Sandberg, Mary Sanders, Kenneth Schaffer, Korstiaan Schipper, Marc Schneider, Steven Schwartz, Georg Schukat, Matthias Schulz, Venkat Sharma, James Shaw, Mike Siemens, Todd Simi, Dino Sims, Don Sinkiewicz, Dan Smeltz, James Smith, Larry Smith, Eli Sokal, Carl Sopchak, Paulo Soromenho, Gerhard Speck, Bob Staples, David Stevenson, Bill Stewart, Jim Swinny, Cary Swoveland, Dan Taysom, John Tengwall, Alex Thomas, Peter Thompson, Bob Thornthwaite, Mike Thorp, Mike Tills, Scott Trautman, Jeff Trembath, David Tucker, Rainer Uhr, Chris Ulaky, Arnold Van Kampe, Frank Van Gilluwe, Gino Van Nauw, Scott Vivian, Stephen Walker, Ruby Waters, Bruce Weaver, Bennett Weber, Ron Wheeler, Philip Whirley, Christopher Wiencek, Martin Willingha, Walter Willmertinger, Don Winterhalter, Heinz Wittenbecher, Richard Wooden, Ira Woolery, John Wymant, Don Young.

Thanks to Tom Melvin who provided me with the shell script that I used as a basis for the script in Chapter 14.

Thanks to my neighbor, Rainer Kurberg, for many last minute tips on the hardware section.

I would also like to thank my new co-workers for making me feel so welcome: Bernd Bätz, Jürgen Bernschneider, Stephan Gesell, Torsten Höhlein, Susi Hofmann, Andreas Hoger, Michael Karsch, Achim Knauer, Falko Lameter, Ralf Linortner, Hartmut Lorenz, Holger Ranft, Thomas Propst, Ralf Schwarz, Wolf Siegemund, Jürgen Thauer, and Peter Werhahn.

Lastly, thanks to you for being an SCO customer and giving me the reason to write this book.

Although there were a lot of people who provided technical information and reviewed my material, any mistakes that may appear are solely my responsibility. I tried to test everything and check everything I said, but I'm only human. Therefore, there just might be something in here that's wrong. If you find something that you believe is inaccurate, please contact me. Also, please tell me what you might have added, left out, or changed in this book. Most of all, I would like to find out how much you learned from this book and if my efforts were worth it. I can be reached at: jimmo@blitz.de or 100542.2677@compuserve.com.

# Introduction

One of the questions that you are probably asking is that from all the UNIX books on the market, why should you buy this one? You probably have SCO UNIX or one of the bundled products such as Open Desktop or the latest product, Open Server. Therefore, you were probably drawn to the fact that the title itself says that this book is about SCO UNIX. But why this one? Why should you give out your hard earned money for this book instead of another?

Well, if you are looking for a hand-holding, step-by-step introduction to all the commands, utilities, and functions, then I have to disappoint you. This book is not for you. If your looking for a first aid book, that will list the 1000 most common problems and their solutions, then I have to disappoint you again. If you are looking for a how-to book that tells you step-by-step how to configure printers, install a new hard disk, and add users, then this book is also not for you. So why buy this book?

There are already many books on the market that provide the commands and the hand-holding. In order to make you want to buy this book, I have to give you something different. There is already a good introduction to the SCO commands and utilities: the SCO UNIX documentation. In addition, O'Reilly and Associates has published *SCO UNIX in a Nutshell,* by Ellie Cutler. This provides more than a quick reference to all the commands, utilities, and functions. There is also *Essential SCO System Administration* by Keith Vann, published by Prentice Hall. This is a quick reference to the administration side of an SCO UNIX system. Repeating what is in either of these books hurts you more than helps you as you now need to worry about which one you should buy. So why buy this one?

There are other UNIX books on the market that deal with system administration, using the shell, TCP/IP, and a dozen other aspects on a SCO system. Buying them all would cost you a fortune and you would have to spend months, if not years, to read them all. The SCO documentation covers all this to a certain degree as well as many other books. So, why buy this one?

If you are looking for a book that tells you what files change when you configure a printer and what is happening when you install that hard disk and what a user really is to the system, then you have come to the right place. What I am going to show you here is not only the inside of an SCO UNIX system, but also how things interact with the system as well as each other. In other words, I will not only show you the anatomy of an SCO UNIX system, but the physiology as well.

It is very common that when customers call a company for technical support, they lack the basic information and knowledge required to not only get the answer they need, but to understand the causes and implications of the problem. A great deal of time is wasted when technical support representatives need to explain basic computer and UNIX issues in order to gather the information they need to solve the customer's problem or answer their question. This book provides that missing information along with how it relates to SCO UNIX systems.

In the four years I worked in SCO Technical Support, I constantly heard the complaint that basic information was not provided in SCO documentation. The purpose of software documentation is to describe the function and behavior and not the underlying concepts, just as an automobile handbook does not describe the details of the internal combustion engine. However, should the car need a tune-up, basic knowledge of the internal combustion engine is useful, if not essential. Books are available that describe how to repair particular models, while explaining the basic concepts of how the car operates. No other book provided that level for SCO UNIX systems—until now.

Based on my experiences in SCO Support and what I have seen both in Internet newsgroups and in the CompuServe SCO forum, it became obvious to me that SCO users were having trouble accomplishing some very fundamental system installation and maintenance tasks, such as managing user accounts, installing hardware devices, and managing system security. I realized that a book was needed that focused in on the very problems people were having.

The computer industry is like no other in that most customers are not trained to use the product they are purchasing. Therefore, they are not even aware of how little they know about the subject or what information is needed or knowledge is required to accomplish what they intend. Additionally, the computer industry is like no other in that customers feel that software and hardware vendors are somehow obligated to provide free support on even the most basic issues.

This book will provide you with the information necessary to limit the need for calling SCO Technical Support or wherever you might have a support agreement. In addition, you will have the knowledge and tools to solve problems yourself and in a much shorter time than if you had to call support. Also, by limiting the need to call for support, you will have a much better relationship to the product and feel more comfortable with it; just as a car owner feels better about his car if it is not regularly in the repair shop. That's what I hope to achieve with this book.

There are other advantages to a book of this type. First, you will gain new insights into the product that is not available in current SCO documentation, thereby increasing the usefulness of the product. Second, with these new insights, you will be better able to use the tools and information already on the system to solve problems and implement solutions on your own. Third, should the issue or problem be too complex for a typical user or administrator to handle, this book will provide you with the information needed to call SCO Technical Support and quickly get the proper solution.

One of the things that I have always felt was missing from both the SCO documentation as well as other sources, is that you either get the introduction or the nuts and bolts. You don't find the middle ground that tells you how the nuts and bolts fit together. This is comparable to a book about cars. You might get an introduction that tells you that pressing the gas pedal makes the car go faster. Another book explains what is happening chemically inside each cylinder as the gas is mixed with air and ignited. You don't find a book that makes the connection between the gas pedal and internal combustion.

Actually, there are books about cars that make these connections. However, there is nothing on SCO that does this—until now. What I am going to try to do in the following pages is to not only explain to you the basics and what goes on inside, but to show you how each end of the spectrum is connected. I am going to show you the relationships and interactions and just what happens when you click the OK button or press enter.

This is not an easy task. Entire books have been written on many of the subjects we will cover. Therefore, I cannot tell you all the gory details on every subject I want to address. However, I can give you the tools you need to *understand* what is happening on your system. If that "something" is undesirable, then you will have the understanding to know what can be done about it.

Most books on the market today address only the two extremes: users or administrators. There are few books that attempt to bridge the gap. Because SCO prides itself on providing a system that "anyone" can install or run, system administrators are often people with very limited computer experience. In fact, many have less knowledge than what would be classified as a "knowledgeable user." However, they are expected to administer an SCO UNIX system. In order to allow the user to advance to the point where he or she can adequately administer the system, it is essential that there be a bridge like the one discussed.

Books exist on the market that cover general PC hardware, while others cover UNIX usage or administration. However, few or none combine the two or describe their relationship. It is often very difficult to explain solutions to customers if they are unfamiliar with these relationships or if they do not understand their significance. This book provides you with the necessary understanding of those relationships.

In addition, there is no book on the market that addresses SCO specific issues regarding use and administration in this fashion. Although SCO UNIX is based on System V, there are many differences that limit the value of generic UNIX books. However, much of the information provided is useful no matter what dialect of UNIX you have.

This brings up another question: why me? Why should you trust me to not only give you the information that you need to know, but also trust that what I tell you is not taken from a science fiction novel? I spent four years as a support engineer in SCO's technical support department. I had been thinking about a project of this type for years before I began making notes and considering this a viable project. Aside from taking notes on the technical side of things, I was taking notes on what has become a key aspect of this book. That is, what information is it that people are lacking most. What pieces of the SCO puzzle are missing?

The information provided in the book is based on those four years of experience in SCO tech support. Common issues arose when dealing with customers that this book addresses. If addressed at all in existing documentation, users and administrators needed to wade through several different manuals and third party references to get their answers. This book provides a single source that addresses the important issues and their relationship to each other and the SCO UNIX system.

While on the phone in SCO Support, I encountered many of the same problems. Users were trying to accomplish some task and they lacked the basic knowledge to go beyond what was explained in the SCO documentation. When they wanted to go beyond the basics or expand on the examples provided, they couldn't. Many people simply called SCO support for the answers, while others would get themselves into situations that they couldn't easily back out of.

After a couple of years of these kinds of phone calls, it became obvious that many users lacked information about the various aspects of their system. Information is available from many different sources, but nowhere was all of the essential information gathered in one place—until now.

In the following pages I hope to give you that information. Not as a list of facts that you store away somewhere, but rather as a collection of interworking processes. Like your body, SCO Unix is a system that works together to reach a common goal. When one part fails, the whole system can collapse.

What this book is not, is a first-aid handbook. I am not going to list out specific issues and specific problems with an explanation of what you need to do to implement that functionality or solve that problem. These books annoy me because they will list 100 things you can do or 100 problems. However, I end up having problem 101 and the book does not go into enough details to solve the problem.

This book is also not a cookbook. I do not provide step-by-step instructions, telling you what to input in what field, what button to press and what menu option to select. Although cookbooks are good to tell you how to bake a cake, they don't cut it when it comes to administering your computer system. On the other hand, a cookbook that explains how flour, eggs, and milk interact with each other when you stick them in the oven enables you to not only bake a cake, but a pie, and bread as well. That's what we're going to do here.

This book is intended to be used by the entire range of SCO UNIX users, from the novice to the system administrator. The novice will see how the commands he or she uses behave aside from simply returning a particular output. This way, the user will be better able to use those commands and the UNIX environment as a whole. The system administrator will also have a better understanding of things "behind the scenes," thereby making it easier to identify problems and find solutions.

Because customers calling into support often lack basic computer knowledge, this book assumes a very minimal level. For example, I will assume you know what a hard disk is, but not that you know the difference between SCSI and IDE.

The information is presented in language that even beginners can understand to give them the tools to understand what is happening and why. I intentionally tried to avoid "buzz-words" and "techno-speak" in an effort to bring my message across to the most people. Because of that, some of the more knowledgeable readers will see places where I oversimplify or gloss over something. This was unavoidable.

I also tried to make this "easy reading." I did not want to bog you down with long drawn out explanations, but rather show you key concepts. My intention was to provide a book that you could read on the living room couch without feeling as if you had to have a computer in front of you.

By using real world examples, you will see that the solution to any problem is within your reach. In this way you will be able to take a completely new situation and solve the problem on your own. This is a book that, unlike the product documentation, focuses not on the features of the operating system, but rather on real world problems and situations that real world people are experiencing.

The decision on where to put things and in what order was hard. I tried to put things in an order that would form blocks upon which subsequent sections and chapters would build. One of the major problems that kept cropping up was the chicken-egg/cart-horse business. Often, I thought I had to explain one thing first before I started something, then later switched things around to limit the number of times I had to repeat myself.

Unfortunately that is the nature of the business. Hardware and software work together. You can't have one without the other. You can't explain one without explaining the other. Somewhere along the line you either make assumptions about what people already know, and leave things out, or you repeat yourself. I did both. However, I feel that I left out those things that were easily accessed from other sources and only repeated myself when I absolutely had to.

A single book cannot do everything in this regard. I tried to cover the issues that represented the majority of the calls to SCO Support and the problems I saw on CompuServe. I also attempted to address those issues where people lack knowledge of basic relationships.

I felt that the assumption of certain base knowledge would be more useful than starting with an explanation of bits and bytes. There are enough books on that kind of thing and I didn't want to waste precious space. I also tried not to rehash things that you could find in SCO manuals. However, in order to make sense in many places it was necessary to repeat the SCO documentation.

The book begins with basic concepts of both UNIX in general and the SCO implementation. Subsequent chapters provide information needed on a user level and then progress into the more advanced topics that would be needed by a system administrator. The material is presented in a way that relates to the actual use of the products rather than simply describing programs and their behavior. Many real situations with customers are used as examples of how the information is useful.

The book is based on Open Desktop 3.0 *and* the current release, OpenServer 5. However, one important aspect of this book is that I point out to you those places where the two products differ. This not only helps you avoid problems, it helps you understand the product better if you know that something has changed. The decision not to base this book entirely on OpenServer is because there are many thousands of installations that will remain with previous releases for some time.

So, what am I going to talk about? Well, Chapter 1 is an introduction to operating system concepts. This is the foundation of all subsequent chapters. This chapter provides you with a basic understanding of key operating system concepts and how they relate to SCO UNIX.

In Chapter 2, I go into what makes up the SCO product. Here, as in most chapters, I refer to *both* Open Desktop 3.0 (ODT) and the newest member of the SCO family, OpenServer 5.

Chapter 3 goes into most users' first interface to the system: the shell. Here, we talk about what the shell is and how it reacts to the input that we give it. Here we'll talk about the basic concepts of inputting the commands and getting output. We'll also talk about a few key tools that you can use to create your own commands and utilities: `vi`, `sed`, and `awk`. At the end of the chapter we'll talk about the process of creating your own commands.

In Chapter 4 we talk about users and how they interact with the system. This not only covers what a user account is, but also how the user account interacts with the system. This includes logging into the system, the user's environment, and just what the user can or can't do on the system. This means that here we will also be covering system security and how it is implemented in SCO.

In Chapter 5 we open up the hood and take an inside look at the operating system and it's environment. We'll go into details about the concepts we talked about in Chapter 1 and discuss the life of a program and how it interacts with the system. Here, too, we'll talk about the device files, which is the way the system accesses the physical hardware.

In Chapter 6 we talk about files and filesystems. We'll talk about the physical structure on the hard disk as well as how the system represents these structures and how we (as users) see them. Plus, we'll go into some details about the newer SCO filesystems and what they can do for you.

Chapter 7 describes the process of starting and stopping your system. We'll go into the details of what is happening from the moment you flip the power switch, up to the time when you finally get to log into the system. On the other end, we'll talk about how to shutdown the system.

Since most systems will need to put words on paper, this book would not be complete without talking about printers. That's what Chapter 8 is about. As in other chapters, we'll talk about the interactions of the different components. We'll also go over the way the system accesses printers and ways that you can adapt that to your needs.

Chapter 9 addresses one of the hottest topics in the computer business today: networking. We'll go into the basic concepts of what makes up a network and how your SCO system uses them. This includes the different types of networks you can have and the tools you use to access them.

Without hardware, an SCO system is just a CD-ROM sitting in a box. So, that's what we'll be covering in Chapter 10. Here we talk about what hardware you have available to you and how to configure that hardware to allow your SCO to access it.

Chapter 11 is the first chapter of the "hands-on" section. This chapter is on installing and upgrading your system. This appears this far into the book for two reasons. First, if you're like me, you buy a book on a software product after it's already installed. Therefore, installing or upgrading is not high on your list of priorities. Second, there are many concepts and issues that we must address first, before we can really address the issue of installing.

Chapter 12 talks about making the network components of your system work. We'll address some of the key configuration issues as well as emphasize some of the areas in which users commonly have trouble.

A common thing done after the operating system is installed is adding new hardware to your system. We talked about what kinds of hardware is available already, so Chapter 13 talks about adding this hardware to an existing system. We'll go into many of the problems and other issues that are frequently encountered when adding hardware.

Chapter 14 is about system monitoring. This vague heading discusses the tools you can use and the files that you can look at to get a picture of the way your system is behaving and how it is configured. At the end of the chapter, I provide you with a script that can gather much of this information for you.

Chapter 15 also has the vague heading of "problem solving." Here we talk about the tools available to you to determine if your system is behaving correctly and what you can do about it.

So, what happens if all that you learned in the first 15 chapters is not enough? I realize that this book cannot address every issue. Therefore, there may come a time when you need to get help from elsewhere . That's what Chapter 16 is all about. Here we talk about other places that you can get answers to your questions.

As I said, this book will not cover everything. It cannot be everything to everyone and answer all your questions. However, I am sure that after reading it you will have gained the understanding to go beyond this book and find answers for yourself.

Throughout the book you will find several symbols. The first symbol looks like a mountain. The mountain is supposed to represent Mount Everest. Everest is the code name used for SCO OpenServer 5 prior to shipping. Therefore, anytime that you see this symbol, there is something that is different between Open Desktop 3.0 and OpenServer 5.

The next symbol is a note tacked onto the page . This is used to indicate something that you should jot down or take a closer look at. Often I used it to indicate pieces of information that are "neat" or interesting.

The last symbol is a caution sign. I used this symbol to represent those issues that you need to watch out for.

Throughout the book I tell you stories about my experiences in SCO Support. Often the customer I am talking about may appear like an idiot or it may seem like I am trying to make fun of him or her. This is *not* the case. I am trying to use these examples to demonstrate the problems that arise when you do not understand the principles behind what is happening on your system. Once you are done reading this book, you won't have these problems any more.

I hope you enjoy reading and using this book as much as I enjoyed working on it.

Best Regards,


jimmo
Untersiemau, Germany
May 1996

# CHAPTER
# 1

- What is an Operating System?
- Processes
- Files and Directories
- Operating System Layers

# Introduction
# to Operating
# Systems

I t is a common occurrence to find users who are not aware of what operating system they are running. On occasions, you also find an administrator who may know the name of the operating system, but nothing about the inner workings of it. For many, they have no time as they are often clerical workers or other personnel reluctantly appointed the system administrator.

Being able to run a Santa Cruz Operation (SCO) UNIX system does not mean you have to understand the intricate details of how it functions internally. However, there are some operating system concepts that will help you not only interact better with the system, but also serve as the foundation for many of the issues we're going to cover in this book.

In this chapter we are going to go through the basics of what makes an operating system. First we'll talk about what an operating system is and why it is important. We are also going to address how the different components work and work together.

My goal is not to make you an expert on operating system concepts. Instead, I want to provide you with a starting point from which we can go on to other topics. If you want to go into more details about operating systems I would suggest *Modern Operating Systems* by Andrew Tanenbaum, published by Prentice Hall and *Operating System Concepts* by Silberschatz, Peterson, and Galvin, published by Addison Wesley.

## What is an Operating System?

In simple terms, the operating system is a manager. It manages all the resources available on a computer. These resources can be the hard disk, a printer, or the monitor screen. Even memory is a resource that needs to be managed. Within an operating system are the management functions that determine who gets to read data from the hard disk, what file is going to be printed next, what characters appear on the screen, and how much memory a certain program gets.

Once upon a time, there was no such thing as an operating system. The computers of forty years ago ran one program at a time. The computer programmer would load the program he (they were almost universally male at that time) had written and run it. If there was a mistake that caused the program to stop sooner than expected, the programmer had to start over. Since there were many other people waiting for their turns to try their programs, it may have been several days before the first programmer got a chance to run his deck of cards through the machine again. Even if the program did run correctly, the programmer probably never got to work on the machine directly. The program (punched cards) was fed into the computer by an operator who then passed the printed output back to the programmer several hours later.

As technology advanced, many such programs, or jobs, were all loaded onto a single tape. This tape was then loaded and manipulated by another program, which was the ancestor of today's operating systems. This program would monitor the behavior of the running program and if it misbehaved (crashed) the monitor could then immediately load and run another. Such programs were called monitors.

In the 1960s, technology and operating system theory advanced to the point that many different programs could be held in memory at once. This was the concept of 'multiprogramming.' If one program needed to wait for some external event such as the tape to rewind to the right spot, another program could have access to the CPU. This improved performance dramatically and allowed the CPU to be busy almost 100% of the time.

By the end of the 1960s, something wonderful happened: UNIX was born. It began as a one man project design by Ken Thompson of Bell Labs and has grown to become the most widely used operating system. In the time since UNIX was first developed, it has gone through many different generations and even mutations. Some differ substantially from the original version. BSD (Berkeley Software Distribution) UNIX and others, such as SCO UNIX, still contain major portions that are based on the original source code. (A friend of mine described UNIX as the only operating system where you can throw the manual onto the keyboard and get a real command.)

SCO UNIX is an operating system like many others, such a DOS, VMS, OS/360, or CP/M. It performs many of the same tasks in very similar manners. It is the manager and administrator of all the system resources and facilities. Without it, nothing works. Despite this, most users can go on indefinitely without knowing even which operating system they are on, let alone the basics of how an operating system works.

For example, if you own a car, you don't really need to know the details of the internal combustion engine to understand that this is what makes the car move forward. You don't need to know the principles of hydraulics to understand what isn't happening when pressing the brake pedal has no effect.

An operating system is like that. You can work productively for years without even knowing what operating system you're running on, let alone how it works. Sometimes things go wrong. If you work in a company, you probably have a service number to call when problems arise. You tell them what happened and they deal with it.

If the computer is not back up within a few minutes, you get upset and call back, demanding to know when, "that damned thing will be up and running again." When the technician (or whoever has to deal with the problem) tries to explain what is happening and what is being done to correct the problem, the response is usually along the lines of, "Well, ya, I need it back up now."

The problem is that many people hear the explanation, but don't understand it. It is not unexpected for people not to acknowledge that they didn't understand the answer. Instead, they try to deflect the other person's attention away from that fact. Had they understood the explanation, they would be in a better position to understand what the technician is doing and that they are actually working on the problem.

By having a working knowledge of the principles of an operating system, you are in a better position to understand not only the problems that can arise, but also what steps are necessary to find a solution. There is also the attitude that you have a better relationship with things you understand. Like in a car, if you see steam pouring out from under the hood, you know that you need to add water. This also applies to the operating system.

In this section, that's what we're going to talk about. What goes into an operating system and what does it do? How does it do it? How are you, the user, affected by all this?

Because of advances in both hardware design and performance, computers are able to process increasingly larger amounts of information. The speed at which computer transactions occur is often talked about in terms of *billionths* of a second. Because of this speed, today's computers can give the appearance of doing many things simultaneously by actually switching back and forth between each task extremely fast. This is the concept of multitasking. That is, the computer is working on multiple tasks "at the same time."

Another function of the operating system is to keep track of what each program is doing. That is, the operating system needs to keep track of whose program, or task, is currently writing its file to the printer or which program needs to read a certain spot on the hard disk, etc. This is the concept of multi-user, as multiple users have access to the same resources.

## Processes

One of the basic concepts of an operating system is the process. If we think of the program as the file stored on the hard or floppy disk, and the process as that program in memory, we can better understand the difference between a program and a process. Although these two terms are often interchanged or even misused in "casual" conversation, the difference is very important for issues that we talk about later.

A process is more than just a program. Especially in a multi-user, multitasking operating system such as UNIX, there is much more to consider. Each program has a set of data that it uses to do what it needs. Often this data is not part of the program. For example, if you are using a text editor, the file you are editing is not part of the program on disk, but is part of the process in memory. If someone else were to be using the same editor, both of you would be using the same program. However, each of you would have a different process in memory.

Under UNIX, many different users can be on the system at the same time. In other words, they have processes that are in memory all at the same time. The system needs to keep track of what user is running what process, which terminal the process is being run on, and what other resources the process has (such as open files). All of this is part of the process.

When you log into a UNIX system, you usually get access to a command line interpreter, or shell. This takes your input and runs programs for you. If you are familiar with DOS, then you already have used a command line interpreter. This is the COMMAND.COM program. Under DOS, your shell gives you the C:> prompt (or something similar). Under UNIX, the prompt is usually something like $, #, or %. This shell is a process and it belongs to you. That is, the in-memory (or in-core) copy of the shell program belongs to you.

If you were to start up an editor, your file would be loaded and you could edit your file. The interesting thing is that the shell has not gone away. It is still in memory. Unlike what operating systems like DOS do with some programs, the shell remains in memory. The editor is simply another process that belongs to you. Since it was started by the shell, the editor is considered a "child" process of the shell. The shell is the parent process of the editor. (A process has only one parent, but may have many children.)

An example might be encountered by a system administrator performing a backup. When you log in, you have the shell. From the shell you enter the commands for the sysadmsh utility, which starts a new process. When you choose the *Backups* option, a third process is started. Once you have chosen the parameters for the backup, the backup process calls the cpio command, which starts a fourth process and starts the backup. Figure 1–1 shows how this might look graphically.

The nice thing about UNIX is that while the administrator is backing up the system, you could be continuing to edit your file. This is because UNIX knows how to take advantage of the hardware to have more than one process in memory at a time. (Note: It is not a good idea to do a backup with people on the system as data may become inconsistent. This was only used as an illustration.)

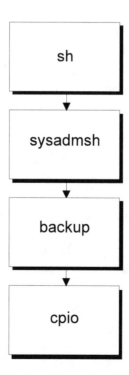

**Figure 1–1**   Relationship of multiple processes.

As you continue to edit, you delete words, insert new lines, sort your text, and write it out occasionally to the disk. All this time, the backup is continuing. Someone else on the system may be adding figures to a spreadsheet, while a fourth person is inputting orders into a database. No one seems to notice that there are other people on the system. For them, the processor is working for them alone. Well, that's the way it looks.

As I am writing this sentence, the operating system needs to know whether the characters I press are part of the text or commands I want to pass to the editor. Each key that I press needs to be interpreted. Despite the fact that I can clip along at about thirty words per minute, the Central Processing Unit (CPU) is spending approximately 95% of its time doing nothing.

The reason for this is that for a computer, the time between successive keystrokes is an eternity. Let's take my Intel 80486 running at a clock speed of 50Mhz as an example. The clock speed of 50Mhz means that there are 50 million(!) clock cycles per second. Since the 80486 gets close to one instruction per clock cycle, this means that within one second, the CPU can get close to executing 50 million instructions! No wonder it is spending most of its time idle. (Note: This is an over-simplification of what is going on.)

A single computer instruction doesn't really do much. However, being able to do 50 million little things in one second allows the CPU to give the user an impression of being the only one on the system. It is simply switching between the different processes so fast that no one is aware of it happening.

Each user, that is each process, gets complete access to the CPU for an incredibly short period of time. On SCO UNIX 3.2v4 and later, this period of time, (referred to as a *time-slice*) is 1/100th of a second! That means, at the end of that 1/100th of a second, it's someone else's turn and your process is *forced* to give up the CPU. (In reality it is much more complicated than this and we'll get into more details later.)

Compare this to an operating system like standard Windows (not Windows NT or Windows 95). The program will hang onto the CPU until it decides to give it up. An ill-behaved program can hold onto the CPU forever. This is the cause of many of the system hangs, since nothing, not even the operating system itself, can gain control of the CPU.

Depending on the load of the system (how busy it is) a process may get several time-slices per second. However, after it has run for its time-slice, the operating system checks to see if some other process needs a turn. If so, that process gets to run for a time-slice and then it's someone else's turn; maybe the first process, maybe a new one.

As your process is running, it will be given full use of the CPU for the entire 1/100th of a second unless one of three things happens. Your process may need to wait for some event. For example, the editor I am writing this in is waiting for me to type in characters. I said that I type about 30 words per minute, so if we assume an average of 6 letters per word, that's 180 characters per minute or 3 characters per second. That means that on the average, a character is pressed once every 1/3 of a second. Since a time-slice is 1/100th of a second, over 30 processes can have a turn on the CPU between each keystroke! Rather than tying everything up, the program waits until the next key is pressed. It puts itself to sleep until it is awoken by some external event, such as me pressing a key. Compare this to a "busy loop" where the process keeps checking for a key being pressed.

When I want to write to the disk to save my file, it may appear that it happens instantaneously, but like the "complete-use-of-the-CPU myth" this is only appearance. The system will gather requests to write to or read from the disk and do it in chunks. This is much more efficient than satisfying everyone's request when they ask for it.

Gathering up requests and accessing the disk at once has another advantage. Often times the data that was just written is needed again, for example in a database application. If the system wrote everything to the disk immediately, you would have to perform another read to get back that same data. Instead the system holds that data in a special buffer, it "caches" that data in the buffer. This is called the *buffer cache*.

If a file is being written to or read from, the system first checks the buffer cache. If on a read it finds what it's looking for in the buffer cache, it has just saved itself a trip to the disk. Since the buffer cache is in memory it is substantially faster to read from memory than from the disk. Writes are normally written to the buffer cache, which is then written out in larger chunks. If the data being written already exists in the buffer cache, it is overwritten. How this looks graphically we see in Figure 1–2.

When your process is running and you make a request to read from the hard disk, you can't do anything until you have completed the write to the disk. If you haven't completed your time-slice yet, it would be a waste not to let someone else have a turn. That's exactly what the system does. If you decided you need access to some resource that the system cannot immediately give to you, you are "put to sleep" to wait. It is said that you are put to sleep waiting on an event; the event being the disk access. This is the second case where you may not get your full time on the CPU.

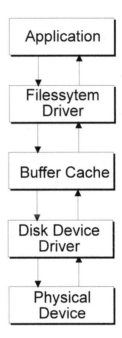

**Figure 1–2**    The flow of file access.

The third way that you might not get your full time-slice is also the result of an external event. If a device (such as a keyboard, the clock, hard disk, etc.) needs to communicate with the operating system, it signals this need through the use of an interrupt. When an interrupt is generated, the CPU itself will stop execution of the process and immediately start executing a routine in the operating system to handle interrupts. Once the operating system has satisfied this interrupt, it returns to its regularly scheduled process. (Note: Things are much more complicated than that. The "priority" of both the interrupt and the process are a factor here. We will go into more detail later.)

As I mentioned earlier, there are certain things that the operating system keeps track of as a process is running. The information the operating system is keeping track of is referred to as the process' *context*. This might be the terminal you are running on or what files you have open. The context even includes the internal state of the CPU, that is, what the content of each register is.

What happens when a process' time-slice has run out or for some other reason another process gets to run? Well, if things go right (and they usually do) eventually that process gets a turn again. However, to do things right the process must be allowed to return to the exact place where it left off. Any difference could result in disaster.

You may have heard of the classic banking problem when deducting from your account. If the process returned to a place *before* it made the deduction, you would have it deducted twice. If it hadn't yet made the deduction, but the process started up again at a point after it would have made the deduction, it appears as if the deduction was made. Good for you, not so good for the bank. Therefore, everything must be put back the way it was.

The processors used by SCO UNIX (Intel 80386 and later) have built-in capabilities to manage both multiple users and multiple tasks. We will get into the details of this in later chapters. For now, just be aware of the fact that the CPU *assists* the operating system in managing users and processes. Figure 1–3 shows how multiple processes might look in memory.

In addition to user processes, such as shells, text editors, and databases, there are system processes running. These are processes that were started by the system. Several of these deal with managing memory and scheduling turns on the CPU. Others deal with delivering mail, printing, and other tasks that we take for granted. In principle, both of these kinds of processes are identical. However, system processes can run at much higher priorities and therefore run more often than user processes.

Many of these system processes are referred to as daemon processes or background processes as they run behind the scenes without intervention for users. It is also possible for a user to put one of his or her processes "in the background." This is done by using the ampersand (&) metacharacter at the end of the command line. (I'll talk more about metacharacters in the section on shells.)

What normally happens when you enter a command is that that the shell will wait for that command to finish before it will accept a new command. By putting a command in the background, the shell does not wait, but rather is ready immediately for the next command. If you wanted, you could put the next command in the background as well.

I have talked to customers who have complained about the system grinding to a halt after they put dozens of processes in the background. The misconception is that since they didn't see the process running, it must not be taking up any resources. (Out of sight, out of mind.) The issue here is that even though the process is running in the background and you can't see it, it still behaves like any other process.

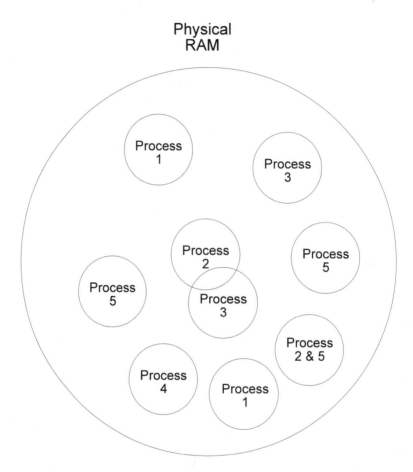

**Figure 1–3**    Multiple processes in memory.

## Files and Directories

Another key aspect of any operating system is the concept of a file. A file is nothing more than a related set of bytes on disk or other media. These bytes are labeled with a name, which is then used as a means of referring to that set of bytes. In most cases, it is through the name that the operating system is able to track down the file's exact location on the disk.

There are three kinds of files that most people are familiar with: programs, text files, and data files. However, on a UNIX system there are other kinds of files. One of the most common is a device file. These are often referred to as *device files* or *device nodes*. Under UNIX, every device is treated as a file. Access is gained to the hardware by the operating system through the device files. These tell the system what specific device driver needs to be used in order to access the hardware.

Another kind of file is a *pipe*. Like a real pipe, stuff goes in one end and out the other. Some are named pipes; that is they have a name and are located permanently on the hard disk. Others are temporary and are unnamed pipes. Although these do not exist once the process using them has ended, they do take up physical space on the hard disk. We'll talk more about these later.

Unlike operating systems like DOS, there is no pattern for file names that is expected or followed. DOS will not even attempt to execute programs that do not end with .EXE, .COM or .BAT. UNIX. On the other hand, it is just as happy to execute a program called program as it is a program called program.txt. In fact, you can use any character in a file name except for "/" and NULL.

However, completely random things can happen if the operating system tried to execute a text file as if it were a binary program. To prevent this, UNIX has two mechanisms to ensure that text does not get randomly executed. The first is the file's permission bits. The permission bits determine who can read, write, and execute a particular file. You can see the permissions of a file by doing a long listing of that file. What the permissions are all about, we get into a little later. The second is that the system must recognize a *magic number* within the program indicating it is a binary executable.

Even if a file was set to allow you to execute it, the beginning portion of the file must contain the right information to tell the operating system how to start this program. If that information is missing, it will attempt to start it as a shell script (similar to a DOS batch file). If the lines in the file do not belong to a shell script and you try to execute the program, you end up with a screen full of errors.

What you name your file is up to you. You are not limited by the eight-letter name and three-letter extension as you are in DOS. You can still use periods as separators, but that's all they are. They do not have the same "special" meaning that they do under DOS. For example, you could have files called:

```
letter.txt
letter.text
letter_txt
```

```
letter_to_jim
letter.to.jim
```

Only the first one is valid under DOS, but all are valid under SCO UNIX. Note that even though names prior to SCO UNIX 3.2.v4.0 you were limited to fourteen characters in file name, all of these are still valid. With SCO UNIX 3.2.v4.0 and later, file names can be as long as 254 characters.

There is one naming convention that does have special meaning in SCO UNIX, and that is creating "dot" files. These are files where the first character is a '.' (dot). If you have such a file, it will by default be invisible to you. That is, when you do a listing of a directory containing a "dot" file, you won't see it. However, unlike the DOS concept of "hidden" files, "dot" files can be seen by simply using the -a (all) option to ls, as in ls -a. (ls is a command used to list the contents of directories.) One thing to note is that the Superuser (root) is magic. It can see these files whether it uses the -a or not, because ls recognizes that you are root and adds the -a.

The ability to group your files together into some kind of organization is very helpful. Instead of having to wade through thousands of files on your hard disk to find the one you want, SCO UNIX, along with other operating systems, allows you to group the files into a *directory*. Under SCO UNIX, a directory is actually nothing more than a file itself with a special format. It contains the names of the files associated with it and some pointers or other information to tell the system where the data for the file actually resides on the hard disk.

Directories do not actually "contain" the files that are associated with them. Physically, (that is how they exist on the disk) directories are just files in a certain format. The directory structure is imposed on them by the program you use. For example, the hd program in ODT 3.0 will output the contents of a directory "file" without regard to the format that might be imposed by something like ls. (Note that the hd  program in OpenServer does not do that any more and is, in my mind, broken.)

The directories have information that points to where the real files are. In comparison, you might consider a phonebook. A phonebook does not contain the people listed in it, just their names and telephone numbers. A directory has the same information: the names of files and their numbers. In this case, instead of a telephone number there is an information node number, or *inode* number.

The logical structure in a telephone book is that names are grouped alphabetically. It is very common for two entries (names) that appear next to each other in the phone book to be in different parts of the city. Just like names in the phonebook, names that are next to each other in a directory may be in distant parts of the hard disk.

As I mentioned, directories are logical groupings of files. It is common to say that the directory "contains" those files or the file is "in" a particular directory. In a sense this is true. The file that is the directory "contains" the name of the file. However, this is the only connection between the directory and file, but we will continue to use this terminology.

One of the kinds of files a directory can contain is more directories. These, in turn, can contain still more directories. The result is a hierarchical tree structure of directories, files, more directories, and more files. Directories that contain other directories are referred to as the *parent* directory of the *child* or subdirectory that they contain. (Most references I have seen refer only to parent and subdirectories. Rarely have I seen references to child directories.)

When referring to directories under UNIX, there is often either a leading or trailing slash ("/"), and sometimes both. The top of the directory tree is referred to with a single "/" and is called the "root" directory. Subdirectories are referred to by this slash followed by their name, such as `/bin` or `/dev`. As you proceed down the directory tree, each subsequent directory is separated by a slash. The concatenation of slashes and directory names is referred to as a path. Several levels down, you might end up with a path such as `/usr/jimmo/letters/personal/chris.txt`, where `chris.txt` is the actual file and `/usr/jimmo/letters/personal` is all of the directories leading to that file. The directory `/usr` contains the subdirectory `jimmo`, which contains the subdirectory `letters`, which contains the subdirectory `personal`. This directory contains the file `chris.txt`.

Movement up and down the tree is accomplished by the means of the cd (change directory) command, which is part of your shell. Although this is often difficult to grasp at first, you are not actually moving anywhere. One of the things that the operating system keeps track of within the context of each process is that process' *current directory*, also referred to as *current working directory*. This is merely the name of a directory on the system. Your process has no physical contact with this directory; just that it is keeping its name in memory.

When you change directories, this portion of the process' memory is changed to reflect your new "location." You can 'move' up and down the tree or make jumps to completely unrelated parts of the directory tree. However, all that really happens is that the current working directory portion of your process gets changed.

Although there can be many files with all the same name, each *combination* of directories and file name must be unique. This is because the operating system refers to every file on the system by this unique combination of directories and file name. In the example above, I have a personal letter called `chris.txt`. I might also have a business letter by the same name. It's path would be: `/usr/jim/letters/business/chris.txt`. Someone else might also have a business letter to Chris. Their path might be: `/usr/john/letters/business/chris.txt`. This is shown graphically in Figure 1–4.

One thing to note is that John's business letter to Chris may be the exact same file as Jim's. I am not talking about one being a copy of the other. Rather, I am talking about a situation where both names point to the same physical locations on the hard disk. Since both files are referencing the same bits on the disk, they must therefore be the same file.

This is accomplished through the concept of a *link*. Like a chain link, a file link connects two pieces together. I mentioned above the "telephone number" for a file was its inode. This number actually points to a special place on the disk called the *inode table*, with the inode number being the offset into this table. Each entry in this table not only contains the file's physical location on this disk, but the owner of the file, the access permissions and the number of links, as well as many other things. In the case where the two files are referencing the same entry in the inode table, these are referred to as *hard links*. A *soft link* or *symbolic link* is where a file is created that contains the *path* of the other file. (We get into details about this in Chapter 6.)

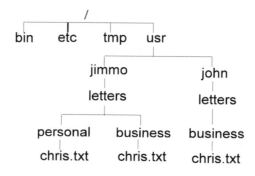

**Figure 1–4**    Diagram of directory tree structure.

However, it does *not* contain the name of the file. The name is *only* contained within the directory. Therefore, it is possible to have multiple directory entries that have the same inode. Just as there can be multiple entries in the phone book, all with the same phone number. We'll get into a lot more detail about inodes in the section on filesystems. A directory and where the inodes point to on the hard disk might look like Figure 1–5.

Let's think about the telephone book analogy once again. Although it is not too common for an individual to have multiple listings, there might be two people with the same number. For example, if you were sharing a house with three of your friends, there might be only one telephone. However, each of you would have an entry in the phone book. I could get the same phone to ring by dialing the telephone number of four different people. I could get the same inode with four different file names.

Under SCO UNIX, files and directories are grouped into units called *filesystems*. A filesystem is a portion of your hard disk that is administered as a single unit. Filesystems exist within a section of the hard disk called a *partition*. Each hard disk can be broken down into multiple partitions and each partition can be broken down into multiple filesystems. Each has a specific starting and end point that is managed by the system.

In an operating system such as SCO UNIX, the file is more that just the basic unit of data. Instead, almost everything is either treated as a file or is only accessed

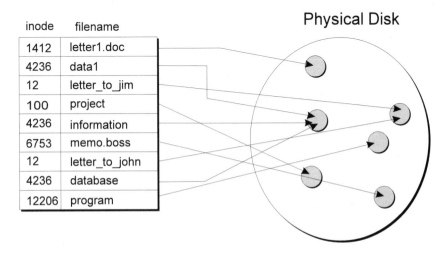

**Figure 1–5**   Files and inodes in a directory.

through files. For example, in order to read the contents of a data file, the operating system must access the hard disk. SCO UNIX treats the hard disk as if it were a file. It opens it like a file, reads it like a file and closes it like a file. The same applies to other hardware such as tape drives and printers. Even memory is treated as a file. The files used to access the physical hardware are the device files that I mentioned earlier.

When the operating system wants to access any hardware device, it first opens a file that "points" toward that device (the device node). Based on information it finds in the inode, the operating system determines what kind of device it is and can therefore access it in the proper manner. This includes opening, reading, and closing, just like any other file.

If, for example, you a reading a file from the hard disk, not only do you have the file open that you are reading, but the operating system has open the file that relates to the filesystem within the partition, the partition on the hard disk, and the hard disk itself (more about these in later chapters). There are three additional files that are opened every time you log in or start a shell. These are the files that relate to input, output, and error messages.

Normally, when you log in, you get to a shell prompt. When you type a command on the keyboard and press enter, a moment later something comes onto your screen. If you made a mistake or the program otherwise encounters an error, there will probably be some message on your screen to that effect. The keyboard where you are typing in your data is the input, referred to as standard input (standard in or *stdin*) and that is where input comes from by default. The program displays a message on your screen, which is the output, referred to as standard output (standard out or *stdout*). Although it appears on that same screen, the error message appears on standard error (*stderr*).

Although stdin and stdout appear to be separate physical devices (keyboard and monitor), there is only one connection to the system. This is one of those device files I talked about a moment ago. When you log in, the file (device) is opened for reading so you can get data from the keyboard, and for writing so that output can go to the screen and you can see the error messages.

These three concepts (standard in, standard out, and standard error) may be somewhat difficult to understand at first. At this point, it suffices to understand that these represent input, output, and error messages. We'll get into the details a bit later.

## Operating System Layers

Conceptually, the SCO UNIX operating system is similar to an onion. It consists of many layers, one on top of the other. At the very core is the interface with the hardware. The operating system must know how to communicate with the hardware or nothing can get done. This is the most privileged aspect of the operating system.

Because it needs to access the hardware directly, this part of the operating system is the most powerful as well as the most dangerous. What accesses the hardware is a set of functions within the operating system itself (the kernel) called *device drivers*. If it does not behave correctly, a device driver has the potential for wiping out data on your hard disk or "crashing" your system. Since a device driver needs to be sure that it has properly completed its task (such as accurately writing or reading from the hard disk), it cannot quit until it has finished. For this reason, once a driver has started, very little can get it to stop. We'll talk about what can stop it in the section on the kernel.

Above the device driver level is what is commonly thought of when talking about the operating system. Here are the management functions. This is where the decision is made about what gets run and when, and what resources are given to what process.

In our previous discussion on processes, we talked about having several different processes all in memory at the same time. Each gets a turn to run and may or may not get to use up its time-slice. It is at this level that the operating system determines who gets to run next when your time-slice runs out, what should be done when an interrupt comes in, and where it keeps track of the events that a sleeping process may be waiting on. It's even the alarm clock to wake you up when you're sleeping.

The actual processes that the operating system is managing are at levels above the operating system itself. Generally, the first of these levels is for programs that interact directly with the operating system, such as the various shells. These interpret the commands and pass them along to the operating system for execution. It is from the shell that you usually start application programs such as word processors, databases, or compilers. Since these often rely on other programs that interact directly with the operating system, these are often considered a separate level. What the different levels or layers of the operating system look like graphically we see in Figure 1–6.

Under SCO UNIX, there are many sets of programs that serve common functions; this includes things like mail or printing. These groups of related programs

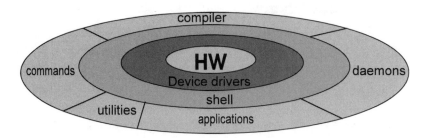

**Figure 1–6**     Operating system layers.

are referred to as "System Services." Whereas individual programs such as vi, custom, or fdisk are referred to as utilities. Programs that perform a single function such as ls or date are referred to as commands.

## Moving On

You now have an understanding of the basics of how SCO UNIX works. We talked about the different functions that the operating system is responsible for, what it manages, and a little about how everything fits together. As we move on through the book, we'll build on these ideas and concepts to give you an understanding of a complete SCO UNIX system.

I do need to make one general comment about UNIX before I let you move on. Always remember that UNIX is not DOS; nor is it any other operating system for that matter. UNIX is UNIX and SCO UNIX is SCO UNIX. As you go through this book, keep that in mind.

I came from the DOS world before I started on UNIX. I had many preconceptions about the way an operating system "should" behave and react. The way DOS did things was the "right" way. As I learned SCO UNIX I began to see a completely different world. The hardest part was not that I had to learn a whole new set of commands, but rather that I was fighting myself since I was so used to DOS.

For example, I believed that the way commands are given arguments or options was better in DOS. Every time I used a UNIX command, I grumbled about how wrong it was to do things like that. As I learned more about UNIX, I came to realize that many of the decisions on how things work or appear is completely arbitrary. There is no right way of doing many things. There is a DOS way and a UNIX way. Neither is right. You might be used to the DOS way or whatever system you use. However, that does not make it right.

If you are fairly new to UNIX, while you are reading this book you should keep in mind that there are many differences. The way UNIX does them is not the same way DOS does them. If you are new to SCO, also keep in mind that there are going to be differences. If you keep this in mind, you will have a much more enjoyable time learning the SCO way.

# CHAPTER 2

- What SCO is all About

- Reading All About It—SCO Documentation

# Basics
# of SCO UNIX

**M**any companies have point-of-sales systems hooked up to an SCO host. For the users at the cash register, they never see what is being run. Often, there is really no need for you to go into details about your system for any other reason than pure curiosity.

On the other hand, if you do have access to the command line or interact with the system by some other means, knowing how the system is put together is useful information. Knowing how things interact helps expand your knowledge. Knowing what's on your system is helpful in figuring out just what your system can do.

That's what this chapter is about: what's out there. We're going to talk about what makes up the SCO Open Desktop and OpenServer products. Part of this includes the different components that make up each product. The components are related to the different processes that go on in a computer system, such as printing and accessing a network.

Each of these components is composed of individual files and programs. What each of these programs is and what it does may provide you with new tools to make your life easier. This goes for both the user and the administrator.

## What SCO is all About

### A Guided Tour

Unless you are on familiar ground, you usually need a map to get around any large area. To get from one place to another, the best map is a road map (or street map). If you are staying in one general area and are looking for places of interest, you need a tourist map. Since we are staying within the context of SCO and we're looking for things of interest, what I am going to give you now is a tourist map of SCO UNIX directories.

In later chapters, we'll go into detail about many of the directories that we are going to encounter here. For now, I am going to briefly describe where they are and what their function is. As we get into different sections of the book, it will be a lot easier to move and know how files relate if we have an understanding of the basic directory structure.

The top-most directory is the root directory. In verbal conversation, you say "root directory," whereas it may be referred to in text as simply "/". Under root, there are several subdirectories with a wide range of functions (see Figure 2–1). This representation does not depict every subdirectory of /, just the more significant ones. In subsequent diagrams I will continue to limit myself to the most significant directories in order to keep from losing perspective.

In order to talk about the root directory, we actually need to talk about two directories at the same time. With ODT 3.0, the programs needed to boot and load the operating systems were located in the root directory. OpenServer changed that with the introduction of the /dev/boot filesystem. The programs needed to boot are now located here. Rather than repeating this explanation for every file, I will simply refer to them without any path. Unless otherwise noted, these files are in / on ODT 3.0 and in /stand on OpenServer.

One of these files, one could say, is the single *most* important file: unix. This file is the operating system proper. It contains all the functions that make everything go. When referring to the file on the hard disk, one refers to /unix whereas the in-memory executing version is referred to as the *kernel*. On OpenServer this file resides in /stand, but there is a symbolic link to it in /.

The next file is actually accessed before unix. This is the boot program. For those of you who are familiar with SCO UNIX systems, it is the boot program that presents the now famous Boot: prompt. It is this program that reads the unix file from the hard disk into memory and begins executing it. We'll get into more details about how the system gets to the boot program and the entire boot process in the section on booting your system.

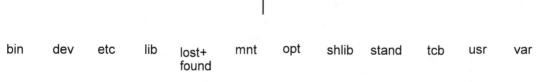

**Figure 2–1**    The root directory.

The dos file can be used to boot the system, as well. Rather than booting UNIX, the dos program finds the primary DOS partition on your system (if you have one) and boots that.

New to the /stand directory are two programs: link and bootos. The /stand/link program is used to install boot-time loadable drivers into your system (these are drivers that normally come with third party products that are needed when booting your system). The /stand/bootos program is used to boot other operating systems. This not only includes DOS as in previous versions, but also Microsoft Windows NT and OS/2. Lastly, there is the sfmt program. This is used to low-level format hard disk connected via an OMTI controller. For more details see the respective man-pages.

In addition to the programs needed to boot the operating system, there are many files located in the root directory that are used by the root user (the system administrator). This is because the / directory is the root user's *home* directory. This is where these files reside. Since the root user does not log in until well after the system has booted, there is no need to have these files in /stand. Therefore, on both ODT 3.0 and OpenServer, they only exist in /.

The first directory we get to is /bin. Its name is derived from the word *bin*ary. Often the word binary is used to refer to executable programs or other files that contain nonreadable characters. The /bin directory is where many of the system-related binaries are kept, hence the name. Although several of the files in this directory are used for administrative purposes and cannot be run by normal users, everyone has read permission on this directory, so you can at least see what is here.

The /dev directory contains the device nodes. As I mentioned in our previous discussion on operating system basics, device files are the way both the operating system and users gain access to the hardware. Every device has at least one device file associated with it. If it doesn't, you can't access it. For more details on each of the individual device files, take a look at Chapter 5.

The /etc directory serves as sort of a dumping ground for programs that don't seem to belong anywhere else. Its name comes from the common abbreviation *etc.* for etcetera. This means "and so on." Normal users do not normally execute programs in /etc. Although there are a few programs that can be executed by normal users, most of what is kept here is generally for system or administrative use.

Under /etc are several subdirectories of varying importance to both administrators and users. Figure 2–2 shows what the subdirectories of /etc would look like graphically.

The /etc/auth subdirectory contains security or authorization related information. The name "auth" comes from "authorization." Normal users do not have

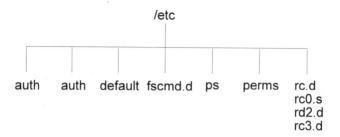

**Figure 2–2**    Subdirectories of `/etc`.

access to this directory (for obvious reasons). However, if you'd like to take a peek at its insides, take a look at Chapter 4.

Although normal users can move around inside of it, the `/etc/conf` directory is primarily of use to the system administrator. The name "conf" is short for "configuration." Underneath `/etc/conf` are several more subdirectories. Combined with a few programs scattered around the system, these directories are collectively called the link kit. These are the files and programs used to add new devices to the system, change system parameters, and combine them all into a new copy of the operating system: `/unix`. (`/stand/unix` on OpenServer).

One subdirectory that is of importance to both users and administrators is the `/etc/default` directory. As its name implies, it contains default information. In general, the files in this directory are readable by everyone, so the users on a system can take a look at the defaults themselves. Most of the files in this directory either have their own man-page or are associated with programs that do.

The `/etc/fscmd.d` directory is another one that is of interest only to administrators. The name "fscmd" is from "filesystem commands" and the ".d" at the end is a standard convention to indicate a directory. In practice, even administrators do not need to go into this directory. This is where the filesystem-specific programs exist, which are actually called by their generic namesakes. For example, the program used to clean (ensure the integrity of) a filesystem is called `fsck`. When invoked by the system administrator, the `fsck` program first determines what type of filesystem is being cleaned, then executes the appropriate program in `/etc/fscmd.d`. Rather than having one monolithic program that contains the code for all the filesystems, there is one small front-end that calls the others.

When you run the `ps` (process status) command, rather than hunting through several system files, it simply reads the information in the files in the `/etc/ps` directory. If you have written permission in this directory (for example, as an administrator) you can remove these files and see how much longer the `ps` command takes to run as it must first gather the information stored in `/etc/ps`.

In the `/etc/perms` directory are files containing lists of all the files that come with the installed products; sort of a packing list, you might say. In addition to file and directory names and where they end up, there is also the name of the owner, group, and default permissions on each file. The name "perms" comes from "permissions." In OpenServer, the `/etc/perms` directory is not used in the same way. We go into more details about that later. For more information, see both the `custom` (ADM) and `fixperm` (ADM) man-pages.

The `/etc/rc.*` directories contain files that the system uses when starting up or shutting down. Which files are read depends on whether the system is being started or shutdown. We'll talk more about these directories and their associated files in the section on starting up and shutting down the system.

Moving back up to the root directory, we next find the `/lib` directory (for library). If the SCO Development System has been installed on your system then this directory will contain the libraries needed for program development. Hence the directory name "lib." In addition, there are usually some of the programs necessary for a kernel rebuild.

The `/shlib` directory contains the *shared libraries* used by the system. For those of you who are not programmers, a shared library is a means of providing uniformity across programs as well as saving space. For example, almost all of the programs that users and administrators use accept input from the keyboard and write output to the screen. Rather than each program having copies of the necessary functions to do this, a single copy is stored in a shared library. Since the code for performing this I/O is not in the program itself, the program can be smaller and thereby save space. If ever this code needs to be changed, it can be changed in one place and you don't run the risk of forgetting to change it somewhere.

The `/tcb` directory is used in conjunction with the `/etc/auth` directory. TCB is an abbreviation for Trusted Computing Base. The `/etc/auth` directory contains just data files, but the `/tcb` directory contains both data files and support programs used to manage and administer system security. We will be covering system security in more detail in Chapter 4.

The `/usr` directory contains many user-related subdirectories. Note the 'e' is missing from "user". In general, one can say that the directories and files under `/usr` are used by and related to users. There are programs and utilities here that users use on a daily basis. Unless changed, `/usr` is where users have their home directory. Figure 2–3 shows what the subdirectories of `/usr` would look like graphically.

Whereas `/bin` contains programs that are used by both users and administrators, `/usr/bin` contains files that are almost exclusively used by users. (However, like everything in UNIX, there are exceptions.) Here again, the `bin` directory contains binaries.

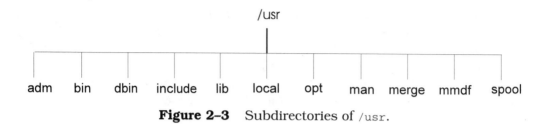

**Figure 2–3**    Subdirectories of `/usr`.

The `/usr/adm` directory contains mostly administrative data. The name "adm" comes from "administration." There are three key files stored here. The first is the `messages` file that contains all the system services, kernels, and device driver messages. Next is the `hwconfig` file. This is where the `hwconfig` program gets its information. Last, is the `syslog` file. This is where the system logs messages from the `syslogd` daemon. For more information, see the respective man-page.

There is also an important directory here: `sar` (`system activity reporter`). This is were the `sar` utility gets and writes its information. Many of the files in this directory are data files, so you really can't go looking through them with a text editor. Check out the `sar (ADM)` man-page for more details.

The `/usr/include` directory and its various subdirectories contain all the include files. For a normal user and even most system administrators, the information here is more a place to get one's curiosity satisfied. However, for me that is enough. This directory, and its various subdirectories contain information that both the kernel needs when being recreated and programs need when being compiled. (For those of you who know that this is dramatic simplification, all I can say is that you already know what this directory is for anyway.)

Many system parameters and values are stored inside the files underneath `/usr/include`. Because of the information provided in many of the files, I will be making reference to them through the book. Rather than spelling out the full path of the directory I will make a reference to the files relative to the `/usr/include` directory, the same way that is done in C source code. For example, when I refer to something like `<sys/proc.h>`, I mean the full path `/usr/include/sys/proc.h`. When you see something enclosed in the angle brackets like this, you can make the expansion yourself.

The `/usr/lib` directory is difficult to explain. Without belittling its significance, I have to say that it's pretty much a dumping ground for things that don't fit elsewhere (didn't I say that about `/etc`?). We could say that it contains the user related library files (based on its name). However, that still does not accurately de-

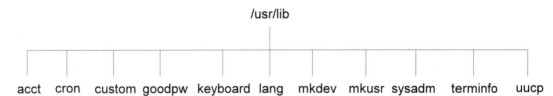

**Figure 2–4**    Subdirectories of `/usr/lib`.

scribe the complete contents. One thing it contains is the library files that are less general than those you find in `/lib`. These include the libraries for cross compilation in DOS and OS/2. Figure 2–4 shows what the subdirectories of `/usr/lib` look like graphically.

A little known aspect of SCO UNIX is that it has built-in (albeit limited) abilities to do system accounting. You can keep track of system resources on the system on a per user basis and charge them for that usage. All the associated files are kept in `/usr/lib/acct`. The name "acct" comes from "accounting."

The `/usr/lib/cron` directory contains the data files that the `cron`, `at`, and `batch` utilities use when running noninteractive jobs. Not only does it contain the commands to be run and the schedule to adhere to, but it also contains configuration information for the jobs as they run. This is also where the access lists for the three utilities are stored.

For a normal user, the `/usr/lib/custom` directory is of little value. It contains information which `custom` uses when installing or removing software packages. In addition, it contains a history file (`/usr/lib/custom/history`) that lists all the software that has been added or removed using the `custom` utility. Here you will also find all the removal scripts for the installed packages.

Every time you run `passwd` to try to change your password, the system determines if your password is "good." "Good" is determined by both the `/etc/default/goodpw` file and the files in `/usr/lib/goodpw`. It is possible through configuring the files in this directory to restrict it far beyond the defaults. For more details see the `goodpw (ADM)` man-page.

The `/usr/lib/keyboard` directory contains files that are used to configure the system console keyboard. Through these files, you can configure your keyboard to accommodate one of several different languages. You can even configure them for dialects of the same language, such as the German keyboard as used in Switzerland or Germany. You can also change these files to create some totally new keyboard layout, such as the Dvorak. For more details see the `keyboard (F)` man-page.

In keeping with the internationalization theme, we next look at the /usr/lib/ lang directory. Here we have the file used to determine language specific things such as the collation sequence, decimal and thousand's separator, or the names of the months and days of the week. For more details on this, look at the locale (C) man-page.

The /usr/lib/mkdev is normally only of interest to system administrators. The name "mkdev" comes from "make device" and the scripts in this directory are used to add devices to your system. Adding devices to the system is done by using the /etc/mkdev utility. The argument passed to it is the name of the device that you want to add, which turns out to be the name of one of the scripts in this directory. The scripts then ask the necessary questions to install that device and may relink the kernel. We'll talk a lot more about adding devices in Chapter 5.

The /usr/lib/mkuser directory is usually never accessed directly. Instead, the files here are used every time you run the system administration shell (sysadmsh in ODT or scoadmin in OpenServer). The files in here are accessed when you add or "make" a user. Along with the information in the /etc/default/authsh file, the system creates user accounts based on the values input in the sysadmsh. We'll talk more about these files in Chapter 4.

The /usr/lib/sysadm directory contains information used by the system administration shell. Here the data files are located that are used to create all the menus as well as other programs that the sysadmsh calls to actually get the work done. Keep in mind that if you are running SCO OpenServer, the sysadmsh has been replaced with scoadmin.

The /usr/lib/terminfo directory contains both the source files and compiled versions of the terminfo database. Terminfo is the mechanism by which the system can work with so many different types of terminals and know which key is being pressed. For more information, see the terminfo (M) man-page.

When configuring UUCP, all the necessary files are contained in the /usr/lib/uucp directory. Not only are the configuration files here, but this is also home for most of the uucp programs. UUCP (UNIX-to-UNIX Copy) is a package that allows you to transfer files and communicate with remote systems using serial lines. We'll talk in more details about this directory in the section on networking.

One directory that I didn't mention above requires special attention: /usr/lib/sh. It contains a single file and that file is a gold mine. Well, it's a gold mine if you are a shell programmer. It contains a dozen shell functions that can be used in many different circumstances. If you are a shell programmer, take a look at this file and you will learn a load of new tricks. I'll talk more about this file and those tricks in the section on shells and shell programming.

Moving back up to the /usr directory, we find the /usr/local subdirectory. This may or may not contain anything. In fact, there are no rules governing its contents. It is designed to contain programs, data files, and other information that is specific to your local system, hence the name. There is often a bin directory that contains local programs and a lib directory that contains data files or libraries used by the programs in /usr/local/bin.

Also in the /usr directory is /usr/man. This is where the man-pages and their respective indices are kept. This directory contains the index files, which you could search through to find a command you are looking for. You can also create and store your own manual pages here.

The /usr/mmdf directory contains all the programs and configuration files for MMDF. MMDF is SCO UNIX's default mail system. We will get into details about MMDF in later chapters. By default, the subdirectories in here are readable by everyone, so you can poke around a little and see what it's all about.

The /usr/spool directory is the place where many different kinds of files are stored temporarily. The word "spool" is an acronym for *s*imultaneous *p*eripheral *o*peration *off-l*ine. This is the process whereby jobs destined for some peripheral (printer, modem, etc.) are queued to be processed later.

There are several subdirectories that are used as holding areas for the applicable programs. For example, the /usr/spool/cron directory contains the data files used by cron and at. The /usr/spool/lp directory not only contains the print jobs as they are waiting to be printed, it also contains the configuration files for the printers.

As you might guess, since MMDF is SCO's primary mail system, the /usr/spool/mmdf directory contains mail messages that are being processed (waiting to be sent). The same thing applies for /usr/spool/uucp. The two directories /usr/spool/uucplogins and /usr/spool/uucppublic are used by UUCP when communicating with other systems via UUCP. We'll talk about these in later chapters.

Lastly is a pair of directories that work together: /opt and /var/opt. Although these directories did exist in ODT 3.0, they were essentially empty. However, these two directories are key components of OpenServer. These directories are used by the Static Storage Objects (SSOs), which I will talk about in a moment.

Okay, so that's about it. There were many directories that I skipped (as I said I would at the beginning of this section). Think about the comparison that I made to a tourist map. We visited all the museums, 200-year-old churches, and fancy restaurants, but I didn't show you where the post office substations were.

Granted that such offices are necessary for a large city, but you really don't care about them when touring the city; just as there are certain directories and files that are not necessary for an appreciation and understanding of the SCO UNIX directory structure.

### What is SCO UNIX Made Of?

There are many aspects of the SCO UNIX operating system that are difficult to put labels on. We can refer to individual programs as either utilities or commands, depending on the extent of their functions. However, it is difficult to label collections of files. Often the labels we do try to place on these collections do not accurately describe the relationship of the files, however, I am going to try.

If you have been working with an SCO system for a while, there are certain aspects of the operating system that you may have heard of, but have not fully understood. In this section we're going to talk about functions that the system performs in some of the programs and files that are associated with these functions. We're also going to talk about how many of the system files are grouped together into what are referred to as "packages" and we will discuss some of the more important packages.

In our tour of the SCO UNIX directory structure, I talked about the `/etc/perms` directory and described it as sort of a packing list. It is in the files of the `/etc/perms` directory that the packages are defined. Each file in `/etc/perms` has a name that reflects its function and the packages it contains. I will go into more detail about the contents of these files in the section on installing your system. However, I need to talk about some of these packages in order to set the stage for many of the topics I will be covering later. How the different components fit together we see in Figure 2–5.

Why is it important to know the names of the different packages? Well, for the average user, it really isn't. However, the average user logs on, starts an application and has very little or no understanding of what lies under the application. The mere fact that you are reading this book says to me that you want to know more about the operating system and how things work together. Since these packages are the building blocks of the operating system (at least in terms of how it exists on the hard disk), knowing about them is an important part of understanding the whole system. First, let's talk about how the packages are broken down in ODT. You can get the names of all the packages by running this command:

```
grep '#!' /etc/perms/*
```

In order to be able to do any work on an SCO UNIX system, you have to first install software. Most people think of installing software as adding a word process-

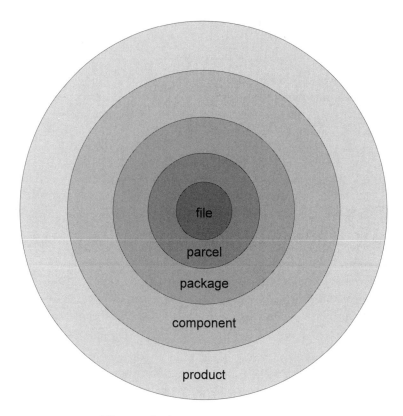

**Figure 2–5**   SCO product units.

ing program or database application, but any program on the operating system needs to be installed at one time or another. Even the operating system itself must be installed.

Earlier, I referred to the SCO UNIX operating system as all the files and programs on the hard disk. For the moment, I want to restrict the definition of "operating system" to just those files that are necessary for "normal" operation. SCO has defined that set of programs and files as the Run-Time System or RTS. Although there are many files in the RTS that can be left out to have a running system, this is the base set that SCO installs.

The list of the files that compose the RTS package are in two files: /etc/perms/rts and /etc/perms/rtsmd. If you examine these files, you see a major separation in functionality. Whereas both contain very basic programs, the /etc/perms/rtsmd contain files and programs that are related to the hardware or the machine itself. These are dependent on the machine, hence the name

`/etc/perms/rtsmd` (RTS *Machine Dependent*). (Note that these files do not change if you have a different machine or architecture, but rather the files are, for the most part, directly related to the hardware.)

Perhaps the next most significant package is the extended utilities, or EXT package. These cover a wide range of areas such as printing, mail, backups, and adding users. Like the RTS, the extended utilities have two files: `/etc/perms/ext` and `/etc/perms/extmd`. Also like the RTS, the file `/etc/perms/extmd` contains machine dependent (machine related) programs and files. The `/etc/perms/rtsmd` file contains only the link kit, which is the collection of files used to create a new kernel. We will talk about the link kit in much more detail later.

SCO has defined a set of files that it considers the base set of extended utilities. This package is called BASE and contains such things as an unlimited precision calculator (`bc`), a calendar (`cal`), and a disk copying program (`diskcp`).

One would be pressed to find an SCO system where users don't print. Printing is one of the more common operations on a system. If one is talking about the act of printing, the files and programs that allow users to print are collectively called the "print spooler." If one is talking about the files and programs themselves, these files are referred to as "the LPR package." This is what we will be talking about here.

Contained within the LPR package are the programs that the system uses to manage the printing process. These include the program that schedules specific print jobs for specific printers: the print scheduler; as well as the programs that actually send the files to the printers. There are, of course, other programs that check the status of the print process, and stop and start the print schedule. We'll be talking in more detail about all of this in the section on printing.

Another commonly used package is MAIL, which contains the files used to communicate between users via electronic mail (what else). This includes the mail program itself and its related programs, but it also contains the MMDF files. Although MMDF, is actually part of the MAIL package, it is often (although incorrectly) referred to as a package of its own.

Saying that the MAIL package contains just the files for communication between users via electronic mail is not entirely true. The MAIL package also contains a few other programs (`write`, `hello`, and `mesg`) that are used to communicate directly between users. This shows how files are sometimes just lumped together in somewhat arbitrary packages. For more information see the respective man-pages.

Similar terminology applies to the UUCP package. It contains more than just UUCP. The UUCP (UNIX-to-UNIX Copy) package can be used in conjunction with mail, but can also be used on its own to transfer files between systems. This package also contains the modem configuration and access files (referred to as "dialers," as they dial the phone). However, the UUCP package contains more than just programs to copy file between systems. There is also the ability to start programs on the remote system (uux), as well as a simple terminal program (cu).

The SYSADM package contains system administration programs. This, however, does not contain the system administration shell, which is considered part of the RTS.

What the SYSADM package does contain is "supplemental" administrative tools. This includes programs like last which reports on the last time a user was logged in, or ncheck, which can be used to find out what file is associated with a particular inode. The package also contains the tunesh or Tune-Shell program.

The BACKUP package, like the SYSADM package, does not contain most of the files that do the actual backup, but rather contains supplemental files, such as those used for scheduling backups. The "real" backup programs, such as tar and cpio are part of the RTS.

There are other packages that are less obvious, such as DOS, which contain programs to access DOS disks; or CSH, which contains the C-shell and its support files.

Is that all? No, on an ODT or OpenServer system with the SCO Development System installed, there are well over a hundred packages. Many are rarely used. Many contain just a few files and are related to a single entity such as the VI package that contains only vi and its related files.

Administering over a hundred packages is a big task. To make things a little simpler, the packages themselves are grouped into larger units called Service Components. These components are then grouped into Services. Whereas the separation of files into packages occurs in the files in /etc/perms, the separation of packages into services and service components happens in the files in /etc/perms/bundle.

Except for the entire Operating System of the RTS, each of these services, service components, and packages can be removed from or installed on the system. The officially supported way to remove these files is by using the custom utility. It is important to use custom to remove the files in a package, service component, or service. If files are removed or installed by hand, inconsistencies can develop, making it impossible to add or remove anything without completely corrupting your system.

The newest shipping SCO operating system, OpenServer, has a redesigned product organization. Some of the changes help in cutting down software piracy, while others were implemented to help in remote distribution of software. In this new organization, there is still the basic concept of a "product." This is the unit of software that you buy such as SCO OpenServer. This unit has its own version number.

Each product is broken down into *components*. This is the largest unit of functionality. TCP/IP cannot be (or rather is not) broken down further for sale. However, it could be sold as a stand-alone product, as it was before. Like products, components have their own version number. Smaller than the component is the *package*. This is the smallest unit of software that can be installed or removed (not counting single files).

**Software Storage Objects—SSO.**   Under OpenServer, the central concept of the new product structure is the *Software Storage Object* (SSO). SCO designed the SSO structure based on its concept of software management, which covers installing, updating, removing, and administering already installed software packages. The files that make up a product can be separated into those that remain unchanged (such as binaries) and those that do change (such as configuration files). Each represents a particular package and since there is one unique SSO for each package, you can have copies of different versions of the same software. Which is used is dependent on the configuration and the connection to the SSO is made through the use of what are called *symbolic links* (more on those later).

Although divided into products and components like ODT, these units take on greater significance in OpenServer in view of the importance of the SSO. It is these components that are the "objects" of the SSO. Because of the design of the SSO architecture, it is even more important that components be more "self-contained" units than in previous releases.

These components are broken down even further, like ODT and previous releases. This is the concept of the package. These packages may contain files or other packages. New to the SSO model is the idea of a *parcel*. This is used for more complex products, when breaking them into components and packages does not provide enough "granularity." Therefore, a parcel is a unit of the product smaller than the package. However, the distinction of a parcel is not as clear cut. The OpenServer Enterprise product contains the Graphics parcel, for example. It is also possible for parcels to cover portions of multiple components. For example, the man-pages and other documentation may be thought of as a parcel.

An SSO is essentially broken down into two parts. There is a part that is shared and other machines have access to it. These are kept under the /opt directory. The other part belongs to one specific client and is not accessed by other machines. These are kept in /var/opt. Here, a client is any machine that uses the SSO, including the local machine.

Files within the SSO have several characteristics. A *shared file* is one that clients can read only. The only copy of a shared file is in the original location within the

/opt directory. Why make copies when they aren't going to get changed anyway? As you might guess, *nonshared files* are ones that can be modified by the client. To keep these separate from the shared files, these files are copied into /var/opt. These files now belong to the client.

*Public files* are visible and accessible outside of the SSO. These are made available to the rest of the world (users and other SSOs) as links. Almost exclusively, these are symbolic links, which have grown to become one of the primary administrative tools in OpenServer. These links make the real location of the file transparent to the system and applications. *Private files* are only visible to that SSO. The relationship between private/public and shared/non-shared is shown in Table 2–1.

This provides a very important advantage. Let's first consider files that are not modified by the clients, that is, the shared files. These generally consist of the programs (versus data or configuration files) belonging to a particular package. Every client with a particular version of a package will be using the same programs and utilities. The nonshared files are the data and configuration files. These are the aspects of that package that are applicable only to that particular client. Why should other clients have access or even care what is in these files?

By keeping these two separate, all you need to do when updating a package is to update the program portion and leave the data portion alone. This essentially eliminates problems with updating packages; configuration files would often get overwritten during the update. Since only the program files are getting updated, there is less fear of overwriting the data files.

This is one reason why things are done with symbolic links. Like a regular link, a symbolic link is just another name for a given file. However, symbolic links do not need to point to anything "real." It is not until the file is accessed that something needs to be there. We can then overwrite the real file, without the symbolic link being affected. In addition, this scheme allows us to backup the data components without having to backup the program files.

We now have an idea of how everything works. Now let's take a look at where everything is. To find the actual files, you need to dig deep. To help, let's

**Table 2–1**   Relationship of Static Storage Object Properties

|         | Shared | Nonshared |
|---------|--------|-----------|
| Private | Reside in /opt. Not linked to an external directory. | Copied to /var/opt on each client. Not linked to an external directory. |
| Public | Reside in /opt. Linked to an external directory. | Copied to /var/opt on each client and linked to an external directory. |

take a look at a road map. The program files for a particular component are found in

`/opt/K/VendorCode/ComponentCode/ComponentVersion`.

The data files are found in

`/var/opt/K/VendorCode/ComponentCode/ComponentVersion`.

This directory is called a component's *SSO root*. For example, the SSO root for the SCO Operating System, version 5.0.0d, is /opt/K/SCO/UNIX/5.0.0d.

So, what's with the *K* and *P*? Well, the single letters were chosen in order to keep the names as short as possible. Second, *P* refers to both products and packages. As for the K, well that stands for component. Originally, this was a C, which was often confused with the C programming language. Instead they used K. Urban legend has it that one of the members of the SCO SSO development team is Norwegian and "Komponent" is the Norwegian spelling of "component."

In order to allow different vendors to use the same component name without conflicts, the *vendor code* defines a unique vendor. In this case, the vendor code is *SCO* as we are referring to SCO products. The *component code* is used to uniquely identify a component. The *version number is*, as one might guess, the version of that particular component. By including version numbers in this scheme, it is possible for different versions of the same component to exist.

### SCO UNIX Capabilities

On any operating system there is a core set of tasks that are performed. On multi-user or server systems such as SCO UNIX, these tasks include adding and configuring printers, adding and administering users, and adding new hardware to the system. Each of these tasks could take up an entire chapter in this book. In fact, I do cover all of these, and many others, in a fair bit of detail later on.

I think it's important to briefly cover all of the basic tasks that an administrator needs to perform in one place. There are a couple of reasons for this. First, many administrators of SCO UNIX systems are not only novice administrators, they are novice users. Usually, they get into the position because they are the only ones in the company or department with computer experience (they've worked with DOS before). By introducing the varied aspects of system administration here, I hope to lay the foundation for later chapters. I first tell you that a car has a motor, brakes, a steering wheel and a transmission. Then, I tell you how each works.

Second, the average user may not want to get into the details that the later chapters provide. So here, I give an overview of the more important components. Hopefully, this will give you a better understanding of what goes into an operating system as well as just how complex the job is that your system administrator does.

One of the first things that gets done is that users are added to the system. Access is gained to the system only through user accounts. Although it may be all that a normal user is aware of, these accounts consist of substantially more than just a name and password. Each user must also be assigned one of the shells, a home directory, and a set of privileges in order to access system resources.

Although the system administrator could create a single user account for all users to log in as, this ends up creating more problems than it solves. Each user has their own password and home directory. If there was a single user, everyone's files would be stored in the same place and everyone would have access to everyone else's data. This may be fine in certain circumstances, but not in most.

Users are normally added to the system through the system administration shell (sysadmsh in ODT ) or the Account Manager portion of scoadmin in OpenServer. Here, when adding a user, you can input that user's default shell, their home directory, as well as their access privileges. Should you need to change any of that for a particular user, you can do this through the sysadmsh/SCOAdmin. In addition, they are also used to "retire" or remove a user.

One of the key aspects of a user account on an SCO UNIX system is the concept of privileges. Starting with SCO UNIX 3.2.4.0, there are four levels of security that, among other things, specifies the range of tasks the user is authorized to do. The higher the security level, the less a user can do by default. If the security level does not allow access to a particular function by default and the user must have access, the system administrator has the ability to change this through the sysadmsh or the Account Manager.

Another very common function is the addition and configuration of system printers. This includes determining what physical connection the printer has to the system, what characteristics the printer has (in order to choose the appropriate model printer) as well as making the printer available for printing.

Adding a printer is accomplished in three ways. As you would guess, the first is through the system administration shell. The second is by running the command /usr/lib/sysadm/lpsh or mkdev lp on ODT 3.0 or running the Printer Manager or mkdev lp on OpenServer. Why so many different ways? Well, both lpsh and mkdev lp are the same under ODT 3.0 and mkdev lp and the Printer Manager are the same on OpenServer. The program that is called in the end is the same one every time. It is simply to make things easier for administrators who may have come from older systems without the new front-ends.

What happens when you want to remove a file and inadvertently end up removing the wrong one (or maybe all of them)? If you are like me with my first computer, you're in big trouble. The files are gone, never to show their faces again. I learned the hard way about the need to do backups. If you have a good system

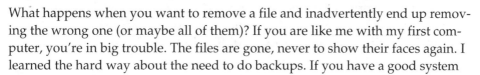

administrator, he or she either has probably already learned the lesson and makes regular backups of your system.

There are several ways of making backups and several different utilities for doing them. Which program to use and how often to make backups is completely dependent on the circumstances. The system administrator needs to take into account things like how much data needs to get backed up, how often the data is changed, how much can be lost, and even how much will fit on the backup media.

Using the *versioning* capabilities of SCO OpenServer, even the hassle of restoring from backups has been eliminated. With versioning turned on, you can undelete files that you have removed as well as automatically save multiple copies (versions) of files.

There are things that an administrator may need to accomplish at regular intervals such as making backups, cleaning up temporary directories, or calling up remote sites to check for incoming mail. One of the basic utilities in every UNIX version is cron. Cron (the 'o' is short) is a program that sits in the background and waits for specific times. When these times are reached, it starts predefined programs to accomplish various, arbitrarily defined tasks. These tasks can be set to run at intervals ranging from once a minute to once a year, depending on the needs of the system administrator.

Cron "jobs" (as they are called) are grouped together into files, called *cron tables* or *crontabs*, for short. There are several that are created by default on your system and many users and even system administrators can go quite a long time before they notice them. Crontabs monitor certain aspects of system activity, clean up temporary files, and even check to see if you have UUCP jobs that need to be sent.

What about a program that you only want to run one time at a specific time and then never again? SCO UNIX provides a mechanism for this: at. Like cron, at will run a job at a specific time, but once it has completed, the job will never be run again.

There is a third command that relates to cron and at. This is the batch command. This differs from the other two in the fact that batch gets around to running the job you submit, whenever it has time; that is, when the system load permits.

### What Goes with SCO UNIX?

Throughout this book, we are going to be talking a great deal about what makes up the SCO UNIX operating system. Up until the newest release it could be purchased as a single product under the name SCO UNIX System V/386 Release 3.2 Operating System Version 4.2. This product contains, the run-time system and the extended utilities (including UUCP, MMDF, LPR, etc).

For many companies or businesses, that's enough. You may have a single computer with several serial terminals attached, running a word processor, database, or some other application. However, when a single computer is not enough, the SCO UNIX product does not provide everything that you need.

Suppose you want to be able to connect all the computers in your company into a computer network. The base SCO UNIX product does provide them with a certain networking capability with UUCP. However, this is limited to exchanging files, remotely executing programs, and simple terminal emulation. However, for the most part, this is limited to serial lines and the speed at which data can be transferred is also limited.

So it was in dark recesses of ancient computer history. Today, products exist that allow simultaneous connection between multiple machines with substantially higher performance. One such product is SCO's TCP/IP (Transmission Control Protocol/Internet Protocol). So, if a company decides it needs an efficient network it might decide to install TCP/IP, which has become the industry standard for connecting not only UNIX Systems, but other systems as well.

The SCO TCP/IP Runtime System allows users to log into remote systems, transfer files, use printers anywhere on the network, as well as send and receive electronic mail. Plus, the group of protocols that composes TCP/IP serves as the bases for many other programs and products.

There is a problem with TCP/IP that many companies run into. Suppose you want everyone in the company to be able to access a specific set of files. With TCP/IP you could devise a scheme that copies the files from a central machine to the others. However, if the files need to be changed, you need to ensure that the updated files are copied back to your source machine. This is not only prone to errors, but it is also inefficient.

Instead, why not have a single location where the source files themselves can be edited? This way, changes made to a file are immediately available to everyone. The problem is that TCP/IP by itself has nothing built in to allow you to share files. You need a way to make a directory (or set of directories) on a remote machine *appear* as if it was local to your machine.

Like many operating system vendors, SCO provides an answer: NFS (Network File System). With NFS, directories or even entire filesystems can appear as if they are local. One central computer can have the files physically on its hard disk and make them available via NFS to the rest of the network.

Soon you discovered the wonders of a graphical user interface (GUI). Maybe at home you use Microsoft Windows or have a Macintosh and are used to being able to point and click or having multiple sessions or terminals on the screen at the same time. SCO provides a solution in the form of X Windows. This was available separately as the X-Sight product. However, the new OpenServer has X bundled with every version of it.

If you just switched to SCO UNIX, you still have quite a few DOS applications that you probably can't live without. Rather than making you junk all of your DOS applications, SCO provides a solution: SCO Merge.

SCO Merge actually runs MS-DOS 5.0 in ODT and 6.2 in OpenServer. Each of these is licensed directly from Microsoft. Merge can support most character-based MS-DOS applications on terminals or the system console, as well as graphical MS-DOS applications on the system console or X11 graphics terminals. Since it behaves like a real MS-DOS machine, SCO Merge provides access to thousands of MS-DOS applications, even many that bypass MS-DOS and access the hardware directly.

The only limitation is that since it is a software emulation, SCO Merge cannot run programs in 386 protected (enhanced) mode. This includes running MS-Windows in enhanced mode. However, this isn't a problem as you can run it under Merge in standard mode just fine. In fact, you can start SCO Merge from within X Windows and then start MS-Windows. You end up with windows within windows.

Okay, you bought the operating system. Soon you discovered that was not enough, so you got TCP/IP and then NFS. A short time later, you wanted the best of both worlds so you got X Windows and SCO Merge. Each time you had to lay out several hundred dollars.

After running for a few months, you discovered that SCO offers all of these products together in a package called Open Desktop. You're annoyed that you had to install everything individually, and when you see how much you could have saved by buying everything at once in the form of Open Desktop, you get angry.

Phone calls to your distributor and then to SCO have little effect. You bought separate products, each with their own price, so it only makes sense that you pay the price for separate products; just as power steering costs more when you get it installed after you have the car than it would if it came equipped with it.

You got penalized for not considering all the options when you first purchased your system. That's the nature of the business. That's the nature of any business. If you buy more at once, it usually comes out being cheaper. At least that was the way it was originally.

Well, SCO thought this type of policy was wrong. By "forcing" you to buy something you may not need just because you can get it cheaper is great for business, but only for short term business. It looks good on paper, but when your customers never come back because your "hard sell" put them off, you lose in the long run. SCO came up with a way of allowing you to ergonomically let your system grow as your needs change.

When you purchase the SCO UNIX operating system on tape or CD-ROM, the media already comes with the other products. If you purchase one set of products and later discover you need more, you can easily purchase the missing components for only the difference between the product you have and the product you want. You don't pay for what the products would cost separately.

One company might only need the networking capabilities so there is no need to by X Windows or SCO Merge. So, SCO created the "Network Bundle" that contains only the network products such as TCP/IP and NFS. Perhaps a user needs a workstation capable of running X Windows across a network. The solution is ODT Lite, which contains only X Windows and TCP/IP. If you decide that you need everything including the kitchen sink, there is the SCO OpenServer Enterprise System (including your choice of Captain Kirk or Picard). With the right kind of trickery you could pull off the components that you want but didn't pay for. However, there are some problems with this. First, it would be software piracy. It would be the same as if you copied software from someone else. You would be using software that you didn't pay for.

Second, you won't get support for it. SCO can tell what product was purchased and what components that product has. Suppose you bought the Network Bundle and figured out a way to extract the files to make it the OpenServer. If you call into SCO Support for help, they will know what is going on.

Finally, the serial number and activation key are matched to the product you have. If you purchase the Network Bundle and try to install X Windows, for example, you can't. The serial number and activation key you have won't work with X Windows. Also if you try to use that same serial number on a machine that just has the operating system, in an effort to get TCP/IP, that won't work either.

SCO's newest product line can be broken down into three separate products. Although the base operating system is the same in each case, the components each has is based on the intended purpose. The Host System product is intended for "turnkey" solutions as well as other situations were networking is not required. An example of this would be a point-of-sales system. Despite the lack of networking, the Host System contains full X Windows capabilities.

Next is the Desktop System. As its name implies, this system is intended to sit on your desktop and is designed as a single-user workstation. It does contain full networking and graphical support. One added feature of SCO OpenServer is their new Desktop filesystem. Here, a compressed filesystem allows up to 1 Terabyte (a Mega-Megabyte) of data!

At the top of the line is the Enterprise System. Due to the recent and long over-due demise of his predecessor, this version of the Enterprise System only comes in the Picard version. (Okay, the joke's getting old.) This is a superset of the tools and functionality of the Host System. In addition, it has built-in networking in the form of TCP/IP, NFS, IPX/SPX, Netware Gateway, as well as LAN Manager Client support. The Enterprise System also enables you to do network installs. This means the actual files used for an installation exist on a server on your net-work and are copied to the machine you are installing on.

A major change since ODT 3.0 is the distribution media. For those of you who still only have a 5.25" floppy, you are out of luck. None of the new SCO products are available on 5.25". In fact, the only one that is available even on 3.5" floppies is the Host System. Although you do get a single 3.5" to boot from, both the Desktop System and the Enterprise System are available only on CD-ROM or 150MB cartridge tape. Earlier releases fit on 60Mb cartridge tape. However, even with compressing things, the operating system no longer fits on the 60Mb tapes.

SCO has also decided to reduce the number of printed manuals that come with the system. Each product will be shipped with *Release Notes* and the *SCO OpenServer Handbook*. However, the remainder of the documentation is shipped on-line. This is all written in the Hypertext Markup Language (HTML). Hyper-text is the concept whereby you click on many of the words and phrases, which then jumps you to other parts of the documentation or even other documents.

The basic format of the on-line documentation reader is the same as MOSAIC, which many net surfers are familiar with. This provides not only a history mech-anism, but allows you to define "bookmarks" that you can use to immediately jump to places that you access regularly. The only major shortcoming is its searching abilities. As of this writing you are limited to single word searches, so you need to be careful with what you search for. We'll talk more about the docu-mentation reader in the section on SCO documentation.

If, like me, you find that you cannot live without hardcopy documentation, most of the on-line documentation is available in printed format in two sets. The first set contains the *Operating System User's Guide* and the *System Administrator's Guide*. The second set contains the man-pages.

Another major change that I find particularly neat is the fact that many add-on products are included on your distribution media. This includes SCO Symmetri-cal Multiprocessing (SMP—the successor to MPX), SCO Virtual Disk Manager, SCO Merge, SCO Windows Application Binary Interface (Wabi), and the SCO OpenServer Development System. Some, like SCO Wabi and the SCO Develop-ment System, contain additional on-line documentation.

At first this seemed odd to me. Without even asking for it, let alone paying for it, SCO provides you the software for all sorts of wonderful tools. They will even allow you to install it. However, having it run is a different matter. This is all accomplished by the SCO License Server.

The SCO License Server is a set of programs that runs on your system and "allows" other programs to run. Each system has a license database that allows licensed (purchased) products to run. All the licenses are all contained in a database. When a program starts, it first checks the license server to see if it is licensed. If so, all is well. If the product is not licensed, the system will tell you and won't allow you to run. A single license server can manage multiple machines, thereby allowing licenses to be used where needed and not restricted to single machines.

Each product has a License Number, which is a unique number identifying each SCO product. There is a License Code, which is used to activate the product. The third piece of information provided with your license is your License Data. This is not always present on the Certificate of License and Authenticity and is, therefore, not required in those cases.

I think the License Server is something that could have been left out. However, the marketing people have a very strong voice in any company the size of SCO. As a result, you are now required to register your product within a predefined grace period. If you don't, you get annoying messages when you login that says the software is unregistered.

As the system boots, you will get a message saying that you have to register and that the reason is to prevent software piracy and to keep you informed on updates. Although, you are not actually forced to register, if you don't, "reminders" will continue to appear at system start-up and even after you have logged in. Generically this is referred to as "nag-ware."

When your system is installed, a SCO System ID is generated. This is a unique number, specific to your machine, that is used to identify your SCO OpenServer installation. Since it is generated each time your system is installed, a new SCO System ID is generated if you reinstall your SCO OpenServer system. You can find out your system ID by running the License Manager.

When you register, the Registration Center will issue you a Registration Key for each product. Another very annoying feature is that The Registration Key is tied to the SCO System ID and therefore you must re-register your SCO products if you reinstall your SCO OpenServer system.

## Reading All About It—SCO Documentation

Software documentation is a very hot subject. It continues to be debated in all sorts of forums from CompuServe to user groups. Unless the product is very intuitive, improperly documented software can be almost worthless to use. Even if intuitive to use, many functions are hidden unless you have decent documentation. Unfortunately for many, UNIX is not very intuitive. Therefore, good documentation is essential to be able to use SCO UNIX to its fullest extent.

Despite what many customers may believe, SCO provides good documentation. Well over half of all the calls to Support can be avoided by following the step-by-step procedures in the appropriate section or sections in the manual. A large part of the remainder of problems can be avoided by not just following the steps, but by understanding what is being done and not just blindly following instructions.

Unfortunately, few administrators and very few users take the time to read the manuals. This is not good, for two important reasons. The first is obviously the wasted time spent calling support for help on things that are expained in the manual. The second is that you miss many of the powerful features of the various programs. When you call to support, you usually get a quick and simple answer. Tech support does not have the time to train you on how to use a particular program. Two weeks later when you try to do something else with the same program, you're on the phone again.

The biggest problem is that people see the stack of manuals that come with a SCO UNIX system and are immediately intimidated. They would rather spend the money to have support explain things rather than spend time "wading" through all the documentation. Some customers do that and they pay a price. Most companies cannot afford the thousands of dollars needed to get that kind of service.

The nice thing is that you don't have to. You neither have to wade through the manuals nor spend the money to have support hold your hand. The SCO manuals are like most books; they have a table of contents, chapters that are logically grouped, and at the end of almost every manual is an index. In SCO OpenServer the manuals are on-line. This makes searching that much easier. In fact, you can search every manual at once, if you like. You can even bounce between difference places, using what are called "hypertext links."

Since knowing where to look is the biggest problem, that's the issue we are going to address. I don't need to teach you how to read, or understand a table of contents, or how to interpret an index entry. However, by making you more familiar with how the documentation is laid out and where to look, you have a much better chance of finding out the answers on your own.

There is no law that says to list a directory the command that you *must* use is `ls` or the way to add a user *has* to be added through the `sysadmsh` or SCOAdmin. These are merely conventions that SCO has adopted. If you are new to this environment, then many of the commands and utilities seem very obscure to you. In order to be able to fully utilize them, you need to know what they do. Often, the reverse is true as well. The user (or administrator) knows there is a tool on the system to do a certain thing, but doesn't know where it is.

This is where good documentation comes in. By looking at the appropriate manual, you can quickly find what you are looking for. As those of us who have been in the business for a while know, this is easier said than done. SCO Documentation provides a wealth of information. Almost any task that you need to get accomplished is possible through reading the documentation. Often, documentation is not effectively used because the user or administrator isn't sure where the information he or she wants is located.

There are two major groups of documentation in SCO systems. The first group is the "guides." These include the *System Administrator's Guide* and *User's Guide*, which give step-by-step, often very detailed instructions on procedures and activities on the system. In the table of contents, each section heading is listed along with its page number. A quick glance through the table of contents can quickly point you to the right place. If that doesn't work, there is an extensive index.

The *User's Guide* is user oriented, although a beginning administrator would find the information here to be very useful. The *User's Guide* provides explanations of the various shells and file manipulation programs such as `vi`, `sed`, and `awk`. There are also chapters on communication with other users with mail or other sites using UUCP.

For the administrator, there is a *System Administrator's Guide*. Although it contains many of the same subjects, such as mail and UUCP, these are from the administrative perspective. They describe how to set up and configure these programs and services. In most cases, they provide step-by-step instructions for basic installation and configuration. If that is not sufficient, there is enough supplemental information for you to understand how things are configured and interact to enable you to configure your system far beyond the basics.

Supplemental to the guides are the "references." These include the *System Administrator's Reference* and the *User's Reference*. Since these are simply descriptions of various commands and utilities, often limited to a few pages, they are commonly referred to as manual pages or man-pages for short. In many places, including this book, you are encouraged to read the man-page for a particular command. This is what we are talking about when we tell you to read the man-page.

Unfortunately, the breakdown of commands listed in the man-pages is not as clear cut as is described in the *Administrator's* or *User's Guide*. Often, commands that serve administrative functions are listed in the *User's Reference* or commands that users need are listed in the *Administrator's Reference*.

The nice thing is that you usually don't have to know whether a particular command is considered to be an administrator's command or a user command. The system will tell you. Unless they have been removed or intentionally not installed, man-pages exist on-line on your system. They are part of the base installation and must either be explicitly removed or intentionally not installed.

Built into the system is a command to read these man-pages: man. By typing man <command> you can find out many details about the command <command>. There are several different options to man that you learn about by typing man  man, which will bring up the man man-page (or the man-page for man).

Often, there are entries in multiple sections. For example, in the C section (where the commands are found) there is an lp entry that explains the various options to the lp command. Additionally, there is an lp man-page in the HW (hardware) section that describes the various parallel port possibilities. There is a man-page for tar in the C section that talks about how to use the tar command. In the F (file format) section, there is a man-page for tar that describes the format of a tar archive. At the front of both the *User's Reference* and *Administrator's Reference* is an alphabetical list of all the commands found in that book, along with a brief description of their function.

With OpenServer things are even different still. The only document that is delivered is the *SCO OpenServer Handbook*. This is comparable to the *Release Notes* and *Installation Guide* in previous releases. If you want hard copies of the other documentation you need to order it. Keep in mind that all the documentation is already on-line.

Should you have Open Desktop installed or one of the extension products, there are additional man-page for these products. If the SCO Development System is installed, there are also several different man-page categories available. Also, SCO ODT comes with additional documentation such as the *Graphical Environment Administrator's Guide* which contains information about customizing and administering the graphical portion of ODT.

You will see in SCO Documentation, when referring to a particular command, the name followed by a letter in parenthesis, such as ls(C). This indicates that the ls command can be found in the C section of the man-pages. By including the section, you can more quickly find what you are looking for. I will be making reference to files as examples. I will not be adhering to that practice. I will only say what section they are in when I explicitly point you toward the man-page.

One very useful aspect of the man-pages is their reference to other man-pages. At the bottom of many of the man-pages is a "See Also" section. This points to man-pages that are related in some way. The reference might be to a command with similar functionality; the rm (remove) command has a reference to the rmdir (remove directory) command. In other cases, the reference is to the same heading in a different section; the tar(C) man-pages refers you to the tar(F) man-page.

The references and guides that I talked about are not all there is to SCO documentation. There are several other books that are supplied with your product that contain different pieces of information. Some of it can only be found in these books, while other pieces are overviews and reviews of what appears elsewhere.

One common piece of documentation that is overlooked is the *Release Notes*. The people that most often overlook the *Release Notes* are those that have either been with SCO for some time or are familiar with other UNIX dialects. Their attitude is that they "know it all" or at least they know everything of importance and the manuals cannot tell them anything new. This is not an exaggeration. On many occasions I received calls from customers saying that they, "know how to do an SCO install." When they run into problems they call support, only to find the solution in the *Release Notes*.

Of all the books that can prove them wrong, the *Release Notes* is the most significant. One of the key things that the *Release Notes* talks about is the difference between previous releases and the current one. (Get it? They are notes about this release.)

I lost track of all the customers who called in saying that there was a bug in the new version (SCO UNIX 3.2. version 4.0 and later) because it didn't recognize their parallel or serial port. In that the freshly installed or upgraded system did not recognize these ports, they were 100% accurate. Where they were off target was in the fact that it wasn't a bug. The *Release Notes* clearly state that this is the case.

The reason that these drivers are intentionally left out is an issue of space. With the release of SCO UNIX 3.2. version 4.0, there was a substantial increase in the number of devices that it supported. Many of them, such as SCSI host adapters, needed to be recognized during the installation. To be able to do this they needed to be included in the kernel on the installation disks. As a result, the kernel became too large to fit on a floppy, so something had to go. What else make sense other than something that is not absolutely needed during installation such as serial or parallel ports?

In the *Release Notes* there is a list of all the documentation that comes with the product. Here the *Release Notes* are described as, "crucial information for Open Desktop installation and configuration." In many cases this is true. For example, if you have only SCSI hard disks in your system you must tell the system CMOS that there are *no* hard disks. If you don't, the hardware will be looking for an IDE or ESDI hard disk and you'll never be able to install. (This is *crucial* because if you don't do it right, you can't boot.)

Another piece of documentation that is ignored and contains a wealth of information is the *Installation and Update Guide* or the *SCO OpenServer Handbook*. Often, the user's have the attitude that this can't tell them anything new. This is more likely to be true for someone who has been working with SCO for a long time. However, if this is the first time you are working with a particular release, there will definitely be something here that's new.

This book is especially important to people who are new to SCO. Countless customers will call support saying that after installation, they are missing half of their hard disk. I have even dealt with people on CompuServe who claim the same problem. Within a minute on the phone, or by reading the CompuServe message, I know that, no, the space is not missing, they just didn't read the *Installation and Update Guide*. If they had, they would have known that the "missing" hard disk space is now part of a /u you filesystem and they have to tell the system to go look at it.

If the customer does take up support on this offer (or they already have a support contract) they then get to talk to support analysts. When they are told that this is clearly documented, the reaction is often that they don't have time to read *all* the manuals. Well, they aren't expected to, just the one relevant to the task at hand: installation. The ironic part is that they have the time to call up support and wait to talk to a support engineer, but don't have the time to look for things in the manual.

Accompanying the *Release Notes and Installation Guide* is the *Hardware Configuration Guide*. This gives a lot of hardware-specific information that can help during installation. In addition, this is a very useful piece of documentation when you decide to add hardware to an existing system. Information about supported hardware is also available from SCO sales *before* you buy your system.

Once the system is installed, a good place to start reading is the Tutorial. If you are new to SCO, or UNIX in general, this gives a quick overview of the system. Even if you are an experienced SCO user, you might learn a few tricks.

The documentation provided in SCO OpenServer took a giant leap forward. Unless you specifically request hardcopy versions, then the majority of SCO documentation only comes in its on-line version. At first, I was bothered by this, as I like having the doc in front of me. However, the only documentation that you *really* need to have in hardcopy format is the *Release Notes* and *Installation Guide*, and that's what you get.

The fundamental structure of `scohelp` is the same as the MOSAIC interface developed by the National Center for Supercomputing Applications (NCSA) that many people use for their World Wide Web browser. As with the WWW browser, documents, images, and other items are connected via "hypertext" links. Because if this similar and the use of the http daemon, `scohelp` can also provide file across the network.

Each of the hundreds of files composing the SCO Documentation Library is conceptually the same as pages and form what are referred to as "virtual" books. These books are what we normally think of as documentation, such as the *Administrator's Guide*.

The files themselves are written in the hypertext markup language (HTML), which can be used to link not only text but graphics and even photographic images to documents. A document may contain a reference to a particular image, which appears automatically on the screen with the page that is displayed. There may also be highlighted lines or text that when you click on them you are brought to a different document. These are called "hypertext links."

Hypertext links do not have to point to images. They can also point to other documents, as well. Using this technique you can move between different areas of the documentation, reviewing related topics and then returning to your starting point. Because the documentation is composed of individual files that are connected via these hypertext links, changes can be made to individual pages without having to redo the entire document. When updates or patches are installed, new or corrected pages can be installed into the SCO Documentation Library without anyone noticing. Because of the way the links are defined, someone could be currently using `scohelp` and, provided he or she is not using that exact page, the changes would be in effect when they move to that page.

Also built into `scohelp` is the ability to define "book marks." These are pages (documents) that you have called-up and want to remember. Like a real bookmark, these mark your place within a particular book, allowing you to jump back to that exact page at the click of a button. Although very limited in ability, `scohelp` does provide a search mechanism.

## What's Next?

After two chapters we know what an operating system does and what goes into making the SCO UNIX product. With the understanding of how things interact and what components are available, we can now start thinking about what the system can do for us. We are now ready to begin working with the system to see just what we need to do to get the system to work for us.

# CHAPTER

# 3

# Shells
# and Basic
# Utilities

**M**ost UNIX users are familiar with "the shell." This is where you input commands and get output on your screen. Often, the only contact users have with the shell is logging in and immediately starting some application. Some administrators, however, have modified the system to the point where users may never even see the shell, or in extreme cases have eliminated the shell completely for the users.

If you never get to the point where you can actually input commands and see their output, then this chapter may be a waste of time. If your only interaction with the operating system is logging in, then most of this entire book can only serve to satisfy your curiosity. However, if you are like most users, understanding the basic workings of the shell will do wonders to improve your ability to use the system to its fullest extent.

Up to this point, we have referred to the shell as an abstract entity. In fact, that's the way it is often referred to, as there are many different shells that you can use. Each has its own characteristics (or even quirks), but all behave in the same general fashion. Since the basic concepts are the same, I will avoid talking about specific shells until later.

In this chapter, we are going to cover the basic aspects of the shell. We'll talk about issue commands and how the system responds. Along with that, we'll cover how commands can be made to interact with each other to provide you with the ability to make your own commands. We'll also talk about the different kinds of shells, what each has to offer, and some details of how particular shells behave.

## Talking to SCO UNIX: The Shell

As I mentioned in Chapter 1, the shell is essentially the users' interface to the operating system. The shell is a Command Line Interpreter. Through it, you issue commands that are interpreted by the system which carry out certain actions. Often the state where the system is sitting at a prompt, waiting for you to type input, is referred to (among other things) as being at the shell prompt or at the command line.

For many years before the invention of graphic user interfaces such as X Windows, the only way to input commands to the operating system was through a command line interpreter, or shell. In fact, shells themselves were thought of as wondrous things during the early days of computers, since prior to them, users had no direct way to interact with the operating system.

Most shells, be it under DOS, UNIX, VMS, or other operating systems, have the same input characteristics. In order to get the operating system to do anything, you have to give it a command. Some commands, such as the `date` command under UNIX, do not require anything else to get them to work. If you type in `date` and press return, that's what appears on your screen: the date.

Some commands need something else to get them to work. This is called an *argument*. Some commands, like `mkdir` (used to create directories) can work with only one argument: as in `mkdir directory_name`. Others, like `cp` (to copy files) require multiple arguments: as in `cp file1 file2`.

In many cases, you can pass flags to commands to change their behavior. These flags are generally referred to as *options*. For example, if you wanted to create a series of subdirectories without creating every one individually, you could run `mkdir` with the `-p` option like this:

`mkdir -p one/two/three/four`.

In principle, anything added to the command line after the command itself is an argument to that command. Using the terminology discussed, some arguments are optional and some options are required. The convention is that an option changes the behavior, whereas an argument is acted upon by the command. Generally, options are preceded by a dash (-), whereas arguments are not. I've said it before and I will say it again, nothing is certain when it comes to UNIX. By realizing that these two terms are often interchanged, you won't get confused when you come across one or the other. I will continue to use *option* to reflect something that changes the command's behavior and *argument* to indicate something that is acted upon.

Each program or utility has its own set of arguments and options, so you will have to look at the manual pages or *man-pages* for the individual commands. You can call this up from the command line by typing in

```
man <command_name>
```

where `<command_name>` is the name of the command you want information about. Also, if you are not sure what the command is, OpenServer has the `whatis` command that will give you a brief description.

Many commands require that the option appear immediately after the command and before any arguments. Others have options and arguments interspersed. Again, look at the man-page for the specifics of a particular command.

If you need a quick reminder what a command does, you can use the `whatis` command. This gives you a one line description of the command. For more details see the `whatis(C)` man-page.

Often you just need a quick reminder as to what the available options are and what their syntax is. Rather than going through the hassle of calling up the man-page, a quick way is to get the command to give you a *usage message*. As its name implies, a usage message reports the usage of a particular command. I normally use `-?` as the option to force the usage message as I cannot think of a command where `-?` is a valid option.

### The Search Path

It may happen that you know there is a program by a particular name on the system, but when you try to start it from the command line, you are told that the file is not found. Since you just ran it yesterday, you assume the file has gotten removed or you don't remember the spelling.

The most common reason for this is that the program you want to start is not in your search path. Your search path is a predefined set of directories in which the system looks for the program you type in from the command line (or is started by some other command). This saves time since the system does not have to look through every directory trying to find the program. Unfortunately, if the program is not in one of the directories specified in your path, the system cannot start the program unless you explicitly tell it where to look. To do this you would have to specify either the full path of the command or a path relative to where you are currently located.

Let's look at this issue for a minute. Think back to our discussion of files and directories. I mentioned that every file on the system can be referred to by a unique combination of path and file name. This applies to executable programs as well. By inputting the complete path, you can run any program, whether it is in your path or not.

Let's take a program that is in everyone's path like `date` (at least it should be). The `date` program resides in the `/bin` directory, so its full path is `/bin/date`. If you wanted to run it, you could type in /bin/date, press enter, and you might get something that looks like this:

```
Sat Jan 28 16:51:36 PST 1995
```

However, since date is in your search path, you need only input its name, without the path, to get it to run.

You could also start a program by referencing it through a *relative path*. This is simply the path in relation to your current working directory. In order to understand the syntax of relative paths we need to backtrack a moment. As I mentioned, you can refer to any file or directory by specifying the path to that directory. Since they have special significance, there is a way of referring to either your *current directory* or its *parent directory*. The current directory is referenced by '.' and it's parent by '..' (often referred to in conversation as 'dot' and 'dot-dot').

Since directories are separated from files and other directories by a /, a file in the current directory could be referenced as ./file_name, and a file in the parent directory would be referenced as ../file_name. You can reference the parent of the parent by just tacking on another ../, and then continue on to the root directory if you want. So the file ../../file_name is in a directory two levels up from your current directory. This slash (/) is referred to as a *forward-slash* as compared to a *back- slash* (\) which is used in DOS to separate path components.

When interpreting your command line, shell interprets everything up to the first / as a directory name. Assume that we were in the root (upper-most) directory. We could access date in one of several ways. The first two, date and /bin/date, we already know about. Using the fact that ./ refers to the current directory means we could also get to it like this: ./bin/date. This is saying, relative to our current directory (./) to look in the bin subdirectory for the command date. If we were in the /bin directory, we could start the 'date' command like this: ./date. This is useful when the command you want to execute is in your current directory, but the directory is not in your path.

We can also get the same results from the root directory by starting the command like this: bin/date. If there is a ./ at the beginning, it knows that everything is relative to the current directory. If all that's there is a /, the system knows that everything is relative to the root directory. If no slash is at the beginning, the system searches until it gets to the end of the command or encounters a slash, whichever comes *first*. If there is a / there (like in our example) it translates this to be a subdirectory of the current one. So executing the command bin/date is translated the same as ./bin/date.

Let's now assume that we were in our home directory, /usr/jimmo (for example). We could obviously access the date command simply as date since it's in our path. However, to access it by a relative path, we could say `../../bin/date`. The first `../` moves up one level into `/usr`. The second `../` moves us up another level to `/`. From there we look in the subdirectory `bin` for the command `date`. Keep in mind that throughout this whole process, our current directory does not change. We are still in `/usr/jimmo`.

Searching your path is only done for commands. If we were to enter `vi` (`vi` is a text editor) `file_name` and there was no file called `file_name` in our current directory, `vi` would start editing a new file. If we had a subdirectory called `text` where `file_name` was, we would have to access either as `vi ./text/file_name` or `vi text/file_name`. Of course, we could access it with the absolute path of `vi /usr/jimmo/text/file_name`.

One problem that regularly crops up for users coming from a DOS environment is that the *only* place UNIX looks for commands is in your path. However, even if not specified in your path, the first place DOS looks is your current directory. This is not so for UNIX. UNIX only looks in your path.

For most users this is not a problem, as the current directory is included in your path by default. Therefore, the shell will still be able to execute something in your current directory. Root does not have the current directory in its path. In fact, this is the way it should be. If you want to include the current directory in root's path, make sure it is the last entry in the path so that all "real" commands are executed before any one a users might try to "force" on you.

Assume a malicious user created a program in his directory called `more` that actually did something bad. If root were to run `more` in that user's directory, the incorrect one would run, with potentially disastrous results. (Note that the current directory normally always appears at the end of the search path. So, even if there was a program called `more` in the current directory, the one in `/usr/bin` would probably get executed first. However, you can see how this could cause problems for root.)

It is common to have people working on SCO systems that have *never* worked on a computer before or have only worked in pure windowing environments like on a Macintosh. When they get to the command line they are lost. On more than one occasion, I have talked to customers where I have asked them to type in `cd /`. There is a pause and I hear: `click-click-click-click-click-click-click-click-click-click-click-click` "Hmmm," I think to myself, "that's too many characters." So I ask them what they typed. They respond, "cdspaceslash."

There are some conventions we need to adhere to throughout this book in order to make things easier. One is that commands that I talk about will be in your path unless I say otherwise. Therefore, to access them all you need to do is input the name of the command without the full path.

The second convention is the translation of the phrases "input the command," "enter the command," and "type in the command." These are translated to mean "input/enter/type in the command and *press enter*." I don't know how many times I have talked with customers and have said, "Type in the command . . ." and then ask them for what happens and their response is, "Oh, you want me to press enter?" Yes! Unless I say otherwise, always press enter after inputting, entering, or typing in a command.

All this time we have been talking about finding and executing commands, but there is one issue that I haven't mentioned. That is the concept of permissions. In order to access a file, you need to have permission to do so. If you want to read a file, you need to have read permission. If you want to write to a file you need to have write permission. If you want to execute a file you have to have execute permission.

Permissions are set on a file using the chmod command or when the file is created. The details of which I will save for later. You can read the permissions on a file by using either the l command or ls -l. At the beginning of each line will be ten characters, which can either be dashes or letters. The first position is the type of file, whether it is a regular file (-), a directory (d), a block device file (b), and so on. Below are some examples of the various file types:

```
-rw-rw--r-   1 jimmo     support    1988 Sep  15 10:05   letter.txt
crw-------   1 root      terminal    0,0 Jul   2 10:05   /dev/tty01
brw-------   1 sysinfo   sysinfo     1,0 Mar   8 07:34   /dev/hd00
drwxr-xr-x   3 bin       bin        3584 May  26 14:15   /bin
p-w--w----   1 root      lp            0 Jul   2 09:48   /usr/spool/lp/fifos/FIFO
lrwxrwxrwx   1 root      root         37 Mar  28 15:45   /etc/custom ->/opt/K/SCO/
Unix/5.0.0Cd/custom/custom
```

- - regular file
c - character device
b - block device
d - directory
p - named pipe
l - symbolic link

We'll get into the details of these files later. If you are curious about the format of each entry, you can look at the ls(C) man-page for more details.

The next nine positions are broken into three groups. Each group consists of three characters indicating the permissions. They are, in order, read(r), write(w), and execute(x). The first group indicates what permissions the owner of the file has. The second group indicates the permissions for the group of that file. The last group indicates the permissions for everyone else.

If a particular permission was not given, there will be a dash (-) here. For example, rwx means all three permissions have been given. In our example above, the symbolic link /etc/custom has read, write, and execute permissions for everyone. The device nodes /dev/tty01 and /dev/hd00 have permissions rw- only for the owner, this means only read and write, but not execute permissions have been given. The directory /bin has read and execute permissions for everyone (r-w), but only the owner can write to it (rwx) (see Figure 3–1).

For directories, the situation is slightly different than for regular files. If you do not have read permission on a directory, you cannot read the contents of that directory. Also, if you do not have write permissions on a directory, you cannot write it. This means that you cannot create a new file in that directory. Execute permissions on a directory mean that you can search it. That is, even if you could not see the contents of a particular directory, you could still access a file there if you knew its name.

Write permission on a directory also has an interesting side effect. Since you need to have write permissions on a directory to create a new file, you also need to have write permissions to remove an existing file. Even if you do not have write permissions on the file itself, if you can write to the directory, you can erase the file. At first this sounds odd. However, remember that a directory is nothing

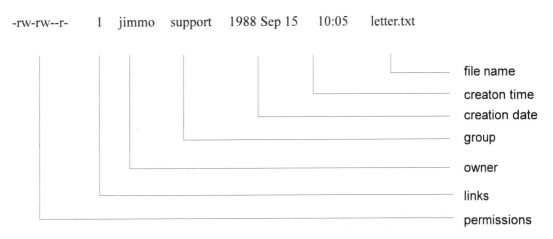

**Figure 3–1**   Breakdown of file permissions.

more than a file in a special format. If you have write permissions to that directory file, you can remove the references to other files, thereby removing them.

### Shell Variables

Before we talk about specific shells, there are some general shell concepts we need to talk about. The first thing we should talk about is the shell's environment. This is all the information that the shell will use as it runs. This includes such things as your command search path, your *logname* (the name you logged in under), and the terminal type you are using. Collectively they are referred to as your *environment variables* and individually as the "so-and-so" environment variable, such as the TERM environment variable which contains the type of terminal you are using.

When you log in, most of these are set for you in one way or another. (The mechanism that sets all environment variables is shell dependent, so we will talk about it when we get to the individual shells.) Each can be viewed by simply typing `echo $VARIABLE`. For example, if I type `echo $LOGNAME`, I get

```
jimmo
```

Typing `echo $TERM`, I get

```
ansi
```

One of the most important environment variables is the PATH variable. Remember that the PATH tells the shell where it needs to look when determining what command it should run. One of the things the shell does to make sense of your command is to find out exactly what program you mean. This is done by looking for the program in the places specified by your PATH variable.

Although it is more accurate say that the shell looks in the directories specified by your PATH environment variable, it is commonly said that the shell, "searches your path." Since this is easier to type, I am going to use that convention here.

If you were to specify a path in the command name, the shell does not use your PATH variable to do any searching. That is, if you issued the command `bin/date`, the shell would interpret that to mean that you wanted to execute the command `date` that was in the `bin` subdirectory of your current directory. If you were in / (the root directory), all would be well and it would effectively execute `/bin/date`. If you were somewhere else, the shell might not be able to find anything that matched.

If you do not specify any path (that is, the command does not contain /) the system will search through your path. If it finds the command, great, if not you get a message saying the command was not found.

Let's take a closer look at how that works by looking at my path variable. From the command line, if I type `echo $PATH`, I get

```
/bin:/usr/bin:/usr/dbin:/usr/ldbin:/usr/jimmo/bin:.⇐watch the dot!!
```

If I type in `date`, the first place that the shell looks is the `/bin` directory. Since that's where `date` resides, it is executed as `/bin/date`. If I type in `vi`, the shell looks in `/bin`, doesn't find it, then looks in `/usr/bin`, where it does find `vi`. Now I type in `getdev`. ( This is a program I wrote to translate major device numbers into the driver name. Don't worry if you don't know what a major number is. You will.) The shell looks in `/bin` and doesn't find it. It then looks in `/usr/bin`—still not there. It then tries `/usr/dbin` and `/usr/ldbin` and still can't find it. When it finally gets to `/usr/jimmo/bin` it finds the `getdev` command and executes it. (Note that since I wrote this program, you probably won't have it on your system.)

What happens if I had not yet copied the program into my personal `bin` directory? Well, if the `getdev` program is in my current directory, the shell finds a match with that last `.` (dot) in my path. (Remember that the `.` (dot) is translated to the current directory so the program is executed as `./getdev`.) If that final `.` (dot) was missing or the `getdev` program was somewhere else, the shell could not find it and would tell me so with something like

```
getdev: not found
```

### Regular Expressions and Metacharacters

Often the arguments that you pass to commands are file names. For example, if you wanted to edit a file called `letter`, you could enter the command `vi letter`. In many cases, typing the entire name is not necessary. Built into the shell are special characters that it will use to expand the name. These are called *metacharacters*.

The two most common metacharacters are `*` and `?`, which are often referred to as *wildcards*. The `*` is used to represent any number of characters including zero. For example, if we have a file in our current directory called `letter` and we input `vi let*` the shell would expand this to be `vi letter`. If we had a file simply called `let`, this would match as well.

Instead, what if we had several files called `letter.chris`, `letter.daniel`, and `letter.david`? The shell would expand them all out to give me the command

```
vi letter.chris letter.daniel letter.david
```

We could also type in `vi letter.da*` which would be expanded to:

```
vi letter.daniel letter.david
```

If we only wanted to edit the letter to chris, we could type it in as `vi *chris`. However, if there were two files, `letter.chris` and `note.chris`, the command `vi *chris` would have the same results as if we typed in:

```
vi letter.chris note.chris
```

In other words, no matter where the asterisk appears, the shell will expand it to match *every* name it finds. If files existed in my current directory with matching names, the shell would expand them properly. However, if there were no matching names, then file name expansion could not take place and the file name would be taken literally.

For example, if there was no file name in our current directory that began with letter, then the command `vi letter*` could not be expanded so we would end up editing a new file called (literally) `letter*`, including the asterisk—not what we wanted.

What if we have a subdirectory called `letters`? If there were the three files `letter.chris`, `letter.daniel`, and `letter.david`, we could get to them by typing `vi letters/letter*`. This would expand to be

```
vi letters/letter.chris letters/letter.daniel letters/letter.david
```

The same rules for path names with commands also apply to file names. The command `vi letters/chris.letter` is the same as `vi ./letters/letter.chris` which is the same as `vi /usr/jimmo/letters/letter.chris`. This is because the shell is doing the expansion before it is passed to the command. Therefore, even directories are expanded. Therefore, the command `vi le*/letter.*` could be expand as both `letters/letter.chris` and `lease/letter.joe`.

The next wildcard is `?`. This is expanded by the shell as one, and only one, character. For example, the command `vi letter.chri?` is the same as `vi letter.chris`. However, if we were to type in `vi letter.chris?` (note that the `?` comes after the `s` in `chris`), the result would be that we would begin editing a *new* file called (literally) `letter.chris?`. Again, this is not what we wanted. Also, if there were two files, `letter.chris1` and `letter.chris2`, the command `vi letter.chris?` would be the same as

```
vi letter.chris1 letter.chris2
```

Another commonly used metacharacter is actually a pair or characters: `[ ]`. The square brackets are used to represent a list of possible characters. For example, if we were not sure whether our file was called `letter.chris` or `letter.Chris`. We could type in the command as `vi letter.[Cc]hris`. So, no matter if the file was called `letter.chris` or `letter.Chris` we would find it. What happens if both files exists? Just as with other metacharacters, both are expanded and passed to `vi`. Note that in this example `vi letter.[Cc]hris` is the same as `vi letter.?hris`, but it is not always so.

The list that appears inside the `[ ]` does not have to be upper- and lowercase versions of the same letter. They can be any letter, number, or even punctuation.

(Note that some punctuation marks have special meaning, such as `*`,`?`, `[,]` which we will cover shortly). For example, if we have five files, `letter.chris1-letter.chris5`, we could edit to all of them with `vi letter.chris[12435]`.

A nice thing about this list is that if it is consecutive, we don't need to list them all. Instead, we can use a dash (-) inside the brackets to indicate that we meant a range. So, the command `vi letter.chris[12345]` could be shortened to be `vi letter.chris[1-5]`. What if we only wanted, the first three and the last one? No problem, we could specify it as `vi letter.chris[1-35]`. This does not mean that we want files `letter.chris1` through `letter.chris35`! Rather, we want `letter.chris1`, `letter.chris2`, `letter.chris3`, and `letter.chris5`. This is because these are all seen as individual characters.

Inside the brackets, we are not limited to just numbers or just letters. We can use both. The command `vi letter.chris[abc123]` has the potential for editing six files: `letter.chrisa`, `letter.chrisb`, `letter.chrisc`, `letter.chris1`, `letter.chris2`, and `letter.chris3`.

If we are so inclined, we can mix and match any of these metacharacters any way we want. We can even use them multiple times in the same command. Let's take as an example the command `vi *.?hris[a-f1-5]`. Should they exist in our current directory, that would match *all* of the following:

```
letter.chrisa    note.chrisa
                 letter.chrisc    letter.chrisb    note.chrisb
note.chrisc      letter.chrisd
                 note.chrise      note.chrisd      letter.chrise
letter.chris1    note.chris1
                 letter.chris3    letter.chris2    note.chris2
note.chris3      letter.chris4
                 note.chris5      note.chris4      letter.chris5
letter.Chrisa    note.Chrisa
                 letter.Chrisc    letter.Chrisb    note.Chrisb
note.Chrisc      letter.Chrisd
                 note.Chrise      note.Chrisd      letter.Chrise
letter.Chris1    note.Chris1
                 letter.Chris3    letter.Chris2    note.Chris2
note.Chris3      letter.Chris4
                 note.Chris5      note.Chris4      letter.Chris5
```

Also, any of these names without the leading `letter` or `note` would match. Or if we issued the command `vi *.d*`, this would match

```
letter.daniel    note.daniel         letter.david    note.david
```

Remember, I said that the shell expands the metacharacters only with respect to the name specified. This obviously works for file names as I described above, however, it also works for command names as well.

If we were to type `dat*` and there was nothing in our current directory that started with `dat`, we would get a message like

```
dat*: not found
```

However, if we were to type `/bin/dat*`, the shell can successfully expand this to be `/bin/date`, which it would then execute. The same applies to relative paths. If we were in `/` and entered `./bin/dat*` or `bin/dat*`, both would be expanded properly and the right command would be executed. If we enter the command, `/bin/dat[abcdef]` we get the right response as well since the shell tries all six and finds a match with `/bin/date`.

An important thing to note is that the shell expands as long as it can before it attempts to interpret that command. I was reminded of this fact by accident when I input `bin/l*`. This yielded the output

```
-r-xr-xr-t   6   bin    bin      23674   Mar   15   1993     /bin/lc
-rwx--x--x   1   bin    bin      33172   Jan   19   1993     /bin/ld
-r-xr-xr-t   6   bin    bin      23674   Mar   15   1993     /bin/lf
-rwx--x--x   1   bin    bin      1070    Mar   15   1993     /bin/line
-rwx--x--x   1   bin    bin      40920   Jan   19   1993     /bin/list
-rwx--x--x   4   bin    bin      22394   Mar   15   1993     /bin/ln
-r-x------   1   root   bin      79014   Mar   15   1993     /bin/login
-rwxr-xr-x   1   root   other    88988   Jan   04   10:26    /bin/lone-tar
-rwxr-xr-x   1   bin    bin      2518    Jan   19   1993     /bin/lorder
-r-xr-xr-t   6   bin    bin      23674   Mar   15   1993     /bin/lr
-r-xr-xr-t   6   bin    bin      23674   Mar   15   1993     /bin/ls
-r-xr-xr-t   6   bin    bin      23674   Mar   15   1993     /bin/lx
```

At first, I expected each one of the files in `/bin` that began with an `l` (ell) to be executed. Then I remembered that expansion takes place *before* the command is interpreted. Therefore, the command that I input, `/bin/l*` was expanded to be

```
/bin/l /bin/lc /bin/ld /bin/lf /bin/line /bin/list /bin/ln/bin/login
/bin/lone-tar/bin/lorder /bin/lr /bin/ls /bin/lx
```

Since `/bin/l` was the first command in that list, I ended up with a long listing of all the files in that list. The same kind of thing happened when I input `/bin/l?` . However, the output looked like this

`/bin/ld /bin/lf /bin/ln /bin/lr /bin/ls /bin/lx`

This is because the command was interpreted to be

`/bin/lc /bin/ld /bin/lf /bin/ln /bin/lr /bin/ls /bin/lx`

Or, when I input `/bin/l[abcdef]`, I got

`/bin/ld /bin/lf`

This was expanded as

`/bin/lc /bin/ld /bin/lf`

Keep in mind that the shell interprets the first thing on each line as being the command. The only way for the shell to see each of these as individual commands would be to type them all out with a semicolon ( ; ) to separate them. For example,

`/bin/lc; /bin/ld; /bin/lf`

This would cause the system to execute `/bin/lc` followed by `/bin/ld` and then by `/bin/lf`.

I first learned about this aspect of shell expansion after about a couple of hours of trying to extract a specific subdirectory from a tape that I had made with the `cpio` command. Since I made the tape using absolute paths, I attempted to re-store the files as `/usr/jimmo/letters/*`. Rather than restoring the entire directory as I expected, it did nothing. It worked its way through the tape until it got to the end and then rewound itself without extracting any files.

At first I assumed I made a typo, so I started all over; this time checking the command before I sent it on its way. After half an hour or so of whirring, the tape was back at the beginning. Still no files. Then it dawned on me, I hadn't told the `cpio` to overwrite existing files unconditionally. So I started it all over again.

Now those of you who know `cpio` realize that this wasn't the issue either. At least not entirely. When the tape got to the right spot, it started overwriting everything in the directory (as I told it to). However, the files that were missing (the ones that I really wanted to get back) were still not copied from the backup tape.

The next time, I decided to just get a listing of all the files on the tape. Maybe the files I wanted were not on this tape. After a while it reached the right directory and lo and behold, there were the files that I wanted. I could see them on the tape, I just couldn't extract them.

Well, the first idea that popped into my mind was to restore *everything*. That's sort of like fixing a flat by buying a new car. Then I thought about restoring the entire tape into a temporary directory where I could then get the files I wanted. Even if I had the space, this still seemed like the wrong way of doing things.

Then it hit me. I was going about it all the wrong way. The solution was to go ask someone what I was doing wrong. I asked one of the more senior engineers (I had only been there less than a year at the time). When I mentioned that I was using wildcards, it was immediately obvious what I was doing wrong (obvious to him, not to me).

Let's think about it for a minute. It is the *shell* that does the expansion, not the command itself. When I ran /bin/1* the shell interpreted the command as starting with /bin/1. Therefore, I got the listing of all the files in /bin that started with 'l'. With cpio, the situation is similar.

When I first ran it, the shell interpreted the files (/usr/jimmo/data/*) before passing them to cpio. Since I hadn't told cpio to overwrite the files, it did nothing. When I told cpio to overwrite the files, it only did so for the files that it was told to; that is, only the files that the shell saw when it expanded /usr/jimmo/data/*. In other words, cpio did what it was told. I just told it to do something that I hadn't expected.

The solution is to find a way to pass the wildcards to cpio. That is, have the shell ignore the special significance of the asterisk. Fortunately, there is a way. By placing a back-slash ' \ ' before the metacharacter, you remove its special significance. This is referred to as "escaping" that character.

So, in my situation with cpio, when I referred to the files I wanted as /usr/jimmo/data/\*, the shell passed the arguments to cpio as /usr/jimmo/data/*. It was then cpio that expanded the * to mean all the files in that directory. Once I did that, I got the files I wanted.

Another interesting thing happens as a result of this wildcard expansion. The maximum number of characters that the shell can process on the command line is 5120. This seems like a lot (and it is), but some circumstances cause commands to run into this limit. SCO recognized this as a problem and increased the limit to 100,000 bytes by default. Let's look at the directory /usr/include/sys. This contains files that are used by the system when making a copy of the kernel as well as by programmers. On my system, this directory contains over 200 files. If I change directories and do a listing (ls), I see all the files and directories under /usr/include/sys. If I do an ls *, I also see a list of all the files and directories. All is as it should be.

Now, if we run ls /usr/include/sys. What do we get? What we expect: a list of all the files and directories in /usr/include/sys. If, however, we run ls /usr/include/sys/* we get

```
sh: /bin/ls: arg list too long
```

What happened?

Well, it all has to do with the wildcard expansion. Whenever we run `ls` with no arguments, as with `ls /usr/include/sys`, or change directories and simply run `ls`, it is up to `ls` to scan the directory to give me the output. However, whenever we use wildcards, the *shell* must first process the command *before* it's handed off to `ls`. When we are in `/usr/include/sys`, and run `ls *`, there is no problem. Each of the files in `/usr/include/sys` is expanded as if we had typed in

```
1 Sdsk.h Srom.h ... vwdisp.h
```

All told, this works out to less than 2500 characters (at least on my system).

On the other hand, if we run `ls /usr/include/sys/*` this is the same as if we had typed in

```
1 /usr/include/sys/Sdsk.h /usr/include/sys/Srom.h ... usr/include/sys/vwdisp.h
```

The total number of characters here is over 5700. This is well over the maximum number of characters per line. (Actually, it's the `exec()` system call that fails and not the shell itself. If that doesn't mean anything to you, don't worry, it is not important to understand this limitation.)

Another aspect of this is what happens when you use this same example on a smaller directory. For example if we did a listing like this

```
ls /etc/default
```

all we would see is the names of the files. If instead, we did it like this

```
ls /etc/default/*
```

we see the directory names as well. This is as if we had done:

```
ls /etc/default/accounts /etc/default/authsh ...
```

In OpenServer, things are slightly different. The shell interacts with the command that is being executed. If the system finds that an asterisk is appropriate to pass to the command, it will do so and the asterisk is expanded by the command, not the shell.

Another symbol that has special meaning is the dollar sign ($). This is used as a marker to indicate that something is a variable. I mentioned earlier in this section that you could get access to your log in name environment variable by typing

```
echo $LOGNAME
```

The system stores your log in name in the environment variable LOGNAME (note no '$'). The system needs some way of knowing that when you input this on the command line, you are talking about the variable LOGNAME and not the literal string LOGNAME. This is done through the '$'. There are several variables that are set by the system. You can also set variables yourself and use them later on. I get into more details about shell variables later on.

So far we have been talking about metacharacters used for searching the names of files. However, metacharacters can often be used in the arguments to certain commands. One example is the grep command, which is used to search for strings within files. The name grep comes from Global Regular Expression Print. As its name implies, it has something to do with regular expressions. Let's assume we have a text file called documents and we wish to see if the string "letter" exists in that text. The command might be

```
grep letter documents
```

This will search for and print out every line containing the string letter. This includes such things as "letterbox," "lettercarrier," and even "love-letter." However, it will not find "Letterman," since we did not tell grep to ignore upper- and lowercase (using the -i option). To do so using regular expressions, the command might look like this

```
grep [Ll]etter documents
```

Now, since we specified to look for either "L" or "l" followed by "etter," we get both "letter" and "Letterman." We can also specify that we want to look for this strings only when it appears at the beginning of a line using the caret (^) symbol. For example,

```
grep ^[Ll]etter documents
```

This searches for all strings that start with the "beginning-of-line" followed by either "L" or "l" followed by "etter". Or, if we want to search for the same things at the end of the line, we would use the dollar sign to indicate the end of the line. Note at that the beginning of a string, the dollar sign will be treated as the beginning of a string, whereas at the end of strings, it indicates the end of the line. Confused? Let's look at an example. Let's define a string like this:

```
VAR=^[Ll]etter
```

If we echo that string we simply get ^[Ll]etter. Note that this includes the caret at the beginning of the strings. When we do a search like this

```
grep $VAR documents
```

it is equivalent to

```
grep ^[Ll]etter documents
```

Now, write the same command like this:

```
grep $VAR$ documents
```

This says to find to the strings defined by the VAR variable(^[Ll]etter), but only if it is at the end of the line. Here were have an example, where the dollar sign has *both* meanings. Take it one step further:

```
grep ^$VAR$ documents
```

This says to find the strings defined by the VAR variable, but only if it takes up the entry line. In other words, the line consists only of the beginning of the line (^), the string defined by VAR, and the end of the line ($).

### *Quotes*

One last issue that causes its share of confusion is quotes. In SCO UNIX there are three kinds of quotes. They are referred to as *double- quotes* ("), *single- quotes* ('), and *back-quotes*(`) (also called back-ticks). On most US keyboards, the single- and double-quotes are on the same key, with the double-quotes accessed by pressing shift and the single-quote key. Usually this is on the right side of the keyboard next to the enter key. The back-quote is usually in the upper left hand corner of the keyboard, next to the '1'.

To best understand the difference between the behavior of these quotes, I need to talk about them in reverse order. We will first talk about the back-quotes or back-ticks.

When enclosed inside of back-ticks, the shell interprets that as meaning, "the output of the command inside of the back-ticks." This is referred to as *command substitution* as the output of the command inside the back-ticks is substituted for the command itself. This is often used to assign the output of a command to a variable. As an example, let's say we wanted to keep track of how many files are in a directory. From the command line we could say

```
ls | wc
```

The wc command gives me a word count, along with the number of lines and number of characters. Here, the command might come up as

```
7    7    61
```

However, once the command is finished and the value has been output, we can only get it back again by rerunning the command. Instead, If we said

```
count=`ls |wc'
```

then the entire line of output would be saved in the variable count. If we then say echo $count, we get

```
7    7    61
```

showing me that count now contains that line. If we wanted, we could even assign a multiline output to this variable, we could use the ps command, like this:

```
trash=`ps`
```

Then type in

```
echo $trash
```

which gives me:

```
PID TTY TIME COMMAND 209 06 0:02 ksh 1362 06 0:00 ps
```

This is different from the output that `ps` would give when not assigned to the variable `trash`:

```
PID    TTY    TIME    COMMAND
209    06     0:02    ksh
1362   06     0:00    ps
```

The next kind of quote, the single-quote ( ' ), tells the system not to do *any* expansion at all. Let's take the example above, but this time turn the quotes around and use single quotes:

```
count='ls|wc'
```

If we were to now type `echo$count`, we get

```
ls|wc
```

What we got was exactly what we expected. The shell did no expansion and simply assigned the literal string "ls | wc" to the variable `count`. This even applies to the variable operator '$'. For example, if we simply say

```
echo '$LOGNAME'
```

What comes out on the screen is

```
$LOGNAME
```

No expansion is done at all and even the `'$'` is left unchanged.

The last set of quotes is the double-quote. This has partially the same effect as the single-quotes, but to a limited extent. If we include something inside of double-quotes, everything loses its special meaning except for the variable operator ($), the back-slash (\), the back-tick (`), and the double-quote itself. Everything else takes on its absolute meaning. For example, we could say

```
echo "`date`"
```

which gives us

```
Wed Feb 01 16:39:30 PST 1995
```

This is a round-about way of getting the date, but it is good for demonstration purposes. Plus, I often use this in shell scripts, when I want to log something. Remember that the back-tick first expands the command (by running it) and then the echo echoes it to the screen.

This wraps up the characters that have special meaning to the shell. You can get more details from the *User's Guide* if you need it, but the best way to see what's happening is to try a few combinations and see if they behave as you would expect.

I mentioned that some punctuation marks had special meaning. We already know about the special meaning of *, ?, and [ ]. What about the others? Well, in fact, most of the other punctuation marks have special meaning. I will discuss them in more detail when I talk about shell programming.

### Pipes and Redirection

Perhaps the most commonly used character is |, which is referred to as the pipe symbol, or simply pipe. This enables you to pass the output of one command through the input of another. For example, say you would like to do a long directory listing of the /bin directory. If you simply type ls -l then press return, the names flash by much too fast for you to read. When it finally stops, all you see is the last twenty or so.

If instead we ran the command ls -l | more, we say that the output of the ls command is "piped through more." In this way we can scan through the list one screenful at a time.

Recall our discussion of standard input and standard output in Chapter 1. Standard input is just a file that usually points to your terminal. Standard output is also a file that usually points to your terminal in this case. The standard output of the ls command is changed to point to the pipe and the standard input of the more command is changed to point to the pipe as well.

The way this works is that when the shell sees the pipe symbol it creates a temporary file on the hard disk. Although it does not have a name or directory entry, it does take up physical space on the hard disk. Since both the terminal and the pipe are seen as files from the perspective of the operating system, all we are saying is that the system should use different files instead of standard input and standard output.

Under SCO UNIX (as well as other UNIX dialects) there exist the concepts of standard input, standard output, and standard error. When you log in and are working from the command line, standard input is your terminal keyboard and both standard output and standard error are the terminal screen. In other words, the shell expects to be getting its input from the keyboard and show the output (and any error messages) on the terminal screen.

Actually, the three (standard input, standard output, and standard error) are references to files that the shell automatically opens. Remember that in UNIX everything is treated as a file. When the shell starts, the three files it opens are usually the ones pointing to your terminal.

When we run a command like cat, it gets input from a file that it displays to the screen. Although it may appear that the standard input is coming from that file, the standard input (referred to as stdin) is still the keyboard. This is why when the file is large enough and more stops after each page, you can continue by pressing either the spacebar or enter key. That's because *standard* input is still the keyboard.

As it is running, more is displaying the contents of the file to the screen. That is, it is going to standard output (stdout). If you try to do a more on a file that does not exist, the message

```
file_name: No such file or directory
```

shows up on your terminal screen as well. However, although it appears to be the same place, the error message was written to standard error (stderr). We'll show this difference shortly.

One pair of characters that is used quite often, < and > also deal with stdin and stdout. The more common of the two, >, redirects the output of a command into a file. That is, it changes standard output. An example of this would be ls /bin > myfile. If we were to run this command, we would have a file (in my current directory) named myfile that contained the output of the ls /bin command. This is because stdout is the file myfile and not the terminal. Once the command completes, stdout returns to being the terminal.

Now, we want to see the contents of the file. We could simply say more myfile, but that wouldn't explain about redirection. Instead, we input more <myfile. This tells the more command to take its standard input from the file myfile instead of the keyboard or some other file. (Remember, even when stdin is the keyboard, it is still seen as a file.)

What about errors? As I mentioned, stderr *appears* to be going to the same place as stdout. A quick way of showing that it doesn't is by using output redirection and forcing an error. If wanted to list two directories and have the output go to a file, we run this command:

```
ls /bin /jimmo > /tmp/junk
```

We get this message:

```
/jimmo not found
```

However, if we look in /tmp, there is, indeed, a file called junk which contains the output of the ls /bin portion of the command. What happened here was that we redirected stdout into the file /tmp/junk. It did this with the listing of /bin. However, since there was no directory /jimmo (at least not on my system), we got the error /jimmo not found. In other words, stdout went into the file, but stderr still went to the screen.

If we want to get the output and any error messages to go to the same place, we can do that. Using the same example with ls, the command would be:

```
ls /bin /jimmo > /tmp/junk 2>&1
```

The new part of the command is 2>&1. This says that file descriptor 2 (stderr) should go to the same place as file descriptor 1 (stdout). By changing the command slightly to,

```
ls /bin /jimmo > /tmp/junk 2>/tmp/errors
```

we can tell the shell to send any errors some place else. You will find quite often in shell scripts thoughout the system that the file that error messages are sent to is /dev/null. This has the effect of ingoring the messages completely. They are neither displayed on the screen nor sent to a file. Figure 3–2 shows what this might look like graphically.

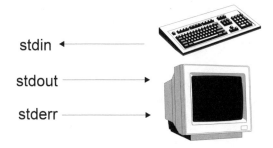

redirection with:  *command 2> error.file*

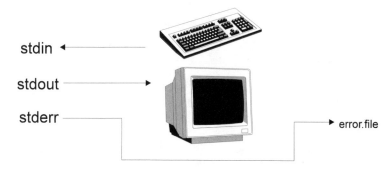

**Figure 3–2**   File redirection.

Note that this command does not work as you think:

```
ls /bin /jimmo 2>&1 > /tmp/junk
```

The reason is that we redirect stderr to the same place as stdout *before* we redirect stdout. So, stderr goes to the screen, but stdout goes to the file specified.

Redirection can also be combined with pipes like this:

```
sort < names | head
```

or

```
ps | grep sh > ps.save
```

In the first example, the standard input of the `sort` command is redirected to point to the file `names`. Its output is then passed to the pipe. The standard input of the `head` command (which takes the first ten lines) also comes from the pipe. This would be the same as the command

```
sort names | head
```

In the second example, the `ps` command (process status) is piped through `grep` and the output of the whole thing is redirected to the file `file.save`. What this looks like graphically we see in Figure 3–3.

If we want to redirect stderr, we can. The syntax is similar, but it differs slightly from shell to shell. Therefore, I am going to hold this explanation until I talk about the individual shells.

It's possible to input multiple commands on the same command line. This can be accomplished by using a semicolon (;) between commands. I have used this on occasion to create command lines like this:

```
man ksh | col -b > man.tmp; vi man.tmp; rm man.tmp
```

This command redirects the output of the man-page for `ksh` into the file `man.tmp`. (The pipe through `col -b` is necessary because of the way the man-pages are formatted.) Next, we are brought into the `vi` editor with the file `man.tmp`. After I exit `vi`, the command continues and removes my temporary file `man.tmp`. (After about the third time doing this, it gets pretty monotonous, so I create a shell-script to do this for me. I'll talk more about shell-scripts later.)

### Interpreting the Command

One question that I had was "in what order does everything gets done?" We have shell variables to expand, aliases and functions to process, "real" com-

**Figure 3–3**    Data flow through a pipe.

mands, and pipes and input/output redirection. There are a lot of things that the shell has to consider when figuring out what to do and when.

For the most part this is not so important. Commands do not get so complex that knowing the evaluation order becomes an issue. However, on a few occasions I have run into situations were things did not behave as I thought they should. By evaluating the command myself (as the shell would) it became clear what was happening. Let's take a look.

The first thing that gets done is for the shell to figure out how many commands there are on the line. (Remember, you can separate multiple commands on a single line with semicolon.) This process determines how many *tokens* there are on the command line. In this context a token could be an entire command or it could be a control word such as "if". Here, too, the shell has to deal with input/output redirection and pipes.

Once it determines how many tokens, it checks the syntax of each of the tokens. Should there be a syntax error, the shell will not try to start *any* of the commands. If the syntax is correct, it begins interpreting the tokens.

The first thing it checks for is aliases. Aliases are a way for some shells to allow you to define your own commands. If any of the tokens on the command line is actually an alias that you have defined, it is expanded before the shell proceeds. If it happens that an alias contains another alias, they are expanded before continuing with the next step. Here, functions are expanded. Like functions in programming languages like C, a shell function can be thought of as a small subprogram. We'll discuss both aliases and functions shortly.

Once aliases and functions have all been completely expanded, the shell evaluates variables. Finally, it uses any wildcards to expand them to file names. This is done according to the rules we talked about previously.

After it has evaluated everything, it is *still* not ready to run the command. It first checks to see if the first token represents a command built into the shell or an external one. If it's not external, the shell needs to go through the search path.

At this point, it sets up the redirection, including the pipes. These obviously have to be ready before the command starts since the command may be getting its input from some place other than the keyboard and may be sending it somewhere other than the screen. Figure 3–4 shows how the evaluation looks graphically.

This is an oversimplification. Things do happen in this order, however there are many more things that occur in and around the steps I have listed here. What I am attempting to describe is the general process that occurs when the shell is trying to interpret your command.

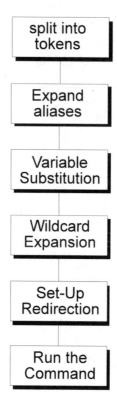

**Figure 3–4**   Evaluating a command.

Once the shell has determined what each command is and has determined that it is an executable *binary* program (not a shell script) the shell makes a copy of itself using the fork() system call. This copy is a child process of the shell. It then uses the exec() system call to overwrite itself with the binary it wants to execute. (We talked more about the fork-exec pair earlier). Keep in mind that even though the child process is executing, the original shell is still in memory, waiting for the child to complete (assuming the command was not started in the background with &).

If the program that needs to be executed is a shell script, the program that is fork-exec'ed() is another shell. This new shell starts reading the shell script and interprets it, one line at a time. This is why a syntax error in a shell script is not discovered when the script is started, but rather when the erroneous line is first encountered.

Understanding that a new process is created when you run a shell script helps to explain a very common misconception under UNIX. When you run a shell script and that script changes directories, your original shell knows nothing about the change. This confuses a lot of people who are new to UNIX as they come from the DOS world where changing the directory from within a batch file *does* change it. This is because DOS does not have the same concept of a process as UNIX.

Look at it this way: The subshell's environment has been changed in that the current directory is different, but this is *not* passed back to the parent. Like "real" parent-child relationships, only the children can inherit characteristics from their parent, not the other way around. Therefore, any changes to the environment, including directory changes, are not noticed by the parent. Again, this is *different* from the behavior of DOS .bat files.

You can get around this by either using aliases or shell functions (assuming that your shell has them). Another way is using the dot (.) command in front of the shell script you want to execute. For example,

```
. myscript   ←notice the dot
```

This script will then be interpreted directly by the current shell, *without* forking a subshell. If the script makes changes to the environment, then it is *this* shell's environment that is changed.

You can use this same behavior if ever you need to reset your environment. Normally, your environment is defined by the startup files in your home directory. On occasion, things get a little confused (maybe a variable got changed or removed) and you need to reset things. By using the . (dot) command you can reset your environment. For example, with either sh or ksh you can do it like this:

```
. $HOME/.profile
```

Or, using a function of ksh you can also do

```
.~/.profile
```

This uses the tilde (~), which I haven't mentioned, yet. Under the ksh, this is a shortcut way of referring to a particular user's home directory. I'll talk more about this in the section on ksh.

If you have csh, the command is issued like this:

```
source $HOME/.login
```

### The Different Kinds of Shells

The great-grandfather of all shell is /bin/sh, called simply sh or the Bourne-Shell (named after its developer Steven Bourne). This is the standard shell and the one that you will find on every version of UNIX (at least all the ones I have seen). Although many changes have been made to UNIX, sh has remained basically unchanged.

All the capabilities of the shell I've talked about so far apply to `sh`. Anything I've talked about that `sh` can do, the others can do as well. So rather than going on about what `sh` can do (which I already did), I am going to talk about the characteristics of the other two shells, `csh` and `ksh`.

SCO includes both a visual/menu driven shell, `scosh`, as well as restricted versions of the other shells. I think of `scosh` as more of an application than a shell, like `sh`, `ksh`, or `csh`. Therefore, we will leave it for another time and place. The restricted versions of each shell all have the same basic characteristics of their nonrestricted counterpart. I get into this a little in Chapter 4. In addition, there are many different shells that are either available as public domain, shareware, or commercial products that can be installed on SCO UNIX. However, since they are not provided with the base system, we will skip them.

In the section on shell basics, we talked about environment variables. As I mentioned, these are set up for you as you are logging in or you can set them up later. The shell you use, the files used, and where they are located is a different story. Some variables are made available to everyone on the system and are accessed through a common file. Others reside in the user's home directory. Normally, those residing in the user's home directory can be modified. If they can't, then maybe the system administrator has a reason or there is some other problem.

One convention I will be using here is how I refer to the different shells. Often I will say "the `csh`" to refer to the C-Shell as a concept and not the program `/bin/csh`. I will use "the `sh`" to refer to the "Bourne Shell" as an abstract entity and not specifically to the program `/bin/sh`.

Most of the issues I am going to address here are detailed in the appropriate man-pages and other docs. Why cover them here? Well, in keeping with the basic premise of this book, I want to show you the relationships involved. In addition, many of the things I will discuss are not emphasized as much as they should. Often, users will go for months or years without learning the magic that these shells can offer. Since they "looked at" the manuals but never read them cover to cover, the user missed some of these things. These are things I feel are too exciting to miss out on.

There is one oddity that really needs to be addressed. This is the behavior of the different shells when moving through symbolic links. As I mentioned before, symbolic links are simply pointers to files or directories elsewhere on the system. If you change directories into symbolic link, then your location on the disk is different than what you might think. In some cases, the shell understands the distinction and hides from you the fact that you are somewhere else. This is where the problem lies.

Although the concept of symbolic links exists in ODT, it is not as widespread as in OpenServer. OpenServer uses the symbolic link as a key administrative tool. The directories I will be talking about here as symbolic links only exist in OpenServer. Let's take the directory /usr/adm as an example. Since it contains a lot of administrative information it is a useful and commonly accessed directory. This is actually a symbolic link to /var/adm. If we are using sh as our shell, when we do a cd /usr/adm and then pwd, the system responds with /var/adm. This is where we are "physically" located, despite the fact that we did a cd to /usr/adm. If we do cd .. (to move up to our parent directory) we are now located in /var. All this seems logical. This is also the behavior of csh.

If we use ksh, things are different. This time when we do a cd /usr/adm and then pwd, the system responds with /usr/adm. This is where we are "logically". If we now do a cd .., we are located in /usr. Which of these is the "correct" behavior? Well, I would say *both*. There is nothing to define what the "correct" behavior is. Depending on your preference, either is correct. I tend to prefer the behavior of ksh since I wanted to be in /usr/adm and not /var/adm. However, the behavior of sh and csh is also valid.

### The C-Shell

One of the first "new" shells to come around was the csh or 'C-Shell'. It is so named because much of the syntax it uses is very similar to the C programming language. This isn't to say that this shell is only for C programmers, or programmers in general. Rather, knowing C makes learning the syntax much easier. However, it isn't essential. (Note: The csh syntax is *similar*, so don't get your dander up if it's not *exactly* the same.)

The csh is normally the shell that users get on UNIX systems. Every place I ever got a UNIX account, it was automatically assumed that I wanted csh as my shell. When I first started out with UNIX, that was true. In fact, this is true for most users. Since they don't know any other shells, the csh is a good place to start.

As you log in with csh as your shell, the system first looks in the global file /etc/cshrc. Here, the system administrator can define variables or actions that should be taken by every csh user. Next, the system reads two files in your home directory: .login and .cshrc. The .login file normally contains the variables you want set and the actions you want to occur each time you log in. This can include setting your terminal type or warning you that your password is about to expire.

In both of these files, settings variables has a syntax unique to the csh. This is one *major* difference between the csh and the other two shells and a reason why it is not a good idea to give root csh as its default shell. The syntax for csh is

```
set variable_name=value
```

Whereas for the other two it is simply

```
variable=value
```

Once the system has processed your `.login file`, your `.cshrc` is processed. The `.cshrc` contains things that you want executed or configured every time you start a `csh`. At first, I wasn't clear with this concept. If you are logging in with the `csh`, don't you want to start a `csh`? Well, yes. However, the reverse is not true. Every time I start a `csh` I don't want the system to behave as if I were logging in.

Let's take a look at this for a minute. One of the variables that gets set for you is the SHELL variable. This is the shell you use any time you do a *shell escape* from a program. A "shell escape" starts a shell as a subprocess of that program. Remember that in our discussion of operating system basics we talked about the concept of processes. As a rather contrived example, I described a case where you would start `vi`, then "jump out." This "jumping out" is called a shell escape as you "escape" from your current program to get to a shell.

When you do a shell escape, the system starts a shell as a new (child) process of whatever program you are running at the time. As we talked about earlier, once this shell exits, you are back to the original program. Since there is no default, the variable *must* be set to a shell. If set to something else, you end up with an error message like `vi` gives you

```
invalid SHELL value: <something_else>
```

`<something_else>` is whatever your SHELL variable is defined as.

If you are running `csh` and your SHELL variable is set to `/bin/csh`, every time you do a shell escape the shell you get is `csh`. If you have a .cshrc file in your home directory, not only is this started when you log in, but *any time* you start a new `csh`. This can be useful if you want to access personal aliases from inside subshells.

What are personal aliases? No, this isn't the ability to call yourself Thaddeus Jones when your real name is Jedediah Curry. However, it is the ability to use a different name for a command. In principle, they can be anything you want. They are special names that you define to accomplish tasks. These aren't shell scripts, as a shell script is external to your shell. To start up a shell script, you type in its name: The system starts a shell as a child process of your current shell in order to run the script.

Aliases, too, are started by typing them in. However, they are internal to the `csh`. That is, they are internal to your `csh` process. Instead of starting a subshell, the `csh` executes the alias internally. This has the obvious advantage of being quicker, as there is no overhead of starting the new shell or searching the hard disk.

Another major advantage is the ability to create new commands. You can do this with shell scripts (which we get into later), but the overhead of creating a new process does not make it worthwhile for simple things. Aliases can be created with multiple commands strung together. For example, I created an alias, 't', that shows me the time. Although the date command does that, all I want to see is the time. So, I created an alias 't', which I defined like this:

```
alias t='date | cut -c12-16'
```

When I type in 't', I get the hours and minutes, just exactly the away I want it.

Aliases can be defined in either the .login or the .cshrc. However, as I described above, if you want them for all subshells, they need to go in .cshrc. If you are running a Bourne-Shell, aliasing may be the first good reason to switch to another shell.

The sh does have the means of creating new commands. This is done by creating shell functions. Shell functions are just like those in a programming language. A set of commands is grouped together and jointly called by a single name. The csh can create them as well.

The format for functions is the same for all three shells:

```
function_name()
{
    first thing to do
    second thing to do
    third thing to do
}
```

Functions can be defined anywhere; this includes from the command line. All you need to do is simply type in the lines one at a time, similar to the example shown above. The thing to bear in mind is that if you type from the command line, once you exit that shell, the function is gone.

Be careful when creating aliases or functions so that you don't redefine existing commands. You may end up forgetting the alias or there may be some other program that uses the original program and fails since the alias gets called first. I once got a call where the customer had a system where he could no longer install software. The custom program was failing. We tried replacing the custom program, but that didn't work. We tried replacing the files in /etc/perms, but that didn't work. Since it was an SCO product he was trying to install, I assumed that it was defective media. Fortunately, he had another copy of that same product, but custom died with the same error. It didn't seem likely that the copy was bad media, too. At this point, I had been with him for almost an hour, so I decided to hand off the problem to someone else. (Often a fresh perspective is all that is needed.)

About an hour later one of the other engineers came into my cubie with the same problem. He couldn't come up with anything either (which kind of relieved me). So, he decided that he needed to research the issue. Well, he found the exact message in the custom source code and it turned out that this message comes when custom cannot run the sort command. Ah, a corrupt sort binary. Nope! Not that easy. What else was there. As it turned out, the customer had created an alias called sort which he used to sort directories in a particular fashion. Since custom couldn't work with this version of sort, it died.

So, why use one over the other? Well, if there is something that can be done with a short shell script, then it can be done with a function. However, there are things that are difficult to do with an alias. One thing is making long, relatively complicated commands. Although you can do this with an alias, it is much simpler and easier to read if you do it with a function. I will go into some more details about shell functions later in the section on shell scripting. You can also find out more details in the csh man-page.

I mentioned that aliases are a good reason to switch from sh to csh. However, that's not the only reason. Another advantage that the csh has is its ability to repeat, and even edit, previous commands. Commands are stored in a shell "history list", which, by default, contains the last twenty commands. This is normally defined in your .cshrc file or you can do so from the command line. The command set history=100 would change the size of your history list to 100. One thing to keep in mind is that everything you type at the command line is saved in the history file. Even if you mis-typed something, the shell tosses it into the history file.

What good is the history file? Well, the first thing is that by simply typing 'history' with nothing else, you get to see the contents of your history file. That way if you can't remember the exact syntax of a command you typed in five minutes ago, you can check your history file.

This is a nice trick, but it goes far beyond that. Each time you issue a command from the csh prompt, the system increments an internal counter that tells you how many commands have been issued up to that point. If you have a default csh, then your prompt is probably a number followed by a '%: that number is the current command. You can use that number to repeat those previous commands. This is simply done with an exclamation mark (!) followed by the command number as it appears in the shell history.

For example, if the last part of your shell history looked like this

21 date

22 vi letter.john

23 ps

24 who

you could edit the letter again by simply typing in !22. This repeats the command vi letter.john and adds this command to your history. After you get done editing the file, this portion of the history file would look like this:

21 date

22 vi letter.john

23 ps

24 who

25 vi letter.john

Another neat trick that's built in to this history mechanism is the ability to repeat the commands without using the numbers. If you know that sometime within that history you edited a file using vi, you could edit again by simply typing !vi. This searches backward though the history file until it finds the last time you used vi. If there were no other commands since the last time you used vi you could also start it with !v. If you want to redo the command you just entered, you could do so simply by typing in !!.

This history mechanism can also be used to edit previously issued commands. Let's say that instead of typing vi letter.john, we had typed in vi letter.jonh. Maybe we know someone named jonh, but that's not who we meant this letter to be addressed to. So rather than typing in the whole command, we can edit it. The command we would issue would be !!:s/nh/hn/.

At first, this seems a little confusing. The first part, however, should be clear. The "!!" tells the system to repeat the previous command. The colon (:) tells the shell to expect some editing commands. The s/nh/hn/ says to substitute for pattern nh the hn. (If you are familiar with vi or sed you understand this. If not, we get into this syntax later.)

What happens if we had edited a letter to john, done some other work, and then decided we wanted to edit a letter to chris instead. We could simply type !22:s/john/chris/. Granted, this is actually more key strokes than if we had typed everything over again however, you should see the potential here. Check out the csh man-page for many different tricks for editing previous commands.

In the default .cshrc are two aliases that I found quite useful. These are pushd and popd. These aliases are used to maintain a directory "stack." When you run pushd <dir_name> your current directory is pushed onto (added to) the stack and you change the directory to <dir_name>. When you use popd it pops (removes) the top of the directory stack and you change directories to it.

Like other kinds of stacks, this directory stack can be several layers deep. For example, let's say that we are currently in our home directory. A 'pushd /bin' makes our current directory /bin with our home directory the top of the stack. With 'pushd /etc' we are now in /etc. If we do it one more time with pushd /usr/bin and we are now in /usr/bin. The directory /usr/bin is now the top of the stack.

If we run popd (no argument), then /usr/bin is popped from the stack and /etc is our new directory. Another popd and /bin is popped and we are now in /bin. One more pop brings me back to our home directory. (In all honesty, I have never used this to do anything more than to switch directories, then jump back where I was. Even that is a neat trick.) How this might look graphically we see in Figure 3–5.

There is another neat trick built into the csh for changing directories that is very useful. This is the concept of a directory path. Like the execution search path, the directory path is a set of values that are searched for matches. Rather than searching for commands to execute, the directory path is searched for directories to change into.

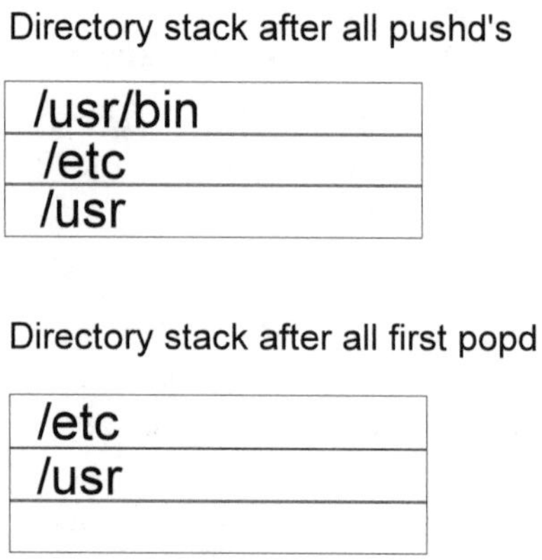

Directory stack after all pushd's

| /usr/bin |
| --- |
| /etc |
| /usr |

Directory stack after all first popd

| /etc |
| --- |
| /usr |
| |

**Figure 3–5**   Changes in a directory stack.

The way this works is by setting the `cdpath` variable. This is done like any other variable in `csh`. For example, if, as system administrator, we wanted to check up on the various spool directories, we could define `cdpath` like this:

```
set cdpath = /usr/spool
```

Then, if we entered

```
cd lp
```

and if the shell can't find a subdirectory or current one named `lp`, it looks in the `cdpath` variable. Since it is defined as `/usr/spool` and there is a `/usr/spool/lp` directory we jump into `/usr/spool/lp`. From there, if we type

```
cd mail
```

we jump to `/usr/spool/mail`. We can also set this to be several directories like this:

```
set cdpath = ( /usr/spool /usr/lib /etc )
```

In doing so, each of the three named directories will be searched.

The `csh` also can make guesses about where you might want to change directories. This is accomplished through the `cdspell` variable. This is a Boolean variable (true/false) that is set simply by typing:

```
set cdspell
```

When set, the `cdspell` variable tells the `csh` that it should try to guess what is really meant when we misspell a directory name. For example, if we typed

```
cd /sur/bin
```

instead of

```
/usr/bin
```

the `cdspell` mechanism will attempt to figure out what the correct spelling should be. You are then prompted with the name that it guessed as being correct. By typing in anything other than 'n' or 'N' you are changed into this directory. There are limitations, however. Once it finds what it thinks is a match it doesn't search any further.

For example, we have three directories 'a', 'b', and 'c'. If we type 'cd d', all three could be the one we want. The shell will make a guess and choose one, which may or may not be correct.

### The Korn Shell

When I first started at SCO, I was given a `csh` and once I figured out all it could do, I enjoyed using it. I found the editing to be cumbersome from time to time, but it was better than retyping everything.

One of my co-workers, Kamal, was an avid proponent of the Korn Shell (ksh). Every time he wanted to show me something on my terminal he would grumble when he forgot that I wasn't using ksh. Many times he tried to convert me, but learning a new shell wasn't high on my list of priorities.

I often complained to Kamal how cumbersome vi was (at least I thought so). One day I asked him for some pointers on vi, since every time I saw him do something in vi it looked like magic. He agreed with one condition, that at least I try the ksh. All he wanted to do was to show me one thing, and if after that I still wanted to use the csh, that was my own thing—not that he would stop grumbling, just that it was my own thing.

The one thing that Kamal showed me convinced me of the errors of my ways. Within a week I had requested the system administrator to change my login shell to ksh.

What was that one thing that Kamal had shown me? Well, from what I told you above, you know that the csh allows you to edit previous commands. What if there was a way to edit the commands as if you were in vi? As it turns out, there is. Once Kamal showed me how to do it, I felt like the csh editing mechanism was like using a sledge hammer to pound in a nail—it does what you want, but it is more work than you need.

Like the csh, the ksh has a history mechanism. The ksh history mechanism has two major advantages over that of the csh. First, the information is actually saved to file. This is either defined by the HISTFILE environment variable *before* the shell is invoked or it defaults to .sh_history in your home directory. At any point you can edit this file and make changes to what the ksh perceives as your command history.

This could be useful if you knew you were going to be issuing the same commands every time you logged in and you didn't want to create aliases or functions. If you copied a saved version of this file (or any other text file) and named it .sh_history then you would immediately have access to this new history. (Rewriting history? I shudder at the ramifications.)

The next nice trick is the ability to edit directly from the commands line any of the lines in your .sh_history file. If you have your EDITOR environment variable set to vi or you use the set -o vi command, you can edit previous commands using many of the standard vi editing commands.

To enter edit mode you press ESC. You can now scroll through the lines of your history file using the movement keys from vi (h-j-k-l). Once you have found the line you are looking for you can use other vi commands to delete, add, change, whatever. If you press 'v', you are brought into the full-screen version of vi .

(I found this out by accident) For more details, check out the `vi` or `ksh` man-page or the section later on `vi`.

In the section above on `csh`, I talked about using `pushd` and `popd` to keep track of what directories you are in. Unfortunately, the `ksh` cannot maintain a directory stack. However, it does keep track of your *last* directory in the `OLDPWD` environment variable. Whenever you change directories, the system saves your current directory in `OLDPWD` *before* it changes you to the new location.

You can use this by simply entering `cd $OLDPWD`. Since the variable `OLDPWD` is expanded before the `cd` command is executed, you end up back in your previous directory. Although this is more characters that just `popd`, it's easier since the system keeps track of this. Also, since it's a variable, I can access it in any way that I can access other environment variables.

For example, if there was a file in our old directory that we wanted to move to our current one, we could do this by entering

```
cp $OLDPWD/<file_name> ./
```

However, things are not as hard as they seem. Typing in `cd $OLDPWD` is still a bit cumbersome. Why isn't there something like that in the `ksh`? There is. In fact, it's much simpler. When I first found out about it, the adjective that first came to mind was "sweet." To change directories to your previous directory, simply type in `'cd -'`.

Another predefined "variable" is the tilde (~), which is a shortcut way of referring to a particular user's home directory. By itself, it refers to the home directory of the user using it. If you follow it with a user's name, then it refers to the home directory of that user. For example, `~jimmo` refers to the home directory of the user jimmo.

## Commonly Used Utilities

There are hundreds of utilities and commands plus thousands of support files in a normal SCO ODT or OpenServer installation. Very few people I have met know what they all do. As a matter of fact, I don't know anyone who knows what they all do. Some are obvious and we use them every day, such as `date`. Others are not so obvious and I have never met anyone who has used them, like `xtd`.

Despite the overwhelming number of them and their often cryptic names and even more cryptic options, there are many commands that are very useful and very powerful.

I have often encountered users, as well as system administrators, who will combine many commands into something relatively complicated. This type of elaborate combining is often unnecessary.

In this section we are going to cover some of the more common commands. I am basing my choice on a couple of things. First, I am going to cover those commands that I personally use on a regular basis. These are ones that I use to do things I need to do, or those that I help end-users use to get done what they need to. Next, I will cover the SCO UNIX system itself. There are dozens of scripts scattered all through the system that contain many of these commands. By talking about them here, you will be in a better position to understand existing scripts, should you need to expand or troubleshoot them.

Since utilities are usually part of some larger process (such as installing a new hard disk or adding a new user), I am not going to talk about them here. I will get to the more common utilities as we move along. For a wonderful overview, see Ellie Cutler's *SCO UNIX in a Nutshell* from O'Reilly & Associates.

### *Looking for Files*

There are many ways to do the things that you want. Some use a hammer approach and force results out of the system. In many cases, there are other commands that do the exact same thing without all the gyrations. So, what I am going to try to do here is step through some of the logic (and illogic) that I went through when first learning SCO UNIX. That way we can all laugh together at how silly I was and maybe you won't make the same mistakes I did.

Every dialect of UNIX that I have seen uses the `ls` command. This gives a directory listing of either the current directory, if no argument is given, or a listing of what every files or directories are specified as arguments. The default behavior under SCO UNIX for the `ls` command is to list the names of the files in a single column. Try it and see.

It is a frequent (maybe not common) misconception for new users to think that they have to be in a particular directory to get a listing of it. They will spend a great deal of time moving up and down the directory tree looking for a particular file. Fortunately, they don't have to do it that way. This issue with this misunderstanding is that every command is capable of working with paths, as it is the operating system that does the work. Recall our discussion of SCO basics. Paths can be relative to our current directory such as `./directory`, or absolute such as `/usr/jimmo/directory`.

For example, assume you have a subdirectory of your current working directory called `letters`. In it are several subdirectories for the type of letter, such as `business`, `school`, `family`, `friends`, and `taxes`. To get a listing of each of this directories, you could use

```
ls ./letters/business
ls ./letters/school
ls ./letters/family
ls ./letters/friends
ls ./letters/taxes
```

Since the `ls` command allows you to have multiple commands on the same line, you could have issued the command like this:

```
ls ./letters/business ./letters/school ./letters/family
   ./letters/friends ./letters/taxes
```

Both will give you a listing of each of the five directories. Even for five directories, typing all of that is a pain. You might think you can save some typing if you simply entered

```
ls ./letters
```

Well, this gives you a listing of all the files and directories in `./letters`, not the subdirectories. Instead, if you entered

```
ls ./letters/*:
```

the shell will expand the wildcard (*) and give you a listing of both the `./letters` directory as well as the directories immediately below `./letters`, like the second example above. If each of the subdirectories is small, then this might fit onto one screen. If, on the other hand, you have fifty letters in each of these subdirectories, they are not all going to fit on the screen at once. Remember our discussion on shell basics? You can use the pipe (`|`) to send the command through something like `more` or `pg` so you could read it a page at a time.

What if the `taxes` directories contained a subdirectory for each year for the past five years, and each of these contained a subdirectory for each month, and each of these contained a subdirectory for federal, state, and local taxes, and each of these contained ten letters?

If we knew that the letter we were looking for was somewhere in the `taxes` subdirectory, the command `ls ./letters/taxes/*` would show us the subdirectories of `taxes` (`federal`, `local`, `state`), and it would show their contents. We could then look through this output for the file we were looking for.

What if the file we were looking for was five levels deeper? We could keep adding wildcards (*) until we reached the right directory, as in,

```
ls ./letters/taxes/*/*/*/*/*
```

This might work, but what if the files were six levels deeper? Well, we add an extra wildcard. What if it were ten levels deeper? Well, we could fill the line with wildcards. Even if we had too many, we would still find the file we were looking for.

Fortunately for us, we don't have to type in ten asterisks to get what we want. We can use the -R option to ls to do a recursive listing. The -R option also avoids the "argument list too long" error that we might get with wildcards. So, the solution here is to use the ls command like this:

```
ls -R ./letters/taxes | more
```

The problem with this is that we now have 1800 files to look through. Piping that through more and looking for the right file will be very time consuming. If knew that it was there, but we missed it on the first pass, we would have to run through the whole thing again.

The alternative is to have more search for the right file for you. Because the output is more than one screen, more will display the first screen and at the bottom display --More--. Here we could type a slash (/) followed by the name of the file and enter. More will now search through the output until it finds the name of the file. Now we know that the file exists.

The problem here is the output of the ls command. We can find out whether a file exists by this method, but we cannot really tell where it is. If you try this, you will see that more jumps to the spot in the output where the file is (if it is there). However, all we see is the file name, not what directory it is in. Actually, this problem also exists even if we didn't search for it.

An alternative would be to pipe the output through pg. Both pg and more have the ability to search for specific text. If not used as a pipe, but using the name of a file as an argument, both can jump to a specific line number. For example, the command

```
pg +42 file_name
```

will jump to line 42 of the file file_name before displaying any output. If, however, we use more or pg as the end of the pipe, the plus-sign (+) will move us forward so many *screens*.

There are a couple advantages that pg offers. First it has the ability to move *backward*. In contrast to the --More-- from more, pg uses a colon (:) as its prompt. Here, we can use a minus (–) to move *backwards* screens.

However, more does have one advantage over pg that I use quite often. This usually occurs when I have several files in a directory that contain some information I need to edit. I could use more to search the files until I found the right one, then use vi to edit the file. However, more makes things easier. Once I get the --More-- prompt, I simply press 'v' and that brings me into vi. (I found this out by accidentally pressing 'v', when I wanted to press the space bar to move down one screen.) Note that this does not work when using more as the end of a pipe. You cannot edit standard input, and that's where more is getting its input from.

If you use more as the command and not the end of a pipe, instead of just seeing --More--, you will probably see something like this:

```
--More--(16%)
```

This means that you have read 16% of the file.

However, we don't need to use more for that. Since we don't want to look at the entire output, rather just for a particular file, we can use one of three commands that SCO UNIX provides to do pattern searching: grep, egrep, and fgrep. The names sound a little odd to the SCO UNIX beginner, but grep stands for *global regular expression print*. The other two are newer versions that do similar things. For example, egrep searches for patterns that are full regular expressions and fgrep searches for fixed strings and is a bit faster.

Let's assume that we are tax consultants and have fifty subdirectories; one for each client. Each is then broken down by year and type of tax (state, local, federal, sales, etc.). A couple years ago, a client bought a boat. We have a new client who also wants to buy a boat and we need some information in that old file.

Since we know the name of that file we can use grep to find it, like this:

```
ls -R ./letters/taxes | grep boat
```

Even if the file was called boats, boat.txt, boats.txt, or letter.boat, the grep will find it. The reason is because grep is only looking for the pattern boat. Since that pattern exists in all four of those file names, all four would be potential matches.

The problem is that the file may not be called boat.txt, but rather Boat.txt. Remember, unlike DOS, UNIX is case-sensitive. Therefore, grep sees boat.txt and Boat.txt as different things. The solution here would be to tell grep to look for both.

Remember our discussion on regular expression in the section on shell basics? Not only can we use regular expressions for file names, we can often use them in the arguments to commands. The term *regular expression* is even part of grep's name Using regular expressions, the command might look like this:

```
ls -R ./letters/taxes | grep [Bb]oat
```

This would now find both boat.txt and Boat.txt.

Some of you many see a problem with this. Not only does SCO UNIX see a difference between boat.txt and Boat.txt, but also between Boat.txt and

BOAT.TXT. In order to catch all possibilities, we would have to have a command something like this:

```
ls -R ./letters/taxes | grep [Bb][Oo][Aa][Tt]
```

Although this is perfectly correct syntax and it will find it no matter what case the word 'boat' is in, it is too much work. The programmers who developed grep realized that people would want to look for something regardless of what case they were in. Therefore, they built in the -i option. This simply says *ignore* the case. Therefore, the command

```
ls -R ./letters/taxes | grep -i boat
```

will not only find boats, boat.txt, boats.txt, and letter.boat, but it will also find Boat.txt and BOAT.TXT as well.

If you've been paying attention, you might have noticed something. Although the grep command will tell you about the existence of a file, it won't tell you where it is. This is just like piping it through more, only we're filtering out something. Therefore, it still won't tell you the path.

Now, this isn't grep's fault. It did what it was supposed to. We told it to search for a particular pattern and it did and then it displayed that pattern for us. The problem still exists that the ls command is not displaying the full paths of the files, just their names.

Instead of ls, let's use a different command. Let's use find instead. Just as its name implies, find is used to find things. What it finds is files. If we change the command to look like this:

```
find ./letters/taxes -print | grep -i boat
```

this finds what we are looking for and gives us the paths as well.

Before we go on, let's look at the syntax of the find command. There are a lot of options and it does look foreboding, at first. It is easiest to think of the command in this way:

```
find <starting_where> <search_criteria> <do_something>
```

In this case, the "where" is ./letters/taxes. Therefore, find started its search in the ./letters/taxes directory. Here, we had no search criteria, we simply told it to do something. That something was to -print out what it finds. Since the files it finds all have a path relative to ./letters/taxes, this is included in the output. Therefore, when we pipe it through grep, we get the path to the file we are looking for.

We also need to be careful since the find command we are using will also find directories named boat. This is because we did not specify any search criteria. If instead, we wanted it *just* to look for a regular file (which is often a good idea), we could change the command to look like this:

```
find ./letters/taxes -type f -print | grep -i boat
```

Here we see the option `-type f` as the search criteria. This will find all the files of type `f` for regular files. This could also be a `d` for directories, `c` for character special files, `b` for block special files, and so on. Check out the `find(C)` man-page for other types that you can use.

Too complicated? Let's make things easier by avoiding `grep`. There are many different things that we can use as search criteria for `find`. Take a quick look at the man-page and you will see that you can search for specific owner, groups, permissions, and even names. Instead of having `grep` do the search for us, let's save a step (and time) by having `find` do the search for us. The command would then look like this:

```
find ./letters./taxes -name boat -print
```

This will then find any file named `boat` and list its respective path. The problem here is that it will only find the file named `boat`. It *won't* find the files `boat.txt`, `boats.txt` or even `Boat`.

The nice thing is that `find` understands regular expression so we could issue the command like this:

```
find ./letters./taxes -name '[Bb]oat' -print
```

(Note that we had to include the single-quote (') to avoid the square brackets (`[]`) from being first interpreted by the shell)

This command told `find` to look for all files named both `boat` and `Boat`. However, this won't find `boat`. We are almost there.

We have two alternatives. One is to expand the `find` to include all possibilities as in,

```
find ./letters./taxes -name '[Bb][Oo][Aa][Tt]' -print
```

As in the example above, this will find all the files with any combination of those four letters and print them out. However, it won't find `boat.txt`. Therefore, we need to change it yet again. This time we have,

```
find ./letters./taxes -name '[Bb][Oo][Aa][Tt]*' -print
```

Here we have passed the wildcard (*) to `find` to tell it to find anything that starts with 'boat' (upper- or lower-case) followed by anything. If we add an extra asterisk, as in

```
find ./letters./taxes -name '*[Bb][Oo][Aa][Tt]*' -print
```

we not only get `boat.txt`, but also `newboat.txt`, which the first example would have missed.

This works. Is there an easier way? Well, sort of. There is a way that is easier in the sense that there are less characters to type in. This would be:

```
find ./letters/taxes -print | grep -i boat
```

Isn't that the same command that we issued before? Yes, it is. In this particular case, this combination of `find` and `grep` is the easier solution, since all we are looking for is the path to a specific file. However, these examples show you different options to `find` and different ways that you can use it.

### Looking Through Files

Let's assume for a moment that none of the commands we issued came up with a file. There was not a single match of *any* kind. This might mean that we removed the file. On the other hand we might have named it `yacht.txt` or something similar. What can we do to find it?

We could jump through the same hoops for yacht as we did for boat. However, what if the customer had a canoe or a junk. Are we stuck with searching every possible word for boat? Yes, unless we know something about the file, even if that something is *in* the file.

The nice thing is that `grep` doesn't have to be the end of a pipe. One of the arguments can be the name of a file. If you want, you can put several files, since `grep` will take the first argument as the pattern it should look for. If we were to enter

```
grep [Bb]oat ./letters/taxes/*
```

we would search the contents of all the files in the directory `./letters/taxes` looking for the word Boat or boat.

If the file we are looking for happens to be in the directory `./letters/taxes`, then all is well. If we have dozens of directories to look through, this is impractical. So, we turn back to `find`.

One of the useful options to find is `-exec`. When a file is found, you use `-exec` to execute a command. We can therefore use `find` to find the files, then use `-exec` to run `grep` on them. Since you probably don't have dozens of files on your system related to taxes, let's use an example from files that you most probably have.

Let's find all the files in the `/etc` directory containing `/bin/sh`. This would be run as:

```
find ./etc -exec grep /bin/sh {} \;
```

The `{}` substitutes the file found by the search, so the actual `grep` command would be something like

```
grep /bin/sh ./etc/filename
```

The `"\;"`, is a flag saying that this is the end of the command.

The `find` command searches for all the files that match the specified criteria (in this case there was no criteria so it found them all), then run `grep` on them searching for the pattern `[Bb]oat`.

Do you know what this tells me? It says that there is a file somewhere under the directory `./letters/taxes` that contains either 'boat' or 'Boat'. It *doesn't* tell me what the file name is called. The reason is the way the `-exec` is handled. Each filename is handed off one at a time, replacing the `{}`. It would be as if we had entered individual lines for

```
grep '[Bb]oat' ./letters/taxes/file1
grep '[Bb]oat' ./letters/taxes/file2
grep '[Bb]oat' ./letters/taxes/file3
```

If we had entered

```
grep '[Bb]oat' ./letters/taxes/*
```

the `grep` would have output the name of the file in front of each matching line it found. However, since each line is treated separately when using `find`, we don't see the file names. We could use the `-l` option to `grep`, but that would only give me the file name. That might be okay if there was one or two files. However, if the line in the file mentioned a "boat trip" or a "boat trailer", these might not be what we were looking for. If we used the `-l` option to `grep` we wouldn't see the actual line—catch-22.

In order to get what we need, we have to introduce a new command: `xargs`. By using it as one end of a pipe, we can repeat the same command on different files without actually having to input it multiple times.

In this case, we would get what we wanted by typing

```
find ./letters/taxes -print | xargs grep [Bb]oat
```

The first part is the same as we talked about earlier. The `find` command simply prints all the names it finds (all of them in this case, since there was no search criteria) and passes them to `xargs`. Next, `xargs` processes them one at a time and creates commands using `grep`. However, unlike the `-exec` option to `find`, `xargs` will output the name of the file before each matching line.

Obviously, this example does not find those instances where the file we were looking for contained words like yacht or canoe instead of boat. Unfortunately, the only way to catch all possibilities is to actually specify each one. So, that's what we might do. Rather than list the different possible synonyms for boat, let's just take the three: boat, yacht, and canoe.

To do this we need to run the `find | xargs` command three times. However, rather than typing in the command each time, we are going to take advantage of a useful aspect of the shell. In some instance, the shell knows when you want to continue with a command and gives you a *secondary prompt*. If you are running `sh` or `ksh`, then this is probably '>'.

For example if we typed

```
find ./letters/taxes -print |
```

the shell knows that the pipe (|) cannot be at the end of the line. It then gives me a > or ? prompt where we can continue typing:

```
> xargs grep -i boat
```

The shell interprets these two lines as if we had typed them all on the same line. We can use this with a shell construct that lets me do loops. This is the `for/in` construct for `sh` and `ksh`, and the `foreach` construct in `csh`. It would look like this:

```
for j in boat ship yacht
> do
> find ./letters/taxes -print | xargs grep -i $j
> done
```

In this case, we are using the variable `j`, although we could have called it anything we wanted. When we are putting together such quick little commands, we save ourselves a little typing by using single letters as variables.

In the `sh/ksh` example, we need to enclose the body of the loop inside the `do-done` pair. In the `csh` example we need to include the `end`. In both cases this little command we have written will loop through three times. Each time, the variable `$j` is replaced with one of the three words that we used. If we thought up another dozen or so synonyms for boat, then we could have included them all. Remember that the shell knows that the pipe (|) is not the end of the command, so this would work as well:

```
for j in boat ship yacht
> do
> find ./letters/taxes -print |
> xargs grep -i $j
> done
```

Doing this from the command line has a drawback. If we want to use the same command again, we need to retype everything. However, using another trick, we can save the command. Remember that both the `ksh` and `csh` have history mechanisms to allow you to repeat and edit commands that you recently edited. However, what happens tomorrow when you want to run the command again? Granted, `ksh` has the .sh_history file, but what about `sh` and `csh`?

Why not save this in a file that we have all the time? We could use `vi` or some other text editor. However, we could take advantage of a characteristic of the `cat` command, which is normally used to output the contents of a file to the screen. You can also redirect the `cat` to another file.

If we wanted to combine the contents of a file we could do something like this:

```
cat file1 file2 file3 >newfile
```

This would combine `file1`, `file2`, and `file3` into `newfile`.

What happens if we leave the names of source files out? Our command would look like this:

```
cat >newfile
```

Now, `cat` will take its input from the default input file: `stdin`. We can now type in lines, one at a time. When we are done, we tell `cat` to close the file by sending it an end of file character, CTRL-D. So, to create the new command we would issue the `cat` command as above and type in our command:

```
for j in boat ship yacht
do
find ./letters/taxes -print |
xargs grep -i $j
done
<CTRL-D>
```

Note that here the secondary prompt (>) does not appear here since it is `cat` that is reading our input and not the shell. We now have a file containing the five lines that we typed in that we can use as a shell script.

However, right now all that we have is a file named `newfile` that contains five lines. We need to tell the system that it is a shell script, so that it can be executed. Remember in our discussion on operating system basics I said that a file's permissions need to be set in order to be able to execute a file. In order to change the permissions, we need a new command: `chmod`. (Read: "change mode" since we are changing the mode of the file.)

The `chmod` command is used to not only change access to the file, but also to tell the system that it should *try* to execute the command. I said "try" because the system reads that file, line-by-line, and tries to execute each line. If we typed in some garbage in a shell script, the system would try to execute each line and would probably report `not found` for every line.

To make a file execute, we need to give it execute permissions. To give everyone execution permissions, you use the `chmod` command, like this:

```
chmod +x newfile
```

Now the file `newfile` has execute permissions, so, in a sense, it is executable. However, remember that I said the system would *read* each line. In order for a shell script to function correctly, it also needs to be readable by the person executing it. In order to read a file, you need to have read permission on that file. More than likely, *you* already have read permissions on the file since you created it. However, since we gave everyone execution permissions, let's give them all read permissions as well, like this:

```
chmod +r newfile
```

You now have a new command called `newfile`. This can be executed just like any the system provides for you. If that file resides in a directory somewhere in your path, all you need to do is type it in. Otherwise, (as we talked about before) you need to enter in the path as well. Keep in mind that the system does not need to be able to *read* binary programs. All it needs to be able to do is execute them. Now you have your first shell script and your first self-written UNIX command.

What happens if after looking though all of the files, you don't find the one you are looking for? Maybe you were trying to be sophisticated and you used "small aquatic vehicle" instead of boat. Now, six months later, you cannot remember what you called it. Looking through every file might take a long time. If only you could shorten the search a little. Since you remember that the letter you wrote was to the boat dealer, if you could remember the name of the dealer, you could find the letter.

The problem is that six months after you wrote it, you can no more remember the dealer's name than you can remember whether you called it a "small aquatic vehicle" or not. If you are like me, seeing the dealer's name will jog your memory. Therefore, if you could just look at the top portion of each letter, you might find what you are looking for. You can take advantage of the fact that the address is always at the top of the letter and use a command that is designed to look there. This is the `head` command and we could use it something like this:

```
find ./letters/taxes -exec head {} \;
```

This will look at the first ten (the default for `head`) lines of each of the files that it finds. If the addressee is not in the first ten lines, but rather in the first 20 lines, we could change it to

```
find ./letters/taxes -exec head -20 {} \;
```

The problem with this is that twenty lines is almost an entire screen. If you ran this is would be comparable to running `more` on every file and hitting `q` to exit after it showed the first screen. Fortunately we can add another command to restrict the output even further. The `tail` command is just the opposite of `head`, as it shows you the bottom of the file. So, if we knew that the address resided on lines 15–20, we could run a command like this:

```
find ./letters/taxes -exec head -20 {} \; | tail -5
```

This command passes the first 20 lines of each file the pipe and then `tail` displays the last 5 lines of that. So you would get lines 15–20 of every file, right? Not quite.

The problem is that the shell sees these as two *tokens*; that is, two separate commands in `find ./letters/taxes -exec head -20 {} \;` and `tail -5`. All of the output of the `find` is sent to the pipe and it is the last five lines of this that `tail` shows. Therefore, if the `find | head` had found 100 files, we would not see the contents of the first 99!

The solution is to add two other shell constructs: `while` and `read`. This carries out a particular command (or set of commands) `while` some criteria is true. The `read` can read input either from the command line, or as part of a more complicated construction. So, using `cat` again to create a little command like we did above, we could have something like this:

```
find ./letters/taxes -print | while read FILE
do
echo $FILE
head -20 $FILE | tail -5
done
```

In this example, the `while` and `read` work together. The `while` will continue so long as it can read something into the variable `FILE`, that is, so long as there is output coming from the `find`. Here again, we also need to enclose the body of the loop within the `do-done` pair.

The first line of the loop simply `echoes` the name of the file so we can keep track of what file is being looked at. Once we have found the correct name, we could use it as the search criteria for a `find | grep` command. This does require looking through each file twice, however, if all you need to see is the address, then this is a lot quicker than doing a `more` on every file.

## Basic Shell Scripting

By now we have a pretty good idea of how commands can be put together to do a wide variety of tasks. However, in order to create more complicated scripts, we need more than just a few commands. There are several shell constructs that you need to be familiar with in order to make complicated scripts. A couple (the `while` and `for-in` constructs) we already covered. However, there are several more that can be very useful in a wide range of circumstances.

There are several things we need to talk about before we can jump into things. The first is the idea of arguments. Like binary programs you can pass arguments to shell scripts and have them use these arguments as they work. For example, let's assume we have a script called `myscript` that takes three arguments. The first is the name of a directory, the second is a file name, and the third is a word to search for. The script will then search for all files in that directory with any part of their name being the filename and then search in those files for the word specified. A very simple version of the script might look like this:

```
ls $1 | grep $2 | while read file
do
     grep $3 ${2}/${file}
done
```

The syntax is

```
myscript directory file_name word
```

We discussed the `while-do-done` construct at the beginning of the chapter when we were talking about different commands. The one difference here is that we are sending the output of a command through a second pipe before we send it to the `while`.

This also brings up a new construct: `${2}/${file}`. By enclosing a variable name inside of curly brackets, we can combine variables. In this case we take the name of the directory ( `${2}` ), tack on a `'/'` for a directory separator followed by the name of a file that the `grep` had found ( `${file}` ). This builds up the path name to the file.

We run the program like this:

```
myscript /usr/jimmo trip boat
```

The two arguments `/usr/jimmo`, `trip`, and `boat` are assigned to the *positional parameters* 1, 2, and 3, respectively. "Positional" because the number they are assigned is based on what position they appear in the command. Since the positional parameters are shell variables, we need to refer to them with the leading dollar sign ($).

When the shell interprets the command, what is actually run is

```
ls /usr/jimmo | grep trip | while read file
do
     grep boat /usr/jimmo/${file}
done
```

If we wanted we could make the script a little more self-documenting by assigning the values of the positional parameters to variables. The new script would look like this:

```
DIR=$1
FILENAME=$2
WORD=$3
ls $DIR | grep $FILENAME | while read file
do
                grep $WORD ${DIR}/${file}
done
```

If we started the script again with the same arguments, first /usr/jimmo would get assigned to the variable DIR, trip would get assigned to the variable FILE-NAME, and boat would get assigned to WORD. When the command was interpreted and run, it would still be evaluated the same way.

Being able to assign the positional parameters to variables is useful for a couple of reasons. First, we face the issue of self-documenting code. In this example, the script is very small and since we know what the script is doing, we probably would not have made the assignments to the variables. However, if we had a larger script, then making the assignment would be very valuable in terms of keeping track of things.

The next issue is that you can only reference ten positional parameters. The first $0, refers to the script itself. What this can be used for, we'll get to in a minute. The others, $1–$9, refer to the arguments that are passed to the script. Well, what happens if you have more than nine arguments? This is where the shift instruction comes in. It moves the arguments "down" in the positional parameters list.

For example, let's assume we changed the first part of the script like this:

```
DIR=$1
shift
FILENAME=$1
```

On the first line, the value of positional parameter 1 is /usr/jimmo and we assign it to the variable DIR. The next line, the shift moves every positional parameter down. Since $0 remains unchanged, what was in $1 (/usr/jimmo) drops out of the bottom. Now the value of positional parameter 1 is trip which is assigned to the variable FILENAME and positional parameter 2 (boat) is assigned to WORD.

If we had ten arguments, the tenth would initially be unavailable to us. However, once we do the shift, what was the tenth argument shifts down and becomes the ninth. It is now accessible through the positional parameter 9. If we had more than ten, there are a couple of ways to get access to them. First, we could issue enough shifts until the arguments all moved down far enough. Or, we could use the fact that `shift` can take as an argument the number of shifts it should do. Therefore, using

```
shift 9
```

makes the 10th argument positional parameter 1.

What about the other nine arguments? Are they gone? Well, if you never assigned them to a variable, then yes, they are gone. However, by assigning them to a variable *before* you make the shift, you still have access to their values.

Being able to shift positional parameters comes in handy in other instances. This brings up the issue of a new parameter: $*. This refers to all the positional parameter (except for $0). So, let's assume we have ten positional parameters and do a `shift` 2 (ignoring whatever we did with the first two). Now the parameter $* contains the value of the last eight arguments.

What if we wanted to search for a *phrase* and not just a single word in our sample script above? We could change the script to look like this:

```
DIR=$1
FILENAME=$2
shift 2
WORD=$*
ls $DIR | grep $FILENAME | while read file
do
     grep "$WORD" ${DIR}/${file}
done
```

The first change was that after assigning positional parameters 1 and 2 to variables, we shifted twice, effectively removing the first two arguments. We now assign the remaining argument to the variable WORD (WORD=$*) Since this could be a phrase, we need to enclose the variable in double-quotes ("$WORD"). We can now search for phrases as well as single words. If we did not include the phrase in double-quotes, the system would see it as individual arguments to grep.

Another useful parameter keeps track of the total number of parameters: $#. In the script above, what would happen if we only had two arguments? Well, the grep would fail because there would be nothing for it to search for. Therefore, it would be a good thing to keep track of the number of arguments.

We need to first introduce a new construct. This is the if-then-fi construct. This is similar to the while-do-done construct, where the if-fi pairs mark the ends of the block (fi is simply if reversed). The difference is that instead of repeating the commands within the block while the specific condition is true, we only do it once *if* the condition is true. In general, it looks like this:

```
if [ condition ]
then
     do something
fi
```

The conditions are all defined in the `test(C)` man-page and can be string comparisons, arithmetic comparisons, and even conditions where we test specific files (such as if they are writeable or not). Check out the `test(C)` man-page for more examples.

Since we want to check the number of arguments passed to our script, we will do an arithmetic comparison. We can check if the values are equal, the first is less than the second, the second less than the first, the first greater than or equal to the second and so on. In our case, we want to ensure that there are *at least* three arguments, since having more is valid if we are going to be searching for a phrase. Therefore, we would want to compare the number of arguments and check if it is greater than or equal to 3. So, we might have something like this:

```
if [ $# -ge 3 ]
then
     body_of_script
fi
```

If we only have two arguments, then the test inside the brackets is false, the `if` fails, and we do not enter the loop. Instead the program simply exits silently. However, to me, this is not enough. We want to know what's going on, therefore, we use another construct: the `else`. When used with the `if-then-fi` we are saying that if the test evaluates to true, do one thing, otherwise do something else. In our example program, we might have something like this:

```
DIR=$1
FILENAME=$2
shift 2
WORD=$*
if [ $# -ge 3 ]
then
ls $DIR | grep $FILENAME | while read file
do
     grep "$WORD" ${DIR}/${file}
done
fi
else
     echo "Insufficient number of arguments"
fi
```

If we only put in two arguments, the if fails and the commands between the else and the fi are executed. To make the script a little friendly, we usually tell the user what the correct syntax is, therefore we might change the end of the script to look like this:

```
else
    echo "Insufficient number of arguments"
    echo "Usage: $0 <directory> <file_name> <word>"
fi
```

The important part of this change is the use of the $0. As I mentioned a moment ago, this is used to refer to the program itself. Not just it's name, but rather the way it is called. Had we hardcoded the line to look like this:

```
echo "Usage: myscript <directory> <file_name> <word>"
```

then no matter how we started the script, the output would always be

```
Usage: myscript <directory> <file_name> <word>
```

However, if we use $0 instead, we could start the program like this:

```
/usr/jimmo/bin/myscript /usr/jimmo file
```

and the output would be

```
Usage: /usr/jimmo/bin/myscript <directory> <file_name> <word>
```

On the other hand, if we started it like this:

```
./bin/myscript /usr/jimmo file
```

the output would be

```
Usage: ./bin/myscript <directory> <file_name> <word>
```

One thing to keep in mind is that the else needs to be within the matching if-fi pairs. The key here is the word *matching*. We could nest the if-then-else-fi several layers if we wanted. We just need to keep track of things. The keys issues are that the ending fi matches to the *last* fi and the else is enclosed within an if-fi pair. Here is what multiple sets might look like:

```
if [ $condition1 = "TRUE" ]
then
    if [ $condition2 = "TRUE" ]
    then
        if [ $condition3 = "TRUE" ]
          echo "Conditions 1, 2 and 3 are true"
        else
          echo "Only Conditions 1 and 2 are true"
        fi
    else
echo "Only Condition 1 is true"
fi
```

```
echo "No conditions are true"
else
fi
```

Now, this doesn't take into account the possibility that `condition1` is false but `condition2` or `condition3` are true. However, hopefully, you see how to construct nested conditional statements.

What if we had a single variable that could take on several values? Depending on what value that was, the program would behave differently. This could be used as a menu, for example. Many system administrators build such a menu into their users' `.profile` (or `.login`) so that they never need to get to a shell. They simply input the number of the program that they want to run and away they go.

In order to do something like this, we need to introduce yet another construct. This is the `case-esac` pair. Like the `if-fi` pair, `esac` is the reverse of `case`. To implement a menu, we might have something like this:

```
read choice
case $choice in
a) program1;;
b) program2;;
c) program3;;
*) echo "No such Option";;
esac
```

If the value of `choice` that we input is either a, b, or c, then the appropriate program is started. The things to note are the `in` on the first line, the expected value is followed by a closing parenthesis, and there are two semicolons at the end of each block.

It is the closing parenthesis that indicates the end of the possibilities. If we wanted, we could include other possibilities for the different options. In addition, since the double semicolons mark the end of the block, we can simply add other commands before we get to the end of the block. For example, if we wanted our script to recognize either upper or lowercase, we could change it to look like this:

```
read choice
case $choice in
    a|A) program1
         program2
         program3;;
    b|B) program2
         program3;;
    c|C) program3;;
    *) echo "No such Option";;
esac
```

If necessary, we could also include a range of characters

```
case $choice in
    [a-z] ) echo "Lowercase";;
    [A-Z] ) echo "Uppercase";;
    [0-9] ) echo "Number";;
esac
```

Now, whatever is called as the result of one of these choices does not have to be a UNIX command. Since each line is interpreted as if it were executed from the command line, we can include anything that we could if we had executed the command from the command line. Provided they are known to the shell script, this also includes aliases, variables, and even shell functions.

A shell function behaves similarly to functions in other programming languages. It is a portion of the script that is set-off from the rest of the program and is accessed through its name. These functions are the same as the functions we talked about in our discussion of shells. The only apparent difference is that functions created inside of a shell script will disappear when the shell exits. To prevent this, start the script with a . (dot).

For example, if we had a function inside a script called `myscript` we would start it like this:

```
. myscript
```

The result is that although the script executes normally, a sub-shell is not started. Therefore, anything you set or define remains. This includes both functions and variables.

Shell functions behave like small shell scripts in that they can accept arguments like a shell script and the positional parameters behave in the same way. Actually, they don't have to be small, at all. In fact, the only limitations we can find are the same that apply to shell scripts in general such as the length of the command line and overall size of the file. However, one thing to keep in mind is that the functions need to appear in the script *before* they are called.

The basic syntax of the function is

```
function_name()
{
   what the function does
}
```

When you call a function, you simply use its name, just as you would from the command. If the function takes any arguments, these are passed just like shell scripts. In fact, shell functions have positional parameters, just like the shell script. Added to that, they are different from those belonging to the shell script. For example, let's look at this script, called (what else?) `myscript`:

```
funct1()
{
     echo $1
}
funct1 two
```

If we started it like this:

```
myscript one
```

the output would be

```
two
```

This is because the positional parameter 1 inside of the function `funct1()` refers to the arguments used to call the function. So, if `funct1` was called with no arguments, then $1 would not be set when we got inside of `funct1`.

One thing I commonly use functions for is to clean up for me when things go wrong. In fact, there are quite a few shell scripts on a standard SCO system containing "clean-up" functions. Such functions are necessary to return the system to the state it was in before the shell script was started. What happens when the user hits the delete key in the middle of a script. Unless it has been disabled or *trapped*, the script will terminate immediately. This can leave some unwanted things lying around the system. Instead, we can catch or *trap* the delete key and run a special clean-up function before we exit.

This is done with the `trap` instruction. The syntax is

```
trap 'command' signals
```

where `command` is the command to run if any of the signals listed in `signals` are received. For example, if we wanted to trap the delete key (signal 2) and run a cleanup function, the line might look like this:

```
trap 'cleanup' 2
```

After we start the script, any time we press the delete key it will first run the function cleanup. We can also set up different traps for different signals, like this:

```
trap 'cleanup1' 1
trap 'cleanup2' 2
```

So, now you know some of the basic commands and how to put them together into a script. The biggest problem up to this point is figuring out how to create that script. You could continue to use `cat`. However, that will get old fast, especially if you make a lot of typos or want to make changes to your scripts. Therefore, you need a better tool. What you really need is a text editor, which is the subject of the next section. Table 3–1 contains a list of some of the more common commands.

**Table 3–1**    Commonly Used Commands

### FILE MANAGEMENT

| command | function |
| --- | --- |
| cd | change directory |
| chgrp | change the group of a file |
| chmod | change the permissions (mode) of a file |
| chown | change the owner of a file |
| cp | copy files |
| file | determine a file's contents |
| l, lc, lf, ls, lx | list files or directories |
| ln | make a link to a file |
| mkdir | make a directory |
| mv | move (rename) a file |
| rm | remove a file |
| rmdir | remove a directory |

### FILE MANIPULATION

| command | function |
| --- | --- |
| awk | pattern-matching language |
| cat | display a file |
| cmp | compare two files |
| csplit | split a file |
| cut | display columns of a file |
| diff | find differences in two files |
| dircmp | compare two directories |
| find | find files |
| head | show the top portion of a file |
| more | display screenfuls of a file |
| pg | display screenfuls of a file |
| sed | noninteractive text editor |
| sort | sort a file |
| tail | display bottom portion of a file |
| tr | translate chracters in a file |
| uniq | find unique or repeated lines in a file |
| xargs | process multiple arguments |

In a shell script (or from the command line for that matter), you can input multiple commands on the same line. For example,

```
date; ls | wc
```

would run the date command and then give the word count of the `ls` command. Note that this does not write the output of both commands on the same line. This just allows you to have the multiple commands on the same line. First the date command is executed and then the `ls | wc`. Each time, the system creates an extra process to run that program.

We can prevent the system from creating the extra process by enclosing the command inside of parenthesis; for example,

```
(date; ls | wc )
```

This is run by the shell itself and not as subshells.

### Odds and Ends

You can get the shell to help you debug your script. If you place a `set -x` in your script, each command with the corresponding arguments are printed as they are executed. If you want to just show a section of your script, include the `set -x` before that section and then a `set +x` at the end. The `set +x` turns off the output.

If you want, you can capture the output into another file, without having it go to the screen. This is done using the fact that output generated as a result of the `set -x` is going to stderr and not stdout. If you redirect stdout somewhere, the output from the `set -x` still goes to the screen. On the other hand, if you redirect stderr, stdout still goes to your screen. To redirect sterr to a file, start the script like this:

```
mscript 2>/tmp/output
```

This says to send file descriptor 2 (stderr) to the file `/tmp/output`.

If you want to create a directory that is several levels deep, you do not have to change directories to the parent and then run `mkdir` from there. The mkdir command takes as an argument the path name of the directory you want to create. It doesn't matter if it is a subdirectory, relative path, or absolute path. The system will do that for you. Also, if you want to create several levels of directories, you don't have to make each parent directory before you make the subdirectories. Instead, you can use the `-p` option to `mkdir`, which will automatically create all the necessary directories.

For example, we want to create the subdirectory `./letters/personal/john`, however, the subdirectory `letters` does not exist, yet. This also means that the subdirectory `personal` doesn't exist. If we run `mkdir` like this:

```
mkdir -p ./letters/personal/john
```

then the system will create `./letters`, then `./letters/personal` and then `./letters/personal/john`.

Assume that you want to remove a file that has multiple links; for example, `ls`, `lc`, `lx`, and `lf` are links to the same file. The system keeps track of how many names reference the file through the *link count* (more on that later). Such links are called hard links. If you remove one of them, then the file still exists, as there are other names that reference it. Only when we remove the last link (and with that the link count goes to zero) will the file be removed.

There is also the issue of symbolic links. A symbolic link (also called a soft link) is nothing more than a path name that points to some other file, or even directory. It is not until the link is accessed that the path is translated into the "real" file. This has some interesting effects. For example, if we create a link like this:

```
ln -s /usr/jimmo/letter.john /usr/jimmo/text/letter.john
```

you would see the symbolic link as something like this:

```
drw-r--r-- 1 jimmo support 29 Sep 15 10:06 letter.john-> /usr/jimmo/letter.john
```

Then the file `/usr/jimmo/text/letter.john` is a symbolic link to `/usr/jimmo/letter.john`. Note that the link count on `/usr/jimmo/letter.john` doesn't change, since the system sees these as two separate files. It is easier to think of the file `/usr/jimmo/text/letter.john` as a text file that contains the path to `/usr/jimmo/letter.john`. If we remove `/usr/jimmo/letter.john`, then `/usr/jimmo/text/letter.john` will still exist. However, it points to something that doesn't exist. Even if there are other hard links that point to the same file as `/usr/jimmo/letter.john` did, that doesn't matter. The symbolic link `/usr/jimmo/text/letter.john` points to the *path* `/usr/jimmo/letter.john`. Since the path no longer exists, the file can no longer be accessed via the symbolic link. It is also possible for you to *create* a symbolic link to a file that does exist, as the system does not check until you access the file.

When you create a file, the access permissions are determined by their *file creation mask*. This is defined by the UMASK variable and can be set using the umask command. One thing to keep in mind is that this is a mask; that is, it masks out permissions rather than assigning them. If you remember, permissions on a file can be set using the `chmod` command and a three digit value; for example,

```
chmod 600 letter.john
```

explicitly sets the permissions on the file `letter.john` to 600 (read and write permission for the user and nothing for everyone else). If we create a new file, the permissions might be 660 (read/write for user and group). This is determined by the UMASK. To understand how the UMASK works, you need to remember that the permissions are octal values, which are determined by the permissions *bits*. Looking at one set of permissions we have

```
bit:         2    1    0
value:       4    2    1
symbol:      r    w    x
```

This means that if the bit with value 4 is set (bit 2), the file can be read. If the bit with value 2 is set (bit 1), the file can be written to. If the bit with value 1 is set (bit 0), the file can be executed. If multiple bits are set, their values are added together. For example, if bits 2 and 1 are set (read/write), the value is $4 + 2 = 6$. Just as in the example above. If all three are set, we have $4 + 2 + 1 = 7$. Since there are three sets of permissions (owner, group, other), the permissions are usually used in triplets, just as in the chmod example above.

The UMASK value *masks* out the bits. The permissions that each position in the UMASK masks out is the same as the file permissions themselves. So, the left-most position masks out the owner permission, the middle position masks the group, and the right-most masks out all others. If we have a UMASK=007, then the permissions for owner and group are not touched. However, for others we have the value 7. This value is obtained by setting all bits. Since this is a mask, then all bits are unset.

The problem many people have is that the umask does *not* force permission, but rather it limits them. For example, if we had a UMASK=007, then we could assume that any file created has permissions of 770. However, this depends on the program that is creating the file. If the program is creating a file with permissions 777, then the umask will mask out the last bits and the permissions will, in fact, be 770. However, if the program creates permissions of 666, then the last bits are still masked out. However, the new file will have permissions of 660, *not* 770. Some programs, like the C compiler, generate files with the execution bit (bit 0) set, however, most do not. Therefore, setting the UMASK=007, does not force creation of executable programs (unless the program creating the file does itself).

Let's look at a more complicated example. Assume UMASK=047. If our program creates a file with permissions 777, then our UMASK does nothing to the first digit, but masks out the 4 from the second digit, giving us 3. Then since the last digit of the UMASK is 7, this masks out everything, so the permissions here are 0. As a result, the permissions for the file are 730. However, if the program creates the file with permissions 666, then the resulting permissions are 620. The easy way to figure out the effects of the UMASK are to subtract the UMASK from the default permissions that the program sets. Note that all negative values become 0.

As I mentioned, one way the UMASK is set is through the environment variable UMASK. You can change it any time using the umask command. The syntax is simply

```
umask <new_umask>
```

Here the `<new_umask>` can either be the numeric value (for example, 007) or symbolic. For example, to set the umask to 047 using the symbolic notation we have

```
umask u=,g=r,o=rwx
```

This has the effect of removing no permissions from the user, removing read permissions from the group, and removing all permissions from others.

## Interactively Editing Files with vi

### Basics

SCO UNIX provides a handful of programs used to edit files. Depending on the circumstances, each one could be useful. The two I most frequently use are the full screen editor `vi` and the stream editor, `sed`.

The use and benefits of any editor like `vi` is almost religious. Often the reasons people choose one over the other is purely a matter of personal taste. Each offers its own advantages and functionality. Some versions of UNIX provide other editors, such `emacs`. However, the nice thing about `vi` is that every dialect of UNIX has it. You can sit down at any UNIX system and can edit a file. For this reason, more than any other, I think it is worth learning.

One of the problems `vi` has is that it is very intimidating. I know, I used to not like it. I frequently get into discussions with people who have spent less than ten minutes using it and rant about how terrible it is. Often I see them spending hours trying to find a free or relatively cheap add-on so they don't have to learn `vi`. The problem with this approach is that if you spend as much time learning `vi` as you do trying to find an alternative, you can actually become quite proficient with `vi`.

There is more to `vi` than just its availability on different UNIX systems. To me, `vi` is magic. Once you get over the initial intimidation, then you will see that there is a logical order to the way the commands are laid out and fit together. Things fit together in a pattern that is easy to remember. So, as we get into it, let me tempt you a little.

Among the "magical" things `vi` can do:

- Automatically correct words that you misspell often
- Allow you to create your own `vi` commands
- Insert the output of UNIX commands into the file you are editing
- Automatically indent each line
- Shift sets of lines left or right
- Check for pairs of {}, (), and [] (Great for programmers)
- Automatically wrap around at the end of a line
- Cut and paste between documents

I am not going to mention every single command. Instead, I am going to show you a few and how they fit together. At the end of this section, there is a table containing the various commands you can use inside of `vi`. You can then apply the relationships to the commands I didn't mention.

In order to see what is happening when you enter commands, what don't you find a file that you can poke around in. Make a copy of the `termcap` file (`/etc/termcap`) in your home directory and then edit it (`cd /tmp; cp /etc/termcap; vi termcap`).

Before we really can jump into the more advanced features of `vi`, I need to cover some of the basics; not command basics, but rather some behavior basics. In `vi`, there are two modes: command mode and input mode. While you are in command mode, every key stroke is considered part of a command. This is were you normally start when you first invoke `vi`. The reverse is also true. While in input mode, everything is considered input.

Well, that isn't entirely true and we'll talk about in a minute. However, just remember that there are two modes. If you are in command mode, you go into input mode using a command to get you there, such as append or insert (we'll talk about these in a moment). If you want to go from input mode to command mode, you press ESC.

When, `vi` starts it goes into full-screen mode (assuming your terminal is set-up correctly) and it essentially clears the screen. If we started the command as `vi search`, at the bottom of the screen you see `"search" [New file]`. Your cursor is at the top left-hand corner of the screen, and there is a column of tildes (~) down the left side to indicate that these lines are nonexistent.

### Basic Editing and Movement Commands

Most editing and movement commands are single letters and are almost always the first letter of what they do. For example, to insert text at your current cursor position you press 'i'. To append text you press 'a'. To move forward to the beginning of the next word, you press 'w'. To move back to the beginning of the previous word you press 'b'.

The capital letter of each has a similar behavior. An 'I' will start you inserting at the beginning of a line. An 'A' will start the append from the end of the line. To move "real" words, use a 'W' to move forward and a 'B' to move back.

Real words are those terminated by whitespaces (space, tab, newline). Assume we wanted to move across the phrase 'static-free bag'. If we start on the 's', pressing 'w', will move me to the '-'. Pressing 'w' again, we move to the 'f' and then to the 'b'. If we are on the 's' and press 'W', we jump immediately to the 'b'. That is, to the next "real" word.

Moving in vi is also accomplished in other ways. Depending on your terminal type, you can use the traditional method of arrow keys. If vi doesn't like your terminal type, you can use the keys h-j-k-l. If we want to move to the left we press 'h'. This makes sense since this key is in on the left end of these four characters. If we want to move right we press 'l'. Again, this makes sense as the 'l' is on the right end of the row.

Movement up and down is not as intuitive. One of the two remaining characters (j and k) will move us up and the other will move us down. But which one? Unfortunately, I don't have a very sophisticated way of remembering. If you look at the two letters physically, then maybe it helps. If you imagine a line running through the middle of these characters, then you see that the 'j' hangs down below that line. Therefore, use the 'j' to move down. On the other hand, the 'k' sticks up above the middle, so you use the 'k' to move up. However, in most cases the arrow keys work, so you don't need to remembering. However, it is nice to know them, so as you can then leave your fingers on the keyboard.

As I mentioned, some keyboard types will allow you to use the arrow keys. However, you might be surprised by their behavior in input mode. This is especially true if you are used to word processors where the arrow and other movement keys are the same all the time. The problem lies in the fact that most keyboards actually send more than one character to indicate something like a left-arrow or page-up key. The first of these is normally an escape (ESC). When you press one of these characters in input mode, the ESC is interpreted as your wish to leave input mode.

If you want to move to the first character on a line, press '0' (zero) or '^'. To move to the last character, press '$'. Now these are not all that intuitive. However, if you think back to our discussion on regular expressions, you'll remember that the '^' (caret) represents the beginning of a line and the '$' (dollar sign) represents the end of a line. Although, these two characters do not necessarily have an intuitive logic, they do fit in with other commands and programs that you find on an SCO UNIX system.

We can also take advantage of the fact that vi can combine movement with its ability to count. By pressing a number before the movement command, vi will behave as if we had pressed the movement key that many times. For example, 4w will move us forward four words or 6j will move us six lines down.

If we want to move to a particular line we input the number and the G. So, to move to line 43, we would press 42G, kind of like 42-Go!. If instead of G we pressed <ENTER>, we would move ahead that many lines. For example, if we were on line 85, pressing 42<ENTER> would put us on line 127. (No, you don't have to count lines, vi can display them for you, as we'll see in a minute.)

As you might have guessed, we can also use these in conjunction with the movement keys (all except CTRL-u and CTRL-d). So, to delete everything from your current location to line 83, you would input d83G (note that Delete begins with 'd'). To change everything from the current cursor position down twelve lines, you would input c12+ or c12<enter>.

There are a couple of other special editing commands. Pressing dd will delete the entire line you are on. 5dd will delete five complete lines. If you want to open up a line for editing, press o to open it up after the line you are currently on and O for the line before. The letter x will delete the character that the cursor is on and can also be used with numbers.

When we want to move something we just deleted, we put the cursor on the spot where we want it. Then either press p to put that text after the current cursor position or P to put it before the current position. A nice trick that I always use to swap characters is xp. The x deletes the character you are on and the p immediately inserts it. The result is that you swap characters. So if I had typed the word 'into' as 'inot', I would place the cursor on the 'o', and type xp, which would swap the 'o' and the 't'.

If we wanted to repeat an edit we just did, be it deleting 18 lines or inputting "I love you", we could do so by pressing '.' (dot) from command mode. In fact, any edit command can be repeated with the dot.

**Changing Text.** To make a change you press c followed by a movement command or number and movement. For example, if you wanted to change everything from where you are to the next word, press cw. To change everything from where you are to the end of the line, press c or c$. If you do that, then a dollar sign will appear indicating how much you intend to change.

If you go back into command mode (press ESC), before you reach the dollar sign, then everything from the current position to the dollar sign is removed. When you think about this, it is actually logical. If you press 'C', you tell vi that you want to change everything to the end of the line. When you press ESC, you are basically saying that you are done inputting text, however, the changes should continue to the end of the line, thereby deleting the rest of the line.

If you want to undue the last edit, what should you press? Well, what's the first letter of the word 'undue'? Keep in mind that pressing u only does the last change. For example, let's assume we enter the following:

```
o             (to open a new line and go into input mode)
I love
ESC           (to go back to command mode)
a             (to append from current location)
you
ESC           (to return to command mode)
```

The result of what we typed was to have a new line with the text, "I love you." We see it as one change, however, from the perspective of vi, there were two changes. First we entered 'I love', then we entered 'you'. If we were to press u, only the 'you' would be removed. However, if u undoes that last change, what command do you think returns the line to its original state? What else, U. As you are making changes, vi keeps track of the original state of that line. When you press U, the line is returned to the original state.

**Searching and Replacing.**    If you are trying to find a particular text you can get vi to do that for you. You can tell vi that you want to enter a search pattern by pressing '/'. This will bring you down to the bottom line of the screen where you will see '/'. You then can type in what you want to look for. When you press <enter>, vi will start searching from your current location down toward the bottom of the file. If you use press '?' instead of '/', then vi will search from your string toward the top of the file.

If the search is successful, and the string is found, you are brought to that point in the text. If you decide that you want to search again, you have three choices. Either you can press '/' or '?' and input the search string again. Or, you could press 'n' which is the first letter of the word 'next'. Or you could simply press '/' or '?' with text following it, and vi would continue the search in the applicable direction. If you wanted to find the next string that matches but is in the opposite direction, what do you think would be the command? (Hint: what is the capital form of 'n'?)

Once you have found what you are looking for, you can edit the text all you want and then continue searching. This is because the search string you entered is kept in a buffer. So, when you press '/', '?' , 'n', or 'N', the system remembers what you were looking for.

You can also include movement commands in these searches. First you enclose the search pattern with the character used to search (/ or ?), then add the movement command. For example, if you wanted to search backward for the phrase "hard disk" and then move up a line, you would enter `?hard disk?-`. If you wanted to search forward for the phrase "operating system" and then move down three lines, you would enter `/operating system/+3`.

All this time, you have been referring to it as a search string. As you just saw, you can actually enter phrases. In fact, you can use any regular expression you want when searching for patterns. For example, if you wanted to search for the pattern SCO, but only when it appears at the beginning of a line, you would enter `/^SCO`. If you wanted to search for it at the end of the line, you would enter `/SCO$`. You can also do more complicated searches such as `/^new [Bb][Oo][Aa][Tt]`, which will search for the word 'new' at the beginning of a line, followed by the word 'boat' with each letter in either case.

No good text editor would be complete without the ability to search for text and also replace it. One way of doing this is to search for the pattern and then edit the text. Obviously, this starts to get annoying after the second or third instance of the pattern you want to replace. Instead, you could combine several of the tools you learned so far.

For example, let's say that throughout the text you wanted to replace 'Unix' with 'UNIX'. First, do a search on Unix with /Unix, tell `vi` that you want to change that word with `cw`, then input UNIX. Now search for the pattern again with /. Now simply press '.'. The dot repeats your last command. Now do the search and press the dot again.

Actually, this technique is good if you have a pattern that you want to replace, but not every time it appears. Instead, you may want to do this selectively. You can just press 'n' (or whatever) to continue the search without carrying out the replacement.

What if you know that you want to replace every instance of the pattern with something else? Are you destined to search and replace all fifty occurrences? Of course, not. Silly you. There is a way.

Here we introduce what is referred to as escape or ex-mode, since the commands you enter are the same as in the `ex` editor. To get to ex-mode you press ' : '

(colon). Like with searches, you are brought down to the bottom of the screen, but this time you see the ' : '. The syntax is

```
:  <scope>  <command>
```

An example of this would be

```
:45,100s/Unix/UNIX/
```

This tells vi that the scope is lines 45 *through* 100. The command is s/Unix/UNIX/ which says you want to substitute (s) the first pattern (Unix) with the second pattern (UNIX). Normally in English we would want to say, "substitute UNIX for Unix." However, the order here is in keeping with the UNIX pattern of source first, then destination (or what it is first, and what it will become second; like mv source destination).

Note that this only replaces the first occurrence on each line. In order to get all of them we need to include a 'g' for global at the end of each line, like this:

```
:45,100s/Unix/UNIX/g
```

A problem arises if you want to modify only some occurrences. You could add the modifier c for confirm. The command would then look like this:

```
:45,100s/Unix/UNIX/gc
```

This causes vi to ask for confirmation before it makes the change.

If you want to do the search and replace every line in the file you could specify every line, such as :1,48, assuming there were 48 lines in the file (oh, by the way, use CTRL-g to find out what line you are on and how many lines there are in the file). Instead of having to check how many lines there are each time, you could simply use the special character $ to indicate the end of the file. (Yes, it also means the end of the line, but in this context it means the end of the file.) So, the scope would be :1,$.

Once again, the developers of vi made life easy for you. They realized that making changes throughout the file is something that is done a lot. They included a special character to mean the entire file: %. Therefore, % = 1,$.

Here again, the search patterns can be regular expressions. For example, if we wanted to replace every occurrence of boat (in either case) with the word 'ship', the command would look like this:

```
%s:/[Bb][Oo][Aa][Tt]/ship/g
```

As with regular expressions in other cases, you can use the asterisk (*) to mean any number of the preceding character, or a period ( . ) to mean any single character. So, if you wanted to look for the word 'boat' (again in either case), but only when it was at the beginning of the line and only if it was preceded by at least one dash, the command would look like this:

```
%s:/^--*[Bb][Oo][Aa][Tt]/ship/g
```

The reason you have two dashes is that the search criteria specified *at least* one dash. Since the asterisk can be *any* number, including zero, you have to consider the case where it would mean zero. That is, where 'boat' was at the beginning of the line and there were no spaces. If you didn't care what the character was as long as there was at least one, you could use the fact that in a search context a dot means any single character. The command would look like this:

```
%s:/^..*[Bb][Oo][Aa][Tt]/ship/g
```

This ex-mode also allows you to do many things with the file itself:

- `:w` to write the file to disk
- `:q` to quit the file (`:q!` if the file has been changed and you don't want to save the changes)
- `:wq` to write the file and quit
- `:e` to edit a new file (or even the same file)
- `:r` read in a new file starting at the current location

**Buffers.**    Remember when we first started talking about searching, I mentioned that whatever expression you were looking for was held in a buffer. The same thing can be made to happen here. In this case, whatever was matched by `/[Bb][Oo][Aa][Tt]` can be held in a buffer. We can then use that buffer as part of the replacement expression. For example, if we wanted to replace every occurrence of UNIX with SCO UNIX, we could do it like this:

```
:%s/UNIX/SCO UNIX/g
```

The scope of this command is defined by the %, the shortcut way of referring to the entire text. Or you could first save UNIX into a buffer, then use it in the replacement expression. To enclose something in a buffer, enclose it within matching pairs of \( and \). This defines the extent of a buffer. You can even have multiple pairs that define the extent of multiple buffers. These are reference by \#, where # is the number of the buffer.

In this example,

```
:%s/\(UNIX\)/SCO \1/g
```

the text UNIX is placed into the first buffer. You then reference this buffer with \1 to say to vi to plug in the contents of the first buffer. Since the entire search pattern is the same as the pattern buffer you could have written it like this:

```
:%s/\(UNIX\)/SCO &/g
```

as the ampersand represents the entire search pattern.

This obviously doesn't save much typing. In fact, in this example, it requires more typing to save UNIX into the buffer and then use it. However, If what you wanted to save was longer, you would save time. You also save time if you want to use the buffer twice. For example, assume you have a file with a list other files. Some are C language source files. All of them end in '.c'. You now want to change just the names of the C files so the ending is 'old' instead of .c. To do this you have to insert an mv at the beginning of each line as well as produce two copies of the file name: one with .c and one with .old. You could do it like this:

```
:%s/^\(.*\).c/mv \1.c \1.old\g
```

In English, this line says

- For every line (%)

- substitute (s)

- for the pattern starting at the beginning of the line (^) consisting of any number of characters ( \(.*\) ) (placing this pattern into the buffer #1) followed by a .c

- and use the pattern mv  followed by the contents of buffer #1 (\1) followed by a .c,  which is again followed by the contents of buffer #1 (\1) followed by .old

- and do this for every line (g), (i.e. globally).

Now each line is of the form

```
mv file.c file.old
```

I can now change the permissions to make this a shell script and execute it. We could then move all the files as I described above.

Using numbers like this is useful if there is more that one search pattern that you want to process. For example, assume that you wanted to be able to change the order in which columns appear in a three column table. For simplicities sake, let's also assume that each column is separated by a space so as not to make the search pattern too complicated.

Before we start we need to introduce a new concept to vi, but one that you have seen before: [ ]. Like the shell, the [ ] pair inside of vi is used to limit sets of characters. Inside of the brackets, the caret (^) takes on a new meaning. Rather than indicating the beginning of a line, here it negates the character we are searching for. So we could write

```
%s/\([^ ]*\) \([^ ]*\) \([^ ]*\)/\3 \1 \2/g
   |_____||_____|
```

Here we have three regular expressions all referring to the same thing: `\([^ ]*\)`. As we discussed above, the `\( \)` pairs delimits each of the buffers, so everything inside is the search pattern. Here, we are searching for `[^]*`, which is any number of matches to the set enclosed within the brackets. Since the brackets are limiting a set, the set is `^`, followed by a space. Since the `^` indicates the negation, we are placing any number of characters that is *not* a space into the buffer. In the replacement pattern, we told `vi` to print pattern3, a space, pattern1, another space, and then pattern2.

In the first two instances we followed the pattern with a space. As a result, those spaces were not saved into any of the buffers. We do this because we may want to define our column separator differently. Here we just used another space.

I have often had occasion to want to use the pattern buffers more than once. Since they are cleared after use, you can use them as many times as you want. Using the example above, if we change it to

```
%s/\([^ ]*\) \([^ ]*\) \([^ ]*\)/\3 \1 \2 \1/g
   |_____||_____|
```

we would get pattern3, then pattern2, then pattern2, and at the end pattern1 again.

Believe it or not, there are still more buffers. In fact there are dozens that we haven't touched on. The first set is the numbered buffers, and they are numbered 1–9. These are used when we delete text and they behave like a stack. That is, the first time we delete something, say a word, it is placed in numbered buffer 1. We next delete a line which is placed in buffer 1 and the word that was in buffer 1 is now in buffer 2. Once all the numbered buffers all full, any new deletions push the oldest ones out the bottom of the stack and are no longer available.

To access them, we first tell `vi` that we want to use one of the buffers by pressing the double-quote (`' " '`), then the number of the buffer (say 6), then either `p` or `P` to put it (as in `"6p`). When you delete text and then do a put without specifying any buffer, it automatically comes from buffer 1.

There are some other buffers, in fact 26 of them, that you can use by name. These are the named buffers. If you can't figure out what their names are think about how many of them there are (26). With these buffers, we can intentionally and specifically place something into one of these buffers. First, we say which buffer we want by preceding its name with a double-quote ("); for example, "f. This says we want to place some text in the named buffer f. Then, we place the data in the buffer; for example by deleting the whole line with dd or deleting two words with d2w. We can later put the contents of that buffer with "fp. Until we place something new in that buffer, it will contain that deleted line.

Now if you want to put something into a buffer without having to delete it, you can. You do this by "yanking it." Okay, folks, another pop quiz. What letter do we use to "yank" text?

To yank an entire line you could do one of several things. You could use yy or Y. You could use y, followed by movement commands as in y+4, which would yank the next 4 lines (including the current one) or y/expression, which would yank everything from your current position up to and including the specified expression and put it into the default buffer (numbered buffer 1).

If you want to place it into a named buffer, it is the same procedure as deleting it. For example if we wanted to yank the next twelve lines into named buffer h, we would do "h12yy. Now those twelve lines are available to us. Keep in mind that we do not have to store full lines. Inputting "x12yw will put the next twelve words into the buffer h.

Some of the more observant readers might have noticed that since there are 26 letter and each has both an upper- and lowercase, we could have 52 named buffers. Well, up to now the uppercase letter did something different. If uppercase letters were different buffers, then they wouldn't follow the pattern. Have no fear, they do.

Instead of being different buffers than their lowercase brethren, the upper case letters are the *same* buffer. The difference is that the yanking or deleting something into the uppercase buffer appends the contents rather that overwriting it.

You can also have vi keep track of up to twenty-six different places with the file you are editing. These function just like bookmarks in other word processors. Pop Quiz: If there twenty-six of them, what are their names?

To mark a spot, move to that place in the file, type m for mark (what else?), then a single backquote ('), followed by the letter you want to use for this bookmark. To go back to that spot, press the backquote (') followed by the appropriate letter. So, to assign book mark q to a particular spot, you would enter 'q. Keep in mind that reloading the current file or editing a new one makes you lose the book marks.

 **vi Magic.**   I imagine that long before now, you have been wondering how to turn on all that magic I said that vi could do. Okay, let's do it.

The first thing I want to talk about is abbreviations. You can tell `vi` that when you type in a specific set of characters it is supposed to automagically change it to something else. For example, we could have `vi` always change USA to United States of America. This is done with the `abbr` command.

To create a new abbreviation you need to get into ex-mode by pressing the colon (:) in command mode. Next, type in `abbr` followed by what you want to type in, then what `vi` should change it to; for example,

`:abbr USA United States of America.`

Note that the abbreviation cannot contain any spaces, since `vi` interprets everything after the second word as being part of the expansion.

If we later decide we don't want that abbreviation any more, we enter

`:unabbr USA`

Since it is likely that we will want to use the abbreviation USA, it is not a good idea to use an abbreviation that would normally occur. It would be better, instead, to use an abbreviation that doesn't occur normally, like Usa. Keep in mind, that abbreviations only apply to complete words. Therefore, something like the name Sousa, won't get translated to SoUSA. In addition, when your abbreviation is followed by a space tab, ENTER, or ESC, the change is made.

Let's take this one step further. What if you were always spelling 'the' as 'teh'. You could then create an abbreviation:

`:abbr teh the`

Every time you misspelled 'the' as 'teh', `vi` would automatically correct it for you. What if we had a whole list of words that we regularly misspelled and created similar abbreviations. Then every time we entered one of these misspelled words, it would get replaced with the correctly spelled word. Wouldn't that be automatic spell correction?

If we ever want to "force" the spelling to be a particular way (that is, turn off the abbreviation momentarily), we simply follow the abbreviation with a CTRL-V. This tells `vi` to ignore the special meaning of the following character. Since the next character is a whitespace which would force the expansion of the abbreviation (which makes the whitespace special in this case), "turning off" the whitespace keeps the abbreviation from being expanded.

We can also use `vi` to remap certain sequences. For example, I have created a command so that all I need to do to save a file is do CTRL-W for write. If I want to save the file and quit, I enter CTRL-X. This is done with the 'map' command.

The most common maps that I have seen have always been using control characters, since most of the other characters are already taken up. Therefore, we need to side step a moment. First, we need to know how to access control characters from within vi. This is done in either command mode or input mode by first pressing CTRL-V, then pressing the control character we want. So to get the CTRL-W, I would type CTRL-V then CTRL-W. This would appear on the screen as ^W. This looks like two characters, but if you inserted it into a text and moved over it with the cursor, you would realize that vi sees it as only one. Note that although I pressed the lowercase 'w', it will appear as uppercase on the screen.

So, if you wanted to map CTRL-W so that every time you pressed it, you would write the current file to disk, the command would be

```
map ^W :w^M
```

This means that when we press ctrl-W, vi interprets it as if you actually pressed :w followed by an <ENTER> (the CTRL-M, ^M). The <ENTER> at the end of the command is a good idea, since you usually want the command to be executed right away. Otherwise you would have to press enter yourself.

Also keep in mind that this can also be used with the function keys. Since I am used to many Windows and DOS applications where the F2 key means to save, I map my F2 with CTRL-V then F2. It then looks like this:

```
map ^[[N :w^M     (The ^[[N is what the F2 key displays on the screen.)
```

If we want, we can also use shifted function characters. Therefore, we can map SHIFT-F2 to something else. Or, for that matter, we can also use shifted and control functions keys.

It has been my experience that, for the most part, if you use shift and control with nonfunction keys, vi only sees the control and not the shift. Also, the ALT may not work since on the system console, ALT plus a function key tells the system to switch multiscreens.

I try not to use the same key sequences that vi already uses. First, it confuses me since I often forget that I remapped something. Second, the real vi commands are then inaccessible. However, if you are used to a different command set (that is, from a different editor), you can "program" vi to behave like that other editor.

Never define a mapping that contains its own name, as this ends up recursively expanding the abbreviation. The classic example is: :map! n banana. Every time you typed in the word banana, you'd get the following:

```
babababababababababababababababababa . . .
```

Depending on what version you run, `vi` would catch the fact that this is an infinite translation and stop.

**Inserting Command Output.**   It often happens that you want the output of UNIX commands in the file you are editing. The sledgehammer approach is to run the command and redirect it to a file, then edit that file. If that file containing the command's output already exists, you can use the `:r` from ex-mode to read it in. But, what if it doesn't yet exist? For example, I often want the date as the in text files as log of when I input things. This is done with a combination of the `:r` (for read) from ex-mode and a *shell escape*.

A shell escape allows you to go from one program and jump out of it (escape) to a shell. Your original program is still running, but you are now working in a shell that is a child process of that program.

To do a shell escape, you need to be in ex-mode. Next, press the exclamation mark followed by the command. For example, if you want to see what time it was, you could do `:!date`. You then get the date at the bottom of the screen with the message to press any key to continue. Note that this didn't change your original text, just showed us the output of the date command.

In order to read in that output, you need to include the `:r` command, as in `:r!date`. Now, the output of the date is read into the file (it is *inserted* into the file). You could also have it replace the current line by pressing '!' twice as in '!!date'. Note that you are brought down to the last line on the screen and there is a single '!'.

If you want you can also read in other commands. What is happening is that `vi` is seeing the output of the command as a file. Remember that `:r <file_name>` will read a file into the one you are editing. Why not read from the output of a file? With pipes and redirection, both stdin and stdout can be files. Why not here as well? In fact, that is basically what is happening.

You can also take this one step further. Image you are editing a file containing a long list. You know that many lines are duplicated and you also want the list sorted. You could do `:%!sort`, which is a special symbol meaning all the lines in the file. These are then sent through the command on the other side of the '!'. Now you can do

`:%!uniq`

to remove all the duplicate lines.

Remember that this is a shell escape. From the shell you can combine multiple commands using pipes. You can here as well. So to save time, you could enter

```
:%!sort | uniq
```

Which would sort all the lines and remove all duplicate ones. If you only wanted to sort a set of lines, you could do that like this:

```
:45,112!sort
```

which would sort lines 45 through 112. You can take this one step further by either writing line 45–112 to a new file with `:45,112w file_name` or reading in a whole file to replace line 45-112 with `:45,112r file_name`.

### More vi Magic

If you want, you can start editing a file at a point part of the way through it, rather than at the beginning. This is done from a command line like

```
vi +# filename
```

where # is the line number to start with. If you leave off the number, `vi` will start editing at the end of the file. This is great for handwritten logs and the like. If you want `vi` to first find a particular phrase and jump there, this is just as easy; as in `vi +/expression`. If you need to, we can also edit multiple files with this command:

```
vi file1 file2 file3
```

Once you are editing we can switch between files with `:n` for the next file and `:p` for the previous one. Keep in mind that the file names do not wrap around. In other words, if you keep pressing `:n` and get to file3, doing it again does not wrap around and bring you to file1. If you know the name of the file, you can jump directly there, with the ex-mode edit command as in,

```
:e file3
```

The ability to edit multiple files has another advantage. Do you remember those numbered and named buffers? They are assigned for a single instance of `vi` and not on a per-file basis. Therefore you can delete or yank text from one file, switch to the next, and then insert it. This is a crude, but effective cut and paste mechanism between files.

You can specify line numbers to set your position within a file. If you switch to editing another file (using :n or :r), or reload the original file (using `:rew!`), the contents of the deletion buffers are preserved so that you can cut and paste between files. The contents of all buffers are lost, however, when you quit `vi`.

**Odds and Ends.**   You may find yourself re-using the same `vi` commands over and over again. Here too, `vi` can help. Since the named buffers are simply sequences of characters, you can store commands in them for later use. For example, when editing files in `vi` I need to mark new paragraphs in some way as my word processor normally sees all the end-of-line characters as new paragraphs. Therefore, I created a command that entered a `para` marker for me.

First, I needed to create the command. I did this by opening up a new line in my current document and typed in the text

`Para`

Had I typed this from command mode, this would have inserted the text 'Para' at the beginning of the line. I then loaded it into a named buffer with `"pdd`. This deletes the line and loads it into buffer `'p'`. To execute it I entered `@p`. The at-sign (`@`) is what tells `vi` to execute the contents of the buffer.

Keep in mind that many of the commands and abbreviations are transitive. For example, when I want to add a new paragraph I don't write `"Para"` as the only characters on the line. Instead, I use something less common: `{P}`. I am certain that I will never have `{P}` at the beginning of a line, however, there are contexts where I might have `"Para"` at the beginning of a line. Instead I have an abbreviation `"Para"` that translated to `{P}`.

Now I can type in `Para` at the beginning of a line in input mode and it will be translated to `{P}`. When I execute the command I have in buffer `'p'`, it inserts `"Para"` which is then translated to `{P}`

So why don't I just have `{P}` in the buffer `'p'`? Because the curly brackets are one set of movement keys that I did not mention, yet. The `'{'` moves you back to the beginning of the paragraph and the `'}'` moves you forward. Since paragraphs are defined by `vi` as being separated by blank lines or delimited by `nroff` macros, I never use them (`nroff` is an old UNIX text processing language). Because `vi` sees the brackets as something special in command mode, I need to use this transitivity.

If you are a C-programmer you can take advantage of a couple of nifty tricks of `vi`. The first is the ability to show matching pairs of parenthesis `( )`, square brackets `[ ]`, and curly brackets `{}`. In ex mode (:), type `set showmatch`. Afterwards, every time you enter the closing one (`)`, `]`, or `}` ), you are bounced back to its match. This is useful in checking whether or not you have the right number of each.

You can also jump back and forth between these pairs by using the percent sign (%). No matter where we are within a `{ }` pair, pressing `%` once moves us to the first (opening) one. Press `%` again and you are moved to its match (the closing one). You can also place the cursor on the closing one and press `%` to move to the opening one.

As a programmer, you may like to indent blocks of code to make things more readable. Sometimes changes within the code make you want to shift blocks to the left or right to keep the spacing the same. To do this use the `<<` (two less-than signs) to move the text one "shift-width" to the left and >> (two greater-than signs) to move the text one "shift-width" to the right. A "shift-width" is defined in ex mode with `set shiftwidth=n`, where n is some number. When you shift a line, it moves left or right n characters.

If you want to shift multiple lines, input a number before you shift. For example, if you input `23>>`, you would shift the next 23 lines one "shift-width" to the right.

There are a lot of settings that can be used with `vi` to make your life easier. These are done in ex mode, using the `set` command. For example, use `:set autoindent` to have `vi` automatically indent. This, along with other `set` commands, can be abbreviated. See the `vi(C)` man-page for more details. Other useful `set` commands:

- `wrapmargin=n`  Automatically "word wrap" when you get to within *n* spaces of the end of the line

- `showmode`  Tells you if you are in insert mode or not

- `number`  Displays line numbers at the left-hand edge of the screen

- `autowrite`  Saves any changes that have been made to the current file when you issue a `:n`, `:rew`, or `:!` command

- `ignorecase`  Ignores the case of text while searching

- `list`  Prints end-of-line characters as "$", and tab characters as "^I"; these characters are normally invisible

- `tabstop=n`  Sets the number of spaces between each tab stop on the screen to n

- `shiftwidth`  Sets the number of spaces << and >> shift each line

### Configuring vi

Since we started talking about `vi`, I mentioned that there were a lot things that we could do to configure it. There are mappings and abbreviations and settings that we can control. The problem is that once we leave `vi`, everything we added will be lost.

Fortunately, there is hope. Like may programs, `vi` has its own configuration file: .exrc (note the dot at the front). Normally this file does not exist by default, so `vi` just takes its standard settings. If this file resides in our home directory, it will be valid every time we start `vi`. The exception is when we have an `.exrc` file in our current directory. This will then take precedence. Having multiple `.exrc` files is useful when doing programming as well as editing text. When writing text, I don't need line numbers or autoindent like I do when programming.

The content and syntax of the lines is exactly the same as in `vi`, however we don't have the leading colon. Part of the `.exrc` file in my text editing directory looks like this:

```
map! ^X :wq
map x :wq
map! ^W :w
map w :w
set showmode
set wm=3
abbr Unix UNIX
abbr btwn between
abbr teh the
abbr refered referred
abbr waht what
abbr Para {P}
abbr inot into
```

**The Next Step.**   No one can force you to learn `vi`. Just as no one can force you to do backups. However, in my opinion, doing both will make you a better administrator and programmer. There will come a time when having done regular backups may save your career. There may also come a time when knowing `vi` may save you the embarrassment of having to tell your client or boss that you can't accomplish a task because you need to edit a file and the only editor is the one that comes default with the system: `vi`.

## Noninteractively Editing Files with sed

Suppose you have a file that you need to make some changes in. You could load up `vi` and make the changes that way. What if what you wanted to change was the output of some command before you sent it to a file? You could first send it to a file and then edit that file. You could also use `sed`, which is a **Stream EDitor** and is specifically designed to edit data streams.

If you read the previous section or are already familiar with either the search and replace mechanisms in `vi` or the editor `'ed'`, you already have a jump on learning `sed`. Unlike `vi`, `sed` is not interactive, but can handle more complicated editing instructions. Since it is noninteractive, commands can be saved in text files and used over and over again. This makes debugging more complicated and `sed` constructs that much easier. For the most part, `sed` is line oriented which allows it to process files of almost any size. However, this has the disadvantage that `sed` cannot do editing that is dependent on relative addressing.

Unlike the section on `vi`, I am not going to go into as many details about `sed`. However, `sed` is a useful tool and I use it very often. The reason I am not going to cover it in too much detail is three-fold. First, much of what is true about pattern searches, addressing, and so on, that is true in `vi` is also true in `sed`. Therefore, I don't feel a need to repeat. Second, it is not that important that you become a `sed` expert for you to be a good system administrator. There are a few cases where scripts on an SCO UNIX system will use `sed`. However, they are not that difficult to understand, provided you have a basic understanding of `sed` syntax. Lastly, `sed` is like any programming language. You can get by with simple things. However, to get really good you need to practice and we just don't have the space to go beyond the basics.

In this section we are going to talk about the basics of `sed` syntax, as well as some of the more common `sed` commands and constructs. If you want to learn more in order to write your own or just because you are curious, I recommend getting *sed & awk* by Dale Dougherty from O'Reilly and Associates. This will also help you in the section on `awk` coming up next.

The way `sed` works is that it reads input a line at a time and then carries out whatever editing changes you specify. When it has finished making the changes it writes them to stdout. Like commands, such as `grep` and `sort`, `sed` acts like a filter. However, with `sed` you can create very complicated programs. Since I normally use `sed` as one end of a pipe, most of the `sed` commands that I use have the following structure:

```
first_cmd | sed <options> <edit_description>
```

This is useful when the edit descriptions that you are using are fairly simple. However, if you want to perform multiple edits on each line, then this way is not really suited. Instead, you can put all of your changes into one file and start up `sed` like this:

```
first_cmd | sed -f editscript
```

or

```
sed -f editscript <inputfile
```

As I mentioned before, the addressing and search replace mechanism within `sed` is basically the same as within `vi`. It has this structure:

```
[address1[,address2]] edit_description [arguments]
```

As with `vi`, addresses do not necessarily need to be line numbers, but can be regular expressions that `sed` needs to search for. If you leave the address off, `sed` will make the changes globally, as applicable. The `edit_description` tells `sed` what changes to make. There are several arguments that can be used and we'll get to them as we move along.

As `sed` reads the file, it copies each line into its *pattern space*. This pattern space is a special buffer that `sed` uses to hold to the line of text as it processes it. As soon as it has finished reading the line, `sed` begins to apply the changes to the pattern space based on the edit description.

Keep in mind that although `sed` will read a line into the pattern space, it will only make changes to addresses that match the addresses specified. `Sed` does not print any warnings when this happens. In general, `sed` either silently ignores errors, or terminates abruptly with an error message as a result of a syntax error, not because there were no matches. If there are no lines that contain the pattern, no lines match and the edit commands are not carried out.

Because you can have multiple changes on any given line, `sed` will carry them each out in turn. When there are no more changes to be made, `sed` sends the result to its output. The next line is read in and the whole process starts over. As it reads in each line, `sed` will increment an internal line counter, which keeps track of the *total* number of lines read, not lines per file. This is an important distinction if you have multiple files that are being read. Assume you had two 50-line files. From `sed`'s perspective, line 60 is the 10th line in the second file.

Each `sed` command can have 0, 1, or 2 addresses. A command with no addresses specified is applied to every line in the input. A command with one address is applied to all lines that match that address. For example,

```
/mike/s/fred/john/
```

substitutes the first instance of "john" for "fred" only on those lines containing "mike". A command with two addresses is applied to the first line that matches the first address, then to all subsequent lines until a match for the second address has been processed. An attempt is made to match the first address on subsequent lines, and the process is repeated. Two addresses are separated by a comma. For example,

```
50,100s/fred/john/
```

substitutes the first instance of "john" for "fred" from line 50 to line 100 inclusive. (Note that there should be no space between the second address and the s command.) If an address is followed by an exclamation mark (!), the command is applied only to lines that do not match the address. For example,

```
50,100!s/fred/john/
```

substitutes the first instance of "john" for "fred" everywhere except lines 50 to 100 inclusive.

Sed can also be told to do input and output based on what it finds. The action it should perform is identified by an argument at the end of the sed command. For example, if we wanted to print out lines 5–10 of a specific file, the sed command would be

```
cat file | sed -n '5,10p'
```

The -n is necessary so that every line isn't output in *addition* to the lines that match.

Remember the script we created in the first section of this chapter where we wanted just lines 5–10 of every file. Now that we know how to use sed, we can change it to be a lot more efficient. It will now look like this:

```
find ./letters/taxes -print | while read FILE
do
echo $FILE
cat $FILE | sed -n '5-10p'
done
```

Rather than sending the file through head and then the output of that through tail, we send the whole file through sed. It can keep track of what line it is on and then print the necessary lines.

In addition, sed allows you to write lines that match. For example, if we wanted all the comments in a shell script to be output to a file, we could use sed like this:

```
cat filename | sed -n '/^#/w filename'
```

Note that there must be exactly one space between the w and the name of the file. If we wanted to read in a file, we could do that as well. Instead of a w to read, we use an r to write. The contents of the file will be appended after the lines specified in the address. Also keep in mind that writing to or reading from a file are independent of what happens next. For example, if we write every line in a file containing the name John, but in a subsequent sed command change John to Chris, the file will contain references to John, as no changes are made. This is logical since sed works on each line, and the lines are already in that file before the changes are made.

Keep in mind that every time a line is read in, the contents of the pattern space are overwritten. In order to save certain data across multiple commands, sed provides what is called the "hold space." Changes are not made to the hold space directly, rather the contents of either one can be copied into the other for processes. The contents can even be exchanged if needed. Table 3–2 contains a list of the more common sed commands, including what commands are used to manipulate the hold and pattern spaces.

**Table 3–2**   `Sed` Commands

| Command | Function |
|---------|----------|
| a | appends text to the pattern space |
| b | branches to a label |
| c | appends text |
| d | deletes text |
| D | deletes all the characters from the start of the pattern space up to and including the first newline |
| g | overwrites the pattern space with the holding area |
| G | appends the holding area to the pattern space, separated by a newline |
| h | overwrites holding area with the pattern space |
| H | appends the pattern space to the holding area, separated by a newline |
| i | inserts text |
| l | lists the contents of the pattern space |
| n | adds a newline to the pattern space |
| N | appends the next input line to the pattern space, lines are separated by newline |
| p | prints the pattern space |
| P | prints from the start of the pattern space up to and including the first newline |
| r | reads in a file |
| s | substitutes patterns |
| t | branches only if a substitution has been made to the current pattern space |
| w | writes to a file |
| x | interchanges the contents of the pattern space and the holding area: the maximum number of addresses is two |

# Programming with awk

Another language that SCO provides and is standard on many (most?) UNIX systems is `awk`. The abbreviation `awk` is an acronym composed of the first letter of the last names of its developers: Alfred Aho, Peter Weinberger and Brian Kernighan. Like `sed`, `awk` is an interpreted, pattern matching language. In addition, `awk`, like `sed`, can read stdin as well as be passed the name of a file containing its arguments.

One of the most useful aspects of awk (at least useful for me and the many SCO scripts that use it) is its idea of a field. Like sed, awk will read whole lines, but awk can immediately break into segments (fields) based on some criteria. Each of the fields is separated by *field separator*. By default, this is a space. By using the -F option on the command line or the FS variable within an awk program you can specify a new field separator. For example, if you specified a colon (:) as a field separator, you could read in the lines from the /etc/password file and immediately break it into fields.

A programming language in its own right, awk has become a staple of UNIX systems. The basic purpose of the language is manipulation and the processing of text files. However, awk is also a useful tool when combined with output from other commands, allowing you to format that output in ways that might be easier to process further. One of the major advantages of awk is that it can accomplish in a few lines what would normally return dozens of lines in sh or csh shell script, or may even require writing something in a lower-level language like C.

The program awk appears in three forms on SCO UNIX systems. The binary /usr/bin/awk is the program that ought to be called from scripts or from the command line and may be linked to either /usr/bin/oawk (Old awk) or /usr/bin/nawk (New awk). On SCO OpenServer systems, all three are linked together. Although there are slight differences between the behavior with oawk and nawk, they do not interfere with the basic functionality of the language. Therefore, I am not going to address them. If you want details about the differences, check out the awk(C) man-page.

The basic layout of an awk command is

```
pattern { action }
```

where the action to be performed is included within the curly braces. Like sed, awk reads input a line at a time, but awk sees this line as a record broken up into fields. Fields are separated by an input Field Separator (FS), which by default is a tab or a space. The FS can be changed to something else, for example a semicolon, with FS=;. This is useful when we want to process text that contains blanks; for example, data of this form:

```
Blinn, David;42 Clarke Street;Sunnyvale;California;95123;33
Dickson, Tillman;8250 Darryl Lane;San Jose;California;95032;34
Gibberson, Suzanne;102 Truck Stop Road;Ben Lomond;California;26
Holder, Wyliam; 1932 Nuldev Street;Mount Hermon;California;95431;42
Nathanson, Robert;12 Peabody Lane;Beaverton;Oregon;97532;33
Richards, John;1232 Bromide Drive;Boston;Massachusettes;02134;36
Shaffer, Shannon;98 Whatever Way;Watsonville;California;95332;24
```

Here we have name, address, city, state, zip code, and age. Without using ; as a field separator, Blinn and David;42 would be the two fields. Here, we would want to treat each name, address, city, and so on as a single unit, rather than multiple fields.

The basic format of an awk program or awk script, as it is sometimes called, is a pattern followed by a particular action. Like sed, each line of the input is checked by awk to see if it matches that particular pattern. Both sed and awk do well when comparing string values, However, whereas checking numeric values is difficult with sed, this functionality is an integral part of awk.

If we wanted we could output only the names and cities of those people under 30. First we need an awk script, called awk.scr, that looked like this:

```
FS=;   $6 < 30 { print $1, $3 }
```

Next, assume that we have a data file containing the seven lines of data above, called awk.data. We could process the data file in one of two ways:

```
awk -f awk.scr awk.data
```

The -f option, tells awk that it should read its instructions from the file that follows. In this case, awk.scr. At the end, we have the file that awk need to read its data from. Alternatively, we could start it like this:

```
cat awk.data | awk -f awk.scr
```

We can even make string comparisons, as in

```
$4 == "California" { print $1, $3 }
```

Although, it may make little sense, we could make string comparisons on what would normally be numeric values, as in

```
$6 == "33" { print $1, $3 }
```

This prints out fields 1 and 3 from only those lines where the sixth field equals the string "33".

Not to be outdone by sed, awk will also allow you to use regular expressions in your search criteria. A very simple example is one where we want to print every line containing the characters 'on'. (NOTE: These have to be adjacent and in the appropriate case.) This line would look like this:

```
/on/ {print $0}
```

However, the regular expressions that awk uses can be as complicated as those in sed. One example would be

```
/[^s]on[^;]/ {print $0}
```

This says to print every line containing 'on', but only if it is *not* preceded by an 's' nor followed by a semi-colon(;). The trailing semicolon eliminates the two town names ending in "on" (Boston and Beaverton) and the leading 's' eliminates all the names ending in 'son'. When we run awk with this line, our output is

```
Gibberson, Suzanne;102 Truck Stop Road;Ben Lomond;California;96221;26
```

Hmmm. Doesn't the name "Gibberson" contain "son"? Shouldn't it be ignored along with the others? Well, yes. However, that's not what matched. The reason this line was printed out was because of the 'on' in Ben Lomond.

We can also use addresses as part of the search criteria. Assume we wanted to print out only those lines, where the first field name (i.e., the person's last name) is in the first half of the alphabet. Since this list is sorted, we could look for all the lines between those starting with A and those starting with M. Therefore, we could use a line like this:

```
/^A/,/^M/ {print $0}
```

When we run it, we get

Hmmm. What happened? There are certainly several names in the first half of the alphabet. Why didn't this print anything? Well, it printed exactly what we told it to print. Like the addresses in both vi and sed, awk *searches* for a line that matches the criteria we specified. So, what we really said was, "Find the first line that starts with an 'A' and then print all the lines up to and including the last one starting with an 'M'." Since there was no line starting with an 'A', the start address didn't exist. Instead, the line to get what we really want should look like this:

```
/^[A-M]/ {print $0}
```

This is to print all the lines whose first character is in the *range* A–M. Since this checks every line and isn't looking for starting and ending addresses, we could have even used an unsorted file and would have gotten all the lines we wanted. The output then looks like this:

```
Blinn, David;42 Clarke Street;Sunnyvale;California;95123;33
Dickson, Tillman;8250 Darryl Lane;San Jose;California;95032;34
Gibberson, Suzanne;102 Truck Stop Road;Ben Lomond;California;96221;26
Holder, Wyliam; 1932 Nuldev Street;Mount Hermon;California;95431;42
```

If we did want to use a start and end address, we would have to specify the start letter of a name that actually existed in our file; for example,

```
/^B/,/^H/ {print $0}
```

Since printing is a very useful aspect of awk, it's nice to know that there are actually two ways of printing with awk. The first we just mentioned. However, if you use printf instead of print, you can get much more detailed in the way your output can be formatted. If you are familiar with the C programming language, then you already have a head start as the format of this printf is essentially the same as in C. However, there are a couple of differences that you will see immediately if you are a C programmer.

For example, if we wanted to print out both the name and age with this line:

```
$6 >30 {printf"%20s %5d\n",$1,$6}
```

the output would look like this:

```
Blinn, David          33
Dickson, Tillman      34
Holder, Wyliam        42
Nathanson, Robert     33
Richards, John        36
```

The space used to print out each name is 20 characters long, followed by 5 spaces for the age.

Since awk reads each line as a single record and blocks of text in each record as fields, it needs to keep track of how many records there are and how many fields. These are denoted by the NR variable.

Another useful way of using awk is the end of a pipe. You may have the multiple-line output from one command or another, but we only want one or two fields from that line. For example, we may only want the permissions and file name from an ls -l output. We would then pipe it through awk like this:

```
ls -l | awk '{ print $1" "$9 }'
```

The output might look something like this:

```
-rw-r--r-- mike.letter
-rw-r--r-- pat.note
-rw-r--r-- steve.note
-rw-r--r-- zoli.letter
```

This brings up the concept of variables. Like other languages, awk allows you to define variables. A couple are already predefined and come in handy. For example, what if we didn't know off the top of our head that there were nine fields in the ls -l output? Since we know that we wanted the first and the last field, we could have used the variable that specifies the number of fields. The line would then look like this:

```
ls -l | awk '{ print $1" "$NF }'
```

In this example the space enclosed in quotes is necessary, otherwise awk would print $1 and $NR right next to each other.

Another variable that awk has is used to keep track of the number of records read so far: NR. This can be useful, for example, if you only wanted to see a particular part of the text. Remember our example at the beginning of the section where we wanted to see lines 5–10 of a file? (This was to look for an address in the header.) In the last section, we showed you how to do it with sed, now I'll show you with awk.

We can use the fact that the NR variable keeps track of the number of records. Since each line is a record, the NR variable also keeps track of the number of lines. So, we tell awk that we want to print out each line between 5–10, like this:

```
cat datafile | awk '{NR >=5 && NR <= 10 }'
```

This brings up four new issues. The first is the NR variable itself. The second is the use of the double ampersand (&&). Like in C this means a logical "and." That both the right side and the left side of the expression must be true in order for the entire expression to be true. In this example, if we read a line and the value of NR is greater than or equal to 5 (that is, we have read in at least 5 lines) *and* the number of lines read must be no more than 10. The third issue is that there is no print statement. The default action of awk when it doesn't have any additional instructions is to print out each line that matches the pattern.

The last issue is the use of the variable NR. Note that here, there is no dollar sign ($) in front of the variable. This is because we are looking for the value of NR; not what it points to. This is because you do not need to prefix it with $ unless it is a field variable. Confused? Let's look at another example.

Let's say we wanted to print out only the lines where there were more than nine fields. We could do it like this:

```
cat datafile | awk '{ NF > 9 }'
```

Compare this:

```
cat datafile | awk '{ print $NF }'
```

which prints out the last field in every line.

Up to now we've been talking about one line awk commands. These all have performed a single action on each line. However, awk has the ability to do multiple tasks on each line as well as tasks before it begins reading and after it has finished.

We use the BEGIN and END pair as markers. These are treated like any other pattern. Therefore, anything appearing after the BEGIN pattern, is done before the first line is read. Anything after the END pattern is done after the last line is read. Let's look at this script:

```
BEGIN { FS=";"}
{printf"%s\n", $1}
{printf"%s\n", $2}
{printf"%s, %s\n",$3,$4}
{printf"%s\n", $5}
END {print "Total Names:" NR}
```

Following the BEGIN pattern we define what the field separator is. Therefore, this is done before the first line is read. Each line is processed four times, where we print a different set of fields. When we get done, we have output that looks like this:

```
Blinn, David
42 Clarke Street
Sunnyvale, California
95123

Dickson, Tillman
8250 Darryl Lane
San Jose, California
95032

Gibberson, Suzanne
102 Truck Stop Road
Ben Lomond, California
96221

Holder, Wyliam
1932 Nuldev Street
Mount Hermon, California
95431

Nathanson, Robert
12 Peabody Lane
Beaverton, Oregon
97532

Richards, John
1232 Bromide Drive
Boston, Massachusettes
02134

Shaffer, Shannon
98 Whatever Way
Watsonville, California
95332

Total Names:7
```

Aside from having a predefined set of variables to use, awk allows us to define variables ourselves. If in the last awk script we had wanted to print out, let's say, the average age, we could add a line in the middle that looked like this:

```
{total = total + $6 }
```

**Table 3–3**   awk Comparison Operators

| Operator | Meaning |
|---|---|
| < | less than |
| <= | less than or equal to |
| == | equal to |
| != | not equal to |
| >= | greater than or equal to |
| > | greater than |

Since $6 was the age of each person, every time through the loop, it is added to the variable `total`. Unlike other languages, like C, we don't have to initialize the variables, awk will do that for us. Since are initialized to the null string and numeric variables are initialized to 0.

After the END, we can include another line to print out our sum, like this:

```
{print "Average age: " total/NR}
```

Is that all there is to it? No. In fact, we haven't even touched the surface. awk is a very complex programming language and there are dozens more issues that we could address. Built into the language are mathematical functions, if and while

**Table 3–4**   Default Values of awk Built-in Variables

| Variable | Meaning | Default |
|---|---|---|
| ARGC | number of command-line arguments | - |
| ARGV | array of command-line arguments | - |
| FILENAME | name of current input file | - |
| FNR | record number in current file | - |
| FS | input field separator | space or tab |
| NF | number of fields in the current record | - |
| NR | number of records read | - |
| OFMT | numeric output format | %.6g |
| OFS | output field separator | space |
| ORS | output record separator | newline |
| RS | input record separator | newline |

loops, the ability to create your own functions, strings and array manipulation, and much more. Table 3–3 shows us what comparison operators we can use and Table 3–4 shows us the variables that are built into `awk`.

Unfortunately, this is not a book on UNIX programming languages. Some readers may be disappointed that I do not have the space to cover `awk` in more detail. I also am disappointed. However, I have given you a basic introduction to the constructs of the language to enable you to better understand the over 100 scripts on your system that use `awk` in some way.

## Putting Things Together

Since I wasn't trying to make you shell or `awk` programming experts, there are obviously things that we didn't have a chance to cover. However, I hope I have given you the basic tools to create your own tools and configure at least your shell environment the way you need or want it.

Like any tool or system, the way to understand it is to practice with it. Therefore, my advice is that you play with the shell and programs on the system to get a better feeling for how they behave. By creating your own scripts, you will become more familiar with both `vi` and shell script sytnax, which will help you create your own tools and understand the behavior of the system scripts. As you learn more, you can add `awk` and `sed` components to your system to make some very powerful commands and utilities.

# CHAPTER 4

- User Accounts
- Security

# Users
# and User
# Accounts

I t is uncommon to find an SCO system that does not have users on it. Although there are "system" users that have the same characteristics as human users, these are not what we normally think of when talking about users. For us, a user is a person that interacts with the system. This can be anything from logging in and getting to a shell prompt or accessing files on a remote system by using various networking programs.

Users are what computers are made for. One of the key advantages that UNIX has over operating systems is that it was designed to run with multiple users, all accessing the same system and resources. It is important that the system not only be able to distinguish between different users, but also make decisions about what each user can and cannot do.

In this chapter, we are going to talk about what makes a user. We'll look at what the operating system sees as a user. In other words, what files, values, and data go into the system's interpretation of a user. We'll also talk about what a user can and cannot do, plus the mechanisms that are in place to prevent a user from doing something he or she shouldn't. This is the whole idea behind system security.

## User Accounts

Users gain access to the system only after the system administrator has created *user accounts* for them. These accounts are more than just a user name and password, but they also define the environment the user works under including the amount of access he or she has.

Users are added to SCO UNIX Systems by one of two ways. The most common way is through the System Administration Shell (sysadmsh) in ODT 3.0 and the Account Manager in OpenServer. Here the system administrator can define the basic aspects of a user's account. The other way is by means of the `addxusers`, which is used to add users when moving from SCO XENIX, or from other systems that do not have the level of security as SCO UNIX. Although this does not allow you the detail of control you get when adding users the "official" way, you do have the ability to incorporate this command into a shell script to automate adding users. We'll talk more about both of these a little later.

Adding a user to an SCO UNIX system is often referred to as "creating a user" or "creating a user account." The terms "user" and "user account" are often interchanged in different contexts. For the most part, the term "user" is used for the person actually working on the system and "user account" is used to refer to the files and programs that create the user's environment when he or she logs in. However, these two phrases can be interchanged and people will know what you are referring to.

When an account gets created, a shell is assigned along with the default configuration files that go with that shell. Users are also assigned a home directory, which is their default directory when they log in. This is usually of the form `/usr/<username>`. Note that the parent of the users' home directories may be different.

When user accounts are created, each user is assigned a User Name (login name or logname), which is associated with a User ID (*UID*). Each is assigned to at least one group, with one designated as their *login group*. Each group has an associated Group ID (*GID*). The UID is numbers that are used to identify the user. The GID is a number used to identify the login group of that user. Both are used to keep track of that user and determine what files he or she can access.

In general, programs and commands that interact with us humans report information about the user by logname or group name. However, most identification from the operating systems point of view is done through the UID and GID. The UID is associated with the logname of the user. The GID is associated with the login group of the user. In general, the group a user is a part of is only used for determining access to files.

With the exception of the security related information (which we cover in detail in the next section), all the user information is kept in two files: `/etc/passwd` and `/etc/group`. For details of the contents of these files, see the `passwd(F)` and `group(F)` man-pages.

If you look on your system you will see that both of these files are readable by everyone. My first reaction was that this was a security problem, but when I was told what this was all about, I realized that it was necessary. I was also concerned that passwords may be accessible, even in encrypted format. Since I know what my password is, I can compare my password to the encrypted version and figure out the encryption mechanism, right? Nope! It's not that easy.

At the beginning of each encrypted password is a *seed*. Using this seed, the system creates the encrypted version. When you log in, the system takes the seed from the encrypted password and encrypts the password that you input. If this matches the encrypted password, you are allowed in. There is *nowhere* on the system that stores the unencrypted password, nor do any of the utilities or commands generate it.

Next, let's talk about the need to be able to access this information. Remember that the operating system knows only about numbers. When we talked about operating system basics, I mentioned that the information about the owner and group of a file was stored as a number in the inode. However, when you do a long listing of a file (`ls -l`) you don't see the number, but rather a name. For example, if we do a long listing of `/bin/mkdir`, we get

```
-rwx--x--x  1 root    sys     7558 Mar 15 1993 /bin/mkdir
```

The entries are

```
permissions links owner group size date filename
```

Here we see that the owner of the file is `root` and the group is `sys`. Since the owner and group are stored as numerical values in the inode table, the system *must* be translating this information before it displays it on the screen. Where does it get the translation? From the `/etc/passwd` and `/etc/group` files. You can see what the "untranslated" values are by doing an `ls -ln /bin/mkdir`, which gives us

```
-rwx--x--x  1 0     3       7558 Mar 15 1993 /bin/mkdir
```

If we look in `/etc/passwd`, we see that the 0 is the UID for `root` and if we look in `/etc/group` we see that 3 is the GID for the group `sys`, which are the numbers we got above. If the `/etc/passwd` and `/etc/group` files were not readable by everyone, then no translation could be made like this, without some major changes to most of the system commands and utilities. Keep in mind that the GID only has meaning in terms of accessing files.

If the SCO UNIX system you are working on was installed with a high level of security, some other files come onto the scene. If you have any security level other than "low," the encrypted password is stored in the file `/etc/shadow`. This file is readable only by `root` and contains the user name and encrypted password, as well as longevity information about the password. Because the encrypted password is stored in the `/etc/shadow` file, an 'x' will appear in the `/etc/passwd` file in place of the encrypted password. For more details, see the section on security and the `shadow(F)` man-page.

Although they exist at all security levels, the files of the Protected Password Database become an issue at levels above "low". These files contain information about privileges that each user has on the system. (We talk more about this in the section on security.) In addition to user specific information, there are system defaults related to logging in and passwords that are defined in `/etc/default/login` and `/etc/default/passwd`.

On a number of occasions, I have talked to customers that claimed to have experienced corruption when transferring files from one system to another. Sometimes it's with `cpio` and sometimes with `tar`. In every case, files have arrived on the destination machine and have had either "incorrect" owners or groups and sometimes both. Sometimes, the "corruption" is so bad that there are no names for the owner and group, just numbers.

Numbers, you say? Isn't that how the system stores the owner and group information for the files? Exactly. What does it use to make the translation from these numbers to the names that we normally see? As I mentioned, `/etc/passwd` and `/etc/group`. When you transfer files from one system to another, the only owner information that gets transferred are the numbers. When the file arrives on the destination machine, weird things can happen. Let's look at an example.

At SCO, my user name was jimmo and I had UID 12709. All my files were stored with 12709 in the owner field of the inode. Let's say that I create a user on my machine at home, also named jimmo. Since there are far fewer users on my system at home than at SCO, jimmo ended up with UID `200`. When I transferred files from work to home, the owner of all "my" files was 12709. That is, where there was normally a name when I did a long listing, there was the number 12709, not jimmo.

The reason for this is that the owner of the file is stored as a number in the inode. When I copied the files from my system at work, certain information from the inode was copied along with the file. This included the owner. Not the user's name, but the numerical value in the inode. When the files were listed on the new system, there was no user with UID 12709, therefore no translation could be made from the number to the name. The only thing that could be done was to display the number.

This makes sense because what if there were no user `jimmo` on the other system? What value should be displayed in this field? At least this way there is some value and you have a small clue as to what is going on.

In order to keep things straight I had to do one of two things: either create a shell script that changed the owner on all my files when I transferred them, or figure out some way to give jimmo UID 12709 on my system at home. And that's what I did.

Here, too, there are two ways I can go about it. I could create the 12508 users on my system and then the 12709th would be jimmo. (Why 12508? By default the system starts with a UID 200 for normal users.) This bothered me because I would first have to remove the user jimmo with UID 200 then create it again. I felt that this would be a waste of time.

The other alternative was to change the system files. Now, there is nothing that SCO provided that would do that. There were many aspects of the user jimmo that I could change; the UID was not one of them. After careful consideration, I realized there was a tool that SCO provided to make the changes: `vi`. Since this information is kept in simple text files, you can use a text editor to change them. After reading the remainder of the chapter you should have the necessary information to make the changes yourself.

Note that when you create a user you are offered a value for the UID. This is usually one higher than the previously assigned UID. However, you do not have to accept this value. You can give any value you want provided it has not already been assigned.

When the first customer called with the same situation, I could immediately tell him why it was happening, how to correct it, and assure him that it worked.

You can also change a user's group if you want. However, you don't have to go through all that, since this *is* one of the changes you can make through the `sysadmsh`. Remember, however, that all this does is change the `GID` for that user in `/etc/passwd`. Nothing else! Therefore, all files created before you make the change will still have the old group.

There is a way of changing your UID while you are working. This is done with the `su` command. What does `su` stand for? Well, that's a good question. I have seen several different translations in books and from people on the net. I personally say that it means "switch UID" as that's what it does. However, other possibilities include "switch users" and "super-user." What this command does is set your UID to a new one. The syntax is

```
su <user_name>
```

where `<user_name>` is the logname of the user whose UID you want to use. After running the command you have a UID of that user. However, there is more to it than just that. The system also keeps track of the UID that you logged in under. This is your login UID or LUID. The LUID is maintained by the process and all of its descendants for as long as they run. Nothing can change it. To check your LUID, run this command:

```
id -l
```

We can also change our GID, as well. This is done with the `newgrp` or `sg` commands. The `sg` command is new and has many more options than `newgrp`.

We need to remember that a shell is the primary means by which the users gain access to the system. Once they do gain access, their ability to move around the system (in terms of reading files or executing programs) is dependent on a couple of things: permissions and privileges.

Permissions are something that most people are familiar with if they have ever worked on an SCO UNIX (or similar) system before. Based on what has been granted, different users will have different access to files, programs, and directories. You find out what permissions a particular file has by doing a long listing of it. The permissions are represented by the first ten characters on the line. This is something that we covered in a fair bit of detail in the section on shell basics, so there is no need to repeat it here.

Privileges or authorizations are given at the time the user is created, but can be changed later. Although you *could* do this by editing the files directly, it is better (read: safer) to use the tools that are provided for that purpose: `sysadmsh` on ODT 3.0 and `scoadmin` on OpenServer. Be very careful when granting privileges to users. Unless there is a very compelling reason, you should not give users anything more than what the default is. On a system with a lower security level, the privileges granted to users are quite extensive. If you seem to be giving users more that what the default is, then maybe your security level is too high. See the section on system security for more details on this.

A very dramatic example in ODT 3.0 is the "auth" system privilege. This privilege is usually giving to root and user of the type "administrator." By itself, it does have limited power. However, there is a catch. Anyone with "auth" system privileges has the ability to change any password on the system. I repeat *any* password. So, although this user may not have root privileges, all the user needs to do is to change root's password and log in as root.

### Logging into the System

Through user accounts, users gain access to the system. This is the first level of security. Although it is possible to configure applications that start directly on specific terminals, most everyone has logged into an SCO UNIX system at least once. More than likely if you are one of those people who never log in, you never see a shell prompt and are probably not reading this book.

Most SCO UNIX systems have a very standard log in. What this log in process looks like you can see in Figure 4–1. You see the name of the system, followed by a brief message (the contents of `/etc/issue`), and the log in prompt, which usually consists of the system name and the word login. In OpenServer, the `/etc/issue` is no longer present, by default. Instead, information is taken from the file (`/etc/default/banner`). Rather than be a straight, hardcoded text file

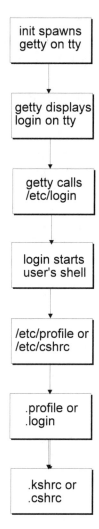

**Figure 4–1**   The log in process.

like `/etc/issue`, `/etc/default/banner` allows you to present "dynamic" information. The banner string is defined in `/etc/default/banner` as a set of variables that the system reads prior to presenting the log in. Afterwards you see the log in prompts, such as

`scoburg!login:`

If you do have something in both `/etc/default/banner` and `/etc/issue`, you will see the banner defined by `/etc/default/banner` followed by the contents of `/etc/issue`.

When you log in, you are first asked your user name and your password. Having been identified and password verified, you are allowed access to the system. This often means that the system starts a shell for you. However, many programs can be used in place of a shell.

One of the entries in the password file is your home directory. This is the directory that you have as your current directory when you log in. This is also the place that the shell returns you to if you enter cd with no arguments.

After determining your log in shell and placing you in your home directory, the system will set up some systemwide defaults. If you have a Bourne or Korn shell, these are done through the /etc/profile file. If you have ksh as your log in shell, the system runs through the commands stored in the .profile in your home directory, then the .kshrc file, provided they exist. If you have sh, then there is no equivalent for the .kshrc file. If you have a C-shell, the system defaults are established in the /etc/cshrc file. The system then executes the commands in the .cshrc and .login files in your home directory; again, provided they exist. See the appropriate man-page and the section on shell basics for more details.

During the log in process, you are shown several pieces of information about the local system. Prior to the login prompt, you usually see the contents of the /etc/issue file, as I mentioned above. After your log in is successful, you will normally see a message about the last successful and unsuccessful logins, several copyright messages, and the message of the day. This is the contents of the file /etc/motd.

There may be cases where all of this information is bothersome. For example, many businesses have either menus that their users log into, or applications that start from their users' .profile or .login. In this case, the information about copyrights and last log in is of little value.

There are cases where even knowing that this is an UNIX system could be a problem. There are many hackers in the world who would just love the chance to try and crack your security. By not even telling them what kind of system you have, you reduce the temptation. As least, that's one more piece of information that they need to figure out. Therefore, we need a way to disable these messages.

The two obvious ones are /etc/issue (/etc/default/banner in OpenServer) and /etc/motd. By default, both of these contain information about your system. By either changing the contents or removing all the files, you can eliminate that source of information.

The next is the log in prompt itself. Again, by default, this contains the name of your system. This may not be of concern to most system administrators; however, in cases where security is an issue, you might like to disable it. This comes from the `/etc/gettydefs` file. The `gettydefs` file contains information used by the `getty` program when starting the login program on a terminal. The more common lines in the `gettydefs` file contain an entry that looks like this:

```
@!login:
```

Take a look at the login prompt and you will see that it also contains `!login:` immediately following the name of the system. The name of the system comes from the `@`. By changing either one of the parts (or both) you can change the appearance of your login prompt; even removing the name of the system if you want.

At this point we are left with the last log in messages and the copyrights. Unfortunately, these are not contained in files that are as easily removed as `/etc/motd` and `/etc/issue`. However, by *creating* a file we can remove them. This is the file `.hushlogin` in your home directory. It has no contents, rather the existence of this file is the key. You can create it simply by changing to a users home directory (yours, if you are that user) and running

```
touch .hushlogin
```

It's possible that your system administrator (if that's not you) has disabled the `hushlogin` capabilities for the entire system. In which case, you can create `.hushlogin` files all day and you will still see the login messages. If you want to check, look for the ALLOWHUSH entry in `/etc/default/login`. If this is set to NO, then hushlogins are disabled systemwide.

Often administrators want to keep users' knowledge of the system as small as possible. This is particularly important for systems with a high level of security where users start applications and never see the shell prompt. One "give-away" as to what kind of system you are on is in the two lines when you login:

```
Last successful login for user...
Last unsuccessful login for user...
```

System administrators would regularly call into support asking for a way to turn this off. Fortunately, this can be disabled by creating the `.hushlogin` file. Once this functionality is enabled, you can simplify things by having this file created every time a new user is created. This is done by editing the file `/usr/lib/mkuser/lib/mkuser.lib`. Search for the line

```
mkuser_mkdir "$homedir" home
```

This will be within a function called `mk_home`. You need to add the line:

```
touch ${homedir}/.hushlogin
```

This will then create the file `.hushlogin` in the user's home directory. For more details on this, take a look at the part of this chapter on creating users as well as the *System Administrator's Guide*.

One thing to consider before you turn this off, is that watching when the last unsuccessful log in attempt was made may indicate a security problem. If you repeatedly see unsuccessful log in attempts when you are not there, this is not a good thing. It may indicate someone is trying to break into your account.

### Adding Users

As I mentioned before, there are two standard ways of adding users to the system. The most common method is through the menuing interfaces provided. In ODT 3.0 this was `sysadmsh`, in OpenServer this is the Account Manager. In order to ease the transition from SCO XENIX there is also the `addxusers` command.

Although this alleviates many problems, it does not help administrators who have brand new systems and need to create dozens or even hundreds of users at once. Going through either the `sysadmsh` or Account Manager with even a few dozen users can be very tedious. If you were an experienced administrator, you could write a shell script, combining some of the techniques that you learned in the section on `sed` and `awk`, that would edit the necessary files and add the appropriate entries.

Fortunately, there is an answer in OpenServer. Three new commands were included that allow you to add, remove, and modify user accounts. These are, respectively, `useradd`, `userdel`, and `usermod`. Despite the introduction of these commands, and despite the different programs used in each operating system, what lies behind the scenes when adding (or removing) a user remains the same.

The most obvious (or at last most familiar) thing is the addition of lines to both the `/etc/passwd` and `/etc/group` files. As I mentioned before, if your system is at a security level higher than "low", an entry will also be created in `/etc/shadow`. However, entries are created in the security database at every level.

Entries are also made into the security database, *regardless* of the security level. I go into details about the security databases in the section on security. However, we have one of those chicken-egg situations. In order to understand the process of adding a user I need to jump ahead a little to talk about the security databases.

There are two databases that divide the privileges each user has into two different perspectives. One contains a set of files, one *per user*, that lists the privileges that particular user has. The other is also a set of files, but here there is one file *per privilege*, listing which user has that privilege. This redundancy is to ensure the integrity of the security database as well as to make access to the necessary information easier.

As I mentioned before, each user is given a home directory. This may be one that already exists, or a new one. If the directory is new, the system will automatically make copies of the shell start-up files in that directory based on which shell is selected. Then, that user is made the owner, and his or her group is made the group of those files. The originals of these start-up scripts are kept in subdirectories in /usr/lib/mkuser. There is one directory for each of the possible log in shells. These can be easily modified by the system administrator to make changes to the default shells.

As the user is created, there are a set of defaults that are assumed. These are found in /etc/default/authsh. They include, the home directory, the shell, the permissions on the home directory, and the type of user. Since this file is readable, any user can see what the defaults are. In OpenServer, this is, instead, the file /etc/default/accounts.

### Terminal Settings

Applications are governed by a couple of processes. If you have a serial terminal, the flow of data is controlled by the serial line characteristics. This includes the baud rate, the number of data bits, parity, and so on. One aspect that is often forgotten or even unknown to many users is the terminal characteristics. The terminal characteristics are used to control the physical appearance on the screen.

As I mentioned previously, the serial line characteristics are initially determined by the gettydefs file. These are often changed from within the user's startup scripts (.profile, .login, etc.). In addition, you can change them yourself by using the stty command. Rather than jumping to changing them let's take a look at what our current settings are, which is also done with the stty command. With no arguments, stty might give us something like this:

```
speed 9600 baud;   ispeed 9600 baud;   ospeed 9600 baud;
-parity hupcl
swtch = ^@; susp = <undef>;
brkint -inpck -istrip icrnl onlcr
echo echoe echok
```

This shows the more "significant" terminal (stty) settings. The top line shows us the input and output speeds; 9600 in both cases. On the second line, we see that parity is turned off (-parity) and the system sends a hangup signal on the last close of this port. This is useful on modem connections to ensure that the connection is actually broken and you don't end up with large phone bills.

The switch (swtch) character tells us what is used to switch between different shell layers. Here it is defined as CTRL-@. We can tell this, because in the output of stty, the caret (^) indicates a control character. See the `shl`(C) man-page for more details.

The suspend character (`susp`) tells the system what key is pressed to suspend the current job. This is only valid for shells that support job control. When you suspend a job it is comparable to putting the process in the background, although it does not continue working. This process can be returned to foreground operation with the `fg` command, or can be restarted in the background with the `bg` command.

The other settings include echoing every character that is typed (`echo`), on input map carriage returns to new lines (`icrnl`) and on output map new lines to carriage returns (`onlcr`). Characteristics can be specifically turned off by including a minus in front of them, such as `-istrip` which says not to strip input characters to seven bits.

Setting these values is very straightforward. For settings that are Booleans (on or off), the syntax is simply

```
stty <setting>
```

to turn it on, or

```
stty -<setting>
```

to turn it off.

For example, if I wished to turn on input stripping, the command would look like this:

```
stty istrip
```

Settings that require a value have the sytnax

```
stty <setting> <value>
```

So, to set the speed (baud rate) to 19200 the syntax would look like this:

```
stty speed 19200
```

or to set the suspend character to CTRL-Z we would enter

```
stty susp ^Z
```

Note that ^Z is not two separate characters. Instead, when you type it you hold down the CTRL key and press 'z'. The letter appears as capital although we pressed the lowercase letter.

If there are characteristics that the default output does not show, you can use the `-a` option to show all the characteristics. You might end up with output like this:

```
speed 9600 baud;  ispeed 9600 baud;  ospeed 9600 baud;  line = 0(tty);
intr = DEL; quit = ^\; erase = ^H; kill = ^U; eof = ^D; eol = ^@;
swtch = ^@; susp = <undef>; start = ^Q; stop = ^S;
```

```
-parenb -parodd cs8 -cstopb hupcl cread -clocal -loblk
-ortsfl -ctsflow -rtsflow
-ignbrk brkint ignpar -parmrk -inpck -istrip -inlcr -igncr icrnl -iuclc
ixon ixany -ixoff
isig icanon -xcase echo echoe echok -echonl -noflsh
-iexten -tostop -xclude
opost -olcuc onlcr -ocrnl -onocr -onlret -ofill -ofdel
isscancode xscancode -cs2scancode
```

For details on what each of these entries mean, please see the `stty(C)` man-page.

If you want to be able to save your `stty` settings, change some, and then restore the original values, you can use the `-g` option. This outputs the `stty` settings as a string of hexadecimal values. For example, I might get something like this:

```
stty -g
500:5:d050d:3b:7f:1c:8:15:4:0:0:0:0:0:1a:11:13:0:0:0:0:0:0:0:0:0
```

We can run the `stty` command to get these values, make the changes, then run `stty` again and use these values as the argument. No, we don't have to type in everything by hand, we simply take advantage of the fact that variables are expanded by the shell before being passed to the command. Let's look at the example in the SCO doc:

```
echo "Enter your secret code: \c"
old='stty -g'
stty -echo intr '^-'
read code
stty $old
```

We assign the output of the `stty` command to the variable old. We then change the `stty` settings so that the characters we input are not echoed to the screen and the interrupt key is disabled. We then read a line from the keyboard and then reset the `stty` settings to their old value.

**Terminal Capabilities.**   If you are interacting with the system solely through command line input, then you have few occasions to encounter the terminal capabilities. As the name implies, terminal capabilities determine what the terminal is capable of. For example, can the terminal move the cursor to a specific spot on the screen?

The terminal capabilities are defined by one of two databases. Older applications such as SCO's Lyrix use termcap, while newer ones use terminfo. For the specifics on each, please see the appropriate man-page. Here, we are going to talk about the concept of terminal capabilities and what it means to you as a user.

Within each database is a mapping of what character or character sequence the terminal expects for certain behavior. For example, on some terminals pressing the backspace key sends a CTRL-H character. On others, a CRTL-? is sent. When your TERM environment variable is set to the correct one for your terminal, pressing the backspace key sends a signal to the system which, in turn, tells the application that the backspace characteristic was called. It is then up to the application to determine what is to be done.

The key benefit of a system like this is that you do not have to recompile or rewrite your application to work on different terminals. Instead, you link in the appropriate library to access either termcap or terminfo and listen for what capability the OS is sending you. When the application receives that capability, it reacts accordingly.

There are three types of capabilities. The first are Boolean, which determine if that terminal has a particular feature. For example, does the terminal have an extra "status" line? The next type is numeric values. Examples of this are the number of columns and lines the terminal can display. In some cases, this may not remain constant as terminals such as the Wyse 60 can change between 80- and 132-column mode. Lastly, are the string capabilities which provide a character sequence to be used to perform a particular operation. Examples of this are clearing the line from the current cursor position to the end of the line or deleting the contents of an entire line (with or without removing the line completely).

Despite the fact that there are hundreds of possible capabilities, any given terminal will have only a small subset of them. In addition, many of the capabilities do not apply to terminals, but rather to printers.

Both the termcap database and the terminfo database have their own advantages and disadvantages. The termcap database is defined by the file /etc/termcap. This is an ASCII file that is easily modified. In contrast to this is the terminfo database which starts out as an ASCII file, but must be "compiled" before it can be used. The default source file is /usr/lib/terminfor/terminfo.src. To compile the entries you use the terminfo compiler: tic. The tic utility will then place the compiled version in a directory under /usr/lib/terminfo based on the name of the terminal. For example, the ansi terminal ends up in /usr/lib/terminfo/a and Wyse terminals end up in /usr/lib/terminfo/w. SCO also provides you with a tool to convert existing termcap entries to terminfo: captoinfo.

## Security

The term *security* is common enough. On a personal basis we think of it as freedom from risk or danger; being safe. We also think of this as the methods we undertake to prevent someone from breaking into our house.

If we talk about being safe from risk when working with computers, we are often talking about things like regular backups and reliable hardware. Although these are very important issues, these are not what is generally meant when referring to security. On computer systems, security refers to preventing someone from breaking into the system. The definition can be expanded by saying computer security is preventing someone from doing something that they are not allowed to do. This could be anything from reading other people's mail to stopping the printers.

In this section we are going to be talking about what mechanisms exist to keep people from poking around and doing things they shouldn't. We'll talk about what tools SCO UNIX provides to control access, change what users can access, and how to make sure users are not even trying to do things they shouldn't.

In any information system, whether it is a computer or filing cabinet, there are some basic security issues that need to be considered. First, there is one aspect of security that no operating system can help you with: the physical security of your system. You might have all the security implemented that SCO UNIX provides, but if someone can walk off with your computer, even the highest levels of operating system security won't do any good; just as a security policy in an office has no effect if someone can just walk away with sensitive files.

One of the easiest and most effective types of physical security is simply a locked door. This prevents the "crime of opportunity" from ever happening (such as someone walking away with pieces of equipment, or the whole machine for that matter). The only thing that can prevent this kind of theft are more elaborate security measures that are beyond the scope of this book. However, it is something that you must give serious thought to. Locking the door to the computer can also prevent people from breaking into the system. Anyone who has a set of installation disks or an emergency boot disk set can gain access to your system if they have access to the computer itself.

Access to the all powerful root account may be an issue. On an SCO system root can do anything. Although it is possible to restrict roots access to certain functions, a knowledgeable user with root priviliges can overcome that. There are many instances when you may have several people administering some aspect of the system, such as printers or the physical network. One person always says, "Well, he has root access, why can't I?"

Access to the root account should be limited for a couple of reasons. First, the more people with root access, are the more people who have *complete* control over the system. This makes access control difficult.

Also, the more people that have root access, the more fingers get pointed. I know from experience that there are people who will deny doing anything wrong. Often this results in a corrupt system. Since everyone has the power to do everything, someone will do something that messes up the system somehow and no one will admit. Sound familar?

The fewer people that have root, the fewer fingers need to be pointed and the less people can pass the buck. Mistakes happen, and if there are few people with root access and something goes wrong, tracking down the cause is much easier.

Rather than several users all having the root password, some people think that it is safer to create several users all with the UID of root. Their belief is that since there are several lognames, it's easier to keep track of things. Well, the problem in this thinking is that the system keeps track of users by the UID. There is no way to keep these users separate, once they log in.

My personal suggestion is that if several users need root powers, make it company policy that no one logs in as root. Instead, grant each required user the su system privilege. They can log in with their own account and do an su to root. Although everything is still done as root, there is a record of who did the su in /usr/adm/sulog.

Another aspect of physical security is access to the machine itself. It may be impractical for someone to walk off with your computer. However, a knowledgeable user with root access to a comparable SCO system can gain access to yours if they have physical access. Even without access to another system, if that user has access to the installation floppies, they can get into your system.

The next issue is privacy. This can be the company's privacy or that of individuals. You don't want unauthorized users to have access to payroll records or to other employees personal files. One of the most commonly ignored aspects of this is the power of small pieces of information. As individual items, these pieces may have no significance at all. However, when taken in context they can have far reaching implications. Police use this same concept to investigate crimes and intelligence agencies like the CIA use it as well. Extending this to the business world, such techniques are useful for corporate spies.

What if someone changed an important piece of information? For example, an employee thinks he is underpaid and changes his salary. Whether this information is on paper or in a computer, the integrity of the data is an important part of security. Along the same lines is the consistency of the data. You want the same behavior from the system in identical situations. For example, if salary is based on position, inconsistent data could mean that the night watchman suddenly gets paid as much as the company president.

An aspect of note is the concept of auditing. Like an audit of a company's books, in a computer security sense it is a record of the *transactions* or *events* that occurred on the system. This allows the system administrator to follow the tracks of suspected perpetrators and maybe catch them in the act.

Regardless of what security issue you are talking about, any breach in security can be prevented by limiting access to the system. Now, this can be taken to extremes by not letting *anyone* have access. However, by limiting access to the system only to authorized users, you substantially lower the risk of breaches in security. Keep in mind that there is no such thing as a secure system. This is especially important when you consider that the most serious threat comes from people who already have an account on that system.

Access control has been a part of UNIX for a long time. It is a fundamental aspect of any multi-user system. The most basic form of access control is in the form of user accounts. The only way you should be able to gain access to an SCO UNIX system is through an account. Users usually gain access to the system when they have an account set up for them. Each user is assigned an individual password that allows them access. In some cases, this password may be blank, meaning the user only need press enter. In other cases it can be removed altogether so you are never even prompted to input your password.

Removing the password may not always be a good idea. In fact, SCO UNIX allows the system administrator the option to prevent users from either having no password or having to just press return. Since we are talking here about security, and accounts without passwords are not very secure, we'll restrict ourselves to talking about accounts that have passwords.

Built into SCO UNIX are some enhancement to simple passwords that prevent one of the more common security breaches: letting someone get access to your password. If you write your password on a Post-It® and stick it on your monitor, then no operating system in the world can do anything about it. But what cases where you inadvertently give someone your password?

This happens when users choose passwords that are easily guessed by someone trying to break in. Often users will choose passwords that are easy to remember, such as their license plate number or spouse's birthday. SCO UNIX cannot do anything to keep you from using your license plate number as a password. However, it does have some built in features to limit what you can use.

Words that can be found in a dictionary are not good choices for passwords. With just a few lines of code, you could write a simple program that searches through a list of words and tries them all as passwords. However, if activated, SCO UNIX will prevent you from choosing any of these as your passwords. It also prevents you from making simple changes to the password like rotating (*strawberry* becomes *awberrystr*) or reversing (*yrrebwarts*).

Depending on how the system administrator implements it, SCO UNIX can also prevent you from using things like the name of the system, the word UNIX, and several other things. This can even be expanded by the system administrator to prevent you from using things like the company's name as passwords. To help you in your choice, the SCO UNIX passwd program provides a password generator to create easy to remember, but nonsensical passwords. Well, at least that's what the SCO doc says. Personally, I have found the generated password more of a problem than "obvious" ones. Because the generated ones are nonsensical, users are more likely to forget them. For more details on this, check out the goodpw(ADM) and passwd(ADM) man-pages.

Although this password protection stops most attempts to gain unauthorized access to the system, many security issues involve users that already have accounts. Unchecked, curious users could access payroll information and find out what their boss gets paid. Corporate spies could steal company secrets. Disgruntled workers could wreak havoc by destroying data or slowing down the system.

Once logged in, SCO UNIX (among other UNIX dialects) provides a means of limiting the access of "authorized" users. This is in the form of file permissions, which we already talked about. File permissions are one aspect of security that most people are familiar with in regard to UNIX security.

The first thing we need to talk about is the concept of a file *owner*. Each file has an owner, whether or not some user explicitly went out there and "claimed" ownership. It's a basic characteristic of each file and is imposed upon them by the operating system. The owner of the file is stored, along with other information, in the inode table in the form of a number. This number corresponds to the User ID (UID) number from /etc/passwd.

Normally, files are initially owned by the user who creates them. However, there are many circumstances that would change the ownership. Ownership may be intentionally changed. Only the owner of the file and root can change its ownership. If you are the owner of a file, you can, in essence, "transfer ownership" of the file to someone else. Once you do, you are no longer the owner (obviously) and have no more control over that file.

Another characteristic of a file is its *group*. Like the owner, the file's group is an intrinsic part of the file's characteristics. The file's group is also stored in the inode as a number. The translation from this number to the group name is made from the `/etc/group` file. As we talked about in the section on users, the concept of a group has real meaning only in terms of security; that is, who can access which files.

What this means is that only "authorized" users can access files in any of the three manners: read, write, and execute. It makes sense that normal users cannot run the `fdisk` utility, otherwise they would have the ability to repartition the hard disk, potentially destroying data. It also makes sense that normal users do not have write permission on the `/etc/passwd` file, otherwise they could change it so that they could have access to the root account. Since we talked about it in the section on shell basics and on users, there is no need to go into more details here.

### System Security under SCO

In early versions of UNIX, account passwords and file permissions were the only types of security implemented. As computers became more widespread and users who wanted to gain unauthorized access became more devious, it became apparent that this was not enough. Since the US government was steadily increasing the number of agencies that had computers, the level of system security needed to be increased as well.

In 1985, the National Security Agency's National Computer Security Center (NCSC) created a set of computer security standards for the Defense Department titled, *Trusted Computer Systems Evaluation Criteria.* This is commonly known as the *Orange Book,* as it was published with an orange cover. (This is part of a series of documents by the DOD related to computer security, all with different colored covers.)

Within the *Orange Book,* there are four broad classes of security levels for computers:

- D  Minimal security
- C  Discretionary protection
- B  Mandatory protection
- A  Verified protection

The C class contains two sublevels: C1 and C2, with C2 offering slightly more security than C1. Class B offers three sublevels: B1, B2, and B3.

Traditional PC-based operating systems, like DOS and Windows fall within class D. This minimal protection does not mean there is no security, just that it is not as high as the C class. You can buy add-on products to add passwords to your system or change the file attributes to prevent accidental erasure.

Class C systems include the features and functions to employ *discretionary protection*. That means that it is up to the system administrator's discretion to decide how much access system users may have. Class C1 systems offer enough security to let users keep their data private from other users and prevent it from being accidentally read or destroyed. As we've already discussed, standard UNIX already provides this level of security in the form of user passwords and file permissions.

Class C2 demands tighter log in procedures, auditing of security related events, and isolation of system resources. This is the level that is *provided* by SCO UNIX. Since it is at the discretion of the system administrator, it may not be in place on your system.

Class B systems implement *mandatory protection*. That is, the system administrator cannot turn it off if he or she likes. Class B1 systems have *labeled protection*. This means that security procedures and *sensitivity labels* are required for each file. (A sensitivity level is basically a security classification.) Class B2 adds the requirement that the system must be able to account for every code in the system. This helps to prevent such security holes as *Trojan horses*. Class B3 deals with the security of data access, in terms of preventing tampering and notification of security-relevant events.

The most secure class, Class A1, requires *verified* designs. Although they are functionally the same as B3 systems, A1 systems have also been formally defined, as well as *proven*, by tests.

The set of files that contain the security privileges on an SCO UNIX system is referred to as the *Trusted Computing Base* (TCB). It consists of a database of information that is accessed by both utilities and the SCO UNIX kernel to prevent unauthorized use of the system. Since you need a user account to get access, and TCB privileges are determined by the user account, you can say that the TCB also prevents unauthorized access.

When implementing these security functions, an SCO UNIX system is referred to as *trusted* rather rather than *secure*. A computer system can never be completely secure, but by implementing these features, it can be trusted to provide a specific amount of protection.

SCO UNIX allows C2 security to be relaxed. Both trusted and relaxed security use the TCB database. Both feature log in security, command restriction, and data encryption. A trusted system goes one step further and audits the use of certain commands, logins and logouts, database events, and use of *authorization*. It also allows greater command restriction.

As I mentioned above, the C2 level of security allows the system administrator to decide what should be protected and what not. This is the concept of *discretionary access control* (DAC). On traditional UNIX systems, this discretion is only in the form of file permissions. (Who gets an account is also at the discretion of the system administrator.)

Under C2 security as implemented by SCO, this is expanded to include *authorizations* and *protected subsystems*. Authorizations are broken down into two categories: *kernel* and *sub-system*. Subsystem authorizations (also called privileges) are assigned to users to *allow* them to perform various tasks on the system. For example, a user must have authorization to stop or start the print scheduler.

Kernel authorizations are associated with processes. Although the processes are acting on behalf of the users, there is a slight difference in the effect it has on access. For example, certain commands under SCO UNIX will change the UID temporarily as it's running. These are called SUID programs as they set the uid. Without the *execsuid* kernel authorization you cannot run such a program *even if* the file permissions allow you to.

Protected subsystems are collections of files that provide common functionality; access to which is normally controlled as a group not as individual files. For example, administering printers consists of accessing several different (but related) programs. Therefore, `lp` is considered a protected subsystem.

Starting with SCO UNIX Version 3.2. Release 4.0, there are four levels of security: low, traditional, improved, and high. Each offers more security than the one before it. During installation, the level of security is one of the questions asked. As described above, this determines the *default* access user's have to the system.

Note that I said *default*. There are two things to keep in mind. First, authorizations and access to protected subsystems are on a *per user* basis. Once they are set, the system defaults do not affect them. Therefore, if you change the default and want existing users changed, you must change them by hand.

The second thing is that you can use `relax`(ADM) to change to any security level. However, you should only use it to change to a *less* secure level. The reason for this is that you must then change the access on all existing users to reflect the new level. It's safe to think, for example, that a system changed to traditional, with trusted level users, is still traditional security. However, a system with traditional security remains so, even if you "improve" it to trusted. This is because there are still users with privileges at the traditional security level.

### The TCB

The files that form the basis for system security reside in two separate directories: `/etc/auth` and `/tcb`. The `/etc/auth` directory contains the system and subsystem related database files as well as the system defaults.

The /tcb directory contains binaries, libraries, and user-related database files. The /tcb/bin directory contains the binaries that are used by both the operating system and the system administrator to insure system integrity and security. The more important ones we'll talk about in a minute. The /tcb/lib directory contains TCB library files.

One of the key things to note is that although these directories represent different perspectives (/etc/auth is from a system perspective and /tcb is from a user perspective), both directories contain much of the same information. This is *not* a duplication of effort, rather it provides a check to ensure that there is no corruption in the database as well as making access to the data easier.

Users can't look in the files, so understanding how these files are laid out is of little use to them. Since the files are created automatically, even system administrators rarely need to look in these files. However, on those occasions where something does go wrong with the TCB database (such as a user losing privileges), knowing what these files say can be very useful. In addition, I feel that understanding what these files contain and how they work together aids in understanding SCO's implementation of system security.

*System privileges* allow users (user processes) to gain access to specific operating system services. Most users are familiar with the chown command, which changes the ownership of the specified file. The chown command makes use of the chown() system call, which, in this case, is the operating system service in question. Without the chown privilege, you cannot use the chown() system call and therefore cannot use the chown command. Another commonly used service is accessed through programs that are set-UID; that is, those that change the user-ID of the process when they run. Without the execsuid privilege, you cannot run SUID programs. Table 4–1 contains a list of the system privileges.

**Table 4–1**    System Privileges

| Privilege | Ability |
| --- | --- |
| configaudit | configure audit subsystem parameters |
| writeaudit | write audit records to the audit trail |
| execsuid | run set-UID programs |
| chmodsugid | set the set-UID and set-GID bit on files |
| chown | change the owner of an object |
| suspendaudit | suspend operating system auditing of the process |

The TCB is actually composed of several different databases, each related to a different aspect of the system. The Protected Subsystem Database contains those files that are related to subsystem authorizations. This database is broken down by subsystem authorization, listing each user with that authorization. These files are located in `/etc/auth/subsystems`. This directory contains files whose names are the *primary* subsystem authorization they represent. For example, the users with the UUCP authorization are in the file `/etc/auth/subsystems/uucp`. Each file contains a list of users and what *primary* and *secondary* authorizations each user has. If a user is listed here, but the privilege is not specified for that user in the Protected Password Database security (more on that in a moment), then the database is *inconsistent*.

By dividing the authorizations in this way, the "powers" that were once reserved only for the root user are now divided into subsystems, enabling the system administrator to assign only the privileges that each user should have. Secondary authorizations are then used to limit these capabilities even further, if necessary.

Keep in mind two things. First, certain SCOAdmin managers require more than one authorization. For example, to use the Filesystem Manager you need the `sysadmin` and `backup` authorizations. Second, be careful of the privileges you assign. The `auth` subsystem authorization allows users to make changes to any account, including root. Other authorizations, such as `backup`, `sysadmin`, or `passwd` can be similarly abused.

Let's take a look at one of these files. For example, the file `/etc/auth/subsystem/lp` might look like this:

```
adm:printqueue,printerstat
audit:printqueue,printerstat
auth:printqueue,printerstat
bin:printqueue,printerstat
daemon:printqueue,printerstat
lp:lp
sys:printqueue,printerstat
root:lp
jimmo:printqueue
```

Each line begins with the name of a user who is to be given the particular subsystem authorization. In this case, the primary authorization is `lp` and the secondary authorizations are `printqueue` and `printerstat`. Some users, such as `lp` and `root` are given just the primary authorization. By giving a user just the primary authorization, you give them all the secondary authorizations. In this case, there are only the two secondary authorizations, so it will have to be sufficient to give those users the `lp` primary authorization instead.

So what's the difference? Well, in many cases, there are no secondary authorizations, for example, the mem authorization. However, where there are secondary authorizations, you can further limit the access each user has. In our example above, those users with just the `printqueue` authorization are able to see everyone's print job, without it they could only see their own. However, in order to enable or disable printers, they need the `printerstat` authorization. Table 4–2 contains a list of primary authorizations and Table 4–3 contains a list of the secondary authorizations. Where the secondary authorizations are defined is `/etc/auth/system/authorize`. The left side of this file is the primary authorization and the right side is the corresponding secondary authorization(s).

The Terminal Control Database contains information about terminals (both physical and pseudo) that are used to log in. This includes information about who logged in last and whether or not the terminal is locked. Two files compose the Terminal Control Database. The `/etc/auth/system/ttys` file contains entries for the terminals on the system. Each entry describes characteristics of a physical device, such as the name of the device, the UID of the last user to log in on this terminal, and if the terminal is locked. For a complete list of the characteristics, look at the `ttys(F)` man-page. The `/etc/system/devassign` file makes name assignments for different device names that represent the same physical device. This is so that you don't need to specify every device in `/etc/auth/system/ttys`.

**Table 4–2**   Primary Authorizations

| Authorization | Scoadmin Manager | What is Permitted |
|---|---|---|
| mem | — | access to system data tables (i.e., list all processes) |
| terminal | — | unrestricted use of the `write` command |
| lp | Printer Manager | administer printers |
| backup | Backup Manager | perform backups |
| auth | Account Manager | administer user accounts |
| audit | Audit Manager | audit administrator |
| cron | Cron Manager | control use of `cron`, `at`, and `batch` |
| root | — | allows use of commands in `/tcb/files/rootcmds` |
| sysadmin | Filesystem Manager | alter mount configuration |
| passwd | Account Manager | change user passwords |

**Table 4–3**  Secondary Authorizations

| AUTHORIZATION | | |
| --- | --- | --- |
| **Secondary** | **Primary** | **What is Permitted** |
| audittrail | audit | generate audit reports on one's own activities |
| backup_create | backup | create (but not restore) backups |
| restore | backup | restore (but not create) backups |
| queryspace | backup | use df command to query disk space |
| printqueue | lp | view all jobs in queue using lpstat |
| printerstat | lp | enable/disable printers |
| su | auth | access to the root account and other accounts (still requires a password) |
| shutdown | root | use Shutdown Manager or shutdown command. |

The File Control Database contains a list of files and directories along with their permissions, owner, and group. This is contained within the /etc/auth/system/files file. The purpose of this database is to ensure that programs do not grant more access than they should (for example, granting root privileges through the SUID bit) and ensuring that data files can only be accessed by the right users (such as ensuring that /etc/passwd cannot be written to by everyone). Two support programs are used to ensure the files match their entries in the File Control Database: integrity and fixmog. For details on the format, check out the files(F) man-page.

However, in /etc/auth/system/files, many groups of files are listed only by the directory they are in. In other words, every file in certain directories is expected to have certain permissions. In most cases this is fine, however, in SCO UNIX 3.2.2 this wasn't and problems arose. SCO UNIX 3.2.4.0 corrected this, as well as the problem that permissions didn't match between the two (/etc/perms and /etc/auth/system/files).

The Protected Password Database contains the information related to users on the system, such as their encrypted password and the subsystem authorizations they have. The information here is used in conjunction with the /etc/passwd (or /etc/shadow) file and the protected subsystem database. The user specific TCB database files reside in /tcb/files/auth. They include much more than the password. In this directory are twenty-six subdirectories, one for each letter of the alphabet. These letters represent the first character of every log in on the system. (Note there are only twenty-six, since a user account name cannot begin with a number, a non-English character, or a capital letter.) Within the respective directories are files with the names of each user.

The files in these directories contain some information that is stored elsewhere like the user name, UID, and even the user's encrypted password. The structure of these files is somewhat difficult to understand at first. So we ought to take a quick look at how these files are put together.

### Reading TCB Files

Although it may not appear that way, each file contains only a single line. At the end of each line is a backslash (\) which indicates that the line continues. (Note that the backslash must not appear on the last line.) Each field is separated with a colon (:) and with the exception of the user name at the very beginning, the entries can appear in any order.

If lines are split in multiple virtual lines, then the last entry on the first line must be followed by a colon and the first entry on the next line must be preceded by one. The `chkent` field indicates the end of that entry. For example,

```
entry_name:cap1:cap2:cap3:chkent
```

could be split into

```
entry_name:\
     :cap1:cap2:\
     :cap3:chkent
```

These capabilities (or characteristics) can take one of three forms. Capabilities requiring a string are followed by an equal sign (=) and then the string. Capabilities requiring a numeric value, are followed by a pound sign (#) and then the numeric value. Boolean capabilities (those that are either on or off) are unchanged if on, and followed by an at sign (@) if off.

Let's take a look at what the entry for an account looks like in the Protected Password Database:

```
jimmo:u_name=jimmo:u_id#12709:\
     :u_pwd=aaIOFIofdmlIMmZTsBdj3vds:\
     :u_type=general:u_succhg#784410590:u_pswduser=jimmo:\
     :u_suclog#793204347:\:u_suctty=tty06:u_unsuclog#792886734:\
     :u_unsuctty=tty05:u_lock@:chkent:
```

The first entry is my user name, `jimmo`. However, so is the second entry (`u_name`). At first this appears like redundant information, however it does make things easier when the system is reading this file to build its internal tables. The `u_id` is my user ID as it appears in `/etc/passwd`. Note the backslash, just after my UID. As I mentioned before, this indicates that this is a single logical line, although it spans multiple physical lines in the file.

The next entry (u_pwd) is my encrypted password. As I mentioned before, if this system has a low security level, then this will be the same as in /etc/passwd. In all but the lowest security level, the encrypted password is not stored in /etc/passwd, but rather /etc/shadow. (For more details see the shadow(ADM) man-page.)

Think back to the problem of transferring files and mixing up the UIDs. This is the place, along with the /etc/passwd file, where you would make the changes. After making the changes, run authck to ensure the integrity of the TCB.

What kind of user I am is determined by the u_type entry. Here, I am just your average user, which is referred to as "general" in the TCB database (although this is referred to as an "individual" user in the sysadmsh if you have ODT 3.0). This is determined when the user is first created. (Note that the descriptions here do not always match the ones in the sysadmsh in ODT 3.0 or the usermod command in OpenServer.)

The next few entries deal with your password. The u_succhg is the last time you successfully changed your password. The u_pswduser entry is who can change my password. In this case I can. However, if root wanted to keep me from changing the password; for example if this account was shared by several users there would be some other user name here.

Next, we have records of my last log ins. The entries u_suclog and u_suctty say when, and on what tty, the last time I successfully logged in. The entries u_unsuclog and u_unsuctty say when and on what tty the last time I unsuccessfully logged in.

The u_lock entry says whether my account is locked or not. This could be the result of too many unsuccessful attempts at logging in, or the system administrator thinks I work too hard and wants to keep me out. Because this is a Boolean value and there is an @, this means my account is not locked. Finally, chkent indicates the end of the entry. If you were paying attention, you'll notice that I never once mentioned what privileges I have. In this case, I didn't need to. When the user account jimmo was created, I was given *default* system privileges. Therefore, there is no need to store this information here. Instead it's kept in /etc/auth/system/default.

Should a user get created that has privileges other than the default, *all* the privileges the user has are listed here. Not just the ones that are different than the default. This is necessary for a couple of reasons. First, there are cases where a user has less than the default. There is nothing built in to indicate that a user does not have particular privileges. In order to do so, you would have to have a separate entry to indicate which ones have been removed. Instead you have a list of which privileges have been given.

Second, there is no entry to say that the user has the default, other than the fact that there is nothing specifically listed. There could be a specific entry to signify the user had the default, *plus* whatever was listed. We could reference the user's entry in `dflt_users`. However, this is not in keeping with the separation of the files in `/etc/auth` being system oriented and the files in `/tcb/files/auth` being user oriented.

Should the privileges be listed here, they will be in the `u_cmdpriv` and `u_syspriv` entries. The `u_cmdpriv` entry lists the subsystem authorizations the user is given and the `u_syspriv` entry lists the kernel authorizations the user is given.

Note that if no `u_cmdpriv` or `u_syspriv` entries are listed, this does *not* mean that the user has default privileges. This is a safety mechanism to ensure that the privileges match. The file `/etc/default/subsystems/dflt_users`, contains a list of users with default privileges. If there is either a `u_cmdpriv` or `u_syspriv` entry for a user that is listed in `dflt_user`, the TCB database is considered inconsistent.

There are a dozen more entries that can find their way into the protected password database files. Many are added depending on changes made to the user account through the `sysadmsh`. Should you have the SCO UNIX or SCO ODT Development System installed, you can find a list of all the entries in `/usr/include/prot.h`. If not, Table 4–4 contains a list of them.

As I mentioned earlier, the entries in `/tcb/files/auth/*` are user related. They correspond indirectly to the files in `/etc/auth/subsystem`. The `u_cmdpriv` entries contain a list of the subsystem authorizations that user has. Simply having them in these files is not enough. The files in `/etc/auth/subsystem` also list details of what user has what privilege, but from the privilege perspective. These two *must* be consistent.

### Issues with TCB Files

Up to this point we've talked about how the files interact and that the TCB database is considered in "inconsistent" if the files don't match. However, up until now I have intentionally left things a little vague. This is because I wanted to talk about correcting problems all at once, not just correcting the individual files.

**Table 4–4**   Fields in `/tcb/files/auth` files

| Entry Name | Function |
|---|---|
| u_priority | The default nice value `login` run at |
| u_minchg | The minimum length of time before user's password can be changed |
| u_maxlen | The maximum length of a generated password |
| u_exp | How long a password lasts until it expires. |
| u_life | How long after the password has expired until the account is locked |
| u_pickpw | Can the user pick their own password? (Boolean) |
| u_genpwd | Can the user use the password generator? (Boolean) |
| u_restrict | Should the user's password be checked for obviousness? (Boolean) |
| u_nullpw | Is a user allowed to have a null password? (Boolean) |
| u_maxtries | Maximum number of unsuccessful attempts to log in before account is locked. |
| u_lock | Is the account locked by default? (Boolean) |
| u_integrity | Can duplicated account information be inconsistent between `/etc/passwd` and the Protected Password database? (Boolean) |
| u_tcbpw | Is `TCB` the master for inconsistent fields? (Boolean) |
| u_pwseg | Maximum significant length of cleartext passwords in units of 8 characters. If this is 1, then only the first 8 characters are significant. |
| t_maxtries | Maximum number of unsuccessful attempts to log in to a terminal before locking the terminal. |
| t_login_timeout | Length of time (in seconds) to complete a successful log in before the log in times out. |

Even if the system was installed correctly and the TCB database files were managed correctly, it is possible for the files within the different TCB databases to become corrupt or inconsistent. This is usually the result of abnormal events such as hardware failure or system crashes. If this happens, the system does have a built-in mechanism to prevent inappropriate access.

This mechanism is the rule that states if things are inconsistent, a user gets the least amount of privilege possible. For example, let's assume the user jimmo was given backup subsystem privileges. This means I have the secondary subsystem authorization "queryspace", which means I can see how much disk space is being used. If suddenly my name is removed from the Protected Subsystem Database (the file `/etc/auth/subsystems/backup`) I would lose this privilege although it was still in the protected password database (`/tcb/files/auth/j/jimmo`).

What to do? Which is correct? How do you even know something is wrong in the first place? The first way is that the user tells you. All of a sudden the user can no longer perform a task that they could a few minutes ago. There will usually be some message about insufficient authorizations, which usually tells you what's missing.

Well, the most obvious way to solve the problem is to restore from backups. Using the information I provided above you can see what subdirectories are needed (`/etc/auth` and `/tcb/files/auth`). You then do a selective restore of those directories. Unfortunately, time limitations may not always allow you to do this. Depending on the speed of your tape drive and the type of backup you did, it may be an hour or so before you are back to where you were. Fortunately, SCO UNIX has some built-in tools that will check and correct most of the problems you will encounter.

Assume you had a situation like we mentioned above, where the two databases were inconsistent. You can use the program `/tcb/bin/authck` (authentication check), which will check all the databases for consistency. There is a particular option to `authck` to check each of the databases. However, you can check everything at once with the -a option. If you are concerned (or curious) about what changes are being made you can use the `-v` (verbose) option, as well. This provides a "running diagnoses."

Because of the importance of having the databases be consistent, this system actually runs `authck` each time the system goes into multi-user mode. Look at the `/etc/inittab` file. One of the first few lines starts with `ack`. If you look at that line you see the program it runs is `/etc/authckrc`. This is the program that actually runs `authck`. (Check the `inittab(F)` man-page and the chapter on Starting and Stopping Your System for more details.)

Next, look at `/etc/authckrc`, which is just a simple shell script. About midway through the script you will see the message

```
Checking tcb...
```

This message is echoed to your screen just before `authck` runs and indicates the first phase of checking the entire TCB database. Here the `authckrc` script runs `/etc/tcbck`, which does a basic "sanity check" of the TCB database. It looks for missing files as well as ones that might be in an invalid state as the result of a crash or something else.

Toward the bottom of the `authckrc` script you will see several lines that you may have noticed as the system is booting into multi-user mode:

```
Checking auth database ...
Checking protected subsystem database ...
```

If you have ODT 3.0 and look in /etc/authckrc, you will also see that just after the system echoes these messages, it runs authck—the first time with the -p option to check the protected password database and the second time with the -s option to check the protected subsystem database. In OpenServer, authck is called once, with *both* the -p and -s options.

Just before it exits, you see authckrc echoing

```
Checking ttys database ...
```

Just afterwards, it runs /tcb/bin/ttyupd. At first it surprised me that authckrc just didn't run authck -t to check it. Well, that's just the point. The -t option to authck just checks the values in /etc/auth/system/ttys for "reasonable" values. However, it takes the /etc/ttyupd program to correct problems.

A common problem that administrators run into with a lot of users on their system is the fact that running authck takes a long time. First, it is run with the -p option and then again with the -s option. This means that for every user on the system, authck is run twice. (NOTE: This is only for ODT 3.0.)

There are two ways around this. First you can create the file /etc/default/ security which contains the single line

```
TCBFILES=OFF
```

I don't recommend doing this, since it turns off all checking. That is, authck is not run at all. If the TCB database is corrupt, you may not notice it until it is too late. Therefore, a good idea would be to edit authckrc and comment out the two lines running authck, then add a new one that runs authck on all databases. It would look like this:

```
/tcb/bin/authck -av
```

(The -v option tells the system to report things as it's making corrections.)

### Odds and Ends

The TCB is the primary mechanism for controlling system access, despite the fact that it is permissions that allow users to run programs and access files. The permissions on these programs remain constant, regardless of what security level you have. However, the privileges that a user has change. It is for this reason that it is essential that changes to the TCB be made with the appropriate tools and not by editing the files directly, despite what I showed you how to do in the previous section.

# CHAPTER
# 5

- **The Kernel—The Heartbeat of SCO UNIX**

- **Devices and Device Nodes**

- **The Link Kit**

# The Operating System and Its Environment

I n this chapter we are going to go into some details about what makes up an SCO UNIX operating system. I am not referring to the product SCO UNIX or either of the bundled products ODT or OpenServer. I am talking strictly about the software that manages and controls your computer.

Since an operating system is of little use without hardware and other software, we are going to discuss how the operating system interacts with other parts of the ODT and OpenServer products. We will also talk about what goes into making the kernel, what components it is made of, and what you can do to influence the creation of a new kernel.

Much of this information is far beyond what many system administrators are required to know for their jobs. So why go over it? Because what is required and what the administrator should know are two different things. Many calls I received while in SCO support could have been avoided if the administrator understood the meaning of a message on the system console or the effects of making changes. By going over the details of how the kernel behaves, you will be in a better position to understand what is happening.

## The Kernel—The Heartbeat of SCO UNIX

If any single aspect of the SCO product could be called "UNIX," then it would be the kernel. So what is the kernel? Well, on the hard disk it is *represented* by the file /unix. (On SCO OpenServer, this is a symbolic link to /stand/unix). Just as a program like /bin/date is a collection of bytes that isn't very useful until it is loaded in memory and running, the same applies to /unix.

However, once the /unix program is loaded into memory and starts its work it becomes "the kernel" and has many responsibilities. Perhaps the two most important are process management and file management. However, the kernel is responsible for many other things. One aspect is I/O management, which is essentially the accessing of all the peripheral devices. The kernel is also responsible for security; that is, ensuring that only authorized users gain access to the system and that they only do what they should.

### Processes

From the user's perspective, perhaps the most obvious aspect of the kernel is process management. This is the part of the kernel that ensures that each process gets its turn to run on the CPU. This is also the part that makes sure that the individual processes don't go around "trouncing" on other processes by writing to areas of memory that belong to someone else. To do this, the kernel keeps track of many different structures that are maintained both on a per user basis as well as systemwide.

A process is the running instance of a program (a program simply being the bytes on the disks). One of the most powerful aspects of SCO UNIX is its ability to not only keep many processes in memory at once, but to switch to them fast enough to make it appear as if they are all running at the same time.

As a process is running, it works within its *context*. It is also common to say that the CPU is operating within the context of a specific process. The context of a process is all of the characteristics, settings, and values used by that particular program as it runs, as well as those that it *needs* to run. Even the internal state of the CPU and the contents of all its registers are part of the context of the process. When a process has finished having its turn on the CPU, and another process gets to run, the act of changing from one process to another is called a *context switch*, which we see graphically in Figure 5–1.

We can say that a process' context is defined by its *uarea* (also called its *ublock*). The uarea contains information such as the effective and real UID, effective and real GID, system call error return value, and a pointer to the system call arguments on that process' system stack.

The structure of the uarea is defined by the `user` structure in `<sys/user.h>`. There is a special part of the kernel's private memory that holds the uarea of the currently running process. When a context switch occurs, it is the uarea that is switched out. All other parts of the process remain where they are. The uarea of the next process is copied into the *exact* same place in memory as the uarea for the old process. This way the kernel does not have to make any adjustments and knows exactly where to look for the uarea. It will always be able to access the uarea of the currently running process by accessing the same area in memory.

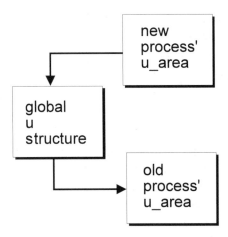

**Figure 5–1**   Context switch.

One of the pieces of information that the uarea contains is the process' *Local Descriptor Table* (LDT). A descriptor is a 64-bit data structure that is used by the process to gain access to different parts of the system; that is, different parts of memory or different *segments*. Despite a common misunderstanding, SCO UNIX uses a segmented memory architecture. In older CPUs, segments were used as a way to get around memory access limitations. By referring to memory addresses as offsets within a given segment, more memory could be addressed than if memory was looked at as a single block. The key difference with SCO UNIX is that each of these segments are 4GB and not the 64K they were originally.

The descriptors are held in *descriptor tables*. The LDT is used to keep track of a process' segments, also called regions. That is, these are descriptors that are *local* to the process. The *Global Descriptor Table* (GDT) keeps track of the kernel's segments. Since there are many processes running, there will be many LDTs. These are part of the process' context. However, there is only one GDT, as there is only one kernel.

Within the area (also called *ublock*) is a pointer to another key aspect of a process' context: its *Task State Segment* (TSS). The TSS contains all the registers in the CPU. It is the contents of all the registers that defines the state that the CPU is currently running in. In other words, the registers say what a given process is doing at any given moment. Keeping track of these registers is obviously vital to the concept of multitasking.

By saving the registers in the TSS, you can reload them when this process gets its turn again and continue where you left off. This is because all of the registers are reloaded to their previous value. Once reloaded, the process simply starts over where it left off, as if nothing had happened. If you are curious about what the TSS holds, take a look in `<sys/tss.h>`.

This brings up two new issues: system calls and stacks. A system call is a programming term for a very low-level function. These are functions that are "internal" to the operating system and are used to access the internals of the operating system, such as in the device drivers that ultimately access the hardware. Compare this to library calls, which are made up of system calls.

A stack is a means of keeping track of where a process has been. Like a stack of plates, objects are *pushed* onto the stack and *popped* off the stack. Therefore, things that are pushed onto the stack *last* are the *first* things popped off. When calling routines, certain values are pushed onto the stack for safe-keeping. These include the variables to be passed to the function, plus the location the system should return to after completing the function. When returning from that routine, these values are retrieved by popping them off the stack.

If you look in `<sys/user.h>` at the size of the system called argument pointer (u_ap) you will see it is only large enough to hold six arguments, each four bytes long. Therefore, you will never see a system call with more than six arguments.

Part of the uarea is a pointer to that process' entry in the process table. The process table, as its name implies, is a table containing information about all the processes on the system, whether that process is currently running or not. Each entry in the process table is defined in `<sys/proc.h>`. The principle that a process may be in memory, but not actually running is important and we will get into more details about the life of a process shortly.

In ODT 3.0 and earlier, the size of this table was a set value and determined by the kernel parameter NPROC. Although you could change this value, you needed to build a new kernel and reboot for the change to take effect. If all the entries in the process table are filled and someone tries to start a new process, it will fail with the error message

```
newproc - Process table overflow ( NPROC = x exceeded)
```

where x is the defined value of NPROC.

One nice thing is that if all but the last slot is taken up, only a process with the UID of root can take it. This prevents a process from creating more and more processes and stopping the system completely. Thus, the root user has one last chance to stop it. OpenServer changed that with the introduction of dynamically configured parameters. Many of the parameters that had to be configured by hand, will now grow as the need for them increases.

Just how is a process created? Well, the first thing that happens is that one process uses the fork() system call. Like a fork in the road, it starts off as a single entity and then splits into two. When one process uses the fork() system call, an *exact* copy of itself is created in memory and the uareas are essentially identical. The value in each CPU register is the same, so both copies of this process are at the exact same place in their code. Each of the variables also have the exact same value. There are two exceptions: the process ID number and the return value of the fork() system call. Graphically, this looks like Figure 5–2.

Like users and their UID, each process is referred to by its process ID number, or PID. This is a unique number which is actually the process' slot number in the process table. When a fork() system call is made, the value returned by the

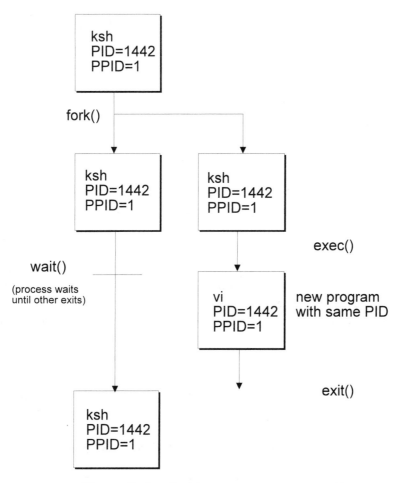

**Figure 5–2**   Creating a new process.

fork() to the calling process is the PID of the newly created process. Since the new copy didn't actually make the fork() call, the return value in the copy is 0. This is how a process *spawns* or *forks* a *child* process. The process that called the fork() is the *parent process* of this new process, which is the child process. Note that I intentionally said *the* parent process and *a* child process. A process can fork many child processes, but has only one parent.

Almost always, a program will keep track of that return value and will then change its behavior based on that value. One of the most common things is for the child to issue an exec() system call. Although it takes the fork() system call to create the space that will be utilized by the new process, it is the exec() system call that causes this space to be overwritten with the new program.

At the beginning of every executable program is an area simply called the "header." This header describes the contents of the file: how the file is to be interpreted. This could be information to tell the system that the file is a 286 or 386 binary, the size of the text and data segments, or where the symbol table is. The symbol table is basically the translation from variable names that we humans understand to the machine language equivalents.

The header contains the locations of the text and data segments. As we talked about before, a segment is a portion of the program. The portion of the program that contains the executable instructions is called the text segment. The portion containing *pre-initialized* data is the data segment. Pre-initialized data are variables, structures, and arrays that have their value already set even before the program is run. The process is given descriptors for each of the segments. These descriptors are referred to as *region descriptors* and under SCO UNIX segments are more commonly referred to as *regions*.

In contrast to other operating systems running on Intel-based CPUs, SCO UNIX has only one region (or segment) each for the text, data, and stack. The reason that I didn't mention the stack region until now is because the stack region is created when the process is created. Since the stack is used to keep track of where the process has been and what it has done, there is no need create it until the process starts.

Another region that I haven't talked about until now is not always used. This is the shared data region. Shared data is an area of memory that is accessible by more than one process. Recall from our discussion on operating system basics that I said that part of the job of the operating system is to keep processes from accessing areas of memory that they aren't supposed to. So, what if they *want* to? What if they are *allowed* to? That is where the shared data region comes in.

If one process tells the other where the shared memory region is (by giving a pointer to it), then *any* process can access it. The way to keep unwanted processes

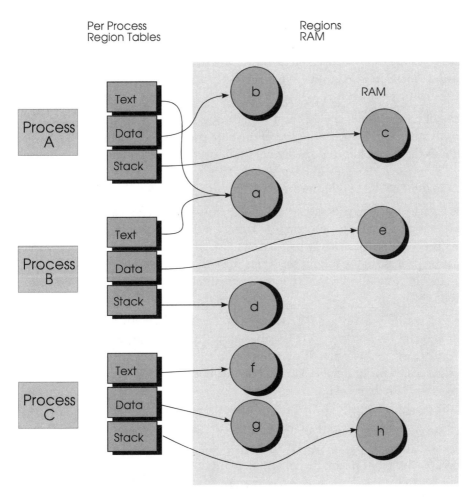

**Figure 5–3**   Process regions.

away is simply not to tell them. In this way, each process that is allowed can use the data and the region only goes away when that last process disappears. Figure 5–3 shows how several processes would look in memory.

If we take a look at Figure 5–3, we see three processes. In all three instances, each process has its own data stack regions. However, process A and process B share a text region; that is, process A and process B have called the same executable off the hard disk. Therefore, they are sharing the same instructions. Note that in reality, this is much more complicated since the two processes may be not be executing the exact same instructions at any given moment.

Each process has at least a text, data, and stack region. In addition, each process is created in the same way. An existing process will (normally) use the `fork()`-`exec()` system call pair to create another process. However, this brings up an interesting question, similar to, "Who or what created God?" If *every* process has to be created by another, then who or what created the first process?

When the computer is turned on, it goes through some wild gyrations that we will talk about later. At the end of the boot process the system loads and executes the `/unix` binary—the kernel itself. One of the last things the kernel does is to "force" the creation of a single process, which then becomes the great-grandparent of all the other processes.

This first, primordial process is the `sched` process, also referred to as the swapper. It has a PID of 0. Its function is to free memory, by hook or by crook. If another process can spare a few pages it will take those. If not, `sched` may swap out an entire process to the hard disk; hence the name. `Sched` is only context-switched in when the amount of free memory is less than the running process needs.

The first *created* process is `init`, with a PID of 1. All other processes can trace their ancestry back to `init`. `Init`'s job is basically to read the entries in the file `/etc/inittab` and execute different programs. One of the things it does is to start the `getty` program on all the log in terminals, which eventually provides every user with their shell.

Another system process is `vhand`, whose PID is 2. This is the paging daemon or page stealer. If free memory on the system gets below a specific low water mark (the kernel tunable parameter GPSLO), then `vhand` is allowed to run every clock interrupt. (Whether it runs or not will depend on many things which we will talk about later.) Until the amount of free memory gets above a high water mark (GPGSHI), `vhand` will continue to "steal" pages.

Next is `bdflush`, with a PID of 3. This is the buffer flushing daemon. Its job is to clean out any "dirty" buffers inside of the system's buffer cache. A dirty buffer is one that contains data that has been written to by a program, but hasn't yet been written to the disk. It is the job of `bdflush` to write this out to the hard disk (probably) at regular intervals. These intervals are defined by the kernel tunable parameter BDFLUSHR, which has a default of 30 seconds. The kernel tunable parameter NAUTOP specifies how long the buffer must have been dirty before it is "cleaned." (Note that by cleaning, I don't mean that the data is erased. It is simply written to the disk.)

All processes, including the ones I described above, operate in one of two modes: user or system mode. In the section on the CPU we will talk about the privilege levels. An Intel 80386 has four privilege levels (0–3). SCO UNIX uses only the two most extreme: 0 and 3. Processes running in user mode are running at privilege level 3 within the CPU. Processes running in system mode are running at privilege level 0.

In user mode, a process is executing instructions from within its own text segment, it references its own data segment and uses its own stack. Processes switch from user mode to kernel mode by making system calls. Once in system mode, the instructions executed are those within the kernel's text segment, the kernel's data segment is used, and a system stack is used within the process' uarea.

Although the process is going through a lot of changes when it makes a system call, keep in mind that this is *not* a context switch. This is still the same process. The process is operating at a higher privilege. What this looks like graphically we see in Figure 5–4.

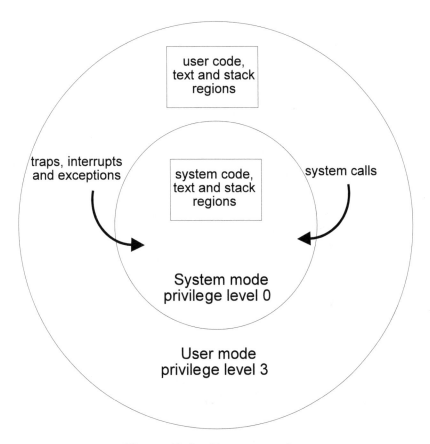

**Figure 5–4**  Process modes.

### The Life Cycle of Processes

From the time a process is `forked` into existence, until the time it has completed its job and disappears from the process table, it goes through many different states. The state a process is in changes many times during its "life." These changes can occur, for example, when the process makes a system call, it is someone else's turn to run, an interrupt occurs, or the process asks for a resource that is currently not available.

A commonly used model shows processes operating in one of eight separate states. However, in the file `<sys/proc.h>` there are only seven separate processes listed. However, to understand the transitions better, the following eight states are used:

1.  executing in user mode

2.  executing in kernel mode

3.  ready to run

4.  sleeping in main memory

5.  read-to-run, but swapped out

6.  sleeping, but swapped out

7.  newly created, not ready to run and not sleeping

8.  issued exit system call (zombie)

The states listed here are intended to describe what is happening conceptually and not to indicate what "official" state a process is in. The official states are listed in Table 5–1.

In my list of eight states there was no mention of a processes actually being on the processor (SONPROC). Processes that are running in kernel mode or running

**Table 5–1**    Process States

| State | | Description |
|---|---|---|
| SLEEP | — | awaiting an event |
| SRUN | — | running |
| SZOMB | — | terminated but not waited for |
| SSTOP | — | process stopped by a debugger |
| SIDL | — | process being created |
| SONPROC | — | process on the processor |
| SXBRK | — | process needs more memory |

in user mode are both in the SRUN state. Although there is no 1:1 match-up, hopefully you'll see what each state means as we go through the following description. Figure 5–5 shows what this looks like graphically.

A newly created process enters the system in state seven. If the process is simply a copy of the original process (a `fork` but no `exec`), it then begins to run in the same state as the original process (1 or 2). (Why none of the other states? It has to be running in order to fork a new process.) If an `exec()` is made, then this process will end up in kernel mode (2). It is possible that the `fork()-exec()` was done in system mode and the process *never* goes into state 1. However, this is highly unlikely.

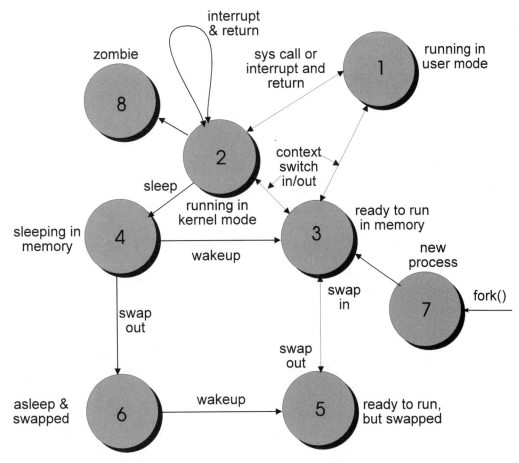

**Figure 5–5**   Process states.

When running, an interrupt may be generated (more often than not this is the system clock) and the currently running process is pre-empted (3). This is the same state as state 3, since it is still ready-to-run and in main memory. The only difference is that the process gets kicked off the processor.

When the process makes a system call while in user mode (1), it moves into state 2 where it begins running in kernel mode. Assume at this point that the system call made was to read a file on the hard disk. Since the read is not carried out immediately, the process goes to sleep. It waits for the *event* that the system has read to the disk and for the data to be ready. It is now in state 4. When the data is ready, the process is woken up. This does not mean it runs immediately, but rather it is once again ready to run in main memory (3).

If sched discovers that there is not enough memory for all the processes, it may decide to swap out one or more processes. The first choice is with those that are sleeping, since they are not ready to run. Such a process now finds itself in state 6; it is sleeping, but swapped out. It is also possible that there are no processes that are sleeping, but a lot of processes that are ready to run, so sched needs to swap one of those out instead. Therefore, a process could move from state 3 (ready to run) to state 5 (ready to run, but swapped out). However, as we'll see in a moment, most processes are sleeping.

If a process that was asleep is woken up (perhaps the data is ready), it moves from state 4 (sleeping in main memory) to state 3 (ready to run). However, a process cannot move directly from state 6 (sleeping, but swapped) to state 3 (ready to run). This requires two transitions. Since it is not effective to swap in processes that are not ready to run, sleeping processes will *not* be swapped in. This is simply because the system has no way of knowing which processes will be awoken soon, since swapping and waking are two separate actions. Instead, the system must first make the process ready to run, so it moves from state 6 (sleeping, but swapped) to state 5 (ready to run, but swapped). When the process is swapped back in, it returns to where it was. This can be either user mode (1) or kernel mode (2).

Processes can end their life by either explicitly calling the exit() system or having it called for them. The exit() system call releases all the data structures that the process was using. One exception is the slot in the process table. This is the responsibility of the init process. The reason for hanging around is that the slot in the process table is used for the exit code of the exiting process. This can be used by the parent process to determine if the process did what it was supposed to or if it ran into problems. The process shows that it has terminated by putting itself into state 8; it becomes a "zombie." Once here, it can never run again as nothing exists other than the entry in the process table.

This is the reason why you cannot "kill" a zombie process. There is nothing there to kill. In order to kill a process, you need to send it a signal. Since there is nothing there to receive or process that signal, trying to kill it makes little sense. The only thing to do is to let the system clean up.

If the exiting process has any children, they are "inherited" by `init`. One of the values stored in the process structure is the PID of that process' parent process. This value is (logically) referred to as the *parent process ID* or PPID. When a process is inherited by init, the value of their PPID is changed to 1 (the PID of `init`).

A change in the state of a process can cause a context switch in several different cases. One is when the process voluntarily goes to sleep. This can happen when the process needs a resource that is not immediately available. A very common example of this is when you log in. You type in a command, the command is executed, and you are back to a shell prompt. Between the time the command is finished and you input your next command a very long time could pass—at least two or three seconds.

Rather than constantly checking the keyboard for input, the shell puts itself to sleep to wait for an event. That event is an interrupt from the keyboard to say, "Hey! I have input for you." When a process puts itself to sleep, it sleeps on a particular *wait channel* (WCHAN). When the event occurs that is associated with that wait channel, *every* process waiting on that wait channel is woken up.

There is probably only one process waiting on input from your keyboard at any given time. However, many processes could be waiting for data from the hard disk. If so, there might be dozens of processes all waiting on the same wait channel. All are awoken when the hard disk is ready. It may be that the hard disk has read only the data for a subset of the processes waiting. Therefore, (if the program is correctly written) the processes check to see if their data is ready for them. If not, they put themselves to sleep on the same wait channel.

When a process puts itself to sleep, it is *voluntarily* giving up the CPU. It may be that this process had just started its turn when it noticed that it didn't have some resource it needed. Rather than forcing the other processes to wait until the first one gets its "fair share" of the CPU, the process is being "nice" and is letting some other process have a turn on the CPU.

Because the process is being so nice to let others have a turn, the kernel is going to be nice to the process. One of the things the kernel allows is that a process which puts *itself* to sleep can set its own priority when it awakens. Normally, the kernel process scheduling algorithm calculates the priorities of all the processes. However, in exchange for voluntarily giving up the CPU, the process is allowed to choose its own priority.

### Process Scheduling

Scheduling processes is not as easy as finding the one that has been waiting the longest. Older operating systems used to do this kind of scheduling. It was referred to as "round-robin." The processes could be thought of as sitting in a circle. The scheduling algorithm could then be thought of as a pointer that moved around the circle getting to each process in turn.

The problem with this type of scheduling is that you may have ten processes all waiting for more memory. Remember from our discussion that the sched process is responsible for finding memory for processes that don't have enough. Like other processes, sched needs a turn on the processor before it can do its work. If every process had to wait until sched ran, then those that run right before sched may never run.

This is because sched would run and free up memory. By the time the system got around to the processes just before sched, all the free memory would be taken. The processes that come after sched would have to wait again. When sched runs again it frees memory, which is then take up by the other process.

Instead, SCO UNIX uses a scheduling method that takes many things into consideration, not just the actual priority of the process itself or how long it has been since it had a turn on the CPU. The priority is a calculated value, based on several factors. The first factor is what priority the process already has.

Another factor is recent CPU usage. The longer a process runs, the more it uses the CPU. Therefore, to make it easier for faster jobs to get in and out quickly, the longer a process runs the lower its priority. For example, a process that is sorting a large file needs a longer time to complete the date command. If the process executing the date command is given a higher priority due to the fact that it is relatively fast, it leaves the process table quickly so there are less processes to deal with and every process gets a turn more often.

Keep in mind that the system has no way of knowing in advance just how long the date command will run. Therefore, the system can't *give* it a higher priority. However, by the fact that it *gives* the sort processes a lower priority after it has been running a while, the date command appears to run faster. I say "appear" since the date command needs the same number of CPU cycles to complete. It just gets them sooner.

SCO UNIX also allows you to be nice to your fellow processes. If you feel that your work is not as important as someone else's, you might want to consider being nice to them. This is done with the nice command. The syntax of which is

```
nice <nice_value> <command>
```

For example, if you wanted to run the date command with a lower priority, it could be run like this:

```
nice -10 date
```

This has the effect of decreasing the start priority of the date command by 10. Note that only root can increase a process' priority; that is, use a negative nice value. The nice value only affects running processes, but child processes inherit the nice value of their parent. By default, processes started by users have a nice value of 20. This can be changed within `sysadmsh` in ODT 3.0 and with the `user-mod` command in OpenServer. Therefore, using the `nice` command in the example above increases the startup priority to 30. OpenServer has provided a tool (`renice`) which allows you to change the priority of *running process*. See the appropriate man-pages for more details.

The formula used to determine a process' priority is

```
priority = ( recent_cpu_usage /2) + nice_value + 40
```

Note that the value 40 is hardcoded in the calculation. This is because the highest priority a user process can have is 40. Those of you who have been paying attention might have noticed something odd. If you add the recent CPU usage to the nice value, then add 40, you have a larger number. Therefore, the longer the process is on the CPU the *higher* the priority. Well, sort of.

The numeric value calculated for the priority is the opposite of what we normally think of as priority. A better way of thinking about it is to compare it to the pull-down numbered tickets you get at the ice cream store. The lower the number, the sooner you get served; so it is for processes.

Because of the way the priority is calculated, process scheduling in SCO UNIX has a couple of interesting properties. First, as time passes the priority of a process running in user mode will decrease. The decrease in priority means that it will be less likely to run the next time there is a context switch. Conversely, if a process hasn't run for a long time, the *recent* CPU usage is lower. Since it hasn't used the CPU much recently, its priority will increase. Such processes are more likely to run than those that just got their turn (assuming all other factors are the same). Figure 5–6 shows three processes as they run and their priorities. This will give you an idea of how priorities change over time.

This table makes several assumptions, which are probably not true for a "real" system. The first is that these are the only three processes running on your system. Since even in maintenance mode, you have at least four running, this is unrealistic. The second assumption is that all processes start with an initial priority of 40 and nothing has changed their nice value of 20. We also assume that there is

| Time (Secs) | Process A | | Process B | | Process C | |
|---|---|---|---|---|---|---|
| | priority | CPU | priority | CPU | priority | CPU |
| 0 | 60 | 0 | 60 | 0 | 60 | 0 |
| | | 1 | | | | |
| | | . | | | | |
| 1 | | 80 | | | | |
| 1 | 80 | 40 | 60 | 0 | 60 | 0 |
| | | | | 1 | | |
| | | | | . | | |
| 2 | | | | 80 | | |
| 2 | 70 | 20 | 80 | 40 | 60 | 0 |
| | | | | | | 1 |
| | | | | | | . |
| 3 | | | | | | 80 |
| 3 | 65 | 10 | 70 | 20 | 80 | 40 |
| | | 11 | | | | |
| | | . | | | | |
| 4 | | 80 | | | | |
| 4 | 80 | 40 | 65 | 10 | 70 | 20 |
| | | | | 11 | | |
| | | | | . | | |
| 5 | | | | 80 | | |
| 5 | 70 | 20 | 80 | 40 | 65 | 10 |
| | | | | | | 11 |
| | | | | | | . |
| 6 | | | | | | 80 |

**Figure 5–6**  Changes in process priority.

nothing else on the system that would change the flow of things such as an interrupt from a hardware device.

Another assumption is that each process gets to run for a full second. The maximum time a process gets the CPU is defined by the MAXSLICE kernel tunable, which by default is 1 second. The number of times the clock interrupts per second, and therefore the numbers of times the priority is recalculated is defined by the HZ system variable. This is defined by default to be 100HZ, or 100 times a second. However, we are assuming that the priorities are only calculated once a second instead of 100 times.

If we look at process A, which is the first to run, we see that between second 0 and 1, its CPU usage went from 0 to the maximum of 80. When the clock tick occurred (the clock generated an interrupt), the priorities of all the processes are recalculated. Since our CPU usage is at 80, it is the first to decay; we cut it in half to get 40, add the nice value of that to the 40 that's hard coded to give 80 as the new priority for Process A. Since Processes B and C haven't run yet, their CPU time is 0. We only add their nice value of 20 to the static value of 40 to keep them at 60.

Since Process A is now at priority 80, both Process B and Process C have higher priorities. Let's say B runs. Between seconds 1 and 2, process B changed just like Process A did between seconds 0 and 1.

When the clock tick occurs, Process B's priority is calculated just like Process A's. Process B is now at 80. However, Process A had its priority recalculated as well. It is now at 70.

All this time, Process C was not on the CPU, therefore its priority hasn't changed from the original 60. Since this is the lowest value, it has the highest priority and now gets a turn on the CPU. When its turn is finished (at the end of second 2) and priorities are recalculated, Process C is at 80. Process B is at 70, but Process A has been recalculated to be 65. Since this is the lowest, Process A get a chance to run again.

In reality, things are not this simple. There are dozens of processes competing for the CPU. There are different start-up priorities, different nice values, and different demands on the system. These demands include requests for services from peripherals such as hard disks. Responding to these requests can almost instantly change which process is running.

Interestingly enough, sudden changes in who is on the CPU are, in part, due to the priority. However, all this time I intentionally avoided mentioning the fact that regardless of what a process' priority is, it will not run unless it is in the *run queue*. This is the state of SRUN. A process in the run queue does not mean that it is running, just that it *can* run if it has the highest priority.

Remember when I said that user processes can never have a lower priority value than 40? Well, in case you hadn't guessed (or didn't already know) system processes like `sched`, `vhand`, and `init` almost exclusively operate with priority values less than 40. Well, if they always have a lower priority why don't they always get to run? Simple. They aren't always in the run queue.

### Interrupts, Exceptions, and Traps

Normally, processes like `sched`, `vhand`, and `init`, as well as most user processes are sleeping waiting on some event. When that event happens, these processes are called into action. Remember, it is the responsibility of the `sched` process to free up memory when a process runs short of it. So, it is not until memory is needed that `sched` starts up. How is it that `sched` knows?

In Chapter 1, we talked about virtual memory and I mentioned page faults. When a process makes reference to a place in its virtual memory space that does not yet exist in physical memory, a page fault occurs.

Faults belong to a group of system events called *exceptions*. An exception is simply something that occurs outside of what is normally expected. Faults (exceptions) can occur either before or during the execution of an instruction.

For example, if an instruction needs to be read that is not yet in memory, the exception (page fault) occurs *before* the instruction starts being executed. On the other hand, if the instruction is supposed to read data from a virtual memory location that isn't in physical memory, the exception occurs *during* the execution of the instruction. In cases like these, once the missing memory location is loaded into physical memory, the CPU can start the instruction.

Traps are exceptions that occur *after* an instruction has been executed. For example, attempting to divide by zero will generate an exception. However, in this case it doesn't make sense to restart the instruction since every time you try to run that instruction, it still comes up with a `Divide-by-Zero` exception. That is, all memory references are read in before you start to execute the command. It is also possible for processes to generate exceptions intentionally. These programmed exceptions are called software interrupts.

When any one of these exceptions occurs, the system must react to the exception. In order to react, the system will usually switch to another process to deal with the exception—this means a context switch. In our discussion of process scheduling, I mentioned that with every clock tick the priority of every process is recalculated. In order to make those calculations, something other than those processes have to run.

In both ODT 3.0 and OpenServer the system timer (or clock) is programmed to generate a hardware interrupt 100 times a second. (This is defined by the HZ system parameter.) The interrupt is accomplished by sending a signal to a special chip on the motherboard called an interrupt controller. (We go into more details about these in the chapter on hardware.) The interrupt controller then sends an interrupt to the CPU. When the CPU gets this signal it knows that the clock tick has occured and it jumps to a special part of the kernel that handles the clock interrupt. Scheduling priorities are also recalculated within this same section of code.

Because the system might be doing something more important when the clock generates an interrupt, there is a way to turn them off. In other words, there is a way to *mask* out interrupts. Interrupts that can be masked out are called *maskable interrupts*. An example of something more important than the clock would be accepting input from the keyboard. This is why clock ticks are lost on systems with a lot of users who are inputting a lot of data. As a result, the system clock appears to slow down over time.

Sometimes events occur on the system that you want to know about *no matter what*. Imagine what would happen if memory was bad. If the system was in the middle of writing to the hard disk when it encountered the bad memory, the results could be disastrous. If the system recognizes the bad memory, the hardware generates an interrupt to alert the CPU. If the CPU was told to ignore all hardware interrupts, it would ignore this one. Instead, the hardware has the ability to generate an interrupt that cannot be ignored or *masked out*. This is called a *non-maskable interrupt*. Non-maskable interrupts are generically referred to as NMIs.

When an interrupt or an exception occurs, it must be dealt with to ensure the intergrity of the system. How the system reacts depends on whether it was an exception or an interrupt. In addition, what is done when the hard disk generates an interrupt is going to be different than when the clock generates one.

Within the kernel is the *Interrupt Descriptor Table* (IDT). This is a list of descriptors (pointers) that point to the functions that handle the particular interrupt or exception. These functions are called the *interrupt* or *exception handlers*. When an interrupt or exception occurs, it has a particular value called an identifier or vector. Table 5–2 contains a list of the defined interrupt vectors. For more information see `<sys/trap.h>`.

The reserved identifiers currently are not used by the CPU, but are reserved for possible future use. Interrupts that come from one of the interrupt controllers are assigned to the identifiers 64 through 79. Identifiers 32–63 and 80–255 are not currently used by SCO UNIX. These identifiers are often referred to as vectors and the Interrupt Descriptor Table (IDT) is often referred to as the Interrupt Vector Table.

These numbers are really indices into the IDT. When an interrupt, exception, or trap occurs, the system knows which number corresponds to that event. It then uses that number as an index into the IDT, which in turn points to the appropriate area of memory for handling the event. What this looks like graphically is shown in Figure 5–7.

**Table 5–2**    Interrupt Vectors

| Identifier | Description |
|---|---|
| 0 | Divide error |
| 1 | Debug exception |
| 2 | Nonmaskable interrupt |
| 3 | Breakpoint |
| 4 | Overflow |
| 5 | Bounds check |
| 6 | Invalid opcode |
| 7 | Co-processor not available |
| 8 | Double fault |
| 9 | (reserved) |
| 10 | Invalid TSS |
| 11 | Segment not present |
| 12 | Stack exception |
| 13 | General protection fault |
| 14 | Page fault |
| 15 | (reserved) |
| 16 | Co-processor error |
| 17 | Alignment error (80486) |
| 18–31 | (reserved) |
| 32–255 | External (HW) interrupts |

It is possible for devices to share interrupts. That is, there are multiple devices on the system that are configured to the same interrupt. In fact, there are certain kinds of computers that are designed to allow devices to share interrupts (we'll talk about them in the hardware section). If the interrupt number is an offset into a table of pointers to interrupt routines, how does the kernel know which one to call?

Well, as it turns out there are two IDTs; one for shared interrupts and one for nonshared interrupts. During a kernel relink (more on that later), the kernel determines if the interrupt is shared or not. If it is, it places the pointer to that interrupt routine into the shared IDT. When an interrupt is generated, the interrupt routine for each of these devices is called. It is up to the interrupt routine to check to see if the associated device really generated an interrupt or not. The order in which they are called is the order in which they are linked.

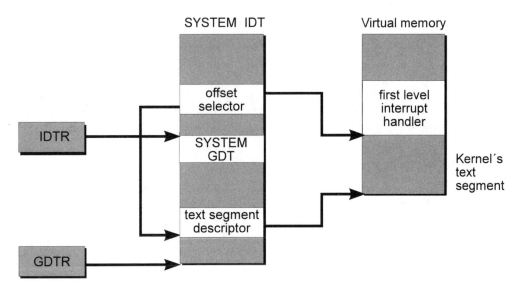

**Figure 5–7**   First-level interrupt handler.

When an exception happens in user mode, the process passes through something called a *trap gate*. At this point, the CPU no longer uses the process' user stack, but rather the system stack within that process' uarea (each uarea has a portion set aside for the system stack). At this point, that process is operating in system (kernel) mode. That is, at the highest privilege level, 0.

Before the actual exception can be handled, the system needs to ensure that the process can return to the place in memory where it was when the exception oc-cured. This is done by a *low-level interrupt handler*. Part of what it does is to push (copy) all of the general purpose registers onto the process' system stack. This makes them available again when the process goes back to using the user stack. Graphically this looks like Figure 5–7.

The low-level interrupt handler also determines whether the exception occurred in user mode or system mode. If the process was already in system mode when the exception occurred, there is no need to push the registers onto the process' system stack, as this is the stack that the process is already using.

The kernel treats interrupts very similarly to the way it treats exceptions. All of the general purpose registers are pushed onto the system stack and a common interrupt handler is called. The current interrupt priority is saved and the new priority is loaded. This prevents interrupts at lower priority levels from interrupting the kernel as it is handling this interrupt. Then the real interrupt handler is called.

Since an exception is not fatal, the process will return from whence it came. It is possible that immediately upon return from system mode, a context switch occurs. This might be the result of an exception with a lower priority. Since it could not interrupt the process in kernel mode, it had to wait until it returned to user mode. Since the exception has a higher priority than the process when it is in user mode, a context switch occurs immediately after the process returns to user mode.

If another exception occurs while the process is in system mode, this is not a normal occurrence. Exceptions are the result of software events. Even a page fault can be considered a software event. Since the entire kernel is in memory all the time, a page fault should not happen. When a page fault does happen in kernel mode, the kernel panics. There are special routines built into the kernel to deal with the panic to help the system shutdown as gracefully as possible. Should something else happen that causes another exception while the system is in panic, a double panic occurs.

This may sound confusing, as I just said that a context switch could occur as the result of another exception. What this means is that the exception occurred in user mode, so there needs to be a jump to system mode. This does *not* mean that the process continues in system mode until it is finished. It may (depending on what it is doing) be context-switched out. If another process runs before the first one gets its turn on the CPU again, that process may generate the exception.

There are a couple of cases where exceptions in system mode do not cause panics. The first is when you are debugging programs. In order to stop the flow of the program, exceptions are raised and you are brought into special routines within the debugger. Since exceptions are expected in such cases, it doesn't make sense to have the kernel panic.

The other case is when page faults occur as data is being copied from kernel memory space into user space. As I mentioned above, the kernel is completely in memory. Therefore, the data will have to be in memory to copy from the kernel space. However, it is possible that the area that the data needs to be copied to is not in physical memory. Therefore, a page fault exception occurs, but this should *not* cause the system to panic.

Unlike exceptions, it is possible that another interrupt occurs while the kernel is handling the first one (and therefore is in system mode). If the second interrupt has a higher priority than the first, a context switch will occur and the new interrupt will be handled. If the second interrupt has the same or lower priority, then the kernel will, "put it on hold." These are not ignored, but rather saved to be dealt with later.

### Signals

Signals are a way of sending simple messages to processes. Most of these messages are already defined and can be found in `<sys/signal.h>`. However, signals can only be processed when the process is in user mode. If a signal has been sent to a process that is in kernel mode, it is dealt with immediately upon returning to user mode.

Many signals have the ability to immediately terminate a process. However, most of these signals can be either ignored or dealt with by the process itself. If not, the kernel will take the default action specified for that signal. You can send signals to processes yourself by means of the `kill` command as well as the delete key and Ctrl-/. However, you can only send signals to processes that you own. Or, if you are root, you can send signals to any process.

It's possible that the process that you want to send the signal to is sleeping. If that process is sleeping at an *interruptable* priority, then the process will awaken to handle the signal. Processes sleeping at a priority of 25 or less are not interruptable. The priority of 25 is called PZERO.

The kernel keeps track of pending signals in the `p_sig` entry in each process' process structure. This is a 32-bit value, where each bit represents a single signal. Since it is only one bit per signal, there can only be one signal pending of each type. If there are different kinds of signals pending, the kernel has no way of determining which came in when. It will therefore process the signals starting at the lowest numbered signal and then move up.

### System Calls

If you are a programmer, you know what a system call is and have used them many times in your programs. If you are not a programmer, you may not know what they are, but you still use them thousands of times a day. All low-level operations on the system are handled by system calls. These include such things as reading from the disk or printing a message on the screen. System calls are the user's bridge between user space and kernel space. This also means that it is the bridge between a user application and the system hardware.

Collections of system calls are often combined into more complex tasks and put into *libraries*. When using one of the functions defined in a library you *call* a *library function* or make a *library call*. Even when the library routine is intented to access the hardware, it will make a system call long before the hardware is touched.

Each system call has its own unique identifying number that can be found in <sys.s>. The kernel uses this number as an index into a table of system call entry points. These are pointers to where the system calls reside in memory along with the number of arguments that should be passed to them.

When a process makes a system call, the behavior is similar to that of interrupts and exceptions. Entry into kernel space is made through a *call gate*. There is a single call gate which serves as a guardian to the sacred area of kernel space. Like exception handling, the general purpose registers and the numbers of the system call are pushed onto the stack. Next, the system call handler is invoked, which calls the routine within the kernel that will do the actual work.

After entering the call gate, the kernel system call dispatcher "validates" the system call and hands control over to the kernel code that will actually perform the requested function. Although there are hundreds of library calls, each of these will call one or more system calls. In total, there are about 150 system calls, all of which have to pass through this one call gate. This ensures that user code moves up to the higher privilege level at a specific location within the kernel (a specific address). Therefore, uniform controls can be applied to ensure that a process is not doing something it shouldn't.

When the system call is complete, the system call dispatcher returns the result of the system and status codes (if applicable). As with interrupts and exceptions, the system checks to see if a context switch should occur upon the return to user mode. If so, a context switch takes place. This is possible in situations where one process made a system call and an interrupt occurred while the process was in system mode. The kernel then issues a `wakeup()` to all processes waiting for `date` from the hard disk.

When the interrupt completes, the kernel may go back to the first one that made the system call. But, then again, there may be another one with a higher priority.

### Paging and Swapping

In Chapter 1, we talked about how the operating system uses capabilities of the CPU to make it appear as if you have more memory than you really do. This is the concept of virtual memory. In Chapter 12, we'll go into details about how this is accomplished; that is, how the operating system and CPU work together to keep up this illusion. However, in order to make this section on the kernel complete, we need to briefly talk about this concept from a software perspective.

One of the basic concepts in the SCO UNIX implementation of virtual memory is the concept of a *page*. A page is a 4Kb area of memory and is the basic unit of memory that both the kernel and the CPU deal with. Although both can access individual bytes (or even bits), the amount of memory that is managed is usually in pages.

If you are reading a book, you do not need to have all the pages spread out on a table for you to work effectively; just the one you are currently using. I remember many times in college when I had the entire table top covered with open books, including my notebook. As I was studying I would read a little from one book, take notes on what I read and if I needed more details on that subject, I would either go to a different page or a completely different book.

Virtual memory in SCO UNIX is very much like that. Just as I only needed to have open the pages I was currently working with, a process needs only to have those pages in memory that it is working with. If the process needs a page that is not currently available (not in physical memory), it needs to go get it (usually from the hard disk).

To continue the analogy, if another student came along and wanted to use my table, there might be enough space for him or her to spread out books as well. If not, I would have to close some of my books (maybe putting book marks at the pages I was using). If another student came along or the table was fairly small, I might have to put some of the books away. SCO UNIX does this as well. If the textbooks represent the unchanging text portion of the program and the notebook represents the changing data, things might be a little clearer.

It is the responsibility of both the kernel *and* the CPU to ensure that I don't end up reading someone else's textbook or writing in someone else's notebook. That is, they ensure that one process does not have access to the memory locations of another process (a discussion of cell replication would look silly in my calculus notebook). The CPU also helps the kernel by recognizing when the process tries to access a page that is not yet in memory. It is the kernel's job to figure out which process it was, what page it was, and to load the appropriate page.

It is also the kernel's responsibility to ensure that no one process hogs all available memory; just like the librarian telling me to make some space on the table. If there is only one process running (not very likely) then there may be enough memory to keep the *entire* process loaded as it runs. More likely there will be dozens of processes in memory and each will get a small part of the total memory. (Note, depending on how much memory you have, it is still *possible* that the entire program is in memory.)

Processes generally adhere to the *principle of spatial locality*. This means that over a short period of time, processes will access the same portions of their code over and over again. The kernel could establish a *working set* of pages for each process. These are the pages that have been accessed with the last $n$ memory references. If *n* is small, then processes may not have enough pages in memory to do their job. Instead of letting processes work, the kernel is busy spending all of its time reading in the needed pages. By the time the system has finished reading in the needed pages, it is some other process' turn. Now, some other process needs more pages, so the kernel needs to read them in. This is called *thrashing*. Large values of *n* may lead to cases where there is not enough memory for all the processes to run.

However, SCO UNIX does not use the working set model, but does use the concept of a *window*. When the amount of available (free) memory drops below a certain point (which is configurable), the vhand process is awakened and put on the run queue. Using this window does not mean that thrashing cannot occur on an SCO system. When memory gets so full of user processes that the system spends more time freeing up memory and swapping processes in and out, even SCO will thrash.

As I mentioned, the number of free pages is checked at every clock tick. If this gets below the value set by the kernel tunable GPGSLO, vhand, the "page stealer" process, is woken up. When it runs, vhand searches for pages that have not been recently accessed by a process.

If a page has not been referenced within a predetermined time, it is "freed" by vhand and added to a list of free pages. In order to keep one area from having pages stolen more often than others, vhand remembers where it was and starts with a different area the next time it runs. When vhand has freed up enough pages so there are more than GPGSHI pages available, it puts itself back to sleep. This is the reason why vhand does not always run, even though it has a high priority.

If a page that vhand steals is part of the executable portion of a process (the text), it can easily free up the page, since it can always get it back from the hard disk. However, if the page is part of the process' data this may be the only place where that data exists. The simplest solution is to just say that data pages cannot be stolen. This is a problem, since you may have a program that needs more data than there is physical memory. Since you cannot keep it *all* in memory at the same time, you have to figure out a better solution. How sched and vhand work together we see in Figure 5–8.

The solution is to use a portion of hard disk as a kind of temporary storage for data pages that are not currently needed. This area of the hard disk is called the *swap space* or *swap device* and is a separate area used solely for the purpose of holding data pages from programs. Copying pages to the swap space is the responsibility of the system process swapper.

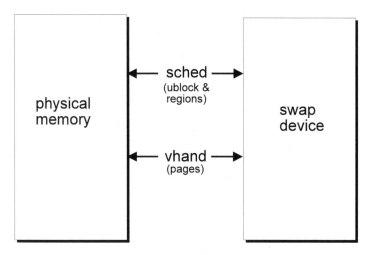

**Figure 5–8**  sched and vhand working together.

The size and location of the swap device is normally set when the system is first installed. Afterwards, more swap space can be added if needed. (This is done with the swap command.) Occupied and free areas of the swap device are managed by a map, where a zero value says the page on the swap device is free and a nonzero value is the number of processes sharing that page.

If the system is short of memory and pages need to be swapped out, the swapper process needs to determine just what processes can be swapped out. It first looks for processes in the states of either SSLEEP (process is sleeping) or SSTOP (process is stopped by a debugger). If there is only one, the choice is easy, if not, the swapper needs to calculate which one has the *lowest* priority.

Often times, there are no processes that fit these criteria. Although this usually happens only on systems that are heavily loaded, the system needs to take into account cases where there are no processes in either SSLEEP or SRUN. Therefore, the swapper needs to look elsewhere to find a process to swap out. It then considers processes in the state SRUN (read-to-ready) or SXBRK (needs more memory) and tries to find the processes with the lowest priority in these states.

If the swapper is trying to make room for a process that is already swapped out, then that process must have been on the swap device for at least two seconds. The two-second threshold is to keep the system from spending all of its time thrashing and not getting any work done.

If we find a suitable process to swap out, sched locks the process in memory. Hmmm, why lock a process into memory that we are just going to swap out? Remember that `sched` is just another process. It could be context-switched out if an interrupt (or something else) occurs. What happens if `sched` gets context-switched out, but `vhand` runs before the `swapper` gets a chance to run again? It could happen that `vhand` steals pages from the first process. When `vhand` gets switched back in, the pages it wanted to steal may already be gone. Either `sched` has to again figure out what pages are to be swapped out, or `vhand` steals pages that `sched` just brought in. Instead, it locks the pages in memory.

Next, space is allocated on the swap device for the process' uarea. If there is no space available, the `swapper` generates an error indicating swap space is running low and will try to swap out other parts of the process. If it can't, the system will panic with an, "out of swap" message. Remember that a panic is when something happens that the kernel does not know how to deal with. Since the kernel has a process that needs to run and it cannot make more memory available by swapping out a process, the kernel doesn't know what to do; therefore, it panics.

All regions of the process are checked. If a region is locked into memory it will not be swapped. If a region is for private use, such as data or stack, all of the region will be swapped out. If the region is shared, only the *unreferenced* pages will be swapped. That is, only those pages that have not been referenced within a certain amount of time will be swapped.

Note that swapping may not require a physical write to the swap device. This is due to the fact that once an area is allocated for a process, it remains so allocated until the process terminates. Therefore, it can happen that a page is swapped back in to be read, but never written to. If that page later needs to be swapped out again, there is no need to swap it out as it already exists in the correct state on the hard disk.

Eventually, the process that got swapped out will get a turn on the CPU and will need to be swapped back in. Before it can be swapped back in, the `swapper` needs to ensure that there is enough memory for at least the uarea and a set of structures called *page tables*. Pages tables are an integral part of the virtual memory scheme and point to the actual pages in memory. We talk more about this when we talk about the CPU in the hardware section.

If there isn't enough room, `sched` looks for the process that has been waiting for memory the longest (SXBRK) and tries to allocate memory for that process. If there are none in this state, `sched` goes through the same procedures as it does for processes that are already in main memory. It's possible for `sched` to make memory available to other processes in addition to the original one. Up to ten processes in the SXBRK state can have memory allocated and up to five can be swapped back in during a pass of the `swapper`.

Often you don't want to swap in certain processes. For example, it doesn't make sense to swap in a process that is sleeping on some event. Since that event hasn't occurred yet, swapping it in means that it will just need to go right back to sleep. Therefore, only processes in the SRUN state are eligible to be swapped back in. That is, only the processes that are *runnable* are swapped back in. In addition, these processes must have a priority of less than 60. If the process has a higher priority value (therefore a lower priority) the odds are that there are other processes that will be run first. Since you are already swapping, it is more than likely that this process will be swapped out again.

When being swapped back in, the pages that are not pages of the uarea or page tables are left on the swap device. It is not until the process actually needs them that they will be swapped back in. This will happen in pretty short order, since anything the process wants to do will cause a page fault and cause pages to be swapped back in.

Keep in mind that accessing the hard disk is hundreds of times slower than accessing memory. Although swapping does allow you to have more programs in memory than the physical RAM will allow, using it does slow down the system. If possible, it is a good idea to keep from swapping by adding more RAM.

### *Processes in Action*

If you are like me, knowing how things work in theory is not enough. You want to see how things are working on *your* system. SCO provides several tools for you to watch what is happening. The first is perhaps the only one that the majority of users have ever seen. This is the ps command, which gives you the process status of particular processes. Depending on your security level, normal users can even look at every process on the system. (They must have the mem subsystem privilege.)

Although users can look at processes using the ps command, they cannot look at the insides of the processes themselves. This is because the ps command is simply reading the process table. This contains only the control and data structures necessary to administer and manage the process and not the process itself. Despite this, using ps can not only show you a lot about what your system is doing, but it can give you insights into how the system works. Because much of what I will talk about is documented in the ps man-page, I want to suggest in advance that you take a look there for more details.

If you start ps from the command with no options, the default behavior is to show the processes running on our current terminal, something like this:

```
PID    TTY     TIME      CMD
608    ttyp0   00:00:02  ksh
1147   ttyp0   00:00:00  ps
```

This shows us the process ID (`PID`), the terminal that the process is running on (`TTY`), the total amount of time the process has had on the CPU (`TIME`) and the command that was run (`CMD`). If the process had already issued an `exit()`, but hadn't finished it yet by the time the `ps` read the process table, we would probably see `<defunct>` in this column.

Although this is useful in many circumstances, it doesn't say much about these processes. Let's see what the long output looks like. This is run as `ps -l`:

| F | S | UID | PID | PPID | C | PRI | NI | ADDR | SZ | WCHAN | TTY | TIME | CMD |
|---|---|-----|-----|------|---|-----|-----|------|-----|--------|-------|----------|-----|
| 20 | S | 0 | 608 | 607 | 1 | 73 | 24 | fb11b9e8 | 140 | fb11b9e8 | ttyp0 | 00:00:02 | ksh |
| 20 | O | 0 | 1172 | 608 | 14 | 42 | 24 | fb11c0a0 | 184 | - | ttyp0 | 00:00:00 | ps |

Now this output looks a little better. At least there are more entries, so maybe it is more interesting. The columns `PID`, `TTY`, `TIME`, and `CMD` are the same as in the previous output.

The first column (`F`) are flags in *octal* to tell us *some* information about the state of the process. For example, a 01 here would be for a system process that is always in memory, such as `vhand` or `sched`. The 20 in both cases here means that the process is in main memory.

The `S` column is one of the "official" states that the process can be in. These states are defined in `<sys/proc.h>` and can be one of the following values:

- O   Process is currently on the processor (SONPROC)
- S   Sleeping (SSLEEP)
- R   Ready to run (SRUN)
- I   Idle, being created (SIDL)
- Z   Zombie state (SZOMB)
- T   Process being traced, used by debuggers (SSTOP)
- B   Process is waiting for more memory (SXBRK).

Here we see that the `ksh` process (line 1) is sleeping. Although we can't tell from the output, I know that it is waiting for the completion of the `ps` command. One indication I have is in the `PID` and `PPID` columns. These are, respectively, the Process ID and Parent Process ID. Notice that the PPID of the `ps` process is the *same* as the PID of the `ksh` process. This is because I started the `ps` command from the `ksh` command line and the `ksh` had to do a `fork()`-`exec()` to start up the `ps`. This makes `ps` a child process of the `ksh`. Since I didn't start the `ps` in the background, I *know* the `ksh` is waiting on the completion of the `ps`.

We see that the ps process is on the processor (state O-SONPROC). As a matter of fact, I have *never* run a ps command where ps was *not* on the processor. Why? Well, the only way for ps to read the process table is while it is running and the only way for a process to be running is for it to be on the processor.

Since I just happened to be running these processes as root, the UID column, which shows the User ID of the owner of that processes, there is 0 in this column. The owner is almost always the user that started the process. However, you can change the owner of a process by using the setuid() or the seteuid() system call.

The C column is an *estimate* of recent CPU usage. Using this value, combined with the process' priority (the PRI column) and the nice value (the NI column), sched calculates the scheduling priority of this process. The ADDR column is the virtual address of that process' entry in the process table. The SZ column is the size (in kilobytes) of the swappable portion of the process' data and stack.

The WCHAN column is the Wait CHANnel for the process. This is the event that the process is waiting for. Since ps is currently running, it is not waiting for any event. Therefore, there is a dash in this column. The WCHAN that the ksh is waiting for is fb11b9e8. Although, I have nothing here to prove it, I *know* that this event is the completion of the ps.

Although I can't prove this, I can make some inferences. First, let's look at the ps output again, this time let's start ps in the background. This gives us this output:

```
F   S  UID PID  PPID C   PRI  NI   ADDR      SZ   WCHAN    TTY    TIME      CMD
20  S  0   608  607  3   75   24   fb11b9e8  132  f01ebf4c ttyp0  00:00:02  ksh
20  O  0   1221 608  20  37   28   fb11cb60  184  -        ttyp0  00:00:00  ps
```

Next, let's make use of the ability of ps to display the status of processes running on a specific terminal. We can then run the ps command from another terminal and look at what's happening on ttyp0. Running the command

ps -lt ttyp0

we get something like this:

```
F   S  UID  PID  PPID C   PRI  NI   ADDR      SZ    WCHAN    TTY    TIME      CMD
20  S  0    608  1295 3   75   24   fb11b9e8  132   f01ebf4c ttyp0  00:00:02  ksh
```

In the first example, ksh did a fork-exec, but since we put it in the background it returned to the prompt and didn't wait for the ps complete. Instead it was waiting for more input from the keyboard. In the second example, `ksh` did nothing. I ran the `ps` from another terminal and it showed me only the `ksh`. Looking back at that screen, I see that it is sitting there, waiting for input from the keyboard. Notice that in both cases the WCHAN is the same. Both are waiting for the same event: input from the keyboard. However, in the previous example we did not put the command in the background so the WCHAN was the completion of `ps`.

Despite its ominous name, another useful tool is `crash`. Not only can you look at processes, but you can also look at many other things such as file tables, symbol tables, region table, both the global and local descriptor tables, and even the uarea of a process. Because `crash` needs read access to both `/dev/mem` and `/unix`, it can only be run by root. This is because the `crash` command needs to be able to read `/dev/mem`. If a normal user were allowed to read `/dev/mem`, they could read another user's process.

In the chapter on system monitoring, we'll talk about `crash` and all the things it can tell us about our system.

## Devices and Device Nodes

In UNIX nothing works without devices. I mean NOTHING. Getting input from a keyboard or displaying it on your screen both require devices. Accessing data from the hard disk or printing a report also require devices. In an operating system like DOS, all of the input and output functions are almost entirely hidden from you. Drivers for these devices must exist in order to be able to use them, however they are hidden behind the cloak of the operating system.

Although accessing the same physical hardware, device drivers under UNIX are more complex than their DOS cousins. Although adding new drivers is easier under DOS, SCO provides more flexibility in modifying the ones you have. SCO UNIX provides a mechanism to simplify adding these input and output functions. There is a set of tools and utilities to modify and configure your system. These tools are collectively called the Link Kit, or link kit.

The link kit is part of the extended utilities packages. Therefore, it is not a required component of your operating system. Although having the link kit on your system is not required for proper operation, you are unable to add devices or change kernel parameters without it.

Because the link kit directly modifies configuration files and drivers that are combined to create the operating system, a great deal of care must be exercised when making changes. If you are lucky, an incorrectly configured kernel just won't boot rather than trash your hard disk. If you're not . . . is your resumé up to date?

## Major and Minor Numbers

To UNIX, everything is a file. To write to the hard disk you write to a file. To read from the keyboard is to read from a file. To store backups on a tape device is to write to a file. Even to read from memory, is to read from a file. If the file you are trying to read from, or write to, is a "normal" file, the process is fairly easy to understand. The file is opened and you read or write data. If, however, the device being accessed is a special device file (also referred to as a device node), a fair bit of work needs to be done before the read or write operation can begin.

One of the key aspects in understanding device files is in the fact that different devices behave and react differently. There are no keys on a hard disk and no sectors on a keyboard. However, you can read from both. The system, therefore, needs a mechanism whereby it can distinguish between the various types of devices and behave accordingly.

In order to access a device accordingly, the operating system needs to be told what to do. Obviously the manner in which the kernel accesses a hard disk will be different from the way it accesses a terminal. Both can be read from and written to, but that's about where the similarities end. In order to access each of these totally different kinds of devices, the kernel needs to know that they are, in fact, different.

Inside the kernel are functions for each of the devices the kernel is going to access. All the routines for a specific device are jointly referred to as the device driver. Each device on the system has its own device driver. Within each device driver are the functions that are used to access the device. For devices such as a hard disk or terminal, the system needs to be able to (among other things) open the device, write to the device, read from the device, and close the device. Therefore, the respective drivers will contain the routines needed to open, write to, read from, and close those devices (among other things).

In order to determine how to access the device, the kernel needs to be given instructions. Not only does the kernel need to be told what kind of device is being accessed, but any special information such as the partition number if it's a hard disk or density if it's a floppy, for example. This is accomplished by the major and minor number of that device.

The major number is actually the offset into the kernel's device driver table, which tells the kernel what kind of device it is; that is, whether it is a hard disk or a serial terminal. The minor number tells the kernel special characteristics of the device to be accessed. For example, the second hard disk has a different minor number than the first. The COM1 port has a different minor number than the COM2 port.

It is through this table that the routines are accessed and, in turn, access the physical hardware. Once the kernel has determined what kind of device it is talking to, it determines the specific device, the specific location, or other characteristics of the device by means of the minor number. Figure 5–9 shows what this might look like graphically.

In order to find out what functions can be used to access a particular device, you can take a look in the /etc/conf/cf.d/mdevice file, which contains a list of all the devices in the system. Aside from the function list, mdevice also contains the major numbers for that device. For details on the mdevice file, take a look at the mdevice(F) man-page.

So how do we, let alone the kernel, know what the major and minor numbers of a device are? By doing a long listing of the /dev directory (either with l or ls -l), there are two things that tell us that the files in this directory are not normal files. One thing to look at is the first character on each line. If these are regular files, the first character will be a -. In /dev almost every entry starts with either a b or a c. These represent, respectively, block devices and character devices. (The re-

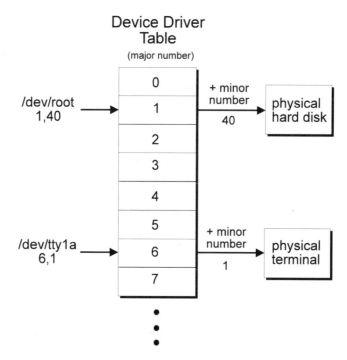

**Figure 5–9**    Process major and minor numbers.

maining entries are all directories and begin with a d. See the ls(C) man-page for additional details on the format of these entries.)

The second indicator that these are not "normal" files is in the fifth field of the listing. For both regular files and directories, this field shows their size. However, device nodes do not have a size. The only place they exist is in their inode (and, of course, the corresponding directory entry). There are no data blocks taken up by the device file, therefore it has no size. For device nodes, there are two numbers instead of one for the size. These are, respectively, the major and minor number of the device.

Like file sizes, major and minor numbers are stored in the file's inode. In fact, they are stored in the same field of the inode structure. File sizes can be up to 2147483648 bytes (2 Gigabytes or $2^{31}$ bytes), but major and minor numbers are limited to a single byte each. Therefore, there can be only 256 major numbers and 256 minor numbers per major.

As I mentioned before, the major number corresponds to whatever is listed in column 5 or 6 of mdevice. Once we have the name of a device, we can scan mdevice to find the name of the corresponding driver. Unlike some dialects of UNIX, SCO has made figuring out what each device does a little easier. Keep in mind that the system does this all internally and does not read mdevice while it is running.

For the most part, the names of devices provide some clue as to their function. Let's take a look at a few to get a better feel for what the names mean. I am going to go into a fair bit of detail about how hard disks are put together since they are the most commonly accessed devices and cause the most problems. Additionally, the hard disk numbering scheme provides a good demonstration of how minor numbers are used.

First, change directories to /dev (cd /dev) and do a long listing of a few files with the command

l hd0*     (Don't forget the asterisk.)

If you have a typical system, this gives you entries that look like this:

| | | | | | | | | | |
|---|---|---|---|---|---|---|---|---|---|
| **brw-------** | 2 | sysinfo | sysinfo | **1,** | **0** | Mar | 23 | 1993 | hd00 |
| **brw-------** | 2 | sysinfo | sysinfo | **1,** | **15** | Mar | 23 | 1993 | hd01 |
| **brw-------** | 2 | sysinfo | sysinfo | **1,** | **23** | Mar | 23 | 1993 | hd02 |
| **brw-rw-rw-** | 2 | sysinfo | sysinfo | **1,** | **31** | Mar | 23 | 1993 | hd03 |
| **brw-rw-rw-** | 2 | sysinfo | sysinfo | **1,** | **39** | Mar | 23 | 1993 | hd04 |
| **brw-------** | 2 | sysinfo | sysinfo | **1,** | **47** | Feb | 26 | 1994 | hd0a |
| **brw-r-----** | 3 | dos | sysinfo | **1,** | **48** | Mar | 19 | 1994 | hd0d |

Immediately, we can tell these are block devices by looking at the first character on each line. If we look at the major number ('1' in each case), we see that each of the listed devices has the same major device number. Therefore, we know that the devices we listed are all accessed using the same driver. In this case it is the device in position 1 of the driver table. If we take a look at `mdevice`, we find that this is the `hd` driver and as you probably guessed, this is the hard disk driver. If we look at the name of each device (the last column) we see that they all begin with `hd`. This is not a coincidence.

Before we talk about what each of these files represent, let's do another long listing of some other files. This time lets do a `l rhd*`. The observant readers will notice that this is almost identical to the command we issued before. However, the extra `r` gave us a slightly different output:

| | | | | | | | | |
|---|---|---|---|---|---|---|---|---|
| **c**rw------- | 2 | sysinfo | sysinfo | **1, 0** | Mar 23 | 1993 | rhd00 |
| **c**rw------- | 2 | sysinfo | sysinfo | **1, 15** | Mar 23 | 1993 | rhd01 |
| **c**rw------- | 2 | sysinfo | sysinfo | **1, 23** | Mar 23 | 1993 | rhd02 |
| **c**rw------- | 2 | sysinfo | sysinfo | **1, 31** | Mar 23 | 1993 | rhd03 |
| **c**rw------- | 2 | sysinfo | sysinfo | **1, 39** | Mar 23 | 1993 | rhd04 |
| **c**rw------- | 2 | sysinfo | sysinfo | **1, 47** | Feb 26 | 1994 | rhd0a |
| **c**rw-r----- | 3 | dos | sysinfo | **1, 48** | Mar 23 | 1993 | rhd0d |

If we look carefully, each line in this output differs from the first only in two letters. As we see, the first character on each line is a 'c', representing a character device. In addition, each name is preceded with an `r`. (That obviously shows up because that's what we listed.) This `r` means that this is a 'raw' device. This tells us that the system reads the device directly and does not use the buffer cache. (The hardware may do some caching of the data, but the operating system does not.) The different devices are more commonly referred to as block and character devices, although the character devices are often referred to as 'raw' devices since there is no caching of their input.

We need to side-step a little here. I mentioned earlier that the kernel maintains a table containing each of the configured devices. Well this is only half true. The kernel maintains two tables, one for each type of device: block and character. The table for the block devices is called the block device switch table (`bdevsw`) and the table for the character devices is called the character device switch table (`cdevsw`). The offset into these tables is the major device. Saying that these are offsets into a table is true, but it is an oversimplification. Each entry in the table is actually a structure of pointers to the different functions that are used to access the device.

As I mentioned, there are only two differences in each line of the `ls` output above. The major and minor numbers are unchanged. Therefore, not only is the same driver being used, but in each case, the same flags are being passed to the driver.

By now, I am sure you are asking, "Just what do all those minor numbers mean?" (Assuming, of course, you don't already know.) Well, as I mentioned, they are flags to the device driver to tell it where to look. The driver knows that this is a hard disk. But since the hard disk can be divided into multiple partitions, an important question to the driver is, "Which partition?" An even better question might be, "What hard disk?" since more than one disk can be configured on the system.

As you might have guessed, which disk is accessed is determined by the minor number. Since each minor number is represented in the inode as a single byte it can only be in the range of 0–255. If we look in `/dev`, we find no device with a minor number (or major number) greater than 255. Therefore, there can only be 256 devices of a particular type. Appendix A contains a quick review of binary counting. Use this as a guide when trying to match minor numbers with the location on the hard disk.

Having 256 hard disks seems like a lot and it doesn't seem all that common for someone to have so many hard disks. The problem lies in the fact that a hard disk minor number does not just tell what hard disk is being accessed, but also what partition and what filesystem. To be able to handle and process this information in an orderly fashion, the system needs some method of encoding it.

This is easily accomplished by accessing the byte that represents the minor as a series of eight bits. In fact, this is exactly what the hard disk (and most other drivers) do. Table 5–3 contains the breakdown of the bits for hard disk minor numbers.

In this scheme, the two high-order bits (7 & 6) tell us what hard disk is beginning accessed. Considered individually, we have the numbers 0–3; exactly like the drive numbers they represent. However, considered in respect to the entire minor number, this represents the values $2^7$ and $2^6$ (128 and 64).

Depending on which bit is set, we end up with the four ranges. If neither bit 6 or 7 is set, the total value of these two bits is 0, and this would be drive 0. This gives us the range of minor numbers 0–63, since this is as high as we can go with bit 0–5. If bit 6 is set we add 64 to this range ($2^6 = 64$), so the range of minor numbers is 64–127 (0 + 64 = 64, 63 + 64 = 127). If bit 7 is set we add 128 to this range ($2^7 = 128$), so the range of minor numbers is 128–191 (0 + 128 = 128, 63 + 128 = 191). Lastly, if bits 6 *and* 7 are set we add 192 to this range (64 + 128 = 192), so the range of minor numbers is 192–255 (0 + 192 = 192, 63 + 192 = 255).

**Table 5–3**   Hard Disk Minor Number Bit Scheme

| | | | BITS | | | | | |
|---|---|---|---|---|---|---|---|---|
| 7 | 6 | 5 | 4 | 3 | 2 | 1 | 0 | **Description** |
| X | X | — | — | — | — | — | — | disk # (0–3) |
| — | — | X | X | X | — | — | — | partition # (1–4) |
| — | — | — | — | — | X | X | X | division # (0–7) |
| — | — | X | X | X | 1 | 1 | 1 | whole partition |
| — | — | 0 | 0 | 0 | 0 | 0 | 0 | whole physical disk |
| — | | 1 | 0 | 1 | — | — | — | active partition |
| — | — | 1 | 1 | 0 | — | — | — | DOS partition (ie. hd0d) |
| — | — | 1 | 1 | 0 | X | X | X | DOS partition (C–J) |

From these numbers we see that any reference to a major number of 1 and a minor number between 0–63 is accessing something on the first hard disk. Anything with a minor number 64–127 is accessing something on the second hard disk, and so on.

The next bits (bits 3–5) represent the partition on the respective hard disk. At first, this seems odd, since there can only be four partitions on a drive and these three bits can represent eight different values. Four of the values are used to represent the individual partitions. Sometimes, it is necessary to refer to the entire disk, regardless of what partitions exist (for example to write the masterboot block). Therefore, a fifth value is needed. The whole disk is referred to when each of these three bits are off.

It is possible that any one of the four partitions can be active. SCO UNIX provides a means to address the active partitions, regardless of how many partitions there are and where they exist. The notion of the active partition is also one of the eight, therefore another set of numbers is used. The active partition is when bits 3 and 5 are *set*. Lastly, since SCO UNIX can access DOS partitions, the systems needs to know that a partition is DOS as well. This is when bits 4 and 5 are set.

If we've counted right, this adds up to seven different values. The eighth one is simply not used. The reason being is the numbering scheme itself. In order to keep things simple, three specific bytes are used for the partition. Since there were not enough specific values to fill all eight, but too many for two bits, one is simply ignored. This is the case when all three bits (3–5) are set.

The actual partition numbers are based on combinations of bits (3–5). The partition number is simply the numeric value of the three bits taken by themselves.

Since there are 3 bits, this can be the range 0–8. So, for example, if bit 3 is set, it would be equivalent to bit 0, if there were only three bits. This is partition 1 ($2^0 = 1$). If bit 4 was set, it would be equivalent to bit 1 being set. This is partition 2 ($2^0 = 2$); and so on.

(Personally, I think it was a wise decision not to start counting the partitions at 0 like with many other things; DOS doesn't. Therefore, if there were a DOS partition on a system, it might get confusing as to which partition was which.)

The last three (lower-order) bits represent the filesystems (also referred to as divisions. Here again, there are eight distinct values. However, there can only be seven divisions within a partition. The eighth value represents the entire partition. This is necessary to write the superblock as well as for certain database applications that require an entire hard disk partition to themselves. Should the partition be DOS, then the last three bytes represent the logical partition (drives C–J).

In the `ls -l` output above, we see the representation of the individual partitions on the hard disk. The breakdown of the individual devices is somewhat difficult to grasp at first. The device `hd00` is the entire first hard disk and we see that it has a minor number of 0. Since it has no partitions, this device uses all of the values 0–7. The devices `hd01-hd04` use the ranges 7–15, 16–23, 24–31, and 32–39 respectively. Divisions (filesystems) within these partitions are sequentially numbered from the start value (7, 16, 24, or 32).

From this we get that the first division of the first partition is 7. This is the start value (7 in this case) plus the division number (0 in this case) or simply 7. The second division is $7 + 1 = 8$, the third $7 + 2 = 9$, and so on. The third division on the fourth partition would be $32 + 3$ or 35 (remember, we started counting at 0 for the divisions).

Next, we have the active partition on the first disk. This is simply one set of eight minor numbers higher, or 40–47 (here bits 3 and 5 are set). The entire partition is represented as the device `/dev/hd0a`. This is the active partition, hence the 'a'. Since we add the division number within the partition to the partition start number, the first division of the active partition would have a minor number of 40.

This might have turned a light on for some of the readers who are more familiar with SCO UNIX. If we look at the root filesystem device (`/dev/root`), it has a major/minor number combination of 1,40. This is no coincidence. Since the root filesystem resides in the first division of the active partition, this matches exactly with the values we just got. Since the swap device is usually the second division, according to our calculations it ends up with a major/minor combination of 1,41. If we look at `/dev/swap`, we see that it has just what we calculated.

On OpenServer, /dev/root is no longer 1,40. Instead it was moved to the division after /dev/swap. Therefore, it is now 1,42. However, the numbers still fit conceptually.

Should the disk have a DOS partition this is represented by the device hd0d (hence the d). This starts at minor number 48 and goes up from there. In older SCO operating systems, you could only have one DOS partition per drive. However, if we take a look at the directory /dev/dsk, we see devices 0sC–0sJ, with minor numbers 48–55. These are the DOS devices for partitions on the first hard disk.

Up to this point, we've only talked about the first hard disk. What happens with multiple hard disks? Well, the calculations are quite easy. Since each disk is given a set of 64 minor numbers, we simply add 64 for each additional hard disk to any of the above values we calculated. Therefore, the entire second disk would be 0 + 64 = 64. The second filesystem on the active partition of the third drive would be 41 + 64 + 64 = 168 and so on. For additional details, take a look at the hd(HW) man-page.

From this scheme, we see that there are only four hard disks of any given type possible on the system. Several years ago, this seemed to be enough. However, as systems got larger, this became a serious bottle-neck. The result was the implementation of a scheme called *extended minor numbers*. To understand this, we need some more background, so I will postpone the discussion until the end of the chapter.

So what does this all have to do with the kernel? Well, when accessing any one of the hard disk partitions or filesystems, the kernel has to know where it is on the disk. By using the minor number it is able to make that determination.

Since hard disks are the only devices that have partitions and divisions, they are obviously the only ones that require a scheme like this. However, other devices use the bits in the minor number in similar ways. In fact, all well-behaved devices follow it to some extent.

If we take a look at the devices representing the first floppy drive, we see some similar patterns. If we change into the /dev directory, an l fd0* gives us the following pattern:

| | | | | | | | | | |
|---|---|---|---|---|---|---|---|---|---|
| brw-rw-rw- | 5 | bin | bin | 2, | 60 | Nov | 09 | 08:03 | fd0 |
| brw-rw-rw- | 5 | bin | bin | 2, | 60 | Nov | 09 | 08:03 | fd0135ds18 |
| brw-rw-rw- | 4 | bin | bin | 2, | 36 | Mar | 23 | 1993 | fd0135ds9 |
| brw-rw-rw- | 5 | bin | bin | 2, | 4 | Mar | 23 | 1993 | fd048 |
| brw-rw-rw- | 3 | bin | bin | 2, | 12 | Mar | 23 | 1993 | fd048ds8 |

| | | | | | | | | | | |
|---|---|---|---|---|---|---|---|---|---|---|
| brw-rw-rw- | 5 | bin | bin | 2, | 4  | Mar | 23 | 1993 | fd048ds9 |
| brw-rw-rw- | 2 | bin | bin | 2, | 8  | Mar | 23 | 1993 | fd048ss8 |
| brw-rw-rw- | 2 | bin | bin | 2, | 0  | Mar | 23 | 1993 | fd048ss9 |
| brw-rw-rw- | 6 | bin | bin | 2, | 52 | Mar | 23 | 1993 | fd096 |
| brw-rw-rw- | 6 | bin | bin | 2, | 52 | Mar | 23 | 1993 | fd096ds15 |
| brw-rw-rw- | 4 | bin | bin | 2, | 36 | Mar | 23 | 1993 | fd096ds9 |

As we see, the major number for floppy devices is 2 and each name begins with `fd` for floppy device. Following that are several characteristics about the device. Like the hard disk, the first digit is the drive number, followed by (possibly) the density (tracks-per-inch), double- or single-sided, and the sectors per track. Note here that floppy device `fd0` and `fd0135ds18` have the same major and minor numbers. This is because the first floppy on my system is a 3.5″ (135-TPI) drive.

Like the hard disks, the bit patterns indicate the drive. However, unlike the hard disk, the floppy devices start at the low-order bit. Therefore, it is bits 0 and 1 that represent the drive number. Bit two, tells us if the floppy is single- or double-sided (0 = single and 1 = double-sided). Bits 3–5 are not as easy to decipher, but still tell us the density and sectors-per-track. 96 and 135-TPI floppies have bit 5 set, 48-TPI have it unset. Drives with 8 sectors per track have bit 3 set, 9 sectors have bits 3 and 4 unset, 15 sectors have bit 4 set, and 18 sectors have bits 3 and 4 set. Because of the fewer "types" of floppies as compared to the disk/partition/division combinations, bits 6 and 7 are not used.

Although floppy disks do not have the same partitions and divisions as a hard disk, the floppy device driver uses minor numbers to tell it characteristics about the device just as the hard disk driver does. These are not the only devices that use this scheme. Any time there is more than one type of device, minor numbers are used to pass information to the driver. Rather than showing you a table for each of the device types, I will just point you to the appropriate man-pages. Many have tables that can make some of the more complicated numbering schemes clearer. In other cases, simply comparing names and functionality will help to clear things up.

### *The Device Directory*

Every UNIX dialect has a device directory. Lucky for us, all of them (at least all the ones I have seen) are called `/dev`. This gives us a little advantage when moving between platforms. Unfortunately, naming conventions are nowhere near uniform and it often takes a great deal of detective work to figure out which device does what. SCO does a good job of naming devices in a consistent and (usually) obvious manner.

Although the naming convention used by SCO makes it easy (easier than most) to figure out what each device does, it helps to have someone hold your hand and explain things. That's what I'm here to do in this section.

Before I start, I again need to point out something. The devices that I make reference to in this section may not be present in your system. All the devices I mention will appear at one time or another on an SCO UNIX system. Many of them only appear if you have certain packages and products installed. This is all based on ODT 3.0 and OpenServer Enterprise systems. If you do not have either of these releases or do not have some of the components installed, this section may refer to things that you do not have on your system. Don't go calling SCO Support saying you're missing things! Also, I will put off talking about the changes made specifically to OpenServer until the end of the section.

There are two ways to approach an examination of the /dev directory. You could go alphabetically through each device type and discuss what they mean. The problem is that some types of devices are not arranged alphabetically. For example, the devices xct0 and rct0 both refer to a tape device. If we were to go through alphabetically, then we would have to jump around a bit in terms of what device types we're talking about.

Instead, I chose to look at each type of device as a group. I will review them somewhat in order of their significance. Some people will have different ideas on what is significant. However, certain assumptions can be made. It is difficult to imagine an SCO UNIX system where a user never accesses the hard disk. However, not having a mouse is a very common situation. Therefore, it makes a certain amount of sense to talk about hard disks first and if you get bored you can stop reading before you get to the section on mice.

What I intend to do here is talk about the structure of the /dev directory and what devices are represented by different sets of files. Since the /dev directory contains subdirectories as well as files, it has a certain structure to it that needs to be discussed. One problem I encountered when deciding how to approach this topic was the fact that the ODT 3.0 and OpenServer /dev/ directories are fairly different. New devices *and* new directories exist that we need to talk about. So, I decided to first talk about what things they have in common and then move on to what's new in OpenServer.

In a default ODT or OpenServer installation, there are literally hundreds of device files. Often devices exist with different names and in different directories despite having the same major and minor number. Therefore, a simple listing is not sufficient to get the whole picture. Let's first take a look at the subdirectories of /dev. I am not going to follow the order that these directories appear, but rather their order of significance. (Here again, significance is relative and the choice really is arbitrary).

There exists a pair of directories `/dev/dsk` and `/dev/rdsk`. If we were to try to pronounce the names of the subdirectories we would not have a clue as to their function. Each contain disk devices, and if we look back at the section on major and minor numbers, we can guess that the `rdsk` subdirectory contains the raw disk devices. If you had bet some money on your guess you would now be up a few bucks, because that's exactly what is going on.

Some of the readers who are more familiar with SCO UNIX might have asked, "Why is there a subdirectory for disk devices when they already exist in `/dev`?" The answer is quite simple: The device files in `/dev` are *not* UNIX devices. Hmm? What are non-UNIX devices doing on a UNIX system?

To understand what's going on here, we need a little history. UNIX is not the first operating system that SCO worked with. It started out with an 8086 version of XENIX, eventually moving to 80286 and 80386 versions. It wasn't until sometime after SCO had been working with XENIX for several years that it started working on UNIX.

One of the conventions used in dialects of UNIX is the device naming scheme. However, SCO had a strong following with XENIX and aside from the logic of the XENIX naming convention, changing names so abruptly was rather difficult. Following the convention, block disk devices reside in `/dev/dsk` and character disk devices reside in `/dev/rdsk`. This is not just for hard disks, but for floppy disks as well.

The next subdirectory of `/dev` that we are going to look at is `/dev/mouse`. For those readers who have already had at least one cup of coffee, it is pretty obvious to see that `/dev/mouse` contains devices specific to mice.

The `/dev/inet` directory is for files related to the `inetd` daemon. Rather than building routines into the applications themselves to access the different network layers, SCO has provided device nodes. For example, to access the IP layer, we have the device `/dev/inet/ip`.

The remaining directories are not as easy to decipher. For example, the `/dev/string` directory itself is unclear. If we look inside we see three devices. These represent various strings that are used or created by the kernel when the system boots. Again we will get into more detail later. The following directories are used by DOS and merge with the respective functionality:

```
vdsp - Virtual display devices
vmouse - Virtual mouse devices
```

```
vkbd - Virtual keyboard devices
vsdsp - Slave virtual display devices
vskbd - Slave virtual keyboard devices
vems - Virtual EMS devices
```

### Hard Disks

Let's talk now about the disk devices. In /dev, these devices exist in name-pairs. For example the first hard disk exists as /dev/hd00 and /dev/rhd00. The first one, /dev/hd00 is the character device associated with the first hard disk and /dev/rhd00 is the block device. I referred to these files as name-pairs because these have similar names, but are *not* the same file. These are *not* links but exist as separate files in that they take up separate inodes. This is shown by using the -i and -1 option to ls as in,

```
ls -li /dev/*hd00
```

which yields

```
167 brw-------  2 sysinfo sysinfo  1, 0 Mar 23 1993 /dev/hd00
162 crw-------  2 sysinfo sysinfo  1, 0 Mar 23 1993 /dev/rhd00
```

We can see that these files have the same major/minor number, but different inode numbers. Therefore, they are different files. For more details on links, see the section on filesystems.

From our discussion of major and minor numbers, we know that the hard disk driver is major number 1. It doesn't matter if the device node is in /dev or somewhere completely different. No matter what its name is, the key is the major and minor number. This *has* to be the case, otherwise the whole major/minor number scheme collapses. If we want to see all the devices using major number 1, that is, all the hard disk devices, we can proceed as follows:

```
l /dev | grep " 1,"
l /dev/dsk | grep " 1,"
l /dev/rdsk | grep " 1,"
```

Note that there is space before the 1 and a comma after it.

If we look at the hard disk devices in /dev/dsk and /dev/(r)dsk we see that they all have more than one link. If we do a long listing of each set of devices, specifying that we also want the inode number we can see that each inode appears more than once. As an example, lets do l -i /dev/hd00/dev/dsk/0s0 and we get the following:

```
167 brw-------  2 sysinfo sysinfo  1, 0 Mar 23 1993 /dev/hd00
167 brw-------  2 sysinfo sysinfo  1, 0 Mar 23 1993 /dev/dsk/0s0
```

then, `l -i /dev/rhd00 /dev/rdsk/0s0`

```
162 crw-------  2 sysinfo sysinfo  1, 0 Mar 23 1993 /dev/rdsk/0s0
162 crw-------  2 sysinfo sysinfo  1, 0 Mar 23 1993 /dev/rhd00
```

As we see, each pair are the same devices and have the same inode. However, the name-pairs `/dev/hd00--/dev/rhd00` and `/dev/dsk/0s0--/dev/rdsk/0s0` do not have the same inode number. The difference is that the SCO (XENIX) devices differentiate between character and block devices in their names and the SysV (UNIX) devices differentiate between them by the directory in which they appear.

Although both can be used and both access the exact same location on the hard disk, the XENIX names are more common in SCO literature. There is something here that I need to point out. The character and block devices are not the same. Not only are they accessed differently, they also have different inode numbers; just the corresponding UNIX-XENIX pairs have the same inode number. However, all four devices have the same major and minor number combination!

Note that because of the way the system determines whether a device is a character or block, the inodes need to be different. The kernel inode structure contains a field that specifies the type of file. This determines what `ls -l` outputs as the file's type. This is the first character of the permissions (b for block, c for character). Since the type of file is a single field in the inode and block and character devices are displayed differently, there must be an inode used for the block device and a separate one for its character equivalent.

As I mentioned in our discussion on major and minor numbers, each hard disk device represents a part of the hard disk. Both the UNIX and XENIX names give an indication as to where they are on the disk. With the UNIX names, the first character represents the physical hard disk and the last character represents the partition. If the last character is a 0, this signifies the entire disk (used to write the master boot block, among other things). So given the device `0s3`, we know that it is the third partition on the first (0th) physical drive. For the XENIX devices, the third character tells us the physical hard disk, and the fourth character tells us the partition. Here again, the physical disks range from 0–3 and the partitions range from 1–4, with 0 reserved for the whole disk. Given the device `hd31`, we know this is the first partition on the fourth physical drive.

In both cases (UNIX and XENIX), if the last character is an `a`, then we know this is the active partition. Although the active partition only has special significance for the first hard disk, partitions on subsequent disks can be made active and the numbering scheme still applies. A final character of `d` means this is a DOS partition. In older versions, SCO UNIX could not access logical DOS partitions, so a single letter was sufficient. However, as soon the drivers were in place to access multiple DOS partitions, additions needed to be made to the device node numbering and naming scheme. As a result, you will find devices in `/dev/dsk` and `/dev/rdsk` for these partitions. Devices `/dev/dsk0sC` through `/dev/dsk/0sJ` represent the first eight DOS partitions per drive.

Up to this point, we've been talking about hard disk devices in very abstract terms. As you may already know, each hard disk is broken up into partitions. Any PC-based operating system needs to create at least one partition on the hard disk. SCO UNIX divides partitions into smaller units called divisions. The most common way of accessing the hard disk is the filesystems that reside within divisions.

Divisions do not necessarily have to have filesystems on them. An example of this would be the swap device. It resides within a division, but does not contain a filesystem. A filesystem is a division that has a particular structure. As the name implies, it is a system of files. All files, including device nodes, exist within the boundaries of a filesystem. The most familiar filesystem is the root filesystem. The device that points to this special location on the disk is `/dev/root` (logical, huh?). The structure of filesystems is discussed in more detail in Chapter 6.

If we look at the device node `/dev/root`, we see that it has a major number of 1, so we know it lies somewhere on the hard disk. The minor number is 40 which we know, from our discussion of major and minor numbers, is on the active partition of the first drive. There is nothing special about this particular location on the disk. In fact, what division the root filesytem is on got changed in SCO OpenServer.

By convention on ODT, the first filesystem on the active partition of the first hard disk is the root filesystem. The system knows that in order to function properly, it needs a device `/dev/root`. However, nothing prevents it from having a different minor number or residing elsewhere on the disk. For example, if there is only one partition on the first disk, the root filesystem could also be referred to with the major/minor number combination 1,8. Where 8 is the first division on the first partition.

Note that if there is only one partition on the first hard disk and it is active, the major/minor number combinations 1,40 and 1,8 are the same place. If there is more than one, then the active partition does not need to be the first one. Therefore, the first filesystem on the active partition may not be 1,8. It may be 1,16 or 1,24 or 1,32. If you were paying attention, you know why the minor number goes up in increments of 8.

For the fun of it, I created multiple partitions with different SCO products (UNIX, XENIX, ODT). Rather than having to change the active partition when I wanted to switch to a different operating system, I left one partition active and passed bootstrings to /boot (see the section on starting your system for more details). Here I referred to the root and swap devices by their absolute minor numbers. In order to be safe, I even changed the device nodes to reflect this. So for the first partition, /dev/root was 1,8 and /dev/swap was 1,9.

In addition to these two devices, it is often common to have a filesystem used exclusively for data, often /dev/u. If you have enough space, you will be prompted to create one during the installation. It is commonly the third division and has a minor number of 42. In addition to these familiar divisions, there is also another division whose function is not commonly known. This is /dev/recover. As its name implies, it is used in recovery processes, specifically when fsck tries to clean filesystems during boot. Since fsck does not know the state of the filesystems being cleaned, it cannot safely write to them when it is trying to clean them (kind of like trying to mop the floor you are standing on). Instead, it writes its outputs to a reserved area of the hard disk called /dev/recover. Each of these also has their own 'raw' counterpart: rroot, rswap, ru, and rrecover.

### Floppy Devices

As with the hard disk devices, there are both XENIX and UNIX floppy devices. The XENIX devices reside in the /dev directory and begin with fd. As I mentioned in the section on major and minor numbers, the characters following the fd tell us characteristics about the device. Let's look at a typical example: /dev/fd0135ds18. The first character following the fd is the drive number. You will normally only find (at most) two floppy drives so this is either a 0 or a 1. At the end is the number of tracks per inch. In this example, we interpret the device as shown in Figure 5–10.

As I mentioned before, both the /dev/dsk and /dev/rdsk directories contain device nodes for SysV disk devices. This includes floppy disks as well. Floppy devices here are recognized by the first character being an 'f'. Subsequent letters relate to specific characteristics of the device.

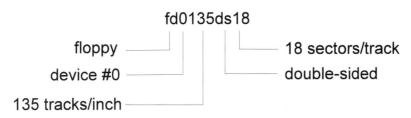

**Figure 5–10**   Explanation of floppy device names.

The second character tells whether it is floppy 0 or 1. The third character tells, not how many tracks per inch, but rather the diameter of the disk. Therefore, a 5 in this column is for a 5.25" floppy and a 3 is for a 3.5" floppy. The fourth column is for the density, with possible values 'h' for high, 'd' for double, and 'q' for quad. The remaining values will vary. The following digits, such as 9, 15, or 18, represent the number of sectors per track. Many of these devices have aliases which represent the same device. For example, `/dev/dsk/f05d9` and `/dev/dsk/fd0d9d` are the same device. For details, see the `fd`(HW) man-page.

There are a few floppy devices that require special attention. These are the `/dev/install`, `/dev/install1`, `/dev/dsk/finstall`, and `/dev/dsk/finstall1` (and, of course, their character device counterparts). Like all the other devices, SCO typically uses the XENIX devices, so only `/dev/install` and `/dev/install1` are more commonly used. As one would guess, these devices are used to install. When running `custom` to install additional software, the system looks at `/dev/install` by default. The really nice thing about these devices, is that it doesn't matter what type of media you have. The floppy device driver will figure out what kind of floppy you have. In fact, if you are unsure of the media you have, accessing `/dev/install` helps you figure it out. Should you need to access the second floppy (for example, if your installation media is a different size), `/dev/install1` provides the same functionality.

### Terminal Devices

Perhaps more common than floppy devices (at least used more often) are terminal devices. The first thing that may come to mind when thinking about terminal devices is serial terminals that are attached to the systems. While these are possibly the ones commonly used, these are not the only ones on the system. In fact, there are a wide range of device types that appear as tty devices in `/dev`.

If we did a directory listing of `/dev`, we would find at least five different tty (terminal) devices. Let's first talk about the serial terminal devices that one might want to attach to a standard serial (COM) port. These are probably the only ones that everyone thinks about when they talk about terminal devices. If we look at some serial devices in the device directory with

```
l /dev/tty[12][a-dA-D]
```

we get something like this:

```
crw-rw-rw-    1    bin   bin   5,    0     Dec   14    20:40   /dev/tty1a
crw-rw-rw-    1    bin   bin   5,    1     Dec   14    20:40   /dev/tty1b
crw-rw-rw-    1    bin   bin   5,    2     Dec   14    20:40   /dev/tty1c
crw-rw-rw-    1    bin   bin   5,    3     Dec   14    20:40   /dev/tty1d
crw-rw-rw-    1    bin   bin   5,    128   Dec   14    20:40   /dev/tty1A
```

| | | | | | | | | | | |
|---|---|---|---|---|---|---|---|---|---|---|
| crw-rw-rw- | 1 | bin | bin | 5, | 129 | Dec | 14 | 20:40 | /dev/tty1B |
| crw-rw-rw- | 1 | bin | bin | 5, | 130 | Dec | 14 | 20:40 | /dev/tty1C |
| crw-rw-rw- | 1 | bin | bin | 5, | 131 | Dec | 14 | 20:40 | /dev/tty1D |
| crw-rw-rw- | 1 | bin | bin | 5, | 8 | Dec | 14 | 20:25 | /dev/tty2a |
| crw-rw-rw- | 1 | bin | bin | 5, | 9 | Dec | 14 | 20:25 | /dev/tty2b |
| crw-rw-rw- | 1 | bin | bin | 5, | 10 | Dec | 14 | 20:25 | /dev/tty2c |
| crw-rw-rw- | 1 | bin | bin | 5, | 11 | Dec | 14 | 20:25 | /dev/tty2d |
| crw-rw-rw- | 1 | bin | bin | 5, | 136 | Dec | 14 | 20:25 | /dev/tty2A |
| crw-rw-rw- | 1 | bin | bin | 5, | 137 | Dec | 14 | 20:25 | /dev/tty2B |
| crw-rw-rw- | 1 | bin | bin | 5, | 138 | Dec | 14 | 20:25 | /dev/tty2C |
| crw-rw-rw- | 1 | bin | bin | 5, | 139 | Dec | 14 | 20:25 | /dev/tty2D |

(NOTE: Most systems will only have tty1a, tty1A, tty2a, and tty2A. The above devices would only exist if you had a 4-port, nonintelligent serial card on both COM1 and COM2.)

If we look closely, we begin to see that, here too, there are patterns in the relationship between device names and major/minor numbers. The most obvious pattern is that each of these devices has a major number of 5. By looking in /etc/conf/cf.d/mdevice, we can see that this is the major number for the serial device driver (sio). The first terminal device in this is tty1a. This is the first terminal attached to COM1, and as you might guess it has a minor number of 0. Each subsequent terminal device increases its minor number by 1 as you would expect. This ends at minor number 3 as there are only four tty devices attached to COM1 in this example.

Following these devices are more terminal devices with very similar names. The only difference is that, rather than using lower case letters, they end with upper-case letters. If we look, we can see that tty1A has a minor number that is 128 above tty1a, tty1B has a minor number that is 128 above tty1b and so on. This is accomplished by simply using the high order bit ($2^7$) as the flag to determine how the device should be accessed. The uppercase letters represent modem-control ports and lowercase letters represent nonmodem-control ports. For more details on the differences, see the section on modems in the chapter on hardware.

If we look at the devices attached to the second COM port (tty2a, tty2A, etc.) and compare them to the devices on COM1 we also see a pattern. In each case, the minor numbers of the COM2 devices are 8 above their COM1 partner. This means that there can be only 8 terminal devices attached to a nonintelligent serial port.

Things change a fair bit when dealing with intelligent multiport boards (those that do the I/O processing themselves). They require their own drivers and therefore use different major numbers. In addition, the numbering scheme is dependent on the manufacturer, but usually follows a similar scheme.

The next kind of terminal devices that most people are aware of are the console multiscreens. Using these devices it is possible to have several different "screens" on the system console. By default there are twelve console multiscreens, and they are accessed through the keyboard combinations ALT-F1 through ALT-F12. For additional details on accessing these, see the multiscreen (M) man-page.

Although each of these get input from the same keyboard and output appears to be going to the same screen, the system treats them as separate devices. When you switch screens, the kernel is actually displaying different parts of its memory. You can see how much memory is reserved for these screens by looking for the %console line in the hardware screen at boot or by running hwconfig. This will probably be set at 64K. When you switch screens, the kernel knows which screen to display by the key combination pressed.

However, there is more to keeping track of each screen than just displaying the right image to the monitor. Each time you log in, you have a totally new process. Input and output are independent of any of the other screens. The kernel maintains an internal table of which process belongs to which screen and manages this through the minor number of the console devices (tty0-11). In addition to the console multiscreens, there are three more console devices that are used at various times.

The terminal device used by the system administrator in single-user (maintenance mode) is /dev/console; next is /dev/systty. This is the device to which system error messages are output. There is also the device /dev/syscon. This device is used by the init process to communicate with the system administrator during system startup and while in single user mode. Note that these three are almost always linked together.

Not quite a console device, but using the same major number (3) and therefore the same driver is /dev/tty. This is a special terminal device that represents the terminal that you are currently on. To be more accurate, this is the control terminal associated with the process group of a given process. It is useful in programs or shell scripts to ensure that output is written to the terminal no matter how the output has been redirected. Try doing a date > /dev/tty. No matter where you are, it will always appear on your screen.

### *Parallel Devices*

Another kind of device that is very familiar to users is printers. Printers are most commonly accessed through either serial or parallel ports, although ones with built-in networking cards are becoming more common.

A serial printer is accessed through one of the tty devices attached to a COM port that we mentioned above (tty1a, tty2a, etc.) A parallel printer is accessed through the devices /dev/lp, /dev/lp0, /dev/lp1, and /dev/lp2. The device /dev/lp is the default and is probably linked to one of the others. (If not, there is something unusual on your system.) On most machines there is only one parallel port and this is probably /dev/lp0. Therefore, /dev/lp is probably linked to /dev/lp0.

Although these are the printer devices that appear by default on your system, they are not the only ones that the system will recognize. By default the system responds to device requests for service through interrupts. On busy systems, interrupts may be missed and printing slows. This is because an interrupt is generated every time the printer wants to tell the operating system to send more characters. In order to speed things up a bit, device nodes can be created that cause the parallel driver to poll the ports (ask them specifically if they have work to be done), rather than relying on interrupts. If polling devices exist, the parallel port devices might look like this:

```
crw-------   2    bin    bin    6,    0    Nov   15    18:28   /dev/lp
crw-------   2    bin    bin    6,    0    Nov   15    18:28   /dev/lp0
crw-------   1    bin    bin    6,    64   Dec   16    20:40   /dev/lp0p
crw-------   1    bin    bin    6,    1    Mar   23    1993    /dev/lp1
crw-------   1    bin    bin    6,    65   Dec   16    20:40   /dev/lp1p
crw-------   1    bin    bin    6,    2    Mar   23    1993    /dev/lp2
crw-------   1    bin    bin    6,    66   Dec   16    20:40   /dev/lp2p
```

Along with the standard parallel devices /dev/lp, /dev/lp0, /dev/lp1, and /dev/lp2, we see three polling devices /dev/lp0p, /dev/lp1p, and /dev/lp2p. The minor numbers for the standard parallel ports start at 0 and go up to 2. Here again, we see devices making use of bit patterns to correspond to different functionality. By turning on the sixth bit for the polling devices, we end up with minor numbers that are 64 above their nonpolling counterparts.

### Tape Drives

A somewhat less well-known, but very important piece of hardware on a UNIX system, is the tape drive. Most end users don't think about this kind of device until they accidentally erase a file and need some way of getting it back. Although tape drives come in all shapes and sizes, both internal and external, the device nodes they are accessed through remain fairly consistent.

The "standard" device is /dev/rct0, which stands for Raw Cartridge Tape 0. It usually has a major and minor number of 10,0. I say "usually" because this is one of the few instances where the major and minor are not always the same. Depending on what kind of tape driver you have, the "real" tape drive is linked to /dev/rct0. As a result, instead of its default major and minor, it has the one appropriate to the tape drive being used. (WARNING: Note the number zero at the end of the device. It is *not* the letter "Oh". I have had many customers who suddenly lost all the space on their hard disks by backing up to /dev/rcto or /dev/rcto. As a result they end up with a 150Mb file called /dev/rcto.)

Let's look at an example. Assume that a QIC-02 tape drive is installed on the system (more details on this in the chapter on hardware). This will be accessed by the device /dev/rct0 with the major and minor numbers 10,0. If I later decide to replace this tape drive with a SCSI, I can install the SCSI tape drive. The system will ask if I want this to be the default tape drive. If I answer yes, the SCSI tape drive (/dev/rStp0) gets linked to /dev/rct0. If I do a long listing with the inode, the two devices look like this:

```
137   crw-rw-rw-   3   root   root   46, 0   Dec  15   17:42   /dev/rStp0
137   crw-rw-rw-   3   root   root   46, 0   Dec  15   17:42   /dev/rct0
```

All of a sudden, the device /dev/rct0 has a different major number and therefore a different device driver. (Note that the major number 46 may not be the same on your system. SCSI devices can be added at any time so they are dynamically assigned major numbers when they are added.)

As you can see, these two device nodes (/dev/rct0 and /dev/rStp0) not only have the same major and minor number, but also the same inode. Therefore, they are the same device (file). If you were looking at /dev/rct0 and didn't see the 10,0 you might think that something was wrong with the system. (Well, at least I did during one of the first calls I took where the customer was having tape drive problems.)

Another commonly used tape device is /dev/xct0. This is used to issue control commands to the tape drive (ioctls for you programmers). By default, this device keeps its major and minor numbers of 10,128. Control commands include things like rewind and retension.

This major/minor number pair causes problems if you have a SCSI tape and you try to issue tape commands. The best thing is to either link your control tape device (i.e. /dev/xStp0) to /dev/xct0 or change the entry in /etc/default/tape to either /dev/rStp0 or /dev/rct0. The minor number for any control tape device is 128. So the major and minor number for a SCSI control tape device would be 46,128. This is what the control device looks like with a SCSI tape drive:

```
144 crw-rw-rw-  1 root    root    46,128 Mar 23 1993 /dev/xStp0
```

In addition to these two, another tape device is /dev/nrct0 (or /dev/nrStp0). The n simply means that this is a non-rewind device. This can be used if you want to store multiple archives on the same physical tape. In the /dev directory the entry would look like this:

```
143 crw-rw-rw-  1 root    root    46, 12 Mar 23 1993 /dev/nrStp0
```

Care needs to be exercised when using this device. Some tape drives will eject (unload) the tape when the tape processes complete successfully. If you are doing backups of multiple volumes, ejecting the tape is not something you want. Therefore, built into this device is a no-unload mechanism. It is bit 3 that determines whether this is a rewind device or not. So, a purely rewind device would have the minor number 8 ($2^3$). A no-unload device is determined by the second bit giving a minor number of 4 ($2^2$). Since the minor number here is 12 (8 + 4), we know that this device is *both* no-rewind and no-unload. Bare in mind that normal cartridge tapes cannot be ejected so there is no need for a no-unload device /dev/nurct0. The no-unload device looks like this:

```
crw-rw-rw-  1 root    root    46, 4 Mar 23 1993 /dev/nurStp0
```

Also for SCSI tape drives, the unload device /dev/urStp0 is automatically linked to /dev/rStp0. That's why there was a '3' in the links column for the listing of /dev/rStp0. The third link is for /dev/urStp0. Should you have OpenServer and your tape drive support error correction, you can use the device /dev/erct0. However, not all tape drives support error correction. So, although this device exists, you may not be able to use it. If so, /dev/erct0 would look like this:

```
crw-rw-rw-  2 root    other   10, 32 Dec 22 16:53 /dev/erct0
```

Other SCSI tape devices such as DAT or Exabyte, simply use the same tape devices as a SCSI cartridge tape, /dev/rStp0.

Another common tape device is those that use the floppy controller. These are the QIC-40, QIC-80, and IRWIN tape drives. The QIC-40 and QIC-80 are referenced by the floppy tape device ft0. Since only one floppy tape drive is support, there will never be a ft1. As with the other tape devices, there is the raw device, /dev/rft0 and the control tape device, /dev/xft0.

Each of these are linked to a 'mini' tape device since QIC-40s and QIC-80s are often referred to as mini tape-drives. Please note that if you are installing one of these, there is a special entry in the mkdev tape. The Mini-Cartridge entry is for Irwin tape drives only.

A long listing of the device nodes for a QIC-40 or QIC-80 might look like this:

```
crw-rw-rw-   2      root   other   13,0    Dec    20    18:46   /dev/rctmini
crw-rw-rw-   2      root   other   13,0    Dec    20    18:46   /dev/rft0
crw-rw-rw-   2      root   other   13,128 Dec    20    18:46   /dev/xctmini
crw-rw-rw-   2      root   other   13,128 Dec    20    18:46   /dev/xft0
```

As you can see here as well, the control tape devices are again 128 above the standard device. In the above example, the tape drive was installed as floppy unit 1, hence the '0' minor number for /dev/rft0. Should the tape drive be installed as device 2, the minor number will be 1, as drive 3 the minor number will be 2, and so on. As with the other kinds of tape drives, 128 will be added to these numbers for the control device.

Although Irwin tape drives have their own drivers, they are physically the same as QIC-40 and QIC-80 tape drives. The device for an Irwin tape drive as unit 1 is /dev/rmc0 with a major and minor number of 33,0. As unit 2, this would be /dev/rmc1 with a major and minor of 33,1. Since both QIC-40/80 and Irwins are referred to as mini-tape devices, either will be linked to /dev/rctmini and /dev/xctmini depending on which one is installed.

### CD-ROM Devices

If you've installed with a CD-ROM or subsequently added one to your system, there will be device nodes for two kinds of CD-ROMs. The first kind is the one most people are familiar with. This kind can be mounted and accessed like any filesystem. The two devices created for a CD-ROM of this type, might look like this:

```
brw-rw-rw-   1 root    other    51, 0 Nov 28 19:48 /dev/cd0
crw-rw-rw-   1 root    other    51, 0 Nov 28 19:48 /dev/rcd0
```

As with hard disks and floppies, the raw device (/dev/rcd0) has the same major and minor number as the block device (/dev/cd0). The other type of CD-ROM device is used only for installation of software. This is the so-called CD-Tape device. The device nodes for this kind of CD-ROM would look like this:

```
crw-rw-rw-   1 root    other    50, 8 Nov 28 19:47 /dev/nrcdt0
crw-rw-rw-   1 root    other    50, 0 Nov 28 19:47 /dev/rcdt0
crw-rw-rw-   1 root    other    50,128 Nov 28 19:47 /dev/xcdt0
```

We see here devices that are similar in name and minor numbering scheme. The t right before the device number indicates that it is the CD tape device. The device with the minor number of 128 is the control device. The third device, /dev/nrcdt0, is similar in functionality to /dev/nrStp0. It is a no-rewind device. However, unloading the CD is not something normally done, therefore this is *not* a no-unload device.

### Mice

For the most, mice are only used on the main console or with X terminals. Rarely are they used in conjunction with anything other than X Windows. However, there is the usemouse utility that allows you to use a mouse with vi or sysadmsh.

There are three basic types of mice. I say "basic types," because there are only three types of drivers that you can install. If the pointing device you are using is commonly referred to as a trackball, the signals it sends to the computer are the same as if it were a mouse. (You roll the ball forward and the cursor moves up. You move the mouse forward and the cursor moves up as well.) The same thing applies for cordless mice.

If you install any mouse on your system, the associated device resides in /dev/mouse. (Logical place, huh?) Should you install a serial mouse, the system will actually use the same serial driver as does a standard COM port. This makes sense as the signals coming from the mouse are essentially the same as if it were a terminal or modem on that port. On my system with a Logitech trackball, I have two devices in /dev/mouse:

```
crw-rw-rw-  2 bin    bin    5, 0 Feb 26 1994 logitech_ser0
crw-rw-rw-  2 bin    bin    5, 0 Feb 26 1994 mouseman_ser0
```

As we can see, these devices have a major number of 5, which is the standard serial driver. Adding a keyboard mouse creates the device /dev/mouse/kb0, with a major number of 20. Bus mice have a major number of 16 and have the name /dev/mouse/bus0 or /dev/mouse/bus1.

In addition to the more well-known mouse devices, there are dozens of additional devices in /dev/mouse. The slave pseudo-mouse device with the name /dev/mouse/mp?, has a major number of 17. The master pseudo-mouse device with the name /dev/mouse/pmp? has a major number of 18. (It is very common for master/slave pairs to have major numbers that are off by 1.)

### Miscellaneous Devices

The directory /dev/string contains special devices that are used as the system is booting. The first thing used is /dev/string/boot. This is the string that is built from user input at the boot: prompt as well as from the contents of /etc/default/boot.

Should you want to install a boot-time loadable driver, the device /dev/string/pkg contains information about the devices being linked in. The last of the three, /dev/string/cfg, contains the concatenation of the configuration strings shown at boot. These are the lines that show up as %disk, %floppy, and so on as the system is booting. Do a `cat` of /dev/string/cfg and compare that to the output of `hwconfig`.

At this point we begin to break into the more esoteric device nodes on the system. (As if the devices in /dev/string are not esoteric enough.) Most users have seen all of the devices we have talked about at one time or another. With over a hundred different devices, there are only a few that the average user has seen before. Although many of these are pretty familiar in terms of being recognizable as part of the system, very few are common enough for even the most seasoned administrator to have cause to use directly.

In most cases there are only a couple devices of each type. Therefore, the minor numbering schemes that we talked about above, just aren't needed. Instead, minor numbers are assigned relatively arbitrarily. It is difficult to decide where to begin, so let's flip a coin and start with the device nodes that represent something physical.

The first set is the video devices, or display adapters. These all have the major number 52. If we look in /etc/conf/cf.d/mdevice we see that major number 52 is the da device, which stands for Display Adapter. These are simply the drivers for your video card. The names are obvious and the devices in this group are: /dev/cga, /dev/color, /dev/colour, /dev/ega, /dev/mono, /dev/monochrome, and /dev/vga.

Next we have memory devices. These have a major number of 4. To access the system's physical memory, use /dev/mem. Its partner, /dev/kmem, is used to access kernel memory. Lastly, we have /dev/null, a.k.a. "the bit bucket." This device essentially represents nonexistence. To send output to never-never land, you redirect it to /dev/null. To destroy the contents of a file you can send the contents of /dev/null into that file.

Another memory device is /dev/ram00. This represents a 16K ramdisk, which is the smallest the system allows. It has a major number of 31. Since this is the smallest size one can make a ramdisk, it is logical that the minor number be 0. However, if you want to create a larger ramdisk you can. You could also create multiple ramdisks of a given size. For more details on ramdisks, see the ramdisk(HW) man-page.

Next are a few devices that access the CMOS and the system clock, these include /dev/clock and /dev/rtc; which both act as interfaces to the hardware real-time clock and have a major number of 8. /dev/cmos is the interface to the system CMOS. /dev/mcapos is the interface to the CMOS clock. Both of these have a major number of 7.

The next device, `/dev/prf`, is used by the operating system profiler and stands alone. It has no other devices related to it. This device is used to interface with profiling information and addresses. Its major number and minor number are 9,0. Another device that stands alone is `/dev/error`. Its major number is 32 and like the other "loner" device, it has a minor number of 0. The purpose of this device is to make error messages available to system daemons.

Should you have system auditing enabled, your system will be able to access the two devices `/dev/auditr` and `/dev/auditw`. These are, respectively, the audit read device and audit write device. The audit daemon uses `/dev/auditr` to get audit collection information. Applications that are authorized to write audit records will write them to `/dev/auditw`. These have the major and minor numbers of 21,0 and 21,1 respectively.

### Changes in OpenServer

The first change I noticed to the device nodes was that `/dev/root` is no longer major/minor 1,40, but rather at 1,42. The reason for this is the introduction of the `/dev/boot` filesystem. The `/dev/boot` device is at 1,40, since during boot things are expected to be in the first filesystem of the active partition. Here is where the `boot` program lies, as well as the kernel itself. Once the kernel is running, access of the root filesystem is made through the device node `/dev/root` and is independent of the major and minor number. Because of this, it was easier to put the `/dev/boot` in the first filesystem and then mount it onto `/boot`, rather than changing dozens of programs to boot somewhere else. There is more significance to `/dev/boot` filesystem that we get into in later sections.

Another change is moving the device `/dev/prf` into `/dev/string`. In doing this, it no longer has a major minor number of 9,0. Instead, it was changed to conform to the pattern of the other devices in `/dev/string`. Now its major number is 34 and its minor number is 4.

New devices within `/dev/byte` provide an unlimited, continuous stream of bytes with a constant value. The minor number they use (23) is for the 'byte' device driver. These devices can be used for testing purposes. Maybe you want to test a serial device, and you want to ensure that the characters coming through the line have the same value. The example in the `byte(HW)` man-page describes sending a stream of `0x07` through `/dev/tty2d`. Since this is the <BELL> character it would make a good test. Once the connection is made, you hear the bell.

In my mind, the man-page is confusing in terms of what value is sent. It says that, "The value of each byte is the same as the minor device number of the file." Okay, what value? If I have a device `/dev/byte/hex/37` with a minor number 37, should the device output a hex 0x37 or decimal 37? It has to be the decimal value. Consider the octal values in particular. If you wanted to send a byte with the decimal value of 255, this would be 377 in octal. Since the minor number cannot be over 255 (they're stored in one byte), there is no way to create a device with that minor number.

The reason for the different directories is to make things easier for humans. For example, if I wanted to send a stream of decimal 37, I could create a node (using the mknod command) in /dev/byte/decimal called 37 with a minor number of 37. If you did a cat of this device, you'd see a stream of percent signs filling up your screen. You could also create a device /dev/byte/hex/25 that would do the same thing.

To make life easier, I could even create a new directory, /dev/byte/ascii, where the names of the device nodes are their ascii names. Using the example above, I could create a device /dev/byte/ascii/%, that looked like this:

```
crw-r--r--  1 root    sys    23, 37 Jun 8 11:24 /dev/byte/ascii/%
```

Catting this device gives me the same stream of percent signs.

There is also a special device /dev/zero that can be used as an unlimited source of zero-value bytes.

Also new to OpenServer is the /dev/table directory. Each device has the major number 34, which is for the tab driver. These devices provide access to various system tables. The minor number of the device determines what table is read. This scheme allows commands and utilities access to the tables without the need to understand where the tables reside in kernel memory. Note that the information that these devices provide is in binary format that the appropriate command knows how to read. What the device nodes are can be seen in Table 5–4.

OpenServer introduced the concept of virtual disks. Although the concept is not new to the computer world, OpenServer is the first SCO release to provide them. Although we get into more details later, we can briefly describe them as areas where you take portions of one or more physical disks and make them appear as if they were one logical (or virtual) drive. The device nodes associated with virtual drives are of the form /dev/rdsk/vdisk# or /dev/dsk/vdisk# where # represents the number of that virtual drive.

Also new to OpenServer is direct support for floptical drives. Floptical drives allow access to normal 3.5" floppies, but also to special magneto-optical floppies that can store up to 21Mb of data. We'll cover the physical characteristics of floptical drives in the section on hardware.

The device driver to access floptical is Sflp, with a minor number of 48. The minor device numbering scheme is similar to that for hard disks and floppies.

**Table 5–4**   Contents of /dev/tab

| Name | Minor Number | Description | Structure |
|------|--------------|-------------|-----------|
| proc | 16 | Processes | proc |
| pregion | 17 | Process regions | pregion |
| region | 18 | Regions | region |
| eproc | 19 | Process extensions | eproc |
| file | 20 | Open files | file |
| inode | 21 | Active i-nodes | inode |
| s5inode | 22 | S5/AFS i-node cache | s5inode |
| diskinfo | 24 | Drive partitioning | diskinfo |
| dkdosinfo | 25 | DOS partitions | dkdosinfo |
| clist | 26 | Character buffers | cblock |
| mount | 28 | Mounted filesystems | mount |
| flckrec | 29 | Outstanding file locks | filock |
| avenrun | 30 | Run averages | short unt |
| sysinfo | 64 | System information | sysinfo |
| minfo | 65 | Paging and swapping | minfo |
| extinfo | 66 | Other information | extinfo |
| v | 48 | System configuration | var |
| tune | 49 | Tunable parameters | tune |

Table 5–5 shows how the bits are defined. The devices themselves reside in /dev/dsk if they are block devices and /dev/rdsk if they are character devices. Device names have the format

```
fp<device_number>3<density>
```

where density is d for 720Kb (double density), h for 1.44Mb (high density), and v21 for 21MB (very high density).

Another new, and in my opinion interesting, set of devices are those accessed through the marriage driver. These devices reside in the /dev/marry directory and allow you to access a regular file as if it were a device node. You can even create filesystems on such devices, mount them, and even run fsck. The only permanent file is /dev/rmarry, with major number of 76 and minor 0. Other devices also have a major number 76, but their minor number is dependent on the order in which they were created. Unless you've established marriages before, then you probably don't have a /dev/marry directory.

**Table 5–5**    Bits for Floppy Device Minor Numbers

| | | | | | BITS | | | | | |
|---|---|---|---|---|---|---|---|---|---|---|
| 9 | 8 | 7 | 6 | 5 | 4 | 3 | 2 | 1 | 0 | Description |
| — | — | — | — | — | — | — | 0 | 0 | 0 | 720KB (DD) |
| — | — | — | — | — | — | — | 0 | 0 | 1 | 1.44MB (HD) |
| — | — | — | — | — | — | — | 1 | 0 | 0 | 21MB (VHD) |
| — | — | — | — | — | 0 | 0 | — | — | — | Reserved |
| — | — | — | — | 0 | — | — | — | — | — | Set to zero |
| — | — | — | 0 | — | — | — | — | — | — | Floppy disk |
| X | X | X | — | — | — | — | — | — | — | Unit # (0–6) |

If your machine is capable for Advanced Power Management (APM), then you may have a /dev/pwr/bios device on your machine. The concept of APM is that your machine can detect when it hasn't been used for a long time and can turn off certain functions. Note that not all machines that have this ability can communicate with the operating system.

If you have a PCI bus on your machine, you can gain access to it using the /dev/pci device, which has major number 22.

In our discussion on shell basics, I talked about the three initial file descriptors (0, 1, and 2) that represent, respectively, standard input, standard output, and standard error. OpenServer provides three device nodes that scripts or programs can access without having to explicitly know where these file descriptors point. These are /dev/stdin, /dev/stdout, and /dev/stderr. All have a major number of 24, which is for the dup driver. Opening one of these devices is equivalent to issue a dup() system call, which makes a duplicate of the file descriptor. The minor numbers of these three devices are the same as the file descriptors they represent. So /dev/stdin has a minor number of 0, /dev/stdout has a minor number of 1, and /dev/stderr has a minor number of 2. The directory /dev/fd is used for duplicates; for file descriptors 0 through 99.

## The Link Kit

One of the major advantages SCO has is that it tries to be as open as possible. This means that SCO tries to support as many different kinds of devices from as many different vendors as possible. SCO supports more different kinds and manufacturers of devices than any other UNIX vendor. For sales people this is a major advantage because they can often sell products based on the fact that certain hardware is "100% compatible" with a name brand that SCO supports. This is not to say that sales people try to deceive you. Rather, the customer often upgrades an operating system for hardware they already have. If the vendor falsely claims compatibility, this can become a nightmare for SCO Support.

For example, SCO has never made the claim that it supports the WonderTrack SCSI Tape Drive[1]. However, since the manufacturer claims that it is "100% compatible" with an Archive 5150, which SCO does support, customers believe that SCO is obligated to help them if things go wrong.

The bottom line on this issue is whether or not the drive is manufactured by Archive. If so, and it just has a different label on it, SCO support assumes that it is an Archive in disguise and they will try to help as best they can.

Unfortunately, things are not always that easy. Many brands claim compatibility, not because they actually are the brand they claim to be, but rather because their engineers used the supported brand as a model and built their new drive based on that model. The result is a crap shoot at best.

However, customers have trouble believing this. Many, if not most, will insist that since the manufacturer claims it is 100% compatible then every operating system vendor is obligated to support it. This goes for SCO as well.

I have talked with at least one customer with this attitude. He suggested that the SCO driver must be defective since SCO SCSI drivers work with almost every other kind of SCSI tape drive, but his. He insisted it wasn't a hardware problem because the tape drive worked fine under DOS. (No need to mention that in the box the tape drive came in was a DOS driver from the drive manufacturer. That obviously had nothing to do with it working under DOS and not under SCO.)

If the drive manufacturer supplied a SCO driver, then it's obviously *not* the same one that SCO supports. Therefore, the customer needed to talk to the manufacturer. Since there was no driver, the customer's assertion was that it worked just like the "real" one and therefore was supported by SCO. Since there was a "bug" in our driver and we support the tape drive that his was compatible with, we were obligated to stay on the phone with him until we had a resolution. At least, that's what he contended.

### The Flow of Things

Anyone who has installed an SCO UNIX system has probably gone through at least one kernel relink. Depending on the speed of the computer (both processor

---

1.    Names changed to protect me from lawsuits.

and I/O subsystem) and the number of devices, this process may take several minutes. During those few minutes very little activity appears on the screen. If it weren't for the flashing hard disk light, you might think that the machine had hung. After a few minutes, you are reassured that the machine has, in fact, not hung, but is continuing the task of building a new kernel.

I have talked with many customers, running ODT 3.0 who believe that there is something wrong with their system because the link kit is reported missing when installing a new device. All this means is that when the system was first installed, whoever did the install just didn't install the link kit. If the installation script for this new device does not ask you if it should install the link kit, you can use `custom` or the Software Manager. The link kit is part of the Extended Utilities package in ODT, but part of the CORE package in OpenServer. Because a kernel relink is needed for the changes to take effect, you cannot change kernel parameters without the link kit being installed.

In the process of a kernel relink (or kernel rebuild as it is often called) several major things take place. One of the first things is construction of tables based on kernel parameters. These parameters are at values that are either set by default or ones that are set by the system administrator. These are commonly referred to as "kernel tunable parameters," or "kernable tunables" for short. (Not really. One of the first UNIX gurus I met in SCO Support used to get tongue-tied when explaining kernel tunable parameters and would often slip and say "kernable tunables". Ever since then it sort of stuck within the support department.)

Another major part of the kernel rebuild is the linking of all the appropriate drivers into the system. I say "appropriate" because some drivers exist on the system, which may have to be *explicitly* linked into the kernel. As I mentioned before, these drivers serve as the interface between the operating system and the hardware. In addition to the drivers, the system must ensure that all the necessary device nodes associated with each driver is present on the system. Remember that the system uses the device nodes to access the physical hardware. What's the point of having a device driver if there is no way to access the device?

For the most part, every system administrator understands that much about a kernel relink. Once the relink is finished, the changes we just made will be a part of the new kernel and once we reboot, these changes will take effect. New drivers are added and old ones are removed. If we need to change kernel parameters, this is the way to do it.

If you are like me, the knowledge that a new kernel is being built is not enough. You want to know more about what is happening during that rebuild. What steps is the kernel going through as it creates a new, slightly modified version of the operating system? In order to better understand the details of a kernel rebuild, we should first look at the big picture.

What good is it to know all this? To answer that, I need to tell you a story from SCO Support. One of my favorite customers was John Esak. Those of you who have been around for a while might remember John as the publisher of *The Guru*. After he decided to stop doing *The Guru*, John became a columnist for *SCO World*. In this position, he often called into SCO Support.

I remember one call late in the afternoon during the last couple of months I was at SCO. John had installed a driver for an SCSI device that seemed to have given his link kit a severe case of indigestion. He had backups, but the only problem he had was that the relink failed miserably. Even after removing the driver, he was still getting errors.

Now John is not a stupid man. In fact, he is quite bright and I enjoy talking with him for that very reason. I know that when he calls, he has gone through all the basics and that the issue is probably somewhat complex. This call was no exception.

One thing that comes in handy is listening to what the system has to tell you. The error messages that the relink generates are often very useful in figuring out what is wrong. Fortunately, this was one of those cases.

During the relink, John was getting error messages about a missing device in `mdevice` (`/etc/conf/cf.d/mdevice`). (We will discuss `mdevice` in a minute.) When we checked `mdevice`, sure enough, the device was missing. I read the line in my `mdevice` file to John and we added this in the right spot in his `mdevice`. Crossing our fingers, we tried the relink again. This time we got the same error message, but referring to a different device.

Rather than replacing and relinking for every conceivable device, we decided to simply go through my `mdevice` file, line-by-line to see what John was missing. As it turned out, the removal script for that driver had removed all references to every other SCSI device on the system! Not a good thing to do. After we had replaced the missing entries, John was able to relink and reboot without any errors at all.

This is also a good case study to remind us that any time you want to make major changes to your system or add unsupported drivers, it's a good idea to do a backup of your system or at least a backup of the link kit.

What does this have to do with the subject at hand? Well, if neither John nor I had an understanding of how a kernel relink worked, we may have been forced to restore from the backups. Since both of us do know, we had the problem solved in about thirty minutes.

Knowing what happens during a kernel relink is not only important for when something goes wrong, but it is also helpful in understanding how the kernel is built: This includes what components go into the kernel and what process the system goes through to create a new kernel. Knowing how your operating system is put together is helpful in administering it. This is also helpful in understanding many of the concepts and processes that we will get into later.

So, what's it all about? Well, the kernel is composed of a few core files, several dozen device drivers and a handful of configuration files. These device drivers are the sets of routines that the kernel uses to access everything else that is not part of itself. Everything from RAM to terminals are accessed through device drivers. The configuration files are used by the kernel to set internal parameters and define the characteristics of the device drivers and other aspects of the system. These files along with the programs used to build a new kernel are jointly referred to as the link kit.

With the exception of a few odds and ends, the link kit resides in the directory /etc/conf. For simplicity, I will make references to files and directories relative to this directory. Among the more significant subdirectories is the bin directory, which contains most of the programs used to build the kernel. The sdevice.d directory contains information about the particular hardware (base address, IRQ) and whether or not it should be linked into the kernel. Paired with this are the subdirectories in pack.d. These directories contain the object code modules for the kernel and device drivers as well as configuration files.

The init.d directory contains information used to create a new inittab file. The inittab file is what the system uses when booting to determine what processes it should start and when. Using the file cf.d/init.base as its starting point, the files in init.d are added to the end of init.base. These normally contain information about terminals that are attached to the system and whether the system should run a getty process on them to allow logins.

The working directory for the kernel build is cf.d. Using files in this directory, the kernel determines such things as which drivers should be included and what kernel parameters need to get changed and to what values. Since the work gets accomplished based on the information in the files in cf.d, this is probably the best place to start. The flow of a relink we will see in Figure 5–11.

The first step in creating a new kernel is the program link_unix. This is found in the /etc/conf/cf.d directory and is started either by the system administrator or automatically by some installation scripts. If you are running SCO OpenServer, you can start a relink through the Hardware/Kernel Manager of SCOAdmin or through the sysadmsh in ODT or in both cases running the com-

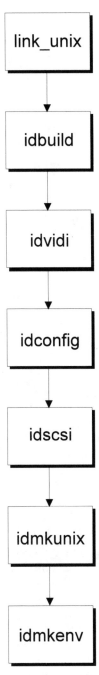

**Figure 5–11**    The flow of a kernel relink.

mand /etc/conf/cf.d/link_unix. (Both sysadmsh and the Hardware/Kernel Manager end up calling link_unix.)

The first thing link_unix does is to remind you that this is a relatively lengthy process and asks you to, "Please wait." After the lights flash and the disk rattles, you are asked a couple of questions and a few moments later a new kernel is resting quietly in your root directory (/dev/stand on OpenServer). What happened? Aside from asking you if you wanted the kernel to boot by default and whether or not you wanted the kernel environment to be rebuilt, the system gave you little indication of what it was doing.

The first place to start is the link_unix program, which resides in /etc/conf/cf.d. Since link_unix is a shell script we can look at it. Because it is a small file, we can look at its entire contents with a simple cat link_unix. However you can use any other viewing tools such as more, pg, or view.

In order to describe the relink process within a reasonable number of pages, I need to make some assumptions. The first is general knowledge about how UNIX command syntax works. The second assumption is that you have a basic understanding of shell programming. These are not required to understand the concepts in this section. If you have trouble with this, take a quick look at the section on shell basics or the sh(C) man-page.

After the initial comments, the link_unix program establishes the environment it will run under. This allows you to rebuild a kernel in a different environment than the one that exists on that machine. For example, you might want to use the kernel on a different system that has different drivers or different kernel parameters. You could even rebuild the kernel for a version of the operating system than was different that the one you were on. This is also useful when you want to test out a new driver or new kernel configurations without destroying your existing link kit.

In establishing the relink environment, we run across one of the first things that is different between the two releases. If you remember from our discussion on SCO basics, one of the key concepts in the new release is the idea of Software Storage Objects (SSOs). Many of the components of the link kit are symbolic links. Since many of the references to file during the relink are relative to the current directory, we have to ensure that all paths are evaluated correctly.

The evaluation of the paths is accomplished through the shell script /etc/conf/bin/path_map.sh which is "dotted" from within link_unix. The functions within path_map.sh are now available to link_unix *and* any script it calls. Rather than sidetracking too much, I will simply suggest that you take a look inside of path_map.sh to see how things get remapped.

In OpenServer, we now have to "build" the paths that were taken for granted in ODT 3.0. The last line of the script does an `exec` of `idbuild`, passing to it all the arguments passed to `link_unix`. Which `idbuild` program is started, depends on the previously built paths. This is really where things get going.

Since the `link_unix` script does an `exec` of `idbuild`, this is a good place to go from here. Luckily, `idbuild` is also a shell script, so we can examine it the same way we did with `link_unix`. Well, not exactly. `Idbuild` is six times larger than `link_unix`, so examining takes a little more work. We could start our examination with the top line and disect everything from there. However, this does little to help in our understanding of what's going on compared to the amount it would annoy and maybe confuse us. Fortunately, there is something built into the shell that we can use. If we put a `set -x` as the first line of `idbuild`, we see the script on our screen as it progresses. If you remember from our discussion on shell basics, this echoes every line to the screen prior to executing it.

However, if you just added the `set -x` and started `link_unix`, when it got to `idbuild` things would be scrolling across the screen. Therefore, we need to slow it down a little. We can do this by piping the output to `more` or `pg`. Remember that the `set -x` sends the output to `stderr`, so to send that through `pg` the command would look like this:

```
link_unix 2>&1 | more
```

Let's start our examination by adding the `set -x` as I described above and then start `link_unix`. If you have a standard 25 line terminal, you only see comments in the first screenful. Although in many scripts the comments tell you little more than copyright information, the comments here give you a quick overview of what's going on. Pressing the space bar once (assuming we are in `more`), brings us the first lines of commands that are executed.

The first few things done are setting up variables to use later. One is the `Pre-serve` variable which determines whether or not intermediate files created during the rebuild should be removed. If set to YES, all the intermediate files are left alone when the rebuild is finished. Otherwise they get removed. Keep in mind that that does *not* mean that the kernel does not have to recompile them the next time. It does. All this means is that there are a lot of .o files lying around which might be useful for debugging drivers or to satisfy your curiosity.

New to OpenServer is the ability to include as well as exclude certain drivers. These are governed by the `Aflag`, `Bflag`, and `Exclude` variables. These variables are used at different times during the kernel rebuild to determine what gets linked into the kernel and what doesn't.

One aspect of the relink that can be changed is the development system used. By default, all the tools the relink uses are relative to the root directory of the system (/). This is defined by the DEVSYS variable. Being able to redefine the development system is useful, for example, when you want to use a different set of programs and libraries to do the relink. You may have a different version of SCO Development System or one from some third party.

In addition to this, we also define the root directory of relink. By default, this is / as well. In ODT 3.0, this is determined by calculating the directory name that is three levels up from where we start link_unix. Since link_unix is started in /etc/conf/cf.d, three levels up is /. Although this is really the same directory, this is three levels up from /etc/conf/cf.d and not /etc/conf/bin, where idbuild resides. This is because we are still in /etc/conf/cf.d, and we start idbuild as ../bin/idbuild.

Let's say we wanted to use an alternate link kit and we started the relink with /test/etc/conf/cf.d/link_unix. Then ROOT=/test. If it does turn out that ROOT is /, it needs to be altered slightly for certain constructs later. As a result, it ends up as ROOT=/., with the period included. This is to prevent the system from thinking that, for example, the file //bin/date is the program /date on the machine //bin as would be the case on a machine running XENIX-Net or Lan Manager. To ensure the names come out right, ROOT is forced to be /./ instead of //. Not to worry. The system interprets these correctly.

In OpenServer, the ROOT variable is checked. If it is set to anything other than /, it is left alone. If set to /, then it is reset to the null string (ROOT="").

Continuing through the file, we find the familiar message about the system rebuild and the request to Please Wait. We have seen that the root directory for the rebuild is not hardcoded. The idbuild script tells us what it has determined ROOT to be with this line:

```
echo "\t Root for this system build is ${ROOT}"
```

After defining a variable used for path definitions (ID) and some locks (IDLCK), idbuild creates a flag that says the relink has begun:

```
>$ROOT/etc/.unix_reconf
```

At first glance, this looks pretty insignificant. All it does is create a zero length file. Although this file has zero length, it is very important as it serves as a flag. If for some reason the rebuild is not successful, the system needs to know that it had started in order to recover properly. We'll talk more about this file later.

Next, idbuild removes files that may have been left lying around and that it will later recreate (the several lines with rm -f). This is done to prevent any of the other utilities and programs from failing, as many of them cannot overwrite existing files.

Then, all the object files are cleared out of the `cf.d` directory. If this is a normal relink, this directory is `/etc/conf/cf.d`. We previously did a cd into `$ID/cf.d` on ODT 3.0 and into `${cf_d}` on OpenServer. If we haven't redefined `$ROOT` to anything for testing, these would be `/etc/conf`. Therefore, we'll end up in `/etc/conf/cf.d` prior to starting to remove these files. However, even if we started the relink as `/test/etc/conf/cf.d/link_unix`, the paths are properly parsed. We would end up with `$ROOT` set to `/test` and `$ID` or `${cf_d}` set to `/test/etc/conf`.

At this point, all the `stubs.o` and `space.o` files are removed from the subdirectories in `/etc/conf/pack.d` as well. The `pack.d` directory contains the object modules for all the drivers on the system as well as relevant configuration information in the form of C-source code modules.

After this clean-up, `idbuild` uses `awk` to process the `mdevice` file (normally `/etc/conf/cf.d/mdevice`). The `mdevice` file is the device driver module description file. It contains descriptions of the characteristics of each of the device drivers. Using the names that `awk` pulled out of the `mdevice` file, `idbuild` creates a new, temporary file, `sdevice.new`, by concatenating the contents of the files in the `sdevice.d` directory. Whereas the `mdevice` file contains descriptions of all the possible device drivers, the `sdevice` file contains information only on the installed drivers.

In OpenServer, the processing of `mdevice` and `sdevice` is different. The primary reason is the ability to include or exclude specific drivers. Here, the flow of `idbuild` changes based on which of the flags is set. For example a normal relink follows one path, whereas one linking in just the base devices would follow another. One reason for just linking in the base devices is trying to get your kernel to fit on a boot floppy. If you link in all the drivers, it may be too large.

After creating the `sdevice.new` entry, the `idbuild` script creates two configuration files in the `cf.d` directory: `sfsys` and `mfsys`. These contain information about the filesystems configured. This is done by `cat`'ing the contents of the files in `/etc/conf/sfsys.d` and `/etc/conf/mfsys.d`.

Next, the video devices available are configured by `idvidi`. The program `idvidi` is also a shell script and sets up for the program `idvdbuild`. Unfortunately, `idvdbuild` is a binary program, and since we don't have access to the source code, we can't take a look inside. Let's just say that the `idvdbuild` program configures the installed video devices. Should this process fail, temporary files left behind are cleaned up and then the `idbuild` script exits.

Next, the `idconfig` program configures all of the drivers in the `sdevice.new` file. The `idconfig` program's primary responsibility is to read the system's configuration files and report any conflicts or errors. Here again, should this process fail, it cleans up temporary files left behind and then exits the `idbuild` script.

Despite the fact that `idconfig` is a binary program, we ought to look at it in some detail. By carefully watching a relink and making some intentional mistakes in some of the configuration files, you can get a feeling for the flow of things.

One thing this program is responsible for is to ensure the overall integrity of the various configuration files. If we look back at `mdevice`, we see that there are nine columns. Should one of the entries have fewer than nine columns, the system has no way of knowing which column is missing. Therefore, it has to stop to avoid creating an unbootable kernel.

As we mentioned earlier, adding or reconfiguring drivers is not the only reason that the kernel needs to be rebuilt. Changing the values of kernel tunable parameters also requires a rebuild of the kernel before the changes can take effect. Ensuring that these values are legitimate is also a function of the `idconfig` program. The first thing read is the `mtune` file. Since this is an 'm-file', this is the master tuning file, and it contains the default values for the tunable kernel parameters. In addition, this file also defines *suggested* maximum and minimum values for these parameters.

Note that in some cases, the maximums can be exceeded and all that happens is that you get a warning during the rebuild. However, I recommend that you only exceed those values where you *personally* know the value will not cause trouble on your system.

Although it is possible to change the default value of a kernel parameter by directly editing the `mtune` file, this is not recommended. Defining *changed* values is the responsibility of the `stune` file. After reading the `mtune` file, `idconfig` reads the `stune` file to determine if any value has been changed. On any system, this file will contain some values, even if you have never made any changes yourself. These values are "changed" during the original installation relink.

As the `idconfig` wraps up its business, one of the last things it does is to create the `conf.c`, `config.h`, `vector.c`, and `fsconf.c` files. Without going into detail, these files are configuration files and are *created* by `idconfig`. The `idconfig` program outputs the individual lines of these files, including all the `#include` statements and the necessary `external declarations` and the arrays that are defined in these files. In fact, `idconfig` generates *everything* in these files.

The `conf.c` file contains `external declarations` and structure initialization for the kernel and driver routines. The header file for this is `config.h` and like other header files, this one contains `#defines`. The `vector.c` file contains information similar to `conf.h`, but it concerns itself solely with the interrupt vector table. Lastly, the `fsconf.c` file contains the file system's routine prototypes. After it has created all these files, the `idconfig` program has finished its work. It then exits, and the flow of the kernel rebuild is now back in the hands of `idbuild`.

One thing that I have to point out is a comment that appears in each of these programs which says

```
/*
 * This file is automatically generated by idconfig(ADM),
 * usually run by idbuild(ADM).   *** DO NOT EDIT ***
 */
```

Listen to it! Do not edit any of these files. If you're *very* lucky, all that will happen is that you will end up with a kernel that won't boot. Why is that lucky? Well, if you are unlucky, you will trash your filesystems.

The next program run from `idconfig` is `idscsi` and as its name implies, it is responsible for the SCSI devices on the systems. The `idscsi` program could have been included in `idconfig`. However, by itself it is half the size of the entire `idconfig` program. From a programmers point of view it's much easier to maintain as two separate programs. There is also the logic that because of the very nature of SCSI devices, it should be handled separately.

For example, in order to access a IDE hard disk, the kernel needs to access the IDE controller. However, to access a SCSI hard disk, the kernel needs to know not only how to access the SCSI hard disk, but also how to access the SCSI host adapter. This is the same level of complexity that applies to any SCSI device. I realize that this is a vast oversimplification. However, this does show how SCSI devices add an additional level of complexity to the system.

The basic configuration file for SCSI devices is `cf.d/mscsi`. It contains information about what SCSI devices are on the system, how they are configured, and what SCSI host adapters they are attached to. However, `mscsi` is not the only file used. As I mentioned early, `mdevice` contains configuration information about all the devices on the system—including SCSI devices. If there is no entry in `mdevice` for a particular SCSI device, `idscsi` issues a warning message. This would also happen if you tried to add an SCSI device to an adapter that didn't exist.

In OpenServer, having the `Bflag` or `Aflag` set changes the flow of things slightly at this point. If either is set, then `idbuild` creates an `mscsi` file based on the installation kernel. This assumes several default values for your SCSI configuration.

After the `idscsi` program is finished, all the preparations for creating a new kernel in ODT 3.0 are finished. However, if you have OpenServer, there are a couple of things left to do. First we create the device registry using the `idmkreg` program. Next we a configuration file necessary for the kernel STREAM linker. This is done by the `/etc/kslgen` script.

At this point `idbuild` begins to compile and link the new kernel. Compile? Link? Don't you need a compiler to do that? Isn't the compiler part of the SCO Development System? Right on both counts. However, in order to allow kernel rebuild, there must be a compiler, linker, and even assembler on the system. These programs are hard to find and even harder to use. They were designed with one task in mind: Create a new kernel.

Experience has told me that there are people out there that are going to try to use these to create programs of their own. I say it three times: *Don't! Don't! Don't!* Using these programs to compile source code is not supported by SCO, so don't even bother calling them. They can't help you. As I said before these programs do one thing and that is to create the new kernel. They have nowhere near the complexity needed for an end user to be able to use them to create run-time applications. Besides, most of you don't have any of the standard libraries, so the compiler is of very little use. If you need to write C programs, get a copy of the SCO Development System.

As a front end (maybe to hide things from foolish users), `idbuild` calls `idmkunix`. This is the program that does all the compiling, assembling, and linking. The most obvious part of the process are the files that were just created by `idconfig`. Since these need to be part of the kernel in order to have any effect, they must be first compiled, which creates the respective .o files.

These .o files are a few of the object modules, which go into the kernel. As I mentioned earlier, each driver exists as an object module in the appropriate directory in `/etc/conf/pack.d` (the `driver.o` files). They too must be linked in. Each driver marked with a `Y` in the `sdevice` file is included.

Those of you who have already poked around may have found out that there are a few object files that find their way into the kernel which are not listed in `mdevice` and `sdevice`. These are the object files that compose the kernel of the kernel and reside in `/etc/conf/pack.d/kernel`. It kind of makes sense that you don't need to tell the kernel to link in these files. It's possible to run without some of the "extras" like hard disk drivers. However, without the basic components of the operating system nothing runs.

In addition to the object files, the majority of the drivers have configuration files associated with them. These are the space.c files; most of which are in the subdirectories of pack.d. Should a driver not need a configuration file, it still needs prototypes and include files. These find their way into the kernel by means of the stubs.c files, which are also in the subdirectories of pack.d.

Once the modules are linked to form the new kernel, idmkunix has finished work. It then exits and flow returns to idbuild, which then does a bit of cleanup. Some of the more observant readers may have noticed references to scodb in the later part of idbuild. This portion of idbuild enables you to create a debuggable kernel. However, this is not important to you unless you are a developer of SCO specific device drivers. Besides, scodb is not a shipping product anyway.

At this point, idbuild creates a file called $ROOT/etc/.new_unix. Note that, as with most things, this is relative to the root of the kernel rebuild. If you have created a directory tree for testing, then this is relative to that root. If not, it is relative to /. The .new_unix file has no contents but simply serves as a flag that a new kernel has been created. Next, idmkdev is called. Since it is a script, we can take a look at it.

One of the first things idmkdev does is to check for the existence of the .new_unix file. If .new_unix doesn't exist, there is no need to continue and the script exits.

If .new_unix does exist, idmkdev begins the process of rebuilding the kernel environment. An important part of the kernel environment is the device nodes. Without them, the programs cannot access devices (at least not well-behaved ones). This is accomplished by the idmknod program, which idmkenv calls. Devices are created based on the entries in the node.d directory.

Let's side-step for a moment and think about what we would normally see on the screen during the relink. One question you are asked is whether or not you want the kernel environment rebuilt. In this context the kernel's environment includes all the device nodes and the /etc/inittab file. Part of the process of rebuilding the kernel environment is the creation of a new /etc/inittab file. A temporary copy is created in /etc/conf/cf.d by combining init.base and the files in /etc/conf/init.d. This copy is then moved into /etc to replace the old inittab. If you choose not to rebuild the kernel environment, /etc/inittab will not get rebuilt. At this point, the kernel rebuild is complete.

It is possible that during the installation of some third party device driver the kernel relink failed miserably. If the rebuild failed, then it is possible that it never created the .new_unix file. So the corresponding section in `idmkenv` was never executed. However, the `/etc/.unix_reconf` file does still exist. It does not get removed until `idmkenv` reaches that section in .new_unix. If .unix_reconf exists, and there is a problem, `idmkenv` will enter the corresponding section and begin to clean-up. The majority of its work is removing temporary and .o files, but an important part of its mission is to remove the last driver that was attempted to be installed. This makes sense because it was probably the addition of the new driver that caused the relink to fail in the first place.

If the reason for the relink is simply changing kernel parameters, there is no need to rebuild the kernel environment. All the required device nodes are there and `inittab` doesn't need to be changed. Therefore, you can answer 'n' when asked whether the kernel environment needs to be rebuilt.

The final line of `idmkenv` is `telinit q`. This tells the system to re-examine the `/etc/inittab` file. The reason for this is that previously in `idmkenv` a new `inittab` was created. If changes had been made to any of the files (`/etc/conf/cf.d/inittab`, `/etc/conf/init.d/*`) then these changes would not take effect until the system is rebooted. By running `telinit q` the changes are immediate.

At this point, `idmkenv` exits and returns control back to `idbuild`. The last line of `idbuild` is simply to exit. Since `idbuild` had been called by `link_unix` with an exec, `idbuild` returns control to the process that called `link_unix`, which is either the user's shell, an installation script, or one of the administration programs. Once you've rebooted, the changes you made will be a part of your new kernel.

Due to the complex nature of both device drivers and the kernel itself, you may have noticed that many issues were glossed over or skipped entirely. This is unfortunate, but necessary due to the limited amount of information you can pack into a book. For more details take a look at the scripts themselves and see what they are doing.

### Key Link Kit Files

**mdevice.**    The `mdevice` file is the device driver module description file. It contains descriptions of the characteristics of each of the device drivers. Let's take a look at part of an `mdevice` file. It consists of dozens of lines in nine columns. Table 5–6 contains a few lines of one `mdevice` file that we can use as reference.

The first column is a mnemonic used by the kernel to identify the particular driver. In simpler terms, it is the internal name of the driver. This is the name used by the system during the relink and is what `awk` is pulling out. By convention, SCO documentation, such as the *Device Driver Writer's Guide* refers to

**Table 5–6**   Examples from `/etc/conf/cf.d/mdevice`

| mnemonic | function list | driver characteristics | handler prefix | block major | block minor | device specific | device specific | DMA |
|---|---|---|---|---|---|---|---|---|
| sio | Iocrwip | iHctk | sio | 0 | 5 | 1 | 100 | −1 |
| aud | Iocrwi | iocr | aud | 0 | 21 | 0 | 0 | −1 |
| fd | Iocrwip | iHODbrcC | fd | 2 | 2 | 1 | 2 | 2 |
| ram | oc | ibk | ram | 31 | 0 | 0 | 0 | −1 |
| vga | — | io | vga | 0 | 0 | 0 | 1 | −1 |
| hd | hoc | irobCcGk | hd | 1 | 1 | 1 | 1 | −1 |
| busmouse | Iocri | iHct | mous | 0 | 16 | 1 | 2 | −1 |
| fp | — | iHor | fp | 0 | 0 | 0 | 1 | −1 |
| ad | I | iHGt | aha | 0 | 3 | 1 | 1 | −1 |
| nmi | I | ios | nmi_ | 0 | 0 | 0 | 1 | −1 |

drivers as *xnamex*. For more information on the naming scheme, take a look at `<sys/cmn_err.h>`.

The second column is a "function list" for the device. For example, if a device has an 'o' in this column, there is a function in its driver to open that device. An example of a device of this type would be a hard disk (`hd`). If there is no device to be opened, there would be no 'o' here. For example, the driver to handle a non-maskable interrupt (`nmi`) only has an initialization routine and there are no hardware-specific functions to be performed when the device is opened. Therefore, there is no open routine in this driver and there is no 'o' in the second column. For details of what functions are possible and what each entry means, see the `mdevice(F)` man-page.

The third column is for the characteristics of that device. Is it a block device like a hard disk or a character device like a terminal? Is this an SCSI device? Does it support 32-bit addresses for DMA-transfers? Is this device even required? All these questions and many more are answered by the characteristics list. This, too, is detailed in the `mdevice(F)` man-page.

The fourth column is the handler prefix of the device. This is the external name for the device and the device driver handler routines associated with this device. This *usually* matches the first column. Since this is normally limited to four characters, it cannot match long names such as `busmouse`. By convention, the driver routines are referred to with the prefix (for example, `xx`) followed by the routine name (for example, `read`). Thus, `xxread()` would be a generic read function and `xxwrite` would be a generic write function. Since the prefix for the floppy driver is `fl`, the floppy read function would be `flread()`. (Here is an example where the driver prefix does *not* match the handler prefix.)

The fifth and sixth columns are the block and character major device numbers. Devices like hard disks and floppies can be accessed as either character or block devices. Therefore, there are entries in both columns of the `hd` and `fd` lines. The serial driver (`sio`) is only a character device, so there is no block major device number. Likewise, the ramdisk driver (`ram`) is only a block device, therefore it has no character major device number. (For more information on major and minor numbers see the section on major and minor numbers.)

The seventh and eighth columns are defined by the device driver. In the case of the Adaptec host adapter driver (`ad`) these are, respectively, the minimum and maximum number of devices that can be associated with the driver. On the serial device driver (`sio`), this value is an offset into a table. In some cases, like the system auditing device (`aud`), these columns are ignored. The last column is the DMA channel used by the device. Should a device not use DMA, like the `vga` driver, there is a -1 in this column.

**sdevice.**    In theory, the "m-files", (`mtune`, `mdevice`) are the "master" files. These should be considered stagnant and unchanging. The "s-files" (`stune`, `sdevice`) are the "system" files and can be changed either directly or with the tools provided by the OS. These files reflect your system's configuration. One of the things contained in the files in `sdevice.d`, is the software priority level (SPL). Since the SPL is in an "s-file," one would think that this is configurable. However, this should not be changed.

Each file in the `sdevice.d` directory has the same structure as the `sdevice` file. This makes sense, since the contents of the files in `sdeviced` are concatenated together to make `sdevice`. If we take a closer look at the files, we can learn details about how specific devices are configured. Let's look at the file `/etc/conf/sdeviced/pa`, as an example. This is the file used to configure the parallel port driver. It should look something like this:

```
pa        Y      1      2      4      7      378      37f      0      0
```

The first field on each line is the name of the device. The second field tells us whether or not the kernel should link in the driver for this device. A `Y` in this column means that the driver should be linked into the kernel. An `N` means that it shouldn't.

It should be noted that in many cases it is *not* sufficient to simply change this Y to an N and have everything work out right. Some devices are defined as *required* (with an r in the third column of mdevice). Changing a Y to an N for a required device causes the relink to halt rather abruptly.

Just like the seventh and eight column in mdevice, the third field in sdevice is driver-specific. The fourth field is the interrupt priority level, which is the same as the system priority level (SPL). A normal value is anything from 1–7. If there is a 0 in this column, the device does not have an interrupt routine.

The fifth field is the type of interrupt the device has. Should the device not have an interrupt routine, this will be 0, like the fourth field. If a driver does have an interrupt routine and the interrupt cannot be shared, there will be a 1 here. If the driver can share an interrupt, a number from 2–6 will be here. This number will be the same for all devices sharing that specific interrupt. The parallel driver has a 4 here, therefore it can share an interrupt with any other driver with a 4 in this column. Like the SPL, this value should not be changed.

Field six is the actual interrupt vector used by the driver. This is the IRQ that the controller is jumped or set to. If the fifth field contains a 0 (that is, no interrupt required), this field is ignored. In this case, we have a 7. As many of you may already know, this is the interrupt vector of the first parallel port.

If we take a look at the output of the hwconfig command or at the hardware screen during boot-up, there is usually at least one entry for a parallel port. If it's configured as lp0 (LPT1), then by default it sits at interrupt 7 and has a base address of 378 to 37f. Looking at the /etc/conf/sdevice.d/pa file, we see in the sixth through eighth column the exact same values. This is no coincidence. (NOTE: The lp driver is not linked in by default so there may not be one present on your system.)

The last two fields are the start and end of start controller memory address which are used by controllers that have internal memory such as some intelligent multiport cards. Some ranges are not allowed. See the sdevice(M) man-page for more details.

**mfsys and sfsys.**  The /etc/conf/cf.d/mfsys file is the configuration file for filesystem types that will be supported when the kernel is relinked. Like many of the other configuration files, mfsys contains a single line for each of the filesystems device drivers that will be included. The source for mfsys is the files in /etc/conf/mfsys.d. Like the mdevice-sdevice pair, the files from mfsys.d that are used are based on the files in /etc/conf/sysfs.d. Each of these files contains a single line with the name of the filesystem to be included and a Y if it should be included and an N if it should not.

The first field is the internal name for the filesystem type. Field 2 is the prefix to the handler functions in the fstypsw structure. The fstypsw structure is functionally the same as the device driver table, except it accesses filesystem device drivers. Field 3 and 4 are flags that are used to fill the fsinfo data structure table entry. Field 5 is a bitmap describing what functions are present.

**mtune and stune.**   As I mentioned before, m-files are the 'master' configuration files and the s-files are those that define the current configuration for your system. So it is with `/etc/conf/cf.d/mtune` and `/etc/conf/cf.d/stune`. The mtune file is the master kernel tunable parameter file and stune contains the parameters that are different on your system. In ODT 3.0 most of these define the absolute size of certain tables and values within the kernel. OpenServer introduced the concept of dynamically configurable parameters, so the parameters in OpenServer define the extent the tables can grow.

The format of the mtune file is as follows:

```
parameter_name          default minimum          maximum
```

Unless changed by the stune file, the relink process takes the name and default value and creates the `#define` entries in `/etc/conf/cf.d/config.c`. If changed in stune, the system will verify that the value specified falls within the range defined by the minimum and maximum defined in mtune. If not, the system will complain during the relink and say that such changes can cause problems. Usually this message can be safely ignored.

In ODT 3.0 it was occasionally necessary to change the maximum value of some of the parameters since the maximum was just not high enough. Without making the change in mtune, the system would complain during the relink. In OpenServer things are a little better. Almost all of the parameters that had to have their maximums increased in ODT 3.0 are now configured dynamically. Therefore, they grow as the need grows. The list of such parameters can be found in mdevice under the heading

```
* Redundant Parameters, required for backward compatibility
```

In most cases, there are new parameters that take the place of the older ones. As I mentioned a moment ago, these new parameters define to what extent the tables can grow and not the absolute value or size.

**node.d.**   The files in the `/etc/conf/node.d` directory are used by idmknod during a kernel relink to create the necessary device nodes (idmknod is called from within idmkenv). Here again, each line has single-line entries which define the devices to be installed. The fields in each line are like this:

```
devicename nodename devicetype minor owner group mode
```

The `devicename` is the same as the first column of the corresponding `mdevice` entry. It is through this connection that the `idmknod` is able to determine what the major number of the node should be.

The `node` name is what the device node will be called when it is created. In some cases (such as `tab`) the new device nodes are created in subdirectories of `/dev`. Therefore, the name of the subdirectory is prepended to the actual device name. In other words, these names are *relative* to the `/dev` directory. If they don't already exist, `idmnod` will create the necessary subdirectories.

The type of file is what will eventually appear as the first entry in the permissions. If a `b`, the new node will be a block device node, a `c` means a character device node, an `l` means a hard link, and an `s` is for a symbolic link.

The minor field is what minor number will be used when this device is created. The owner, group, and mode fields are all optional and define, respectively, the owner, group, and permissions of the new node.

If the new node will be a link then the format of the line will be

```
devicename nodename type oldname
```

where `oldname` is the device node to which this new node should be linked.

### Extended Minor Numbers

So what happens if you have to have more hard disks than will fit within the 256 minor numbers? Well, if some are IDE/ESDI and the rest are SCSI, for example, they can still fit within the 256 values. This is because there are 256 minor numbers for each *driver*. So, if your boot drive is IDE and you have four or less SCSI drives, then the SCSI drives still can be represented by the 256 minor numbers.

A problem arises when you have more than four drives of a *single type*. You then end up banging against the limitation of 256 minor numbers. The reason that there is this limitation is that the original hard disk driver was designed to support ST-506 hard drives. Since you could have two controllers, each with two drives, the 256 values for the minor number were split evenly among the four possible drives. Two bits were then used to represent the possible hard disks. When support was added for ESDI, IDE, and OMTI drives, that scheme still worked nicely.

Then along came SCSI and gummed up the works. Each host adapter could support up to seven drives and you could have multiple host adapters. The result was that the minor numbering scheme was no longer sufficient. That meant that prior to ODT 2.0 and SCO UNIX 3.2.4.0, you could only have four hard disks on your system. This was compounded by the fact that drives were much smaller "in those days."

One solution would have been to redesign the minor numbering scheme. Even taking into account the minor numbers used for the active partition, the whole disk (the "unused partition") you could still use up all the minor numbers. The solution that SCO hit upon was the introduction of *extended minor numbers*. In reality, these are nothing more than another set of minor numbers since they have a *different* major number. Internally, the system translates this "new" major number into the correct one.

When the `mkdev hd` script sees that you are installing the fifth SCSI drive, it uses the `configure` utility to create the new major number and the appropriate extended minor numbers. Therefore, the system administrator doesn't need to do the work themselves. The command would look something like this:

```
./configure -m 1 -b -c -a -X 256
```

The `-m` option is used to create the extended minor number associated with the major number 1. The `-b` and `-c` options configure to create both a block and a character interface to the new driver. The `-a` is used to add the drives. Lastly, `-X` option indicates the *offset* for the new minor numbers. This is the key. When w˄ get done, a new entry exists in `mdevice`. Although not next to each other in the file, the two entries for the hard disk might look like this:

```
hd      hoc     irobCcGk      hd     1      1      1      1      -1
hd      hoc     iobCcGkM      hd     79     79     1      256    -1
```

In our discussion of the `mdevice`, I said that the first column was the name of the driver. In both cases, this is `hd` as both of these entries refer to the same `hd` driver. (Remember that the `hd` driver is just a front-end to the real hard disk driver (wd0, Sdsk, etc.).) The second column was the function list. We see here that both drivers have the same functions. In the third column we see that the `r` is missing from the second entry. This means that it is not required, although the first one is.

The next difference is the `M` in the second entry. This tells the driver that this line is for the extended minor numbers. In turn, this flag changes the meaning of columns seven and eight. Remember that these two columns are device dependent. In this case the seventh column is the "base" minor number (in this case 1) which we know is the hard disk driver. Column eight is the offset.

Let's look at an example. Assume that we have a SCSI boot drive and we want to look at the first file system on the active partition of the fifth drive. Since the fifth drive must be included in the extended minor numbers, it must also have a different major number. Such an entry in the /dev directory might look like this:

```
br--r-----  1 root    backup  79, 40 Sep 26 13:13 /dev/data5
```

When the kernel accesses this filesystem, it sees the major number 79, like it should. Looking at its driver table, offset 79 is for the new hd driver with the extended minor numbers. The minor number here (40) is added to the offset to get the "absolute" minor number. Here we have the offset (256) plus the minor number (40), or an absolute minor number of 296. In binary, this is represented by 100101000.

This binary number is nine digits and not the eight we see with "normal" minor numbers. This makes sense since you can't represent 296 with eight bits. The interesting thing is that, for the most part, the minor numbering scheme is the same. The low order bits represent the division number, the next represent the partition, and the high order represent the physical drive. Graphically it looks like Figure 5–12.

In our example, the binary representation was 100101000. The low order bits are 000, which is obviously 0. This is the 0th division on some partition. The next three bits (indicating the partition) are 101. This is bits 5 and 3 or $2^5 + 2^3 = 40$. The high order bits are 100, which just has bit 9 set, or 256. This gives us $256 + 40 = 296$.

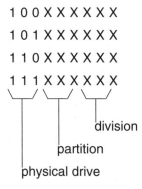

```
1 0 0 X X X X X X
1 0 1 X X X X X X
1 1 0 X X X X X X
1 1 1 X X X X X X
```

division

partition

physical drive

**Figure 5–12**   Extended minor numbers.

We can also look at the high order bits separately. Taken by themselves, the bits 100 represent the number 4. Since we started counting at 0, this is the fifth hard disk. If we added another disk, these higher order bits would be 101, which would be the number 5 or the sixth driver. If we add a seventh and an eighth driver, we would still have enough minor numbers. Once we got to the ninth drive, we would once again run out of minor numbers. No worries, the `mkdev hd` script catches that as well as creates a new set of extended minor numbers. The call to `configure` is the same, but `mdevice` will have a new entry. All three would look like this:

```
hd    hoc    irobCcGk    hd    1    1    1    1    -1
hd    hoc    iobCcGkM    hd    79   79   1    256  -1
hd    hoc    iobCcGkM    hd    82   82   1    512  -1
```

There are two things to note here. First, the minor numbers are not in order. Remember that the minor numbers are allocated based on the order the devices were installed. Since there is a gap between 79 and 82, this implies that other devices were added between the time the fifth drive and the ninth drive were added. The next thing to notice is column eight. In the third entry, the offset is now 512. So when we have a device node like this,

```
br--r-----  1 root    backup  89, 40 Sep 26 13:13 /dev/data9
```

the kernel knows to add 512 to the 40, to give the absolute minor number. In this case, the binary representation of 552 is 1000101001. This has the necessary tenth bit to allow us to get numbers greater than 512. With the high order bits being 1000, this is the number 8, or the ninth drive.

You might think that this tenth digit (a result of the second set of extended minor) will allow you to add eight more drives. While this is correct mathematically, this is not the way the driver works. Before we add the second set, the maximum minor number we can have is 511. Adding 256 to this for the new offset gives us 767. In binary this is 1011111111. In this case, the two high order bits (10) remain the same. Only the two representing the driver number can change. These two bits mean only four new drives can be added. Although this might seem illogical, it does make adding extended minors much simpler to calculate.

So, how many drives can you have? Well, theoretically, there can be 255 major numbers. If you used all the remaining ones times the four for each extended minor number set, you could have several hundred drives. While I was in SCO Support, someone managed to get about two dozen drives on the system. The limitation will probably be the number of slots in your machine. If you have six slots in your machine, and assuming that the video card, serial, and parallel ports were built into the mother board, you could have six host adapters in your machine; this means forty-two drives. Even if you have ten slots, the seventy that are possible is well below the "hundreds" that are theoretically possible.

## The Next Step

Now that you have an understanding of what goes into making the kernel and its environment, where should you go? My recommendation is to go through this chapter again, while sitting in front of a system. With the conception information gained by reading this chapter the first time, you can better understand how your system is configured. Look at the files I talked about. Compare the values you find to what is default or expected. Think about what those changes mean and what effects they have on your system.

# CHAPTER
# 6

- Disk Layout
- Files
- New Filesystems
- Virtual Disks
- Accessing DOS Files

# Filesystems and Files

**A**ny time you access an SCO system, whether locally, across a network, or through any other means, both files and filesystems are involved. Every program that you run starts out as a file. Most of the time you are also reading or writing a file. Since files (whether programs or data files) reside on filesystems, every time you access the system you are also accessing a filesystem.

Knowing what a file is and how it is represented on the disk and how the system interprets the contents of the file is useful to help you understand what the system is doing. You can also use this understanding to evaluate both the system and application behavior to determine if it is proper.

## Disk Layout

In order to be able to access data on your hard disk, there has to be some predefined structure. Without structure, it ends up looking like my desk—there are several piles of papers that I have to look through in order to find what I am looking for. Instead, the layout of a hard disk follows a very consistent pattern. So consistent, that it is even possible for different operating systems to share the hard disk.

Basic to this structure is the concept of a *partition*. A partition defines a portion of the hard disk to be used by one operating system or another. The partition can be any size, including the size of the entire hard disk. Near the very beginning of the disk is the *partition table*. The partition table is only 512 bytes, but can still define where each partition begins and how large it is. In addition, the partition table indicates which of the partitions is *active*. This decides which partition the system should go to when looking for an operating system to boot. The partition table is outside of any partition.

Once the system has determined which partition is active, the CPU knows to go to the very first block of data within that partition and begin executing the instructions there. On an SCO system this is an area called boot0. Although there are only 512 bytes of data in boot0, there are 1024 bytes reserved for it. The code within boot0 is sufficient to execute the code in the next block, boot1. Here, 20Kb are reserved, although the actually code is slightly less. The code within boot1 is what reads the /boot program, which will eventually load the kernel.

Immediately after boot1 is the *division table*. Under SCO, a division is a unit of the hard disk contained within a partition. A division can be any size, including the size of the entire partition. Often, special control structures are created at the beginning of the division that impose an additional structure on that division. This structure makes the division a *filesystem*. In order to keep track of where each division starts and how big it is, the system uses the division table. The division table has functionality similar to that of a partition table, although there is no such thing as an "active" division. There can be up to seven divisions (and therefore seven filesystems) per division, but the size of the division table is fixed at 130 bytes although 1024 bytes are reserved for the table.

Just after the division table is the *bad track table*. A bad track is a portion of the hard disk that has become unusable. Immediately following the bad track table is an area that is used for *alias tracks*. These are the tracks that are used when one of the other tracks goes bad. If that occurs, the operating system marks the bad track as such in the bad track table and indicates which of the alias tracks will be used. The size of the area taken up by the alias tracks is determined by how many entries there are in the bad track table. (There is one alias track per table entry.) You can see the contents of your bad track table by using the badtrk utility. Once the table and alias tracks have been defined, you cannot increase the number without re-installing.

Just after the bad track table are the divisions. If you have one of the older SCO UNIX filesystems (AFS, EAFS), there are two control structures at the beginning of the filesystem: the *superblock* and the *inode table*. The superblock contains information about the type of filesystem, its size, how many data blocks there are, the number of free inodes, free space available, and the location of the inode table.

Many users are not aware of the fact that different filesystems reside on different parts of the hard disk and in many cases on different physical disks. From the user's perspective the entire directory structure is one unit from the top (/) down to the deepest subdirectory. In order to carry out this deception, the system administrator needs to *mount* filesystems. This is done by mounting the device node associated with the filesystem (for example, /dev/u ) onto a *mountpoint* (for example, /u). This can either be done by hand, with the mount command line, or by having the system do it for you when booting. This is done with entries in `/etc/default/filesys`. See the `mount (ADM)` and the `filesys (F)` man-pages for more details.

Conceptually, the mountpoint serves as a detour sign for the system. If there is no filesystem mounted on the mountpoint, the system can just drive through and access what's there. If a filesystem is mounted, when the system gets to the mountpoint it sees the detour sign and is immediately diverted in another direction. Trees and houses still exist on the other side of a detour sign you see in the road. Any file or directory that exists underneath the mountpoint is still there. You just can't get to it.

Let's look at an example. We have the `/dev/u` filesystem which we are mounting on `/u`. Let's say that when we first installed the system and before we first mounted the `/dev/u` filesystem, we created some users with their home directories in `/u`; for example, `/u/jimmo`. When we do finally mount the `/dev/u` filesystem onto the `/u` directory, we no longer see `/u/jimmo`. It is still there, however, only once the system reaches the `/u` directory it is redirected somewhere else.

This brings up an interesting phenomena. When you use `find` to locate a file, it will reach the mountpoint and get redirected. However, `nheck` is not file and directory oriented, but rather filesystem oriented. If you used `find` you would not see `/u/jimmo`. However, you would if you used `ncheck`!

When a filesystem is mounted, the kernel reads the filesystem's superblock into an internal copy of the superblock. This way, the kernel doesn't have to keep going back to the hard disk for this information.

The inode is (perhaps) the most important structure. It contains all the information about a file including, owner and group, permissions, creation time, and, most importantly, where the data blocks are on the hard disk. The only thing it's missing is the name of the file. That's stored in the directory and not in the inode. If you have a Desktop Filesystem (DTFS), then there is no inode table. Rather the inodes are scattered across the disk. How they are accessed, we'll get into later when we talk about the different filesystems.

After the superblock (and inode table, if there is one) you get to the actual data. Data is stored in a system of files within each filesystem (hence the name). As we talked about in the section on SCO basics, files are grouped together into directories. This grouping is completely theoretical in the sense that there is nothing physically associating the files. Not only can files in the same directory be spread out across the disk, it is possible that the individual *data blocks* of a file are scattered as well. Figure 6–1 shows you where all the structures are on the hard disk.

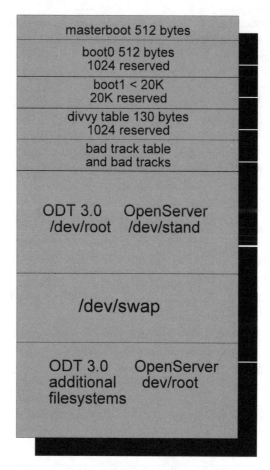

**Figure 6–1**   Boot hard disk layout.

In most systems, there will be at least two divisions on your root hard disk. On ODT 3.0 systems these divisions will contain your root filesystem and your swap space. Although it takes up a division, just like the root filesystem, your swap space is not a filesystem. This is because it has none of the control structures(superblock, inode table) that make it a filesystem. Despite this, there must still be an entry in the division table for it. In OpenServer, there is a new filesystem at the beginning of the partition and the root filesystem is moved into place after the swap space. We'll go into more details later. (NOTE: Whether you have the extra division will depend on what kind of installation you have. We'll cover this in more detail in Chapter 13.)

Up to this point we've talked a great deal about both files and directories, where they reside, and what their attributes (characteristics) are. Now it's time to talk about the concepts of files and directories. We will discuss how the operating system sees files and directories and how the system manages them.

From our discussion of how a hard disk is divided, we know that files reside within filesystems. Each filesystem has special structures that allow the system to manage the files. These are the superblock and inodes. The actual data is stored *somewhere* in the filesystem in *datablocks*. Most SCO UNIX filesystems use a block size of 1024 bytes. If you have OpenServer, the new DTFS has a variable block size.

Every SCO UNIX filesystem uses inodes, which, as I mentioned earlier, contain the important information about a file. (In some books, inode is short for information node and in others it is short for index node.) Although the structure of the inodes is different for each filesystem, they hold the same kinds of information. What each contains can be found in `<sys/ino.h>`, `<sys/inode.h>`, and `<sys/fs/*>`. Each inode has pointers which tell it where the actual data is located. This process is dependent on the filesystem type and we'll get to that in a moment. One piece of information that the inode does *not* contain is the file name. This is contained only within the directory.

If you are running OpenServer, then there are at least three divisions used. The first one (slot 0 in the division table) is used for the `/dev/boot` filesystem. This contains the files that are necessary to load and start the operating system. Although this is what is used to start the system, this is not root filesystem. The root filesystem has be moved to the third division. Once the system has been loaded, the `/dev/boot` filesystem is mounted onto the `/stand` directory and is accessible like any other mounted filesystem, except for the fact that it is normally mounted as read-only. In both ODT 3.0 and OpenServer, the root filesystem normally contains most of the files your operating system uses.

Depending on the size of your primary hard disk and the configuration options you chose during installation, you may have more than just these default filesystems. Common configurations have separate filesystems for users' home directories or data.

Although all of these filesystems are supported, not all are configured into your kernel by default. If you have ODT 3.0, you automatically have support for the three standard UNIX filesystems (EAFS, AFS, and S51K) as well as the XENIX filesystem. In OpenServer, the three UNIX filesystems supported in ODT are included, as well as the XENIX filesystems, and the two new ones: HTFS and DTFS. In order to be recognized they must be first configured in the kernel. How

**Table 6–1**    Filesystems Supported by ODT 3.0

| Type | Description |
| --- | --- |
| EAFS | Extended Acer Fast Filesystem (default) |
| AFS | Acer Fast Filesystem |
| S51K | AT&T UNIX System V 1KB Filesystem |
| HS | High Sierra CD-ROM Filesystem |
| ISO9660 | ISO 9600 CD-ROM Filesystem |
| XENIX | XENIX Filesystem |
| DOS | DOS Filesystem |
| NFS | Network Filesystem |

this is accomplished, depends on what product you are running and what filesystem. Table 6–1 and Table 6–2 show what filesystems are supported.

If you want to use one of the network filesystems such as NFS, SCO Gateway for NetWare, or Lan Manager Client Filesystem, you need to add that product through the Software Manager. This will automatically add support into the kernel for the appropriate filesystem.

**Table 6–2**    Filesystem Supported by OpenServer

| Type | Description |
| --- | --- |
| HTFS | High Throughput Filesystem (default) |
| DTFS | Desktop Filesystem (compression) |
| EAFS | Extended Acer Fast Filesystem |
| AFS | Acer Fast Filesystem |
| S51K | AT&T UNIX System V 1KB Filesystem |
| HS | High Sierra CD-ROM Filesystem |
| ISO9660 | ISO 9600 CD-ROM Filesystem |
| XENIX | XENIX Filesystem |
| DOS | DOS Filesystem |
| NFS | Network Filesystem |
| Rockridge | Rockridge CD-ROM Filesystem |
| NetWare | SCO Gateway for NetWare Filesystem |
| LMCFS | LAN Manager Client Filesystems |

**Table 6–3**   `mkdev` Script Associated with each Filesystem

| Filesystem | mkdev script |
| --- | --- |
| DOS | dos |
| DTFS | dtfs |
| HTFS | htfs |
| High Sierra/ISO9660/Rockridge | high-sierra |
| XENIX | xenix |

If you have ODT 3.0, then you can use `sysadmsh` to add the driver for each of the other filesystems. On OpenServer, you use the Hardware/Kernel Manager. In both cases, there are `mkdev` scripts that will do this. In fact, these scripts are called by `sysadmsh` and the Hardware/Kernel Manager. Table 6–3 shows you which script is run for each filesystem.

## Files

From the filesystem's standpoint, there is no difference between a directory and a file. Both take up an inode, use data blocks, and have certain attributes. It is the commands and programs that we use that impose structure on the directory. For example, `/bin/ls` imposes structure when we do listings of directories.

Keep in mind that it is the `ls` command that puts the file names "in order." Within the directory, the file names do not appear in *any* order. Initially, files appear in the directory in chronological order. As files are created and removed, the slots taken up by older files are replaced by newer ones and even this order disappears.

Other commands, such as `/bin/cat` or `/bin/hd`, allow us to see the directories as files, without any structure. Note that in OpenServer these commands *don't* let you see the structure, which I see as a loss in functionality.

When you do a long listing of a file, (`ls -l` or `l`) you can learn a lot about the characteristics of a file and directory. For example, if we do a long listing of `/bin/date`, we see

```
-rwx--x--x  1 bin   bin    17236 Dec 14 1991 /bin/date
```

This statement describes the file. It indicates the type of file ('-' means regular), the access permissions (`rwx--x--x`), how many links it has (`1`), the owner and group (`bin/bin`), the size(`17236`), the date it was last written to (Dec 14, 1991— maybe the time, as well, if it is a newer file), and the name of the file (`/bin/date`). For additional details on this, see the `ls (C)` man-page.

Unlike operating systems like DOS, most of this information is *not* stored in the directory. In fact, the only information that we see here, which is actually stored in the directory is the file's name. If not in the directory, where is this other information kept and how do you figure out where it is on the hard disk?

As I mentioned before, this is all stored in the inode. All the inodes on each file system are stored at the beginning of that filesystem in the inode table. The inode table is simply a set of these inode structures. If you want, you can see what the structure looks like by taking a peek at <sys/ino.h>.

To access the information in the inode, you need the inode number. Each directory entry consists of an inode number and file name pair. On ODT 3.0 and earlier, the first two bytes of each entry were the inode number. Since a byte can hold 256 values, the maximum possible inode was 256*256, or 65535 inodes per filesystem. The inode simply points to a particular entry in the inode table. This is the *only* connection there is between a filename and its inode, therefore the *only* connection between the filename and the data on the hard disk.

Because this is only a pointer and there is no physical connection, there is nothing preventing you from having multiple entries in a directory pointing to the same file. These would have different names, but have the same inode number, and therefore point to the same physical data on the hard disk. Having multiple file names on your system point to the same data on the hard disk, is *not* a sign of filesystem corruption! This is actually something that is done on purpose.

For example, if you do a long listing of /bin/ls (l /bin/ls) you see this:

```
-r-xr-xr-t  6 bin    bin    23672 Dec 14 1991 /bin/ls
```

Here, the number of links (column 2) is 6. This means there are five other files on the system with the same inode number as /bin/ls. In fact that's all a link is: a file with the same inode on the *same filesystem*. To find out what inode that is, let's add the -i option to give us

```
167 -r-xr-xr-t  6 bin    bin    23672 Dec 14 1991 /bin/ls
```

From this we see that /bin/ls occupies entry 167 in the inode table. There are three ways of finding out what other files have this inode number:

```
find / -inum 167 -print
ncheck -i 167 /dev/root—we're assuming /bin/ls is on the root filesystem
l -iR / | grep '167'
```

Since I know they are all in the /bin directory, I'll try the last one. This gives me the following:

```
167 -r-xr-xr-t  6 bin    bin     23672 Dec 14 1991 l
167 -r-xr-xr-t  6 bin    bin     23672 Dec 14 1991 lc
167 -r-xr-xr-t  6 bin    bin     23672 Dec 14 1991 lf
167 -r-xr-xr-t  6 bin    bin     23672 Dec 14 1991 lr
167 -r-xr-xr-t  6 bin    bin     23672 Dec 14 1991 ls
167 -r-xr-xr-t  6 bin    bin     23672 Dec 14 1991 lx
```

Interesting. This is the entire family of `ls` commands. All of these lines look identical, with the exception of the file name. There are six lines which match the number of links. Each has an inode of 167, so we know that all six names have the same inode and therefore point to the same location on the hard disk. This means that whenever you execute any one of these commands, the same program is started. The only difference is the behavior and that is based on what program you actually start on the command line. Since the program knows what name it was started with, the program can change its behavior accordingly.

There is nothing special about the fact that these are all in the same directory. A name must only be unique within a single directory. You can therefore have two files with the same *basename* in two separate directories; for example, `/bin/mail` and `/usr/bin/mail`. If you take a look, these not only have the same inode number (and are therefore the same file), there are actually three links; the third link being `/usr/bin/mailx`. So, here we have two files in the same directory (`/usr/bin/mailx` and `/usr/bin/mail`) as well as two files with the same basename (`/bin/mail` and `/usr/bin/mail`). All of which have the same inode and are, therefore, all the same file.

The key issue here is that all three of these files exists on the same filesystem, `/dev/root`. As I mentioned before, there may be files on other filesystems that have the same inode. This is the reason why you cannot create a link between files on two different filesystems. With a little manipulation, you might be able to force two files with identical content to have the same inode on two filesystems. However, these are not links (just two files with the same name and same content).

The problem is that it may be necessary to create links across filesystems. You may want to create a path with a much shorter name that is easier to remember. Or perhaps you have several remote filesystems, accessed through NFS, and you want to create a common structure on multiple machines all of which point to the same file. Therefore, you need a mechanism that allows links across filesystems (even remote filesystems). This is the concept of a soft or *symbolic link*.

Symbolic links were first introduced to SCO UNIX in release 3.2.4.0. In SCO OpenServer they are (perhaps) the primary means of referring to installed files. For more information on referencing installed files, see the section on Software Storage Objects. Unlike hard links, symbolic links take up data blocks on the hard disk and therefore have a unique inode number. However, they only need one data block since the contents of that block is the path to the file you are referring to. Note that if the name is short enough, the symbolic link may be stored directly in the inode. See Table 6–4 on page 285 for details on filesystem characteristics.

For example, if I had a file on a `/u` filesystem named `/u/data/albert.letter`, I could create a symbolic link to it as `/usr/jimmo/letters/albert.letter` (no, it doesn't have to have the same name). The one data block assigned to the symbolic link `/usr/jimmo/letters/albert.letter` contains `/u/data/albert.letter`. Whenever I access the file `/usr/jimmo/letters/albert.letter`, the system (the file system driver) knows that this is a symbolic link. The system then reads the full path out of the data block and accesses the "real" file. Since the data file contains only a path, you could have filesystem mounted via NFS where the data is stored on a remote machine. Whatever you are using to access that file (for example, an application, a system utility) cannot tell the difference.

For example, I might have a file in my own `bin` directory that points to a nifty utility on my friend's machine. I have a filesystem from my friend's machine mounted to my `/usr/data` directory. I could create a symbolic like this:

```
ls -s /usr/data/nifty /usr/jimmo/bin/nifty
```

I would therefore have a symbolic link, `/usr/jimmo/bin/nifty` that looked like this:

```
lrwxrwxrwx  1 root other 15 May 03 00:12 /usr/jimmo/bin/nifty ->
/usr/data/nifty
```

We see two ways that this is a symbolic link. The first character of the permissions field is an `'l'`. Next, the name of the file itself is different than we are used to. Next, we see that the name of the file that we use (`/usr/jimmo/bin/nifty`) and a (sort-of) arrow that points to the "real" file (`/usr/data/nifty`). Note that there is nothing here that tells us that a remote filesystem is mounted onto `/usr/data`. The conversion is accomplished by the filesystem driver when the actual file is accessed.

If you were to use just the `ls` command, then you would not see either the type of file (l) or the ->, so there is no way to know that this is a symbolic link. If you use `lf`, then the file is followed by an at sign (@), which tells you that the file is a symbolic link.

Keep in mind that when the system determines that you are trying to access a symbolic link, the system then goes out and tries to access the "real" file and behaves accordingly. Therefore, symbolic links can also point to directories, or any other kinds of files, including other symbolic links. How this looks graphically you'll see in Figure 6–2.

Be careful when making a symbolic link. When you do, the system does not check to see that the source file exists. It is therefore possible to have a symbolic link point back to itself or to point to nothing. Although most system utilities and commands can catch things like this, do not rely on it. Besides, what's the point of having a dog chasing its own tail? It is also advisable not to use any relative paths when using symbolic links. This may have unexpected results when accessing the links from elsewhere on your system.

Let's go back to the actual structure of the directory entries for a minute. Remember that directories are simply files that have a structure imposed on them by something. If the command or utility imposes the (correct) structure, then each directory entry takes the form of 2 bytes for the inode and 14 bytes for the file name itself.

Another change to the system that came in SCO UNIX 3.2.4.0 was the introduction of long filenames. Up to this point, file names were limited to 14 characters. With two bytes for the inode, 64 of these 16 byte structures fit exactly into a disk block. However, with only 14 bytes for the name, this often made giving files

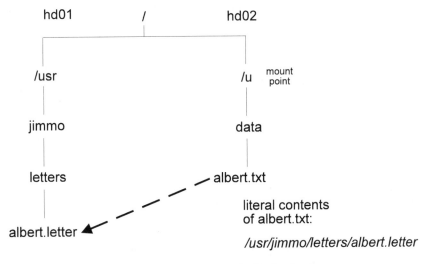

**Figure 6–2**  Symbolic link.

meaningful names difficult. I don't know how many times I personally spent time trying to remove vowels and otherwise squish the name together so that it fit in 14 characters. The default filesystem on SCO UNIX 3.2.4.0 changed all that.

One thing I liked about having 16 bytes was that a directory entry fit nicely into the default output of `hd`. That way you could easily see the internal structure of the directory. I don't know how many times I used `hd` when talking with customers with filesystem problems. However, the `hd` included in the initial release of OpenServer won't let you do this. In my opinion, removing that very useful functionality broke `hd`.

Up to 3.2.4.0, SCO UNIX used the Acer File System (AFS), which had some advantages over the standard UNIX (S51K) filesystem. However, neither can handle symbolic links and long file names. The Extended Acer File System (EAFS) changed that. Since the directory entries of the AFS were 16 bytes long, long file names have to "'spill over" into subsequent entries in the directory. Since a file only has one inode, extended file names beyond 14 characters need to extend into consecutive entries in the directory. Since they are taking up multiple slots, all but the *last* inode entry has the inode number of `'0xffff'`. This indicates that the file name continues on in the next slot. Even with long file names, files names on an EAFS are limited to 255 characters.

When files are removed, the inode entry in the directory is changed to 0. Do an `hd` of the directory (if you're running ODT) and you still see the file name, but the inode is 0. When a new file is created, the file name takes up a slot used by an older, previously removed file *if the name can fit*. Otherwise it must take a new slot. Since long names need to be in consecutive slots, they may not be able to take up empty slots. If so, new entries may need to be created for longer file names.

When you create a file, the system looks in the directory for the first available slot. If this is an EAFS, then it is possible that the file you want to create might not fit in the first slot. Remember that each slot is 16 bytes long—two for the inode number and 14 for the file name. If, for example, slots 16 and 18 are filled, and slot 17 is free, a file name that is longer than 14 characters cannot fit there. This is because the directory entries must be contiguous.

The system must therefore, find a slot large enough or create new slots at the end of the directory. For example, if slots 14 and 18 were taken, but slots 15–17 were free, any file less than 42 characters (14*3) would fit. Anything larger would need to go somewhere else.

If you were to count up all the bytes in the inode structure in `ino.h`, you'd find that each inode is 64 bytes. This means that there are 16 per disk block

(16*64=512). In order to keep from wasting space, the system will always create filesystems with the number of inodes being a multiple of 16.

Inode 1 is always at the start of the third block of the filesystem (bytes 2048–2111) and is reserved (not used). Inode 2 is always the inode of the root directory of any filesystem. You can see this for the root filesystem by doing `ls -id /`. (The `-d` is necessary so you only see the directory and not the contents.)

The total number of inodes on an AFS or EAFS is defined when filesystem is created by `mkfs(ADM)`. Normally, you use the `divvy` command (by hand or through SCOAdmin) in OpenServer to create filesystems. The `divvy` command will then call `mkfs` to create the filesystem for you. The number of inodes created is based on an average file size of 4K. If you have a system that has many smaller files, such as a mail or news server, you could run out of inodes and still have lots of room on your system.

Therefore, if you have a news or mail server, it is a good idea to use `mkfs` to create the filesystem *before* you add any files. Remember that the inode table is at the beginning of the filesystem and takes up as much room as it needs for a given number of inodes. If you want to have more inodes, you must have a larger inode table. The only place for the inode table to grow is into your data. Therefore, you would end up overwriting data. Besides, running `mkfs` 'zeroes' out your inode table so the pointers to the data are lost anyway.

Among other things that the inode keeps track of are file types and permissions, number of links, owner and group, size of the file, and when it was last modified. You will find thirteen pointers (or *triplets*) to the actual data on the hard disk in the inode.

Note that these triplets point to data blocks and not the data itself. Each one of the thirteen pointers to the data is a block address on the hard disk and does not contain the actual data. For the following discussion, please refer to Figure 6–3.

Each of these blocks is 1024 bytes (1k), therefore the maximum file size on an SCO UNIX system is 13Kb. Wait a minute! That doesn't sound right, does it? In fact it isn't. If (and that's a big if) all of the triplets pointed to data blocks, then you could only have a file up to 13Kb. However, there are dozens of files in the /bin directory alone that are larger than 13Kb. How does this work?

Only the first ten of these triplets points to actual data. These are referred to as *direct data blocks*. The eleventh triplet points to a block on the hard disk which actually contains the real pointers to the data. These are the *indirect data blocks* and contain 4-byte values, so there are 256 of them in each block. In Figure 6–3, the eleventh triplet contains a pointer to block 567. Block 567 contains 256 pointers to

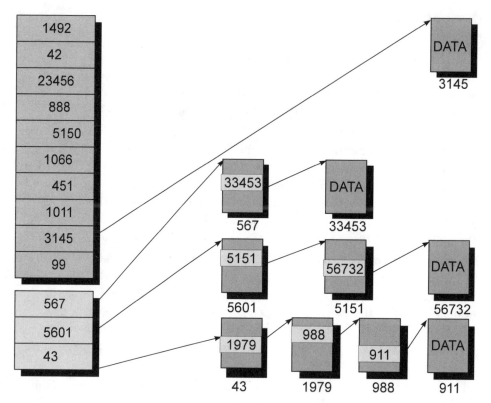

**Figure 6–3**   Inodes pointing to disk blocks.

indirect data blocks. One of these pointers points to block 33453, which contains the actual data. Block 33453 is an indirect data block.

Since the data blocks pointed to by the 256 pointers in block 567 each contain 1K of data, there is an additional 256K of data. So, with the 10K for the direct data blocks and the 256K for the indirect data blocks, we now have a maximum file size of 266K.

Hmmm. Still not good. Although there aren't that many, there are files on your system larger than 266K. A good example is /unix. So, that brings us to triplet 12. This points not to data blocks, not to a block of pointers to data blocks, but to blocks that point to blocks that point to data blocks. These are the *doubly-indirect data blocks*.

In Figure 6–3 the twelfth triplet contains a pointer to block 5601. Block 5601 contains pointers to other blocks; one of which is block 5151. However, block 5151 does not contain data, but more pointers. One of these points to block 56732. It is block 56732 that finally contains the data.

We have a block of 256 entries that each points to a block which each contains 256 pointers to 1024 byte data blocks. This gives us 64Mb, just for the doubly-indirect data blocks. At this point, the additional size gained by the single-indirect and direct data blocks is negligible. Therefore, let's just say we can access over 64Mb. Now, that's much better. You would be hard pressed to find a system with files larger than 64Mb (unless we are talking about large database applications). However, we're not through, yet. We have one triplet left.

So, as not to bore too many of you, let's do the math quickly. The last triplet points to a block containing 256 pointers to other blocks, each of which points to 256 other blocks. At this point, we already have 65536 blocks. Each of these 65536 blocks contain 256 pointers to the actual data blocks. Here we have 16777216 pointers to data blocks, which gives us a grand total of 17179869184 or 16Gb of data (plus the insignificant 64MB we get from the doubly-indirect data blocks). Oh, as you might have guessed, these are the triply-indirect data blocks.

In Figure 6–3 triplet 13 contains a pointer to block 43. Block 42 contains 256 pointers, one of which points to block 1979. Block 1979 also contains 256 pointers, one of which points to block 988. Block 988 also contains 256 points. However, *these* pointers point to the actual data; for example, block 911.

If you are running an ODT 3.0 (or earlier) system, 16Gb is not your actual size limit. This is the theoretical limit placed on you by the number of triply-indirect data blocks. Since you need to keep track of the size of the file and this is stored in the inode table as a signed long integer (31 bits) the actual limit is 2Gb.

As I mentioned a moment ago, when a file is removed the inode is set to 0; however, the slot remains. In most cases this is not a problem. However, when mail gets backed up, for example, there can be thousands of files in the mail spool directories. Each one of these requires a slot within the directory. As a result, the directory files can grow to amazing sizes. I have seen directories with a directory file of over 300,000 bytes. This equates to about 20,000 files.

This brings up a couple of interesting issues. Remember that there are ten direct data blocks for 10Kb, then one single-indirect for 256K for a total of 266Kb for both single- and doubly-indirect data blocks. If you have a case where the directory file is exceptionally large, and the file you are looking for happens to be at the very end of the directory file, the system must first read all ten direct data blocks, then read the eleventh block that points to the singly-indirect data blocks, then read all 64 of those data blocks, then it reads the twelfth block in the inode to find where the data blocks are for the pointers, then reads the blocks containing the pointers, then reads the actual data blocks for the remainder of the directory file. Since a copy of the inode is read into memory, there is no need to go back out to the disk.

On the other hand, remember there are 64 blocks containing the singly-indirect pointers. Each one of them has to be read, *then* each of the blocks they point to has to be read to check to see if your file is there. Then you need to read the data blocks that point to the data blocks that point to where your directory is. Only then do you find out that you mistyped your file name and you have to do it all over again.

Since the system can usually get them all in one read, it is best to keep the number of files in a directory at 638 or less. 638? Sure. Each block can hold 64 entries. There are ten data blocks. The ten direct data blocks can hold 640 entries. Each directory always contains the entries and therefore you can only have 638 additional entries.

The next interesting thing is what happens when you run `fsck` on your system. If the filesystem is clean, there won't be a problem. What happens if your system crashes and your filesystem becomes corrupted? If during the check, `fsck` finds files that are pointed to by inodes, but does not find any reference to them in a directory, it will place them in the `/lost+found` directory. When each file system is created, the system automagically creates 62 files and then removes them. This leaves 62 empty directory slots which gives you 64 total entries times 16 bytes equals 1024 bytes, or one data block.

The reason for the `lost+found` directory is that you don't want the system to be writing anything to a filesystem that you are trying to clean. It is safe enough to be filling in directory entries, but you don't want the system to be creating any *new* files while trying to clean the filesystem. This is what would happen if you had more than 62 "lost" files.

If you have a trashed filesystem and there are more than 62 lost files, they really become lost. The system cannot handle the additional files and has to remove them. Therefore, I think it is a good idea to create additional entries and then remove them whenever creating a new file system. This way you are prepared for the worst. A script to do this would be like this:

```
cd /lost+found
for i in a b c d e f g h i j
do
  for j in a b c d e f g h i j
  do
          for k in a b c d e f g h i j
          do
                  touch $i$j$k
          done
  done
done
rm *
```

This scripts creates 1000 files and then removes them. This takes up about 16K for the directory file, however it allows 1000 files to become "lost", which may be a job saver in the future. Make sure that the rm is done after all the files are created, otherwise you end up creating a file, removing it, then filling the slot with some other file. The result is that you have fewer files than you expected.

If you look in /usr/lib/mkdev/fs (what is actually run when you run mkdev fs) you see that the system does something like this for your every time you add a filesystem. Just after you see the message

Reserving slots in lost+found directory ...

the mkdev fs script does something *very* similar. The key difference is that mkdev fs only creates 62 entries. If you wanted to create 1000 entries every time you ran mkdev fs, you could change that part of mkdev fs to look like the above script.

Something that I have always found interesting was that /bin/cp, /bin/ln, and /bin/mv are all the same binary. That is, they are all links to each other. When you link a file, all that needs to get done is to create a new directory entry, fill it in with the correct inode and then increase the link count in the inode table. Copying a file also creates a new directory entry, but it must also write the new data blocks to the disk.

When you move a file, something interesting happens. First, the system creates a link to the original file. It then removes the old file name by unlinking it. This simply clears the directory entry by setting the inode to 0. However, once the system creates the link, for a brief instant there are two files on your system.

When you remove a file, things get a little more complicated. We need to not only remove the directory entry referencing the file name, but we also need to decrease the link count in the inode table. If the link count at this point is greater than 0, then the system knows that there is another file on the system pointing to the same data blocks. However, if the link count reaches 0, we then know that there are no more directory entries pointing to that same file. The system must then free those data blocks and make them available for other files.

Some of you might have realized that special device files (device nodes) do not take up any space on the hard disk. The only place they "exist" is in the directory entry and inode table. You may also have noticed that in the inode structure there is no entry for the major and minor number. However, if you do a long listing of device node, you will see the major and minor number. Where is this kept?

Well, since you don't have any data blocks to point to, then the 39 bytes used for the data block pointers are unused. This is exactly where the major and minor number are stored. The first byte of the array is the major number and the second byte is the minor number. This is one reason why major and minor numbers cannot be larger than 255.

As with many aspects of the system, the kernel's role in administering and managing filesystem is wide reaching and varied. Among its tasks is the organization of disk space within the filesystem. This function is different, depending on what type of filesystem you are trying to access. For example, if you are copying files to a DOS FAT filesystem, then kernel has to be aware that there are different cluster sizes depending on the size of the partition. (A cluster is a physical grouping of data blocks.)

If you have an AFS (Acer Fast File System) or EAFS (Extended AFS), then the kernel attempts to keep data in logically contiguous blocks called clusters (on most modern hard disks, this also means physically contiguous). By default, a cluster is 16kb, but can be changed when the filesystem is created by using `mkfs`.

When reading data off the disk, the system can read clusters rather than single blocks. Since files are normally read sequentially, the efficiency of each read is increased. This is because the system can read larger chunks of data and doesn't have to go looking for them. Therefore, the kernel can issue fewer (but larger) disk requests. If you have a hard disk controller that does "track caching" (storing previously read tracks), you improve your read efficiency even more.

However, the number of files may eventually grow to the point where storing data in 16K chunks is no longer practical. If there are no more free areas that are at least 16Kb, the system would have to begin moving things around to make a 16Kb block available. This would waste more time than would be gained by maintaining the 16Kb cluster.

Therefore, these chunks will need to be split up. As the file system gets fuller, the amount the chunks are split up (called fragmentation) increases. Therefore, the system ends up having to move to different places on the disk to find the data. Because of this the kernel ends up sending multiple requests and slowing down the disk reads even further. (It's always possible since you can move data blocks from other files. This takes time and is therefore not practical.) What fragmentation might look like graphically you see in Figure 6–4.

The kernel is also responsible for the security of the files themselves. Because SCO UNIX is a multi-user system, it is important to ensure that users only have access to the files that they should have access to. This access is on a per file basis in the form of the permissions set on each file. Based on several discussions we've had so far, we know that these permissions tell us who can read, write, or execute our files. It is the kernel that makes this determination. The kernel also imposes the rule that only the owner or the all-powerful root may change the permissions or ownership of a file.

Allocation of disk blocks is dependent upon organization of what is called the *freelist*. When a file is opened for the first time, its inode is read into the kernels generic inode table. This is a "generic" table, as it is valid for all filesystems. Therefore, on subsequent reads and writes this information is already available and the kernel does not have to make an additional disk read to get the inode information. Remember, it is the inode that contains the pointers to the actual data blocks. If this information were not kept in the kernel, *every time* the file was accessed this information would need to be read from the hard disk.

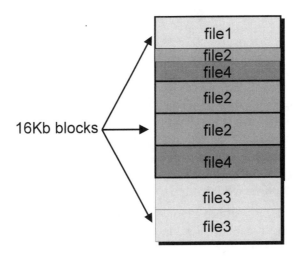

**Figure 6–4**   Disk fragmentation.

Keep in mind that if you have a process that is reading or writing to the disk, it is the kernel that does the actual disk access. This is done through the filesystem and hard disk drivers. Every time the kernel does a read of a block device, the kernel first checks the buffer cache to see if the data already exists there. If so, then the kernel has saved itself a disk read. Obviously if it's not there, the kernel must read it from the hard disk.

At first this seems liked a waste of time. First you must check in one place and then check another. Every single read checks the buffer cache first. So, in many cases, this is wasted time. However, the buffer cache is in RAM. This can be several *hundred* times faster than accessing the hard disk. As a result of the principle of locality, your process (and the kernel as well) will probably be accessing the same data over and over again. Therefore, the existence of the buffer cache is actually a great time saver, since the number of times it finds something in the cache (the hit ratio) is so high.

When writing a file (or parts of a file), the data is first written to the buffer cache. If it remains unchanged for a specific period of time (defined by the BDFLUSHR kernel parameter), the data is then written to the disk. This also saves time because if data is written to the disk, then changed before it is read again, you've wasted a disk write. However, if it stays in the buffer cache forever (or until the file is closed or the process terminates) then you run the risk of losing data if the system crashes. Therefore, BDFLUSHR is set to a reasonable default of 30 seconds.

As I mentioned a moment ago, when a file is first opened, its inode is read into the kernel's generic inode table (assuming it is not already there). This table is the same no matter what kind of file system you have (S51K, AFS, etc.). The structure of this table is defined in <sys/inode.h>. The size of this is configurable in ODT 3.0 with the kernel parameter NINODE.

The entries in the generic inode table are linked into hash queues. A hash queue is basically a set of linked lists. Which list a particular inode will go into depends on its value. This speeds things up, since the kernel does not have to search the entire inode table. It can immediately jump to the relatively smaller hash queue. The more hash queues there are (defined by the NHINODE kernel parameter) the faster things are read since each queue has fewer entries. However, the more queues there are, the more space in memory is required and this gives less room for other things. Therefore, you need to weigh one against the other.

Since there is normally no pattern as to which files are removed from the inode table and when, the free slots in the table are spread throughout the table randomly. Free entries in the generic table are linked onto the freelist so new inodes may be allocated quickly.

One advantage that SCO UNIX provides is the ability to access different kinds of filesystems. Because of this, the kernel must also keep track of filesystem specific information, such as that contained in the inode table. This information is also kept in a kernel internal table, based on the filesystem. The System V dependent inode data structure is defined in `<sys/fs/s5inode.h>`, and is used by S15K, AFS, and EAFS. Other inode tables exist for High-Sierra and DOS. Each time a file is opened an entry is allocated in both the generic and the System V dependent inode table (unless already in memory). The information contained in these inode tables is going to be different, depending on what kind of filesystem you are dealing with.

When a process wants to access a file, it does so using a system call such as `open()` or `write()`. When first writing the code for a program, the system calls that programmers normally use are the same no matter what the file system type. When the process is running and makes one of these system calls, the kernel maps that system call to operations appropriate for that type of FS. This is necessary since the way a file is accessed under DOS, for example, is different than under EAFS. The mapping information is maintained in a table, one per file system and is constructed during a relink from information in `/etc/conf/mfsys.d` and `/etc/conf/sfsys.d`. The kernel then accesses the correct entry in the table by using the FS type as an index into the `fstypesw []` array.

Another table used by the kernel to keep track of open files is the *file table*. This allows many processes to share the same inode information, and is defined in `<sys/file.h>`. Because it is often the case that multiple processes have the same file open, this saves the kernel time by not having to look up inode information for each process individually. Once a file is open and is in the file table, the kernel does not have to reread the inode table.

By the time the kernel actually has the inode number of a file that you are working with, it has gone through three different reference points. The first point is the uarea of your process that has the translation from your personal file descriptors to the entry in the file table. Next, the file table has the references that point the kernel to the appropriate slot in its generic inode table. Last, the generic inode table has the pointers to the file system-specific inode table. At first, this may seem like a lot of work. However, keep in mind that this is all in RAM. Without this mechanism, the kernel would have to go back and forth to the disk all the time. What this could look like graphically you can see in Figure 6–5.

The `open()` system call is implemented internally as a call to the `namei()` function. This is the name-to-inode conversions. `Namei()` sets up both the generic inode table entry and filesystem dependent inode table entry. It returns a pointer to the

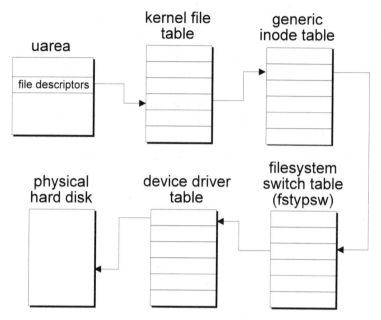

**Figure 6–5** Translation from file descriptions to data.

generic table entry. `Namei()` then calls another function, the routine `falloc()`, which sets up an entry in the file table to point to the inode in the generic table.

The kernel then calls the `ufalloc()` routine, which sets up a file pointer in the uarea to point to the file table entry set-up by `falloc()`. Finally the return value to `open()` is indexed into the file pointer array, known as the file descriptor.

The function of `namei()` is a bit more complicated than just converting a filename to an inode number. `Namei()` converts the filenames to inodes (not to inode numbers). Obviously it must first get the inode number, but this is a relatively easy chore, since it is contained within the directory entry of the file.

In order to find out what inode table to read, `namei()` needs to know on which filesystem a file resides. Simply reading the inode from the directory entry is not enough. As we talked about before, two completely different files can have the same inode provided they are on *different* file systems. Therefore, even though `namei()` has the inode number, it still does not know which inode table to read.

In order to find the filesystem, `namei()` needs to have a complete pathname to the file. A UNIX pathname consists of zero or more directories, separated with '/', terminated by the filename. The total path length cannot be more than 1024 characters. Assuming there is no directory name mentioned when the file is opened (or only a relative path), `namei` has to backtrack a little to get back up to the top of the directory tree.

If not already in memory, the inode corresponding to the first directory in the pathname is read into memory. The directory file is read into memory and the inode/filename pairs are searched for the next directory component. The next directory is read in and the process continues until the actual file is reached. We now have the inode of the file.

With relative paths or no paths at all, we have to backtrack. That is, in order to find the root directory of the filesystem we are on, we have to find the parent directory of our file, then its parent, and so on until we reach the root.

Looking at this, we see the pathname to inode conversion is time consuming. Each time a new directory is read, there must be a read of the hard disk. In order to speed up things, SCO UNIX caches the directories. The size of the cache is set by the S5CACHENT kernel tunable parameter and the entries defined in `<sys/fs/s5inode.h>`. Whenever the kernel searches for a component of the file name, it checks the correct hash queue. In ODT 3.0 the S5CACHENT structures can't hold more than fourteen characters. Therefore, for the long file names possible with EAFS, the kernel must go directly to the disk. Cache hits and misses are recorded and can be retrieved with SAR and can be monitored.

In a S51K (traditional UNIX) filesystem, the superblock contains a list of both free blocks and free inodes. There is room for 50 blocks in the free block list and 100 inodes in the free inode list. The structure of the superblock is found in `<sys/fs/s5filsys.h>`.

When creating a new file, the system examines the array of free inode numbers in the superblock and the next free inode number assigned. Since this list only has 100 entries, they will all eventually get used up. If total number of free inodes drops to zero, the list is filled in with another 100 from the disk. If there ever less than 100 free inodes, then the unused entries are set to 0. In S51K filesystems, the list of free data blocks, the freelist, is ordered randomly. As disk blocks are freed, they are just appended to the end of freelist. During allocation of data blocks, no account is made for physical location of the data blocks. This means that there is no pattern to where the files reside on the disk. This can quickly lead to fragmentation. That is, data blocks from one file can be scattered all over the disk.

In AFS and EAFS the freelist is held as a bitmap, where adjacent bits in the map correspond to logically contiguous blocks. Therefore the system can quickly search for sets of bits representing free blocks and then allocate files in contiguous blocks. Logically contiguous blocks (usually physically contiguous blocks) are known as a cluster.

When the filesystem is first created, the bitmap is created by `mkfs`. There is 1 bit for every data block on the filesystem, so the bitmap is a linear array which says whether a particular block contains valid data or not. Note that this bitmap also occupies disk blocks itself. Actually, there is more than one bitmap. There are several which are spaced at intervals of approximately 8192 blocks throughout the filesystem. Since a block contains 1024 bytes, it contains 8192 bits and can therefore map 8192 blocks. There is also an indirect freelist block, which holds a list of the disk block numbers which actually contain the bitmaps.

When a file is created, the entire cluster is reserved for the file. Although this does tend to waste a little space, it reduces fragmentation and therefore increases speed. When kernel reads a block, it reads the whole cluster the file belongs to as well as the next. This is called read ahead.

When a disk block is needed for a new file, the system searches the bitmap for the first free block. If we later need more data blocks for an existing file, the system begins its search starting from the block number that was last allocated for that file. This helps to ensure new blocks are close to existing ones. Note that when a cluster is allocated, not all of the disk blocks may be free (maybe it is already allocated to another file).

The bitmapped freelist of the AFS and EAFS has some performance advantages. First, files are typically located in contiguous disk blocks. These can be allocated quickly from the freelist using `i80386` bit manipulation instructions. This means that free areas of the disk can be found in just a few instruction cycles and therefore access speeds up.

In addition, the freelist is held in memory. The advantage is that this keeps the system from having to make an additional disk access every time the system wants to write new blocks to the hard disk. When kernel issues an I/O request to read from a single disk block, the AFS maps the request so that the entire cluster contains the disk block and following clusters are read from disk. This is shown in Figure 6–6.

At the beginning of each filesystem is a filesystem-specific structure called the superblock. You can find out about the structure of the superblock by looking in `<sys/fs/*>`. The Sys V superblock is located in the second half of the first block of filesystems (bytes 512–1023). Since the structure is less than 512 bytes, it contains padding to fill out to 512 bytes. When a filesystem is first mounted, its su-

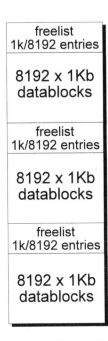

**Figure 6–6**   The AFS freelist.

perblock is read into memory so updates to the superblock don't have to constantly write to the disk.

In order for the structures on the disk to remain compatible with the copies in memory, superblocks and inodes are updated by `sync` which is started at regular intervals by `init`. The frequency of the `sync` is defined by SLEEPTIME in `/etc/default/boot`, with a default of sixty seconds.

## New Filesystems

### *New Concepts*

There are several new concepts in OpenServer. The first is *intent logging*. When this functionality is enabled, filesystem *transactions* are recorded in a log and then committed to disk. If the system goes down before the transaction is completed, the log is *replayed* to complete pending transactions. This scheme increases reliability and recover speed since the system need only read the log to be able to bring the system to the correct state. By using this scheme, the time spent checking the filesystem (and repairing it if necessary) can be reduced to just a few seconds, not the several minutes that was required previously, *regardless* of the filesystem size. There is, however, a small performance penalty since the system has to spend some time writing to the logs.

As changes are being made to any of the control structures (inodes, superblock), the changes are written to a log. Once complete, the transaction is marked as *complete*. However, if the system should go down before the log is written, it is as if the transaction was never started. If the log is complete, but the transaction hasn't finished, the transaction can either be completed or ignored, depending what `fsck` considers possible. Obviously, if the system goes down after the transaction is complete, then nothing needs to be done.

The location of the log file is stored in the superblock. As a real file it resides *somewhere* on the file system, however it is invisible to normal user-level utilities and only becomes visible when logging is disabled.

Intent logging does bring up one misconception in that it does *not* increase the reliability of the system. Only changes to the control structures are logged—data is *not*. The purpose of intent logging is to reduce the time it takes to make the system operational again should it go down.

Another new concept is *checkpointing*. When enabled, the filesystem is marked as "clean" at regular intervals. That is, the pending writes are completed, inodes are updated and, if necessary, the in-core copy of the superblock is written to disk. At this point the filesystem is considered clean. Should the system go down improperly at this point, there is no need to clean the filesystem (using `fsck`) as it is already clean. However, the data is still cached in the buffer cache, so if it is needed again soon, it is available.

If the system goes down, the contents of the buffer cache are lost, but since they were already written to disk, no data is actually lost. Obviously, anything not written between the last checkpoint and the time the system goes down is lost, but checkpointing does decrease the amount lost as well as speed up the recovery process when the system is rebooted. Again, there is no such thing as a free lunch and checkpointing does mean a small performance loss. Checkpointing is turned on by default on High Throughput Filesystem (HTFS) , EAFS, AFS, and S51K filesystems.

For the best reliability and speed of recovery, it's a good idea to have *both* logging and checkpointing enabled. Although they both cause slight performance degradation, the benefits outweigh the performance hit. In most cases, the performance loss is not noticed, only the time required to bring the system back up is a lot quicker.

The idea of sync-on-close for the Desktop Filesystem (DTFS) is another way of increasing reliability. Whenever a file is closed, it is immediately written to disk, rather than waiting for the system to write it as it normally would (potentially thirty seconds later). If the system should do down improperly, you have a better chance of not losing data. Because you are not writing data to the hard disk in large chunks, sync-on-close also degrades performance.

Because I regularly suffer from *digitalus enormus* (fat fingers), I am often typing in things that I later regret. On a few occasions, I have entered `rm` commands with wildcards (`*`, for example) only to find that I left an extra space before the asterisk. As a result, I end up with a nice clean directory. Since I am not *that* stupid, I built an alias so that every time I used `rm` it would prompt me to confirm the removal (`rm-i`). My brother, on the other hand, created an alias where `rm` copies the files into a TRASH directory, which he needs to clean out regularly. Both of these solutions can help you recover from accidentally erasing files.

OpenServer has added a feature whereby you no longer have to create aliases to keep you from erasing things you shouldn't. This is the idea of file *versioning*. Not only does file versioning protect you from *digitalus enormus*, but it will also make automatic copies of files for you.

In order for versioning to be used, it must be first configured in the kernel. There are several kernel tunable parameters that are involved. To change them you either run the program `/etc/conf/cf.d/configure` or click on the "Tune Parameters..." button in the Hardware/Kernel Manager (the Hardware/Kernel Manager calls `configure`). Next, select option ten (Filesystem configuration). Here you will need to set the MAXVDEPTH parameter, which sets the maximum number of versions maintained, and the MINVTIME parameter which sets the minimum time (in seconds) between changes before a file is versioned. Setting MAXVDEPTH to 0 disables versioning. If MINVTIME is set to 0, and MAXVDEPTH to a nonzero value, then versioning will happen no matter how short the time between versions. Versioning is only available for the DTFS and HTFS.

You can also set versioning for a filesystem by using the `maxvdepth` and `minvtime` options when mounting. These can be included in `/etc/default/filesys` (which defines the default behavior when mounting filesystems), or you can specify them on the command line when mounting the filesystem by hand. In addition to that, versioning can be set on a per-directory basis. This is done by using the undelete command; for example,

```
undelete -s /usr/jimmo/letters
```

This command line turns on versioning for all the files in the directory `/usr/jimmo/letters` as well as any child directories. This includes existing files and directories as well as ones created later. Note that even though the filesystem was not mounted with either the `minvtime` or `maxvdepth` options, you can still turn on versioning for individual directories, as long as it is configured in the kernel. Also, using the `-v` option to `undelete`, you can turn on versioning for single files.

When enabled, versioning is performed without the interaction of the users. If you delete or overwrite a file, you usually don't see anything. You can make the existing versions visible to you by setting the SHOWVERSIONS environment variable to 1 and then exporting it.

The means of storing versions is quite simple. The names are appended with a semicolon followed by the version of the file as in,

`letter;12`

This would be the twelfth version of the file `letter` since versioning was enabled on the filesystem. Keep in mind that this does not mean that there are twelve versions. The number of available versions is defined by the MAXVDEPTH kernel parameter or mount option. If higher than twelve, there just might be twelve versions. However, if set to a lower value you will see most MAXVDEPTH versions. Also keep in mind that you are are not just maintaining a list of changes, but rather complete copies of each file.

For example, let's assume I mounted a filesystem with the option `-o maxvdepth=10`. The system will then save, at most, ten versions. After I edit and save a file for a while, the version number might be up to twelve. However, I will not be able to see or have access to versions lower than three, since they are removed from the system.

Different file versions can not only be accessed when making copies or changes to existing files, but also when you remove them. Assume you have the three latest versions of a letter (`letter;10`, `letter;11`, and `letter;12`) as well as the current version `letter`. If you remove `letter`, the three previous versions still exist. These can be seen by using the `-l` (list) option to `undelete`, either by specifying the file explicitly as in

`undelete -l letter`

or if you leave off the file name, you will see all versions of all files. To undelete a versioned file or make the previous version the current one, simply leave off the options. If you repeatedly use `undelete` with just the file name, you can backup and make ever older versions of the current one. Or, to make things easier, simply copy the older version to the current one, as in

`cp letter\;8 letter`

This will make version 8 the current one. (NOTE: The ' \ ' is necessary to remove the special meaning of the semicolon.)

With the first shipping version of OpenServer, there are some "issues" with versioning, in that it does not behave as expected. One of the first things I noticed was that changing the kernel parameters MAXVDEPTH and MINVTIME do not turn on versioning. Instead, they allow versioning to be turned on. Without them, you can't get versioning to work at all. When version is enabled, you still need to use `undelete -s` on the directory.

There is more to it than that. However, I don't want to repeat too much information that's in the manuals. Therefore, take a look at the `undelete(C)` man-page.

There are other changes that have been made to the system. There is the introduction of new filesystem types as well as the addition of new features to the old filesystems. Table 6–4 contains an overview of some of the more significant aspects of the filesystems.

**Table 6–4**    Filesystem Characteristics

| Filesystem Type | Xenix | S51K | AFS | EAFS | HTFS | DTFS |
|---|---|---|---|---|---|---|
| Driver | xx | ht | ht | ht | ht | dt |
| Max. fs size | 2Gb | 2Gb | 2Gb | 2Gb | 2Gb | 2Gb |
| Max. file size | 2Gb | 2Gb | 2Gb | 2Gb | 2Gb | 2Gb |
| Max. inodes | $2^{16}$ | $2^{16}$ | $2^{16}$ | $2^{16}$ | $2^{27}$ | $2^{31}$ |
| Clustering | no | no | yes | yes | yes | yes |
| Long filenames | no | no | no | yes | yes | yes |
| Symbolic links | no | no | no | yes | yes | yes |
| Bootable | yes | yes | yes | yes | no | no |
| **New functionality in OpenServer 5** | | | | | | |
| Symbolic links in inode | no | no | no | no | yes | yes |
| Intent logging | no | no | yes | yes | yes | no |
| Fast filesys. check | no | no | yes | yes | yes | no |
| Lazy block list evaluation | no | yes | yes | yes | yes | no |
| Temporary fs | no | no | yes | yes | yes | no |
| Checkpointing | no | no | yes | yes | yes | yes |
| Versioning | no | no | no | no | yes | yes |

### High Throughput Filesystem

New to OpenServer is the introduction of a new filesystem device driver: ht. This new driver can handle filesystems with 16-bit inodes like S51K, AFS, and EAFS, but also the new HTFS which can handle 32-bit inodes. Although (as of this writing) you cannot boot from an HTFS, it does provide some important performance and functionality gains.

One area that was changed is the total amount of information that can be stored on a single HTFS as the total number of inodes that can be used. Table 6–4 contains a comparison of the various filesystem types and just how much data they can access.

Another new feature of the ht driver is *lazy block evaluation*. Previously, when a process was started with the `exec()` system call, the system would build a full list of the blocks that made up that program. This delayed the actual start-up of the process, but saved time as the program ran. Since a program spends most of its time executing the same instructions, much of the program is not used; that is, many of the blocks are never referenced. Lazy block evaluation builds this list of blocks only as they are needed. This speeds up the start-up of the process and causes small delays when a previously unreferenced block is first accessed.

Another gain is through "transaction based" processing of the filesystem. As activity occurs on the system, processes are gathered together in what is called an *intent log*. If the system stops improperly, the system can use the intent log to make a determination of how to proceed. Since you only need to check the log in order to clean the filesystem, it is quicker and also more reliable.

Another mechanism used to increase throughput is to disable checkpointing. This way, the filesystem will spend all of its time processing requests rather than updating the filesystem structures. Although this increases throughput, you obviously have the disadvantage of potentially losing data.

When dealing with aspects of the system like the print spooler or the mail system when jobs are batch processed, at any given moment it is less likely that data is being processed. Therefore, you do not need the extra overhead of checkpointing.

This is done by treating the filesystem as "temporary." Such filesystems are mounted with the `-o tmp` option. Although checkpointing is new to OpenServer, you can configure both AFS and EAFS filesystems as temporary. Keep in mind that certain applications like `vi` provide their own recovery mechanism by saving the data at regular intervals. If the files are written by `vi`, but not written to disk, a system crash could lose the last update.

When I described the directory structure I mentioned that each inode was represented by two bytes. This allows only for 64K worth of inodes. Since the HTFS can access $2^{27}$ inodes and the DTFS can access $2^{31}$, there needs to be some other format used in the directories. With the two new filesystems, the key word is "extensible." This means that the structure can be extended as the requirement changes. This allows much more efficient handling of long file names, as compared to the EAFS. In most cases, the filesystem driver is capable of making the translation for applications that don't understand the new concepts. However, if the applications read or write the directory directly, you may need a newer version of the application.

The two new filesystems, HTFS and DTFS, can save space by storing symbolic links in the inode. If the path of the symbolic link is 108 characters or less, the DTFS will store the path within the inode and not in a disk block on the disk. For the HTFS, this limit is 52 characters. This saves space since no data blocks are needed, but it also saves time since once you read the inode from the inode table, you have the path and do not need to access the disk.

There are two issues to keep in mind. If you use relative paths instead of absolute paths, then you may end up with a shorter path that fits into the inode. This saves time when accessing the link. On the other hand, think back to our discussion on symbolic links. When crossing the links the behavior of each shell is different. If you fail to take this into account, you may end up somewhere other than you expect.

### Desktop Filesystem

One of the problems with the advances of SCO OpenServer is the increased amount of hard disk space required to install it. On large servers with several gigabytes of space, this is less of an issue. However, on smaller desktop workstations this can become a significant problem.

Operating systems have been dealing with this issue for years. MS-DOS provides a potential solution in the form of its DoubleSpace disk compression program. Realizing the need for such space savings, SCO OpenServer provides a solution in the form of the new DTFS. Among the issues that need to be addressed are the saving of space, and also the reliability of the data and avoiding any performance degradation that occurs when compressed files need to be uncompressed. On fast CPUs with fast hard disks, the preformance hit from compression is noticeable.

The first issue (saving space) is addressed by the DTFS in a couple of ways. The first is that files are compressed before they are written to the hard disk. This can save anywhere from just a small percentage in the case of binary programs to over fifty percent for text files. What you get will depend on the data you are storing.

Space is saved in the way inodes are stored on the disk. With "traditional" filesystems such as S51K or EAFS, inodes are pre-allocated. That is, when the filesystem is first created, a table for the inodes is allocated at the beginning of the filesystem. This is a consistent size no matter how many or how few inodes are actually used. Inodes on a DTFS are allocated as needed. Therefore, there are only as many inodes as there are files.

As a result you never have any empty slots in the inode table. (Actually there is no inode table in the form we discussed for other filesystems. We'll get to this in a moment.) In order to distinguish these inodes from others, inodes on the DTFS are referred to as dtnodes. What the dtnode table looks like you will see in Figure 6–7.

The DTFS has many of the same features as the EAFS filesystem, such as file length up to 255 characters and symbolic links. In addition, the DTFS also has multiple compression algorithms, greater reliability (through the integrated kernel update daemon, which attempts to keep the file system in a stable state), and dynamic block allocation algorithm that can automatically switch between best-fit and first-fit. Best-fit is when the system looks for an appropriately sized spot on the hard disk for the file and first-fit is when the system looks for the first one that is large enough (even if it is much larger than necessary).

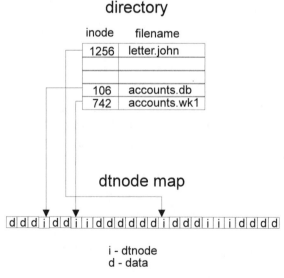

**Figure 6–7**   The dtnode map.

As one might expect, the disk layout is different from other filesystems. The first block (block 0) was historically the "boot block" and has been retained for compatibility purposes. The second block (block 1) is the superblock and like other filesystems it contains global information about the filesystem.

Following the superblock is the block bitmap. There is one block for each 512-byte data block in the filesystem, so the size of the bitmap will vary depending on the size of the filesystem. If the bit is on (1), the block is free, otherwise the block is allocated.

The block bitmap is followed by the dtnode bitmap. Its size is the same as the block bitmap since there is also one bit for each block. The difference is that these bits determine if the corresponding block contains data or dtnodes. A 1 indicates the block contains dtnodes and a 0 indicates data. Following these two bitmaps are the actual data and dtnode blocks. Since the dtnodes are scattered throughout the filesystem, there is no inode table.

Unlike the inodes of other filesystems, dtnodes are not pre-allocated when the filesystem is created. Instead, they are allocated at the same time as the corresponding file. This has the potential for saving a great deal of space since every dtnode points to data in contrast to other filesystems, where inodes may go unused and therefore the space they occupy is wasted.

The translation from dtnode number is straight forward. The dtnode number has the same number as the block number that it resides on. For example, if block 1256 was a dtnode, then that dtnode number would be 1256. This means that since not all blocks contain dtnodes, not all dtnode numbers are used. The one exception to this is that the dtnode number of the root of the filesystem is stored in the superblock. Each dtnode is accessed through the dtnode map.

The contents of the superblock are found in the file location in `<sys/fs/>`. If you take a quick look at it you see several important pieces of information. One of the most important ones is the size of the filesystem. Many of the other parameters included in this structure can be calculated from this value. These include the root dtnode number, start of the bitmaps, the start of the data blocks, as well as the number of free blocks. Although the values can be calculated, it saves time by also storing these values in the superblock.

As I mentioned earlier, the block size of the DTFS varies in increments of 512 bytes between 512 and 4096. The reason for the range is that empirical studies have shown that filesystem throughput increases as the block size increases. However, in an effort to save space (a primary consideration in the DTFS), smaller block sizes were also allowed.

Before being written to the disk, regular files are compressed using one of two algorithms (one being "no compression"). Because of this compression, it is no longer possible to directly calculate a physical block on the hard disk based on the offset in the file. For example, let's consider a file that begins at block 142 of the filesystem. On a noncompressed filesystem, we could easily find byte 712 since block 0 of the file contains bytes 0–511 and block 1 contains bytes 512–1023. Therefore, byte 712 is in block 101 of the filesystem.

However, if we have a compressed filesystem, there is no immediate way of knowing if the compression is sufficient to place byte 712 into block 142, or if it is still in block 143. We could start at the beginning of the file and calculate how much uncompressed data is in each block. Although this would eventually give us the correct block, the amount of time spent doing the calculations more than eliminates advantages gained by the compression.

In order to solve this problem, the structure on the hard disk is maintained in a structure called a B-tree. Without turning this book into a discussion on programming techniques, it is sufficient to say that the basic principle of a B-tree forces the structure to be balanced, therefore the depth of one leaf node is at most one level away from the depth of any other leaf node.

Conceptually the B-tree works like this: Let's assume a block $a$, is the root node. The block offset of every data block that is on the left hand branch of $a$ is smaller than the block offset in $a$. Also, the block offset of every data block that is on the right hand branch of $a$ is larger than the block offset in $a$. This then applies to all subsequent blocks, where the left hand branch is smaller and the right hand branch is larger.

In order to find a particular offset in the file you start at the top of the tree and work down. If the block offset is less than the root, you go down the left hand branch. Likewise, if the block offset is greater, you go down the right hand branch. Although you still have to traverse the tree, the amount you have to search is far less than a pure linear search. Each node has a pointer to both the previous and the next nodes. This allows traversal of the tree in both directions.

Regular files are the only ones that are compressed. Although supported, symbolic links and device nodes are left as they are, since you don't save any space. If a symbolic link is smaller than 192 bytes, the name is actually stored within the dtnode. The size of blocks containing directories is fixed at 512 since directories are typically small. Long names are allowed on the DTFS up to a maximum of 255 characters (plus the terminating NULL). One interesting aspect is the layout of the directory structure. This is substantially different than on the (E)AFS. Among other things there are entries for the size of the filename and size of the directory entry itself.

The DTFS has several built-in features that provide certain protections. The first is a technique called "shadow paging." When a data is about to be modified, extras blocks are allocated that "shadow" the blocks that are going to be changed. The changes are then made to this shadow. Once the change is complete, the changed blocks "replace" the previous blocks in the tree and the old blocks are then freed up. This is also how the dtnode blocks are modified except that the shadow is contained within the same physical block.

If something should happen before the new, changed block replaces the old one, then the system acts as if the change was never started. This is because the file has no knowledge of anything ever happening to it; unlike changes on an EAFS, AFS, and other "traditional" UNIX filesystems, where changes are made to blocks that are already a part of the file. If the system should go down in the middle of writing, then the data is, at best, inconsistent or, at worst, trashed. Obviously, in both cases, once the changes are complete and something happens, the file remains unaffected. We see what this looks like graphically in Figure 6–8.

Also unique to the DTFS is the way the dtnodes are updated. If you look at the structure and count up the number of bytes, you find that the amount of data that each block takes up is less than half the size of the block (512 bytes). The other half is used as the shadow for that dtnode. When it gets updated, the other half is written to first. Only after the information is safely written does the new half become "active." Here again, if the system crashed before the transaction was complete, then it would appear as if nothing was ever started. By comparing the timestamp we can tell which half is active.

Other than saving space, there is another logic to splitting the block in half. Remember that the dtnode points to the nodes that are both above it and below it in the tree. Assume we didn't shadow the dtnode. When one dtnode gets updated, it would get replaced by a new node. Now the nodes above it and below it need to be modified to point to this new node. In order to update them, we have to copy them to new blocks as well. Now, the nodes pointing to these blocks need to get updated. This "ripples" in both directions until the entire tree is updated— quite a waste of time.

Another technique used to increase the reliability is the update daemon (htepi_daemon). Once per second the update daemon checks every writeable filesystem. If the update daemon writes out all the data to that filesystem before another process writes to that filesystem, the update daemon can write out the superblock as well and can then mark the filesystem as clean. If the system were to crash before another process made a write to that filesystem, then it would still be clean and therefore no fsck would be necessary.

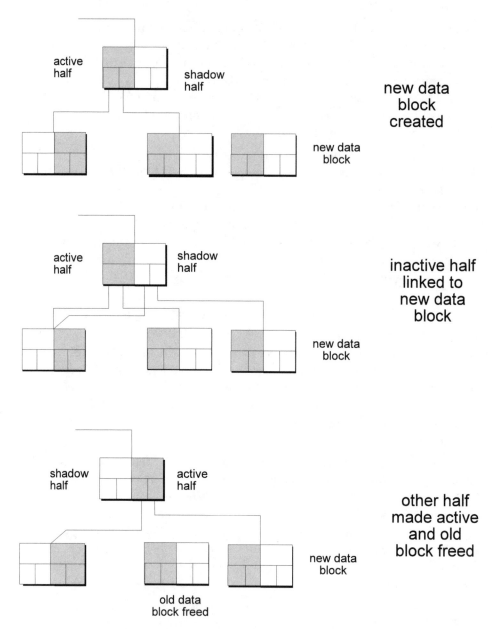

**Figure 6–8**    Updating blocks on a DTFS.

Built into the dtnode is also a pointer to the parent directory of that dtnode. This has a very significant advantage when the system crashes and the directory entry for a particular file gets trashed. In traditional SCO filesystems, if this happened, there would be files without names and when `fsck` ran, they would be placed in `lost+found`. Now, since each file knows who its parent is, the directory structure can easily be rebuilt. That's why there is no more `lost+found` directory.

### High Performance Pipe System

In the section on operating system basics I introduced the concept of a pipe. We all (hopefully) know about pipe through the many commands we have seen in this book. For example, if I want to see the long listing of some directory one screen at a time, I can issue this command:

```
ls -l | more
```

As I mentioned, there are actually data blocks taken up on the hard disk to store the data as the system is waiting for the receiving side to read it. For all intents and purposes this is a real file. It contains data (usually) and it has an inode. The only difference is that, unless it is a named pipe, it has no entry in any directory and therefore no file name. When the system goes down and cannot close the pipes, `fsck` will report them as unreferenced files. This is very disconcerting to many users as they see a long list of unreferenced files when `fsck` runs after a crash.

This represents only one of the problems existing with traditional pipes. The other is the fact that these pipes exist on the hard disk. When the first process writes to the disk, there is a disk access. When the second process reads the disk, there is a disk access. Since disk access causes a bottleneck on most systems, this can be a problem. (NOTE: This ignores the existence of the buffer cache. However, if sufficient time passes between the write and subsequent read, then the buffer cache will no longer contain the data and two disk accesses are necessary.)

SCO OpenServer has done something to correct that. This is the High Performance Pipe System (HPPS). The primary difference between the HPPS and conventional pipes is that the HPPS pipes no longer exist on the hard disk. Instead, they are maintained solely within the kernel as buffers. This corrects the two previously discussed disadvantages of conventional pipes. First, when the system goes down, the pipes simply disappear. Second, since there is no disk interaction, there is never any performance slow-down as a result.

Like traditional pipes, when HPPS pipes are created, an inode is created with it. This inode contains the necessary information to administer that pipe.

## Virtual Disks

One of the major additions to OpenServer is the idea of "virtual disks." These can come in many forms and sizes, each providing its own special benefits and advantages. To the running program (whether it is an application or system command), these disks appear like any other. As a user, the only difference you may see is in the performance improvements that some of these virtual disks can yield.

There are several different kinds of virtual disks which can be used depending on your needs. For example, you may be running a database that requires more contiguous space than you have on any one drive. *Pieces* of different drives can be configured to a single, larger drive. If you need a quicker way of recovering from a hard disk crash, you can *mirror* your disks (one disk is an exact copy of the other). This also increases performance since you can read from either disk. Performance can also be increased by *striping* your disks. This is where portions of the logical disk are spread across multiple physical disks. Data can be written to and read to the disks in parallel, thereby increasing performance. Some of these can even be combined.

Underlying many of the virtual disk types is the concept of RAID. RAID is an acronym for Redundant Array of Inexpensive Disks. Originally, the idea was that you would get better performance and reliability from several, less expensive drives linked together than you would from a single, more expensive drive. The key change in the entire concept is that hard disk prices have dropped so dramatically that RAID is no longer concerned with inexpensive drives; so much so, that the I in RAID is often interpreted as meaning "Intelligent" rather than "Inexpensive."

In the original paper that defined RAID, there were five levels. Since that paper was written, the concept has been expanded and revised. In some cases, characteristics of the original levels are combined to form new levels.

Two concepts are key to understanding RAID. These are *redundancy* and *parity*. The concept of parity is no different than that used in serial communication, except for the fact that the parity in a RAID system can be used to not only detect errors, but *correct* them. This is because more than just a single bit is used per byte of data. The parity information is stored on a drive that is separate from the data. When an error is detected, the information to correct the error is used from the good drives and the parity information. It is also possible to have an entire drive fail completely and still be able to continue working. Usually the drive can be replaced and the information on it rebuilt even while the system is running. Redundancy is the idea that all information is duplicated. If you have a system where one disk is an exact copy of another, one disk is redundant for the other.

In some cases, drives can be replaced even while the system is running. This is the concept of a *hot spare*. This is done from the Virtual Disk Manager. Some hardware vendors even provide the ability to physically remove the drive from the system without having to shut the system down. This is called a *hot swap*. All the control for the hard disks is done by the hard disk controller and the operating system sees only a single hard disk. In either case, data is recreated on the spare as the system is running.

Keep in mind that SCO does *not* directly support hot swapping. This *must* be supported by the hardware in order to ensure the integrity and safety of your data.

SCO's implementation of RAID is purely software. This makes sense since SCO is a software company. Other companies provide hardware solutions. In many cases, hardware implementations of RAID present a single, logical drive to the operating system. In other words, the operating system is not even aware of the RAIDness of the drives it is running on.

In Figure 6–9 we see how the different layers of a virtual drive are related. When an application (vi, a shell, cpio) accesses a file, it makes a system call. Depending on whether you are accessing a file through a raw device or with the filesys-

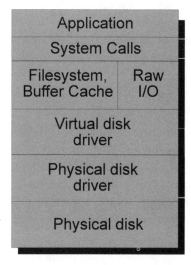

**Figure 6–9** Virtual disk layers.

tem code, the application uses the block or character code within the device driver. The device driver it accesses at this point is for the virtual disk. The virtual disk then accesses the device driver for the physical hard disk.

What device the virtual device driver accesses depends on how it is configured. The virtual disk driver accesses the device in the same way, regardless of what type of disk it is. Accessing the physical disk is the problem of the physical disk driver and *not* the virtual disk driver. It is therefore possible to have virtual disks composed of different types of disks as well as disks on different controllers.

The simplest virtual disk is called (what else) a *simple* disk. With this, you can define all your nonroot filesystem space as a single virtual disk. This can be done to existing filesystems. It not only provides more efficient storage, but using virtual disks instead of conventional filesystems makes it easier to change to the more complex virtual disks. This is because you cannot add existing filesystems to virtual disks. They must be first converted to simple disks.

A *concatenated* disk is created when two or more disk pieces are combined. In this way, you can create logical disks that are larger than any single disk. Disks that are concatenated together do not need to be the same size. The total available space is simply the sum of all concatenated disks. New peices cannot be added to concatenated disks once the filesystem is created. Remember that the filesystem sees this as a logical drive. Division and inode tables are based on the size of the drive when it is added to the system. Adding a new piece would require you to recreate the filesystem.

A *striped array* is also referred to as RAID 0 or RAID Level 0. Here, portions of the data are written to and read from multiple disks in parallel. This greatly increases the speed at which data can be accessed. This is because half of the data is being read or written by each hard disk, which cuts the access time almost in half. The amount of data that is written to a single disk is referred to as the *stripe width*. For example, if single blocks are written to each disk, then the stripe width would be a block. We see this in Figure 6–10.

This type of virtual disk provides increased performance since data is being read from multiple disks simultaneously. Since there is no parity to update when data is written, this is faster than a system using parity. However, the drawback is that there is no redundancy. If one disk goes out, then data is probably lost. Such a system is more suited for organizations where speed is more important than reliability.

Keep in mind that data is written to all the physical drives each time data is written to the logical disk. Therefore, the pieces must all be the same size. For example, you could not have one piece that was 500 MB and a second piece that was

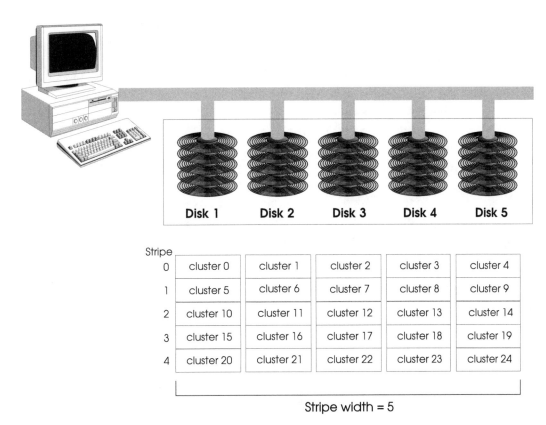

Figure 6–10    Striped array with no parity (RAID 0).

only 400 Mb. (Where would the other 100 be written?) Here again, the total amount of space available is the sum of all the pieces.

Disk mirroring (also referred to as RAID 1) is where data from the first drive is duplicated onto the second drive. When data is written to the primary drive, it is automatically written to the secondary drive as well. Although this slows things down a bit when data is written, when data is read it can be read from either disk, thus *increasing* performance. Mirrored systems are best employed where there is a large database application and availability of the data (transaction speed and reliability) is more important than storage efficiency. Another consideration is the speed of the system. Since it takes longer than normal to write data, mirrored systems are bettered suited to database applications where queries are more common than updates.

As of this writing, OpenServer does not provide for a mirror of the `/dev/stand` filesystem. Therefore, you will need to copy this information somewhere else. One solution would be for you to create a copy of the `/dev/stand` filesystem on the mirror driver yourself. I have been told by people at SCO that an Extended Funtionality Supplement (EFS) is planned to allow you to mirror `/dev/stand` and boot from it, as well.

The term used for RAID 4 is a block-interleaved undistributed parity array. Like RAID 0, RAID 4 is also based on striping, but redundancy is built in with parity information written to a separate drive. The term "undistributed" is used since a single drive is used to store the parity information. If one drive fails (or even a portion of the drive), the missing data can be created using the information on the parity disk. It is possible to continue working even with one inoperable drive since the parity drive is used on-the-fly to recreate the data. Even data written to the disk is still valid since the parity information is updated as well. This is not intended as a means of running your system indefinitely with a drive missing, but rather it gives you the chance to stop your system gracefully. This we see in Figure 6–11.

RAID 5 takes this one step further and distributes the parity information to all drives. For example, the parity drive for block 1 might be drive 5 but the parity drive for block 2 is drive 4. With RAID 4, the single parity drive was accessed on every single data write, which decreased overall performance. Since data and parity is interspersed on a RAID 5 system, no single drive is overburdened. In both cases, the parity information is generated during the write and should a drive go out, the missing data can be recreated. Here again, you can recreate the data while the system is running, if a hot spare is used. We can see this Figure 6–12.

As I mentioned before, some of the characteristics can be combined. For example, it is not uncommon to have to have striped arrays mirrored as well. This provides the speed of a striped array with the redundancy of a mirrored array, without the expense necessary to implement RAID 5. Such a system would probably be referred to as RAID 10 (RAID 1 plus RAID 0). All of these are configured and administered using the Virtual Disk Manager, which then calls the `dkconfig` utility. It is advised that, at first, you use the Virtual Disk Manager since it is easier to use. However, once you get the hang of things, there is nothing wrong with using `dkconfig` directly.

The information for each virtual disk is kept in the `/etc/dktab` file and is used by `dkconfig` to administer virtual disks. Each entry is made up of two lines. The first is the virtual disk declaration line. This is followed by one or more virtual piece definition lines.

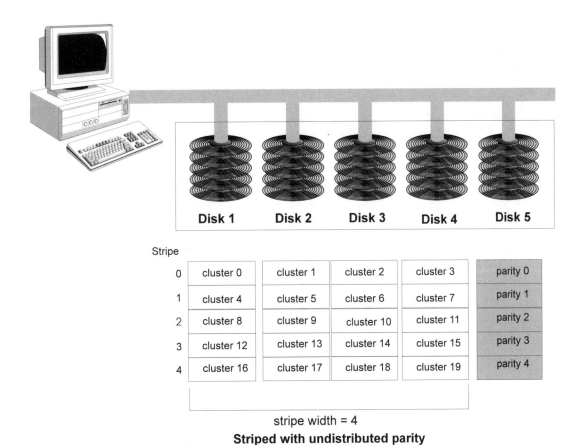

**Figure 6–11**   Striped array with undistributed parity (RAID 4).

This is an example of an entry in a `dktab` file that would be used to create a 1 GB array (this is RAID 5):

```
/dev/dsk/vdisk1        array          5        16
    /dev/dsk/1s1            100      492000
    /dev/dsk/2s1            100      492000
    /dev/dsk/3s1            100      492000
    /dev/dsk/4s1            100      492000
    /dev/dsk/5s1            100      492000
```

The first line is the virtual disk declaration line and varies in the number of fields depending on what type it is. In each case, the first entry is the device name for

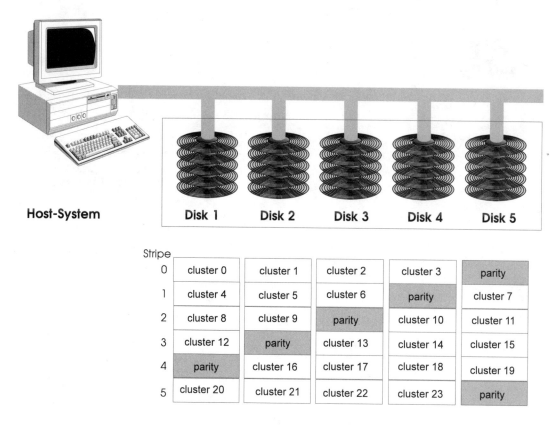

Host-System

| Stripe | Disk 1 | Disk 2 | Disk 3 | Disk 4 | Disk 5 |
|---|---|---|---|---|---|
| 0 | cluster 0 | cluster 1 | cluster 2 | cluster 3 | parity |
| 1 | cluster 4 | cluster 5 | cluster 6 | parity | cluster 7 |
| 2 | cluster 8 | cluster 9 | parity | cluster 10 | cluster 11 |
| 3 | cluster 12 | parity | cluster 13 | cluster 14 | cluster 15 |
| 4 | parity | cluster 16 | cluster 17 | cluster 18 | cluster 19 |
| 5 | cluster 20 | cluster 21 | cluster 22 | cluster 23 | parity |

**Striped with distributed parity**
**(RAID 5)**

**Figure 6–12**    Striped array with distributed parity (RAID 5).

the virtual device followed by what type it is. For example, if you have a simple virtual disk, there is only the device name followed by the type (simple). Here, we are creating a disk array, so we have `array` in the type field.

A simple disk consists of just a single piece. The other types, such as mirror or concatenated, require a third field to indicate how many pieces (simple disks) go into making up the virtual disk. Since we are creating a disk of five pieces, this value is 5.

If you use striped disks or disk arrays, then the fourth field defines the size of the cluster in 512-byte blocks. We are using a value of 16, therefore we have an 8K cluster size. If you have mirrored disks, then the fourth field is the "catch-up" block size and is used when the system is being restored.

The virtual piece definition line describes a piece of the virtual disk. (In this case we have five pieces.) It consists of three fields. The first is the device node of the physical device. Note that in our case, each of the physical drives is a separate physical drive. (We know this because of the device names 1s1-5s1.)

The second field is the offset from the beginning of the physical device of where to start the disk piece. Be sure you leave enough room so you start beyond the division and bad track tables. Here we are using a value of 100 and since the units are disk blocks (512 bytes), we are starting 50K from the beginning of the partitions, which is plenty of room.

The third field is the length of the disk piece. Here you need to be sure that you do not go beyond the end of the disk piece. In our case we are specifying 492000. This is also in disk blocks. Therefore, each of the physical pieces is just under 250Mb. Since the actual amount of storage we get is the sum of all the pieces, we have just under 1000Mb or 1Gb.

To change this array to RAID 4, where there is a single drive that is used solely for parity, we could add a fourth field to one of the virtual piece description lines. For example, if we wanted to turn drive three into the parity drive, we would change it to look like this:

```
/dev/dsk/3s1          100     492000 parity
```

Okay, so you've decided that you need to increase performance or reliability (or both) and have decided to implement a virtual disk scheme. Well, which one? Before you decide, there are several things you need to consider. The *System Administrators Guide* contains a checklist of things to consider when deciding which is best for you.

### Things to Consider

If you create an emergency boot/root floppy on a system with virtual disks, there are a couple of things to remember. First, once you create a virtual disk, you should create a new boot/root floppy set. This is especially important if the virtual disk you are adding is a mirror of the root disk. If you do not and later need to boot from the floppy, then any changes made to the root filesystem will not be made to the mirror. The drives will then be inconsistent.

In order to boot correctly, you need to change the default boot string. Normally, the default boot string points to hd(40) for the root filesystem. Instead, you need to change it to reflect the fact that the root filesystem is mirror. For example, you could use the string

```
fd(60)unix.z root=vdisk(1) swap=none dump=none
```

This tells the system to use virtual disk 1 as the root filesystem.

Note also that the device names are probably different from one machine to another. Therefore, it may not be possible to use the boot/root floppy set from one machine on another.

It's also possible to "nest" virtual drives. For example, you could have several drives that you make into a striped array. This striped array is seen as a single drive, which you can then include in another virtual disk. For example, you could mirror that striped array.

Be careful with this, however. It is not recommended that you nest virtual drivers with redundant drivers (mirrored, RAID 5) *inside* of other virtual disks. This can cause the virtual disk driver to hang, preventing access to *all* virtual drives.

## Accessing DOS Files

Even on a standard SCO UNIX system, without all the bells and whistles of TCP/IP, X-Windows, and SCO Merge, there are several tools that you can use to access DOS filesystems. These can be found on the `doscmd (C)` man-page. Although these tools have some obvious limitations due to the differences in the two operating systems, they provide the mechanism to exchange data between the two systems.

Copying files between DOS and UNIX systems presents a unique set of problems. One of the most commonly misunderstood aspects of this is using wildcards to copy files from DOS to UNIX. This we can do using the `doscp` command, for example,

```
doscp a:*  .
```

One might think that this command copies all the files from the a: drive (which is assumed to be DOS formatted) into the current directory. The first problem is the way that DOS interprets wildcards. Using a single asterisk would only match files without an extension. For example, it would match LETTER, but not LETTER.TXT. So, if we expand the wildcard to include the possibility of the extensions, we get

```
doscp a:*.*  .
```

which should copy everything from the floppy into the current directory. Unfortunately, that's not the way it works either. Instead of the message

```
doscp: /dev/install:* not found
```

you get the slight variation:

```
doscp: /dev/install:*.* not found
```

Remember from our discussion of shell basics that it is the shell that is doing the expansion. Since nothing matches, we get this error. The solution to the problem was a little shell script that does a listing of the DOS device. Before we go on, we need to side-step a little. There are two ways to get a directory listing off a DOS disk. The first is with the dosdir command. This gives you output that appears just as if you had run the dir command under native DOS. In order to use this output, we would have to parse each line to get the file name—not an easy thing. The other is dosls, which gives a listing that looks like the UNIX ls command. Here you have a single column of file names with nothing else—much easier to parse. The problem is that the file names come off in capital letters. Although this is not a major problem, I like to keep my file names as consistent as possible. Therefore, I want to convert them to lowercase.

Skipping the normal things I put into scripts like usage messages and argument checking, the script could look like this:

```
DIR=$1
dosls $DIR | while read file
do
echo "$file"
doscp "$dosdir/$file" 'echo $file | tr "[A-Z]" "[a-z]"' ( Note the back-ticks
done
```

The script takes a single argument which is assigned to the DIR variable. We then do a dosls of that directory which is piped to the read. If we think back to the section on shell programming, we know that this construct reads input from the previous command (in this case dosls) until the output ends. Next, we have a do-done loop that is done once for each line. In the loop, we echo the name of the file (I like to seeing what's going on) and then make the doscp.

The doscp line is more complex. The first part ($dosdir/$file) is the source file. The second part, as you would guess, is the destination file. Remember that the back-ticks mean, "the output of the command." Here, that command is echo | tr. Note that we are echoing the file *name* through tr and not the *contents*. It is then translated in such a way that all capital letters are converted to lowercase. See the tr(C) man-page for more details.

To go the other way (UNIX to DOS), we don't have this problem. Wildcards are expanded correctly, so we end up with the right files. In addition, we don't need to worry about the names, since they are converted for us. The problem lies in names that do not fit into the DOS 8.3 standard. If a name is longer that eight characters or the extension is longer than three characters it is simply truncated. For example, the name letter_to_jim.txt ends up as letter_t.txt, or letter.to.jim becomes letter.to.

One thing to keep in mind here is that copying files like this is only really useful for text files and data files. You *could* use it to copy executables to your SCO system if you are running SCO Merge, for example. However, this process does *not* convert a DOS executable into a form that native SCO can understand.

Be careful when copying files because of conversions that are made. With UNIX text files, each line is ended with a carriage return (CR) character. The system converts this to a carriage return-new line (NL) pair when outputting the line. You can ensure that when copying files from DOS to UNIX that the CR-NL is converted to simply a CR by using the -m option to doscp. This also ensures that the CR is converted to a CR-NL when copying the other way. If you want to ensure that no conversion is made, use the -r option.

You can also make the conversion using either the xtod or dtox commands. The xtod command converts UNIX files to DOS format and the dtox converts DOS format files to UNIX. In both cases, the command takes a single argument and outputs to stdout. Therefore, to actually "copy" to a file you need to redirect stdout.

An alternative to doscp is to mount the DOS disk. Afterwards, you can use standard UNIX commands like cp to copy files. Although this isn't the best idea for floppies, it is wonderful for DOS hard disks. In fact, I have it configured so that all of my DOS file systems are mounted automatically via /etc/default/filesys. To be able to do this, you have to add the support for it in the kernel. Fortunately, it is simply a switch that is turned on or off via the mkdev dos script. Since it makes changes to the kernel, you need to relink and reboot.

Once you have run mkdev dos, you can mount DOS filesystem by hand or, as I said, through /etc/default/filesys. For example, if we wanted to mount the first DOS partition on the first drive, you have two choices of devices: /dev/hd0d or /dev/dsk/0sC. I prefer the latter, since I have several DOS partition; some do not have an equivalent for the first form. Therefore, by using /dev/dsk/0sC, I am consistent in the names I use. If I wanted to mount it onto /usr/dos/c_drive, the command would be

```
mount -f DOS /dev/dsk/0sC /usr/dos/c_drive
```

The only issue with this is that in ODT the file name was all capitalized. In OpenServer, there is the lower option, which is used to show all the file names in lowercase. Therefore, the command would look like this:

```
mount -f DOS -o lower /dev/dsk/0sC /usr/dos/c_drive
```

Although you can use the mkdev fs script to add a DOS filesystem, it displays a couple of annoying messages. Since I think it is just as easy to edit /etc/de-

`fault/filesys`, I do so. There is also the issue that certain options are not possible through the `mkdev fs` script or the Filesystem Manager. Therefore, I simply copy an existing entry and end up with something like this:

```
bdev=/dev/dsk/0sC cdev=/dev/rdsk/0sC \
      mountdir=/usr/dos/c_drive mount=yes fstyp=DOS,lower \
      fsck=no fsckflags= rcmount=yes \
      rcfsck=no mountflags=
```

The key point is the `fstyp` entry. Since we can specify mount options here, I specified the `lower` option so that all filename's would come out in lowercase. Each time I go into multi-user mode, this filesystem is mounted for me. For more details on the options here, check out the `mount(ADM)` man-page or the section on filesystems. (Note: The `lower` option is only available in OpenServer.)

Keep in mind that if the DOS filesystem that you are mounting contains a compressed volume, you will not see the files with the compressed volume. This applies to both ODT and OpenServer.

Another of the DOS commands that I use often is `dosformat`. Although there are a few options (`-v` to prompt for volume name, `-q` for quiet mode, `-f` to run in noninteractive mode), I have never used them. The one thing I need to point out is that you format a UNIX floppy with the raw device (for example, `/dev/rfd0`), but with `dosformat`, you format the block device (for example, `/dev/fd0`).

The remaining files, which I use only on occassion are listed here:

`dosrm` ⇐ Removes files from a DOS filesystem

`dosmkdir` ⇐ makes a directory on a DOS filesystem

`dosrmdir` ⇐ moves directories from a DOS filesystem

## Go Look

As with the kernel components, I suggest you go poke around the system a little. Take a look at the files on your system that we talked about to see what filesystems you have and to find out about your system. Look for different kinds of files. If they are hard links, try to find out what other files are linked to it. If you find a symbolic link, take a look at the file pointed to by that symbolic link.

In every case, look at the file permissions. Think about how they are set and what influence this has on their behavior. Also think about the kind of file it is and who can access it. If you aren't sure of what kind of file it is, you can use the `file` command to do so.

# CHAPTER

# 7

# Starting
# and Stopping
# the System

Almost every user (and many administrators) never sees what is happening as the system is booting. Those that do, often are not sure what is happening. From the time you flip the power switch, to the time you get that first `Login:` prompt, dozens of things must happen. Many things happen long before the system knows that it's SCO UNIX that's running. Knowing what is happening as the system boots (and in what order) is very useful when your system is not starting the way it should.

In this chapter we are going to first talk about starting your system. Although you can get it going by flipping on the power switch and letting the system boot by itself, there are many ways to change the behavior of your system as it boots. How the system boots may depend on the situation. As we move along through the chapter we'll talk about different ways of influencing the way the system boots.

After we talk about how to start your system. There are few choices in terms of how you can stop your system. However, the few that are available allow you to alter the system's behavior when shutting down.

## The Boot Process

The very first thing that happens is the Power-On Self-Test (POST). Here, the hardware checks itself to see that things are all right. One thing that is done is to compare the hardware settings in the CMOS to what is physically on the system. Some errors, like the floppy types not matching are annoying, but your system still can boot. Others, like the lack of a video card can keep the system from continuing. Often times, there is nothing to indicate a problem except for a few little beeps. What the boot process looks like graphically you can see in Figure 7–1.

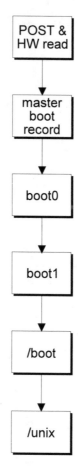

**Figure 7–1**   The stages of booting the system.

Once the POST is completed, the hardware jumps to a specific, predefined location in RAM. The instructions that are located here are relatively simply and basically tell the hardware to go look for a boot device. Depending on how your CMOS is configured, first your floppy is checked and then your hard disk.

When a boot device is found (let's assume that it's a hard disk), the hardware is told to go to the 0th (first) sector (cylinder 0, head 0, sector 0), then load and execute the instructions there. This is the masterboot block, or MBR for you DOS-heads. This 512-byte piece of code is intelligent enough to read the partition table (located just past the masterboot block) and find the active partition. Once it finds the active partition it begins to read and execute the instructions contained within the first block.

It is at this point that viruses can affect/infect SCO systems. The masterboot block is the same format for essentially all PC-based operating systems. All the masterboot block does is to find and execute code at the beginning of the active partition. Instead, the masterboot block could contain code that told it to go to the very last sector of the hard disk and execute the code there. If that last sector contained code that told the system to find and execute code at the beginning of the active partition, you would never know anything was wrong.

Let's assume that the instructions at the very end of the disk are larger than a single, 512-byte sector. If they took up a couple of kilobytes, you could get some fairly complicated code. Since it as at the end of the disk, you would probably never know it was there. What if that code checked the date in the CMOS and if the day of the week was Friday and the day of the month was the 13th it would erase the first few kilobytes of your hard disk? If that were the case, then your system would be infected with the Friday the 13th virus and you could no longer boot your hard disk.

Viruses that behave in this way are called "boot viruses", as they affect the masterboot block and can only damage your system if this is the disk you are booting from. These kinds of viruses can affect all PC-based systems. Some computers will allow you to configure the CMOS (more on that later) so that you cannot write to the masterboot block. Although this is a good safeguard against older viruses, the newer ones can change the CMOS to allow writing to masterboot block. So, just because you have enabled this feature, does not mean your system is safe. However, I must point out that boot viruses can only affect SCO systems if you boot from an infected disk. This will usually be a floppy—more than likely a DOS floppy. Therefore, you need to be especially careful when booting from floppies.

Now back to our story . . .

As I mentioned, the code in the masterboot block finds the active partition and begins executing the code there. On an MS-DOS system, these are the `IO.SYS` and `MSDOS.SYS` files. On an SCO UNIX system, this is referred to as `boot0`. Although `IO.SYS` and `MSDOS.SYS` are "real" files that you can look at and even remove if you want to, the `boot0` program is not. It is part of the partition, but not part of any division. Therefore, it is not part of any filesystem and therefore not a "real" file. Next, `boot0` reads `boot1`. `Boot1`, then reads the first "real" file: `/boot`.

The `/boot` program is not only a file, but it is a program. The key aspect is that it is a "stand-alone" program, often referred to as a *stand-alone loader*, as it must load the specified operating system into memory. Because of this, `/boot` must implement its own system calls and memory management. These are mostly handled by making use of the system BIOS. Once /boot has finished loading the SCO UNIX operating system, UNIX begins to run and the BIOS is no longer used (at least for the most part).

In comparison to the other pieces of code, /boot is a genius. It is /boot that reads the /etc/default/boot file to determine the default boot string (more on that in a moment) and default boot options, such as how long to wait until automatically booting. /boot also displays the now famous boot: prompt.

When you just press ENTER or wait for the time-out to automatically boot, /boot executes the instructions defined in the default boot string. If you look inside of /etc/default/boot, you will see an entry DEFBOOTSTR. This is the default boot string. You will hear it referred to as either "default boot string" or "defbootstr". I am going to talk about some of these options later, but if you want to get more information now, check out the boot(HW) man-page.

In OpenServer, you have a new program: bootos. This can be called from /boot and is used to boot other operating systems, including DOS, Windows NT, and OS/2. Rather than breaking the flow of this discussion, I will get into the bootos program later.

Assuming that you simply pressed <ENTER> or waited for the time-out specified in /etc/default/boot, the first thing is done is "memory sizing." Memory sizing is when the /boot program figures out how much memory you have and displays it on the screen. Such as

```
Memory sizing ............ Memory found: 0k-640k,1m-16m,16m-32m/n
```

In this case, /boot recognized the base 640K (0k-640k) of RAM as well as the rest of my 32Mb(1m-16m,16m-32m). Why didn't it just say 1-32m, rather than splitting it into those two ranges? The answer is in the /n at the end of the line. This says that the range of memory between 16 and 32 megabytes is not DMAable. That is, the Direct Memory Access controller cannot access memory above 16MB. Because of this, all of the kernel's data must be below the 16Mb mark. If you only had 20Mb, this would read: 16m-20m/n. DMA is a way of having a device access memory directly without the intervention of the CPU, which saves time. We talk more about DMA in the chapter on hardware.

Usually what your defbootstr says to do next is to load and execute the /unix program. This is the operating system itself (the kernel). As the system is loading the kernel, you will see several rows of dots moving across the screen. Since the boot procedure takes a few moments, the dots act as an indicator that, yes, it is doing something.

In ODT, each dot represents 4K being loaded. Because the OpenServer kernel is a lot larger, there are more 4K chunks to load in. So, instead of having more dots, each dot in OpenServer represents 3 dots in ODT. Therefore, don't think that your system is loading slower. There's just more to load.

The first set of dots follow the message: `loading .text`. If you remember from the discussion on the kernel internals, the text is the segment of the program that contains the instructions. Next, we see the message `loading .data`. Like other programs, this segment contains the kernel's initialized data. Lastly, we see `loading .bss`. This segment contains the kernel's declared, but uninitialized data.

Shortly thereafter, the screen clears and you see what is referred to as the "hardware screen." At the top is the date, the operating system, the kernel ID number, and a few copyright notices.

Depending on your hardware, you might then see this message:

```
10 bits of I/O address decoding
```

Some buses only have 10 bits to decode I/O address lines. This means that base addresses can only fall into the range of 000h–FFFh. This also means that since there are 6 bits left over, there are 63 "image" addresses that could cause problems with other boards if the lower order 10 bits matched. The above message indicates that on this system, there are only 10 I/O address lines. Therefore, there are only 10 bits for I/O decoding.

Next, we see a table of the hardware devices that the system recognizes. You can see what each of the columns represent by the header at the top of each column. What the individual entries mean in the comments section, we will talk about in the chapter on hardware. This table is basically the same as what you get by running `hwconfig -h`.

We next have a listing of how much memory is in the system and how it is broken down:

```
mem: total = 16256k, kernel = 4852k, user = 11404k
```

This listing is the deciding factor in determining how much your system is running with. Regardless of what the system shows as it boots or what the `/boot` program shows during the memory sizing, this is what the kernel sees. In this case, there are 16 Mb of RAM available. However, I have never seen a case where the hardware reports a different amount of memory than what is displayed here.

Here we can see just how much memory the kernel takes up and how much is left over for users. In this case, not quite 5Mb are being used by the kernel, leaving a little over 11Mb for user processes. Be careful! This can be deceptive.

The amount of user memory does not say how much is left over for users logging in. It would be more informative to refer to it simply as nonkernel memory.

Remember in our discussion of kernel internals, I mentioned that a process can be operated in either user mode or kernel mode. A process that is running in user mode is executing user instructions. This is taking up user memory. Any program that is not the kernel is a process. All system processes, no matter what they do, will take a portion of this remaining 11Mb. This includes such things as `vhand`, `sched`, and `init`.

On my OpenServer system, there are so many system processes that the amount available for "normal" users is almost the exact opposite of what it appears from the message during boot. With nothing running other than the system processes, almost 12Mb is used. (That's why I upgraded from 16Mb to 32Mb.)

We next have details of the import system devices along with their major and minor numbers, such as the root filesystem (`rootdev = 1/40`) and the swap device (`swapdev = 1/41`). The pipe device (`pipedev = 1/40`) is where the system gets the data blocks from creating pipes. We talked about this in the section on files and filesystems. Lastly there is the dump device (`dumpdev = 1/41`). Hope that you never have to use this.

Should something go wrong on your system and it needs to panic (remember our discussion on kernel internals?), the kernel tries to help you figure out what went wrong. It does so by saving an image of all of physical RAM. That way, you can go back and see what the kernel was doing when it panicked.

Have you ever wondered why the SCO doc says that you need at least as much swap as you have RAM? This is the reason. If you panic and there is not enough space on your swap device, you will not get a valid dump image. Granted, you could save some other area of your hard disk for dump and only use the swap area for swap. However, this is a waste of space since during normal operations the dump area is not used and when the system panics, it's not using the swap device.

In addition to being told where the swap device is, we are also told how big it is. In my case, the entry looks like this:

```
nswap = 34000
```

Along with this there is the number of times the clock generates and interrupts per second (`Hz = 100`) and the size of your I/O buffers (`i/o bufs = 1472k`). We talked about these I/O buffers in both the section on device nodes and kernel internals. However, there we used a different name. These I/O buffers are your buffer cache.

When the system boots, you see all the entries in nice, neat little rows, like this:

```
device     address        vector  dma  comment
----------------------------------------------------------
%fpu       -              13       -    type=80387
%serial    0x03F8-0x03FF  4        -    unit=0 type=Standard nports=1
%floppy    0x03F2-0x03F7  6        2    unit=0 type=135ds18
%console   -              -        -    unit=vga type=0 12 screens=68k
%adapter   0x0330-0x0332  11       5    type=ad rev=01 ha=0 id=7 fts=s
%tape      -              -        -    type=S ha=0 id=2 lun=0 bus=0 ht=ad
%disk      -              -        -    type=S ha=0 id=0 lun=0 bus=0 ht=ad
%Sdsk      -              -        -    cyls=1170 hds=64 secs=32 fts=sb
mem: total = 16256k, kernel = 4852k, user = 11404k
swapdev = 1/41, swplo = 0, nswap = 50000, swapmem = 25000k
rootdev = 1/42, pipedev = 1/42, dumpdev = 1/41
kernel: Hz = 100, do bufs = 1472k
```

The column headers are the type of device, base address range in hexadecimal, the interrupt vector (IRQ), DMA channel, and comments (which contains other details about the hardware).

This is also how the file /usr/adm/messages (where this boot information eventually ends up) looks on an OpenServer system. However, if you look in /usr/adm/messages on an ODT 3.0 system, things look a lot sloppier:

```
D 10 bits of I/O address decoding
Sat Feb 26 14:35:16
g
E device                   address        vector dma comment
-----------------------------------------------------------
%fpu                       -              13      -   type=80387
F0 F1 F2 F3 F4 F5 %serial  0x03F8-0x03FF  4       -   unit=0 type=Standard nports=1
F6 F7 %floppy              0x03F2-0x03F7  6       2   unit=0 type=135ds18 %floppy
                           -              -       -   unit=1 type=96ds15
F8 F9 F10 %console         -              -       -   unit=vga type=0 12 screens=68k
F11 F12 %adapter           0x0330-0x0332  11      5   type=ad ha=0 id=7 fts=s
F13 F14 F15 F16 F17 F18 %tape -           -       -   type=S ha=0 id=2 lun=0 ht=ad
F19 G H0 H
Sat Feb 26 14:35:17
1 H2 H3 H4 H5 H6 %disk     -              -       -   type=S ha=0 id=0 lun=0 ht=ad fts=s
%Sdsk                      -              -       -   cyls=1170 hds=64 secs=32
H7 H8 H9 H10 H11 H12 H13 I0 mem: total = 16256k, kernel = 3428k, user = 12828k
J K L M rootdev = 1/40, swapdev = 1/41, pipedev = 1/40, dumpdev = 1/41
nswap = 34000, swplo = 0, Hz = 100
kernel: i/o bufs = 600k
```

Interspersed among the information that we already talked about, you will see sets of letters, with some followed by numbers. These are essentially checkpoints that the kernel has reached as it checks the hardware it expects to find on your system, as well as when it first mounts the root filesystem, prints the hardware configuration information above, and other things it must do at start-up. Because some of the start-up procedures occur rather quickly, you may not see the letter for that stage, however it is there. You may see this information as the system boots. Table 7–1 contains the boot letters you see as your system is coming up.

It is around here that the kernel loads and starts the `init` program. One of the first things that `init` does is reads the `/etc/inittab` file. It looks for any entry that should be run when the system is initializing (the entry has a `sysinit` in the third field) and then executes the corresponding command. (See the `inittab` `(F)` man-page for more details).

The first thing `init` runs out of the `inittab` is `/etc/bcheckrc`. This is a shell script, so you can take a look at it if you want. The first thing it does is to determine if you have a memory dump image on your swap device. If you should have the misfortune of having your system panic, you may have the good fortune to have the system spill its guts into the dump device (usually the same as the swap device). This contains a complete image of what was in physical mem-

**Table 7–1**   Boot Letters

| Boot phase | Description |
|---|---|
| D | Check for 10 bits of I/O decoding and perform certain machine-specific initializations |
| E | Print configuration information for the math coprocessor if there is one |
| F | Initialize I/O devices and pseudo-device |
| G | Initialize the PICs and multiprocessors as well as configure the root disk driver and reset keyboard |
| H | Initialize various system resources such as the kernel inode table, streams, and c-lists |
| I | Print machine-specific information, start certain devices, and print the total kernel and user memory |
| J | Initialize floating point emulator |
| K | Open the swap device and add the swap file table |
| M | Initialize machine-specific memory ECC support, as well as display the primary devices (root, pipe, and dump) , clock interrupt rate (HZ), kernel I/O buffers( the buffer cache), and additional CPUs found |

ory at the time the system panicked. There is useful information here that can often be used to determine why the system panicked.

Obviously, the system needs some place to put the memory image. As I mentioned before, this is the dump device. Unless you have changed it, this will be the same place as the swap device. Because the system needs to dump all memory in order to ensure it got everything it needed, the dump device must be at least the same size as the amount of RAM you have. Since the dump and the swap device are usually the same thing, this is one reason why the swap device must be at least the same size as RAM.

If the system panics and is successful in writing the memory image to dump device, you will probably see the following message when the system reboots:

```
There may be a system dump memory image in the swap device.

Do you want to save it? (y/n)
```

If you respond n, you are then asked if you want to delete the image; enter y to save the image and continue.

Another likely possibility when the system panics is that one or more filesystems will be "dirty", which could mean that they are in an inconsistent state. In many cases no serious problems arise as a result. However, in order to access the filesystem, it must be checked first as the system has no way of knowing if there are any problems until it has checked and the problems are corrected. This is referred to as *cleaning* the filesystem.

If the system was not shutdown properly (through a panic or by simply turning off the power) then every mounted filesystem will need to be cleaned. Depending on how you configured them initially, nonroot filesystems could be cleaned automatically. However, unless you changed the default, cleaning of the root filesystem will need to be done manually. At the very least, you will be prompted to start `fsck`. Look at the chapter on filesystems for a discussion of `fsck`. See the `filesys(F)` man-page for more details on cleaning filesystems automatically.

Checking to see if the root filesystem is dirty is another function of the `/etc/bcheckrc` script. The indication that the filesystem was not unmounted correctly occurs at boot time when you see this message:

```
fsstat: root filesystem needs checking

OK to check the root filesystem (/dev/root) (y/n)?
```

To clean the filesystem, enter y (for yes), this starts the `fsck` utility, which cleans the filesystem. The extent the `fsck` utility goes through to clean the filesystem is dependent on the extent of the problems. We'll get into details about this later.

If you have intent logging enabled on your filesystem in OpenServer, the cleaning process is shortened considerably. Normally, `fsck` must look through every directory and check every file in the inode table to ensure things are consistent. If intent logging is enabled, the log can be replayed and outstanding transactions completed. As a result, the time spent to both check and clean the filesystem is only a fraction of what it was previously (seconds compared to minutes).

After we have cleaned the root filesystem, `bcheckrc` adds the root filesystem to the mount table by hand and then exits. It is here that we are at the point we would have been if we hadn't needed to clean the filesystem. Since `bcheckrc` is now finished, we need to look in `inittab` again to see what is run next. Here we find `/etc/smmck`.

It is the responsibility of `/etc/smmck` to ensure that files in the TCB are in a consistent state. Many TCB programs create temporary files as they work. It is the job of `smmck` to determine which of these temporary files is the 'correct' one.

Next, `init` looks through `inittab` for the line with `initdefault` in the third field. The `initdefault` entry tells the system what run-level to enter initially. It is here we are given the prompt

```
INIT: SINGLE USER MODE
Type CONTROL-d to continue with normal startup,
(or give the root password for system maintenance):
```

This allows us to choose one of two operating modes. If you were to type in the root password you would enter *system maintenance mode*. Since the root user is the only one who has access to this mode, it is also referred to as *single-user mode*.

In maintenance mode, virtually nothing is going on in the system. There are, of course, the system processes such as `init`, `sched`, `vhand`, and `bdflush`. However, that's about it. As a result, what we might consider as normal operations such as printing or network access are not active. This allows the system administrator to work on the system without fear that his or her actions will conflict with those of others on the system.

Well, what kind of actions? One with the most impact is adding new or updating software. There are often cases where new software will impact the old software in such a way that it is better not to have other users on the system. In such cases, the installation procedures for that software should keep you from installing unless you are in maintenance mode.

This is also a good place to configure hardware that you added or change kernel parameters. Although these rarely impact users, you will have to do a kernel re-link. This takes up a lot of system resources and overall performance is degraded. In addition, some utilities such as ps do not work after a kernel relink until the system is rebooted. The flow of the system from single-user mode to multi-user mode we see in Figure 7–2.

If the changes you made do not require you to relink the kernel (say, adding new software), you can go directly from single-user to multi-user mode. This is done by pressing CTRL-D from the command prompt. You also enter multi-user mode when you press CTRL-D at the prompt

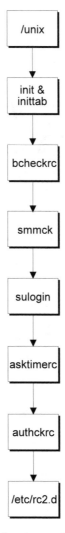

**Figure 7–2**   The flow from single-user to multi-user.

```
Type CONTROL-d to continue with normal startup,

(or give the root password for system maintenance):
```

It kind of makes sense, doesn't it?

The very next thing that happens is that you are told that you are now entering a new "run level", with this message:

```
INIT: New run level: 2
```

We now go back to `inittab` file. `Init` looks for any entry that has a 2 in the second field. This 2 corresponds to the *run-level* we are currently at. Run-level 2 is the same as multi-user mode. The first thing `init` finds is the program `/etc/ask-timerc`. This is a shell script that asks you to input the system time, like this:

```
Current System Time is Fri May 12 16:56:58 MET 1995

Enter new time ([YYMMDD]hhmm[ss]):
```

The time the system is displaying here is what it obtained from the hardware clock. In most cases, you can simply press enter, as the hardware clock is correct. If not, then you need to enter the correct time. At a minimum, you need to enter the hour and minutes (`hhmm`) using a 24 hour clock and specify two digits for each. If you want you can also include the year (`YY`), the month (`MM`), *and* the day (`DD`) or the seconds (`SS`).

There are a couple of things to note here. First, you can't just specify the year or month. You need to specify all three (year, month, and day). Otherwise, the system has no way of determining which one you mean. Also, the ability to set the seconds is new to SCO OpenServer. In previous releases, you could only get minute accuracy. The `asktime` utility can also be used to set the system clock after the system has started. See the `asktime` (ADM) man-page for details on the format of these values.

The next thing `init` finds in `inittab` is `/etc/authckrc`. This script checks the security databases. As it is doing this, you see four messages on your screen if you have ODT 3.0:

```
Checking tcb ...

Checking auth database ...

Checking protected subsystem database ...

Checking ttys database ...
```

and three if you have SCO OpenServer:

```
Checking tcb ...

Checking protected password and protected subsystems databases ...

Checking ttys database ...
```

The change is because the middle two under ODT are the same program (`/tcb/bin/authck`), which was actually run twice. If you had a lot of users on your system, running it twice took a long time. In SCO OpenServer, `authck` is run simply with the `-a` for "all." Rather than having to load the table twice, they are already there and that saves time.

The reason for these checks is to ensure the integrity of the TCB itself. If the system goes down unexpectedly, your file system could be damaged. One of the things that could be damaged are the TCB files. If that is the case, and `authck` cannot correct the problem, you are advised of the situation and told to restore from backups. If you have OpenServer, what might be damaged is just the symbolic link and you simply need to restore the link.

If the system can correct problems in the Protected Password Database (perhaps the name exists in `/etc/passwd` but there is no TCB file), `authck` asks you if it should correct the problem:

```
There are errors for this user

Fix them (y/n)?
```

Next, the Protected Subsystem Database files are compared to the Protected Password Database to check for discrepancies. You then see this message:

```
Checking ttys database ...
```

This message is shown just prior to the `/etc/ttyupd`. The `ttyupd` command is run to ensure that all `ttys` in `/etc/inittab` have entries in the Terminal Control Database (`/etc/auth/system/ttys`). If any files were reported missing, you must now log in on the override terminal to restore them. By default, the override terminal is defined as `tty01`, also known as the first multiscreen. If you removed the default entry in `/etc/default/login`, you will have to shut the system off, reboot, and enter single-user mode, where you can restore the files that are missing or corrupt. When you log in on the override `tty`, this message is displayed:

```
The security databases are corrupt.

However, root login at terminal tty01 is allowed.
```

The next line in `inittab` is to simply cat the contents of the files in `/etc/copyrights`. As you would guess, these are files contain copyright information. Normally, there is one line per file. Because of the large number of components in OpenServer, it is no longer practicle to display all of the copyrights. Instead, you can use the `copyright` command to display them.

The last thing `init` reads out of `inittab` is `/etc/rc2`. This is a shell script and does several things. First, it executes all the scripts in `/etc/rc2.d`. (Note that very often a `.d` at the end of a name indicates the directory associated with a particular command or function) It is in these files that most all of the system processes get started. For example, it is here where `cron`, the print spooler, and the networking processes are started.

The `/etc/rc2` executes each startup script within a for-loop. Each startup script is started with a command line like this:

```
/bin/sh ${f} start
```

We see here that each of this scripts is started with the Bourne shell. Therefore, it is important that any changes made to these scripts maintain the Bourn shell syntax. The `${f}` is the variable used to keep track of the file name. The key is the trailing start. This is passed as an argument to the start-up script.

Well, if it's a "start-up" script why do we need to tell the script that we want to start? If you look in `/etc/rc2.d`, you'll see that each file has multiple lines. In virtually every case, these are linked to files in `/etc/rc0.d`. So when the system goes into run-level 0 (shutdown), the scripts in `/etc/rc0.d` are called. They started in similar fashion from `/etc/rc0`. The difference is that when the system is shutdown, the scripts are called with stop and not start. In each script, the flow of execution is controlled by the argument passed to it. If start, the script starts things up. If stop, the script stops everything.

Next `/etc/rc2` executes the commands in `/etc/idrc.d`. In most cases this directory is empty and is provided for compatibility reasons. After that there are the scripts in the `/etc/rc.d` directory. These carry out a few more system initialization functions and are mostly there for compatibility reasons. This also applies the `/etc/rc` script, which is the last thing run by `/etc/rc2` before it says

```
The system is ready.
```

After it has completed running `/etc/rc2`, now runs a getty on all enabled ports. This is what finally gives us our login prompt.

## Run-Levels

Most users are only familiar with two run-states or run-levels. The one that is most commonly used is referred to as multi-user mode. This is where logins are enabled on terminals, the network is running, and the system is behaving "normally." The other run-level is system maintenance or single-user mode, where there is only a single user on the system (root) who is probably doing some kind of maintenance tasks.

It is generally said that the "system" is in a particular run-level. However, it is more accurate to say that the `init` process is in a particular run-level, as it is `init` that determines what other processes get started at each run-level.

In addition to the run-levels most of us are familiar with, there are several others that the system can run in. Despite this fact, few of them are hardly ever used. For more details on what these run-levels are, take a look at the init(M) man-page.

The system administrator can change to a particular run-level by using that run-level as the argument to init. For example, running init 2 would change the system to run-level 2. To determine what processes to start in each run-level, init reads the /etc/inittab file. This is defined by the second field in the /etc/inittab file. Init reads this file and executes each program defined for that run-level in order.

The fields in the inittab file are as follows:

- id          uniquely identify for that entry
- rstate      run-level in which this entry will be processed
- action      tells init how to treat the process specifically
- process     what process will be started

When the system boots, it decides what run-level to go into based on the DEFAULT_LEVEL variable in /etc/default/boot. If this is not set, then the /bin/sulogin program is run which asks whether the system should be brought into maintenance or multi-user mode. If brought into maintenance mode, this is run-level S. If, for whatever reason, the /etc/inittab is corrupt or otherwise unreadable, then this is the only valid run-level.

Keep in mind that you do not have to reboot the system in order enter run-level S. You can do so by passing S as an argument to init. In addition, you can use the shutdown command to enter a specific run-level, which will ultimately use init.

If you are in maintenance mode (run-level S) and type in exit, this will kill the shell you are running and the system returns you to this prompt:

```
Type CONTROL-D to proceed with normal startup
```

Here, you can press CTRL-D to begin the startup into run-level 2 or multi-user mode. If you want, you can simply type in init 2, which will start the process of bringing the system into run-level 2. I have also typed exit or CTRL-D in single user mode and found myself in run-level 2 without a prompt.

If we look in /etc/inittab, we see quit a few entries that have a 2 in the second column. Many of these are the same programs we talked about earlier when we described the boot process in general. The /etc/inittab file is where they originate.

One thing I need to point out is that the entries in inittab are not run *exactly* according to the order they appear. If you are entering a run-level other than S for the first time since boot-up, init will first execute those entries with a boot or bootwait in the *third* column. These are the processes that should be started before users are allowed access to the system, such as checking the status of the filesystems and then mounting them.

In run-level 2, a `/etc/getty` process is started on the terminals specified. It is the `getty` process that gives you your `login:` prompt. When you have entered your logname for the first time, `getty` starts the `login` process which asks you for your password. If incorrect, you are prompted to input your logname again. Note that this time the prompt is different. The first time you (usually) see the system name as part of the prompt. If you input an incorrect logname or password, the second `login:` prompt will not contain the system name. This is because it is the `login` process that is giving you the prompt the second time, not `getty`.

If your password is correct, then the system starts your "login shell." Note that what gets started may not be a shell at all, but some other program. The term "login shell" is the generic term for whatever program is started when you log in. This is defined by the last field of the appropriate entry in `/etc/passwd`.

Keep in mind that you can move in either direction, that is, from a lower run-level to a higher run-level or from a higher to a lower without having to first re-boot. `Init` will read the `inittab` and start the necessary processes. If a particular process is not defined at a particular run-level then `init` will kill it. For example, assume you are in run-level 2 and switch to run-level 1. Many of the processes defined do not have a 2 in the second field. Therefore, they and all their children will be stopped.

Once we are in multi-user mode, we can return to maintenance mode either through the `shutdown` command or by running `init` directly. I need to emphasize that running `init` directly is not really a good idea. The `shutdown` script is designed to be a little more gentle. By running, for example, `init S`, the system is suddenly in maintenance mode. No warning is given, all user processes simply cease to exist. Since `shutdown` at least gives some warning, this is less likely to have angry co-workers calling you.

If we have shutdown from run-level 2 into run-level 1, for example, we see two entries in `inittab` with a 1 in the second field:

```
r1:1:wait:/etc/rc1  1> /dev/console 2>&1 </dev/console
co1:1:respawn:/bin/sh -c "sleep 20; exec /etc/getty tty01 sc_m"
```

The first entry (`r1`), runs the script `/etc/rc1`. If we look inside that script, we see at the end that what happens is that all processes are stopped (`/etc/killall 9`) and all filesystems are unmounted (`/etc/umountall`). The very last thing it does is to run `init` and switch to run-level S. Here is where we see a difference between run-level 1 and run-level S. Although they are functionally the same for most users, it is the transition to run-level 1 that unmounts the filesystem. So, if you shutdown into run-level S, all your filesystems will remain mounted.

To shutdown the system immediately, you could run

```
init 0
```

which brings the system immediately into run-level 0. If we look in `/etc/inittab`, we find that there are only two lines that have a 0 in the second column. These are

```
r0:056:wait:/etc/rc0  1> /dev/console 2>&1 </dev/console
sd:0:wait:/etc/uadmin 2 0 >/dev/console 2>&1 </dev/console
```

The first thing that is processed is the `r0` line which runs the `/etc/rc0` script. If we look in that script, we see that it runs the `killall` command that stops (almost) all other processes on the system; shortly thereafter, it exits.

At this point, `init` continues with the next entry that is for the specified run-level, in our case run-level 0. This line runs the program `uadmin`, which is what actually shuts the system down. This means nothing is running and the system stops. Note that `uadmin` can only be executed from the system console.

Let's back up and look at that first line again:

```
r0:056:wait:/etc/rc0  1> /dev/console 2>&1 </dev/console
```

Here there are three numbers in the second column and not just one. This means that if `init` changes to any one of those three, this line will get executed. If you look in `/etc/inittab`, you will see that there are several lines that are started in multiple run-levels.

After it has started the necessary process from `inittab`, `init` just hangs out and waits. When one of it's "descendants" dies (a child process of a child process of a child process . . . of `init`, started by a process that `init` started), `init` rereads the `inittab` to see what should be done. If, for example, there is a `respawn` entry in the third field, `init` will start the specified process again. This is the reason you immediately get a new `login:` prompt when you log out.

Because `init` just hangs around waiting for processes to die, you cannot simply add an entry to `inittab` and expect the process to start. You have to tell `init` to go and reread the `inittab`. However, you can force `init` to reread the `inittab` by running `init` (or `telinit q`). This is the only time you should use the `init` program yourself.

In addition to the run-levels we discussed here, there are several more that are possible. Unfortunately, this is one of those cases where I have to put off further discussion since these other run-levels are rarely, if ever, used. If you're curious, take a look at the `init(M)` man-page.

## Boot Magic

A very useful facet of SCO UNIX is the ability to boot in many different ways. At the beginning of this section I mentioned the default bootstring (DEFBOOTSTR). As its name implies, this contains the default parameters the system uses to boot. Sometimes it is necessary to change the behavior of the system when it boots; that is, change the default.

One alternative is to edit the DEFBOOTSTR (in /etc/default/boot). This is useful if the changes you want to make are somewhat permanent. This is not necessarily a good idea when you want to make a quick test, as you need to change the file again once you're done. The other disadvantage is that there is always the possibility of mistakes. If you make a mistake, then you have to type in a boot string at the boot prompt anyway, so why not type it in by hand the first time?

One of the more common things that I do when changing how the system boots is to define specific memory ranges. I do this in a couple of cases. The first is when I suspect anti-caching. Anti-caching occurs when you do not have enough cache for the amount of RAM you have. Normally, this is 64k of cache per 16Mb of RAM. If, for example, you had 32Mb of RAM, but only 64K of cache, you wouldn't have enough. Some motherboards recognize this and then disable *all* cache—including the internal cache on the CPU. This has a dramatic effect on the performance since every instruction must now be taken from main memory and not the cache. You thought that adding RAM was going to speed things up, but instead it slowed things down. See the section on hardware for more details.

Rather than pulling out the extra memory, you can tell the kernel only to use a particular part of memory with different boot strings. This is the mem= option. To tell the kernel that you want it only to use the RAM below 16Mb, the bootstring would look like this:

```
boot : defbootstr mem=1-16m
```

The defbootstr tells the kernel to read the default boot string from /etc/default/boot, but to use the memory from 1-16Mb. Note that we don't need to specify the memory below 640K since the kernel will use that anyway. If we specified this boot string and the system ran faster, despite the fact that we had less memory, then this would indicate anti-caching.

I also use the mem= option to exclude chunks of memory when I suspect that I have bad RAM. In certain motherboards, like the one I have, you cannot just pull out a SIMM to see if your memory problems go away. This is because each bank needs to be completely full in order for things to work. However, if you tell the kernel to skip a certain range, you might be able to figure out which SIMM is bad.

For example, lets say I have four 4MB SIMMs and have a bad spot of memory somewhere. If I tell the kernel at boot to avoid the 3rd SIMM (as in `mem=1-8m,12-16m`) and my problem goes away, then this is the bad SIMM.

There is a problem with checking for bad RAM like this. Some motherboards read memory from all SIMMs in parallel, not sequentially. That is, they read 32 bits at a time, eight from each SIMM rather than reading the first SIMM completely before starting on the second.

If you have a system that reads from memory in parallel, then blocking out segments at boot probably won't work. This is because you are blocking out portions of every SIMM and not just one. Unless you know that the system reads in parallel, this is worth a try. However, the only way you can be certain is if you get a positive result; that is, the problem goes away.

Another very common thing to do is to boot different kernels. Very often adding a new driver will toast your kernel to the point that it cannot be booted. Your new kernel may be beyond the 1024th cylinder and therefore can no longer boot. By typing in the name of another kernel you can boot that. More than likely there is a `unix.old` if you just relink the kernel. SCO OpenServer maintains a couple of copies such as `unix.install` and `unix.safe`.

One useful trick that I have used is the ability to specify your root filesystem and swap device as well as the kernel that I want to boot. When I was working in SCO Support. I needed quick access to many different operating systems and environments. Rather than having several different machines, I had only one, with the different operating systems on different filesystems or partitions. When I needed to boot one, I could simple type in the appropriate boot string.

You tell the `/boot` program where to look by specifying the driver name, the minor number, and the program in this form:

`driver(minor)program`

Even in SCO OpenServer the only two driver names it accepts are `hd` (for the hard disk) and `fd` (for the floppy). See the section on major and minor numbers or the `hd(HW)` and `fd(HW)` man-pages for details on what minor numbers are all about.

To specify other devices, the format is like this:

`device=driver(minor)`

Now, let's assume that my hard disk contains only two partitions. The first is for SCO UNIX and the second for SCO XENIX. Since the UNIX partition is active, it has minor numbers in the range 40–47. This was also the first partition, so it has minor numbers in the range 8–15. The second partition had minor numbers in the range 16–23.

Originally, my default boot string simply said `hd(40)unix`. This meant it would load the UNIX program from the hd device with a minor number of 40. Once I started adding the other operating systems, I expanded my boot string to specify each of the devices explicitly, as in

```
hd(40)unix root=hd(40) swap=hd(41)
```

Normally, the UNIX program is located on the root filesystem. That's why they both have a minor number of 40. I could also have specified the absolute minor numbers, as in

```
hd(8)unix root=hd(8) swap=hd(9)
```

To boot by SCO XENIX system, the boot string would look like this:

```
hd(16)unix root=hd(16) swap=hd(17)
```

After the third or fourth time you enter one of these strings, you realize that it is bothersome. Fortunately, there is an easier way. You can actually assign names to these strings and have `/boot` make the translation for you. This is done in the `/etc/default/boot` file and is called *boot aliasing*. Accessing the different file-system is shown in Figure 7–3.

By default, there is already one boot string alias: `DEFBOOTSTR`. Although this is what `/boot` looks for by default, you could just as easily type in `defbootstr` at the boot prompt. The syntax is the same as variable definitions in `sh` or `ksh`: `variable_name=value`. In the case of the default boot string, the variable name is `DEFBOOTSTR` and the value is `hd(40)` (or something similar). You can type in `defbootstr` and then add something else, such as

```
defbootstr Stp=ad(0,3,0)
```

This uses the default boot string and tells the system to add a SCSI tape drive to the ad (Adaptec) driver at host adapter 0, SCSI ID 3, and LUN 0.

In my `/etc/default/boot` file, I created two additional aliases. One is for my SCO UNIX partition:

```
UNX=hd(8)unix root=hd(8) swap=hd(9)
```

One is for my SCO XENIX partition:

```
XNX=hd(16)unix root=hd(16) swap=hd(17)
```

If you are running OpenServer, you can also use the System Startup Manager or change the `DEFBOOTSTR` in `/etc/default/boot`. This way you can define aliases for boot strings that are fairly complicated, but you don't have to type them in. For example, the two I have on my hard disk are

```
OS5=hd(40)unix swap=hd(41) dump=hd(41) root=hd(42)
ODT=hd(24)unix swap=hd(25) dump=hd(25) root=hd(24)
```

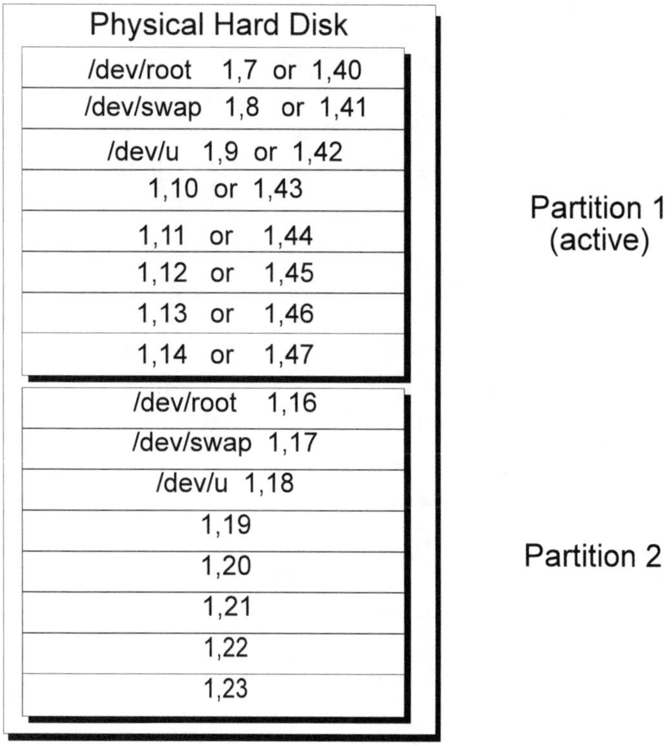

| Physical Hard Disk | |
|---|---|
| /dev/root   1,7 or 1,40 | |
| /dev/swap  1,8  or  1,41 | |
| /dev/u  1,9  or  1,42 | Partition 1 |
| 1,10  or  1,43 | (active) |
| 1,11   or   1,44 | |
| 1,12  or   1,45 | |
| 1,13   or   1,46 | |
| 1,14  or   1,47 | |
| /dev/root   1,16 | |
| /dev/swap  1,17 | |
| /dev/u  1,18 | |
| 1,19 | |
| 1,20 | Partition 2 |
| 1,21 | |
| 1,22 | |
| 1,23 | |

**Figure 7–3**   Loading the system from different filesystems.

When I want to start up OpenServer, I type in OS5. This is interpreted by /boot as if I had typed in

```
hd(40)unix swap=hd(41) dump=hd(41) root=hd(42)
```

I really don't need to include all these values. However, to make sure things are set the way they are supposed to, I aliased it like this.

When I want to start up ODT 3.0, I use the ODT entry. Notice that I don't use the same minor numbers. OpenServer is installed on the active partition and if you remember from the discussion of major and minor numbers, the range for minor numbers on the active partition of the first drive is 40–47. Since ODT 3.0 is not on the active partition, I have to used the absolute minor numbers. Although I could have used absolute minor numbers with OpenServer, this shows me right way which partition is active.

## The `bootos` Program

I remember a rather "excited" message on the SCOFORUM on CompuServe. The message poster was quite upset at what he percieved as a major shortcoming in SCO. Despite the fact that SCO simply reads and writes a standard bootblock and partition table, he was upset that this prevented him from booting into his OS/2 boot manager. This was a case where a little bit of preparation could have saved him some heartaches.

A major advance of OpenServer is the ability to not only boot DOS, like ODT, but to boot other operating systems, such as Windows NT, OS/2, and even CP/M. This is accomplished by the `bootos` program, which is called from `/boot`, depending on the boot options you give it. The `bootos` program is started simply by entering it at the `Boot:` prompt. One very useful option is the `?`; for example, this would be started like this:

```
bootos ?
```

This displays your partition table and includes details such as whether the partition is active, the type of operating system that is recognized, and the size of the partition. By giving it the number of the partition, `bootos` will attempt to boot the operating system that it finds. The `id=` option can be used to get `bootos` to find the first operating system of that type and boot it, for example,

```
bootos id=dos_12
```

looks for the first DOS 12-bit filesystem. Or we try

```
bootos id=os2
```

which causes `bootos` to look for an OS/2 filesystem. Note that OpenServer cannot distinguish between a Windows NT NTFS, OS/2 filesystem, or OS/2 HPFS, so the above example could also be specified as

```
bootos id=nt
```

or

```
bootos id=os2_hpfs
```

Therefore, if you have both an OS/2 and an NT partition, you will need to specify the partition number.

For those of us who have had DOS partitions on our systems, we are used to being able to start-up by simply typing `dos` at the boot prompt. This option is still available, however, this is equivalent to starting the system with:

```
bootos dos
```

For more details on this, see the `bootos(HW)` man-page.

## Stopping the System

For those of you who hadn't noticed, neither SCO ODT nor SCO OpenServer is like DOS. Despite the superficial similarity at the command prompt, they have little in common. One very important difference is the way you stop the system.

Under DOS, you are completely omnipotent. You know everything that's going on. You have complete control over everything. You can decide that you've had enough and flip the power switch. However, with dozens of people working on an SCO UNIX system and dozens more using its resources, simply turning off the machine is not something you want to do. Despite the fact that you will annoy quite a few people, it can cause damage to your system depending on exactly what was happening when you killed the power. (Okay, you could also create problems with a DOS system, but with only one person, the chances are less likely.)

In order to make sure that things are stopped safely, you need to shutdown your system "properly." SCO provides several tools to stop the system and allows you to decide what is proper for your particular circumstance. Flipping the power switch is *not* shutting down properly.

The first two stop processes are actually two links to the same file: /etc/haltsys and /etc/reboot. These are shell scripts, so you can take a look at the insides and see what they do.

The first thing is to flush the buffer cache and update the superblock with the sync command. If this is not done and the system stops, there is a high probability that what is on the hard disk is not what should be. There are two issues here. First, if you are writing to the disk, more than likely you are going through the buffer cache. If the system stops before that information gets written to the disk, the last changes you made won't have been written to the file.

Second, if you look in either file (haltsys or reboot) you'll see that sync is actually called twice. This was orginally included to ensure that more data is written to the hard disk and things are more likely to be consistent. If something was written as the sync was proceeding, there could still be some information that was not written to the disk. Granted this can catch everything. There is still the chance that after the second sync, something will get written to the buffer cache, however running sync twice decreases the likelihood that something will get lost. It is not only there for historical reasons.

Next, all file systems are unmounted. Part of this process is also to ensure that any pending I/O is completed. This is obviously necessary to prevent any more data loss.

The last thing done is to actually shut the system down using the `/etc/uadmin` command. The arguments that are passed to `uadmin` depend on the command and arguments we use to shut down the system. It's possible to pass an argument to the `haltsys` command that prevents you from rebooting, for example. At this point the system is down and if you started `reboot` instead of `haltsys`, it is rebooted for you. This reboot is one time where SCO does use the BIOS.

One thing to keep in mind is that with both `haltsys` and `reboot`, the system simply stops. You are not given any warning nor are processes allowed to exit gracefully. All processes cease to exist because the system no longer exists.

This is really only an issue if you have other users accessing your system, either logged in locally or using system resources across the net. If, on the other hand, you brought the system into maintenance mode to add a new driver (or whatever) and need to reboot to make the changes take effect, then there is no harm in either using `haltsys` or `reboot`.

When you need to give your user's notice that the system is going to come down or have processes running that need to be stopped gracefully, then neither `haltsys` nor `reboot` is a good idea. A better program is `/etc/shutdown`, which not only gives users notice, but allows programs to stop gracefully, without pulling the rug out from underneath them.

Like `haltsys` and `reboot`, `shutdown` is a shell script. However, it is not linked to the other two but rather to `/tcb/files/rootcmds/shutdown`. This allows it to be used by nonroot users to shutdown the system, if necessary. Putting commands in the `rootcmds` directory is necessary because one of the first things done is to check the UID of the user starting it. If it's not root, then `shutdown` exists.

I won't go into too many details about the various options, since they are all listed in the manual. It suffices to say that you can tell `shutdown` to wait a certain amount of time before stopping the system as well as send a specific message to the users that the shutdown is taking place.

The important thing to note is that `shutdown` does not actually kill any process, rather it lets `init` do it. One of the arguments you pass to `shutdown` is the new `init` state (run-level) you want to run in after warning users that a `shutdown` is coming. `shutdown` calls `init` to bring the system to the specified run-level. If no run-level is specified, it defaults to run-level 0 and the system is brought all the way down.

One advantage this has is the ability to go from normal, multi-user mode (run-level 2) to maintenance mode (run-level S or 1). Is often thought that run-level S and run-level 1 are both the same since the system is brought into single-user mode. Well, it is true that in both cases the only user on the system is root. However, that's where the similarity ends.

Run-level S is essentially the same run-level that we first boot up to go into maintenance mode. Here, only the root filesystem is mounted (all others are unmounted if going from run-level 2 to run-level S) and all processes are killed except those connected to the system console.

If you switch run-levels from run-level 2 to run-level S, then basically the only thing that happens is that users processes are tossed off the system. All file systems remain mounted. For users this means the same thing, although it is useful to keep filesystems mounted without having users on the system. However, as I mentioned before, in run-level 1, all the filesystems are unmounted and it is more like the initial boot-up.

If you decide to shutdown the system completely (run-level 0), all filesystems are unmounted, all processes are killed, and on your screen you see:

```
    ** Safe to Power Off **
             -or-
** Press Any Key to Reboot **
```

The System Shutdown Manager provides a graphic interface to the shutdown command. The functions are the same as from the command line; however, you do get to point and click.

# CHAPTER
8

# Printers
# and Interfaces

The SCO UNIX print spooler, (also called the print service or print scheduler), is a collection of commands and utilities that are used to administer and access printers. These can be printers attached locally to your machine or ones that are attached to remote machines.

The only thing most users think about is what they see: the beginning and ending of the print process. There is the `lp` command, which sends the print request and there is the final output on paper. However, the print spooler does more than just accept the jobs and send the data to the printer. In fact, it has quite a lot to do.

Among the things that the print spooler is responsible for are receiving the data users want to print (either as names of files or the end of a pipe), scheduling the job on the printer, maintaining the status of each job on each printer, interfacing directly with the printer (actually the device node associated with the printer), and sending you messages when things go wrong.

## The Print Process

When you print a file, (either by using the `lp` command to specify a file or as the end of a pipe) the print spooler assigns that request (or job) a unique identifier. This identifier consists of the printer name and the number of the print request. Next, the print spooler puts the job into a *queue* (a waiting line) to be printed. Each job must wait until the printer is ready; that is, each job must wait until the previous job is completed. Otherwise, you end up with jobs printing on top of each other. The process of placing the print job into a "print queue" is called "spooling." Since each printer has its own queue, problems with one printer will not (usually) influence others.

For each job, the print spooler creates two files that describe the job request and places one in the /usr/spool/lp/temp directory and one in the /usr/spool/lp/requests directory. The reason for splitting the files like this is for security reasons. The /usr/spool/lp/temp directory is accessible to everyone. The information contained here is just the necessary information for you to monitor your own jobs. As a normal user you do not have access to the /usr/spool/lp/requests directory.

Once the jobs are printed, these files are removed and the information they contain is combined and placed in the "request log" (/usr/spool/lp/logs/requests). Since the information is the same in the working files and log files, if know how to read one, (that is, what each line means) you know how to read both. The files in temp and request contain the information for just a single job. When combined into the request log, entries are separated by a line starting with an equal-sign and containing the job_ID, UID, GID, total number of bytes, and the data and time the job was queued. Table 8–1 contains a list of what each of these lines mean.

There may come a time when you send a job to a printer and you experience delayed output. You wonder what happened to your print job and you want to take a look at the status. This can be done with the lpstat command or also the Print Job Manager if you are running OpenServer.

If you use lpstat by itself, it will just show you the status of your own jobs. If you use the '-t' option, you will not only see all the jobs, but you will see the complete status information for the entire print spooler. Personally, these are the only two ways I have *ever* used lpstat. However, it does have several different options that may be useful to you in specific circumstances. Therefore, you might want to take a look at the lpstat(C) man-page when you get a chance.

When I run lpstat -t on my system, I get

```
scheduler is running
system default destination: DeskJet
device for DeskJet: /dev/lp0
device for Panasonic: /dev/lp1
DeskJet accepting requests since Tue May 23 20:07:37 1995
Panasonic accepting requests since Fri May 26 16:16:54 1995
printer DeskJet is idle. enabled since Fri May 26 16:00:05 1995.
available.
printer Panasonic is idle. enabled since Fri May 26 16:16:54 1995.
available.
DeskJet-7                  root                  908    May 26 14:54
```

**Table 8–1**    Contents of Printer Spooler Working and Log Files

| Letter | Content of Line |
|:------:|-----------------|
| C | Number of copies. |
| D | Destination. Either a printer or a class of printers (more on that later). |
| F | Name of the file. If a copy is made this will be a name in `/usr/spool/lp/temp`. If no copy is made this will be the full path of the file. If multiple files were queued, then there will be multiple 'F" lines. |
| f | Form name used (if one is specified). |
| H | Special handling, such as resume, hold, or immediate. |
| N | Notification. When the job is finished, should the user get an email message or have a message written to the terminal? |
| O | Options given to `lp` with `-o`. |
| P | Priority of the print job (if applicable). |
| p | List of pages printed. |
| r | Raw processing options (if any) given to `lp`. |
| S | Character set or print wheel used. |
| s | Success of the job, expressed as a combination of bits in hex form: <br> $0 \times 0004$  Slow filtering finished successfully <br> $0 \times 0010$  Printing finished successfully <br> $0 \times 0040$  Request was canceled <br> $0 \times 0100$  Request failed filtering or printing |
| T | Title on the banner page. |
| t | Type of file content. |
| U | User who submitted the print job. |
| x | Slow filter. |
| Y | Special modes to give to the filters. Fast filter. |
| z | Printer used for the request. This only differs from the destination (the D line) if the request was queued for any printer or a class of printers, or if the request is transferred to another printer. |

The first line from `lpstat` tells us whether the print scheduler is running or not. The second line tells us what the system default printer is. The default printer is where the print spooler sends jobs if the user doesn't tell it where the print job should go by using the `-d` option to `lp`. This is useful information because users will sometimes think the spooler swallowed their print jobs because they don't come out where they want. I have had enough calls from customers saying that the spooler worked with only one type of printer or there was some built-in limit to the number of printers. It always turned out that they didn't check to see what the default was—their job was going somewhere they didn't expect.

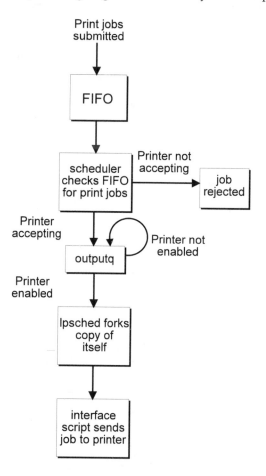

Next is a list of the printers and the associated devices. Keep in mind that just because a device is listed here, does not mean that there is a physical connection to the device or that the device exists at all. It could be that the printer was configured for a particular device that doesn't exist on that system or is now broken. The reason is that `lpstat` does not do any checking of the physical device. It simply reads the configuration file for each printer and outputs the device specified. This information is found in `/usr/spool/lp/admins/lp/printer/<printer_name>` where `<printer_name>` is the name you gave to that printer.

Next is a list of the printers, detailing which are accepting requests/not accepting requests and which are enabled/disabled. Like the information for the device, the print spooler maintains this information in a file. In this case the file is `/usr/spool/lp/system/pstatus`. Each entry is started with a row of equal-signs (=). My file looks like this:

```
==========

DeskJet
disabled
accepting
801501715
801256057
unknown reason
new destination

==========

Panasonic
enabled
accepting
801501414
801501414
new printer
new destination
```

As you can see, my DeskJet is currently disabled. When I disabled it prior to looking at these files, I didn't specify a reason. Therefore, you see the `unknown reason` as the sixth line of this entry. If I were to run `lpstat -t` again, I would get an entry that looked like this:

```
printer DeskJet disabled since Fri May 26 16:21:55 1995. available.
    unknown reason
```

which is essentially the same information as in this file. The entries `new desti-nation` and `new printer` are there because they *are* new. I have never disabled them or rejected requests on them.

If you are a point-and-click person, then this information is obtainable from Printer Manager. If you want to find out the status of print jobs, you need to run the Print Job Manager. Under the `View` menu you can choose to look at the jobs by user or by queue or even all of the jobs if you want. Here, you can also hold jobs, transfer them to other printers, "promote" them by placing them at the head of the queue, and even delete jobs. All of these require commands other than `lpstat`.

The thing that bothers me personally is that the Print Job Manager will only tell you about print jobs. (I guess that's why they called it Print Job Manager.) If you start up the Print Job Manager and see that a job has been waiting for three days to be printed, you get nothing to tell you why. You see what printer the job is destined for (what queue it is in), but in order to find out why that queue is not going anywhere you need to run the Printer Manager. (If the job has been "put on hold" you will see a `held` in the status column in the Print Job Manager.)

I am not knocking either the Print Job Manager or the Printer Manager. Both provide a GUI that makes configuring and administering printers much easier than before. Even the CHARM interface is useful and easy to use. However, when problems arise, I want to see everything in one place. Therefore, I will continue to use my old friend `lpstat`.

Administration of printers has been simplified to a great extent by the graphics interfaces provided by the Print Job Manager and the Printer Manager. Now it is a simple matter of pointing and clicking to delete jobs, move them to other printers, or put them on hold. If you are root or a user with `lp` authorization (see the section on security) you can administer all the jobs on the system, not just your own. If you are just a "regular" user (one without `lp` authorization), then many of the options in the Print Job Manager will be "dimmed." This means that they are inaccessible to you.

When you delete a job under the Print Job Manager (assuming you have the authorization to) the `Status` column briefly changes to `canceled` before the job disappears from display. This is the same thing as if you were to run cancel from the command line.

You may have a print job that is exceptionally large and you want to let other, smaller jobs go first. One alternative is to use the Print Job Manager to promote the other jobs above the large one. If you want just a few printed quickly before "allowing" the larger one to print, then this is a valid option. However, what if there are jobs constantly coming in and you want to wait until lunchtime or the end of the day before you let the job go through?

The answer is to put that job on hold. This means that the job will not be printed until you tell the spooler to do so. This can be accomplished in a couple of ways. First you can use the lp command itself. Either you specify the option as '-H hold' when you submit the print request or you tell the spooler to hold a specific job, as in

```
lp -i DeskJet-42 -H hold
```

The `-i` option is to specify the Job-ID. This example would put on hold job DeskJet-42.

The other alternative is to use the Print Job Manager. First, click on the job you want to hold, then under the `Jobs` menu, find entry `Hold`. If the job is already on hold, or you do not have authorization, then this item is "dimmed" (disabled). Once you have done either of these procedures, then the entries in both the Print Job Manger and `lpstat` change to reflect this.

If we now looked in the status file for this print job, we would see a change in its contents to reflect the fact that the job is being held. For example, if I wanted to put on hold a fifty-page letter to my friend Tillman, the status file might look like this before I put it on hold:

```
C 1
D DeskJet
F /usr/jimmo/letter/tillman
P 20
t simple
U root
s 0x0081
l C
```

and like this, afterward:

```
C 1
D DeskJet
F /usr/jimmo/letter/tillman
H hold
P 20
t simple
U root
s 0x0080
l C
```

Notice that in the first output, there is no reference to being held or anything similar. This is because I didn't specify any hold option. If I later decide that I want to resume the job, I can take it off hold by telling the print spooler to resume. This is done through either the `Resume` entry in the `Jobs` menu of the Print Job Manager or from the command like this:

```
lp -i DeskJet-42 -H resume
```

The status column in the Print Job Manager is cleared and the job will now print. If we look in the status file, we see the `H` entry has changed from

```
H hold
```

to

```
H resume
```

From our perspective, the job is as it was when we started. Therefore, the status file should look the same, shouldn't it? Well, from the spooler's perspective the status of the printer is that it is no longer held, but rather in `resume` status.

Therefore the status of the print job *is* different, from the spooler's point of view.

You can hold jobs that are currently printing, as well as jobs that are further back in the queue. When you resume a job whose turn has passed, it will become the first job to print (after the current one finishes). I have had occasion to use this option when printing a large file that I want to stop in order to print something smaller that I need right away. When I resume the job, it will begin printing from the first page and not where it left off. This is because the print spooler does not keep track of how many pages it has printed. If you want to avoid having to print everything over again, you can use the -P option to lp to tell the spooler what page to start from:

```
lp -i DeskJet-42 -H resume -P 16
```

In this example, the spooler would resume printing job DeskJet-42, but would do so starting on page 16.

Actually, I should say that the spooler "could" resume printing starting on page 16. Remember that I said that the spooler does not keep track of how many pages it printed. In order to start somewhere other than the beginning of the file, you will need a printer filter that can.

The job status files also change when you move a print job to a different printer. It is often necessary to move print jobs. One queue may become backed up, even if you have set up printer classes (groups of printers). I was convinced that there was a built-in mechanism with the print spooler that looked for the *busiest* printer and send all the jobs there. When I was working in SCO support, all the jobs that I submitted ended up going to the printer that was in the process of printing a hundred-page report. This is similar to the phenomena at grocery stores that no matter how many times you change lines, yours is always moving the slowest. However, it was just my bad luck, as the print spooler simply chooses each printer in turn.

There are two ways to move a print job. Either use the Transfer entry in the jobs menu of the Print Job Manager, or use lpmove from the command line. Using either one, you can transfer/move to either a specific printer or to a printer class.

If you look back at the example status file, you will see that the destination (specified by the D) is set to DeskJet. If we move that print job (DeskJet-42) to the Panasonic printer, the entry in /usr/spool/lp/temp/42-0 now looks like this:

```
D Panasonic
```

If we do lpstat or look at the Print Job Manager at this point, the job-ID is still DeskJet-42. The job-ID is given when the job is first queued up. It never changes.

Even when we move the job to a different printer, it keeps the same ID. This often confuses system administrators who expect the job-ID to be dependent on the printer queue.

When I first started talking about putting jobs on hold, I mentioned that you could move jobs up the queue, or promote them. This is done through the print Job Manager. If a job is currently being printed, the only way to get another job to print first is to either cancel or put the first job on hold, then promote the other. One problem exists in that you cannot promote a job over the top of a job that has already been promoted. Well, at least that's what the SCO doc says. This is true when you first promote the job. However, I have found that promoting a job a second time puts it at the top of the queue anyway.

However, putting jobs on hold and promoting them is not the only way of determining the priority of jobs. The print spooler provides a means to predetermine the priority of print jobs on a per user basis. When a user submits a print job, they can assign a priority level, where jobs of higher priority are printed first. These priorities are in the range 0–39, however root (or the `lp` administrator) can set a limit on how high that priority can be. Just like process priorities, users cannot give their jobs a higher priority than allowed, but they can be nice and give themselves a lower priority.

If needed, a default priority can be set so that users who do not have a maximum set for them specifically cannot go too high. Also, a systemwide printer priority can be set. This is done with the `lpusers` command. When starting the job, use the `-q` option to `lp`. By specifying the job-ID with the `-i` option to `lp`, you can change the priority on jobs that are already queued.

## Interface Scripts

Interface scripts are the means by which the system configures and sends data to the printers. As their name implies there are shell scripts that act as the interface to the physical printer. Depending of what kind of printer is being accessed, the interface script can be anywhere from a couple of kilobytes in size to over 10 times that.

The interface script is responsible for almost every aspect of the print process. First, the interface script must configure the port that the printer is connected to. This ensures that the port has the proper settings such as baud rate, parity, and flow control. This is accomplished in the script by using the `stty` command.

Next, the interface script initializes the physical printer. Often this means restoring the printer to a default state. This is necessary in cases where a previous print job made changes to the font, pitch, or page size, and these values are not acceptable for the next job.

After preparing the port and the printer, the interface script is ready to print the file. Often, the first thing it prints is a banner page. This serves as a separator between print jobs. When many different print jobs are sent to a single printer, this can be very useful since the banner page contains information such as the name of the user who printed the file as well as the job-ID.

In each interface script, the format of the banner page is the same and is created "on-the-fly" by the script. It is therefore possible for you to edit the interface script and make any changes you want to the format of the banner page. You can even remove the portion of the script that creates the banner page to prevent it from being printed.

After printing the banner (if told to do so), the interface script now prints the file. Keep in mind that the interface script does not open the device port itself. Rather, the interface script is actually changing the settings and sending the file to stdout. It is the print scheduler that opens the printer port which is then passed to the interface script as stdout. If you look at the interface script (which we'll do in a moment), you'll see that there is no redirection of standard out. When the interface script is started, stdin actually comes from /dev/null.

As the print job progresses, the interface script monitors the progress to see if everything flows smoothly. If there are problems it is the responsibility of the interface script to report the problems back to the print spooler. These are then made available to the user through either lpstat, sysadmsh, or the Print Job Manager.

When you install a printer, you need to choose a particular *model* of printer to use. This refers to the interface script that will be copied from /usr/spool/lp/model to /usr/spool/lp/admins/lp/interfaces with the name you have given to the printer you are installing. If you don't have one of the printers that are listed, you can choose one that comes close. For example, I have an HP DeskJet 540. Since there was no interface script for this printer, I chose the HPDeskJet model and have been very happy with the performance.

If there is nothing that matches even closely, there are two models that are very useful: dumb and standard. The dumb interface script is the smallest and does nothing to prepare either the port or the printer itself. If your application is embedding all the printer configuration commands in the file it's sending, then this is the model to use *even if* the printer you have matches one of the other models. This is so that the configuration commands don't interfere with each other.

Many of the interface scripts (including standard) have special configuration options that you can use to change the behavior of the printer. This is passed with the -o option to the lp and include almost every conceivable characteristic such as characters per inch, font, line spacing, and orientation (portrait or landscape).

In each case these are sequences of characters that tell the printer to change the characteristics. These sequences are then echoed to the printer. For example, if you were using the Epson model interface script and used the option `-obold` to turn on bold output, the Epson interface script would echo the character sequence `\033E\c`. If this same sequence was echoed to the printer port by another shell script or even from the command line, the result would always be to have an Epson printer turn on bold. If you were using the HPLaserJet script, then the character sequence would be different. In most cases, the escape sequences are in the document, so you don't need to worry about them.

If you have a printer that doesn't work right with any of the existing interface scripts, you can modify one of the existing scripts to create one of your own. If one of the existing interface scripts matches closely, but is missing some important characteristics, then modifying the existing script is probably very simple.

To avoid confusion and to allow for the possibility that one day you will have that kind of printer, the best thing is to make a copy of the model interface script. Don't copy this by hand into the `/usr/spool/lp/admins/lp/interfaces` directory. Instead, make a copy in the `/usr/spool/lp/model` directory. That way you can use them again.

Let's assume that you have an Epson compatible printer that has a few more character types than just the standard bold, italic, condensed, and so on. Each of these can be turned on with the `-o` option as in `-obold`, which turns on bold. As I mentioned before, the actual mechanism to turn on each of these characteristics is to simply echo the appropriate character sequence. So, if we know the character sequence for this new typeface (check the printer manual), by using the same means (echoing that character sequence) we can change any characteristic.

The portion of the interface script that does this is a loop that goes through each option and echoes the appropriate character sequence. The `for` loop begins like this:

```
for i in $options; do
    case $i in
    b|nobanner)     banner=no ;;
# Z002 begin \/\/\/\/
    bold)        bold=yes
            echo "\033E\c"
            ;;
```

We see that every option is checked with the `case` statement and if it matches, a variable may be set or something echoes. If we have set the bold option, we see that the interface script then sets the variable `bold` to `yes` and echoes sequence `\033E\c`. If we have a new typeface (let's call it simply `newtype`) that was stated by using the character sequence \033P\c, we could add a new case statement like this:

```
newtype)        newtype=yes
                echo "\033P\c"
                ;;
```

More `case` statements like this can be added if there are more characteristics that you want to add.

## Remote Printing

There are actually several different ways that you can print to remote printers in SCO. In older systems you had a choice of using UUCP to copy files then remotely execute a print command. As networks became the order of the day, then came `rmcd`, `lpd`, and finally the HP Jet Direct EFS; all of which have their uses and all of which we'll get to. SCO supports dialup printers, where you use the UUCP facilities to connect to a remote printer. This has the advantage of not needing any specialized hardware other than a modem (and the printer, of course). SCO also provides support for the Berkeley Remote Printing Daemon, lpd. If the remote site doesn't support `lpd`, we can use a little trick with `rcmd` (remote command) to access the print facilities of remote machines. The HP Jet Direct EFS (which has been subsequently included in the OpenServer product) allows direct access to HP Laser Jet printers, provided they are equipped with the Jet Direct Network card.

### *Printing with* `rcmd`

The first method I want to talk about is perhaps the easiest to configure. Another advantage it has is that it works on most any system that understands the `rcmd` command. This type of remote printing does have a name, per se, other than "printing with `rcmd`". The principle is that we use the rcmd command as the end of a pipe, which accesses the printer service on the remote host. From the command line, if we wanted to print to `scoburg`, it might look like this:

```
cat file_name | rcmd scoburg lp
```

If we wanted, we could also pass options to `lp`, by including the entire command inside double quotes. For example,

```
cat file_name | rcmd scoburg "lp -d printer_name"
```

One advantage this process has is that it does not require any special configuration of the printer on the local side. The only condition is that the remote host can access the local machine. The problem with it is that everyone needs to have access to the remote host (either with user equivalence or .rhost files). They also have to know the syntax of the `rcmd`. The solution is to build this functionality directly into the system. SCO provides an interface script that does the work for you.

This is the network model printer interface script (or `network.ps`, if you have a postscript capable printer). The first step is to create a local printer using this interface. There are a couple of *key* things to watch out for. First, the connection type should be set to "Direct" and the device should be "Hardwired." Next, specify `/dev/null` as the device you are printing to. Although you are not actually printing through this device, you still need to specify some device and `/dev/null` won't cause any problems.

Next, you need to create the file that sets up the command. This is `/usr/spool/lp/remote`, the format of which is

```
printer_name:    remote_command
```

For example, I created one that looks like this:

```
remote:    /usr/bin/rcmd  siemau  /usr/bin/lp -dlaser
```

Here the *local* printer name is `remote`. It will be using the command `/usr/bin/rcmd` to execute the `/usr/bin/lp` command using the destination printer `laser`. Since everything after the local printer name is considered part of the command, it is all passed to the interface script. I can therefore include any options that I want.

Look at the line in the interface script that actually does the work:

```
) | $network -s -ob $lpflags
```

The right parenthesis is the end of a fairly large block of code, the output of which is piped to the `$network` command. The `$network` command is everything that appears after the printer name in the `/usr/spool/lp/remote` file. The `-s` suppresses output messages from the `lp` command and the `-ob` suppresses the banner. This is because the banner may be already generated locally (assuming you don't suppress it there, as well). Finally, the `$lpflags` is any options we passed to the `lp` command from the command line.

Okay. So we are cat'ting the output to the command defined in `/usr/spool/lp/remote`. Does it have to be `rcmd`? No. In fact, we could pipe the output to something like `uux` to get it to a remote print via UUCP. The syntax would be

```
remote: /usr/bin/uux - siemau!/usr/bin/lp -dlaser
```

Here the `'-'` says to take `stdin` as the input file. We then say we want to execute the command `/usr/bin/lp` on the machine `siemau`, using the printer `laser`.

If you are using the first option, then you need to make sure the `rcmd` works as the user lp on the remote side. This is done by either having a `/etc/hosts.equiv` file or a `.rhosts` in the user lp's home directory on `siemau`.

### Printing with `lpd`

Remote printing using the `lpd` daemon falls under that heading of Remote Line Printing (RLP). Although the central program is the `lpd` daemon, I'll continue to use the term RLP as this describes the entire package. RLP adheres to the client-server model, where clients are sending print jobs to the servers that are doing the actual printing.

RLP works differently than "normal" printing. Although you configure the printer in the same way, what happens behind the scenes is different. The first thing is that three of the standard SCO print commands (`lp`, `cancel`, and `lpstat`, with `lpmove` also included in OpenServer) are moved from `/usr/bin` into `/usr/lpd/remote` and replaced by new ones that understand remote printing. When you issue one of these commands, they will check to see if the printer is local or remote. If local, then the copy in `/usr/lpd/remote` was executed. What this looks like you can see in Figure 8–1.

On ODT 3.0, this was a problem. If you "accidentally" ran the configuration script (`mkdev rlp`) twice, the original versions were replaced with the RLP ver-

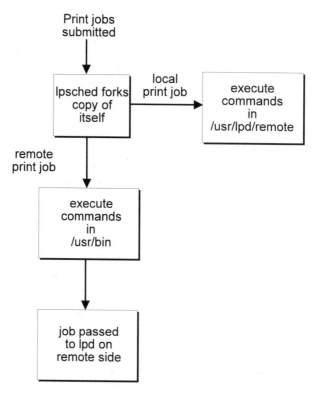

**Figure 8–1**    The flow of LPD print requests.

sions. When you issued one of these print commands, it would check if the printer was local or not and, if so, would call the copy in /usr/lpd/remote. Since this was also the RLP version, it would check if the printer was local or not and, if so, would call the copy in /usr/lpd/remote. Since this was also the RLP version, it would check if the printer was local or not and, if so, would call the copy in /usr/lpd/remote. Since this was also the RLP version . . .

As a result, you would end up will a lot of processes taken up by the program calling itself. There is an option in the mkdev rlp script that removes the RLP functionality and copies the files from /usr/lpd/remote back into /usr/bin. The problem was that this would not do any good as you were copying the RLP files. The only solution was to restore the files from the distribution media.

Assuming you have it configured correctly, when you issue one of these three commands, RLP checks the file /etc/printcap for configuration information about both the local and the remote printer. If the printer is local, you can use any of the standard print commands as the files in /usr/lpd/remote are your original ones (or, at least, should be). If the printer is remote, the print spooler invokes the lpd daemon, which sends the print job over the network to the host specified in /etc/printcap.

Because of the connection across the network, administration and certain printer functionality is limited. First, you cannot do remote administration of the print queue, such as disabling it or moving print jobs to other printers. This must be done locally, either logging in directly or making a network connection using telnet, rlogin, or rcmd. In addition, printer classes are also not supported.

RLP is *installed* using the mkdev rlp script. You configure it using rlpconf. When you run the script you have the choice of installing or removing an existing printer. After creating the /usr/lpd/remote and /usr/spool/lpd directories, the script creates /etc/printcap and copies the three files in /usr/spool/lpd/remote. You are then asked if you want to make changes to the printer description file, which is /etc/printcap, default. It is at this point that the mkdev script calls rlpconf. If you call rlpconf yourself from the command line, you get to this exact same point.

Here you are prompted for the name of the printer and whether it is local or remote. If you say remote, you are prompted for the name of the remote printer. If local, you are asked for the name of the local *device*. Note that this is *not* the name of an existing local printer queue, but the name of a device. When you input this, you are prompted to confirm what you input.

Keep in mind that these are all of the changes the rlpconf command does to /etc/printcap. If there are any special options that you wish to use, you have to edit /etc/printcap by hand. In general the syntax is

```
option=value
```

Take a quick look on one of my machines:

```
# Remote Line Printer (BSD format)
laser2:\
    :lp=:rm=siemau:ex:rp=laser2:sd=/usr/spool/lpd/laser2:
plotter:\
    :lp=/dev/lp:ex:sd=/usr/spool/lpd/plotter:
```

In the first case (laser2), I can tell it is a remote printer. How? Easy. The `lp=` variable tells you the name of the local device. Since it is blank, there is no associated device, therefore it is *not* local. The `rm=` variable says what the name of the remote machine is. Since it equals `siemau` in this case, I know it is remote. In the second case, there is a device defined, but no remote machine; therefore, it is local. In both cases, we see the `ex` option. This is just a Boolean variable that says that `lpd` can handle extended options. If this variable is present, it means that the printer can handle extended options.

In the first entry we have the `rp` variable. This is the name of the remote printer. Since the second entry defines a local printer, there is no remote printer name. The `sd` variable, which is defined in both entries, is the name of the *local* spool directory. There are over a dozen different options you can use. You can find out more about this in the `printcap(SFF)` man-page.

In order for LPD to be working, the remote side needs to allow the local printer to do so. This can be done in several ways and all concern *host equivalence*. Host equivalence is a networking topic that we will discuss in Chapter 12. The issue related to LPD is that you can either set up user equivalence globally using the `/etc/hosts.equiv` file or set it up just for the `lp` user with the file `/etc/hosts.lpd`. This file simply contains a list of the remote machines that are authorized to print to this one using LPD. If you only need equivalence to print, this gives them just what they need and nothing more.

### Multiple Queues to the Same Printer

One common problem when printing is when a single printer needs to be accessed in two separate ways. For example, you may want to print one job in landscape mode and the next in portrait mode. If you have a printer with multiple paper sources, you may want some jobs on company letterhead and others on blank paper. If you have access to the command line, you can pass the necessary options to the `lp` command. Even if the interface is not built with the appropriate functionality, you can add the options to the interface as we talked about earlier.

What happens if you don't have access to the command line? In certain companies, users will never see the command line. Maybe they are brought into a menu to start one of several applications. Maybe the application doesn't have the ability to switch between different formats. Therefore, you need to rely on the operating system to do the work for you.

We go from the assumption that there is no access to the command line in order to print the file. The basic idea is that we need to create names for the same printer. This is based on the idea that from the operating system's standpoint, a printer is only different in terms of its name and *not* the device.

So what does that mean? Well, when you print to a printer, your print job is queued. The print schedule sends it to the physical port "when it gets around to it." What physical port is used is defined in the `configuration` files in `/usr/spool/lp/admins/lp/printers/<printer_name>`. Jobs being sent to a particular printer name are scheduled one after the other. Such is the behavior of any queue.

If there are two printer names going though the same physical port, the printer scheduler has no way of knowing. What could then happen is two files are being sent to the same printer at the same time. The result is that one job is interspersed with another. So, how do you get two printer names to go to the same port? We can see this all graphically in Figure 8–2.

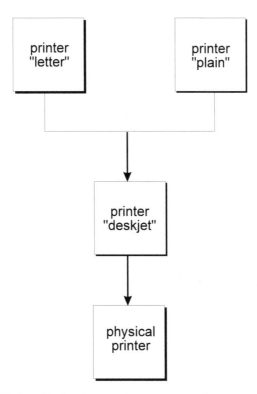

**Figure 8–2**   Multiple print queues to the same printer.

Well, one solution that I came up with while at SCO Support was to create two printers, just as you normally would. In each case you specify the same device. In order to avoid the situation you need to edit the appropriate interface script and have one printer first disable the other, print the file, then re-enable the other. The first line of the interface script runs `disable`. Since the interface script is run as the `lp` user, the script has the authority to disable any printer. After finishing the print job, `enable` is called to re-enable that printer.

This mechanism is simple and fairly easy to implement. Although unlikely, there is a potential for this mechanism to fail. What *could* happen is that the interface script starts, but before the first line is executed (the one disabling the other printer), the process is context-switched out. If the other script is run, it disables the first printer. However, it's too late. The interface script has already started and the `disable` command only affects the print scheduler and not the running process. When the first job is context-switched back in, it disables the second printer. Again, this is too late. As a result, you have two printers sending output to the same physical port at the same time.

Keep in mind that this situation is highly unlikely. I have talked with customers, and even on systems with "constant" printer use, they have never seen merged print jobs. However, it is theoretically possible.

So, how do you prevent this? Well, you don't. The only way to keep the system from merging print jobs like this is to have only a single printer access the port. The principal behind this is that you have multiple "virtual" printers that each print to a single printer, which, in turn, prints to the physical port. The virtual printers are then configured to perform the needed functions.

For this, let's assume we have two paper sources. One containing letterhead, which we will call "letter," and the other containing plain paper, which we will call "plain." Changing paper bins is not something that is contained within the interface scripts that SCO provides. Therefore, we also need to assume that we have made some changes to an interface script to allow this functionality. Let's say that we have letterhead in the top bin, so that the option to access this bin will be `-otop` and the plain paper is in the bottom bin, which we access with `-obottom`. Let's call the real printer "deskjet."

The two virtual printers need to be configured using the network interface and print to the device `/dev/null`. This allows us to edit the file `/usr/spool/lp` `/remote` to print to the real printer with the necessary options. If `/usr/spool/` `lp/remote` does not exist, you will need to create it. In any event, add the lines

```
letter: lp -ddeskjet  -otop
plain:  lp -ddeskjet  -obottom
```

If you remember from the discussion on network printing, you know that when we use the network interface we are actually piping the output through a command. The command is what we have defined in `/usr/spool/lp/remote`. In both of these cases the command we are using is simply `lp`. The key is that we are sending each job to the same printer, but with different options. Therefore, if your application cannot specify which paper bin, you print to `letter` to get letterhead or to `plain` to get plain paper.

## When Things Go Wrong

Printers have problems. Some of them can be solved by remaining calm and looking at your system. Others require very simple changes. Unfortunately, not all problems fall into this set. Sometimes there are printer problems that cannot be quickly resolved. Although I do not advocate it as the only solution to printer problems, removing and reinstalling the printer package is a relatively quick answer and solves a lot of problems.

If you really want to find the cause of your problem, then obviously removing the print package is not the answer. However, most of the time, the customers I talked to did not want to know why it happened, just what they could do to get printing again. I made it a rule that I would work on a printer problem for the same length of time that it would take to remove and reinstall the printer package. Normally, this is only about twenty minutes. If I was nowhere nearer the solution than when I started, reinstalling was a good alternative.

Obviously, if you have fifty printers configured then removing and reinstalling the printer package is probably not the best solution. You probably spent hours configuring the printers and spending an hour to solve the printer problem is a good investment.

If you decide that removing and reinstalling the printer package is your best choice, there are a couple of things to consider. If you are running RLP, then I would suggest that you first remove RLP before you remove the entire print package. This is done by running `mkdev rlp` and saying that you want to delete remote printing. This ensures that the commands used for remote printing end up in the right place.

The next issue is your existing printers. If you are using the default interface scripts, then you are okay. However, if you have made any modifications to the interface scripts, then you should make copies of them. When you reinstall the printer package, you can simply replace the new interface scripts with your old ones. As a side note, if you are upgrading from SCO Xenix, you can take interface scripts from Xenix and use them on SCO UNIX, usually with no modifications.

Another thing to consider is that you do not need to go through sysadmsh or the Printer Manager. The lpadmin command will allow you to create printers from the command line. For example, if I wanted to use the HPDeskJet interface and create a printer called DeskJet, which is attached to /dev/lp0, the command might look like this:

```
/usr/lib/lpadmin -p DeskJet -m HPDeskJet -o nobanner -v /dev/lp0
```

The -p option is the name of the printer. The -m option is the model printer we want to use. The -o option is printing options that we want by default. In this case, we specified nobanner to supress the banner page. The -v says what device the printer is attached to.

By creating a shell script that contains several lines, each creating a new printer; you can quickly recreate all the printers you removed. Doing it like this, even fifty can be recreated quickly. For more details, see the lpadmin(ADM) man-page.

A common problem (that does *not* require you to reinstall) is that the printer output appears to "stairstep." That is, when the file is output, the text reached the end of the line, drops down to the next line, and continues printing without starting at the beginning of the line. In other words, there is a new line without a carriage-return. This normally happens on serial printers and the reason for this is that the serial driver will reset the stty settings on the line when that line is closed for the last time.

The solution is to create a script that keeps the line open. Such a script is called a "hold-open" script. Actually, it is only a single line that you can incorporate into an existing startup script or one that you start by hand. A common place is /etc/rc.d/8/userdef. Since this is one of the last scripts executed before going into multi-user mode, there is nothing that will interfere with it. The line should look like this:

```
(stty  <stty_settings> ; while : ; do sleep 3600; done) < /dev/ttyXX &
```

Some suggestions for the <stty_settings> include the baud rate, ixon, ixoff, and -ixany. You could also explcitly tell the port to add a carriage-return after all new lines with the setting onlcr. We have enclosed the entire first portion within parenthesis so that it is treated as a single command. Therefore, the stty settings are made, and we go into a loop where we sleep for 3600 seconds (1 hour). We then go to the top of the loop and sleep for another hour. This holds the port (/dev/ttyXX) open and holds the stty settings the way we want them. We then place the entire command in the background.

Another common problem is the print scheduler stops. Although this is not a problem that happens regularly, it is common in the sense that it results in calls to SCO Support. The administrator may see that the print scheduler has stopped and try to restart it. Unfortunately, this does not work.

The key to this problem is the file /usr/spool/lp/SCHEDLCK. This file is simply a flag to indicate that the scheduler is running and so prevents it from being started again. If the scheduler has stopped and won't restart, make sure that this file does not exist. If it does, simply remove it.

On other occasions, none of these things fix your problem. It is often difficult to find the solution when you cannot see what is happening at each step. Since the print spooler is run behind the scenes, you rarely get a glimpse of what it is doing. However, we can force the system to tell us what it is doing with a simple little trick.

If you remember in Chapter 3, I mentioned placing a set -x in a script to have it display each command as it is executed. Remember that this goes to stderr and not stdout. As the print spooler is executing the interface script, there is no stderr like from a script started from the command line. So, instead of displaying each line to the screen, the output is *mailed* to you. There is a mail file for each print job that you submit. You can then examine the mail files to figure out what is happening.

If you are using RLP to do remote printing, there are a couple of things to cover. If you submit a job that is destined to be printed on a remote machine, but never arrives, the first place to look is the local machine. First check to see if you can print at all from the local machine. If not, it is unlikely that remote printing will work. If you can print locally, make sure that the printer is enabled and accepting requests.

If the local printer is enabled and accepting requests, it's still possible for the problem to be local. Make sure that lpd is running on *both* sides. The local side needs to be able to send the file and the remote side needs to be able to accept the file. For remote printing, there is also the rlpstat command, which gives you information similar to lpstat. Also check /usr/spool/lpd/<printer_name>/status. This file gives you status information on the specific printer, which is usually helpful in tracking down the problem.

The print scheduler itself, lpsched, has the ability to do its own debugging. To enable debugging, you need to start lpsched with the -d option. This is easily accomplished by editing the print scheduler start-up script in /etc/rc2.d (probably S80lp). Note that this option *does* exist in ODT, but it is not listed in the lpsched(ADM) man-page. Information is displayed to the screen when lpsched starts up and other information is placed in files in /usr/spool/lp/logs.

There will be three files of primary interest. The messages file will contain all messages between lp and lpsched. The requests file will contain information on all requests submitted. The exec file contains information on all commands executed by lpsched.

# CHAPTER
# 9

- UUCP

- TCP/IP

- NFS

- Serial Network Protocols

- Mailers

- Mosaic and the Web

- Network Technologies

- Stay Tuned

# Talking
# to Other
# Machines

Long ago (at least in terms of the history of electronic data processing) having two computers was something you read about in science fiction novels. As systems became more common, the time did come when a company or university would have two computers. The need then arose for data to be exchanged between the two machines. This was the beginning of SNEAKER-Net (Slow, Non-Electrical Activity, Keeping Everyone Running), which was developed in the 1950s. With SNEAKER-Net, the technician would copy data onto a tape or other media and, using his sneakers, would run the tape over to the other machine to be loaded. In many organizations, SNEAKER-Net is still employed today as this is often the only type of network they think they can afford.

In 1976, researchers at AT&T Bell Laboratories came to the rescue. Bell developed a serial line protocol to exchange data between UNIX machines, which came to be known as UUCP, for UNIX-to-UNIX copy. Over the years there were several changes, upgrades, and revisions. In 1983, AT&T released a new version that came to be known as Honeydanber UUCP, as it had been developed by Peter **Honey**man, **D**avid **A**. **N**owitz, and **B**rian **E**. **R**edman. This is the version currently employed on SCO systems.

Although, UUCP was a good thing, it was limited by the speed of the serial line connecting the two computers. Since the system could only be as fast as its slowest component, there needed to be a way to speed up that slowest component. Well, serial line speeds increased, but that still was not enough. In the 1970s, Xerox came out with *Ethernet*, which made high speed communication between computers possible. It was now possible for users to access remote computers and expect response times comparable to being logged in locally, rather than experiencing delays as was common with the serial line communication of the day. (We'll get into more details on Ethernet later.)

Today, both are still widely spread. Although prices have dropped to the point that Ethernet networks are commonplace (I even have one in my house), UUCP is still used regularly when distances prevent other types of connection, or when the connection is going to be quick or short-term and the administrator doesn't want the added hassle of first installing the Ethernet cards.

We are going to talk about both in this chapter. First, we'll talk about UUCP, as this is a set of programs that everyone has on their SCO system even if they don't have ODT or OpenServer. Later, we'll talk about networking principles, especially TCP/IP and the treasure chest (or Pandora's box) of tools and programs that go with it.

## UUCP

Perhaps the oldest form of UNIX computer networking is UUCP. UUCP stands for UNIX-to-UNIX copy and stems from the time when even the ability to copy files directly between computers was a big deal. Today, UUCP is still widely used in systems where more complex networking is either not necessary or not possible. UUCP also provides the ability to remotely execute jobs as well as interactively log in to remote sites.

UUCP and most of its associated programs are batch oriented. This means that transfers and remote execute requests are "spooled" to be carried out later. The user submits a request and waits for the request to be carried out. There is often little control over when the transfer actually takes place. This is essentially the same way the print spooler works. Jobs are done when the system gets around to it. In most cases, communications between remote systems is carried out according to specific schedules, usually when the phone rates are cheaper.

Because of its complex nature and the large number of support programs, UUCP can be considered a system service. UUCP is not only the name of the package or service within SCO, but is also the name of one of the programs within the package. The uucp command is perhaps the most commonly used of the commands, with the interactive login program (cu) a close second. The remote execution command, uux, also places in the top three.

Built into UUCP are several levels of security. The first level is normal file permissions that everyone must adhere to, whether local or a remote. The next is the system level security that allows or denies access to your system or to a remote system. There is also the ability within UUCP to restrict access to specific directories and commands. This means that although the permissions on a file or directory might give you access to it and you have a valid UUCP account on that system, you still cannot access it. With UUCP you can not only limit access to certain directories, but also to certain commands that can be executed. (Remember UUCP also allows remote execution.)

The SCO UUCP package is essentially the same between ODT and OpenServer. The differences really show themselves when you are trying to configure and administer UUCP, so we will wait until we talk about configuration to talk about these differences. The SCO UUCP package provides two programs for copying files between systems: `uucp` and `uuto`. The `uucp` command is the more common of the two and provides more flexibility. On the other hand, `uuto` is a little easier to use. Personally, I have never used `uuto` other than to test a user's command to see if they were doing it right.

For the purpose of this discussion, we're going to assume that there is a valid UUCP connection between the two machines. In the second half of the book, when we talk about configuring and troubleshooting UUCP, we talk about problems and what to do. We'll also assume that we have three machines, all of which use UUCP. The local machine is scoburg. It connects via modem to the machine siemau. Siemau is connected via a direct serial line to the machine vesta.

The reason we are including this third machine is that it is possible to transfer files to and from machines via UUCP to which there is no connection. So, if you have connection to one machine (in our case scoburg can talk to siemau) and the second machine can talk to the third (siemau and vesta) you can use the second machine as a bridge between the other two.

Before we start, we need a crash course in the basics. There are three primary files, all of which are located in `/usr/lib/uucp`. First the Systems file contains a list of which sites (machines) are known to you. The device that UUCP uses to connect to the remote machine is defined in the Devices file. What each machine can do in terms of copying or remotely executing commands is defined in the local Permissions file. For example, what siemau is authorized to do on scoburg is defined in *scoburg's* Permissions file regardless of who called whom.

Let's assume that we were on scoburg and we wanted to transfer a file to siemau. We start up UUCP which looks in the Systems file to see if it can find siemau. When it does, it then checks to see if this is a proper time to call (also defined in Systems). It then looks through the Devices file for an appropriate device (serial port). Once it finds the device UUCP can then begin calling siemau.

In order for scoburg to be able to log into siemau, an account has to be established. For UUCP to log in, it goes through the same procedure as "real" users: It needs both a valid logname (an account) and a password. When UUCP on scoburg gives the correct logname and password, UUCP is started up on siemau and the two UUCPs begin to talk to each other. When they start talking, UUCP on scoburg tells UUCP on siemau that it wants to send a file and where it wants to put that file. UUCP on siemau checks its Permissions file to see if scoburg has authorization to send files in the first place and if so, whether UUCP on siemau can send the file to the location specified. If it can, then the file is copied (actually the work is done by the program `uucico`).

By default, ODT 3.0 and OpenServer provides a UUCP login account: `nuucp`. The default Permissions file also allows every `uucp` login to be able to write to the `/usr/spool/uucppublic` directory. This directory is available on many different versions of UNIX as a common, generally accessible directory for transferring files. This allows you to easily transfer files with new sites, without having to establish special accounts for them. On the other hand. If every site shares the same UUCP account, they all have access to the same files. Therefore, if security is a concern, then you should consider individual accounts.

### *Copying Files*

So let's get to it. Just keep in mind something I have been saying all along. This book is not a tutorial. I want to show you relationships and how things fit together. In order to do that I need to establish some base level understanding, which is what I am going to do with UUCP. We're going to quickly go through some basic UUCP commands to get a feel for how they work. Then we are going to go into the details of what happens behind the scenes.

The primary (most used) command in UUCP is `uucp`. Surprised? This command allows you to copy files from one UNIX machine to another. UUCP has spread itself so widely throughout the computer world that many vendors supply UUCP for non-UNIX machines, such as is provided in the MKS Toolkit from Mortice-Kern Systems for DOS.

The syntax of the `uucp` is essentially the same as the "normal" UNIX copy command: `command source destination`. The only difference is that normally you want to specify a machine name in the source or destination name (or both). However, this is not a requirement. If you want, you could leave the machine name out completely and use UUCP to copy files on your local machine.

Let's say I wanted to copy a letter I have from my home directory on scoburg and put in the `uucppublic` directory on siemau. The syntax would be

```
uucp /usr/jimmo/letter siemau!/usr/spool/uucppublic/letter
```

The first thing to notice is that the machine name (siemau) is followed by an exclamation mark. This is a flag to UUCP to signify that this is a machine name and not part of the file name. (If you are using the C-shell, you should switch to the `ksh`.) If you really don't want to switch (or can't) then you need to be careful because (remember the chapter on shell basics?) the exclamation mark means something to the C-shell. Therefore, you need to escape it. The syntax for the C-shell would be

```
uucp /usr/jimmo/letter siemau\!/usr/spool/uucppublic/letter
```

As in other sections, I am not going to give you both `csh` and `(k)sh` syntax. Instead, I will just say that when you use `csh` you need to be careful about the exclamation mark.

Just like the normal `cp` command, the tilde (~) also has special significance for UUCP. By itself, it refers to the `/usr/spool/uucppublic` directory. Therefore, the above command could be written as

```
uucp /usr/jimmo/letter siemau!~/letter
```

Not only does this save time in typing, you don't have to worry (too much) about misspelling anything. When I don't use the tilde, I often have only one 'p' in the middle of `uucppublic` and my UUCP request will fail.

You can also use the tilde with a user name so it expands to mean their home directory. Therefore, I could have written the above command as:

```
uucp ~jimmo/letter siemau!~/letter
```

which saves me a whole four characters. However, some systems I have seen with hundreds of users have the home directories scattered across several filesystems. Using this mechanism, you don't have to know what filesystem a user is on in order to get the file to or from their home directory.

Keep in mind that although you can specify a pathname with this short-cut, you do not automatically have access to that directory—even if it is your own account. The problem is that UUCP does not know that you are you. To UUCP these are two different accounts, even if they have the same UID and GID. Also, keep in mind that you as the submitter of this job *must* have access to the source file. However, it is UUCP that needs to have access to the destination.

Another way of specifying the file is with relative paths or no paths, provided I am specifying a file in that directory. If I were already in `/usr/jimmo`, the above command could look like this:

```
uucp letter siemau!~/letter
```

or

```
uucp ./letter siemau!~/letter
```

This also works for relative paths, such as

```
uucp ../jimmo/letter siemau!~/letter
```

When the job is submitted to UUCP it will create the appropriate full path name for that file. Also, if you specify the home directory for a user on a remote machine, that user need not exist locally for the expansion to take place. The reason is that the path name is not expanded locally. Rather, the system sends the path name you specify to the remote machine. It is there that the expansion takes place. Because there is no rule as to when and where the expansion takes place, it is best not to use relative paths when specifying files on a remote machine.

Just as you can copy files from one directory to another, although neither is your current directory, you can copy files from one machine to another, although neither is you local machine. For example, assume our local machine is scoburg, which knows about both the source machine, siemau, and the destination machine, vesta. We can copy files from siemau to vesta with the following command:

```
uucp  siemau!/usr/spool/uucppublic/file  vesta!/usr/spool/uucppub-
lic/file
```

We see from this example that the source machine is remote (remember that we are assuming that the local machine is scoburg). We are taking a file from siemau and copying it to vesta. What would happen if we left out the reference to a remote machine when we specified the destination for the file? We would be taking a file from the remote machine and copying it to our local machine. That is, we would be copying from siemau to scoburg.

We can take this one step further and specify multiple machines in our destination; for example,

```
uucp /etc/motd siemau!vesta!~/filename
```

Since the local machine (scoburg) does not know about vesta, this is actually the way we would have to run the command. If we tried the first example on scoburg, UUCP would have complained immediately that it did not know about vesta.

There are a couple of commonly used options in UUCP. For example, you can use the -j option to print out the job-ID. If you later decide that you really don't want to send the file (or remotely execute the command), you can use this job-ID to cancel the request.

The -m option can be used to send mail to the requester that the file has been transferred or the job executed. Or if you want to notify someone on the remote machine, you can use the -n option followed by that user's name.

Depending on how your system is configured, the actual transfer of the file might not take place immediately. As I mentioned before, the Systems file contains information on what is an appropriate time to call. Often, calls are only permitted during certain hours to either reduce the traffic on the line or to limit calls to times when the phone rates are less expensive. It may also be the case that your system is configured to *never* call the other system. Transfer is dependent on the other system calling you. Therefore, as a user, if your request does not go through as quickly as you want, talk to your administrator to find out how UUCP has been configured. If you are an administrator and the request doesn't go through as quickly as you expect, then you probably configured something incorrectly.

Requests are "spooled." This is essentially the same as for the print spooler. There is a special holding area for spooled UUCP jobs. At what time UUCP decides to send the message is dependent on your system configuration, and we'll get to that a little later.

As with spooled print jobs, there will probably be a time when you would like to find out the status of your spooled UUCP requests. To check the status in the print spooler, you use the `lpstat` command. To check the status in the UUCP spooler, you use the `uustat` command.

If I run `uustat` after submitting the request

```
uucp /etc/motd siemau!~/filename
```

the output of `uustat` would look like this:

```
siemauN522d  05/28-14:45 S siemau jimmo 90 /etc/motd
```

In this example, there is only one output line. Like `lpstat` when several print jobs are queued, `uustat` will also show information on multiple UUCP jobs that are queued. The entries in each line are

```
job-ID date/time type_of_job remote machine requester size_of_file
file_name
```

If we take a more complicated example, then the output of `uustat` gets more complicated as well. For example, let's say we want to copy a file from siemau to vesta. Assume there is nothing in the queue and we issue the following `uucp` command:

```
uucp siemau!/etc/motd vesta!~/filename
```

When we run `uustat`, we now get

Nothing. Hmmm. What happened? Well, it has to do with the default behavior of `uustat`. Just as the default behavior of `lpstat` is to only show us our pending jobs, `uustat` only shows us the pending `uucp` jobs. As a result we don't see anything. Because we are actually creating a local `uux` job that sets up a `uucp` job on vesta.

Instead we need to use the `-a` option to `uustat`, which says to show us all queues, not just `uucp`. This time we get

```
vestaN6451  05/28-14:56 S vesta uucp uucp -C siemau!/etc/motd
!/tmp
```

The biggest change is that instead of a size and file name at the end of the line, we have what appears to be a uucp command. This is exactly what it is. What we said was that we wanted to copy a file from siemau to vesta. What happens is that UUCP actually creates a job for remote execution on *vesta* which says to go get the file from siemau. This is why we don't get any output from uustat. It is no longer considered a uucp request, but rather a uux request. If we look in /usr/spool/uucp/vesta we will see both a control file (C.) and a data file (D.)

### Remote Execution

Just as uucp allows you to copy to and from different sets of machines, uux allows you to execute commands across sets of machines. For example, I want to print a file on a printer attached to vesta, but the file I want to print is on siemau. I could do this with the command

```
uux vesta!lp siemau!/etc/motd
```

This would actually create two UUCP jobs. This first would transfer the file /etc/motd from siemau to vesta. The second then prints out the file on vesta. In principle we can use uux to execute any command on a remote system. There are two limitations. First, uux is an SUID program, so it is run as the user uucp. Therefore, the user uucp needs to have permission to run the command. Second, the commands that can be remotely executed may be limited by the Permissions file on the remote machine.

### Interactive UUCP Connections

There is one interactive program included in the UUCP package: cu (call UNIX). Its purpose is to access the modem and to dial the number specified, either through the Systems file or directly on the command line. Once the remote modem has answered, cu's work is over. cu serves as a kind of terminal emulator as it displays the output from the remote system on your screen, however it responds to your commands and does nothing on its own. Because cu is simply echoing the output of the remote system, you don't even have to be calling another UNIX system!

If the system you called was like UNIX, where you eventually got to a command prompt, then the commands you input would actually be executed on the remote system. Built into cu is also the ability to execute commands on your local system, even though you are attached to (logged into) the remote system.

The format of cu is

```
cu [options] destination
```

As I mentioned above this destination can either be a phone number or the name of a system from the Systems file. If you use a telephone number you can use a special character to represent secondary dial-tones (=), or pauses (-).

Let's assume the phone number for siemau was 555–6501. To use cu to connect to it I could do so in two ways:

```
cu siemau
```

or

```
cu 5556501
```

You can also tell cu to access a particular device using the -l option, rather than trying to dial a phone; for example,

```
cu -l tty2a dir
```

This would connect me to the modem attached to /dev/tty2a (assuming there is a modem there).

Built into cu are several commands that are accessed by preceding the command with a tilde (~). Normally cu passes everything to the remote machine. However, if the first character on a line is the tilde, the line is interpreted as a command for cu.

A tilde followed by an exclamation mark (~!) tells cu that you want to execute a shell on the *local* machine. Although you are still connected to the remote machine, everything you now input is executed on the local machine. To return to the cu session, simply type exit. You can include a command name with the ~!. This will execute the command locally and immediately return you to the cu sessions.

Two other important tilde commands are ~%take and ~%put. These allow you to *take* a file from the remote machine and copy it to a local file, or *put* a file onto the remote system from the local system. The syntax is

```
~%command source destination
```

So, if I wanted to copy the remote file file_name and copy it to new_file on my local machine, the command would be

```
~%take file_name new_file
```

Keep in mind that this really only works for ASCII (text) files. The reason for this is that the cu command was designed for 7-bit communication. cu treats every 7 bits as a character. However, the bytes that compose a binary file are 8 bits long. You end up having everything garbled. However, there is a nifty trick that you can use with one of the other UUCP commands: uuencode.

The primary function of uuencode is to convert a set of 8-bit characters to 7-bit and then back again. Well, to the uninitiated, the syntax for uuencode is a bit

confusing. The first thing to note is that by default, `uuencode` sends the results of its work to stdout. You do give it two names as arguments, but one is the destination name and not the place that the output goes. Confused? Well, lets look at an example.

Assume I have a program that I want to transfer named `newprg`. To `uuencode` it I might be tempted to input

```
uuencode newprg newprg.uue
```

I am using the convention of .uue as an extension to indicate that this is a `uuencoded` file. Well, if I were to use this command, I would get screen after screen of characters scrolling by. As I said, the output of `uuecode` is `stdout`, not the filename we give as an argument. To understand this, let's look at the first line of the output:

```
begin 711 newprg.uue
```

The first part of the line is the word `begin`. When we finally get around to decoding the file, this is a flag to tell `uudecode` where to start. This allows us to include `uuencode`'d messages as part of email.

Next we have `711`. This is the permissions the resulting file will have. At the end of the line is `newprg.uue`. This is what we input, expecting to be the output file name. This is actually the name of the resulting file when we *decode* the file. In order to get this into a file so we can transfer it, the command would actually be

```
uuencode newprg newprg > temp.uue
```

Now we have a file (`temp.uue`) that contains the output of the previous command. If we look at the first line, we see that it is the same as the previous one except that the resulting file name is now `newprg` and not `newprg.uue`. We now have a 7-bit file that we can transfer using either `~%put` or `~%take`. When we are done, we can terminate the `cu` session by inputting tilde-dot (`~.`).

The best way to learn about something is to do tech support for it. That's how I learned about UUCP. One of the first calls I had with UUCP was, fortunately for me, a very basic call. The user was simply having trouble communicating with another machine.

We checked all the configuration files on the local machine and everything made sense. That is, all the files had the right values in the right place. One of the first things to try is `cu`, which provides an interactive login. If `cu` works, then you know that the physical connection between the two sites and the software configuration is correct; that is, the modems are set up correctly, you are going through the right device, and you have the correct system name and phone number.

We tried to call, but we just couldn't communicate. The biggest problem was that the user didn't have access to the other machine. He was relying on the fact that the administrator from the remote side said that everything was configured correctly. However, we were still not communicating.

After about twenty minutes of checking our configuration and trying to call a site with which we could communicate, we both agreed that it *had* to be something on the remote side, despite what the other administrator said. So, the user called him on another phone and had him watch and listen as we tried to communicate with him.

Well, we heard the phone ring on the remote side. It rang and rang and rang. Finally, UUCP gave us an error saying it couldn't connect. So we had the other administrator turn the modem on and off to make sure that it had not gotten into some "weird" state. We tried it again. The phone rang and rang and rang.

Fortunately, there was a set of lights on the front of the modem. One of them was the AA light, for Auto-Answer. The other administrator failed to notice, or failed to tell us, that this light was off. This meant that no matter how hard we tried, the modem wouldn't answer. We were trying to communicate with another site that just wasn't listening. After setting the modem to Auto-Answer, we could communicate with no problems.

Oh, you wonder what organization had this communications problem where only one side was listening? The United Nations.

### The Flow of Things

Most UUCP files can be found in one of two directories. The /usr/lib/uucp directory contains the UUCP configuration files and many of the support programs. The /usr/spool/uucp directory is the working directory for UUCP. There are several subdirectories here with various functions, which we'll get to in a moment.

There are three key programs that manage as well as supervise UUCP communication. The first, uucico, is perhaps the workhorse of the UUCP package. It is the responsibility of uucico to determine what device should be used to make the connection, start up the modem dialer programs, log into the remote site, and perform the actual transfer of the data. We see what this looks like in Figure 9–1.

Part of the configuration process of UUCP is to establish UUCP accounts. With these accounts, remote sites can access through the uucico program (among others). When uucico calls a remote site, it logs as a predefined user. This user should have been established as a UUCP user on the remote site. If so, that user does not have a log in shell as we know it, but rather has uucico. When your uucico logs into the remote site, the remote uucico starts up and the two start to talk to each other.

**Figure 9–1**   The flow of UUCP.

To be able to communicate with each other, the two uucico programs need to determine whether they both speak the same language. The language they speak is called a protocol and the process they go through is called *negotiating the protocol*. The most common one used in SCO UNIX systems is the 'g' protocol. This comes in two flavors: G and g.

The entire time it is attempting to log in and afterwards as it is processing and carrying out requests, uucico is maintaining its supervisory roll. It is the responsibility of uucico to ensure that files and commands are only accessed if the system allows it.

To execute commands on a remote machine, you use the uux command. It searches for requests for remote execution, but is also concerned with security and can only execute them if the remote site allows it.

If the connection cannot be made (we'll get into that later), the job remains in the spool directory. Like the print spooler, the files in the UUCP spool directory are the only record the system has of pending jobs. If they get removed, then the job must be resubmitted. This is obviously not a good thing if the files are removed accidentally, however it does allow you to remove files that may be causing problems.

If the remote computer or the device selected to make the connection to the remote computer is unavailable, the request remains queued in the spool directory. This is also what happens when you either tell uucp to specifically hold onto the job or the time permitted to call hasn't been reached.

By default, there are several entries in the UUCP user's crontab that are related to job scheduling. At 9 and 39 minutes after each hour, cron will start the /usr/lib/uucp/uudemon.hour program. Why it is called uudemon.hour when it runs every half hour is beyond me. Maybe uudemon.half-hour was a bit too much to write. Actually, the reason is the number of characters. UNIX file names are restricted to fourteen characters on the traditional UNIX filesystems. Therefore, they *couldn't* have a file called uudemon.half-hour.

The uudemon.hour program is actually a shell script that contains two commands:

```
/usr/lib/uucp/uusched &
/usr/lib/uucp/uuxqt &
```

The uusched program (often called a daemon) checks for pending jobs and schedules them for execution by uucico. The uuxqt program is the remote end of uux, in that it is what executes the jobs that have been submitted for remote execution. It is the uusched program that eventually starts up uucico on the local machine.

To get a better understanding of what happens, let's look at an example. Let's assume your local machine is scoburg and you wish to send a file to the remote machine siemau. The command you would enter would be

```
uucp file_name siemau!/usr/spool/uucppublic
```

Remember from our discussion on the various shells that the exclamation mark means something to the C-shell. Therefore you have to escape it by placing a backslash in front of it, as in

```
uucp file_name siemau\!/usr/spool/uucppublic
```

Work files are created in the `/usr/spool/uucp/siemau` directory. Each system will have its own subdirectory under `/usr/spool/uucp`, but these are not created until the first request is submitted. There is a control file, whose name has the format `C.siemau#xxxx`, where # is the grade, or processing priority of the request and `xxxx` is the job number of that particular request. The grade is a single alphabet character (letter) and grades are processed in order from A–Z and then from a–z. The default under SCO OpenServer is 'N'.

After submitting the above job we might have a file in `/usr/spool/uucp/siemau` that looked like this:

```
-rw-r--r--  1 uucp    sys      41 May 27 10:49 C.siemauN5214
```

Since this file is readable by everyone, we could look at it no matter who submitted the job. Its contents look like this:

```
S /use/jimmo/file_name /tmp jimmo -dc D.0 644 jimmo
```

The format of this file is as follows:

*Type of request.* Here we have an 'S' for Send a file to the remote machine. This could also be an 'R' to request a file. If we want to remotely execute a job, this would be an 'S' as we are sending a request for remote execution.

*Source path name of the file.* If we specified a relative path (or no path) `uucp` will determine the full path and use the full path here. If we had specified a path relative to the home directory of a particular user (with the `~username`), then the entry would also appear here in that form. In this case we are sending the file `/usr/jimmo/file_name`. If we are requesting remote executing, the source file is the data file (D.).

*Destination path.* Here too, if we specified a relative path (or no path) `uucp` will determine the full path and use the full path here. If we had specified a path relative to the home directory of a particular user, then the entry would also appear here in that form. Here we are simply sending it to the `/tmp` directory. UUCP will ensure that it gets the right name, in this case `motd`. This is the same behavior as the `cp` command. If we are requesting remote execution, the destination name is the same as the control file, but will have an X instead of a C.

*The login name of the sender.*

*List of command options specified to either uucp or uux.* Here we have `-dc`. These are the defaults. The `-d` says to create directories necessary to copy the file. The `-c` says not to copy the local file into the spool directory prior to transferring. Instead the file will be copied directly from the source, in this case `/usr/jimmo/file_name`. (Copy the file if you don't want to change permission.)

*Name of the data file.* Here is the default of D.0. This means that UUCP will copy the file directly from the source. If I had chosen to copy the file into the spool directory this would point to that file.

*Mode of the source file in octal.* This is only used when sending files. Check the `chmod(C)` man-page for details on the octal format of file permissions.

*Who to notify.* The default is the sender. However, if you used either the `-n` or `-m` options.

In this example, I am copying the file directly from the source, in this case `/usr/jimmo/file_name`. If I had specified the `-C` option, `uucp` would have first copied the file into the spool directory. Check the permission here as well. You see that they are 644. That means that everyone, including UUCP has the right to read the file. If UUCP did not have the right to read the file, it would matter whether I specified a copy or not. UUCP would automatically make a copy of that file in the spool directory for me.

The file created by UUCP is referred to as the data file. Its name begins with a D and has the format

```
D.siemauXXXXzzz
```

where `XXXX` is the sequence/ID number of that job and is the same as the job number on the control file, and `zzz` is a number used to identify any additional data files associated with that job. This is used when there are several data (D.) files created for a single control file. The format of the files is a single character to identify the type of data followed by the data itself. The meaning of each line is as follows:

U   User's name and system.

F   File to transmit. This normally only appears when sending mail since the D. file is the file being transferred in other cases.

I   Identifies standard input.

0    Identifies standard output.

N    If present, prevents mailing acknowledgment of completion of remote execution.

Z    If present, indicates message should only be sent if the job failed.

R    Return address of the requester. This is used by mailers that can forward to more than one hop. This is the user `mmdf` (assuming you are using MMDF).

\#    Comments

After completion of the work files, UUCP can now send the job. If UUCP had been told to simply queue up the job (with the `-r` option), the job will sit and wait until contact is initiated by either side. It is also possible that the system administrator had specified particular times to call that site. So, even if you don't specify the `-r` option, the job will wait in the queue.

First, `uucico` checks the file `/usr/lib/uucp/Systems`. If the system you are trying to reach is not listed or you are not allowed to call at this time, you get an error message.

An entry in the Systems file would look like this:

```
siemau Any ACU 300-2400 5551212 -\r\d-ogin:-\K\d-ogin:-\K\d-ogin:
uusiemau asswd: NoSecret
```

The entries are

```
system time-to-call device-type modem-speed phone-number chat-
script
```

The time-to-call field tells `uucico` what times you can call the remote site. Here we have the entry `Any` which means calls are permitted at any time. We could specify specific times of the day or even days of the week. We'll get into details on this in Chapter 14.

The third entry in the `Systems` file is the device type that should be used to call out. Using this device type, it searches through the file `/usr/lib/uucp/Devices` for a matching entry. For example, I have an entry in my `Devices` file that looks like this:

```
ACU tty1A - 9600-19200 /usr/lib/uucp/atdialHA96
```

The entries are

```
device-type port dialer-line baud-rate dialer
```

Here, `uucico` is looking for an ACU device type. This is an Automatic Call Unit, or modem. Since this is the same device as specified in the `System` file, this line would match. The entry in the `Devices` file also tells what physical device to use and what modem dialer to use. (A modem dialer is a program that is used to access the modem and dial the appropriate number.) Using the telephone number from the `Systems` file, along with the device and dialer from the `Devices` file, `uucico` can now call out.

In order to prevent other UUCP processes from accessing the same device and to prevent them from trying to call the same system, `uucico` creates two lock files in `/usr/spool/uucp`. The port is locked with the file `LCK..ttyxx`, where xx is the nonmodem control device. This is the convention used, although it is usually the modem control device that you are calling out on. In our example, we are calling out on device `tty1A`. therefore the lock file would be `LCK..tty1a`. Check the `serial(HW)` man-page or the section on device nodes for more details on this.

The system lock is in similar form: `LCK..siemau`. In both cases, the LCK file is ASCII and contains the process ID of the process that created the lock. This is useful when trying to figure out who's hogging the modem by downloading dozens of image files when you are trying to transfer your end of month reports.

Now `uucico` can begin calling the remote site. At this point we will assume that the connection can be made and the remote side answers. `Uucico` will attempt to log in using the values defined in the *chat script* portion of the `Systems` file. Essentially, the chat script tells the calling system what to expect the remote system to send it and what it should send in return. We'll get into more details about this in the second part of the book.

Assuming that the logname and password were correct, scoburg has now successfully logged into siemau. One of the first things that siemau needs to do is to create its own lock files. It would not be a good thing if one process started to dial out on the port you were calling in on. These have the same format on siemau as on scoburg, however the system lock (obviously) has the form `LCK..scoburg`.

As I mentioned before, the shell that `uucp` users have is `uucico`. It starts up on siemau and the two `uucico`'s start to talk to each other. One of the first things they do is negotiate the protocol. Keep in mind that there is a lot more to the actual login process than that. However, this covers the main steps and provides a good background for understanding the flow of things.

The `uucico` on siemau needs to ensure that the `uucp` user calling from scoburg is allowed access to where it wants to go. It does so by checking the file `/usr/lib/uucp/Permissions`. Once siemau has determined that the UUCP user calling from scoburg has access it begins transmitting the file in small "packets." These packets are of a specific size. Changing them in SCO ODT 3.0 and earlier was not as straightforward as the `/usr/lib/uucp/Configuration` file in SCO OpenServer. Within each packet is a checksum, If siemau 0 determines that a packet was garbled during transmission, it will ignore (drop) the packet. Since it acknowledges each packet it receives successfully, scoburg will see that this packet was not received and will resend it.

To ensure integrity of the destination file, the `uucico` on siemau writes the file into a temporary file as it is receiving it. This is in the `/usr/spool/uucp/scoburg` directory, with the name TM.xxxx. When the transfer is complete, the file is moved to the specified destination, in this case `/tmp/file_name`. (We hadn't specified the destination file name, so `uucico` assumes that it has the same name.)

As this whole thing is going on, both sides are logging the information. On scoburg there will be a file `/tmp/siemau`. You can watch the progress of the transfer by using

```
tail -f /tmp/siemau
```

The `-f` option tells `tail` to keep reading from the file as new lines are appended to the end. If you are siemau, there is a file `/tmp/scoburg` which you can watch with `tail` as well. The information in these files is for a particular session. Information is logged on a semipermanent basis in `/usr/spool/uucp/.Log/uucp/<system_name>`.

If scoburg has more files to send to siemau, the process continues until there are none left. Scoburg tells siemau that it wants to hang up. If siemau doesn't have any files to send to scoburg, then they shut down communications. If siemau does have files, the roles are reversed and now siemau is the master and scoburg is the slave. The process continues until siemau no longer has files to transfer. Siemau requests to hang up. It's possible that during the time siemau was the master, a new job was submitted on scoburg. It then becomes the master once again. In theory, this could go back and forth indefinitely although I have never seen more than two role reversals.

After the connection is stopped, the `uucico` on both sides can remove the lock files for both the port and the system.

Look back at the beginning of the chapter when we covered the basics of UUCP command syntax. There was an example, where we copied a file from a remote machine to another remote machine:

```
uucp /etc/motd siemau!vesta!~/filename
```

If we change it slightly so that the source is also on a remote machine, we get

```
uucp siemau!/etc/motd siemau!vesta!~/filename
```

UUCP recognizes the fact that both the source and the destination are on a remote machine. It therefore creates a remote execution command and not a simple file transfer. In other words, the local uucp command creates the necessary files so that another uucp command is executed on the remote machine (siemau). This command will copy the local file /etc/motd to the destination "vesta!!/file-name". In this case it happens that there is another remote machine involved (vesta). As a result, the file gets copied from siemau to vesta (assuming all the permissions are set right on siemau and vesta).

## Where Things Live

There are three directories that UUCP uses. The first one, we've talked about in great detail already. This is /usr/spool/uucp. As the /usr/spool/lp directory is for the print spooler, this directory is the working directory for UUCP. Here you'll find all the work files, locks, and log files. There are several subdirectories here as well. These are as follows:

- .Admin      Administrative files. Contain information on transfer statistics and accounting information.

- .Corrupt    Corrupt work and execute files that could not be processed.

- .Log        Log files. One subdirectory for each of uucp, uucico, uux, uuxqt.

- .Old        Old log files.

- .Sequence   System sequence numbers.

- .Status     Status files. One file per system.

- .Workspace  UUCP temporary working area.

- .Xqtdir     Temporary workspace for remote executions.

Plus there is one subdirectory for each system.

Most of the UUCP configuration programs and files are stored in /usr/lib/uucp. Many of them we have already mentioned when going through the example transfer, but I would like to cover them briefly again.

The Systems file contains a list of the remote systems that are known to you. This file determine what kind of device can be used to contact a particular site (modem, direct-line, or TCP), the times that are authorized to call that site, the phone number to call, as well as chat-script, which is used when logging into the remote system.

The Devices file contains information used to access the physical device, usually a serial (tty) device. This file contains such information as the type of device, speed, and the dialer program to use.

The Permissions file contains a list of permissions/authorizations for use when transferring files or requesting remote execution. The entries in this file determine what programs you can run on the remote side, which directories you can access, and whether or not the remote site can request or send files to your site.

 If you are running SCO OpenServer then there is a new file: Configuration. This contains information that determines and configures the protocol used when transferring data. This includes such things as the packet size (how large each data packet is) and the window size (how many packets can be sent before an acknowledgment is required).

## TCP/IP

Before we talk about the details of networking, we should first talk about the process of network communication. Let's take a network program such as `telnet`. The `telnet` program allows you to log in to a remote system. You end up with a shell just as if you had logged in locally. Although you input commands on your local keyboard and the output is appearing on your local screen, all other activity is happening on the remote machine.

To simplify things, we can say that there is a `telnet` program running on each computer. When you input something on your local keyboard, the local copy of `telnet` is accepting input. It passes the information through the network to the `telnet` on the remote machine. The command is executed and the output is handed to the remote `telnet`. That information is passed back through the network to the local `telnet`, which then displays the information on your screen.

Although it may appear as if there is a constant flow of information between your local machine and the remote one, this is not what is happening. At any given time there may be dozens, if not hundreds of programs using the network. Since only one can use the network at a time there needs to be some mechanism to allow each program to have its turn.

Think back on our discussion on the kernel. When we need something from the hard disk, the system does not read everything at once. If it did, one process could hog the computer if it needed to read in a large file. Instead, disk requests are sent in smaller chunks and the program only thinks that it gets everything it wants. Something similar is done with network connections.

Computers are like human beings in that they need to speak the same language in order to communicate. Regardless of how they are connected, be it serial or Ethernet, the computers must know how to talk to each other. The communication is carried out in a predefined manner, called a *protocol*. Like the protocols diplomats and politicians go through, computer protocols determine how each side behaves and how it should react to behavior by its counterpart. Roughly speaking, even the interaction between the computer and the hardware, such as the hard disk, can be considered a protocol.

The most common protocol used by SCO is TCP/IP. However, it is more accurate to call TCP/IP a protocol suite or protocol family. This is because TCP/IP actually consists of several different protocols. Even the name consists of two different protocols. TCP/IP stands for Transmission Control Protocol/Internet Protocol.

TCP/IP is often referred to as protocol *suite* as it contains many different protocols and therefore many different ways for computers to talk to each other. However, TCP/IP is not the only protocol suite. There are dozens, if not hundreds of different ones, although only a small portion have gained wide acceptance. SCO only uses a few itself, although the TCP/IP family is what is delivered by default and most commonly used.

Although the name refers to two specific protocols, TCP/IP actually means an entire suite of protocols and programs. The result of many years of planning and discussion, the TCP/IP suite includes a set of standards which specify how computers ought to communicate. By following these standards, computers "speak" the same language and can therefore communicate. In addition to the actual means of communication, the TCP/IP suite defines conventions for connecting different networks and routing traffic through routers, bridges, and other types of connections.

The TCP/IP suite is result of a Defense Advanced Research Projects Agency (DARPA) research project on network connectivity. However, its availability has made it the most commonly installed network software. Many versions provide source-code which reside in the public domain allowing users to adapt it to many new systems. Most vendors of network hardware (for example, bridges, routers) support the TCP/IP suite.

Whereas the data being transferred to and from the hard disk is talked about in terms of blocks, the unit of information transfer across a network connection is referred to as a *packet*. Depending on the program you are using, this packet can be a different size. In any event they are small enough to send across the network fast enough, so that no one process hogs the network. In addition, the packets go across the network so fast that you don't notice that your data is broken into packets. This is similar to the way the CPU manages processes. Each one gets a very small turn on the processor. Because it switches so fast between processes it appears that you have the processor to yourself.

If we take a step back and look at the process of network communication more abstractly, we see each portion supported by and supporting another. We can say that each portion sits on top of another. Or in other words the protocols are *stacked* on top of each other. Therefore, TCP/IP is often referred to as a *protocol stack*.

Each portion of the stack is referred to as a *layer*. At the bottom of the stack is the layer that is responsible for the physical connection between the two computers. This is the physical layer. Sitting on top of the physical layer is the layer that is responsible for the network portion of the stack. That is, it ensures that packets either stay on the network or get to the right network and at the same time ensures that packets get to the right network address. This is the network layer. What the layers look like we see in Figure 9–2.

On top of the network layer is the layer that ensures that the packets have been transmitted correctly; that is, there are no errors and all packets have been received. This is the transport layer. Finally, at the top of all of this is the layer that the user sees. Since the programs that we use are often called applications, this upper layer is called the application layer.

Conceptually, each layer is talking to its counterpart on the other system. That is, `telnet` on the local machine is passing data to `telnet` on the remote machine. TCP on the remote machine sends an acknowledgment to TCP on the local machine when it receives a packet. IP on the local machine gets information from IP on the remote machine that tells it that this packet is destined for the local ma-

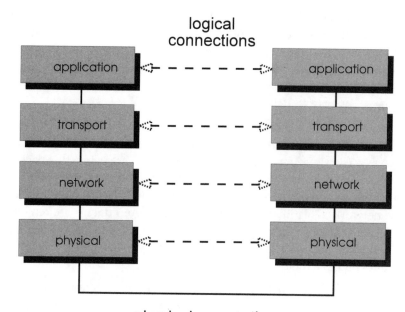

**Figure 9–2**   Network layers.

chine. We also have the network interface cards that communicate with each other using their specific language.

This communication between corresponding layers is all conceptual. The actual communication takes place between the different layers on each machine *not* the corresponding layers on both machines.

When the application layer has data to send. It prepends an *application header* onto the data it needs to send. This header contains information necessary for the application to get the data to the right part of the application on the receiving side. The application then calls TCP to send the information along. TCP wraps that data into a TCP packet, which contains a *TCP header* followed by the application data (including header). TCP then hands the packet (also called a TCP *segment*) to IP. Like the layers before it, IP wraps the packet up and prepends an *IP header*, to create an IP *datagram*. Finally, IP hands it off to the hardware driver; if Ethernet, this includes both an Ethernet header and Ethernet trailer. This creates an *Ethernet frame*.

As we see, it is the TCP layer that the application talks to. TCP sticks the data from the application into a kind of envelope (the process is called *encapsulation*) and passes it to the IP layer. Just as the operating system has a mechanism to keep track of what area of memory belongs to what processes, the network has a means of keeping track of what data belongs to what process. This is the job of TCP. It is also the responsibility of TCP to ensure that the packets are delivered with the correct contents and then to put them in the right order. The entire process of encapsulation you can see in Figure 9–3.

Error detection is the job of the TCP "envelope" which contains a checksum of the data contained within the packet. This checksum information sits in the packet header and is checked on all packets. If the checksum doesn't match the contents of the packet or the packet doesn't arrive at all, it is the job of TCP to ensure that the packet is resent. On the sending end, TCP waits for an acknowledgment that each packet has been received. If it hasn't received one within a specific period it will resend that packet. Because of this checksum and the resending of packets, TCP is considered a *reliable connection*.

Another protocol that is often used is the User Datagram Protocol (UDP). Like TCP, UDP sits on top of IP. However, UDP provides a *connectionless* transport between applications. Services that utilize UDP, such as the Network File Service (NFS), must provide their own mechanism to ensure delivery and correct sequencing of packets. Since it can be either broadcast or multicast, UDP also offers one-to-many services. Because there is no checking by UDP it is also considered unreliable.

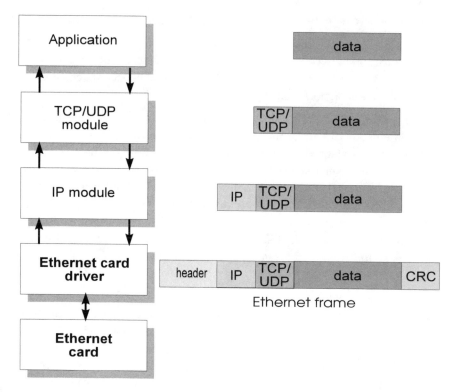

**Figure 9–3**    Encapsulation.

Closest to the hardware level, IP is a protocol that provides the delivery mechanism for the protocols. The IP layer serves the same function as your house address, telling the upper layers how to get to where they need to go. In fact, the information used by IP to get the pieces of information to their destination are called IP addresses. However, IP does not guarantee that the packets will arrive in the right order or that they will arrive at all. Just like a letter to your house requires it to be registered in order to ensure that it gets delivered with the content intact, IP depends on the upper layers to ensure the integrity and sequencing of the packets. Therefore, IP is considered *unreliable*.

Since the hardware (the network cards) does the actual physical transfer of the packets, it is important that they can be addressed somehow. Each card has its own, unique identifier. This is the Media Access Control, or MAC, address. The MAC address is a 48-bit number that is usually represented by six pairs of hexadecimal numbers, separated by (usually) dashes or colons. Each manufacturer of network cards is assigned a specific range of addresses which usually are specified by the first three pairs of numbers. Each card has its own, individual address: the MAC address.

When sending a packet, the IP layer has to figure out how to send the packet. If the destination is on a different physical network, then IP needs to send it to the appropriate *gateway*. However, if the destination machine is on the local network, the IP layers uses the Address Resolution Protocol (ARP) to determine what the MAC address of the Ethernet card is with that IP address.

To figure this out, ARP will broadcast an ARP packet across the entire network asking which MAC address belongs to a particular IP address. Although every machine gets this broadcast, only the one out there that matches will respond. This is then stored by the IP layer in its internal ARP table. You can look at the ARP table at any time by running the command

```
arp -a
```

This would give you a response similar to

```
siemau 194.113.47.147 at 0:0:2:c:8c:d2
```

This has the general format

```
<machine name> (IP address) at <MAC address>
```

Since the ARP table is cached, IP does not have to send out an ARP request every time it needs to make a connection. Instead, it can quickly look in the ARP table to make the IP-MAC translation. Then, the packet is sent to the appropriate machine. This is accomplished by the requesting machine sending out a special message (a broadcast) to all machines in the network asking for a response from whoever "owns" a particular IP address. The machine with that address will then respond with the MAC address of that card. This mapping of an IP address to a MAC address is then stored within the requesting machine's ARP cache and is then available for all subsequent transfers.

Status and error information is exchanged between machines through the Internet Control Message Protocol (ICMP). This information can be used by other protocols to recover from transmission problems or by system administrators to detect problems in the network. One of the most commonly used diagnostic tools, "ping", makes use of ICMP.

At the bottom of the pile is the hardware or link layer. As I mentioned before, this can be represented by many different kinds of physical connections: Ethernet, token-ring, fiber-optics, ISDN, and RS-232 to name a few.

This four-layer model is common when referring to computer networks. This is the model that SCO uses and the one that I will use through the book. There is another model that consists of seven layers. This is referred to as the OSI model, but we won't be using it here.

### Network Services

In the discussion above, I used the `telnet` command as an example of one of the programs that uses TCP/IP. However, there are many others which provide additional services such as transferring files, electronic mail, networking printing, and accessing remote filesystems. Products such as SCO OpenServer can expand upon these basics to provide additional services.

One kind of service that SCO OpenServer provides is remote administration. In contrast to previous versions of SCO products which required you to administer all machines locally, the SCOAdmin suite of programs allows you to administer machines anywhere in your network. Other products, such as database applications may have one central machine containing all the data, and access is gained from the other machines via TCP/IP. Often this access is invisible to the user who just sees the "front end" of the database.

This configuration, where one machine contains the data or resource that an other machine uses is very common in computer networking. The machine with the resource (that it is providing to other machines) is referred to as the server, because it is serving the resource to the other machines. The machine that is using the resource is called the client. This model, where one machine is the server and the other is the client is referred to as a client-server model. The *client-server model* is the primary model used in SCO networks.

Another common network model is the *peer-to-peer model*. In this model, there is no one central machine that has all the resources. Instead, all machines are on equal status. Often times, these two models sort of blend together. In SCO UNIX networks, it is possible to have multiple servers, each providing many of the same resources. In can also happen that multiple machines all have resources that the others need so everyone is acting as both a client and a server, similar to peer-to-peer.

On SCO systems, there are dozens of resources available. Many are well-known such as `telnet`, others, such as `ntp`, are more obscure. Like calling into a large office building with a central switchboard, our server needs to know which numbers are associated with which programs in order to make the proper connection. In the same regard, you need to know what office you want to reach before you call. In some cases you can call and say you want a particular extension. In other cases, you say you want a particular office. In an office building there is a list of available "services," called a phone book. On a SCO UNIX system the phone book is the file `/etc/services`.

The `/etc/services` file contains a list of what services a particular machine may have to offer. The concept of a service is slightly different than the concept of a resource. A machine may provide many resources in the form of login shells that it provides to remote users, however all of them are accessing the machine through the one service: `telnet`.

In addition to what service the machine provides, `/etc/services` also lists the port. To understand the idea of a port, think about this as being the telephone number. When I call in to a machine (say using `telnet`), I am connected to the `telnet` program on the other side through a particular port. This is as if I were calling a large office building with a single switchboard. When I reach that switchboard, I tell the operator which office or person I want to talk to. In the ancient history of telephones, that operator had to manually make the connection between the incoming line and the office.

A port can be thought of as the sockets that the operator plugs the phone lines into. Like in that office building, there may be a set of these sockets, or ports, that are directly connected to a specific person (service). These are *well-known* ports. There may be offices with their own operator (maybe just a receptionist) who passes the incoming phone calls to the right person or may even pick someone themselves to take the call (such as when you call a government agency with a generic question and there is no one person responsible for that area).

On an SCO UNIX system using TCP/IP, the principle is the same. There are dozens of services that one can connect to, but only one way into the system, that's through your network interface card. In order for you to be able to connect to the right service, there has to be something like an operator to make the connection for you. This is the program `/etc/inetd`. This is the "Internet Daemon" and is often referred to as a "super server" since it is `inetd`'s responsibility to wait for requests to access the other servers on your system and pass you along.

Like in our office building, you may know what number you want, that is, which port. When you make the connection to `inetd`, your process tells it what port you want to connect to and `inetd` makes the connection. On the other hand, you may have a program that does not have a well-known port. Therefore a new port needs to be created.

The `inetd` daemon "listens" for the connections. You can say that it is listening on multiple ports in the sense that it manages all the ports. However, it is `inetd` that makes the connection between the incoming connection and the local port, and therefore to the local server. This mechanism saves memory since you don't need to start up the servers you aren't going to use. This is similar to having a central switchboard as opposed to requiring every office to have their own. Graphically this looks like Figure 9–4.

Normally, `inetd` is started during system start-up from a script in `/etc/rc2.d` (normally `/etc/rc2.d/S85tcp`). When it starts, `inetd` reads its configuration file

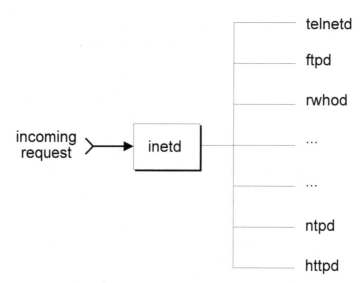

**Figure 9–4**.   The inetd switchboard.

(`/etc/inetd.conf`) to obtain the necessary information to start the various servers. It then builds the logical connection between the server and its respective port (kind of like laying the cable from the central switchboard to the various offices). Technically it creates a *socket*, which is *bound* to the port for that server.

When `inetd` gets a connection request (the phone rings) for a connection-based port, it "accepts" the incoming call which creates a new socket. That is, there is a logical connection between the incoming request and the server. `inetd` can now continue to listen on the original port for additional incoming calls.

If the port is connectionless (UDP), the behavior is dependent on entries in the `/etc/inetd.conf` file. If `inetd` is told to wait (there is a `wait` in the fourth column), then the server that was called must process the incoming message before `inetd` can go on. If told not to wait (there is a `nowait` in the fourth column), `inetd` will continue to process incoming requests on that port. If you look in `/etc/inetd.conf` you see that almost exclusively TCP ports are `nowait` and UDP ports are `wait`.

### Network Standards

We need to discuss what goes into making a standard. Without standards, it makes communication between computers of different types very difficult. For example, bus standards like ISA and PCI help hardware to communicate with the CPU.

In the Internet community, standards are both suggested and established through Request for Comments, or RFCs. To some extent these are the law. If one product claims to comply with a particular RFC, you know that any other applications that does so should be able to communicate with it. However, RFCs include other things such as lists of previous RFCs and basic introductions to things like TCP.

Becoming a standard is a three step process. Usually, the first few paragraphs of an RFC will tell you to what stage it applies—assuming of course, that the RFC is part of a standards proposal. At the first stage, the standard is proposed. Organizations then decide to implement the proposed standard. It requires three separate implementations before the proposal becomes a standard. (Finally, it becomes a standard. This is an oversimplification of the process, since there would also be a lot of discussion about the proposed standard.)

If you need information about a specific network standard, the first place to look is the most current RFC index, which is also published as an RFC. Not only does this list all the RFCs, but it will also tell you if one RFC has been replaced and by which one.

Originally I had planned to include a list of the more commonly used and significant RFCs. I eventually realized that this was an unending task. When I started this book, there were just over 1700 RFCs. The last time I checked before wrapping up this book, there were over 1800. Instead, I will simply tell you where to get them.

You can get RFCs from the "central repository." These are obtainable using `ftp` from ftp.ds.internic.net. There is an `rfc` directory that contains the RFCs in ASCII as well as many in postscript format. If you know what RFC you want, it can be obtained by sending an email message to mailserv@ds.internic.net. List each RFC you want in the format

```
document-by-name rfcXXXX
```

where XXXX is the number of the RFC. You can obtain the index by including the entry

```
document-by-name rfc-index
```

In addition, the RFCs are available from archives all over the Internet. However, rather than tying up the Internet bandwidth with a lot of copy of files you may not need. Check out the Web page www.cdrom.com or mail info@cdrom.com. This is for Walnut Creek CD-ROM and they sell a CD packed with thousands of documents related to the Internet, including the RFCs. Another site with pretty much the same kind of offering is InfoMagic. They can be reached at www.infomagic.com or info@infomagic.com.

For SCO UNIX systems running TCP/IP, one of the most important standards deals with Ethernet. The encapsulation (packaging) of IP datagrams is defined for Ethernet in RFC 894. Developed in 1982 by Digital Equipment Corporation (DEC), Intel and Xerox Ethernet (spelled with a capital) is a standard, rather than a physical entity. Several years later the 802 Committee of the Institute of Electrical and Electronic Engineers (IEEE or I-triple E) published standards of its own that differed in many ways from the original Ethernet standard. Collectively, these are referred to as the 802 IEEE standards. The 802.3 standards cover networks similar to Ethernet. The IEEE 802 encapsulation was defined in RFC 1042. Both of these use an access method called Carrier Sense, Multiple Sense with Collision Detection, or CSMA/CD.

Both of these framing types (RFC 894 and RFC 1042) use a 48-bit addressing scheme. These are generally referred to as the MAC or hardware address. The six bytes of both the destination and source machine are included in the header of both framing types. However, the remainder of the frame is different. As we talked about earlier, this layer is responsible for sending and receiving the IP datagrams. It is also responsible for sending and receiving other kinds of packets as well. These are packets from the Address Resolution Protocol (ARP) and the Reverse Address Resolution Protocol (RARP). We'll talk about both later on.

### IP Addressing

In today's world of interconnected computers, you may have a connection to hundreds of thousands of other machines. Granted there is no single cable connecting all of these computers, however there is a logical connection in that you can use the `telnet` program from your PC in California to connect to a machine in Germany. The problem is, how do the packets get from one end to another. Added to that, how do you keep your local network in California from getting overloaded with packets that are being sent between machines in Germany and at the same time make sure that those telnet packets get through? The answer is provided by the Internet Protocol (IP).

Just as a street address is not always sufficient to get your letter delivered, so the IP is not always sufficient to get the packet delivered. If I sent you a letter, it could be sent to a single, central post office, whose job it was to distribute mail throughout the entire U.S. Because of the incredibly large number of pieces of mail, this is impracticle. Instead, there are thousands of offices, all over the country, whose job it is to route the mail for us.

If we lived in a small town, the local post office could catch a letter destined for a local addresss before it went further. Mail with addresses outside could be sent to other post offices to be processed.

A similar situation applies to IP addresses. In local, self-contained networks, the IP address alone is sufficient. However, when multiple networks are combined, machines spend more time trying to figure out if the packet belongs to them than actually processing information. The solution is a Network Mask. Just as a zip code tells a postal worker whether to process a particular piece of mail locally or not, the Network Mask (or netmask) tells machines whether or not they can simply ignore a packet or process it further.

Every machine on the network, needs to have its own, unique IP address, just like every house has a unique mail address. If that network is connected to the rest of the world, that address must not only be unique within the local network, but unique within the rest of the world, as well. As of this writing, IP addresses are 32-bit values. They are usually represented by four sets of numbers, ranging from 0–255 separated by dots (.). This is referred to as *dotted-decimal notation*. In dotted-decimal notation, an address might look like this:

```
147.132.42.18
```

Since each of these numbers range between 0–255, they can be represented by eight bits and are therefore referred to as an *octet*. This IP address is often thought of as being composed of a network portion (at the beginning) and a node (or machine) portion at the end. This would be comparable to writing a street address as

```
95061.Main_Street.42
```

where 95061 is the zip code, Main Street is the street, and 42 is the address on that street. The reason we write the street address in this fashion, is that it's common to think of the IP address as moving from the general to the more specific.

Currently, there are three classes of networks, which are broken down by both the range used in the first octet and the number of octets used to identify the network. Class A networks are the largest and use the first octet as the network address. Networks in the class will have the first octet in the range 1–126. Class B networks used the first two octets, with the first being in the range 128–192. The smallest networks, Class C, use the first three octets in the network address with the first in the range 192–223. Table 9–1 shows how IP addresses are broken down by the different network classes.

There are a couple of things I would like to point out about this table. First, the network address 127 represents the local computer, regardless of what network it is really on. This is helpful for testing as well as many internal operations. Network addresses 224 and above are reserved for special purposes such as multicast addresses. The terms "possible networks" and "possible hosts per network" are those that are calculated mathematically. In some cases, 0 and 255 are not acceptable values for either the network address or the host address.

**Table 9–1**    IP Address Breakdown by Network

| Class | Range within 1st Octet | Network ID | Host ID | Possible Networks | Possible Hosts per Network |
|-------|------------------------|------------|---------|-------------------|----------------------------|
| A | 1–126 | a | b.c.d. | 126 | 16,777,214 |
| B | 128–191 | a.b | c.d | 16,384 | 65,534 |
| C | 192–223 | a.b.c | d | 2,097,151 | 254 |

Keep in mind that a Class A address does not necessarily mean that having 16 million hosts on a single network is impossible to administrate and would over-burden most network technologies. What normally happens is that a single entity, such as Hewlett-Packard is given a Class A address. They will then break it down futher into smaller *subnets*. We'll get into more details about this shortly.

A network host uses the network ID and host ID to determine which packets it should receive or ignore and to determine the scope of its transmissions (only nodes with the same network ID accept each other's IP-level broadcasts). Because the sender's IP address is included in every outgoing IP packet, it is useful for the receiving computer system to derive the originating network ID and host ID from the IP address field. This is done by using subnet masks, as described in the following section.

### Subnet Masks

Subnet masks are 32-bit values that allow the recipient of IP packets to distin-guish the network ID portion of the IP address from the host ID. Like an IP ad-dress, the value of a subnet mask is frequently represented in dotted-decimal no-tation. Subnet masks are determined by assigning 1's to bits that belong to the network ID and 0's to the bits that belong to the host ID. Once the bits are in place, the 32-bit value is converted to dotted-decimal notation, as shown in Table 9–2.

**Table 9–2**    Default Subnet Masks for Standard IP Address Classes

| Address Class | Bits for Subnet Mask | Subnet Mask |
|---------------|----------------------|-------------|
| Class A | 1111111 00000000 00000000 00000000 | 255.0.0.0 |
| Class B | 1111111 11111111 00000000 00000000 | 255.255.0.0 |
| Class C | 11111111 11111111 11111111 00000000 | 255.255.255.0 |

The result allows TCP/IP to determine the host and network IDs of the local computer. For example, when the IP address is 102.54.94.97 and the subnet mask is 255.255.0.0, the network ID is 102.54 and the host ID is 94.97.

Keep in mind that all of this with the subnet masks is the principle and not necessarily the practice. If you (meaning your company) have been assigned a Class B address, then the the first two octets are assigned to you. You could then breakdown the Class B net into Class C nets. If we take a look at Table 9–1, we see that there are 65,534 possible nodes in that network. That is really too many to manage.

However, if we considered each of the third octets to represent a subnet of our class B network, they would all have 254 possible nodes per subnet. This is basically what a Class C net is anyway. We can then assign each subnet to a department or building and then assign one person to manage each of the Class C subnets, which is a little easier to do.

To keep the different Class C subnets from interfering with each other, we give each subnet a Class C subnet mask, although the first octet is in the range for a Class B network. That way machines on this subnet are only concerned with packets for the subnet. We can also break down the subnets physically so that there is a gateway or router between the subnets. That way the physical network is not overburdened with traffic from 65,534 machines.

Let's look at a concrete example, like SCO, which has been assigned the Class B address 132.147.0.0. The different departments within SCO have been assigned a Class C address that might look like this: 132.147.144.0. Although the first octet (132) says that this is a Class B address, it is really the subnet mask that makes that determination. In this case, our subnet mask would be: 255.255.255.0. Therefore, any packet that is destined for an address other than one starting 132.147.144.0 is not on this network.

It is the responsibility of IP to ensure that each packet ends up going to the right machine. This is accomplished, in part, by assigning a unique address to each machine. This address is referred to as the Internet address or IP address. Each network gets a set of these IP addresses that are within a specific range. In general, packets that are destined for an IP address within that range will stay within the local network. Only when a packet is destined for somewhere outside of the local network is it "allowed" to pass.

In other words, IP is responsible for the delivery of the packet. It functions similar to the Post Office, whereby you have both a sending and receiving address. Often times you have many more letters than a single mail bag can handle. The mail carrier (or someone else at the post office) will break down the number of letters into sets small enough to fit in a bag. This is what IP does.

Since there are many people using the line at once, IP will break down the TCP packets into units of a specific size. Although often referred to as *packets*, the more correct terminology is to refer to IP packets as *datagrams*. Just like bags of mail need to go from one post office to the next to reach their final destination, IP datagrams must often go through different machines to reach their final destination.

Saying that IP routing can be accomplished completely in software isn't entirely accurate. Although, no physical router is needed, IP can't send a packet to someplace where there is no physical connection. This is normally accomplished by an additional network card. With two (or more) network cards a single machine can be connected to multiple networks. The IP layer on that one machine can then be used to route IP packets between the two networks.

Once configured (we'll talk about this in the second part of the book), IP maintains a table of routing information, called (logically) a routing table. Every time the IP layer receives a packet, it checks the destination address.

### Routing and IP Gateways

I mentioned a moment ago that IP is an unreliable, connectionless protocol. It contains no provision to ensure that the packet arrives at the destination correctly, nor is there anything the guarantees that when packets do arrive they arrive in the correct order. Although IP is responsible to ensure that the packets get to the right machine, it has essentially no understanding of the physical connection between the two machines. IP will happily run on machines that are connected with something as simple as a telephone wire, to something as complex as a satellite. IP depends on some other means to "physically" carry it across the network.

What this means is that the system administrator (or network administrator) is responsible for laying the "map" that is used to define which network address goes with which sets of machines and which IP addresses are assigned to individual machines.

One important job that IP does is routing; that is, getting the packet to the right machine. If the source and destination machines are directly connected (that is, on the same network) then routing is easy—essentially there isn't any. IP sees this fact and simply hands the packets off to the data link layer. Otherwise, IP has to figure out how and where to send it.

Usually the 'how' is over a *router*. A router is a piece of hardware that acts like an air traffic controller sending one packet off one way and another off a different way. Often, routers are separate pieces of equipment that can be configured in very detailed ways. The disadvantage to this is that with power comes price. The ability to configure a router in many different ways usually means a high pricetag. Fortunately, many operating systems, including SCO UNIX, allow IP to serve as router software, thereby avoiding the cost of router hardware.

In comparison to the router is the concept of a *gateway*. Like a router, a gateway has knowledge of other networks and how to reach them. In general, we can think of a router as a special piece of hardware that does the work for us. In fact, there are companies that sell equipment called routers. A gateway is more of a concept, in that it is the means by which you go from one network to another. Today, the distinction between a router and a gateway is blurred. Routers can serve as gateways, gateways can serve as routers.

The path the packet takes from one machine to the next is called a *route*. Although each machine can maintain static routes for specific destinations, the default gateway is usually used to find remote destinations. (The default gateway is needed only for computers that are part of an internetwork.) If you have a gateway connected to several other networks, there will (probably) be route definitions for each of those other networks.

Let's look at this process as if we were sending a letter, as we did a little while ago. Each letter we send has an envelope which contains a message. On the envelope we write the source and destination addresses. When we mail the letter it gets to the post office and the person sorting the mail checks the destination zip code. If it's the same as the local zip code, the envelope is sent to one of the carriers for delivery. If the zip code is different, then it is sent to some other location. Perhaps all nonlocal mail is sent to the same place.

If you live across the country from me, the letter probably doesn't go directly from my local post office to yours (assuming I don't live in San Fransisco and you don't live in New York). The same applies to IP packets. My letter first goes to my local post office, if it is destined for a local address it is processed there. If not, it is sent along to a larger post office. If I sent a letter from Santa Cruz, destined for Annsville, Pennsylvania, it will probably go first to San Fransisco and then to New York (or Philadelphia) before it gets sent to Annsville.

Again, the same applies to IP packets. If I were communicating with a network on the other side of the country, my machine would need to know how to get to the other one. This is the concept of a "gateway." A gateway is the first step in the path, or "route," to the remote machine. Just as there are a couple of post offices between Santa Cruz and Annsville, there can be multiple gateways between computers.

Since San Fransisco is the closest "major" city to Santa Cruz, it is possible that all mail bound for points beyond must first go through there. What if I lived in

Fresno, which is about halfway between San Fransisco and Los Angeles? If I sent a letter to Annsville, it could go through Los Angeles or it could go through San Fransisco. To make things easy, it might always get sent through San Fransisco if not destined for a local address. What if the letter is bound for Los Angeles? It seems silly to go through San Fransisco first when it is bound for LA. At the post office in Fresno, they might have a special procedure that says all remote mail goes through San Fransisco, except for those with a zip code in a special range.

Here, too, the same applies to IP addresses. One machine may be defined as the "default" gateway, but if an IP packet was bound for a particular network it could be told to use a completely different gateway. Which gateway to use to get to a particular machine or network is the concept of "routes." If I want all remotely-bound packets to use a particular route, I add that route as a default to my machine. If packets bound for a particular network are to go via a different route, I can add that route as well. A gateway may look like Figure 9–5.

When IP prepares to send a message, it inserts the local (source) and destination IP addresses in the IP header. It then checks whether the network ID of the destination and source match (the zip codes). If so, the packet is sent directly to the

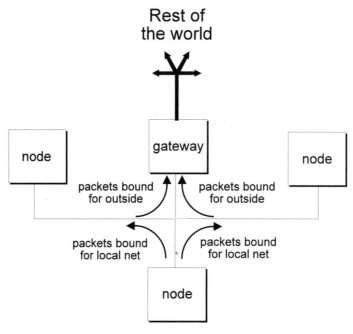

**Figure 9–5**    Network gateway.

destination, since it is on the local network. If the network IDs don't match, the routing table is examined for static routes. If none are found the packet is forwarded to the default gateway.

The default gateway is a computer connected to the local subnet and other networks that has knowledge of the network IDs for other networks and how to reach them. Because the default gateway knows how to reach the other networks, it can forward the packet, either to other gateways or directly to that machine if the gateway is on the same network as the destination. This process is known as routing.

Obviously(?), if you only have a single network, there is no reason to have a gateway, as each machine is directly connected to every other. It's possible that you only want certain machines within your network to go beyond the local net to the outside. In this case, these machines can have a default (or static) route default, while the others have none. However, users can add routes themselves, using the `route` command.

The `telnetd` daemon is a server which supports the `telnet` program. Makes sense, huh? `Telnet` is a terminal program that allows you to work interactively with remote machines, just as if you would with the local machine. When `inetd` receives an incoming `telnet` request, it invokes `telnetd`.

What you then see is no different than if you had logged in locally to that machine (probably). When you are presented with a `login:` prompt, you enter your logname and password. If these are correct, you are then given a shell that you can use to enter commands starts applications, etc.

The way `telnetd` works is that it allocates a pseudo-terminal device for you. This pseudo-terminal has the same behavior as a "normal" terminal in that you input commands and see the results on your screen. Internally the pseudo-terminal is broken down into two parts. The master portion is the side that you see. Since your side is the one that is controlling things, your side is the master. The master side accepts input from your `telnet` program and passes them to `telnetd` on the remote side. As you might guess, the side that has to listen to the master is the slave. The slave side of the pseudo-terminal serves as `stdin`, `stdout`, and `stderr` for the remote application. This is shown in Figure 9–6.

Similar in functionality to `telnet` is `rlogin`. The server for `rlogin` is `rlogind`, and like `telnetd`, is started by `inetd`. One of the primary differences is that, if configured, `rlogind` can provide a connection without the normal log in procedures.

The functionality of `rlogind` is very similar to that of `telnetd`. Pseudo-terminals are allocated and the slave portion becomes the `stdin`, `stdout`, and `stderr`.

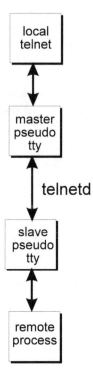

**Figure 9–6**    Pseudo-ttys.

During log in, `rlogind` uses an authentication procedure called "host equivalence," which sets up remote machines as being "trusted." If `rlogind` on the destination machine authenticates the source machine, the user is automatically
logged in. If the authentication fails, the user must go through the normal log in
procedure. We will discuss how to set up host equivalence later.

TCP connections are not the only ones that are managed by `inetd`. Basically, all
network connections are. This can be understood if we go back to the telephone
operator analogy. If the operator (`inetd`) is also the receptionist, we can then
think of TCP connections as incoming telephone calls and UDP packets as incoming letters. Like incoming phone calls, the receptionist is responsible to route the
incoming mail to the right person. (This is a valid analogy since like regular mail,
there is nothing to guarantee the delivery of the message in the letter, although
with TCP connections you can ask your partner to resend the message.) Like TCP
connections, UDP daemons are "listening" on specific ports. Also like TCP, connections for these well-known ports are listed in `/etc/services`.

One common UDP connection is the routing daemon: `routed`. Routed supplies is (as you might have guessed) routing information in the form of routing packets. If your system is serving as a router, then `routed` periodically sends copies of its routing tables to other machines.

One key difference is that `routed` is not actually started by `inetd`. Instead, it is normally started as the system is entering run-level 2 through the `/etc/rc2.d/S85tcp` script. When it starts, `routed` makes the assumption that it will forward packets between all interfaces on the system. This only includes those that are "up" and does not include the loopback driver. (The loopback driver is a special TCP/IP interface that simply loops the packets back to the local machine.) `routed` then transmits a REQUEST packet on each of these interfaces and waits for a RESPONSE packet from any other hosts. Potentially there are other machines on the network that are also sending REQUEST packets, so `routed` can also respond to them.

The response `routed` gives is based on information it has in its *routing tables*. This contains information about known routes, including how far away the destination machine is in terms of *hops* or intermediary machines. When `routed` receives a RESPONSE packet, it uses the information contained in that packet to update its own routing tables. Look at the `routed(NADM)` man-page for more information.

### DNS—Finding Other Machines

If you have TCP/IP installed, by default, your machine is set up to use the `/etc/hosts` file. This is a list of IP addresses and the matching names of the machine. When you try to connect to another machine, you can do it either with the IP address or the name. If you use the name, the system will look in the `/etc/hosts` file and make the translation from name to IP address. The only real drawback with this scheme is that every time a machine is added or removed from the network, you have to change the `/etc/hosts` file on all the machines.

Those of you that have had to administer large networks know that updating every `/etc/hosts` file like this can be a real pain. There is always at least one that you forget or you mistype the name or address and have to go back and change it on every machine—fortunately, there is hope.

Provided with both ODT and OpenServer is a hostname/IP address database called the Berkeley Internet Name Domain (BIND) service. Instead of updating every machine in the network, there is a Domain Name System (DNS) server that maintains the database and provides the client machines with information about both addresses and names. If machines are added or removed, there is only one machine that needs to get changed. This is the Name Server. (Note: The SCO documentation translates DNS as Domain Name Server. Most every other reference I have found calls it the Domain Name System. I have seen it referred to as Domain Name Service also. Since we know what it is, I'll just call it DNS.)

So, when do you use DNS over the `/etc/hosts` file? Well, it's up to you. The first question I would ask is, "Are you connecting to the Internet?" If the answer is "yes," "maybe," or "someday" then definitely set up DNS. DNS functions somewhat like directory assistance from the phone company. If your local directory assistance doesn't have the number, you can contact one in the area you are looking. If your name server doesn't have the answer, it will *query* other name servers for that information (assuming you told it to do so).

If you are never going to go into the Internet, then the answer is up to you. If you only have two machines in your network, the trouble it takes to set up DNS is not worth it. On the other hand, if you have a dozen or more machines, then setting it up makes life easier in the long run.

There are several key concepts that need to be discussed before we dive into DNS. DNS, like so many other aspects of TCP/IP, is client-server oriented. We have the name server containing the IP addresses and names which serves information to the clients. Next, we need to think about DNS operating in an environment similar to a directory tree. All machines that fall under DNS can be thought of as files in this directory tree structure. These machines are often referred to as nodes. Like directories and file names, there is a hierarchy of names with the tree. This is often referred to as the domain name space.

A branch of the DNS tree is referred to as a domain. A domain is simply a collection of computers that are managed by a single organization. This organization can be a company, university, or even a government agency. The organization has a name that it is known by to the outside world. In conjunction with the domains of the individual organizations, there are things called *top-level domains*. These are broken down by the function of the domains under it. The top level domains are as follows:

COM—Commercial

EDU—Educational

GOV—Government

NET—Network

MIL—Military

ORG—Nonprofit organizations

Each domain will fall within one of these top-level domains. For example, there is the domain sco, which falls under the commercial top-level domain. It is thus designated as sco.COM or sco.com. The domain assigned to the White House is whitehouse.gov. The domain assigned to the University of California at Santa Cruz is ucsc.edu. (Note that the dot is used to separate the individual components in the machine's domain and name.)

Keep in mind that these domains are used primarily within the U.S. While a foreign subsidiary *might* belong to one of these top-level domains, for the most part, the top-level domain within most non-U.S. countries is the country code. For example, the geographical domain Germany is indicated by the domain abbreviations de (for Deutschland). I do know some German companies within the com domain. There are also geographic domains within the U.S., such as ca.us for California as compared to just .ca for Canada. This is often for very small domains or nonorganizations, such as individuals. Graphically this might look like Figure 9–7.

Within each domain, there *may* be subdomains. However, there doesn't have to be. You usually find subdomains in larger domains in an effort to break down the administration into smaller units. For example, if SCO Tech Support had a sub-domain it might be support.sco.com.

Keep in mind that these are just the domain names, not the machine or node name. Within a domain there can be (in principle) any number of machines. A machine sitting on the desk in the oval office might be called boss1. Its full name, including domain would be boss1.pres.whitehouse.gov. A machine in SCO Support called darkstar would then be darkstar.support.sco.com. This might be extended further if there was a further division within Support so that the TEAM

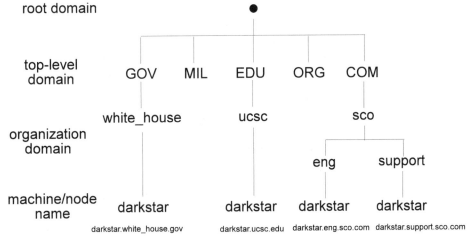

**Figure 9–7**   Internet domains.

support analysts had their own subdomain. The machine might be darkstar.team.support.com. In principle, this can go on quite a ways. Up to now, I have only seen a machine name with five components: the machine name, two subdomains, the company domain, and then the top-level domain. On the other hand, if there was no support subdomain, and everything was under the sco.com domain, the machine's name would be darkstar.sco.com.

You may often see the fully-qualified domain name (FQDN) of a machine listed like this:

```
darkstar.sco.com.
```

including the trailing dot(.). That dot indicates the root domain. This has no name other than root domain or .(read "dot"). This is similar to the way the root directory has no name other than root or /. In some cases this dot is optional. However, there are cases where it is required. We'll get to those in the section on configuring DNS.

Like files, it is possible that two machines have the same name. The only criteria for files is that their full path be unique. The same applies to machines. For example, there might be a machine darkstar at the White House (maybe Bill's a closet Dead Head). Its FQDN would be darkstar.whitehouse.gov. This is obviously not the same machine as darkstar.sco.com any more than 1033 Main Street in Santa Cruz is the same as 1033 Main Street in Annsville. Even something like darkstar.support.sco.com is different from darkstar.sales.sco.com.

A zone is a grouping of machines that may, or may not, be the same as a domain. This is the set of machines over which a particular name server has authority and maintains the data. In our example above, there might be a zone for support, *even if* there was no subdomain. On the other hand, there might be a team.support.sco.com domain, but the zone is still sco.com. Therefore, zones can be subordinate or superior to domains. Basically, zones are used to make the job of managing the name server easier. Therefore, what constitutes a zone depends on your specific circumstances.

In the SCO implementation of DNS, there are five types of servers: primary, secondary, caching-only, slave, and client. Although the SCO doc lists the last one as a server (they also call it a remote server), I hesitate to use that designation. A remote server doesn't serve anyone but itself. It must use the DNS software to resolve all requests through another server.

A primary server is the master server for one or more DNS zones. Each server maintains the database files, and is considered the authority for this zone. It may also periodically transfer data to a secondary server, if one exists for that zone.

DNS functions are carried out by the Internet domain name server: named. When it starts, named reads its configuration file to determine what zones it is responsible for and in which files the data is stored. By default, the configuration file is /etc/named.boot. However, named can be started with the -b option to specify an alternate configuration file. Normally, named is started from /etc/rc2.d/S85tcp.

SCO DNS provides a *stub server*. This is used when a primary server delegates a portion of its name space (like a subzone) to another server. The primary server for the zone needs to know the name service information about the files within that subzone. One way of doing this is by serving as a secondary server to that subzone or serving as a stub server. Note that the concept of a stub server is new to OpenServer so you cannot designate an ODT machine to be a stub server. A stub server is like a secondary server, except that it only caches the NS and SOA records. With this information, it knows what machine is the name server and how long the information is valid.

For example, the primary server for the sco.com domain needs to know about the machines within the support.sco.com domain. It could serve as a secondary server to the support.sco.com domain, whereby it would maintain all the records for the machines within that subdomain. If, on the other hand, it serves as a stub server, the primary for the sco.com need only know how to get to the primary for the support.sco.com subdomain. Note here, that it *is* possible for a server to be primary in one zone and secondary in another.

By moving responsibility to the subzone, the administrator of the parent zone does not need to concern him or herself with changing the configuration files when a machine is added or removed within the subzone. As long as the address of the subzone primary server matches the stub server entry all is well.

A secondary server takes over for the primary, should the primary go down or be otherwise inaccessible. A secondary server maintains copies of the database files and "refreshes" them at predetermined intervals. If it cannot reach the primary to refresh its files, it will keep trying at (again) predetermined intervals. If after another predetermined time, the secondary still cannot reach the primary, the secondary considers its data invalid and flushes it.

Caching-only servers save data in a cache file only until that data expires. The expiration time is based on a field within the data that is received from another server. This is called the time-to-live. Time-to-live is a regularly occurring concept within DNS.

A slave server can be a primary, secondary, or caching-only server. If it cannot satisfy the query locally, it will pass, or forward, the request to a fixed list of forwarders (forwarding server), rather than interacting directly with the primary name servers of other zones. These requests are recursive, which means that the forwarder must answer either with the requested information or by saying it doesn't know. The requesting machine then asks the next server, then the next, and then the next until it finally runs out of servers to check or gets an answer. Slave servers never attempt to contact servers other than the forwarders.

The concept of recursive requests is in contrast to iterative requests. Here the queried server either gives an answer or tells the requesting machine where it should look next. For example, darkstar asks iguana, the primary server for support.sco.com, for some information. In a recursive query, iguana asks boomer, the primary server for sco.com, and passes the information back to darkstar. In an iterative query, iguana tells darkstar about boomer and darkstar then goes and asks boomer. This process of asking name servers for information, whether recursive or iterative, is called *resolution*.

Keep in mind that there is client software running on the server. When an application needs information the client DNS server asks the server for the information, despite the fact that the server is running on the same machine. Applications don't access the server directly.

There is also the concept of a root server. These are servers located at the top of the domain tree that maintain information about the top-level zone. Root servers are positioned at the top, or root, of the DNS hierarchy and maintain data about each of the top-level zones.

### *Your Own IP Address*

If you have a network that is completely disconnected from the rest of the world, then there is no need for you to adhere to any of these conventions. You might be a commericial organization, but still want to use the EDU domain—nothing prevents you. There is also nothing preventing you from using IP addresses that are used by some other organization. However, once you decide to connect to another organization or the Internet at large, you need to ensure that both your names and IP address are unique.

To ensure that you use a unique name and network, the best thing is to contact the Network Information Center, or NIC. Via email, they can be contacted at hostmaster@nic.ddn.mil. The telephone number is 1–800–365–3642 or 1–703–802–4535. By regular mail, use this address:

DDN Network Information Center
14200 Park Meadow Drive, Suite 200
Chantilly, Virginia 22021

If you are not in the United States, the NIC can still provide you with a contact in your area.

If you would like to have one machine that connects to the Internet, but have other machines that cannot, one solution is to use one of the IP addresses defined in RFC 1597. This RFC describes the need for "private" addresses and lists a range of Class A, B, and C addresses that can be used internally within a company.

Some routers will filter out these addresses automatically, others require that they be so configured. This allows you to not only limit access to and from the Internet, but also limits the need for unique addresses. If you only have a handful of machines that need Internet access, some Internet providers will subnet a Class C address and assign you a small block of addresses. See the RFC for more details.

## NFS

The Network FileSystem (NFS) is an industry standard means of being able to share entire filesystems among machines within a computer network. As with the other aspects of networking, the machines providing the service (in this case the filesystem) are the servers and the machines utilizing the service are the clients. Files residing physically on the server appear as if they are local to the client. This enables file sharing without the hassle of copying the files and worrying about which one is the more current.

One difference that NFS has over "conventional" filesystems is that it is possible to allow access to a portion of a filesystem, rather than the entire one. The directory you want the server to make available is said to be *exported*.

Normally, filesystems under NFS are mounted just like any other. The same options apply, and they can be mounted either automatically at boot through entries in /etc/default/filesys or manually by the system administrator. This can be a problem sometimes as the server might not be active when the client boots. Even if the server is active, mounting NFS on boot-up slows down the boot process. What an NFS mount looks like we see in Figure 9–8.

A solution that SCO has provided is automount and as its name implies it can automatically mount NFS. Once configured, any command or program that accesses a file or directory on the remote machine within the exported directory forces the mounting to occur. The exported directory remains mounted until it is no longer needed.

To aid in preventing conflicting access requests to a file, SCO provided the Network Lock Manager (NLM). This consists of a device driver and several daemon

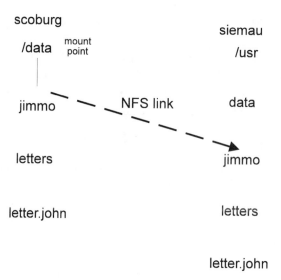

**Figure 9–8**   An NFS mount.

programs that support record and file locking. Remote Execution (REX) is a service that allows users to export their user environments to remote servers in order to execute commands. These commands can access files in the user's current directory and allow for the execution of interactive processes such as full-screen editors.

Keep in mind that NFS is not a stand-alone protocol. It relies on the TCP/IP protocol suite in order to function correctly. NFS uses UDP and not TCP. Therefore, it is up to the programs using NFS to ensure the reliability of the data and not just assume the information coming across is correct. NFS will tell you if the data are there by setting the appropriate failure indicators. This causes your program (such as cp) to fail.

Under ODT 3.0, filesystems are made available for remote mounting by using the exportfs command. Normally this happens at boot, however the system administrator can run it at anytime. When run, exportfs uses information contained in the /etc/exports file to determine directories and their characteristics.

The /etc/exports file is a simple ASCII file and additions or changes can be made with any text editor. There is one line for each directory you want to export. The left side is the *full path* of the directory you want to export and the right side is options you want to apply. For example, you can limit access to the directory to just one machine or make the directory read only. If changes are made, exportfs needs to be run again to make changes take effect.

If your site is on the Internet, the `/etc/exports` file can be a problem. If you export a filesystem, but do not specify who has access, then everyone does. If you are on the Internet, everyone who can access your machine can mount your filesystems. Therefore, I recommend that you explictly list which machines can mount the exported filesystems.

OpenServer provides a graphical interface to this functionality in the form of the Filesystem Manager of SCOAdmin. SCOAdmin can also be used to start the NFS daemons if they are not already running as well as mount and unmount the remote filesystems.

I learned the hard way that configuring a remote filesystem to be mountable through `/etc/default` and automount are mutually exclusive. If both are configured, automount is disabled. This caused me quite a few headaches as I was first learning NFS. You can also use automount with the Network Information System (NIS) in that automount maps are exported along with the other NIS maps. This ensures that each NIS system automatically gets access to the same NFS filesystems. (NIS is a method of automatically exchanging files between different machines.)

The term *exporting* is used to describe how NFS makes local directories available to remote systems. These directories are then said to be *exported*. Therefore, an exported directory is a directory that has been made available for remote access. Sometimes the term *importing* is used to refer to the process of remotely mounting filesystems, although *mounting* is more commonly used.

If you can access a filesystem under OpenServer, you can access it under NFS. This is because the access to the file is a multi-step process. When you first access a file (say opening a text file to edit it), the local system first determines that this is an NFS mounted filesystem. NFS on the local system then goes to NFS on the remote system to get the file. On the remote system, NFS tries to read the file that is physically on the disk. It is at this point that it needs to go through the filesystem drivers. Therefore, if the filesystem is supported on the remote system, NFS should have no problem accessing it.

Once a filesystem has been exported, the client sees the filesystem as an NFS filesystem and therefore its type is *really* irrelevant. The filesystems supported by OpenServer as of this writing are AFS and EAFS, DOS, DTFS, High Sierra (CD-ROM), HTFS, ISO-9660 (CD-ROM), SCO Gateway for NetWare, Rockridge CD-ROM, S51K, and XENIX.

There are a couple of limitations with NFS. First, although you might be able to see the device nodes on a remote machine, you cannot access the remote devices. Think back to the discussion on the kernel. The device node is a file that is opened by a device driver to gain access to the physical device. It has a major and minor number that point and pass flags to the device driver. If you open up a device node on a remote system, the major and minor numbers for that device node point to drivers in the *local* kernel.

Also, NFS-ity is not transitive. That is, you cannot access an NFS file system that is mounted by another machine. Keep in mind, too, that the newer filesystems in OpenServer can have more inodes than those in earlier releases. Since the number of inodes possible is few on older systems, an ODT machine mounting an OpenServer machine via NFS might not see every file.

### The Flow of Things

There are two daemon processes that provide the NFS services on the server: `mountd` and `nfsd`. `Mountd` is responsible for checking access permissions to the exported filesystem. When a client tries to mount a filesystem, `mountd` returns a pointer to the filesystem if the client has permission to mount it.

The workhorse on the server side is the `nfsd` daemon. It has the responsibility of handling all filesystem requests from the clients. Once a filesystem has been mounted, all access to the data on that remote filesystem is made through `nfsd`. Remember that you could be exporting directories and not just entire filesystems. Therefore, it's better to say that access to the *mount point* and below is made through `nfsd`.

On the client side is `biod`, which handles block reads. `Biod` is the Block IO Daemon. Handling just block I/O is an important aspect. If a process is doing operations that do not require block IO, then there is little performance loss by having them each do their own RPC (remote procedure call) system calls. However, when you start moving blocks around, NFS needs to ensure things don't get jammed up and will use the kernel buffer cache. (RPC is a way to execute procedures or functions on a remote machine as if they were local to your machine.)

Also key to this process is the portmapper, `portmap`. The portmapper converts TCP/IP port numbers to RPC program numbers. What this means is that when the NFS starts up, it registers its port with the local portmap process. The clients access the server by asking the portmapper on the server for the port number of `nfsd` and `mountd`. The port number is then used on all subsequent RPC calls.

In principle, mounting a remote filesystem is like mounting a local one. The general syntax is

```
mount <options> <filesystem> <mountpoint>
```

One of the primary differences is that since we are an NFS filesystem, we have to explicitly tell mount by using the `'-f NFS'` option. We can also include other options such as `'-r'` for read only. Let's assume that we have on our two machines scoburg and siemau. On siemau is an NFS filesystem that we want to mount from scoburg. Assuming that the proper entries exist in the `/etc/exports` file on siemau, the command on scoburg might look like this:

```
mount -f NFS siemau:/usr/data /data
```

Like other filesystems, the local `mount` command parses the command into tokens and ensures that entries don't already exist in the mount table (`/etc/mnttab`) for either the filesystem or the directory. Realizing that this is a remote filesystem, `mount` gets the IP address for siemau (by whatever means are configured on the local machine) and gets the port number of `mountd` on siemau. The `mount` command then passes `mountd` the pathname of the requested directory (`/usr/data`).

Now it's the server's turn. To make sure it can service the request, `mountd` must first check `/etc/exports` for the requested filesystem; in this case `/usr/data`. If scoburg is permitted, `mountd` passes back what is called a file handle, or pointer. Now the mount back on scoburg uses that file handle and the mount point (`/data`) as arguments to the `mount()` system call. Finally, an entry is place in the local mount table.

There are two primary NFS configuration files: `/etc/exports` and `/etc/default/filesys`. The `/etc/exports` file exists on the server and lists those files and directories that can be accessed by remote hosts. It can also be configured to allow or deny access to specific hosts. Since these are filesystem, you can manage anything mounted by NFS through `/etc/default/filesys`. This allows you to mount remote filesystems at boot or in any way you can with a "normal" filesystem. One advantage NFS has over local filesystems is that you can configure them to be mounted only when you need them. That is, if the files in the directories are not used, the connection is not made. However, if the files are needed, the connection is automatically made. This is the concept of automounting, which we will get into later.

Accessing files across a network present a whole new set of problems that need to be addressed. One of the important things is that particularly when using NFS, each user and group has to be unique throughout the network. Well, to be quite honest, saying, "has to be unique" is not entirely true—"should be" would be more accurate. Remember that an SCO system only sees the UID as a number. If you have the same LOGNAME on two machines, but two different UIDs, both systems will see these as two separate users. This can run you into trouble when copying files between the two systems. When systems are running NFS, NIS comes in handy to prevent such mismatches.

SCO NFS also gives you the ability to lock files to prevent multiple users from accessing them. The mechanism used allows the system to more effectively cleanup in the event of a system crash or other abnormal shutdown. This is handled by lockd and statd. lockd is the Network Lock Manager and is responsible for file and record locking. lockd runs on both the client and the server, processing both lock requests and lock releases as well as recovers (or at least attempts to recover) in the event of a system crash.

It is the responsibility of the Network Status Monitor (statd) to provide application processes with host status information. Like lockd, statd runs on both the client and server machines to monitor each other's status (as well as their own). Part of the status that is monitored is that of locks. When a state change occurs, lockd needs to be told, which is done by the local statd.

Let's assume that a client were to go down improperly, such as crashing or somehow the network connection dropped. Well, it would be too late for the client statd to do anything. However, when it came back up, the client statd could tell the server statd, "Hey, I just crashed." Since any process that had a lock on a server file no longer exists, the server lockd can free those locks. When the server comes back up after a crash, its statd needs to tell the statd on the clients. The client statds need to tell their lockds which can then "reclaim" the locks still on the server.

### Automounter

Automount provides you with the ability to mount NFS filesystems only when you need them, automatically. They are automatically mounted by automount, hence the name. Actually, conventional NFS mounted filesystems can also be mounted automatically in the sense that you can configure them in /etc/default/filesys and they are automatically mounted as the system boots. Automount filesystems, on the other hand, are mounted when a user tries to access files or directories under the mount point. Also, if the files or directories are not accessed within a specific time, (five minutes by default) they are unmounted, thereby saving network resources. When booting, you also save time since the system is waiting to connect to a remote machine that possibly could be down.

One disadvantage that automount has compared to traditional NFS mounts is that the automounted directories cannot be dynamically added. When changes are made to the configuration, automount must be restarted. Now, this doesn't require a reboot of the system, however it is one extra step. In my opinion this is more than compensated by the fact that whereas traditional NFS mounts are hardcoded (meaning one machine: one mount point), automount can be configured to attempt to mount a secondary system if the first one is not available.

Keep in mind that the server side is oblivious to the fact that the request is coming from automount. As far as it knows it is just your normal everyday NFS mount, therefore automounter can be used with systems that don't know about it.

Don't think of automount as your only means of mounting NFS filesystem just because of its advantages. If you are constantly accessing certain filesystems, then you gain nothing by making them automounted. In fact, you might lose something since each time the connection is made, you need to wait. If mounted in the conventional manner, then you only need to wait once. If you have filesystems that are accessed regularly, but others that are accessed only on occasion, you simply mount some at boot and the rest via automount.

A common use of automount is with NIS. Filesystems mounted via automount are maintained in files, called maps. NIS is used to distribute configuration files from the NIS server across the net to the NIS clients. Why not include the automount maps in the set of files that is being distributed? This could be useful if you wanted to have all the documentation on a single machine to save space and access to the doc is made through automount. Since doc is not being constantly accessed, this saves the problem of having the filesystem containing the doc be continually mounted. Another use is when you want each user to have the same home directory no matter where they are. If mounted by automount and distributed via NIS, every time they logged in, no matter on what machine, they would have the same home directory. There is the problem of not being able to access their home directory if the server is down. However, that problem still applies when logging in to a single machine.

The automount daemon is normally started at boot up via the NFS start-up script, `/etc/rc2.d/S89nfs` (the name may be slightly different), however, it can be started by hand. Usually, automount is started with the -f flag and the name of its configuration file, which by convention is `/etc/auto.master`. This contains a list of mount points and where the configuration information for that mount is found. We'll talk more about these files in the chapter on configuring your network.

In reality, automount behaves very similarly to traditional NFS mounts. The system knows that the specified directory is an NFS mount point. When something is accessed on the other side of the mount point, the automount daemon reacts to the request basically the same way `nfsd` does with a normal NFS filesystem. The automount daemon then checks the `mount` table (`/etc/mnttab`) to see if the filesystem is already mounted and mounts it if it isn't. Once the file system is mounted, requests are handled normally.

One point of interest is the mount points themselves. File systems mounted via automount are not where you think they are. Instead, all automount filesystems are mounted to subdirectories under /tmp_mnt and symbolic links point to these directories from what we see as the mount points. Because of the use of symbolic links, you need to be careful when changing directories up through the mount point when using automounter.

Like other filesystems, an entry is maintained in the system mount table (/etc/mnttab) for all filesystems that have been mounted with automounter. When the timeout has expired (five minutes by default), automounter removes the entry from /etc/mnttab, but still maintains a copy in its memory. This copy is updated whenever mounting or unmounting a filesystem.

There are four types of automount maps: *master*, *direct*, *indirect*, and *built-in*. At first, they are a source of a fair bit of confusion, at least with me and many people I know. A direct mount points to a real directory. The direct maps are used to specify direct mounts. Each of these maps contain a separate entry for each direct mount point. If you need to (or are looking for something to do), you can create nested maps. This is where direct maps point to other maps. The contents of each entry is the full path of the mount point, mount options, and the path to the remote directory (or nested map).

An indirect mount points to a *virtual* directory, which is managed by automount and doesn't really exist. At least that's the way the SCO doc describes it. So, what does it mean? Let's take an example of each and hopefully that will clarify things.

First, let's look at what happens with a direct mount. Let's say we want to set up the system so that help files are accessed through automount on the machine scoburg. This would then be the filesystem scoburg:/usr/lib/scohelp and for simplicity's sake, let's say we are mounting it on the local /usr/lib/scohelp directory. When a local user runs scohelp, the mount point is crossed and automount goes into action.

The first thing it does is to create the mount point if it doesn't already exist. Remember the real mount point is not where we think it is. Instead, in this case, it would be /tmp_mnt/usr/lib/scohelp, which automount may create if necessary. Next, the filesystem is mounted onto /tmp_mnt/usr/lib/scohelp, as if you had issued the command:

```
mount -f NFS scoburg:/usr/lib/scohelp /tmp_mnt/usr/lib/scohelp
```

Since it may be the case that /usr/lib/scohelp does not yet exist, automount would then create a symbolic link from /tmp_mnt/usr/lib/scohelp to /usr/lib/scohelp. Now, whenever you change directories or access a file in /usr/lib/scohelp, you are really accessing them on scoburg.

An indirect mount works differently. (Obviously, since why have two things that behave the same.) Let's say that I not only want to have the help files on a remote machine but the man-pages as well, and I wish to mount them under /usr/lib, as /usr/lib/man (so we know where everything is, for example). We could create multiple direct mounts or we could use the concept of indirect mounts. Basically, what appears to happen is the same as with direct mounts. First, a mount point is created under /tmp_mnt if necessary. Next, automount mounts the remote directory onto the mount point under /tmp_mnt. Finally, the symbolic link is created. Note that automount only does this when something under the mount point is accessed. If, in our example, /usr/lib/man was accessed, only it would get mounted, but /usr/lib/scohelp is untouched.

The interesting thing is that using indirect mounts, the directory /usr/lib/man and /usr/lib/scohelp *do not exist.* If you were to do a listing of /usr/lib, these two directories would not be there. Because of the fact that these directories don't really exist, you can make changes to indirect maps without having to restart automounter.

As I mentioned before the master map points to the files containing the other three maps. It contains the name of the mount point and which file to look in for the configuration information, as well as any mount options. By default this is /etc/auto.master.

Because the mount point directory does not exist for indirect mounts, the map file contains just the name of the parent and not the full path. Therefore, the indirect map is dependent on the master map to tell it where to mount the filesystem.

Built-in automount maps are used to save time and effort if many machines are going to be accessed. One of the maps is -hosts, which is used to mount all exported file systems from all known hosts. Using this option you cannot choose where you want the filesystems mounted as they are all mounted as a unit. All are mounted to a single mount point, which is /net, by convention, but you can choose whatever one you want.

All directories mounted from a single server are mounted in the same fashion. First, there is a subdirectory based on the name of the server from which the filesystems are exported. For example, the filesystems mounted from scoburg would be under /net/scoburg. Next, all directories from that server are mounted at the same time whenever any directory is accessed. Lastly, every directory is mounted with the same options, or default options if none are specified.

The -passwd map is a way of getting automount to automatically mount each user's home directories, to that machine where they log in. The limitation is that all home directories must reside on the same machine. In order to create automount home directories that are on different machines, you will need to create either direct or indirect mounts.

## Serial Network Protocols

### Serial Line Internet Protocol (SLIP)

The first protocol in the TCP family to be developed to run across a serial line was the aptly name Serial Line Internet Protocol (SLIP). One advantage that SLIP provides over PPP is simply its age. There are still many computers that are running comparatively old systems and some do not understand PPP. As a result, the only way to make a serial line TCP connection was SLIP.

Basic to SLIP is the concept of a link, or SLIP link. A SLIP link is a serial communication path between the two computers. It is over this link that the data is transferred as *serialized* IP packets. That is, the system sends the IP packets to the SLIP driver, which then encodes them to be able to be sent across the serial line; in principle, just like PPP. Also like PPP, SLIP can be configured to use either a single serial line connecting the two machines or the machines can be connected via mode across telephone lines.

Improvements have been made to SLIP between ODT and OpenServer. Originally, you were required to have specific IP addresses defined for each end of the link. Although this did not mean that each side had a permanent IP address, but rather the IP address had to be defined as the link was being created. The SLIP implementation in OpenServer provides for dynamic IP address allocation at connect time. It still supports dedicated IP address allocation, as well.

Links are established using the `slattach` command which takes as parameters the local connection (either as a tty name or a UUCP site name), the IP address of both sides of the connection, and other IP and serial line attributes for this link. When the link is established, SLIP has created a *network interface*, which in principle functions the same way as the network interface you have with an Ethernet card or PPP for that matter. Like the other types of network interfaces, a SLIP interface can be monitored with `netstat` and accessed using `telnet`, `rlogin`, `ftp`, or any other network utility.

The SCO implementation of SLIP in OpenServer provides for up to sixty-four simultaneous serial network links. This includes both SLIP and PPP (which we'll talk about shortly). Each of these connections can be initiated from either side and on an "as-needed" basis. Therefore, if you only have one serial line, this can be used for either UUCP, SLIP, or PPP.

There are two ways to make the link "inactive," but only one way I would recommend. The first is to simply mark it down using `ifconfig`. The problem is that this simply makes the link inaccessible, but does not remove it. Since the link is still there, the connection does not stop. Therefore if this link is on a phone line, you can experience some unexpectedly high telephone bills. The safer alternative actually removes the link. This is done by simply killing (with `kill -15`) the `slattach` process. This removes the SLIP interface, so please make sure that there are no more processes accessing the interface, as you are liable to have angry users banging on your door.

The primary command when using SLIP is `slattach` or SLIP Link Attach. SLIP is attached to a serial port and creates either a dedicated, dynamic incoming, or dynamic outgoing link. Each end of the link is given a network (IP) address, based on the parameters passed to `slattach`. Once communication is established, the link functions essentially the same as any other network connection. Applications on both sides of the link can communicate, just as if it were Ethernet, for example. Unlike UUCP that also uses serial lines, multiple processes can be using the connection at the same time.

The newest SCO implementation of SLIP provides a means to identify and filter out specific types of IP packets. This is accomplished through the `/etc/pppfilter` program, which, as you might have guessed from the name, is shared with PPP. This file is created either when the SLIP STREAMS stack is installed or by PPP and, by default, only contains comments until you add the filters you want.

Like the other network protocols, SLIP resolves names either by the `/etc/hosts` file or using the Domain Name Service (DNS). The newest implementation also can be configured to connect to sites listed in `/usr/lib/uucp/Systems`.

A dedicated SLIP connection is one in which communication is made between hosts over a specific (dedicated) link. Either side may initiate the link, however this is (usually) across the same line. This type of connection can only be used with a serial line that is always up and dedicated to a single connection. This can include regular serial cables or leased telephone lines.

A dynamic incoming line is paired with a dynamic outgoing line on the remote line (or vice versa). The incoming line must accept the login and password information forwarded by UUCP to establish the connection. This type of connection allows the local system to accept incoming SLIP connection requests just like normal logins; that is the calling system connects to the destination machine and must get past getty. Therefore, this type of SLIP link requires a login account on the side being called. When SLIP is configured using the Network Configuration Manager, a slip account is created. Rather than a normal shell, this account gets a special shell script that initiates the `slattach`.

On the calling machine (that is, the side initiating the SLIP link) an entry must exist for the destination machine in the `/usr/lib/uucp/Systems` file. This must include the slip account name and password for the remote side.

By default, all packets are allowed through a particular interface. Packet filtering allows you to control which packets pass through the SLIP interface and which do not. It is possible to filter out packets on several different criteria. For example, you may choose to allow only TCP or ICMP packets or you may want to disallow TCP and UDP packets. You could also choose to filter out packets going to a particular destination or those coming from a particular source. Depending on your needs, you can configure filtering for each link, individually talk about `netstat`, and access other network tools.

### Point-to-Point Protocol (PPP)

SCO PPP is another means by which network connections can be made across serial lines. Despite the limitations that might be imposed by serial lines, PPP supports the same programs under TCP/IP that are supported with other media. PPP has certain advantages over faster network connections, such as Ethernet, in that it does not require the specialized hardware. In addition, PPP can be configured to dial across a modem and make the connection only when necessary. This allows network connections anywhere in the world without the cost of other methods. PPP provides advantages over other serial line protocols like UUCP in that multiple, concurrent sessions are possible as well as mixing programs such as `telnet` and `ftp`.

The way PPP works is that the serial lines are linked to the IP layer through what is called the PPP STREAMS stack. This stack consists of several different modules: the packet filter module, the PPP driver, the asynchronous HDLC protocol module, and the STREAMS message to the c-list conversion driver.

Like the other protocols at the physical layer, PPP is responsible for encapsulating the IP packages for transmissions and unpacking them upon receipt. Each connection (local host to remote host) is referred to as a PPP link. Because this link represents the physical connection, each PPP link requires a unique IP address on both sides of the link. Since this is a network link, both sides need to be on the same network.

Like any other network connection, each layer of PPP must be installed. This includes starting the PPP daemon (`pppd`). Normally, `pppd` is started by the `/etc/rc2.d/S85tcp` (which is linked to `/etc/tcp`). However, the PPP configuration file (`/etc/ppphosts`) must be present for `pppd` to start. Starting `pppd` does not necessarily mean that connections are made.

Use of the same PPP link requires only that the applications use the same IP address to specify the remote host. By using different IP addresses to specify the same remote host, two applications can also use individual PPP links to the same host, provided a separate serial line is available for each separate address and both addresses have unique PPP network interfaces. Once a PPP link is established, it remains active until the administrator marks the interface down or the idle timer expires. You can use `ifconfig` to mark an interface down. The idle timer is set in the PPP link configuration.

The version of PPP provided with OpenServer has many improvements over its predecessor. This includes support for up to sixty-four simultaneous links; communication initiated in either direction; dynamic acquisition of the ports (accessed as needed, thereby allowing lines to be shared with UUCP); dynamic IP addressing, including IP address pooling; dynamic reconfiguration which does not require relinking the kernel or rebooting the machine; packet filtering; negotiation of link and IP parameters; authentication of the local host by the remote and of the remote host by the local PPP MIB support (for SNMP).

SCO PPP provides two methods of authentication in the form of two protocols: Password Authentication Protocol (PAP) and Challenge-Handshake Authentication Protocol (CHAP). If authentication is enabled, the administrator can choose either one of these methods (provided the other side also supports it). The authentication is on a per-link basis so you can enable it for some, disable it for others, as well as choose the authentication method you want.

## Mailers

### *MMDF*

If you haven't made changes and are using mail locally, then you are using MMDF. MMDF stands for Multi-channel Memorandum Distribution Facility and is the default mail system used on SCO UNIX systems. It is a collection of programs that allows relatively complex mail configurations to be quickly established and easily maintained.

SCO has a built-in mechanism (`mkdev mmdf`) that allows you to automatically configure MMDF. Often the limitations of this automatic procedure require administrators to go beyond the basics. When this happens, you need to know how the parts of MMDF fit together and interact with the rest of the system.

In this section, we're going to talk about the basics of MMDF. This is more than just an overview of the functionality. We're going to get into the interactions between the various files so that if something goes wrong, you will be in a much better position to find the cause of the problem.

Before we get into things we need to first talk about a couple of terms: *Mail Transport Agent* (MTA) and *Mail User Agent* (MUA). The user agent is the program that the user sees, such as `/bin/mail`. It hands off the message to the transport agent, which does the processing and sends it on its way. The default transport agent on SCO UNIX systems is MMDF and is independent of which user agent is being used. (I will be using the terms "transport agent" and "user agent" because I feel the abbreviations tend to be distractions.)

MMDF provides transport through several different methods. The method used is referred to as a *channel*. Sets of machines are grouped together in domains, which may or may not be equivalent to the Internet domains we talked about earlier. Usually (by default), the MMDF domains are based on what channel is used to get to each machine. However, other criteria such as geographical location is possible.

When a user wants to send a message, he or she starts up whatever program is normally used (the user agent), composes their message, and sends it off. The user agent hands the message off to the submit program. Submit then finds the destination machine by looking through the configured domains and then sends the message into the appropriate channel. Once in the appropriate channel, the deliver program starts the program that will actually do the transfer.

When mail reaches the other end the process is reversed. The receiving end of the transport agent hands the message to deliver to be processed further. If the message is destined for a user on that machine, it is placed in that machine's local channel. If not, it is processed further and sent through the channel appropriate for the next hop. How this all looks graphically you can see in Figure 9–9.

There are three channels that are primarily used on SCO systems: local, uucp, and smtp. The local channel is used for mail between users on the same machine and is configured by default, even if you've never touched MMDF. The uucp channel (logically) uses UUCP to transfer mail between remote machines. MMDF hands the message to UUCP along with a remote execution command to send the job through the remote mail system. The smtp (Simple Mail Transport Protocol) channel is used on systems running TCP/IP.

You might want to log in as either root or mmdf and go into the /usr.mmdf directory. This way you have complete access to all the files we need to look at. Let's start first with an overview of the directory structure. There are two places you will find MMDF files: /usr.mmdf and /usr/spool/mmdf. You only need to look at the spool files when problems arise and you need to start tracking it down. For that reason, I am going to put off talking about them until later.

The /usr/mmdf directory is in the heart of the MMDF subsystem. This contains all the binaries and configuration files that MMDF uses, plus the log files it writes to as it does its work. In this directory is at least one file: mmdftailor. (If you've run mkdev mmdf at least once then there is also mmdftailor-). This is the central MMDF configuration file. Most of the information provided by this file is a result of our responses to questions when we run mkdev mmdf.

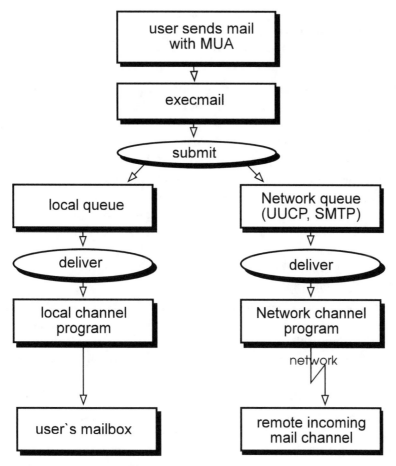

**Figure 9–9**   The flow of MMDF.

Although this file is built by `mkdev mmdf`, it is important to know the structure of this file should it be misconfigured or should you want to enhance your system. Therefore, we are going to take a quick look at it. I will be addressing the entries that you are likely to find on your system but will not give you extensive details on what *could* be there. For details on each of the individual entries, take a look at the `mmdftailor(F)` man-page.

By default, the `mmdftailor` is broken down into four functional areas. Provided they appear in the right order in relationship to each other, there is no absolute order that things must appear. In fact, in SCO UNIX Release 3.2 Version 2, the arrangement was much different than the current release. The order I will be describing below is simply the convention used by SCO. OpenServer changed the layout of `mmdftailor`, once again. Entries are grouped by their type and not by channel. However, the concepts we will address here are the same.

The top portion is the administrative portion. Here, we define the description of our system, such as the host and domain name. It is here that you would define such things as an alternate location for your users' mailboxes (normally it's `/usr/spool/mail`) or set up name hiding. Name hiding is where you hide the name of the machine where the mail originated and simply indicate the domain. We get into this more in the section on configuring MMDF.

The next section is used for aliasing. This is where you define the files, or *tables*, to look through when aliasing user name addresses. This is useful when you want to send mail to people at remote sights without having to remember long addresses. The MTBL lines tell us the names of the alias files to use. The `name=` entries is a kind of alias that will be used in the ALIAS lines to configure that particular alias file. Keep in mind that the `name=` line *must* appear before the others as this defines the alias entry that will be used later.

The ALIAS lines point to files (through the `name=` entry) that are to be used when establishing user aliases. If you look, each line points back to a different alias file. Here only the name of the file is listed, as the system knows to look in `/usr/mmdf/table`. In addition to the file name, there are configuration options for the ALIAS entries.

The next section is where the individual channels are defined and configured. Like alias, there are MTBL entries for each channel, with aliases defined by the `name=` entries. There is one defining the domain file and one defining the channel file. The behavior is the same as for the alias file. An alias is defined for each of the domain or channels files and reference made to the alias. Along with the file name entries there are entries defining the domain specific characteristics (MDMN) and the channel specific characteristics (MCHN).

Even if configured correctly, there are two channels that do not have a corresponding domain. These are the *badhosts channel* and the *baduser channel*. The badhost channel is used whenever you have addressed mail to an address that your local machine does not know about. If configured, the system will try to send to a machine that you have defined as your badhosts machine. This is not necessarily a bad thing. All it means is that you may often need to turn on full trace (FTR) logging. Be careful! If this is turned, on a single *correctly* addressed message will increase the log file by 10K! If you have a busy system, you can quickly have log files that are several megabytes in size.

When doing some MMDF testing with my system while in Support, I came in one Monday morning to find some very disturbing messages on my screen.

Sometime over the weekend my hard disk had filled up and I was now getting messages that the root hard disk was full. When I finally got it, I discovered that I had a 45MB MMDF log file!

That about covers the basic entries that you find in `mmdftailor`. There are dozens of values that can be set, most of which are not set by default or have default values defined within MMDF. Since they are all listed in the `mmdftailor(F)` man-page, I won't go into details about them here. Note that in OpenServer, no logging or locking is defined by default, so each takes on a default value.

Within the `/usr/mmdf` directory, there are several subdirectories. As you would expect, the `bin` directory is where the binary programs are kept. This is where both the `deliver` and `submit` programs reside. The remaining programs serve various functions as MMDF is running its course. Two important ones are `checkque` and `checkaddr`, both of which we discuss in more detail in the section on configuring MMDF.

The `chans` directory contains the channel programs that `deliver` calls to send messages along through the correct channel. The `log` directory is just as its name implies: It is where MMDF writes logging information. Also as its name implies, the `tmp` directory is for temporary files that MMDF creates as it's going about its business.

The last directory, `table`, is where the address oriented configuration information is kept. There are three types of files of importance here: alias files, domain files, and channels files. As it is processing mail, MMDF uses the contents of these files to determine where mail should go.

In our discussion of `mmdftailor`, we talked about the ALIAS, MCHN, and MDMN entries. As you see from their corresponding MTBL entries, these relate to the files in `/usr/mmdf/table`. For example, let's look at the MTBL entry:

```
MTBL name=lalias, file="alias.list", show="Mailing list aliases"
```

This refers to a file `alias.list`. Within the `/usr/mmdf/table` directory there is a file `alias.list`. In this line

```
MTBL name=locdom, file="local.dom", show="Local Domain"
```

there is a reference to the file `local.dom`. There is also a file `local.dom` in the `/usr/mmdf/table` directory. As I mentioned above, the `name =` entry is an alias for that file. In subsequent lines, you see that alias being used.

The alias files (`alias.*`) are used in several instances. For example, if you have someone to whom you regularly send mail and they have a long address that is annoying to type in, you could create an alias for this person that was easier to type. Perhaps you wish to send to one address, but have it be received by ten people. This can be done with alias files as well. Note that in OpenServer, the breakdown on the alias files is substantially different, although the principles are the same. We go into more details in the section on configuring MMDF.

Next are the domain files (*.dom). The domain files contain the names of every machine you want to send mail to and any form of their address that you might want to use. By convention, the machines are grouped by the channel that is used to connect to that machine. However, it is also possible to group them according to other criteria such as geographical location.

The channels files (*.chn) contain the address that will be used to connect to this machine. Since addresses are dependent on the channel being used, the convention here too is that the names of these files is also the name of the channel.

To understand the flow of things, it is important to understand the relationship of these three files to the MMDF system. To do that we need to side track again. When you run `mkdev mmdf`, it calls a program (`dbmbuild`) that combines the data from these files in the order they appear in `mmdftailor` into a database. When you mail something, MMDF doesn't need to look through all of the files, just this one database.

Since all that is being done is a look-up in this database, it is important to maintain the correct format. All three sets of files have the same format:

```
alias: real-name
```

Although I use the words "alias" and "real-name," this format also applies to both the channel and the domain files. The left side is basically what you want to call it and the right side is what it "really" is. How this applies to domain and channel files we'll get into in a moment.

A thing to note is that if there is an entry in an alias file that matches a name, the address will be translated to the alias even if there is a valid user with that name. For example, assume there is a user 'jim' on the system. If there was an entry in the `alias.user` file:

```
jim: james@somewhere.com
```

All mail sent to jim would end up going to james@somewhere.com instead of the local user jim.

At first this may seem a little odd. However, there is some logic behind it. This is the mechanism that allows mail sent to the system users MMDF, UUCP, and so on to end up going to root. If the aliases didn't work like this, then there would be no way to redirect mail from UUCP or MMDF to root. Also, if you have accounts on several machines, you can get your mail on just one.

If there is no defined alias to match, MMDF attempts to deliver mail locally. If there is a user by that name on the local system, all is well. If not, MMDF will attempt to deliver it into the baduser channel. If there is one defined, the processing continues. If there is no baduser channel defined, you end up getting your message sent back with an error saying that this is an unknown user.

If there is a host or domain name with that address, MMDF bypasses the alias entries and looks directly in the domain entries. Because there is no rule as to where machine names go, MMDF must look through all of the domain entries in the database.

To understand how the search is accomplished, let's not look at the database, but rather the source files: the *.dom and *.chn files. Although this is not what happens in reality, it is what happens conceptually and helps in understanding what is happening. In essence, MMDF searches the left side of all the configured domain files until it finds a match.

Note that you often need to specify *every* way you wish to refer to a machine. For example, if you wanted to contact SCO's support bulletin board machine, sosco, you would need entries for sosco, sco.com, and sosco.sco.com (assuming you wanted to be able to use all of them to contact sosco). If you wanted, you could have an entry that simply said 'sco' that pointed to sosco as well.

Once MMDF has found the entry in the domain file, it begins searching all the channel files. Again, this is because there is no rule that says where machine names can go. Theoretically, you could have a machine listed in the local.dom file, but the address in uucp.dom. Once it has found a match in a channel file, it is able to send the message through the appropriate channel.

Note again that this "search" of the *.dom and *.chn files does *not* actually take place. The database is searched. This description is used only as an illustration of what "appears" to happen. The advantage of this method is that once this database is created, MMDF usually needs to only look through a single, relatively small file, instead of several larger ones.

After parsing the database and determining what channel the message needs to be sent through, the message is placed in the appropriate queue directory. These are located in /usr/spool/mmdf/lock/home. There is one directory of the form q.<channel> for each <channel> configured. In addition, there are two other directories here: msg and addr.

The files in q.<channel> are linked to the files in addr and contain administrative information about the message like the sender, recipient, and the queue. At first, it may seem odd to have duplicate files like this. However, this makes sense when you consider the different delivery modes, or "priorities" you can configure MMDF for.

In the MCHN entry for each queue in the `mmdftailor` is a `mod=` entry, which specifies the delivery mode. There are several different kinds of modes, including "imm" for immediate and "reg" for regular. Immediate means just that. Messages will be passed along to the transport agent immediately, even if deliver is not running! Regular means that the message will sit in the queue until delivery starts up again. (The default is once every 10 minutes.)

Although it makes sense for local mail to be sent immediately, it may not make sense for others, depending on the circumstances. Take for example a situation where your only contract to the Internet is via modem through a provider that is not in your local calling area. Once the remote modem answers, the clocks starts ticking. The phone company doesn't care that you are trying to negotiate the protocol. All it cares about is the fact that the phone line is actually being used. If mail through this channel were sent immediately, every message would have to reconnect and waste time. Instead, you queue the messages up, run delivery by hand and then waste the time needed to connect only once. An alternative would be to set the `deliver` program to run at larger intervals, such as every 120 minutes.

What does this have to do with the links in `q.<channel>` and `addr`? Well, if delivery is running on its own, by default it delivers through every channel. To save time, all it needs to do is look through a single directory rather than several. On the other hand, if you want to deliver mail through a single channel, MMDF does not have to search through the files meant for other channels.

The messages themselves, which includes all the header information, is stored in the `msg` directory. This are essentially the same thing you would see when reading your mail. When deliver runs (either as a daemon or starting it by hand) it searches through the various directories here, looking for messages to send. It is at this point that the message is handed off to the channel program. In the case of local mail, deliver passes it off to `/usr/mmdf/chans/local` which appends the message to the user's mailbox. If the message is to be sent through UUCP, delivery starts `/usr/mmdf/chans/uucp` which creates a UUCP transfer job as well as a UUX remote execution job which will start `rmail` on the other end.

### Sendmail

When you compare sendmail to MMDF, it is like comparing shell scripting to C programming. MMDF is quick to configure and easy to maintain. Although you can manage fairly complex mail systems with MMDF, there are some things that you just can't do; just as there are some things you cannot do with shell scripts that you can with C. Because it is the default mailer and requires you to answer just a few simple questions to get a base installation working, MMDF is, by far, the most common mail system on SCO machines.

Because of this and the intrinsic complexity of sendmail, I felt that a detailed discussion of the topic was beyond the scope of this book. If you would like to learn more, both the ODT and OpenServer doc will provide you with a good introduction. There is also a Nutshell Handbook from O'Reilly & Associates called *sendmail* by Bryan Costales with Eric Allman and Niel Rickert that goes into substantial details about sendmail. (It's almost 800 pages!!)

## Mosaic and the Web

It was difficult to decide where to put this topic. You can't have access to the Web without networking, however, it loses much of its impact unless you are using a graphical interface like X. Because the Web is a network of machines accessed in a common manner, I figured the networking chapter would be the best place to talk about it. I think this is a good choice since there are character-based programs that do not require X.

So what *is* the Web. Well, as I just mentioned, it is a network of machines. Not all machines on the Internet are part of the Web, but we can safely say that all machines on the Web are part of the Internet. The Web is the shortened version of World Wide Web, and as its name implies it connects machines all over the world.

Created in 1989 at the internationally renowned CERN research lab in Switzerland, the Web was originally designed as a means of linking physicists from all over the world. Because it is easy to use and integrate into an existing network, the Web has grown to a community of tens of thousands of sites with millions of users accessing it. With the integration of Web access software, on-line services have opened the Web up to millions of people who couldn't have used it before.

The Web really is a vast network of interlinked documents, or resources. These resources may be pure text, but can include images, sound, and even videos. The links between resources are made through the use of the concept of *hypertext*. Now, hypertext is not something new. It has been used for years in on-line help systems; for example, like those in MS-Windows' programs and more recently SCOHelp. Certain words or phrases are presented in a different format (often a different color or maybe underlined). These words or phrases are linked to other resources. When you click on them, the resource that is linked is called. This resource could be the next page, a graphics image, or even video.

When `scohttpd` starts, it reads its configuration files and begins listening for requests from a document viewer (one that uses the HTTP protocol). On OpenServer, this is scohelp, man, and Mosaic. If you are running ODT, then only Mosaic is available. When a document is requested, `scohttpd` checks for the file relative to the DocumentRoot (defined in `/var/scohttp/conf/srm.conf`). By default this is set to `/usr/lib/scohelp`. It is best to leave it like that, otherwise, `scohelp` may not function correctly. If you want to make references to your documents, you can use symbolic links to point to places other than the DocumentRoot. For details on the configuration files, take a look at the `scohttp`(ADM) man-page.

By default, the OpenServer installation sets up the `scohttp` server, which starts the `scohhtp` daemon using the configuration files in `/var/scohttp`. Like TCP, there is actually a script that is used to interface to the `scohttp` daemon: This is `/etc/scohttp`. There are several options that you can pass to it that will start, stop, enable, disable, query the status, or clean-up log files. The daemon itself is `/var/scohttp/scohttpd`. One argument it is passed to is the location of its configuration files. By default these are the files in `/var/scohttp/conf`.

Web pages are written in the Hyptertext Markup Language (HTML). This is a "plain-text" file that can be edited by any editor, like `vi`. Recently, as a result of the increasing popularity of the Web, several commercially available HTML editors have become available. The HTML commands are similar, and also simpler, that those used by `troff`. In addition to formatting commands, there are built-in commands that tell the Web Browser to go out and retrieve a document. You can also create links to specific locations (labels) within that document. Access to the document is by means of a Uniform Resource Locator (URL).

There are several types of URLs that perform different functions. Several different programs can be used to access these resources such as `ftp`, `http`, `gopher`, or even `telnet`. If you leave off the program name, the Web browser assumes that it refers to a file on your local system. However, just like `ftp` or `telnet` you can specifically make references to the local machine. I encourage using absolute names as it makes transferring Web pages that much easier.

For more details on HTML, take a look at the various HTML scripts in both `/usr/man` and `/usr/lib/scohelp`. You can load them into either Mosaic or SCO-Help. You can then select View Source from the File menu. Then compare the output to the source. (You need to set SCOHelp to Web Browser Mode from the Options menu). There is also a very large section on Writing HTML documents in Using Help.

Mosaic has some interesting features that allow you to move around quickly. First, Mosaic keeps track of where you have been. By using the Back button or the Back entry from the Navigate menu, you can backtrack through the pages you already visited. There is also a Forward (and a Forward menu entry) that allows you to move forward through the documents you visited.

If you have some places that you visit often, there is no need to trace through the route that brought you there or remember the URL. Instead, MOSAIC will remember this for you in the form of a Hot List. A Hot List is nothing more than a list of hot places that you've visited. There is a entry under the Navigate menu to add entries to the Hot List as well as to jump directly to the document. The Hot List is stored in $HOME/.mosaic-hotlist-default.

All that you need to access the Web is an Internet connection. If you can do ftp and telnet, then you can probably use the Web. So, assuming you have a Web browser and an Internet connection. The question is where do you go? The question is comparable to, "Given an unlimited value plane ticket, where do you go on vacation?" The sky is the limit.

As I mentioned, the convention is that the Web server's machine name is www.domain.name. To access their home page, the URL would be http://ww.domain.name. For example, to get to SCO's home page, the URL is http://www.sco.com. In order to keep from typing so much, I will simply refer to the domain.name and you can expand it out the rest of the way. In some cases, where the convention is not followed, I'll give you the missing information.

Some sites are commercially oriented such as unidirect.com. This is from the company Unidirect, which provides mail-order UNIX products. The fedex.com site will allow you to track your package. If you are up late, doing some major net surfing, you might want to check out pizzahut.com. Here you can order a pizza on-line. However, as of this writing it was extremely limited in the areas it delivers.

Shortly after SCO came out with their Global Access product for ODT, the comet Schumaker-Levy 9 was making history by plowing into the backside of Jupiter. The Jet Propulsion Laboratory has a Web site, on which they regularly updated the images of Jupiter. I still remember my friends asking me if I had seen the "lastest" images. If they were more than three hours old, I would shrug them off as ancient history.

If you are interested in *free* software (did I say the magic word?), check out www.cdrom.com. You can download gigabytes worth of games and utilities and GIFs and ray-traces and source code and full-text copies of Alice in Wonderland. Most of these are available from sites spread out over the Internet. It's really nice to have them all it one place. The machine www.cdrom.com is the Web server for Walnut Creek CD. Although you could spend weeks downloading their archives, you don't need to. The CDROMs they offer are very reasonably priced. Use the Web site or you can even ftp to ftp.cdrom.com and get access to many of the CDs that they offer. I liked some of those that I found so useful, I subscribed. This saves you about $10 per CD and you get quarterly updates of many of them.

Another place that contains similar information is InfoMagic. While their offering is similar to Walnut Creek CD, InfoMagic does provide a few that Walnut Creek doesn't. They can be reached at www.informagic.com or email them at info@infomagic.com.

One of the CDs that I found very useful was the Internet Info CDROM. This contains a wealth of information about the Internet. This includes standards that are applicable to the Internet like IEEE and RFCs. There are also Frequently Asked Questions (FAQ) from some of the Usenet newsgroups.

The issue of Usenet *newsgroups* opens up a whole can of worms. Without oversimplifying too much, we could say that Usenet was the first, nationwide on-line bulletin-board. Whereas the more commercial services like CompuServe store their messages in a central location, Usenet is based on the "store and forward" principle. That is, messages are stored on a message and forwarded to the next at regular intervals. If those intervals are not all that often, it may be hours or even days before messages are propagated to every site.

Messages are organized into a hierarchical, tree structure, very much like many things in UNIX (although you don't have to be running a UNIX machine to be accessing Usenet). Groups range from things like rec.arts.startrek.fandom to alt.sex.bondage to comp.unix.admin.

Although I would love to go into more details, this really goes beyond the scope of this book. Instead, I would like to recommend *Using UUCP and Usenet* by Grace Todino and Dale Dougherty, and *Managing UUCP and Usenet* by Tim O'Reilly and Grace Todino, both from O'Reilly and Associates. In addition, there is a relatively new book that goes into more details about how Usenet is organized, what newsgroups are available, and some general information about behavior and interaction with others when participating in a Usenet newsgroup. This is *Usenet Netnews for Everyone* by Jenny Fristrup, from Prentice Hall.

## Network Technologies

### Ethernet

SCO supports two of the major network types: Ethernet and token-ring. Ethernet could be labeled as the great-grandfather of all the other network types. It was developed in the 1970s by Xerox for linking computers to printers. Although not very widespread at first, Ethernet has since expanded to be (perhaps) the most widely spread type of network.

The principle behind Ethernet is called Carrier Sensing, Multiple Access with Collision Detection (CSMA/CD). What this means is that every machine on the net sits quietly listening for messages. When one of the machines needs to talk, it waits for a pause and jumps in to send its message. What if two machines simultaneously see the pause and start to send? Well, a collision occurs. This is detected by both machines which wait a random amount of time before they will try again. Although the random amount of time could be the same for both machines, it doesn't happen too often and each machine eventually gets to send its message. The one that didn't get its turn will see that the other one is talking and wait.

Because there is no guarantee that a specific machine will *ever* get a turn on the net, this type of mechanism is referred to as a probabilistic access system, since each machine will probably get access to the system someday. Keep in mind that the busier a network is, the greater the chance for collisions and the greater the likelihood that there will be more waiting. This does not mean that more machines mean more collisions. If I am sitting at my machine doing all of my work locally, then the traffic on the network cause by my machine is minimal. However, once I make a connection, the traffic increases.

Ethernet appears in several different forms, depending on it's physical characteristics. Primarily, these fall into the IEEE specification 802.3, with an average speed of 10MHz. One thing I need to point out is that the original specification developed at Xerox is not what most people think about when they think about Ethernet. Rather it is the IEEE 802.3 standard.

The most popular ways Ethernet appears is 10Base5 (Thicknet), 10Base2 (Thinnet) and 10Base-T (Twisted-Pair). The general format of these labels is *StypeL*, where *S* is the speed of the cable in megahertz, *type* is the transmission system, in this case baseband versus broadband and the *L* is the maximum length of the cable in 100 meters. I have also heard that the last number indicates the thickness of the cable in tenths of an inch. Thicknet, as one would guess, is thicker than thin net, but both are coax cable. Twisted pair is similar is format to normal phone cable, but may often have eight separate wires.

Often times, the topology (layout) of your network is dependent on what kind of cable you are using. Because it requires a central hub, twisted-pair is usually laid out in a star, with the hub at the center. This is a star topology. Thin- and thickwire are usually be spread out in a line, or linear topology. This is also called a bus topology.

### Token-Ring

Token-ring, developed by IBM, is embodied in the IEEE standard 802.5. The key concept in this type of network is the idea of a token. This is similar to a baton in a relay race where each machine must receive the token before it is allowed to go. If a particular machine has nothing to send, it simply passes the token on to the next machine. If it does have something to send, the message is "linked" with the token before it is sent. By seeing the token linked to the message, the other machines know that the token is in use and passes it along to the destination. When the destination machine gets the entire bundle, it puts the token back on the network, with a tag to indicate that it received the packet. It is then passed to the originator as an acknowledgment. The originator then passes the token along to the next machine.

This scheme provides guaranteed access to the network since every machine will eventually get the token. Even if the originator of one packet has more to send, once it gets its acknowledgment back, it must pass the token along. If no others want to send anything, then it can come back to the first machine. However, the others were given the *chance* to send something. This method also provides reliability since the destination machine sends the packet back with an acknowledgment.

### ISDN

For most of the life of electronic/electrical communication, the primary method of communication has been the telephone. As a result, there exists a network of cables and connections throughout the world that dwarfs the Internet in both number of connections and miles of wire. Wouldn't it be wonderful if we could take advantage of the already existing network? Well, we can. This comes to us in the form of a system called Integrated Services Digital Network, or ISDN.

ISDN is one of the fastest growing technologies, particularly in Europe. Local telephone companies are offering it as a replacement (or addition) to conventional telephone lines. As of this writing, the German phone company is offering cash incentives for businesses and private individuals to switch to ISDN. The primary benefit (at least to most end-users) is that you can send data across the same lines as your phone. For example, while you are speaking to a customer, you can be faxing them the spec sheets on your latest product *across the same phone line*. Although such functionality requires ISDN connections on both ends, your phone could be talking to their conventional phone and your fax could be talking to their conventional fax. However, from your office to the phone company is a single telephone connection.

If both sides are using ISDN, they need to be communicating in a fashion similar to a network (like with TCP/IP or IPX/SPX). Therefore, both sides know who is calling. Imagine getting a call from a customer and having your database automatically call up the record on that customer, even before you pick up the phone! This ability to integrate all these different services from voice to fax to data communication gives ISDN its name.

The key concept in ISDN is the idea of a digital data pipe between the end device and the service provider. Note that I didn't say between the two participants.

This allows the service provider (the phone company) to switch between the ISDN connection on one side, to the analog connection on the other. At the receiving end (your office) will be something similar to a switch box. As the packets come in from the service provider, this switch box will route the packets to the appropriate device. Each device is set with a particular ID number. This works conceptually the same way as SCSI IDs.

As of this writing, three types of connections have been standardized. The first is often referred to as the "basic" rate as it provides the necessary service for basic users such as homes and small businesses. This provides two 64 kbps channels for voice or data and one channel for "out-of-band" signaling. The "primary" service provides 23 voices or data channels, instead of just two. In Europe, this is increased to 30 channels. The third type provides a 4 KHz analog phone channel along with a 8 or 16 kbps data channel. This allows you to use your old analog phone along side the new ISDN device.

### SCO Network Drivers

In ODT, network drivers used a concept called Link Level Interface, LLI. With LLI, the network protocol stacks sat directly on top of the LLI layer. This required that the LLI drivers had a certain knowledge of the workings of the protocol stack that was being used.

OpenServer introduced a totally new concept called MAC Driver Interface, MDI. MDI is now isolated from the protocol stacks by the Data Link Provider Interface (DLPI) layer. Therefore, new drivers can be added simply by interfacing them with the AT&T DLPI standard. On the other end, new protocols can be added and old ones modified. Again, simply by interfacing them to the DLPI standard.

Another advantage is that since much of the work of the LLI drivers is taken over by the DLPI layer, MDI drivers are 30–50% smaller. Despite that fact that the driver is smaller, the MDI drivers allow for more detailed driver statistics. Another advantage is that there is only one open on the device. (when the card is initialized) This decreases the likelihood of hangs and other problems, which increases the reliability of the interface.

## Stay Tuned

Believe it or not, that's not all. Networking is more than just understanding what parts are there. You need to be able to configure the parts correctly to make it work. In this chapter we just covered the concepts involved. Later, we're going to go into more details about how to configure your network software. So, stay tuned.

# CHAPTER 10

- Basic Input/Output Services and the System Bus

- The Expansion Bus

- The Small Computer Systems Interface

- Memory

- The Central Processing Unit

- Hard Disks

- Floppy Drives

- Tapes Drives

- CD-ROMs

- Magneto-Optical Drives

- Serial Ports

- Parallel Ports

- Video Cards and Monitors

- Modems

- Printers

- Mice

- Uninterruptable Power Supplies

# The Computer

Hardware is my life. I love working with it. I love installing it. I love reading about it. I am by no means an expert in such a way that I can tell you about every chip on the motherboard. In fact, I enjoy being a "jack-of-all-trades." Of all the trades I am a jack of (of which I am a jack?), I enjoy hardware the most.

It's difficult to say why. There is, of course, the fact that without the hardware nothing works. Software, without hardware, is just words on a page. However, it's something more than just that. I like the idea that it all started out as rocks and sand and now it can send men to the moon and look inside of atoms.

I think that this is what it's all about. Between the hardware and the operating system (I also love operating systems) you pretty much have the whole ball of wax.

During the several years I spent in support, it was common to have people call in without an idea of what kind of computer they had. I remember one conversation with a customer where he answered, "I don't know" to every question I asked about his hardware. Finally, he got so frustrated he said, "Look! I'm not a computer person. I just want you to tell me what's wrong with my system."

Imagine calling your mechanic to say there is something wrong with your car. He asks you whether your car has 4 or 8 cylinders, whether it has fuel injection, whether it is automatic or manual, and whether it uses unleaded or leaded gas. You finally get frustrated and say, "Look. I'm not a engine person, I just want you to tell me what's wrong with my car."

The solution is to drive your car to the mechanic and have it checked. However, you can't always do that with your computer system. You have dozens of people

427

who rely on it to do their work. Without it, business stops. In order to better track down and diagnose hardware problems, you need to know what to look for.

This section should serve as a background for many issues we cover elsewhere. This chapter is designed more to familiarize you with the concepts, rather than make you an expert on any aspect of the hardware. If you want to read more about PC hardware, a good place is the *Winn Rosch Hardware Bible* from Brady Books.

## Basic Input/Output Services and the System Bus

A key concept for this discussion is the bus. So, just what is a bus? Well, in computer terms it has a meaning similar to your local county public transit. It is used to move something from one place to another. A county transit bus moves people. A computer bus moves information.

The information is transmitted along the bus as electric signals. If you ever opened up a computer, you probably saw that there was one central printed circuit board with the CPU, the expansion cards, and loads of chips sticking out of it. The electronic connection between these parts is referred to as a bus.

The signals that move along a computer bus come in two basic forms: control and data. Control signals do just that: they control things. Data signals are just that: data. How this happens and what each part does we will get to as we move along.

In today's PC computer market there are several buses, which have many of the same functions, but approach things quite differently. In this section, we are going to talk about what goes on between the different devices on the bus, what the main components are that communicate along the bus, and then we will talk about the different bus types.

Despite differences in bus types, there are certain aspects of the hardware that are common among all PCs: Basic Input Output System (BIOS), interrupts, Direct Memory Access channels, and base addresses are just a few. Although once the kernel is loaded, SCO UNIX almost never needs the system BIOS, understanding its function and purpose is useful in understanding the process that the computer goes through from the time you hit the power switch to when SCO UNIX has full control of the hardware.

The BIOS stand is the mechanism DOS uses to access the hardware. DOS (or a DOS application) makes BIOS calls, which then transfer the data to and from the devices. Except for the first few moments of the boot process and the last moment of a shutdown, SCO UNIX may never again use it.

The "standard" BIOS for PCs is the IBM BIOS, but that's simply because PC is an IBM standard. However, standard does not mean most common, as there are several other BIOS vendors, such as Phoenix and AMI.

DOS or DOS applications make device-*independent* calls to the BIOS in order to transfer data. The BIOS then translates this into device-*dependent* instructions. For example, DOS (or application) requests that the hard disk read a certain block of data. The application does not care what kind of hard disk hardware there is, nor should it. It is the job of the BIOS to make that translation to something the specific hard drive can understand.

In SCO UNIX, on the other hand, there is a special program called a device driver that handles the functions of the BIOS. As we talked about in the section on the kernel, device drivers are sets of routines that directly access the hardware; just as the BIOS does. It is important to note that although the SCO UNIX kernel accesses devices primarily through devices drivers, there are circumstances where the BIOS *is* accessed. For example, certain video card drivers use it as well as the SCO UNIX kernel itself when it is rebooting the system after you issue the `reboot` or `shutdown` command.

The fact that SCO UNIX by-passes the BIOS and goes directly to the hardware is one reason why some hardware will work under DOS and not under SCO UNIX. In some instances, the BIOS has been specially designed for the machine that it runs on. Because of this, it can speak the same dialect of "machine language" that the rest of the hardware speaks. However, since UNIX does not speak the same dialect, things get lost in the translation.

The Intel 80 × 86 family of processors (which SCO runs on) have an I/O space that is distinct from memory space. What this means is that memory (or RAM) is treated differently than I/O. Other machine architectures, such as the Motorola 68000 family, see accessing memory and I/O as the same thing. Although the addresses for I/O devices appear as "normal" memory addresses and the CPU is performing a read or write as it would to RAM, the result is completely different.

When accessing memory, either for a read or write, the CPU utilizes the same address and data lines as it does when accessing RAM. The difference lies in the M/IO# line on the CPU. For those not familiar with digital electronics, this can also be described as the Memory/Not IO line. That is, if the line is high, the CPU is addressing memory. If it is low, it is addressing an I/O device.

Although the SCO UNIX operating system is much different from DOS, it still must access the hardware in the same fashion. There are assembly language instructions that allow an operating system (or any program for that matter) to access the hardware correctly. By passing these commands the base address of the

I/O device, the CPU knows to keep the M/IO# line low and therefore access the device and not memory.

You can see the base address of each device on the system every time you boot. The hardware screen shows you the devices it recognizes along with certain values such as the base address, the interrupt vector, and the DMA channel. You can also see this same information by running the `hwconfig` command.

Although there are 16 I/O address lines coming from the 80386, some PCs only have 10 of these wired. So instead of having 64K of I/O address space ($2^{16}$), there is only 1K ($2^{10}$). When the system detects this you see the message `10 bits of I/O address decoding` when the system is booting. Some machines have 11 or more address lines and, therefore, have a larger I/O space.

If your motherboard only uses 10 address lines, devices on the motherboard that have I/O addresses (such as the DMA controller and PIC) will appear at their normal address as well as "image" addresses. This is because the high 6 bits are ignored, so any 16-bit address where the lower 10 bits match will show up as an "image" addresses. Since there are 6 bits that are ignored, there are 63 possible "image" addresses (64 minus the one for the "real" address).

These "image" addresses may cause conflicts with hardware that have I/O addresses higher than $0 \times 3FF$ (1023), which is the highest possible with only 10 address lines. Therefore, if your motherboard only has 10 bits of I/O addresses, you shouldn't put devices at addresses higher than $0 \times 3FF$.

When installing, it is vital that no two devices have overlapping (or identical) base addresses. Whereas you can share interrupts and DMA channels on some machines, you can never share base addresses. If you attempt to read a device that has an overlapping base address, you may end up getting information from both devices.

If you are installing a board whose default base address is the same as one already on the system, one of them needs to be changed before they both can work. Additionally, the base address of a card is almost always asked during its installation. Therefore you will need to keep track of this. See the section on troubleshooting for tips on maintaining a notebook with this kind of information.

Table 10–1 contains a list of the more common devices and the base address ranges that they use.

## The Expansion Bus

It is generally understood that the speed and capabilities of the CPU are directly related to the performance of the system as a whole. In fact, the CPU is a major selling point of PCs, especially among less experienced users. One aspect of the

## Table 10–1 Common hex Addresses

| HexRange | Device |
|----------|--------|
| 000–0ff | Motherboard devices (DMA Controller, PIC, timer chip, etc.) |
| 1f0–1f8 | Fixed disk controller (WD10xx) |
| 278–27f | Parallel port 2 |
| 2f8–2ff | Serial port 2 |
| 378–37f | Parallel port 1 |
| 3bc–3bf | Monochrome display and parallel port 2 |
| 3c0–3cf | EGA or VGA adapter |
| 3d0–3df | CGA, EGA, or VGA adapter |
| 3f0–3f7 | Floppy disk controller |
| 3f8–3ff | Serial port 1 |

machine that is less understood and therefore less likely to be an issue is the expansion bus.

The expansion bus, simply put, is the set of connections and slots that allow users to add to, or expand, their system. Although not really an "expansion" of the system, you often find video cards and hard disk controllers attached to the "expansion bus."

Anyone who has opened up their machine has seen parts of the expansion bus. The slots used to connect cards to the system are part of this bus. A thing to note is that people will often refer to this bus as *the bus*. While it will be understood what is meant, there are other buses on the system. Just keep this in mind as you go through this chapter.

Most people are aware of the differences in CPUs. This could be whether the CPU is 16-bit or 32-bit, the speed of the processor, whether there is a math coprocessor, and so on. The concepts of BIOS and interrupts are also very commonly understood.

One part of the machines hardware that is somewhat less known and often causes confusion is the bus architecture. This is the basic way in which the hardware components (usually on the motherboard) all fit together. There are three different bus architectures on which SCO operating systems will run. (Note: Here I am referring to the *main* system bus, although SCO can access devices on other buses.)

The three major types of bus architectures used are the Industry Standard Architecture (ISA), the Extended Industry Standard Architecture (EISA), and the

Micro-Channel Architecture (MCA). Both ISA and EISA machines are manufactured by a wide range of companies, but only a few (primarily IBM) manufacture MCA machines.

In addition to the three mentioned above, there a few other bus types that can be used in conjunction with or supplementary to the three. These include the Small Computer System Interface (SCSI), Peripheral Component Interconnect (PCI) and the Video Electronics Standards Association Local Bus (VL-Bus or VLB).

Both PCI and VLB exist as separate buses on the computer motherboard. Expansion cards exist for both of these types of buses. You will usually find either PCI or VLB in addition to either ISA or EISA. Sometimes, however, you can also find *both* PCI and VLB in addition to the primary bus. In addition, it is possible to have machines that only have PCI, since it is a true system bus and not an expansion bus like VLB. However, as of this writing few machines provide PCI-only expansion buses.

SCSI, on the other hand, compliments the existing bus architecture by adding an additional hardware controller to the system. There are SCSI controllers (more commonly referred to as host adapters) that fit in ISA, EISA, MCA, PCI, or VL-Bus slots.

### Industry Standard Architecture (ISA)

As I mentioned before, most people are generally aware of the relationship between CPU performance and system performance. However, every system is only as strong as its weakest component. Therefore, the expansion bus also sets limits on the system performance.

There were several drawbacks with the expansion bus in the IBM PC. First, it was limited to only 8 data lines. This meant that only 8 bits could be transferred at a time. Second, the expansion bus was, in a way, directly connected to the CPU. Therefore, it operated at the same speed as the CPU. This meant that in order to improve performance with the CPU, the expansion bus had to be altered as well. The result would have been that existing expansion cards would be obsolete.

In the early days of PC computing, IBM was not known to want to cut its own throat. It had already developed quite a following with the IBM PC among users and developers. If it decided to change the design of the expansion bus, developers would have to re-invent the wheel and users would have to buy all new equipment. Instead of sticking with IBM, there was the risk that users and developers would switch to another platform.

Rather than risking that, IBM decided that backward compatibility was a paramount issue. One of the key changes was severing the direct connection between the expansion bus and CPU. As a result, expansion boards could operate at a different speed than the CPU. This allowed users to keep existing hardware and allowed manufacturers to keep producing their expansion cards. As a result, the IBM standard became the industry standard and the bus architecture became known as the Industry Standard Architecture, or ISA.

In addition to this change, IBM added more address and data lines. They doubled the data lines to 16 and increased the address lines to 24. This meant that the system could address up to 16 megabytes of memory; the maximum that the 80286 CPU (Intel's newest central processor at the time) could handle.

When the 80386 came out, the connection between the CPU and bus clocks were severed completely, since no expansion board could operate at the 16MHz or more that the 80386 could. The bus speed does not need to be an exact fraction of the CPU speed, but an attempt has been made to keep it there, since by keeping the bus and CPU synchronized it is easier to transfer data. The CPU will only accept data when it coincides with its own clock. If an attempt is made to speed up the bus a little, the data must wait until the right moment in the CPUs clock cycle before it can pass the data. Therefore, nothing has been gained by making it faster.

One method used to speed up the transfer of data is Direct Memory Access or DMA. Although DMA existed in the IBM XT, the ISA bus provided some extra lines. DMA allows the system to move data from place to place without the intervention of the CPU. In that way, data can be transferred from, let's say, the hard disk to memory while the CPU is working on something else. Keep in mind that in order to make the transfer, the DMA controller must have complete control of both the data and the address lines, so the CPU *cannot* be accessing memory itself at this time. What this looks like graphically you will see in Figure 10–1.

Let's step back a minute. It is somewhat of a misnomer to say that a DMA transfer occurs without intervention from the CPU, as it is the CPU that must initiate the transfer. However, once the transfer is started, the CPU is free to continue with other activities. DMA controllers on ISA-Bus machines use "pass-through" or "fly-by" transfers. That is, the data is not latched or held internally, but rather is simply passed through the controller. If it were latched, two cycles would be needed: one to latch into the DMA controller and the second to pass it to the device or memory (depending on which way it was headed).

Devices tell the DMA controller that they wish to make DMA transfers through the use of one of three DMA request lines, numbered 1–3. Each of these lines is given a priority based on its number, with 1 being the highest. The ISA-Bus includes two sets of DMA controllers. There are four 8-bit channels and four 16-bit channels. The channels are labeled 0–7, with 0 having the highest priority.

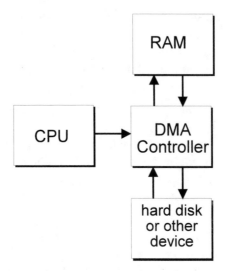

**Figure 10–1**   Direct Memory Access.

Each device on the system that is capable of doing DMA transfers is given its own DMA channel. The channel is set on the expansion board usually by means of jumpers. The pins that these jumpers are connected to are usually labeled DRQ, for DMA Request.

The two DMA controllers (both Intel 8237), each with four DMA channels, are cascaded together. The master DMA controller is the one that is connected directly to the CPU. One of its DMA channels is used to connect to the slave controller. Because of this, there are actually only seven channels available.

Everyone who has had a baby knows what an interrupt driven operating system like SCO UNIX goes through. Just like a baby when it needs its diaper changed, when a device on the expansion bus needs servicing it tells the system by generating an interrupt. For example, when the hard disk has transferred the requested data to, or from memory, it signals the CPU by means of an interrupt. When keys are pressed on the keyboard, the keyboard interface also generates an interrupt.

Upon receipt of such an interrupt, the system executes a set of functions commonly referred to as an Interrupt Service Routine, or ISR. Since the reaction to a key being pressed on the keyboard is different from the reaction when data is transferred from the hard disk, there need to be different ISRs for each device. Although the behavior of ISRs is different under DOS than UNIX, their functionality is basically the same. For details of how this works under SCO, see the chapter on the kernel.

On the CPU there is a single interrupt request line. This does not mean that every device on the system is connected to the CPU via this single line. Just like there is a DMA controller to handle DMA requests, there is also an interrupt controller to handle interrupt requests. This is the Intel 8259 Programmable Interrupt Controller, or PIC.

On the original IBM PC, there were five "Interrupt Request" lines, numbered 2–7. Here again the higher the number the lower the priority. (Interrupts 0 and 1 are used internally and are not available for expansion cards.)

The ISA-Bus also added an additional PIC, which is "cascaded" off the first one. With this addition, there were now 16 interrupt values on the system. However, not all of these were available to devices. Interrupts 0 and 1 were still used internally, as well as interrupts 8 and 13. Interrupt 2 was something special. It was reserved for system use, but instead of being a device of some kind, an interrupt on line 2 actually meant that an interrupt was coming from the second PIC; similar to the way cascading works on the DMA controller.

A question that I brought up when I first started learning about interrupts was, "What happens when the system is servicing an interrupt and another one comes in?" Well there are two mechanisms for helping in this.

Remember that the 8259 is a "programmable" interrupt controller. There is a machine instruction called 'Clear Interrupt Enable' or CLI. If a program is executing what is called a *critical section* of code (one that should not be stopped in the middle), the programmer can call the CLI instruction and disable acknowledgment of all incoming interrupts. As soon as the critical section has left, the programmer should execute a Set Interrupt Enable, or STI instruction within a timely manner.

I say "should" because the programmer doesn't have to. There could be a CLI instruction in the middle of a program somewhere and if the STI is never called, no more interrupts will be serviced. Nothing, aside from common sense, prevents him or her from doing this. Should the program take too long before it calls the STI, interrupts could get lost. This is common on busy systems when characters from the keyboard disappear.

The second mechanism is that the interrupts are priority based. The lower the interrupt request level, or IRQ, the higher the priority. This has an interesting side effect since the second PIC (or slave) is bridged off the first PIC (or master) at IRQ2. The interrupts on the first PIC are numbered 0–7 and on the second PIC 8–15. However, interrupt 2 is where the slave PIC is attached to the master. Therefore, the actual priority is 0,1,8–15,3–7. Table 10–2 contains a list of the standard interrupts.

One consideration is needed when dealing with interrupts. On XT machines, IRQ 2 was a valid interrupt. On AT machines, IRQ 2 was bridged to the second PIC.

**Table 10–2**  Default Interrupts

| IRQ | Device |
| --- | --- |
| 0 | System timer |
| 1 | Keyboard |
| 2 | 2nd level interrupt |
| 3 | COM 2 |
| 4 | COM 1 |
| 5 | Printer 2 |
| 6 | Floppy |
| 7 | Printer 1 |
| 8 | Clock |
| 9 | Not assigned |
| 10 | Not assigned |
| 11 | Not assigned |
| 12 | Not assigned |
| 13 | Math co-processor |
| 14 | Hard disk |
| 15 | Hard disk |

So, in order to ensure that devices configured to IRQ 2 worked properly, the IRQ 2 pin on all the expansion slots was connected to the IRQ 9 input of the second PIC. In addition, all the devices attached to the second PIC, have a IRQ value associated with where they are attached to the PIC, plus the fact they generate IRQ 2 on the first PIC.

The PICs on an ISA machine are *edge-triggered*. This means that they react only when the interrupt signal is transitioning from low to high. That is, it is on a transition *edge*. This becomes an issue when you attempt to share interrupts. This is where two devices use the same interrupt.

Assume you have a serial port and floppy controller both at interrupt 6. If the serial port generates an interrupt, the system will "service" it. If the floppy controller generates an interrupt before the system has finished servicing the interrupt for the serial port, the interrupt from the floppy gets lost. There is another way to react to interrupts called "level-triggered" which we will get to shortly.

As I mentioned earlier, a primary consideration in the design of the AT Bus (as the changed PC bus came to be called) was that it maintained compatibility with it predecessors. It maintains compatibility with the PC expansion cards, but takes advantage of 16-bit technology. In order to do this, connectors were not changed only added. Therefore, cards designed for the 8-bit PC bus could be slid right into a 16-bit slot on the ISA-Bus and no one would know the difference.

### Micro-Channel Architecture (MCA)

The introduction of IBM's Micro-Channel Architecture (MCA) was a redesign of the *entire* bus architecture. Although IBM was the developer of the original AT architecture, which later became ISA, there were many companies producing machines that followed this standard. The introduction of MCA meant that IBM could produce machines that it alone had the patent rights to.

One of the most obvious differences is the smaller slots required for MCA cards. ISA cards are $4.75 \times 13.5$ inches, compared with the $3.5 \times 11.5$ inches of MCA cards. As a result, the same number of cards can fit into a smaller area. The drawback is that ISA cards cannot fit into MCA slots and MCA cards cannot fit into ISA slots. Although this might seem like IBM had decided to cut its own throat, the changes made in creating MCA made it very appealing.

Part of the decrease in size was a result of surface mount components or surface mount technology (SMT). Previously, cards used "through-hole" mounting where holes were drilled through the system board (hence the name). Chips were mounted in these holes or into holders that were mounted in the holes. Surface mount components do not use this and as a result look "flattened" by comparison. This not only saves space, but also time and money as SMT cards are easier to produce. In addition, the spacing between the pins on the card ( 0.050") corresponds to the spacing on the chips. This makes designing the boards much easier.

Micro-channel also gives increases in speed since there is a ground on every fourth pin. This reduces interference and as a result, MCA bus can operate at ten times the speed of non-MCA machines and still comply with FCC regulations in terms of radio frequency interference.

Another major improvement was the expansion of the data bus to 32 bits. This meant that machines were no longer limited to 16 megabytes of memory, but could access 4 gigabytes.

One of the key changes in the MCA architecture was the concept of *hardware-mediated bus arbitration*. With ISA machines, devices could share the bus, and the OS was required to arbitrate who got a turn. With MCA, that arbitration is done at the hardware level, freeing the OS to work on other things. This also enables multiple processors to use the bus. To implement this, there are several new lines to the bus. There are four lines that determine the *arbitration bus priority level*, which represents 16 different priority levels that a device could have. Who gets the bus, is dependent on the priority.

From the user's perspective, installation of MCA cards is much easier than for ISA cards. This is due to the introduction of the Programmable Option Select, or POS. With this, the entire hardware configuration is stored in the CMOS. When new cards are added, you are required to run the machine's *reference disk*. In addition, each card comes with an *options disk* which contains configuration information for the card. With the combination of the reference disk and option disk, conflicts are all but eliminated.

Part of the MCA spec is that each card has its own unique identifying number encoded into the firmware. When the system boots, the settings in the CMOS are compared to the cards that are found on the bus. If one has been added or removed, the system requires you to boot using the reference disk to ensure things are set up correctly.

As I mentioned, on each options disk is the necessary configuration information. This is contained within the Adapter Description File (ADF). The ADF contains all the necessary information to get the expansion card to be recognized by your system. Because it is only a few kilobytes in size, many ADF files can be stored on a floppy. This is useful in situations like we had in SCO Support. There were several MCA machines in the department, with dozens of expansion cards, each with their own ADF file. Rather than having copies of each of the diskettes, the analysts who supported MCA machines (myself included) each had a single disk with all the ADF files. (Eventually that too became burdensome, so we copied the ADF files into a central directory where we could copy them as needed.) Any time we needed to add a new card to our machines for testing, we didn't need to worry about the ADF files, as they were all in one place.

Since each device has its own identification number and this number is stored in the ADF, the reference diskette can find the appropriate one with no problem. All ADF files have names such as @BFDF.ADF, so it isn't obvious what kind of card the ADF file is for, just by looking at the name. However, since the ADF files are simply text files, it is easy to figure out by looking at the contents.

Unlike ISA machines, the MCA architecture allows for *interrupt sharing*. Since many expansion boards are limited to a small range of interrupts, it is often difficult, if not impossible to configure every combination on your system. Interrupt sharing is possible on the MCA machine because it uses something called *level-triggered interrupts* or *level-sensitive interrupts*.

With edge-*triggered interrupts*, or edge-sensitive interrupts, that the standard ISA-bus uses, an interrupt is generated and then drops. This sets a flag in the PIC, which figures out which device generated the interrupt and services it. If interrupts were shared with edge-triggered interrupts, any interrupt that arrived between the time the first one is generated and serviced would be lost. This is because the PIC has no means of knowing that a second one occurred. All it sees is that an interrupt occurred. Figure 10–2 shows what this looks like graphically.

With level-triggered interrupts, when an interrupt is generated it is held high until the PIC forces it low after the interrupt has been serviced. If an other device were on the same interrupt, the PIC would *try* to pull down the interrupt line, however, the second device would keep it high. The PIC would then see that it was high and would be able to service the second device.

Despite the many obvious advantages of the MCA, there are a few drawbacks. One of the primary drawbacks is the interchangeability of expansion cards between architectures. MCA cards can only fit in MCA machines. However, it is possible to use an ISA card in an EISA machine.

### Extended Industry Standard Architecture (EISA)

In order to break the hold that IBM had on the 32-bit bus market with the Micro-Channel Architecture, a consortium of computer companies, led by Compaq, issued their own standard in September, 1988. This new standard was an extension of the ISA bus architecture and was (logically) called the Extended Industry Standard Architecture (EISA). EISA offered many of the same features as MCA, but with a different approach.

Although EISA provides some major improvements, it has maintained backward compatibility with ISA boards. Therefore, existing ISA boards can be used in EISA machines. In some cases, such boards can even take advantage of the features that EISA offers.

In order to maintain this compatibility, EISA boards are the same physical size as their ISA counterparts. EISA boards also provide connections to the bus in the

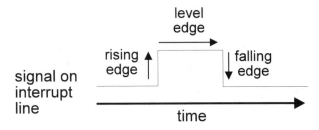

**Figure 10–2**   Interrupt signal.

same locations. The original design called for an extension of the bus slot, similar to the way the AT slots were an extension on the XT slots. This was deemed impractical as some hardware vendors had additional contacts that extended beyond the ends of the slots. There was also the issue that in most cases, the slots would extend the entire length of the motherboard. This meant that the motherboard would need to be either longer or wider to handle the longer slots.

The solution called for the additional connections to be "intertwined" with the old ones and to be extended lower. In what used to be gaps between the connectors, there are now leads to the new connectors. Therefore, EISA slots are deeper than those for ISA machines. By looking at EISA cards you can easily tell them from ISA cards by the two rows of connectors. Figure 10–3 shows what the ISA and EISA connections look like. Note that this is not to scale.

Another major improvement of EISA over ISA is the issue of *bus arbitration*. Bus arbitration is the process by which devices "discuss" whose turn it is on the bus

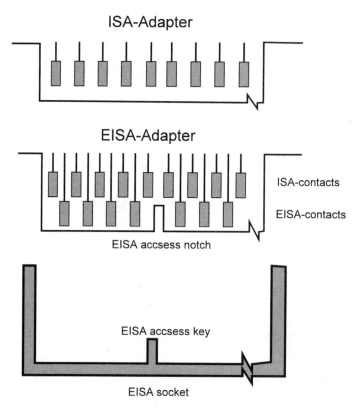

**Figure 10–3**    Comparison of ISA and EISA connections.

and then let one of them go. In XT and AT class machines, control of the bus was completely managed by the CPU. EISA includes additional control hardware to take this job away from the CPU. This does two important things. First, the CPU is now free to carry on more important work and second, the CPU gets to use the bus only when its turn comes around.

Hmmm. Does that sound right? Since the CPU is the single most important piece of hardware on the system, shouldn't it get the bus whenever it needs it? Well, yes and no. The key issue of contention is the use of the word "single." EISA was designed with multiprocessing in mind; that is, computers with more than one CPU. If there is more than one CPU, which *one* is most important?

The term used here is *bus arbitration*. Each of the six devices that EISA allows to take control of the bus, has its own priority level. A device signals its desire for the bus by sending a signal to the Centralized Arbitration Control (CAC) unit. If conflicts arise (multiple requests), the CAC units resolve them according to the priority of the requesting devices. Certain activity such as DMA and memory refresh have the highest priority, with the CPU following close behind. Such devices are called "bus mastering devices" or "bus masters" as they become the master of the bus.

The EISA DMA controller was designed for devices that cannot take advantage of the bus mastering capabilities of EISA. The DMA controller supports ISA, with ISA timing and 24-bit addressing as the default mode. However, it can be configured by EISA devices to take full advantage of the 32-bit capabilities.

Another advantage that EISA has is the concept of dual buses. Since cache memory is considered a basic part of the EISA specification, the CPU can often continue working for some time even if it does not have access to the bus.

A major drawback of EISA (as compared with MCA) is that in order to maintain the compatibility to ISA, EISA speed improvements cannot extend into memory. This is because the ISA bus cannot handle the speed requirements of the high-speed CPUs. Therefore, EISA requires separate memory buses. This results in every manufacturer having its own memory expansion cards.

In our discussion on ISA we talked about the problems with sharing of level-triggered interrupts. MCA, on the other hand, uses edge-triggered which allows interrupt sharing. EISA uses a combination of the two. Obviously, it needs to support edge-triggered to maintain compatibility with ISA cards. However, it allows EISA boards to configure that particular interrupt as either edge- or level-triggered.

As with MCA, EISA allows each board to be identified at boot up. Each manufacturer is assigned a prefix code to ease identification of the board. EISA also provides a configuration utility, similar to the MCA reference disk to allow configuration of the cards. In addition, EISA supports automatic configuration which allows the system to recognize the hardware at boot-up and configure itself accordingly. This can present problems for the SCO system as drivers in the kernel rely on the configuration to remain constant. Since each slot on an EISA machine is given a particular range of base addresses, it is necessary to modify your kernel prior to making such changes. This is often referred to as the EISA-config, EISA Configuration Utility, or ECU.

### VESA Local Bus (VLB)

As I've said before, the system is only as good as its weakest part. With computer systems, that weakest link has been the IO subsystem for many years. CPUs got faster, but the system was still limited by slow communication with the outside world. The 32-bit buses of MCA and EISA made significant advances and increased throughput by a factor of 5 or more; however, this was not enough.

The Video Electronics Standards Association, or VESA, ( a consortium of over 120 companies) came up with an immediate solution to this problem. Although originally intended as a means of speeding up video transfer, the VESA local bus, or VL-Bus can achieve data transfer speeds that make it a worthy partner to fast 80386, 80486 CPUs, and even the Intel Pentium.

Like EISA, the VL-Bus is a hybrid. That is, it is not a complete change from ISA as MCA is. Whereas EISA interleaves the new connections with the old, the VL-Bus extends the existing slots, something EISA decided *not* to do. Because of the load put on the system by the VL-Bus, usually only three slots on the motherboard have the VL-Bus extension. The other remain just ISA, EISA, or MCA.

The reason for the three card limit is one of performance. There is the slight cost increase for adding the extra connectors and traces, however the lure of the increased performance would outweigh the cost. Alas, things are not that easy. The CPU is directly accessing the control, address, and data pins of the VL-Bus cards (that's why it's called *local*). However, unless you want to reduce the speed of the CPU, (ya, right) the CPU just can't handle more than three external loads. In practice, this means that although there are three slots, the CPU can't have more than one or two at speeds greater than 33MHz.

However, it is relatively inexpensive to change an existing ISA or EISA design into a VL-Bus. There are a few new chips, a couple of new traces on the motherboard, and two or three new connectors. There isn't even a change to the BIOS.

VL-Bus is not intended as a replacement for ISA, although MCA and EISA sell themselves as such (or a replacement for each other, depending on whose literature you read). Current technology doesn't seem to allow it. As I mentioned, you can only have one or two VL-Bus devices before you have to consider reducing your CPU speed. Therefore, you have to have some other kind of bus slots, as well.

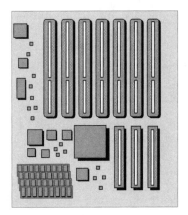

ISA or EISA
bus slots

VL-Bus
expansion
slots

**Figure 10–4**  Comparison of ISA/EISA bus slots to VLB.

In Figure 10–4 we see standard ISA/ESIA slots are the same length, with VLB slots hanging down "below" them. Because the VL-Bus slots are an extension of the existing slots, it is not necessary to leave those slots empty if you have only one or two VL-Bus cards. In fact, all the slots with the VL-Bus extension can be filled with other cards (ISA, EISA, or MCA).

Watch out for machines that are advertised as "local bus." It is true that they might be, however there is a catch. Sometimes they have an SVGA chip or hard disk controller built onto the motherboard. These are connected directly to the CPU and are therefore "local," but they do not adhere to the VL-Bus specifications.

### Peripheral Component Interconnect (PCI)

More and more machines you find on the market today are being included with PCI local buses. One advantage that PCI offers over VL-Bus is the higher performance, automatic configuration of peripheral cards and superior compatibility. A major drawback with the other bus types (ISA, EISA, MCA) is the I/O bottleneck. Local buses overcome this by accessing memory using the same signal lines as the CPU. As a result, they can operate at the full speed of the CPU as well as utilizing the 32-bit data path. Therefore, I/O performance is limited by the card and not the bus.

Although PCI is referred to as a local bus, it actually lies somewhere "above" the system bus. As a result it is often referred to as a "mezzanine bus" and has electronic "bridges" between the system bus and the expansion bus. As a result, the PCI bus can support up to five PCI devices, whereas the VL-Bus can only support two or three. In addition, the PCI bus can reach transfer speeds four times that of EISA or MCA.

Despite PCI being called a mezzanine bus, it could replace either ISA, EISA, or MCA buses; although in most cases, PCI is offered as a supplement to the existing bus type. If you look at a motherboard with PCI slots, you will see that they are completely separate from the other slots. Whereas VLB slots are extensions of the existing slots (see Figures 10–4 and 10–5).

PCI offers additional advantages over the VLB as the VLB cannot keep up with the speed of the faster CPUs, especially if there are multiple VLB devices on the system. Because PCI works together with the CPU it is much more suited to multitasking operating systems like UNIX. Whereas the CPU cannot work independently if a VLB device is running.

Like EISA and MCA, PCI boards have configuration information built into the card. As the computer is booting, the system can configure each card individually based on system resources. This configuration is done "around" existing ISA, EISA, and MCA cards on your system.

To overcome a shortcoming PCI has when transferring data, Intel (designer and chief proponent of PCI) has come up with a PCI-specific chip, set which allows data to be stored on the PCI controller, freeing the CPU to do other work. Although this may delay the *start* of the transfer, once the data flow starts, it should continue uninterrupted.

A shortcoming of PCI, (at least from SCO's perspective) is that ISA and EISA cards can be swapped for VLB cards, without any major problems. This is not so for the PCI cards. Significant changes need to be made to both the kernel and device drivers to account for the differences.

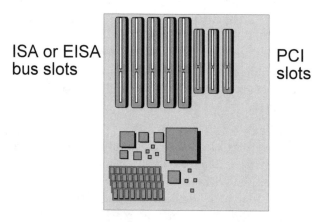

**Figure 10–5**    Comparison of ISA/EISA bus slots to PCI.

## The Small Computer Systems Interface (SCSI)

The SCSI bus is an extension of your existing bus. A controller card, called a host adapter, is placed into one of your expansion slots. A ribbon cable, containing both data and control signals then connects the host adapter to your peripheral devices.

There are several advantages to having SCSI in you system. If you have a limited number of bus slots, then the addition of a single SCSI host adapter allows you to add up to seven more devices by taking up only one slot with older SCSI systems and up to 15 devices with wide-SCSI. SCSI has higher throughput than either IDE or ESDI. SCSI also supports many more different types of devices.

There are five different types of SCSI devices. The original SCSI specification is commonly referred to as SCSI-1. The newer specification, SCSI-2 offers speed and performance increases over SCSI-1 as well as adds new commands. Fast-SCSI increases throughput to over 10MB/second. Fast-Wide SCSI provides a wider data path and throughput of up to 40MB/second and up to fifteen devices. The last type, SCSI-3 is still being developed as of this writing and will provide the same functionality as Fast-Wide SCSI as well as support longer cables and more devices.

Each SCSI device has its own controller and can send, receive, and execute SCSI commands. As long as it communicates with the host adapter using proper SCSI commands, internal data manipulation is not an issue. In fact, most SCSI hard disks have an IDE controller with a SCSI interface built onto them.

The fact that there is a standard set of SCSI commands, allows new and different kinds of devices to be added to the SCSI family with little trouble. However, IDE and ESDI are limited to disk type devices. Because the SCSI commands need to be "translated" by the device, there is a slight overhead. This is compensated for by the fact that SCSI devices are intrinsically faster than non-SCSI devices. SCSI devices also have higher data integrity than non-SCSI devices. The SCSI cable consists of fifty pins, half of which are ground. Since every pin has its own ground, it is less prone to interference, therefore it has higher data integrity.

On each SCSI host adapter there are two connectors. One is at the top of the card (opposite the bus connectors) and is used for internal devices. A flat ribbon cable is used to connect each device to the host adapter. On internal SCSI devices, there is only one connector on the device itself. Should you have external SCSI devices, there is a connector on the end of the card (where it attaches to the chassis). Here SCSI devices are daisy-chained together.

The SCSI bus needs to be *closed* in order to work correctly. By this I mean that each end of the bus must be terminated. There is usually a set of resistors (or slots for resistors) on each device. The device that is physically at either end of the SCSI bus needs to have such resistors. This is referred to as terminating the bus and the resistors are called terminating resistors.

It's fine to say that the SCSI bus needs to be terminated. However, that doesn't help in your understanding of the issue. As with other kinds of devices, SCSI devices react to commands sent to them along the cable. Unless otherwise impeded, the signals reach the end of the cable and bounce back. There are two outcomes, both of which are undesirable: either the bounced signal interferes with the valid one or the devices react to a second (unique in its mind) command. By placing a terminator at the end of the bus, the signals are "absorbed" and therefore, don't bounce back.

Figure 10–6 and Figure 10–7 show examples of how the SCSI bus should be terminated. Note that Figure 10–6 says that it is an example of "all external devices." Keep in mind that the principle is still the same for internal devices. If all the devices are internal, then the host adapter would still be terminated as well as would be the last device in the chain.

If you don't have any external devices (or only external) then the host adapter is at one end of the bus. Therefore, it too must be terminated. Many host adapters today have the ability to be terminated in software, therefore there is no need for terminating resistors (also known as resistor packs).

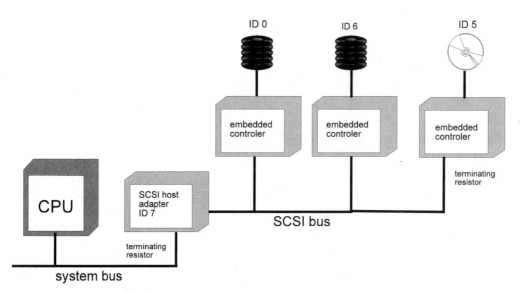

**Figure 10–6**  Example of SCSI bus with all external devices.

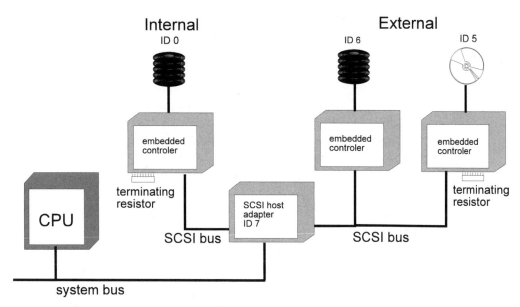

**Figure 10–7**   Example of SCSI bus with both external and internal devices.

Each SCSI device is "identified" by a unique pair of addresses. The controller address is also referred to as the SCSI ID and is usually set by jumpers or dip switches on the device itself. Keep in mind that the ID is something that is set on the devices itself and is *not* related to location on the bus. Note that in Figure 10–6, on page 446, the SCSI ID of the devices are ordered ID 0, 6, and 5.

Care should be taken when setting the SCSI ID. It is important that you are sure of what the setting is, otherwise the system will not be able to talk to the device. OpenServer supports SCSI host adapters with multiple buses, therefore this is a triplet of numbers rather than a pair. This increases the possibility of mistakes by fifty percent.

This concept seems pretty obvious, but some people don't make sure. They make *assumptions* about what they see on the device as to how the ID is set and do not fully understand what it means. For example, I have an Archive 5150 SCSI tape drive. On the back are three jumpers, labeled 0, 1, and 2.

I have had customers call in with similar hardware with their SCSI tape drive set at 2. After running `mkdev tape` and rebooting, they still cannot access the tape drive. Nothing else is set at ID 2, so there are no conflicts. The system can access other devices on the SCSI bus, so the host adapter is probably okay. Different SCSI devices can be plugged into the same spot on the SCSI cable, so it's not the cable. The SCSI bus is terminated correctly, so that's not the problem.

Rather than simply giving up and saying that it was a hardware problem, I suggested that the customer change the SCSI ID to 3 or 4 to see if that would make a difference. Well, he couldn't. The jumpers on the back only allow him to change the SCSI ID to 0, 1, or 2. Then the problem dawned on me. The jumpers in the back are in binary! In order to set the ID to 2, the jumper needs to be on jumper 1 and *not* jumper 2. Once we switched it to jumper 1 and rebooted, all was well. (Note: I had this customer *before* I bought the Archive tape drive. Went I got my drive home and wanted to check the SCSI ID, I saw only three jumpers. I then did something that would appall most users: I read the manual! Sure enough, it explained that the jumpers for the SCSI ID were binary.)

An additional problem to this whole SCSI ID business is that manufacturers are not consistent. Some might label the jumpers (or switches) 0, 1, and 2. Others label them 1, 2, and 4. Still others label them ID0, ID1, and ID2. I have even seen some with a dial on them with eight settings, which makes configuration a lot easier. The key is that no matter how they are labeled, three pins or switches is binary and their values are added to give you the SCSI ID.

Let's look at Figure 10–8. This represents the jumper settings on a SCSI device. In the first example, none of the jumpers are set, so the SCSI ID is 0. In the second example, the jumper labeled 1 is set. This is $2^1$ or 2, so the ID here is 2. In the last example, the jumpers labeled 2 and 0 are set. This is $2^2 + 2^0 = 4 + 1$ or 5.

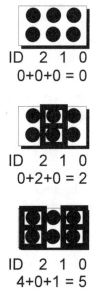

**Figure 10–8**    Examples of binary for SCSI IDs.

On an AT bus, the number of devices added is limited only by the number of slots (the AT bus is limited in how far the slot can be away from the CPU and therefore is limited in the number of slots). However, on a SCSI bus, there can be only seven devices in addition to the host adapter. Whereas devices on the AT bus are distinguished by their base address, devices on the SCSI bus are distinguished by their ID number.

ID numbers range from 0–7 and unlike base addresses, the higher the ID the higher the priority. Therefore, the ID of the host adapter should always be a 7. Since it manages all the other devices, it should have the highest priority. On the newer Wide-SCSI buses, there can be up to fifteen devices, plus the host adapter, with SCSI Ids from 0–15.

Now back to our story . . .

The device address is known as the logical unit number (LUN). On devices with embedded controllers, such has hard disks, the LUN is always 0. All the SCSI devices directly supported by SCO UNIX have embedded controllers. Therefore, you are not likely to see devices set at LUNs other than 0.

In theory, a single-channel SCSI host adapter can support fifty-six devices. There are devices called bridge adapters that connect devices without embedded controllers to the SCSI bus. Devices attached to the bridge adapter have LUNs between 0–7. If there are seven bridge adapters, each with eight LUNs (relating to eight devices), there are fifth-six total devices possible.

The original SCSI-1 spec, only defined the connection to hard disks. The SCSI-2 spec has extended this to such devices like CD-ROMS, tape drives, scanners, and printers. Provided these devices all adhere to the SCSI-2 standard they can be mixed and matched even with older SCSI-1 hard disks.

One common problem with external SCSI devices is the fact that the power supply is external as well. If you are booting your system with the power to that external device turned off, once the kernel gets past the initialization routines for that device (the hardware screen) it can no longer recognize that device. The only solution is to reboot. To prevent this problem, it is a good idea to have all your SCSI devices internal. (This doesn't help for scanners and printer, but since SCO doesn't yet have drivers for them, it's a mute point.)

## Memory

### RAM

There are several ways a computer stores the data it works with. Both are often referred to as memory. Long-term memory, the kind that remains in the system even if there is no power, is called nonvolatile memory and exists in such places as on hard disks or floppies. This is often referred to as secondary storage. Short-term, or volatile memory is stored in memory chips, called RAM, for Random-Access Memory. This is often referred to as primary storage.

There is a third class of memory that is often ignored, or at least not thought of often. This is memory that exists in hardware on the system, but does *not* disappear when power is turned off. This is called ROM, or Read-Only Memory.

We need to clarify one thing before we go on. Read-only memory is as it says, read-only. For the most part it cannot be written to. However, like Random-Access Memory the locations within it can be accessed in a "random" order, that is, at the discretion of the programmer. Also read-only memory isn't always read-only, but that's a different story that goes beyond this book.

The best way of referring to memory to keep things clear (at least the best way in my opinion) is to refer to the memory we traditionally call RAM as "main" memory. This is where our programs and the operating system actually reside.

There are two broad classes of memory: dynamic RAM or DRAM (read Dee-Ram) and static RAM or SRAM (read Es-Ram). DRAM is composed of tiny capacitors that can hold their charge only a short while before they require a "boost." SRAM is static because it does not require an extra power supply to keep its charge. As a result of the way it works internally, SRAM is faster and more expensive than DRAM. Because of the cost, the RAM that composes main memory is typically DRAM.

DRAM chips hold memory in ranges from 64k up to 16Mb and more. In older systems, individual DRAM chips are laid out in parallel rows called banks. The chips themselves were called DIPPs, for Dual In-Line Pin Package. These look like your average, run-of-the-mill computer chip, with two rows of parallel pins, one on each side of the chip. If memory ever went bad in one of these banks, it was usually necessary to replace (or test) dozens of individual chips. Since the maximum for most of these chips was 256 kilobits (32Kb), it took 32 of them for each megabyte!

On newer systems, the DIPP chips have been replaced by Single In-Line Memory Modules, or SIMMs. Technological advances have decreased the size considerably. Whereas a few years ago you needed an area the size of a standard piece of binder paper to hold just a few megabytes, today's SIMMs can squish twice that much into an area the size of a stick of gum.

SIMMs come in powers of 2 (1, 2, 4, 8, etc.) megabytes and are generally arranged in banks of four or eight. Because of the way the memory is accessed, you sometimes cannot mix sizes. That is, if you have four 2Mb SIMMs, you cannot simply add an 8Mb SIMM to get up to 16Mb. Bare this in mind when ordering your system or ordering more memory. You should first check the documentation that came with the motherboard or the manufacturer.

Many hardware salespeople are not aware of this distinction. Therefore, if you order a system with 8 MB that's "expandable" to 128Mb, you may be in for a big surprise. True there are eight slots that can contain 16Mb each. However, if the vendor fills all eight slots with 1 Mb SIMMs to give you your 8 MB, you may have to throw *everything* out if you ever want to increase your RAM.

However, this is not always the case. My motherboard has some strange configurations. The memory slots on my motherboard consist of two banks of four slots each (this is typical of many machines). Originally, I had one bank completely full with four 4Mb SIMMs. When I installed OpenServer this was barely enough. Once I decided to start X Windows and Wabi, this was much too little. I could have increased this by 1Mb by filling the first bank with four 256K SIMMs and moving the four 4Mb SIMMs to the second bank. However, if I wanted to move up to 20Mb, I could use 1Mb instead of 256K. So, here is one example where everything does *not* have to match. In the end, I added four 4 MB SIMMs to bring my total up to 32 MB. The moral of the story: Read the manual!

Another issue that needs to be considered with SIMMs is that the motherboard design may require you to put in memory in either multiples of two or multiples of four. The reason for this is the way the motherboard accesses that memory. Potentially, a 32-bit machine could read a byte from four SIMMs at once, essentially reading the full 32 bytes in one read. Keep in mind that the 32 bits are probably not being read simultaneously. However, being able to read them in succession is faster that reading one bank and then waiting for it to reset.

Even so, this requires special circuitry for each of the slots, called address decode logic. The address decode logic receives a memory address from the CPU and determines which SIMM it's in and where it is located on the SIMM. In other words it decodes the address to determine which SIMM is needed for a particular physical address.

This extra circuitry makes the machine more expensive as this is not just an issue with the memory, but rather the motherboard design as well. Accessing memory in this fashion is called "page mode" as the memory is broken up into sets of bytes, or pages. Because the address decode logic is designed to access memory in only one way, the memory that is installed must fit the way it is read. For example, my motherboard requires each bank to be either completely filled or completely empty. Now, this requires a little bit of explanation.

As I mentioned earlier, DRAM consists of little capacitors for each bit of information. If the capacitor is charged, then the bit is 1. If there is no charge, the bit is 0. Capacitors have a tendency to drain over time, and for capacitors this small, that time is *very* short. Therefore, they must be regularly (or dynamically) recharged.

When a memory location is read, there must be some way of determining if there is a charge in the capacitor or not. The only way of doing that is to discharge the capacitor. If it can be discharged, it means there was a charge to begin with and the system knows the bit was a 1. Once discharged, internal circuitry recharges the capacitor.

Now, assume the system wanted to read two consecutive bytes from a single SIMM. Since there is no practical way for the address decode logic to tell that the second read is not just a reread of the first byte, the system must wait until the first byte has recharged itself. Only then can the second byte be read.

By taking advantage of the fact that programs run sequentially and rarely read the same byte more than once at any given time, the memory subsystem can interleave its reads. That is, while the first bank is recharging, it can be reading from the second, while the second is recharging, it can be reading from the third and so on. Since subsequent reads must wait until previous one have completed, this method is obviously not as fast as simultaneous reads. This is referred to as "interleaved" or "banked" memory.

Since all of these issues are motherboard dependent, it is best to check the hardware documentation when changing or adding memory. Additionally, settings, or jumpers, may need to be adjusted on the motherboard to tell it how much RAM you have and in what configuration.

Another issue that addresses speed is the physical layout of the SIMM. SIMMs are often described as being arranged in a "by-9" or "by-36" configuration. This refers to the number of bits that are immediately accessible. So, in a "by-9" configuration 9 bits are immediately accessible with one used for parity. In a "by-36" configuration, 36 bits are available with four bits for parity (1 for each 8 bits). The "by-9" configuration come on SIMMs with 30 pins, whereas the "by-36" come on SIMMs with 72 pins. The 72-pin SIMMs can read 32-bits *simultaneously*. So, they are even faster than 30-pin SIMMs at the same speed.

There are also different physical sizes for the SIMM. The SIMMs with 30 pins are slightly smaller than those with 72 pins. The larger, 72-pin variety are called PS/2 SIMMs as they are used in IBM's PS/2 machines. Aside from being slightly larger, these have a notch in the center so it is physically impossible to mix up the two. In both cases there is a notch on one end. This fits into a key in the slot on the motherboard, which makes putting the SIMM in backwards almost impossible (see Figure 10–9).

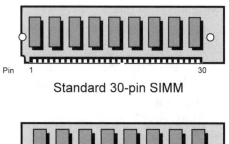

Standard 30-pin SIMM

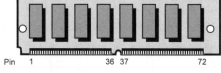

72-pin PS/2 SIMM

**Figure 10–9**    Comparison of 30-pin and 72-pin SIMMs.

SIMMs come in several different speeds, the most common today are between 60-80 nanoseconds. Although there is usually no harm in mixing speeds, there is little to be gained. However, I want to emphasize the word *usually*. Mixing speeds has been known to cause panics. Therefore, if you mix speeds, it is best keep all the SIMMS within a single bank at a single speed. If your machine does not have multiple banks, then it is best not to mix speeds. Even if you do, remember that the system is only as fast as its slowest component.

### Cache Memory

Based on the principle of spatial locality a program is more likely to be spending its time executing code around the same set of instructions. This is demonstrated by the fact that tests have shown that most programs spend 80% of their time executing 20% of their code. Cache memory takes advantage of that.

Cache memory, or sometimes just cache, is a small set of very high-speed memory. Typically it uses SRAM which can be up to ten times more expensive than DRAM, which usually makes it prohibitive for anything other than cache.

When the IBM PC first came out, DRAM was fast enough to keep up with even the fastest processor. However, as CPU technology increased, so did its speed. Soon, the CPU began to outrun its memory. The advances in CPU technology could not be utilized unless the system was filled with the more expensive, faster SRAM.

The solution to this was a compromise. Using the locality principle, manufacturers of fast 386 and 486 machines began including a set of cache memory consisting of SRAM, but still populated main memory with the slower, less expensive DRAM.

To better understand the advantages of this scheme, let's cover the principle of locality in a little more detail. In a computer program we deal with two types of locality: temporal (time) and spatial (space). Since programs tend to run in loops (repeating the same instructions over and over), the same set of instructions need to be read over and over. The longer a set of instructions is in memory without being used, the less likely it is to be used again. This is the principle of temporal locality. Cache memory allows us to keep those regularly used instructions "closer" to the CPU, making access to them much faster.

Spatial locality is the relationship between consecutively executed instructions. We just said that a program spends more of its time executing the same set of instructions. Therefore, in all likelihood, the next instruction the program will be executing lies in the next memory location. By filling cache with more than just one instruction at a time, the principle of spatial locality can be taken advantage of.

Is there really such a major advantage to cache memory? Cache performance is evaluated in terms of *cache hits*. A hit occurs when the CPU requests a memory location and it is already in cache (it does not have to go to main memory to get it). Since most programs run in loops (including the OS), the principle of locality results in a hit ratio of 85%–95%. Not bad!

On most 486 machines, two levels of cache are used. They are called (logically) first level cache and second level cache. First level cache is internal to the CPU. Although nothing (other than cost) prevents it from being any larger, Intel has limited the first level cache in the 486 to 8k (see Figure 10–10).

Second level cache is the kind that you buy extra with your machine. This is often part of the ad you see in the paper and is usually what people are talking about when they say how much cache is in their system. This kind of cache is external to the CPU and can be increased at any time, whereas first level cache is an integral part of the CPU and the only way to get more is to buy a different CPU.

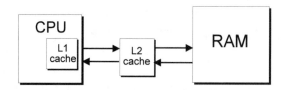

**Figure 10–10**    Level-1 and Level-2 caches.

Typical sizes of second level cache range from 64K–256K. This is usually in increments of 64K.

A major problem exists when dealing with cache memory and that is the issue of consistency. What happens when main memory is updated and cache is not? What happens when cache is updated and main memory is not? This is where the cache's *write policy* comes in.

The write policy determines if and when the contents of the cache are written back to memory. Write-Through cache simply writes the data through the cache directly into memory. This slows things down on writes, but you are assured that the data is consistent. Buffered Write-Through is a slight modification of this, where data is collected and everything is written at once. Write-Back improves cache performance by only writing to main memory when necessary. Write-Dirty is when it writes to main memory only when it has been modified.

Cache (or main memory for that matter) is referred to as "dirty" when it is written to. Unfortunately, the system has no way of telling whether anything has changed, just that it is being written to. Therefore, it is possible, but not likely, that a block of cache is written back to memory even if it is not "really" dirty.

Another aspect of cache is its organization. Without going into detail (that would take most of a chapter itself) we can generalize by saying that there are four different types of cache organizations.

The first kind is fully associative. This means that every entry in the cache has a slot in the "cache directory" indicating where it came from in memory. Usually these are not individual bytes, but chunks of four bytes or more. Since each "slot" in the cache has a separate directory slot, any location in RAM can be placed anywhere in the cache. This is the simplest scheme, but also the slowest since each cache directory entry must be searched until a match (if any) is found. Therefore, this kind of cache is often limited to just 4Kb.

*Direct-mapped* or *1-way set associative cache* requires that only a single directory entry be searched. This speeds up access time considerably. The location in the cache is related to the location in memory and is usually based on blocks of memory equal to the size of the cache. For example, if the cache could hold 4K 32-bit (4-byte) entries, then the block that each entry is associated with is also 4K × 32 bits. The first 32 bits in each block are read into the first slot of the cache. The second 32 bits in each block are read into the second slot, and so on. The size of each entry, or line, usually ranges from 4 to 16 bytes.

There is a mechanism called a tag, to tell us which of the blocks this came from. Also, because of the very nature of this method, the cache cannot hold data from multiple blocks for the same offset. If, for example, slot 1 was already filled with the data from block 1 and a program wanted to read the data at the same location from block 2, the data in the cache would be overwritten. Therefore, the shortcoming in this scheme is when data is read at intervals that are the size of these blocks, the cache gets constantly overwritten. Keep in mind that this does not occur too often due to the principle of spatial locality.

The third type is an extension of the 1-way set associative cache and is called the *2-way set associative*. Here, there are two entries per slot. Again, data can end up in only a particular slot but there are two places to go within that slot. Granted, the system is slowed a little by having to look at the tags for both slots. However, this scheme allows data at the same offset from multiple blocks to be in the cache at the same time. This is also extended to 4-way set associative cache. In fact, the cache internal to 486 and Pentium has a 4-way set associative cache.

Although this is interesting stuff (at least to me), you may be asking yourself, "Why is this memory stuff important as a system administrator?" Well, first, knowing about the differences in RAM (main memory) can aide you in making decisions about your upgrade. Also, as I mentioned earlier, it may be necessary to set switches on the motherboard if you change memory configuration.

Knowledge about cache memory is also important for the same reason, but also because this may be adjustable by you. On many machines, the write policy can be adjusted through the CMOS. For example, on my machine I have a choice of Write-Back, Write-Through, and Write-Dirty. Depending on the applications you are running, you may want to change this to improve performance.

### Odd and Ends

In most memory today, an extra bit is added for each byte. This is a parity bit. Parity is a simple way of *detecting* errors within a memory chip (among other things). If there is an odd number of bits set, the parity bit will be set to make the total number of bits set an even number. Most memory uses even parity. For example, if three bits are set, the parity bit will also be set to make the total set bits equal four.

When data is written, the number of set bits is calculated and the parity bit is set accordingly. When the data is read, the parity bit is also read. If the total number of bits set is even, all is well. However, if there is an odd number of data bits set and the parity bit is not set or if there is an even number of data bits set and the parity bit is set, then a parity error has occurred.

When a parity error occurs in memory, the state of the system is uncertain. In order to prevent any further problems, the parity checking logic generates a Non-Maskable Interrupt (NMI) and the CPU immediately jumps to special codes called the NMI service routine.

When SCO UNIX is interrupted with an NMI as the result of a parity error, it too realizes things are not good and the system panics. The panic causes the system to stop everything and shutdown. Certain machines support ECC RAM and correct parity problems before killing your system.

Even as I wrote this section, the computer industry was shifting away from the old SIMMs toward extended data out RAM or EDORAM. Although as of this writing (May 1996), EDORAM is somewhat more expensive than SIMMS, it is expected that the demand for EDORAM will be such that the price difference will disappear.

The principle behind EDORAM is an extension of the fast page mode (FPM) RAM. With FPM RAM, you rely on the fact that memory is generally read sequentially. Since you don't "really" need to wait for each memory location to recharge itself, you can read the next location without waiting. Since you have to wait until the signal is stabilized, there is still some wait. However, this is much less than waiting for the memory to recharge. At CPU speeds greater than 33 Mhz, the CPU is requesting memory faster than memory can deliver it and the CPU must wait.

EDORAM works by "latching" the memory, which means that secondary memory cells are added. These detect the data being out from memory and store the signals so the CPU can retrieve it. This works at bus speeds of 66Mhz. This process can be sped up by including "burst" EDORAM. This extends the locality principle even further. Since we are going to read sequentially, why don't we anticipate the processor and read more than just that single location? In some cases the system will read 128 bits at once.

Keep in mind, however, you cannot just install EDORAM in your machine and expect it to work. You need a special chip-set on your motherboard. One such chip-set is the Intel Triton chip-set.

## The Central Processing Unit

Sometimes you get people who just don't understand. At first, I thought that they "didn't have a clue," but that was not really the problem. They had a clue, but a single clue doesn't solve a crime, nor does it help you run an SCO UNIX system.

It seems like a simple thing. You use `doscp` to copy a program from a DOS diskette onto an SCO UNIX system. In all likelihood the permissions are already set to be executable. So you type in the name of the program and press enter. Nothing happens or you get an error about incorrect format. Hmmm. The software says it runs on a 386 or higher (which you have), a VGA monitor (which you have), and at least 2 Mb of hard disk space (which you have). Why doesn't it work?

Yes, this is a true story. A customer called in saying that our operating system (SCO UNIX) was broken. This customer had a program that worked fine on his DOS PC at home. It too, was a 386 so there shouldn't be a problem right? Unfortunately, he was wrong. Granted that in both cases the CPU is reading machine instructions and executing them. In fact, they are the same machine instructions. They have to be.

The problem is comparable to German and English. Although both use (basically) the same alphabet, words (sets of characters) written in German are not understandable by someone reading them as English and vice versa. Sets of machine instructions that were designed to be interpreted under DOS are not going to be understood under SCO UNIX. (Actually, the problem is a little more complicated, but you get the basic idea.)

Just like your brain has be told (taught) the difference between German and English, a computer needs to be told the difference between DOS and UNIX programs.

In this section we talk about the CPU; the brains of the outfit. It is perfectly reasonable for users and administrators alike to have no understanding of what the CPU is doing internally. However, a basic knowledge of some of the key issues is important, in order to completely understand some of the issues I get into elsewhere.

It's like trying to tune-up your car. Now you don't really need to know how oxygen mixes with the gasoline in order to be able to adjust the carburetor. However, knowing about it makes adjusting the carburetor that much easier.

I don't go into details about the instruction cycle of the CPU; that is, how it gets and executes instructions. While I like things like that and would love to talk about them, it isn't really necessary to understand what we need to talk about here. Instead we are going to talk mostly about how the CPU enables the operating system to create a scheme whereby many programs can be in memory simultaneously. These are the concepts of paging and multitasking.

Although it is an interesting subject, the ancient history of microprocessors is not really important to the issues at hand. It might be nice to learn how the young PC grew from a small, budding 4-bit system to the gigantic, strapping 64-bit Pentium. However, there are many books that covered this subject and unfortunately I don't have the space. Besides, you can read it elsewhere, and SCO UNIX only runs on Intel 80386 (or 100% compatible clones) and higher processors.

So, instead of setting the Way-Back machine to Charles Babbage and his Analytic Engine, we leap ahead to 1985 to the introduction of the Intel 80386. Even compared to its immediate predecessor, the 80286, the 80386 (386 for short) was a powerhouse. Not only could it handle twice the amount of data at once (now 32 bits), its speed rapidly increased well beyond that of the 286.

New advances were added to increase the 386's power. Internal registers were added as well as an increase in size. Built into the 386 was the concept of virtual memory. This was a way to make it appear as if there was much more memory on the system than there actually was. This substantially increased the system efficiency. Another major advance was the inclusion of a 16-byte, pre-fetch cache. With this, the CPU would load instructions before it actually processed them, thereby, speeding things up even more. Then the most obvious speed increase came by increasing the speed of the processor from 8Mhz to 16Mhz.

Although the 386 had major advantages over its predecessors, at first, its cost seemed relatively prohibitive. In order to allow users access to the multitasking capability and still make the chip fit within their customers' budgets, Intel made an interesting compromise. By making a new chip where the interface to the bus was 16 bits instead of 32 bits, Intel made their chip a fair bit cheaper.

Internally this new chip, designated the 80386SX, is identical to the standard 386. All the registers are there and it is the full 32 bits wide. However, data and instructions are accessed 16 bits at a time, therefore requiring two bus accesses to fill the registers. Despite this short-coming, the 80386SX is still faster than the 286.

Perhaps the most significant advance of the 386 for SCO is its paging abilities. We talked a little about paging in the section on operating system basics so you already have a general idea of what it's about. We will also go into more details about paging in the section on the kernel. However, we need to talk about it a littler here to fully understand the power that the 386 has given us and to see how the CPU helps the OS.

SCO has a product (SCO XENIX) that does run on 286s. In fact, there was even a version of SCO XENIX that ran on the 8086. Because SCO UNIX was first released for the 386, we are not going to go into more details about the 286 nor the differences between the 286 and 386. Instead, I will just describe the CPU used by SCO UNIX as sort of an abstract entity. In addition, since most of what I will be talking about is valid for the 486 and Pentium as well as the 386, I will simply call it "the CPU" instead of 386, 486, or Pentium.

(Note: SCO will also run on non-Intel CPUs. However, the issues we are going to talk about are all common to Intel-based or Intel-derived CPUs.)

I need to take a side-step here for a minute. On PC buses, multiple things are happening at once. The CPU is busily processing while much of the hardware is being accessed via DMA. Although these are multiple tasks that are occurring simultaneously on the system, this is not what is referred to by multitasking.

When we talk about multitasking we are referring to multiple processes being in memory at the same time. Because the time it takes the computer to switch between these processes, or tasks, is much faster than the human brain can recognize, it appears as if they are running simultaneously. In reality, what is happening is that each process gets to use the CPU and other system resources for a brief time and then it's someone else's turn.

As it runs, the process could use any part of the system memory it needed. The problem with this is that a portion of RAM that one process wants may already contain code from another process. Rather than allowing each process to access any part of memory it wants, protections are needed to keep one program from overwriting another one. This protection is built-in as part of the CPU and is called, quite logically, "protected mode." Without it, SCO UNIX could not function.

Note, however, that just because the CPU is in protected mode, does not necessarily mean that the protections are being utilized. It simply means that the operating system can take advantage of the built in abilities if it wants.

Although this capability is built into the CPU, it is not the default mode. Instead, the CPU starts up in what I like to call "DOS compatibility mode." However, the correct term is "real mode." Real mode is a real danger to an operating system like UNIX. In this mode, there are no protections (makes sense since protections exist in protected mode). A process running in real mode has complete control over the entire system and can do anything it wants. Therefore, trying to run a multi-user system on a real mode system would be a nightmare. All the protections would have to be built into the process as the operating system couldn't prevent a process from doing what it wanted.

Also built in is a third mode. This is called "virtual mode." In virtual mode, the CPU behaves to a limited degree like it is in real mode. However, when a process attempts to directly access registers or hardware, the instruction is caught, or trapped, and the operating system is allowed to take over. Let's get back to protected mode as this is what makes multitasking possible.

When in protected mode, the CPU can use virtual memory. As I mentioned, this is a way to trick the system into thinking there is more memory than there really is. There are two ways of doing this. The first is called swapping. Here, the entire process is loaded into memory. It is allowed to run its course for a certain amount of time. When its turn is over, another process is allowed to run. What happens when there is not enough room for both process to be in memory at the same time? The only solution is that the first process is copied out to a special part of the hard disk called the swap space or swap device. Then, the next process is loaded into memory and allowed its turn.

Because it takes such a large portion of the system resources to swap processes in and out of memory, this can be very inefficient. Especially when you have a lot of processes running. Let's take this a step further, what happens if there are too many processes and the system spends all of its time swapping? Not good.

In order to avoid this problem, a mechanism was devised whereby only those parts of the process that are needed are in memory. As it goes about its business, a program may only need to access a small portion of its code. In fact, empirical tests show that a program spends 80% of its time executing 20% of its code. So why bother bringing in those parts that aren't being used? Why not wait and see if they are used?

To make things more efficient, only those parts of the program that are needed (or expected to be needed) are brought into memory. Rather than accessing memory in random units, it is divided into 4K chunks, called pages. Although there is nothing magic about 4K, per se, this value is easily manipulated. In the CPU, data is referenced in 32-bit (4 byte) chunks and 1K (1024) of them is a page (4096). Later you will see how this helps things work out.

As I mentioned, only that part of the process currently being used needs to be in memory. When the process wants to read something that is not currently in RAM, it needs to go out to the hard disk to pull in the other parts of the process; that is, it goes out and reads in new pages. This process is called "paging." When the process attempts to read from a part of the process that is not in physical memory, a "page fault" occurs.

One thing we must bear in mind is the fact that a process can jump around a lot. Functions are called which send the process off somewhere completely different. It is possible, likely for that matter, that the page containing the memory location to where the process needs to jump to is not currently in memory. Since it is trying to read a part of the process not in physical memory, this too is called a page fault. As memory fills up, pages that haven't been used in some time are replaced by new ones. (Much more on this whole business later.)

Assume that a process has just made a call to a function somewhere else in the code, and the page needed is brought into memory. Now there are two pages of the process from completely different parts of the code. Should the process take another jump or return from the function, it needs to know if where it is going is in memory or not. The operating system could keep track of this, however, it doesn't need to. The CPU will keep track for it.

Stop here for a minute! This is not entirely true. The OS must first set up the structures that the CPU uses. However, it is the CPU that uses these structures to determine if a section of a program is in memory or not. Although not part of the CPU, but rather RAM, the CPU administers the RAM utilization through page tables. These tables are simply tables of pages. In other words, they are memory locations in which other memory locations are stored.

Confused? I was at first, so let's look at this concept another way. Each running process has a certain part of its code currently in memory. The system uses these page tables to keep track of what is currently in memory and where it is physically located. To limit the amount the CPU has to work, each of these page tables is only 4K or one page in size. Since each contains a set of 32-bit addresses, a page table can contain only 1024 entries.

Although this would imply that a process can only have 4K*1024 or 4Mb loaded at a time, there is more to it. Page tables are grouped into page directories. Like the page table, the entries in a page directory point to memory locations. However, rather than pointing to a part of the process, page directories point to page tables. Again, to reduce the work of the CPU, a page directory is only one page. Since each entry in the page directory points to a page, this means that a process can only have 1024 page tables.

Is this enough? Let's see. A page is 4K or 4096 bytes, which is $2^{12}$. Each page table can refer to 1024 pages: this is $2^{10}$. Each page directory can refer to 1024 page tables: this is also $2^{10}$. Lets multiply this:

```
page_size * pages_in_page_table * page_tables_in_page_directory
```

or

$$(2^{12}) * (2^{10}) * (2^{10}) = 2^{32}$$

Since the CPU is only capable of accessing $2^{32}$ bytes, this scheme allows access to every possible memory address that the system can generate. Are you still with me?

Inside of the CPU is a register called the Control Register 0 or CR0 for short. There is a single bit in the register that turns on this paging mechanism. If turned on, any memory reference that the CPU gets is interpreted as a combination of page directories, page tables, and offsets, rather than an absolute, linear address.

Built into the CPU is a special unit that is responsible to make the translation from the virtual address of the process to physical pages in memory. It's called (what else?) the Paging Unit. To understand more about the work the Paging Unit saves the operating system or other parts of the CPU, let's see how the address is translated.

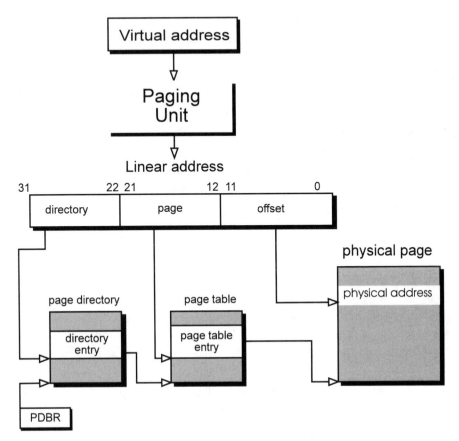

**Figure 10–11** Translation of virtual to physical address.

When paging is turned on, the Paging Unit receives a 32-bit value that represents a virtual memory location within a process. The Paging Unit takes theses values and translates them as shown in Figure 10–11. At the top we see that the virtual address is handed to the Paging Unit which converts it to a linear address. This is *not* the physical address in memory. As you see, the 32-bit linear address is broken down into three components. The first 10 bits (22–31) are the offset into the page directory. The location in memory of the page directory is determined by the Page Directory Base Register (PDBR).

The page directory entry contains 4 bits which point to a specific page table. The entry in the page table, as you see, is determined by bits 12–21. Here again, we have 10 bits, which means each entry is 32 bits. These 32 bits point to a specific page in *physical* memory. Which byte we are referencing in physical memory is determined by the offset portion of the linear address, which is bits 0–11. These twelve bits represent the 4096 (4K) bytes in each physical page.

Keep in mind a couple of things. First, page tables and page directories are not part of the CPU—they can't be. If a page directory was full, it would contain 1024 references to 4K chunks of memory. You would need 4Mb just for the page tables! Since this would create a CPU hundreds of times larger than it is, page tables and directories are stored in RAM.

Next, page tables and page directories are abstract concepts that the CPU knows how to utilize. They occupy physical RAM, and operating systems such as SCO UNIX know how to switch on this capability within the CPU. All the CPU is doing is the "translation" work. When it starts, SCO UNIX turns on this capability and sets up all the structures. The structures are then handed off to the CPU, where the Paging Unit does the work.

As I just said, a process with all of its page directory entries full would require 4Mb just for the page tables. However, this would imply that the entire process is somewhere in memory. Since each of the page table entries points to physical pages in RAM, you would need 16Gb of RAM. I would not mind having that much RAM, but it is a bit costly and even if I had 16Mb SIMMs I would need 1000 of them.

Like pages of the process, it's possible that a linear address passed to the Paging Unit would translate to a page table or even a page directory that was not in memory. Since the system is trying to access a page (which contains a page table and is not part of the process) that is not in memory, a page fault occurs and the system must go get that page.

Since page tables and the page directory are not really part of the process, but are important only to the operating system, a page fault causes these structures to get *created* rather than read in from the hard disk or elsewhere. In fact, as the process is starting up, all is without form and void—no pages, no page tables, and no page directory.

The system accesses a memory location as it starts the process. The system translates the address as we described above and tries to read the page directory. It's not there. A page fault occurs and the page directory must be created. Now that the directory is there, the system finds the entry that points to the page table. Since no page tables exist, the slot is empty and another page fault occurs. So, the system needs to create a page table. The entry in the page table for the physical page is found to be empty, therefore another page fault occurs. Finally, the system can read in the page that was referenced in the first place.

Now this whole process sounds a bit cumbersome, but bear in mind that this amount of page faulting only occurs as the process is being started. Once the table is created for a given process, it won't page fault again on that table. Based on the principle of locality, the page tables will hold enough entries for a while, unless of course the process goes bouncing around a lot.

The potential for bouncing around brings up an interesting aspect of page tables. Since page tables translate to physical RAM in the same way all the time, virtual addresses in the same area of the process end up in the same page tables. Therefore, page tables get filled up since the process is more likely to execute code in the same part of a process than elsewhere (this is spatial locality).

There is quite a lot there, huh? Well, don't get up yet. We're not finished. There are a few issues that we haven't addressed.

First, I often refer to page tables and *the* page directory. Each process has a single page directory (it doesn't need anymore). Although the CPU supports multiple page directories, there is only one for the *entire* system. When a process needs to be switched out, the entries in the page directory for the old process are overwritten by the ones for the new process. The location of the page directory in memory is maintained in the Control Register 3 (CR3) in the CPU.

There is something here that bothered me in the beginning and may bother you. As I described above, each time a memory reference is made, the CPU has to look at the page directory, then a page table, and then calculate the physical address. This means that for *every* memory reference, the CPU has to make two more references just to find out where the next instruction or data is coming from. I thought that this was ridiculous.

Well, so did the designers of the CPU. They have included a functional unit called the Translation Lookaside Buffer, or TLB. The TLB contains thirty-two entries and like the internal and external caches point to sets of instructions, the TLB points to pages. If a page that is being looked for is in the TLB, a TLB hit occurs (just like a cache hit). As a result of the principle of spatial locality, there is a 98% hit rate using the TLB.

When you think about it, this makes a lot of sense. The CPU does not just execute one instruction for a program and then switch to something else. It executes hundreds or even thousands before it is someone else's turn. If each page contains 1024 instructions and the CPU executes 1000 before it's someone else's turn, all 1000 will most likely be in the same page; therefore, they are all TLB hits.

Now, let's take a closer look at the page table entries themselves. Each is a 32-bit value, pointing to a 4K location in RAM. Since it is pointing to an area of memory larger than a byte, it does not need all of the 32 bits to do it. Therefore, it has some bits left over. Since the page table entry points to an area that has $2^{20}$ bytes (4096 bytes = 1 page), there are 12 bits, that it doesn't need. These are the low order 12 bits, and the CPU uses them for other purposes related to that page. A few of them are unused and the operating system can, and does, use them for its own purposes. There are also a couple reserved by Intel and should not be used.

One of the bits, the 0th bit, is the present bit. If this bit is set, the CPU knows that the page being referenced is in memory. If not set, the page is not in memory, and if the CPU tries to access it a page fault occurs. Also, if this is not set, none of the other bits have any meaning. (How can we talk about something that's not there?)

An important bit is the accessed bit. Should a page be accessed for either read or write, the CPU sets this bit. Since the page table entry is never filled in until the page is being accessed, this seems a bit redundant. If that was all there was to it, you'd be right. However, there's more.

At regular intervals the operating system goes around and clears the access bit. If a particular page is never used again, the system is free to reuse that physical page if memory gets short. When that happens all that needs to get done is to clear the present bit and the page is considered "invalid."

Another bit used to determine how a page is accessed is the dirty bit. If a page has been written to, it is considered dirty. Before the system can make a dirty page available, it must make sure that whatever was in that page is written to disk. Otherwise the data is inconsistent.

Finally, we get to the point of all this protected mode stuff. The protection in protected mode essentially boils down to two bits in the page table entry. One bit, the user/supervisor bit, determines who has access to a particular page. If the CPU itself is running at user level, then it only has access to user level pages. If the CPU is at supervisor level it is has access to all pages.

I need to say here that this is the maximum access a process can have. There are other protections that may prevent a user level or even a supervisor-level process from even getting this far; however, these are implemented at a higher level.

The other bit in this pair is the read/write bit. As the name implies, this determines whether a page can be written to or not. This is a single bit, so it is really just an on-off switch. If the page is there you have the right to read it if you can. (That is, either you are a supervisor-level process or the page is a user page.) If the write ability is turned off, you can't write to it, even as a supervisor.

If you have a 386 CPU, then all is well. If you have a 486 and decide to use one of those bits that I told you were reserved by Intel you will run into trouble. Two of these bits that were not defined in the 386 are now defined in the 486. These are Page Write Through (PWT) and the Page Cache Disable (PCD).

PWT determines the write policy (see the section on RAM) for external cache in regard to this page. If set, then this page has a Write-Through policy. If clear, a Write-Back policy is allowed.

PCD decides whether this page can be cached at all. If clear, this page cannot be cached. If set, then caching is allowed. Note that I said "allowed." Having this bit set does not mean that the page will be cached. There are other factors involved that really go beyond what I am trying to get across here.

Well, we've talked about how the CPU helps the OS keep track of pages in memory. We also talked about how the CR3 register helps keep track of which page directory needs to be read. We also talked about how pages can be protected by the use of a couple of the bits in the page table entry. There is one more thing that's missing in order to complete the picture; keeping track of which process is currently running. This is done with the Task Register (TR).

The TR is not where most of the work gets done. It is simply used by the CPU as a pointer to where the important information is kept. This is the Task State Descriptor (TSD). Like the other descriptors that we've talked about, the TSD points to a particular segment. This segment is the Task State Segment, or TSS. The TSD also contains, among other things, the privilege level at which this task is operating. Using this information along with that in the page table entry, you get the protection that "protected mode" allows.

The TSS contains essentially a snapshot of the CPU. When a process' turn on the CPU is over, the state of the entire CPU needs to be saved so that the program can continue where it left off. This information is stored in the TSS. This functionality is built into the CPU. When the OS tells the CPU a task switch is occurring (a new process is getting its turn), the CPU knows to save this data *automatically.*

If we put all of these components together, we get an operating system working together with the hardware to provide a multitasking, multi-user system. Unfortunately, what we talked about here are just the basics. You could spend a whole book just talking about the relationship between the operating system and the CPU and still not be done.

There is one thing I didn't talk about, and that was the difference between the 80386, 80486, and Pentium. With each new processor came new instructions. The 80486 added an instruction pipeline to improve the performance to the point where the CPU could average almost one instruction per cycle. The Pentium has dual instruction paths (pipelines) to increase the speed even further. It also contains *branch prediction logic* which is used to "guess" where the next instruction should come from.

## Hard Disks

You've got to have one. I mean it's one of the minimum hardware requirements to install an SCO system. I guess that with a little trickery, you could get a system up and running from a floppy and RAM disk. I know I could, but what's the point? Life is much better with a hard disk. The larger the better. Right?

A hard disk is composed of several aluminum coated disks with either an "oxide" media (the stuff on the disks) or "thin film" media. Since "thin film" is thinner than oxide, the more dense (read: larger) hard disks are the more likely they are to have thin film. Each of these disks is called a platter and the more platters you have the more data you can store.

Platters are usually the same size as floppies. Older ones were 5.25" in diameter and the newer ones are 3.5" in diameter. (If someone knows the reason for this, I would love to hear it.) In the center of each platter is a hole, through which the spindle sticks. In other words, as they rotate, the platters rotate around the spindle. The functionality is the same as with a phonograph record (remember those?).

The media that is coated onto the platters is very thin—about 30 millionths of an inch. The media has magnetic properties that can change its alignment when exposed to a magnetic field. That magnetic field comes in the form of the hard disk's read/write heads. It is the change in alignment of this magnetic media that allows data to be stored on the hard disk.

As I said, there is a read/write head that does just that: it reads and writes. There is usually one head *per surface* of the platter (top and bottom). That means there are usually twice as many heads as platters. However, this is not always the case. Sometimes the top and bottommost surfaces do not have heads.

The head is moved across the platters that are spinning at several *thousand* times a minute (at least 60 times a second!). The gap between head and platter is smaller that a human hair; smaller than a particle of smoke. For this reason hard disks are manufactured and repaired in rooms where the number of particles in the air is less than 100 per cubic *meter*.

Because of this very small gap and the high speeds that the platters are rotating, should the head come into contact with the surface of a platter, the result is (aptly named) a head crash. More than likely this will cause some physical damage to your hard disk. (Imagine burying your face into an asphalt street going 'only' 20 MPH.)

The heads are moved in and out across the platters by means of the older stepping motors, or the new, more efficient voice-coil motor. Stepping motors rotate and monitor their movement based on notches or indentations. Voice-coil motors operate on the same principle as a stereo speaker. A magnet inside the speaker causes the speaker cone to move in time with the music (or with the voice). Since there are no notches to determine movement, one of the surfaces of the platters is marked with special signals. Because the head above this surface has no write capabilities, this surface cannot be used for any other purpose.

The voice-coil motor allows finer control and is not subject to problems of heat expanding the disk as the marks are expanded as well. Another fringe benefit is that since the voice-coil operates on electricity, once power is removed, the disk moves back to its starting position as it is no longer resisting a "retaining" spring. This is called "automatic head parking."

Physically, data is stored on the disk in concentric rings. The head does not spiral in like a phonograph record but rather moves in and out across the rings. These rings are called tracks. Since the heads move in unison across the surface of their respective platters data is usually stored not in consecutive tracks, but rather from the tracks that are positioned directly above or below it. The set of all tracks that are the same distance from the spindle are called a *cylinder*. Therefore, hard disks read from successive tracks on the same cylinder and not the same surface. Take a look at Figure 10–12.

Think of it this way. As the disk is spinning under the head it is busy reading data. If it needs to read more data than fits on a single track it has to (obviously) get it from a different track. Assume data was read from consecutive tracks. When the disk finished reading from one track, it would have to move in (or out) to the next track before it could continue. Since tracks are rings and the end is the beginning, the delay in moving out (or in) one track causes the beginning of the next track to spin past the position of the head before it can start reading it. Therefore, it must wait until the beginning comes around again. Granted you could stagger the start of each track, but this makes seeking a particular spot much more difficult.

Let's now look at the instance where data is read from consecutive tracks (that is, it reads one complete cylinder before it goes on). Once the disk has read the entire contents of a track and has reached the end, the beginning of the track just below it spins under the head. Therefore, by switching the head it is reading from, it can begin to read (or write) as if nothing was different. No movement needs to take place and the reads occur much faster.

Each track is broken down into smaller chunks, called sectors. The number of sectors that each track is divided into is referred to as sectors per track, or

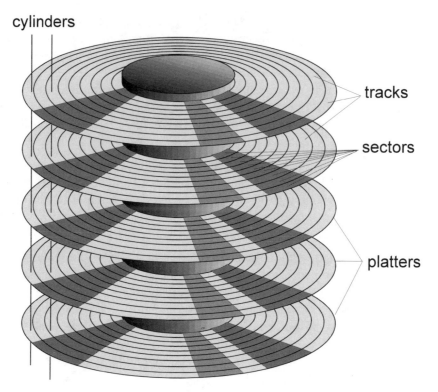

**Figure 10–12**   Logical components of a hard disk.

sectors/track. Although any value is possible, common values for sectors/track are 17, 24, 32, and 64.

Each sector contains 512 bytes of data. However, each sector can contain up to 571 bytes of information. Each sector contains information indicating the start and end of the sector, which is only ever changed by a low-level format. In addition, space is reserved for a checksum contained in the data portion of the sector. If the calculated checksum does not match the checksum in this field, the disk will report an error.

This difference between the total number of bytes per sector and the actual amount of data has been cause for a fair amount of grief. For example, trying to sell you a hard disk, the salesperson might praise the tremendous amount of space that the hard disk has. You might be amazed at the low cost of a one gigabyte drive.

There are two things to watch out for. Computers count in twos, humans count in tens. Despite what the salesperson wants you to believe, a hard disk with 1 billion bytes is *not* a 1 gigabyte drive. It is only $10^9$ bytes. One gigabyte means $2^{30}$ bytes. A hard disk with $10^9$ (1 billion) is only about 950 megabytes. This is five percent smaller!

The salesperson will often state the *unformatted* storage capacity of a drive. This is the number that you would get if you multiplied all the sectors on the disk by 571 (see above). Therefore, the unformatted size is irrelevant to almost all users. Typical formatted MFM drives give the user 85% of the unformatted size and RLL drives give the user about 89%. (MFM and RLL are formatting standards, the specifics of which are beyond the scope of this book. )

On SCO UNIX 324.0, ODT 1.1 and earlier versions, this distinction became a *very* important issue. In these earlier releases, the SCSI commands could only access disks up to 1 Gb (that is $2^{30}$ bytes). Since drive manufacturers often report the unformatted size, a 1 Gb *formatted* drive is a 1.2 Gb *unformatted* drive. The drives that would be reported as problems were those that were 1.2 GB *unformatted*. A customer sees that this larger drive is a problem and since his 1.1 (formatted) drive is smaller than the 1.2 GB, he thinks he's safe. He installs and eventually his data gets corrupted.

This brings up an interesting question. If the manufacturer is telling me that the unformatted size and the formatted size is *about* 85% for MFM and 89% for SCSI/IDE (using RLL), how can I figure out how much useable space there *really* is? Elementary, my dear Watson. It's called multiplication. (Sarcastic, ain't I?)

Let's start at the beginning. Normally when you get a hard disk, it comes with some reference that indicates how many cylinders, heads, and sectors there are per track (among other things). The set of all tracks at the same distance from the spindle is a cylinder. The number of cylinders is simply the number of tracks, since a track is on one surface and a cylinder is all tracks at the same distance. Since you can only use those surfaces that have heads associated with them, we can calculate the number of total tracks by multiplying cylinders times heads. In other words, take the number of tracks on a surface and multiply it by the number of surfaces. This gives you the total number of tracks.

From our discussion of tracks, we know that each track is divided into a specific number of sectors. To find the total number of sectors, we simply multiply the number of total tracks that we calculated above with the sectors per track. Once we have the total number of sectors we multiply this by 512 (the number of bytes *of data* in a sector). This give us the total number of *bytes* on the hard disk. To figure out how many megabytes this is, simply divide this number by 1048576 (1024*1024 = 1 MB).

For those of you who want this as an equation (I always hated word problems myself) consider the following:

$$\text{megabytes} = \frac{\text{cylinders} * \text{heads} * \text{sectors per track} * 512}{1 \text{ Mb}}$$

All PC-based operating systems need to break down the hard disk into units called partitions. A partition can be anywhere from just a couple of megabytes to the entire disk. Each partition is defined in a *partition table* that appears at the very beginning of the disk. This partition table contains information about what kind of partition it is, where it starts, and where it ends. This table is the same whether you have a DOS based PC, UNIX, or both.

Since the table is the same for DOS and UNIX, there can be only four partitions total as there are four entries in the table. DOS gets around this by creating *logical* partitions within one physical partition. This is a characteristic of DOS, *not* the partition table. Both DOS and UNIX must first partition the drive prior to installing the operating system and both provide the mechanism during the installation process in the form of the `fdisk` program. Although their appearance is very different, the DOS and SCO UNIX `fdisk` commands perform the same function.

When you run the SCO UNIX `fdisk` utility, the values you see and input are all in tracks. To figure out how big each `fdisk` partition is, simply multiply that value by 512 times the number of sectors per track. (Remember that each sector holds 512 bytes of data.)

Under SCO UNIX, each partition is broken down even further into *filesystems* or *divisions*. Each partition can contain up to seven filesystems, although a single filesystem can span the entire drive. Since a partition can span (almost) the entire drive, a filesystem that spans the whole partition can span the entire drive as well. (There is a subtle difference between a division and a filesystem. We get into details about this in the section on filesystems.)

Comparable to the partition table, the *division table* contains entries for each of the filesystems within the partition. Each has a name, as well as a starting and ending *block*. The filesystem is the basic unit by which files are grouped under SCO UNIX. (See the section on filesystems.)

To physically connect itself with the rest of the computer, the hard disk has five choices: ST506/412, ESDI, SCSI, IDE, and the newest Enhanced IDE (EIDE). However, the interface the operating system sees for ST506/412 and IDE are identical and there is no special option for an IDE drive. At the hardware level there are some differences that need to be covered for completeness.

To be quite honest, only ESDI and ST506/412 are disk interfaces. SCSI and IDE are referred to as "system-level interfaces" and they incorporate ESDI into the circuitry physically located on the drive.

The ST506/412 was developed by Seagate Technologies (hence the ST) for its ST506 hard disk which had a whopping 5Mb formatted capacity. (Hey! Be fair. This was 1980 when 360K was a *big* floppy.) Seagate later used the same interface in their ST412 which doubled the drive capacity. (Still less hard disk space than I have RAM. Oh, well.) Other drive manufacturers decided to incorporate this technology and over the years it has become a standard. One of its major drawbacks is that it is a fifteen-year-old technology. It can no longer compete with the demands of today's hard disk users.

In 1983, the Maxtor Corporation established the Enhanced Small Device Interface (ESDI) standard. The enhancements provided by ESDI had higher reliability as they had built the encoder/decoder directly into the drive and therefore reduced the noise, had high transfer rates, and the ability to get drive parameters directly from this disk. This means that users no longer had to run the computer set-up routines to tell the CMOS what kind of hard disk it had.

One drawback that I have found with ESDI drives is the physical connection between the controller and the drive itself. Two cables were needed: a 34-pin control cable and a 24-pin data cable. Although the cables are different sizes and can't be (easily) confused, the separation of control and data is something I was never a big fan of. The connectors on the drive itself, were usually split into two unequal halves. In the connector on the cable, a small piece of plastic, called a key, prevented the connector from being inserted improperly. Even if the key is missing, you can still tell which end is which by the fact that the pins on the hard disk are labeled and the #1 line on the cable has a colored stripe down its side. (The may not always be the case, but I have *never* seen one that isn't.)

Another drawback that I have found is that the physical location on the cable determines which drive is which. The primary drive is located at the end of the cable, with the secondary in the middle. The other issue is the number of cables. ESDI hard disk drives require three separate cables. Each drive has its own data cable and they share a common control cable.

Although originally introduced as the interface for hard cards (these were hard disks directly attached to expansion cards) the IDE (Integrated Drive Electronics) interface has grown in popularity to the point where it is perhaps the most commonly used hard disk interface today (rapidly being replaced by SCSI). As its name implies, the controller electronics are *integrated* onto the hard disk itself. The connection to the motherboard is made through a relatively small adapter, commonly referred to as a "paddle board." From here, a single cable is used to attach two hard disks in a daisy-chain. This is similar to the way floppy drives are connected and often IDE controllers have connectors and control electronics for floppy drives as well.

IDE drives often play tricks on systems by presenting a different face to the outside world than is actually the case on the disk. For example, since IDE drives are already preformatted when they reach you, they can have more physical sectors in the outer tracks, thereby increasing the overall amount of space on the disk that can be used for storage. When a request is made to read a particular block of data on the drive, the IDE electronics translates this to the actual physical location.

Because IDE drives come preformatted, you should never low-level format an IDE drive unless specifically permitted by the manufacturer. This has the potential for wiping out the entire drive to the point where it must be returned to the factory for "repair." Certain drive manufacturers, such as Maxtor, provide low-level format routines that accurately and *safely* low-level format your drive. Most vendors that I am aware of today, simply "zero" out the data blocks when doing a low-level format. However, *don't* take my word for it! Check with the vendor.

The next great advance in hard disk technology was SCSI. SCSI is not a disk interface, but rather a semi-independent bus. More than just hard disks can be attached to an SCSI bus. Because of its complex nature and the fact that it can support such a wide range of devices, I talked in more detail about SCSI earlier. However, there are a few specific SCSI issues that relate to hard disks in general and the interaction between SCSI and other types of drives.

The thing to note is that the BIOS inside the PC knows nothing about SCSI; whether this was an oversight or intentional, I don't know. The SCSI spec is over ten years old, so there has been plenty of time to include it. On the other hand, the BIOS is for DOS. DOS makes BIOS calls. In order to be able to access all the possible SCSI devices through the BIOS it must be several times larger. Therefore, every PC-based operating system needs to have extra drivers to be able to access SCSI devices.

Since the BIOS does not understand about SCSI, in order to boot from a SCSI device, you have to trick the PC's BIOS a little. By telling the PC's BIOS that there are no drives installed as either C: or D:, we force it to quit before it goes looking for any of the other types. Once it quits, this gives the BIOS on the SCSI host adapter a chance to run.

The SCSI host adapter obviously knows how to boot from a SCSI hard disk and does so wonderfully. This is assuming that you enabled the BIOS on the host adapter—if not, you're hosed.

There is also the flip side of the coin. The official SCO doctrine says that if you have a non-SCSI boot driver, then you *have* to disable the SCSI BIOS as this causes problems. However, I know customers who have IDE boot drives and still leave the SCSI BIOS enabled. SCO simply reacts as if the SCSI BIOS were not enabled. So, what can you do? My suggestion is to see what works. The only thing I can add is that if you have multiple host adapters, then only one should have the BIOS enabled.

Once the kernel boots from a SCSI device, you lose access to other kinds of drives. Just because it doesn't boot from the IDE (or whatever), does this mean you cannot access it at all? Unfortunately, yes. This is simply the way the kernel is designed. Once the kernel has determined that it has booted off of an SCSI hard disk, it can no longer access a non-SCSI one.

The newest member of the hard disk family is Enhanced IDE or EIDE. The most important aspect of this new hard disk interface is its ability to access more than 504 megabytes. This limitation is because the IDE interface can access only 1024 cylinders, 16 heads, and 63 sectors per track. If you multiply this out using the formula I gave you above, you get 504 Mb.

EIDE also has other advantages such as higher transfer rates, ability to connect more than just two hard disks, as well as attach more than just hard disks. One of the drawbacks that EIDE had at the beginning was part of its very nature. In order to overcome the hard disk size limit that DOS had, EIDE drives employ a method called *logical block addressing* (LBA). This ended up breaking backwards compatibility with the standard IDE/ST-506 interface that SCO used. As a result, up until OpenServer, EIDE was not supported. Although you could disable the logical block addressing (setting the drive to standard IDE) to allow both DOS and ODT to see the drive, you ended up losing the additional size.

The idea behind LBA is that the system's BIOS would "rearrange" the drive geometry so that drives larger than 528Mb could still be booted. Because SCO does not use the BIOS to access the hard disk, the fact that the BIOS could handle the EIDE drive meant nothing. New drivers needed to be added to account for this. This was done for OpenServer.

There are a couple of things to note when dealing with EIDE drives. First, support for multiple drives where some use LBA and some do not, is machine dependent. SCO recommends that either all the drives have LBA enabled or all of them do not. This eliminates many problems.

If you want to use LBA and the drive is new, there is no problem. There is also no problem if the drive was previously used with LBA enabled. Problems arise when it was previously used with LBA disabled and you now want to install

SCO with LBA enabled. In order to do this correctly you need to delete the disk parameter table from the hard disk.

Boot the system with the install floppy and type `tools` at the `Boot:` prompt. Select the option: `Execute a shell on a ramdisk filesystem`. When you get to a prompt type:

```
dd if=/dev/zero of=/dev/rhd00 bs=1b count=1
```

When the command completes, reboot from the install floppy. This command writes a single byte with the value of 0 onto the hard disk, which invalidates the drive information.

## Floppy Drives

A customer once called in to SCO Support with a system that would not boot. For some unknown reason the system crashed and would no longer boot from the hard disk. It got to a particular point in the boot process and hung. Even the copy of `unix.old` hung in the same way.

Fortunately the customer had an emergency boot floppy which allowed him to boot and get access to the hard disk. We stuck the floppy in the drive and pressed the reset button. After a moment, there was the `Boot:` prompt. Since we wanted to make sure things were fine before we continued, I decided to first boot from the floppy to see if we could access the hard disk. So, we pressed enter.

After a moment, the familiar dots went running across the screen. All seemed to go fine until suddenly the dots stops. The customer could hear the floppy drive straining and then came the dreaded `floppy read error`. Rather than giving up I decided to try it again. Same thing.

At that point I started to get concerned. The hard disk booted, but the kernel hung. The floppy booted, but somewhere in the middle of loading the kernel, there was a bad spot on the floppy. This was not a happy situation.

The floppy disk was brand new and they had tested it out immediately after they made it. The most logical thing that cause this problem was having the floppy too close to a magnetic field. Nope! That wasn't the case either. The customer was told to keep his floppy in a safe place and that's what he did.

What was that safe place? He had tacked it to the bulletin board next to the monitor. Not through the hub or at one of the corners, but right through the floppy itself. He was careful not to stick the pin through the media access hole, since he was told never to touch the floppy media itself.

In this section, we're going to talk about floppy disks, lovingly referred to as floppies. They come in different sizes and shapes, but all floppies serve the same basic functions. Interaction with floppies can be a cause of great heartache for the unprepared. So, we're going to talk about what they are like physically, how they are accessed, and what kinds of problems you can have with them.

Although they hold substantially less data, floppies appear and behave very much like hard disks. Like hard disks, floppies are broken down into sectors, tracks, and even cylinders. Like hard disks, the number of tracks tell us how many tracks are on a given surface. Therefore, a floppy described as 40 tracks (such as a 360Kb floppy) actually contains 80 tracks, or 40 cylinders.

Other common characteristics are the header and trailer of each sector, resulting in 571 bytes per sector, of those 512 being data. Floppy disks almost universally use MFM data encoding.

SCO floppy drivers support a wide range of floppies: from the ancient 48 tracks per inch/8 sectors per track, 5.25″ floppies to the newest 135 tracks per inch/36 sector per track, 3.5″ floppies that can hold almost 3Mb of data. The floppy devices found on systems today are somewhere in between.

Because they are as old as PCs themselves, floppies have changed little except for their size and the amount of data that can be stored on them. As a result, very few problems are encountered with floppies. One of the most common problems is that customers are unsure of which floppy device goes to which type of drive. Sometimes customers do know the difference and try to save money by forcing the floppy to format in a higher density than it was designed for. That's where I come in. I carry a keyboard.

It was Thursday, the weather was warm (as always) in Santa Cruz. We were working the afternoon shift on OSD. The boss's name was David, second tier was Wyliam. My name's Mohr. James Mohr.

We had gotten a call from an irate customer claiming there was a bug in our software. She insisted that she immediately talk to an analyst. She wanted help to get data back that was apparently on the floppy that (she claimed) our driver had toasted. Even without a support contract, a customer reporting a bug will always get through. It's part of our job to ensure a quality product.

When I first picked up the phone, the customer seemed angry that it took so long to reach someone. I explained that the queue was on a first come, first served basis. Rather than satisfying her, that seemed to enrage her more.

"There must be a lot a bugs in your software if so many people call in with problems," she said.

I took a sip of coffee and said, "I'm sorry you feel that way ma'am. What can I do to help you?"

The customer continued her tirade on how sloppy the software was and that it was amazing we managed to stay in business so long with such a shoddy product and how we were legally responsible for helping her get her data back.

"Just the facts, ma'am," I said. "Tell me what happened."

"Well, I have been saving data on this floppy to take to our other office. All of a sudden there are errors all over the place."

"It could be a bad floppy," I suggested calmly.

"No sir!" she insisted. "These are high quality floppies. Guaranteed 100% error free."

"How old are they ma'am? You know, floppies do lose their ability to store data over time."

"These are brand new floppies, young man, and don't you going trying to put the blame on the floppies. It's your floppy driver that's the problem."

I took another sip of coffee, realizing that this would not be an easy call. "Could be ma'am, but I need some more information to make that determination. What size floppy is it?"

"Five and a quarter."

"I see. And what device did you use to format it with?"

"I use /dev/rfd096ds15. That's a high density 5¼, you know!"

"Yes, ma'am. Does the floppy have a reinforcement ring in the middle? I mean is there a ring in the center of the floppy that sort of sticks up a little?"

"Why, yes, but I don't see what that has to do with anything," she responded.

"Well, you see ma'am. That's a low density floppy. You can't format those at high density."

"What do you mean? We've been doing this for a long time and we've never had problems before. My boss said that we can do this to save money."

"No, ma'am, you can't. Up to now, you've been lucky. Keep in mind ma'am that floppies can only be formatted as high as the manufacturer allows."

"Oh," she said quietly.

"Have a good day, ma'am."

The story you have just read is true. The names were changed to protect the innocent. Actually the opposite is true. I glorified the story a bit, but the names are true.

The truth of the matter is, that you *can't* format floppies higher than you're supposed to; that is, higher than the manufacturer specifies. To some extent you might get away with punching holes in single sided floppies to make them double sided. However, forcing a floppy to a format at a higher density (if it works) isn't worth risking your data on.

In order to understand why this is so, we need to talk about the concept of coercivity. That is, how much energy (how strong the magnetic field) must be used in order to make a proper recording on a disk. Older floppies had a lower coercivity and therefore required a weaker magnetic field to hold the signal; that is, less energy was required to "coerce" them into a particular pattern.

This seems somewhat contradictory, but look at it another way. As densities increase, the magnetic particles get closer together and start to interfere with each other. The result is to make the particles weaker magnetically. Because the weaker the particles are magnetically, a stronger force is needed to "coerce" them into the proper patterns to hold data. Therefore, high density disks have a higher coercivity.

As the capacity of drives increased, the tracks became narrower. The low density 5.25" floppies had 48 tracks per inch and could hold 360K of data. The high density 5.25" floppies have twice as many tracks per inch and can hold 1.2Mb. The added increase is also due to the fact they have 15 sectors per track instead of nine. Since there are more tracks in a given space, they are therefore thinner. Problems arise if you use a disk formatted at 360K in a 1.2Mb drive. Because, the 1.2Mb drive writes the thinner tracks, not all of the track of the 360K floppy is overwritten. This may not be a problem in the 1.2Mb drive, but if you ever try to read that floppy in a 360K drive the data will run together; that is the larger head will read data from more than one track.

Formatting a 360K floppy as a 1.2Mb usually fails miserably because of the different number of tracks, so you usually can't get yourself into trouble. However, with 3.5" floppies the story is a little different. For both the 720Kb and 1.44Mb floppies, there are 80 tracks per side. The difference is that the 1.44Mb floppies are designed to handle 18 sectors per track instead of just 9. As a result, formatting *appears* to go fine. It is only later that you discover that the data is not written correctly.

The reason for this is that the magnetic media for the lower density 720Kb floppies is less sensitive. By formatting it as 1.44Mb, you subject it to a stronger magnetic field than you should. After awhile, this "overdose" causes the individual magnetic fields to begin interfering with one another. Since high density, 1.44Mb floppies are well below $1.00 a piece, it's not worth risking data by trying to force low density to high density to save money.

While on the subject of money, buying unformatted floppies to save money is becoming less and less the smart thing to do. If you figure that formatting floppies takes at least two minutes a piece and the cost difference between a package of ten formatted floppies and ten unformatted is $2.00, then it would only make sense (or cents) to have someone format these if they were only making $6.00 an hour. Rarely does a company have someone whose sole job it is to format floppies. It usually falls on those people who use them and most of them get more than $6.00 an hour.

(I actually did some consulting work for a company whose president insisted that they buy *unformatted* floppies. Since the only people who used the floppies were his programmers and system administrators, they earned well above $6.00 an hour. In one case, I calculated that turning a package of ten unformatted floppies into formatted ones worked out to costing twice as much for the unformatted as for the formatted ones. That didn't phase him a bit as the system administrators were on salary and getting paid no matter what. By saving the few dollars by buying unformatted ones, his profit margin looked better; at least it did on paper.)

## Tape Drives

For the longest time tape drives literally were a block to me. Although I understood the basic concept (writing to a tape similar to a music cassette) there were just so many that it took me quite a fair bit of time before I felt comfortable with them.

Because this device has the potential for saving your data or opening up career opportunities for you to flip burgers, knowing how to install and use them is an important part of your job as a system administrator. Since the tape device node is usually read/write, regular users can also backup their own data with it.

The first tape drives supported under SCO UNIX were quarter inch cartridge tapes, or QIC tapes. QIC is not just an abbreviation for the size of the media, but is also a standard.

In principle a QIC tape is like a music cassette. Both consist of a long tape consisting of two layers. The 'backing' is usually made of cellulose acetate (photographic film) or polyester (1970s leisure suits) with polyester being more common today. The coating is the actual media that holds the magnetic signals.

The difference is in the way the tapes are moved from the supply reel to the take-up reel. In cassette tapes, movement is accomplished by a capstan and the tape is pinched between two rollers. QIC tapes spread the driving pressure out over a larger area by means of a drive belt. Additionally, more care is taken to ensure that the coating touches only the read/write heads. Another major difference is the size. QIC tapes are much larger (a little bit smaller than a VHS video tape).

The initial size of QIC tapes was 300 feet and it held approximately 30Mb of data. This is a DC300 tape. The tape that next appeared was a DC600, which was 600 feet long and could hold about 60Mb. As with other technologies, tape drives got better and were able to hold more data and tapes got longer. The technology advanced to the point where the same tapes could be used in new drives and could store twice as much as they could before.

There are currently several different QIC standards for writing to tape drives depending on the tape and tape drive being used. Older, 60Mb drives use a QIC-24 format when writing to 60Mb tapes. Newer drives use the QIC-525 format to write to several different kinds of tapes. As a result, different tapes yield different capacity depending on the drive where they are written.

For example, I have an Archive 5150 tape drive that is "officially" designed to work with 150MB tapes (DC6150). However, I can get 120Mb from a DC600. Why? The DC600 is 600 feet long and the DC6150 is just 20 feet longer. However, a tape drive designed to use DC600 tapes only writes in 9 tracks, however, a tape that uses DC6150s (like mine) write in 15 tracks. In fact, there are many different combinations of tapes and drives that can be used.

One thing I would like to point out from a technical standpoint is that there is no difference between 150Mb QIC tape drives and 250Mb QIC drives. When the QIC standard was enhanced to include 1000 feet tapes, 150Mb drives automagically became 250Mb drives. (I wish I had known this before I went out and bought so many DC6150 tapes. Oh, well. Live and learn.)

A similar thing happened with 320 and 525Mb tapes. The QIC-320 standard was based on 600 feet tapes. However, the QIC committee decided to go with the QIC-525 standard based on 1000 feet tape. That's why a 600 foot tape writing with the QIC-525 standard writes 320Mb.

Notice that this entire time, I never referred to QIC-02 tapes. Well, that's because QIC-02 is not a tape standard, but a controller standard.

An interesting side note is just how the data is actually written to the tape. QIC tape drives use a system called "serpentine recording." Like a serpent, it winds its way back and forth along the length of the tape. It starts at one end and writes until it reaches the other end. The tape drive then reverses direction and begins to write toward the other end.

Two other common tape drives are QIC-40 and QIC-80 tape drives, which provide 40Mb and 80Mb, respectively. These provide an inexpensive backup solution. These tape drives are connected to standard floppy controllers and in most cases, the standard floppy cables can be used. The size of the tapes used for this kind of drive is about the same as a pack of cigarettes.

Aside from using the same type of controller, QIC-40/80 tape drives have other similarities with floppy drives. Both use *modified frequency modulation* (MFM) when writing to the device. Sectors are assigned in similar fashions and each tape has the equivalent of a file allocation table to keep track of where each file is on the media.

QIC-40/QIC-80 tapes need to be formatted prior to use, just like floppies. Because the size of data storage is substantially greater than for a floppy, formatting takes substantially longer. Depending on the speed of the tape drive, formatting can take up to an hour. Preformatted tapes are also available and like their floppy counterparts, the prices are only slightly higher than unformatted ones.

Because these tape drives run off the floppy controller, it is often a choice between a second floppy drive and a tape drive. The deciding factor is the floppy controller. Normally, floppy controllers can only handle two drives, therefore this is usually the limit.

However, this limit can be circumvented if the tape drive supports *soft select* (sometimes called "phantom select"), whereby the software chooses the device number for the tape drive when it is using it. The ability to do "soft select" is dependent on the drive. While more and more floppy tape drives support this capability, many of the older drives do not. We get into more details about this in the second part of the book when we talk about installing and using tape drives.

Similar in size and functionality are Irwin tape drives. Although almost identical to QIC-40/QIC-80 tape drives, the behavior of Irwins in regard to the operating system is somewhat different. Therefore there is a special driver that is needed to access Irwin tape drives. There is also a special option in the `mkdev tape` script to do so. This is the option `Mini-Cartridge`.

On larger systems, neither QIC nor mini-tapes can really handle the volume of data being stored. While some QIC tapes can store up to 1.3 Gb, they cannot compare to digital audio tape (DAT) devices. Such devices use Digital Data Storage (DDS) media. Rather than storing signals similar (or analogous) to those coming across the bus, DDS stores the data as a series of numbers or digits on the tape; hence, the name "digital." The result is much higher reliability.

Physically, DAT tapes are the smallest that SCO supports. The actual media is 4mm, hence DAT tapes are sometimes referred to as 4mm tapes.

Hewlett-Packard DAT Tapes can be divided into multiple logical tapes. This is useful when making backups if you want to store different filesystems to different "tapes" and you don't want to use any extra physical tapes. Device nodes are created to represent these different logical tapes. DAT tape drives can quickly scan for the location of subsequent partitions (as they are called), making searches much faster than with backups to single tapes. For more details on this, see the dat(HW) man-page.

One thing to watch out for is that data written to DAT tapes is not as standardized as data written to QIC tapes. Therefore, it is possible that data written on one DAT drive cannot be read on another.

There are two reasons for this problem. This first is the blocking factor. The blocking factor is the minimum space each file will take up. A 1 Kb file with a blocking factor of 20 will have 19 Kb of wasted space. Such a situation is faster in that the tape drive is streaming more, but there is a lot of wasted space. DAT tape drives use either a variable or fixed block size. Each drive has a default blocking factor that is determined by the drive itself.

Another problem is data compression, which if done, is performed at the hardware level. Since there is no standard for data compression, it is very unlikely that two drives from different manufacturers that both do data compression will be able to read each other's tapes.

These are just a couple of the reasons why SCO doesn't provide tape installation media other than QIC tapes.

## CD-ROMs

SCO installation media is becoming more and more prevalent on CD-ROMs. A CD-ROM takes a lot less space than the fifty floppies or even the quarter inch cartridge (QIC) tape, so the media is easier to handle. Added to this, the CD-ROMs are significantly faster than either floppy or tape media. The CD-ROM media is also cheaper. You will save a substantial amount of cash by ordering the CD-ROM media since ODT and OpenServer are several hundred dollars cheaper on CD-ROM than on floppy. If you already have a supported SCSI host adapter in your system, the money you save by ordering CD-ROM media *literally* pays for the cost of the CD-ROM drive. Once installed, the CD-ROM is yours to keep.

OpenServer is available on almost 150 floppies and costs an extra $300. By not paying that much extra for the floppies and buying the CD-ROM version, you can spend the $300 on a CD-ROM drive. Besides, installing from so many floppies would probably take all day and you can install from CD-ROM in less than two hours.

Another important aspect of CDs when it comes to installation media is their size. Therefore, it is possible to get a large number of products on the CD. You can then ship a single CD to a customer and have them pull off what they need. If they later decide they want an additional product, they don't have to wait for the media to be shipped.

CD-ROMs, in fact CD technology in general, has always fascinated me. It amazed me that you could get so much information into such a small place and still have such quick access to your data.

The basic principle behind data storage on a CD is really nothing more than Morse code. A series of light and dark spots (dots and dashes) compose the encoded information on the disk. Commercial CDs, whether music or data, almost universally have data on one side of the disk. Although there is nothing technologically preventing a CD from having a flip side, convention limits data to just a single side. This is enough when you consider that you can get over 600Mb of data on a single CD. As the technology improves, the amount is steadily increasing. In addition, certain manufacturers are working on dual-sided CDs.

In the surface of the disk is a series of "dents" or holes, called "lands." The areas between the lands are called "pits." A laser is projected onto the surface of the disk and the light is either reflected by the pits or scattered by the lands. If reflected, the light reaches a light-sensing receptor, that sends an electrical signal that is received by the control mechanism of the CD-ROM drive. Just as the pattern of alternating dots and dashes form the message when using Morse code, it is the pattern of reflected light and no light that indicates the data being stored on the disk.

When I first thought of CD-ROMs, I conceptualized them as being like WORM drives (Write-Once Read-Many), which they are, sort of. I visualized them as being a read-only version of a hard disk. However, after looking more closely at the way data is stored, the more you look at CDs, the less they have in common with hard disks.

If you remember our discussion of hard disks, each surface is composed of concentric rings called tracks, and each track is divided into sectors. The disk spins at a constant speed as the heads move in and out across the drive's surface. Therefore the tracks on the outer edge are moving faster than those on the inside.

Take, for example, a track that is half an inch away from the center of the disk. The diameter of the circle representing the track is one inch, so the radius of that circle is approximately 3.1415 inches. Spinning sixty times a second, the track goes at a speed of about 190 inches per second. Now, take a track at one inch from the center, or twice as far. The diameter of the circle representing that track is 6.2830 inches. It, too, is going around at sixty revolutions per second. However, since it has to travel twice as far in each revolution it has to be going twice as fast.

A CD-ROM isn't like that. CD-ROMS rotate in a manner called "constant linear velocity." The motor keeps the CD moving at the same speed regardless of where the CD reader is reading from. Therefore, as the light detector moves inward, the disk slows down so that each revolution takes the same amount of time per track.

Let's look at hard disks again. They are divided into concentric tracks that are divided into sectors. Since the number of sectors per track remains constant, the sectors must get smaller toward the center of the disk. (This is because the circumference of the circle representing the track is getting smaller as you move in.)

Again, a CD-ROM isn't like that and there is no reason why it should be. Most CD-ROMs are laid out in a single spiral, just like a phonograph record. There are no concentric circles, so there is no circumference to get smaller. As a result, the sectors in a CD can remain the same size no matter what. The added advantage of sectors remaining the same size means that there can be more on the disk and therefore more data for the user.

ODT only supports SCSI CD-ROM drives that are attached to supported host adapters. However, most newer SCSI CD-ROMs adhere to the SCSI-2 standard. Since the SCO CD-ROM driver (Srom) is issuing standard SCSI commands, there is no reason why SCSI CD-ROMs that are not "officially" supported should not work. In fact, there are very few cases where they don't, as long as they are attached to a supported SCSI host adapter. In addition, OpenServer supports ATAPI/EIDE style CD-ROM drives.

A little known fact about SCO CD-ROM devices that most people are not aware of is that there are actually two different kinds. The first one is what everyone is familiar with. This is the kind that comes as a DOS or UNIX filesystem and can be mounted like any other. These have the ISO-9660 (referred to as High-Sierra under SCO) filesystem format. The second kind of CD-ROM drive is referred to as a CD-Tape drive. This is the device that is being accessed by the system when doing an install. However, this kind cannot be mounted.

It is relatively easy to understand how this is accomplished since, as we mentioned before, the CD is a single spiral. If we were to unwind this spiral, we would have a long "strip" of data, just as if it were a tape. The logic behind this is one of practicality. SCO had been using tapes as its installation media for some time before it started on CDs as installation devices. There were already well-documented procedures to create installation tapes, and there was nothing yet in place to make installation CD-ROMs. Rather than an almost complete redesign of the installation process, a much simpler change was made to the CD-ROM tape driver.

In addition to the CD-Tape format, SCO supports several CD-ROM formats including UNIX filesystems, ISO-9660, and Rockridge formats (which is similar to ISO-9660, but supports things like long file names). Although there are no problems mounting another UNIX filesystem, adding an ISO-9660 format filesystem has a unique set of problems.

When installing a CD-ROM drive, you have two options. The first option is to install a normal CD-ROM and the other is to install a CD-Tape device. The CD-Tape device has one purpose; to install SCO software. The standard CD-ROM allows you to access both UNIX filesystems as well as the ISO-9660 format.

In order to access the ISO-9660 format, you need to add the right driver to the system. Since this is necessary to access the standard CD-ROM, you are asked during the installation if you want to add it.

## Magneto-Optical Drives

Similar in operation to hard disks, magneto-optical (or just MO) drives are very different in the way the data is written to and read from the drive. One of the key differences is that MO drives write to a much smaller area than a regular hard disk. In order to accomplish this they rely on a laser to get the data area down to a much smaller size than a hard disk.

Because the media they are written to has a higher coercivity, the data on MO disks have a much longer lifetime than normal hard disks. Manufacturers of MO drives estimate that the magnetic fields holding the data on MO will remain at "useable" levels for 10–15 years. (Interesting speculation when you consider the MO technology is not that old.)

Ever placed a floppy near a magnetic field (for example, a stereo speaker) and have it lose data? Because of the MO disk's very high coercivity this is less likely to happen. Remember that coercivity is basically the force needed to put the magnetic field in the correct pattern to represent data. If it takes a lot of force to turn it into data. It takes a lot of force to make it garbage. Therefore, MO disks are much less affected by stray magnetic fields.

There is a problem here as well. How do you get a strong enough magnetic field to whip the MO disk into shape? Well, there is an interesting aspect of magnetism called the *Curie temperature*. Each media has a specific Curie temperature. Close to this temperature, it takes almost *no* force to change the magnetic field. That is, the coercivity gets close to zero.

By using the laser to heat up a spot close to the Curie temperature, a weaker magnetic field is needed. Even though the field created by the head covers a wide area, only the pinpoint spot generated by the laser is hot enough to be affected.

MO drives have one major disadvantage compared to conventional hard disks: a longer access time when writing data. The design of the MO drive cannot change the orientation (polarity) of the field fast enough. As a result, the drive must make two passes over the same area. The first pass aligns the field in an area to be written in a single direction. The second pass then aligns it the way the data would have it. Adding the slower rotational speed gives access times that are two or three times longer than conventional hard disks.

Reading the disk is slightly different. Whereas the writing process uses a self-generated magnetic field to orient the particles, reading uses the laser. The photons in the laser are aligned with respect to each other. When they enter the magnetic field generated by the disk, their alignment changes. This change can be noticed and is what allows us to read the data.

## Serial Ports

Most machines that are sold today come with two serial ports attached. These can either be built into the motherboard, part of a serial/parallel card, or part of an "all-in-one" card that has serial ports, parallel ports, a games port, and even hard disk and floppy controllers.

A serial board is an expansion card that translates the parallel bus signals (at least eight bits at a time) to serial signals (one bit at a time). These bits are encapsulated into groups of one byte. The encapsulation contains other signals that represent the start and end of the byte, as well as a parity bit. Additionally, the number of bits that are used to represent data can either be 7 or 8.

Parity is the mechanism with which single bit errors can be detected during transmission. The number of bits set to one is counted and based on whether even or odd parity is used, the parity bit is set. For example, if even parity is used and there are 3 bits that are set, then the parity bit is also set to make the total number of bits set an even number. However, if odd parity is used, the number of bits set is already odd, therefore the parity bit is left unset. When you are using some other means to detect errors, parity can be turned off and you are said to be using no parity. This is the default for modems in SCO UNIX.

Serial communication parameters must be agreed upon by both ends. These parameters are often referred to in triples, such as 8-1-N (read eight-one-none). In this instance there are eight data bits, 1 stop bit, and no parity is used. This is the default for SCO UNIX systems.

One of the key elements of a serial board is the Universal Asynchronous Receiver-Transmitter, or *UART*. The transmitter portion takes a byte of parallel data written by the serial driver to the card and transmits it one bit at a time (serially). The receiver does just the opposite. It takes the serial bits and converts them into parallel data that is sent down the bus and is read by the serial driver.

Although SCO only provides drivers for standard serial ports, intelligent ones are often installed to allow many more logins (or other connections) to the system. The most significant difference is that intelligent serial boards (often referred to as smart serial boards) have a built-in CPU. This allows it to take all of the responsibility for processing the signals away from the system CPU.

In addition, intelligent serial boards can better buffer incoming signals that keep them from getting lost. With nonintelligent boards, the system may be so busy that it does not get time to read characters of the board. Although the 16550 UART common on most serial boards today contains 16-byte buffers, this is often not enough. Under heavy load, the serial driver does not react fast enough and characters are overwritten.

Serial board performance is also increased by intelligent boards. Since signals are buffered and sent in large chunks, there is less overhead on a per character basis. With nonintelligent boards, single characters are often transmitted, so the per-character overhead is much larger. In fact, most nonintelligent boards generate an interrupt and the associated overhead with *each* character.

Because there is a lot of processing done on the board itself, intelligent serial boards require special drivers from the manufacturer. Since SCO does not have access to the drivers and cannot determine what is and what is not correct behavior, support for these devices is often difficult. As with other devices, if the device driver is not included with the product, then SCO is under no obligation to support it. This doesn't mean they won't. SCO has very good official and nonofficial relationships with many vendors and both sides are willing to help out the other.

It is possible to obtain supported serial boards that have multiple ports. Although such boards have multiple UARTs, they do not have the performance of intelligent boards, but do provide a low cost alternative. For a discussion on the device nodes used for such boards, see the section on the device directory.

Originally designed to connect mainframe computers to modems, the RS-232 standard is use exclusively for serial ports on PCs. Two kinds of devices are considered with RS-232: *Data Terminal Equipment* or *DTE* and *Data Communication Equipment* or *DCE*. DTE is the serial port side and DCE is the modem side.

Two types of connections are used: DB25 (with 25 pins) and DB9 (with 9 pins). Although they serve the same basic function, the numbering of the pins is slightly different. Tables 10–3 and 10–4 list the main pins, their functions, and a mnemonic that is commonly used to refer to them.

Note that on a DB25 connector, pin 1 is *chassis ground*, which is different from signal ground. Chassis ground ensures that both serial connectors are operating at the same electric potential and keeps you from getting a shock. See Figure 10–13 for a comparison of the two kinds of connectors.

**Table 10–3**  Common Pins on DB-25 Connector

| Pin | Function | Mnemonic |
|---|---|---|
| 2 | Transmit | TXD or TX |
| 3 | Receive | RXD or RX |
| 4 | Request to Send | RTS |
| 5 | Clear to Send | CTS |
| 6 | Data Set Ready | DSR |
| 7 | Signal Ground | GND |
| 8 | Carrier Detect | CD |
| 20 | Data Terminal Ready | DTR |
| 22 | Ring Indicator | RI |

In order to communicate properly, the DTE device must say that it is ready to work by sending a signal on the DTR line. The DCE device must also do the same on the DSR line.

One side indicates that it has data by sending a signal on the RTS line (it is requesting to send data). If ready, the other side says that it is ready by sending a signal on the CTS line (the sender is clear to send the data). What happens when the receiving side can't keep up? What happens if the sending side is sending too fast? If the receiving side needs to stop (perhaps a buffer is full), it stops the CTS signal (meaning the sender is no longer clear to send the data). This causes the

**Table 10–4**  Pins on DB-9 Connector

| Pin | Function | Mnemonic |
|---|---|---|
| 1 | Carrier Detect | CD |
| 2 | Receive | RXD or RX |
| 3 | Transmit | TXD or TX |
| 4 | Data Terminal Ready | DTR |
| 5 | Signal Ground | GND |
| 6 | Data Set Ready | DSR |
| 7 | Request to Send | RTS |
| 8 | Clear to Send | CTS |
| 9 | Ring Indicator | RI |

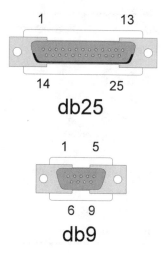

**Figure 10–13**    Physical layout of pins on serial cables.

sending side to stop. This is referred to as *hardware handshaking, hardware flow control,* or *RTS/CTS flow control.*

Problems arise when connecting other types of devices. Some devices, such as printers, are themselves DTE devices. If you tried to connect a standard RS-232 cable, TX is connected to TX, RX is connected to RX, DSR is connected to DSR, and DTR is connected to DTR. The result is that nothing happens. The solution is a *cross-over* cable which internally swaps the appropriate signals and makes sure they end up going to the right place.

If you have a terminal, things are easier. First off, although the data is going in both directions, the data coming from the terminal will never exceed the speed of the serial port (I'd like to see you type at 240 characters per second). Data heading toward the terminal is displayed on the screen, which will display it as fast as it comes. Therefore, you only need three signals: send, transmit, and ground.

Should the terminal be displaying the data too fast for you to read, you can stop it by sending an XOFF character back to the system. This is usually a CTRL-S and unless turned off, this will stop incoming data. To turn the flow of data back on again, you send the system an XON (CTRL-Q) character. This type of flow control is called *software flow control* or *XON/XOFF flow control.* In some cases, depending on how the terminal is configured, sending *any* character.

Both the serial(HW) man-page and the *System Administrator's Guide* provide additional information on serial ports, especially how they work as terminal devices. We will also be talking more about serial devices later when we talk about modems.

## Parallel Ports

Parallel ports are a common way printers are attached to an SCO UNIX system. Although there are many different problems that arise with printers attached to parallel ports, there are not many issues that arise with parallel ports. First, let's take a look at how parallel ports work.

One of the key differences between parallel and serial ports is the way data is sent. From our discussion of serial ports, you know that data goes across a serial line one bit at a time across a single data line. Parallel ports send data across a byte (eight bits at a time) across eight data lines.

Another key difference is the cable. Looking at the computer end, it is easily confused with a serial connector. Both have 25 pins in the same layout. On the printer end is where things are different. Here is a special kind of 36-pin connector called a *Centronics* connector named after the printer manufacturer Centronics. A cable that has a 25-pin *D-shell* connector on one end and a 36-pin on the other is called a Centronics or parallel cable. Unlike serial cables, there are not different kinds of cables (like straight-through or crossed). Because of this, all that usually needs to get done is to plug in the cable at both ends and go (see Figure 10–14).

Although some devices allow communication in both directions along a parallel, SCO UNIX does not support any of these. In fact, the only thing that SCO directly supports on parallel ports are printers.

Because there is no guarantee that all the data bits will arrive at the port at the same time, there needs to be some way of signalling the printer that the data is

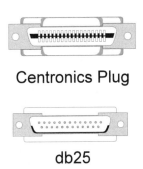

**Centronics Plug**

**db25**

**Figure 10–14**   Comparison of Centronic and DB-25 connectors.

ready. This is done with the *strobe* line. Once a character (or any byte of data) is ready, the system sends a signal along the strobe line. The use of the strobe line also prevents characters from being read more than once.

Often the printer cannot keep up with the data flow from the parallel port. Just like RTS-CTS flow control on serial ports, parallel ports also need a way to be told to stop. This is done with the *busy* line. Actually, the busy line is set after each character, in case the printer cannot process the character fast enough. Once the character is processed, the printer can turn off the busy signal.

However, this is not enough to get the parallel port to send the next character. The printer must first tell the parallel port it has received the character by sending a signal along the *acknowledge* line. Note that this acknowledge occurs after *every* character.

There are other control lines the printer uses. One is the *select* line that indicates that the printer has been selected, or is "on-line." There is also a special line to say when the paper source is empty. This is the *paper empty* line. If the problem is unknown, the printer can send a signal along the *fault* line that basically says that "something" is wrong.

One thing that comes up regularly is the confusion as to what physical parallel port is related to what lp device. In order to work correctly, it is necessary to configure your parallel ports according to the following Table 10–5.

If parallel port is configured with the correct addresses, but with the wrong interrupt, the parallel port will be recognized, but will not work. Note that the hardware screen and `hwconfig` show you the interrupt that it *expects* the port to have and *not* what it is actually configured at. This is true for all devices.

The use of two devices with the same interrupt is not supported on ISA machines. This means that a system with both /dev/lp0 and /dev/lp1 installed is not supported. The result could be any one (or more) of the following:

- Attempting to access either port generates the error message
  "cannot create"
  "no such device or address"

**Table 10–5**  Default Parallel Port Devices

| Device Name | Address | IRQ |
|-------------|---------|-----|
| /dev/lp0 | $0 \times 378$ | 7 |
| /dev/lp1 | $0 \times 3BC$ | 7 |
| /dev/lp2 | $0 \times 278$ | 5 |

- Attempting to access either port hangs with no error message
- Attempting to access both ports at the same time causes either one or both ports to hang or to print extremely slowly.

On the other hand, I have heard of systems working with all three parallel ports enabled, provided they are not all accessed simultaneously.

## Video Cards and Monitors

Without a video card and monitor you don't see anything. In fact, every PC that I have ever seen won't even boot unless there is a video card in it. Granted, your computer could boot and even do work without it being attached to a monitor (and I have seen those), however it's no fun unless you get to see what's going on.

When PCs first hit the market, there was only one kind of video system. High resolution and millions of colors were something you read about in science-fiction novels. Times changed and so did graphics adapters. The first dramatic change was the introduction of color with IBM's color graphics adapter (CGA), which required a completely new (and incompatible) video subsystem. In an attempt to integrate color and monochrome systems, IBM came out with the enhanced graphics adapter (EGA).

But we're not going to talk about those. Why? First, no one buys them any more. I doubt that anyone still makes them. If you could find one, there would be no problem installing them and getting them to work. So, the second reason that I am not going to talk about them is that they are not that common. Since "no one" uses them any more, the time I spent telling you why I won't tell you about them is already too much.

What are we going to talk about instead? Well, the first thing is VGA. VGA (or Video Graphics Array) is the standard by which virtually all video card manufacturers base their products. Although an enhancement to VGA (Super VGA or SVGA) exists, it is all based on VGA.

When talking about VGA, we first need to talk about some basics of video technology. The first issue is just how things work. Digital signals are sent by the operating system to the video card, which sends them through a digital to analog converter (DAC). Usually there is a single chip that contains three DACs, one for each color (red, green, and blue or RGB). The DAC has a lookup table that determines the voltage to be output on each line for the respective color.

The voltage that the DAC has found for a given color is sent to the three electron guns at the back of the monitor's cathode-ray tube(CRT); again, one for each color. The intensity of the electron stream is a result of this voltage.

The video adapter also sends a signal to the *magnetic deflection yoke* which aims the electron beams to the right place on the screen. This signal determines how far apart the dots are as well as how often the screen is redrawn. The dots are referred to as *pixels*, the distance apart they are is the *pitch* and how often the screen is redrawn is the *refresh rate*.

In order to keep the beams precisely aligned, they first pass through a *shadow mask;* a metal plate containing hundreds of thousands of little holes. The dot pitch is how closely aligned the holes are. The closer the holes the higher the pitch. A higher pitch means a sharper image.

The electrons from the electron guns strike the phosphors on the inside of the monitor screen and make them glow. Three different phosphors are used, one for each color. The stronger the beams the more intense is the color. Colors other than RGB are created by changing the amount that each of these three colors is displayed; that is, by changing the intensity of each color. For example, purple would be created by exciting red and blue phosphors, but no green. After the beams stop hitting the phosphor, it will still continue to glow for a short time. To keep the image on the screen, the phosphor must be recharged by the electron beam again.

The electron beams are moved across the screen by changing the deflection yoke. When the beams reach the other side, they are turned off and returned to the starting side, just below the line where they left off. When the guns reach the last line, they move back up to the top. This is called *raster scanning* and it is done approximately sixty times a second.

Some monitor manufacturers try to save money by using less expensive components. The trade-off is that the beams cannot scan every line during each pass. Instead, they scan every other line during the first pass, then they scan the lines they missed during the second pass. This is called interlacing as the scan lines are *interlaced*. Although this provides higher resolutions in less expensive monitors, the images will "flicker" as the phosphors begin to fade before they can be recharged. (This flickering gives me, and other people, a headache.)

For most users, the most important aspect is the *resolution*. Resolution determines the total number of pixels that can be shown on the screen. In graphics mode, standard VGA has a resolution of 640 pixels horizontally and 480 pixels vertically. By convention, you say that your resolution is 640-by-480.

A pixel is actually a set of three phosphors rather than just a single phosphor. In essence, a pixel is a single spot of color on the screen. What color is shown at any given location is an *interaction* between the operating system and the video card. In the early systems, the operating system (or program) had to tell the video card where each dot on the screen was. It had an internal array (or table) of pixels each containing the appropriate color values. Today, some video cards can be told to *draw*. They don't need to know that there is a row of red dots between points A and B. Instead, they are simply told to draw a red line from point A to point B. This results in faster graphics, as much of the work is being taken over by the video card.

In other cases, the system still needs to keep track of which colors are where. If we had a truly monochrome video system, then any given pixel would either be on or off. Therefore a single bit can be used to store that information. If we go up to sixteen colors, we need four bits, or half a byte of information ($2^4 = 16$). If we go to a whole byte, then we can have 256 colors at once ($2^8$). Many video cards use three bytes to store the color data, one for each of the primary colors (RGB). In this way they can get over 16 million(!) colors

Now, 16 million colors seems like a lot, and it is. However, it's actually too much. Humans cannot distinguish that many, so much of the ability is wasted. Added to that, most monitors are limited to just a few hundred thousand colors. So, no matter what your friends tell you about how wonderful their video card is in that it does 16 million colors, you need not be impressed. The odds are that the monitor can't handle them and you certainly can't see them.

However, don't go thinking that the makings of video cards are trying to rip us off. In fact, it's easier to design cards that are multiples of whole bytes. If we had an 18-bit display (needed to get the 250K of colors that monitors could handle) we either use six bits of three different bytes or two whole bytes and two bits of the third. Either way, things are wasted and you spend time processing the bits. If you know that you have to read three whole bytes, one for each color, then there is not as much processing.

How many pixels and how many colors a video card can show are interdependent. When you bought it, your video card came with a certain amount of memory. The amount of memory it has limits the total number of pixels and colors you can have. If we take the standard resolution of a VGA card of $640 \times 480$ pixels, that's 307,200 pixels. If we want to show 16 colors that's $307200 \times 4$ bits or 1,228,800 bits. Dividing this by eight gives you 153,600 bytes needed to display $640 \times 480$ in 16 colors. Since memory is usually produced in powers of two, the next smallest size is 256 Kilobytes; therefore, a video card with 256K of memory is needed.

Maybe this is enough. For me, I don't get enough on the screen with $640 \times 480$ and only sixteen colors looks terrible (at least to me). However, if you never run any graphics applications on your machines, such as X Windows, then there is no need for anything better. Operating in *text mode* your video card does fine.

As I said, I am not happy with this, I want more. If I want to go up to the next higher resolution ($800 \times 600$) with sixteen colors, I need 240,000 bytes. I am still under the 256K I need for $640 \times 480$ and sixteen colors. If, instead, I want 256 colors (which requires 8 bits per pixel), I need at least 480,000. I now need 512K on the video card.

Now I buy a great big monitor and want something closing to "true color". Let's not get greedy, but say I wanted a resolution of 1024 × 768 (the next higher up) and only 65,635 colors. I now need 1,572,864 bytes of memory. Since my video card has only 1Mb of memory, I'm out of luck!

But wait a minute! Doesn't the VGA standard only support resolutions up to 640 × 480? True. However, the Video Electronics Standards Association (VESA) has defined resolutions above 640 × 480 as Super VGA. In addition to the ones mentioned previously (800 × 600 and 1024 × 768), SVGA also includes 1280 × 1024 and 1600 × 1200.

Okay. The mere fact that you have a video card that can handle SVGA resolutions does not mean you are going to get a decent picture (or at least not the picture you want). Any system is only as good as its worst component. This also applies to your video system. It is therefore important to understand a characteristic of your monitor: pitch. I mentioned this briefly before, but it is important to talk about it further.

When shopping for a monitor, you will often see that among the characteristics used to sell it is the pitch. The values you would see could be something like .39 or .28. This is the spacing between the holes in the shadow mask, measured in millimeters. Therefore, a pitch of .28 is just over one-quarter of a millimeter. The lower the pitch, the closer together the holes and the sharper the image. Even if you aren't using any graphics-oriented programs, it's worth the few extra dollars to get a lower pitch and the resulting sharper image.

## Modems

Up to this point, we've talked about things that most every computer user has. We are now moving into a new area. This is where we get one computer to talk to another. In my opinion, this is where computers begin to show their true power.

Perhaps the earliest means of getting computers to talk to one another (at least over long distances) was the modem. Modem stands for *Modulator/Demodulator*, which is its basis of operation. It takes the digital signals that come across the bus from the CPU and converts them into a signal that can be understood by the telephone wires. This process is called *modulation*. On the other end, the signals are converted back from telephone signals into computer signals by a process called *demodulation*. This is shown in Figure 10–15.

Underlying the transmission of data across the telephone line is the concept of a *carrier*. A carrier is a signal running along the phone line that is at a constant

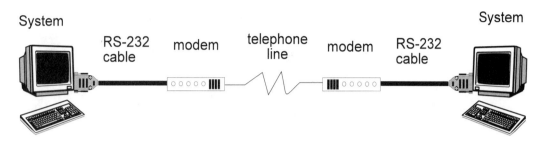

**Figure 10–15** Transfer of data across modems.

strength (amplitude), frequency, and phase. Because all of these are known values, changes in them can be detected. It is the changes that are used to encode the data.

When sending data at relatively low speeds, the exact timing of data being sent is not important. Markers are used within the transmitted data to indicate the beginning at the end of each piece. These are the start and stop bits. (Note: You could have two stop bits.) If each modem is set to the same values, it knows when one piece of data stops and the next one begins. This is called asynchronous transfer.

How big is that piece of data? Usually just a single character. All the modems that I have ever seen either have seven or eight bits for data. That means that there are seven or eight bits between the start-stop bit pairs. This, too, is something that both modems need to agree upon.

Parity works like this: Let's assume that a specific byte has three bits which are set. If you are using even parity, then the parity bit would be set to make the total number set four, which is an even number. If you are using odd parity, the number of the bit is already an odd number (3) and the parity bit would not be set.

When determining the settings for your modem, the order is usually the number of data bits, followed by the number of stop bits, then the parity. By default, SCO UNIX uses eight data bits, one stop bit, and no parity. It is common to refer to this a "eight, one, and none" or 8-1-N. Others might be 7-2-E for seven data bits, two stop bits, and even parity.

Another important characteristic is the speed at which the modem is transmitting the data. Although the exact timing is not critical, signals have to be received within a certain time or there are problems. (You could be waiting for months if the connection suddenly dropped.)

Now, let's go back to the modulated carrier wave. The term for the number of changes in the carrier wave per second is *baud*, named after the French telegraph expert, J.M.E Baudot. One way of encoding data is based on the changes to the carrier wave. This is called *frequency shift keying*, or FSK. The number of changes that can take place per second is the number of bits of information that can be sent per second (one change = one bit).

Let's take a modem connection operating at 2400 baud, 8 data bits, one stop bit, and no parity. This gives us a total of ten bits used for each character sent. (Did you forget the start bit?) Since baud is a measurement of the number of *bits* sent per second, 2400 baud means that 240 characters can be sent per second.

Other encoding methods result in getting more bits per baud. For example, the Bell 212A standard operates at 300 baud. However, since it gets four bits of data per baud, it gets 1200 bits per second for those 300 baud. This rate is accomplished by changing more than just the frequency. If we changed both frequency and amplitude, we have four distinct values that we could use.

Have you ever had someone tell you that you have a 9600 baud modem? Don't believe them! There is no such thing. In fact, the fastest baud rate is only 2400. So what are people taking about when they say their modem goes 9600 or 14400? They are talking about the *bits-per-second* (bps). If you get one bit-per-baud, then these terms are synonymous. However, all 9600 modems get more than that. They operated at 2400 baud, but use a modulation technique that yields 4 bits per baud. Thus a 2400 baud modem gives 9600 bits per second.

### Modem Standards

As with all the other kinds of hardware we've talked about, modems need to have standards in order to be useful. Granted you could have a modem that can only communicate with another from the same manufacturer, but even that is a kind of standard.

Modem standards are like opinions: everyone has one. There are the AT&T standards, the Bell standards, the International Telecommunications Union (ITU) standards (which was formally the Comite Consultatif International Telegraphique et Telephoneique—CCITT) and the Microcom Networking Protocol (MNP) standards.

As of this writing, the two most common standards are the CCITT and MNP. The MNP standards actually work in conjunction with modems that adhere to the other standards and for the most part define technologies rather than speeds or other characteristics.

The CCITT/ITU standards define (among other things) modulation methods that allow speeds up to 9600 bps for the V.32 standard and 1,400 bps for the V.32.bis standard. The new V.34 standard supports 2800bps. One of the newer standards,

V.42 is accepted worldwide and provides error-correction enhancements to V.32 and V.32bis. The V.42 standard also incorporates the MNP 4 standard allowing one modem that supports V.42 to communicate with another that supports MNP 4. For many more details on the different standards look at *The Winn L. Rosch Hardware Bible, Third Edition* and *Modem Reference, Second Edition,* by Michael Banks. Both are published by Brady Books.

One standard we need to go into is the *Hayes command set*. This was developed by and named for the modem manufacturer Hayes and is used by almost every modem manufacturer. It consists of dozens of commands that are used to modify the functionality as well as read the characteristics of your modem. Most of the commands in this set begin with AT (which is short for "attention"), so this is often referred as to the AT command set. Note that the AT and almost every other letter is capitalized.

Several AT commands can be combined in single strings, and this is often used to initialize the modem prior to use. This can set the default speed, whether the modem should automatically answer when someone calls in, and even how many rings to wait for. We'll talk about these in more detail later when we talk about configuring modems.

Modems come in two forms: internal and external. Because a modem is a serial device (it communicates serially as opposed to parallel) it will always take up a serial port. With an external modem, you have to physically make the connection to the serial port, so you are more conscious of the fact that the modem is taking up a port. With internal modems, you are still taking up a serial port, however, this fact is less obvious since you don't actually see the modem. Some users miss the fact that they no longer have a COM1 (or COM2).

External modems are usually connected to the computer via a 25-pin RS-232 connector. Some serial ports have only a 9-pin serial port so you need to get an adapter to convert the 25-pin to 9-pin, since *every* modem I have ever seen has a 25-pin connector.

So, what happens when I want to dial into another site, or send an email message to my sister in Washington? Well, the communications software (maybe cu or uucp) sends a signal (an increase in voltage) along pin 20 (Data Terminal Ready—DTR) to tell the modem that it is ready to transmit data. On the modem, the equivalent pin is #6 (Data Set Ready—DSR).

The modem is told to go "off hook" via the Transmit Data line (TX, line 2). Shortly thereafter the system sends the AT commands to have the modem start dialing either with pulses (ATDP) or with tones (ATDT). Commands are acknowledged by the modem via the line 3 (Receive Data—RX).

The modem dials just like a phone and tries to connect to some device on the other end. This is probably a modem and if *auto answer* is enabled, the modem being called should answer or *pick*-up the modem. When the connection is made, the calling modem sends a high-pitched signal to tell the receiving modem that a modem is calling. The receiving modem sends a higher pitched acknowledgment. You can hear this if your modem has a speaker.

The carrier signal is then established between the two modems, which is kept at a steady, predetermined frequency. It is this signal that is then modulated to actually transmit the data. When the modem begins receiving this carrier signal, it sends another signal back to the system via line 8 (Carried Detect—CD). This is held active for the duration of the call.

The two modems must first decide how they will transmit data. This negotiation is called a handshake. The information exchanged includes many of the things that are defined in the different standards we talked about earlier.

When the system is ready to send data, it first raises line 4 (Request to Send—RTS). If ready, the modem says that it's okay by raising line 5 (Clear to Send—CTS). Data is then sent out on line 2 and received on line 3. If the modem cannot keep up, it can drop the CTS line to tell the system to stop for a moment.

## Printers

Although more and more companies are trying to transform into a "paperless office," you will undoubtedly see a printer somewhere. Even if the office is paperless internally. It will have to use paper of some kind to communicate with the rest of the world.

Printers come in many different shapes, sizes, formats, means of connection to the system, ways of printing characters, speeds, and so on. The two most common ways of connecting printers is by serial or parallel ports. SCO UNIX also supports Hewlett-Packard Laser Jet printers equipped with JetDirect cards. These are cards that allow the printer to be attached directly to a network, thereby increasing its speed. We'll talk more about these later. In addition, although not supported by SCO as of this writing, SCSI printers have shown themselves on the market.

In previous sections, we talked about serial and parallel connections, so I don't need to go into details about them. I do talk about these connections in more details in the second part of the book when we talk about installing and configuring printers.

There are two kinds of printers that, although once very common, are now making way for their more advanced brethren. These are daisy-wheel and chain printers. The distinction that these printers had was that they had preformed characters.

In the case of a daisy-wheel printer, printing was accomplished by means of a wheel, where the characters were at the end of thin "leaves." This made the daisy shape. The wheel was rotated very quickly and as the appropriate letter came into position it was struck with a "hammer" which forced the leaf with the character into the ink ribbon, which then struck the paper. This mechanism is the same principle as a normal typewriter. In fact, there are typewriters that use the same daisy-wheel principle.

Chain printers also have preformed letters. However, instead of a wheel, the letters are on a long strip, called a chain. Instead of rotating, the chains moves back and forth to bring the appropriate letter into position.

Although these printers are fairly quick, they are limited in what they can print. You could get pretty tricky in what characters you use and come up with some rather cute pictures. However, they don't have the ability to do anything very detailed.

The next step was impact dot-matrix printers. These too have hammers, but rather than striking preformed letters, it is the hammers themselves that strike the ink ribbon. Instead of a single hammer, there is a column of usually 9 or 24 hammers, or pins. Such printers are called 9-pin or 24-pin.

As the printer prints, the heads are moved across the page and print out columns of dots. Depending on what character is to be printed, some of the pins do not strike the ink ribbon. For example, when printing a dash, only the middle pin(s) will strike the ribbon. When printing a more complex character like an ampersand (&), the pins strike at different times as the print head moves across the page.

As with monitors, the more dots you have, the sharper the image. Therefore, a printer with 24-pins can produce a sharper image than one with only 9-pins. In most cases, it is obvious the moment you see something that it was printed with a 9-pin printer. Some 24-pin printers require a little closer look before you can tell.

Next, imagine getting rid of the ink ribbon and replacing the pins with little sprayers connected to a supply of ink. Instead of striking something, these sprayers squirt a little dot of ink onto the paper. The result is the same as an impact dot matrix printer. This is what an ink jet printer does.

There are two advantage that ink jets have over impact dot matrix printers; first, is the noise. Since there are no pins striking the ink ribbon, the printer is a lot quieter. Second, by extending the technology a little you can increase the number of jets in each row. Instead of just squirting out black, you could squirt out in color, which is how many color printers work.

The drawback is the nature of the print process itself. Little sprayers, squirting ink all over the place is messy. Without regular maintenance, ink jets can clog up.

Using a principle very similar to video systems, laser printers can obtain very high resolution. A laser inside the printer (hence the name) scans across a rotating drum that has been given a static electric charge. When the laser hits a spot on the drum, that area loses its charge. Toner is then spread across the drum and sticks to those areas that retain their charge. Next the drum rolls across the paper, smashing the toner into the paper. Finally, the toner is fused into the paper by means of a heating element.

Although it may appear as a solid image, laser printers still work with dots. The dots are substantially smaller than those of a 24-pin dot matrix, but they are still dots. As with video systems, the more dots the sharper the image. Because a laser is used to change the characteristics of the drum, the areas affected are very small. Therefore, with laser printers you can get resolutions of even 300 dots-per-inch on even the least expensive printers. Newer ones are approaching 1200 dpi, which is comparable to photographs.

Some laser printers, like HP's LaserJet III and use a technology called resolution enhancement. Although there are still a limited number of dots-per-inch, the size of each dot can be altered, thereby changing the *apparent* resolution.

Keep in mind that printers have the same problem with resolution as do video systems. The more dots that are desired the more memory is needed to process them. An 8½″ × 11″ page with a resolution of 300dpi take almost a megabyte of memory.

With printers such as daisy-wheel and chain printers, you really don't have to deal with this issue. Even a buffer as small as 8K is more than sufficient to hold a whole page of text including *control characters* that can change the way the other characters appear. While such control characters may cause the text to be printed bold or underlined, they are relatively simple in nature. For example, underlining normally consists of printing the character, backing up one space, then printing an underline.

Multiple characters sets or fonts is something that this kind of printer just can't handle. Different character sets (German) or changing their form (italic) can easily be accomplished when the letter is created "on-the-fly" with dot-matrix printers. All that is needed is to change the way the dots are positioned. This is usually accomplished by using *escape sequences*. First, an *escape character* (ASCII 27) is sent to the printer to tell it that the next character (or characters) is a command to change its behavior.

Different printers react differently to different escape sequences. Although there is a wide range of sets of escape sequences, the two most common ones are those for IBM Proprinters and Epson printers. Most dot-matrix printers can be configured to behave like one of these. Some, like my Panasonic KX-P1123, can be configured to behave like *either* one.

The shortcoming with this is that you are limited to a small range of character types and sizes. Some printers, like mine, can get around this limitation by the fact that they can print in graphic modes as well. By viewing the page as one complete image, composed of thousands of dots, they can get any font, any size, and with any attribute (assuming the software can handle this). This is how printers like mine can print charts, tables, and to some extent pictures.

Viewing the page as a complete image works when you have graphics or diagrams, however it's a waste of memory when dealing with straight text. Therefore, most laser printers operate in *character-mapped mode*. The characters are stored in memory and the dots are generated as the page goes through the printer.

Printers are controlled by other means than just escape sequences of treating the page as a single image. One of the most widely used is Adobe System's *Postscript* page description language. It is as much a language as the programming languages C or Pascal, with syntax and vocabulary. In order to utilize it, both the software and the printer have to support it. However, the advantage is that many applications allow you to print Postscript to a file. That file can then be transferred to a remote site with a Postscript printer. The file is then sent to a printer (as raw data) and the output is the same as if it were printed directly from the application. The nice thing is that the remote site does not even have to have the same application, so long as their printer is Postscript capable.

Hewlett-Packard has its own language: *Printer Control Language* or PCL. PCL is a lot simpler than Postscript and was easily incorporated into SCO's printer interface scripts, which are used by the operating system to control printers.

## Mice

Although a mouse can be used with default SCO UNIX programs such as `vi` and `sysadmsh`, it really begins to show its stuff when you have a graphical user interface (GUI) such as X Windows. Although some GUIs (like Microsoft Windows) allow you to run without a mouse, SCO's implementation of X Windows does not. If you ever want to install X Windows or even if you want to use a mouse with `sysadmsh`, then you will need to know about mice.

The basic principle is that by moving the mouse, the cursor (pointer) on the screen is moved in the same manner. Actions can be carried out by clicking one of up to three buttons on the mouse.

As the mouse is moved across a surface, a ball underneath rolls along with it. This ball turns small wheels (usually three of them) inside of the mouse. The amount of movement of each of these wheels can be measured and it is this movement that is translated into movement of the cursor.

Because the ball underneath needs to roll in order to make the mouse work, it has to remain on a flat surface. The surface must also have a certain amount of friction for the ball to roll. Although you can get a certain amount of movement by shaking the mouse, picking it up and expecting the cursor to move is a waste of your time (despite what I have seen some users do).

Originally, mice were connected by a thin cable to the computer. As technology progressed, the cable was done away with and replaced with a light emitting diode (LED) on the mouse and a photodetector near the computer. This has the advantage of not allowing the cable to get buried under a pile of papers and thereby limiting the mouse's movement. The disadvantage is that the LED must remain within line-of-sight of the photodetector in order to function. Some manufacturer's have overcome this by using an alternate form of light that is not dependent on line-of-sight: radio.

Another major problem with all of these kinds of mice is desk space. My desk is not neat. Space is at a premium. Even the small space needed for a mouse pad is a luxury that I rarely have. Fortunately, companies such as Logitech have heard my cries and come to the rescue. The solution is, as an old UNIX guru called it, a dead mouse.

This is a mouse, lying on its back, with its feet (or at least the ball) sticking up in the air. Rather than moving the mouse to move the ball to move the wheels to move the cursor, you simply move the ball. The ball is somewhat larger than the one inside of a mouse, which makes it a lot easier to move. Such a mouse is called a trackball and is very common with laptop computers. Provided the signals sent to the operating system are the same, a trackball behaves functionally the same as a mouse.

The mouse's interface to the operating system can take one of three forms. The mouse is referred to, based on this interface, as either a *serial mouse, bus mouse,* or a *keyboard mouse.*

As its name implies, a serial mouse is attached to your computer through a serial port. Bus mice have their own interface card that plugs into the bus. Keyboard mice, despite their name, usually do not plug into the keyboard. Although I have seen some built into the keyboard, these were actually serial mice. Instead a keyboard mouse is plugged into its own connector, usually next to the keyboard connector, which is then attached directly to the motherboard. These are usually found on IBM PS/2 and some Compaq computers, however more and more computer manufacturers are providing a connector for a keyboard mouse.

When talking about the movement of the mouse, you often hear the term *resolution*. For a mouse, resolution is referred to in terms of clicks per inch or CPI. A click is simply the signal sent to the system to tell it that the mouse has moved. The higher the CPI, the higher resolution. Both mice and trackballs have resolution, since both rely on the movement of a ball to translate to movement of the cursor.

Keep in mind, that despite the way it appears at first, a mouse with a higher resolution is not more precise. In fact, the opposite is almost always true. Higher resolution means that the mouse moves *further* for each given movement on the ball. The result is that the movement is *faster* not more precise. Since precision is really determined by your own hand movements, experience has shown me that you get better precision with a mouse that has a lower resolution.

## Uninterruptable Power Supplies

New to OpenServer is direct support for uninterrupted power supplies (UPS). In previous releases, UPS was supported by third party products such as Power-Chute Plus from American Power Conversion (APC), which would interface directly with APCs various UPSs. Despite the fact that a UPS is not intended to replace your primary power supply, it does provide an interim power source, which allows you to shutdown gracefully.

The first thing I want to address is the concept of uninterruptable power. If we take that term literally we must say that a power supply that goes out at all has been interrupted. In that case, then many UPSs are not correctly named, since there is a brief moment (ca. 30 milliseconds) between the time they notice power has gone out and the time the battery kicks in. This time is too small for the computer to notice, but it is there. (Normally power must be out for at least 300 milliseconds.) As a result, most UPSs should be referred to as stand-by power supply (SPS), since they switch to the battery when the primary supply shuts off. Since Underwriter's Laboratories uses UPS to describe both, that's what I will do here.

The basic UPS provides limited power conditioning (keeping the voltage within a specific range) but no protection against surges and spikes. This is useful if the power goes out, but doesn't protect you if the voltage suddenly jumps (such as the result of a lightning strike). A *double-conversion* model provides the power when the main power fails, but also provides protection against surges. This is done by first passing the power through the batteries. Although this does provide the protection, it is less efficient since power is constantly being drawn from the battery.

# CHAPTER 11

# Installing
# and
# Upgrading

I am sure that you are wondering why the installation chapter appears at this point in the book. Well, it's something that I took a lot of time to think about. I'm betting that you already have an SCO system installed and you bought this book because you want to find out more. If you do need to install something at this point, then it's less likely that its the whole system, but rather something like new hardware or software. That's what the bulk of this chapter is all about. However, because you may (one day) want to install a system from scratch, we're going to talk a little about that.

If you already have ODT, then you are probably not going to do a fresh installation of it. More than likely, the next time you install the OS, it will be to do an install of OpenServer. However, tech support never plays the odds. I can speak from experience when I say that someone out there is going to need to install an ODT system. Perhaps the system needs to be reinstalled because of hardware problems. Maybe there was an unopened ODT box on the shelf and the boss didn't want to waste money buying a copy of the new OS.

In comparison to the installation guide of ODT, the one that comes with OpenServer is wonderful. Not that I am saying the one for ODT is bad. They are simply two completely different books. The installation guide for ODT basically just served the purpose of installing the system. OpenServer guide is called the *SCO OpenServer Handbook,* with the subtitle of *How to Install, Configure, and Start Using an SCO OpenServer System.* It covers much more than just installation and is an invaluable tool for administering your system. There is also the added benefit of having an index. The lack of an index in the ODT installation guide, made it difficult to find information you needed.

Before we jump into things, I'd like to briefly discuss some of the more significant changes to the OpenServer installation. After going through hundreds of installs myself with customers on the phone, I can safely say that the OpenServer installation process is by far the simplest one yet. All of the questions are asked up front and once the files start rolling off the CD-ROM, you can go get some lunch and let the system do the work for you.

One of the most startling differences is that OpenServer only comes with a single floppy. I have been doing installs for years. There is *supposed* to be an N1 *and* N2 floppy, right? The kernel is almost the size of an entire floppy, so how can you get the kernel and the necessary programs to do an install on less than two floppies? You compress them!

Not only is the kernel compressed, but so are the installation programs. Although a certain amount of time needs to be spent uncompressing things, the kernel is uncompressed as it is being loaded. Since you do not have to switch floppies and begin loading that as well, the time you gain more than compensates for the time needed to uncompress things. A RAM disk is created and the root filesystem *image* is loaded into the RAM disk. Like the kernel, this filesystem image is compressed to get it to fit on the floppy. Note that although the files on the floppies are compressed, it is *not* a compressed filesystem.

## Preparing for the Install

Both the *ODT Installation Guide* and *OpenServer Handbook* provide an "installation checklist". One thing I really like about the OpenServer handbook checklist over the one in the ODT installation guide is that it contains comments and references to other pages in the handbook where you can find more information. Although there are comments in the ODT guide, they come *after* the checklist. This means that you have to flip back and forth between pages.

I suggest you make a copy of these pages so you can fill in each entry and include it in a notebook. You will notice that there are some very basic questions concerning keyboard language and time zone. It may seem almost too basic to include this type of information, however, I can speak from experience that the more you have written down, the less prone you are to making mistakes. Even if the information is "basic."

Before you start you need to check out your system. The very first thing you need to check is the hardware itself. The first question to ask yourself is whether or not the hardware is supported. I'm sure there are a few of you out there who are groaning thinking this is an attempt to blow you off. I talked with many customers while I was in SCO Support that went ballistic when I brought up the question of the hardware being supported.

"It works under DOS!" Is a common response. However, as I have said many times, all that really means is that the hardware is probably not broken. I say "probably" because I have seen defective hardware work under DOS, but not on UNIX. Under DOS a lot of hardware is accessed through the system BIOS. The BIOS is often built especially for that machine. It understands the hardware in a way that SCO doesn't. Since the SCO device drivers are accessing the hardware directly, the hardware has to behave in a standard way. Otherwise, the SCO device drivers don't know what to expect.

Does this mean that your no-name hardware won't work? Not at all. My server is running a fair bit of "unsupported" hardware. Much of it is clones of supported hardware (which causes a lot of grief). However, it works. When I tried to install something that wasn't supported and it didn't work, there was no frustration because working was something that wasn't guaranteed (okay, there was a little frustration).

There is also the issue of conflicts. SCO is good about being able to install a wide number of cards at their default. The common place for conflicts is with cards of the same type, such as host adapters. However, having the list in front of you will confirm this before you try to install and have something go wrong.

The key pieces of information are

- base address
- IRQ
- DMA channel
- Memory address

Once you have installed the operating system and it works diligently for six months, the first problems may crop up. Now, what was the model of the hard disk? Rather than digging through a box of papers looking for the invoice, you have it right in front of you.

Okay, knowing that you should fill out the installation checklist is easy. Knowing what to put in each entry is the hard part. Because the OpenServer installation checklist is more detailed and even points you to other places in the installation guide, this may be of more value to people having to install ODT for the first time (if there are any out there). However, I will be going into details of many aspects of the installation that aren't mentioned in the installation guide.

It may already be too late, but an important thing to consider for the installation is the installation media. OpenServer is delivered on CD-ROM and you have to order it extra if you want it on 150MB cartridge tape or floppies. If you like pain, I would definitely suggest getting the floppy version. With 147 floppies, your wrists will get a good workout. If you're the patient kind, but don't like the work, maybe the tape media is best for you. Otherwise, I suggest you stick with the CD-ROM.

Consider the price of CD-ROM drives today. If you buy the CD-ROM version of OpenServer you save hundreds of dollars(!) over the price of floppies. This literally pays for the CD-ROM drive. Now, a friend of mine said that this logic was comparable to his wife's when she went shopping. She would buy a dress that was on sale saying that she saved $30.00, not mentioning she probably would not have bought it if it hadn't been on sale. However, you are going to buy OpenServer even if it's not on sale. So why not get a "free" CD-ROM in the deal? There is also the added benefit of CD-ROMs being faster to access than either tapes or floppies. Once you get the CD-ROM drive you can then get SCO's Skunkware CD, which is loaded with fun stuff.

Doing a CD-ROM install is an arguable point in ODT when you need to install a single file. You can quickly find out what floppy a particular file is on and extract the file within a matter of minutes. It takes longer for you to start custom and have the CD-ROM drive seek to the proper location. With OpenServer, the problem is even worse since you cannot install single files. You must first remove the package and then reinstall it.

During the course of the installation, you will have the choice of several different installation types, from fully automatic to fully configurable. For the more advanced system administrators, the fully configurable allows you control of many different aspects of the install. Fully automatic, basically does everything for you; that is, it evaluates your system and essentially makes all the decisions itself. My recommendation is that if you are a novice administrator *and* there is nothing on the hard disk that you want to save, then the fully automatic is your best choice.

## Preparing for the Worst

One thing that many administrator's don't plan for is the possibility that things will go wrong. Although, good planning and preparation can prevent many disasters, the most devastating are obviously the ones that you are not prepared for. When doing an upgrade, there will come a point in which backing out is no longer possible. If the new operating system doesn't book and you cannot go back to the old one, then you have problems.

One problem that I have had personal experience with is third party device drivers. Although the installation notes for the driver might say that it is for SCO UNIX 3.2. version 4.0 and later, this may not be true. If it is an older card, then what they mean by "and later" is SCO UNIX 3.2 version 4.2 (ODT). In the case of the network card I had it wasn't true. What I had was an NE2000 *compatible* that worked fine in ODT. However, it gave me errors when I tried to relink it under OpenServer.

The problems that my brother encountered where much more dramatic. He has a third party filesystem compression software on his system that he uses for his /u filesystem. Although this is a very stable product and he is completely satisfied with it, the version he has is incompatible with OpenServer. As a result, when he tried to relink, it failed. He then tried to load the backup software he had, only to discover that the install script did not work correctly with the OpenServer custom. The choice was either to wait until he got the OpenServer version of the backup software or reinstall ODT. Since his work depends on timely access to his data, his only choice was to re-install. Since he had a complete backup of his system, he was running again within a couple of hours.

This story illustrates two important issues when doing an upgrade. First, be prepared for the possibility that your third party drivers will not work. It is possible that the device was unsupported in ODT, but is now supported in OpenServer. Installing the manufacturer's driver may not only be unnecessary, it may cause problems. Check the *SCO Hardware Compatibility Guide* or the hardware vendor.

Keep in mind that the compression software is not a "device" in the traditional sense, despite having drivers. Therefore, you will not find it in the *SCO Hardware Compatibility Guide.* The best thing to do in cases like this is to talk to the vendor directly.

The other issue is that you *must* have a **complete** backup of your system before you start. In my brother's case, he did have a complete backup. The problem was that the backup software didn't work in OpenServer. However, since he was prepared before he started the upgrade and had a complete backup, he was running again within a short time. No matter what goes wrong, these backups can get you running again.

One suggestion is to either have the new version of the backup software on hand and *make sure* that it is compatible with OpenServer or use some SCO tool like `tar` or `cpio`. Both the `tar` and `cpio` in OpenServer can read the backups created in ODT.

If you have access to CompuServe, you might want to consider downloading the demo copy of `Lone-Tar` from Library 8. This works with both ODT *and* OpenServer. This is a demo with a limited lifespan, but not limited functionality. I think you might be pleased enough with it to use it as your standard backup tool.

## Upgrading an Existing System

The fact that your computer contains an existing SCO installation, presents its own set of problems. Paradoxically, one of the primary trouble spots is one of the benefits that OpenServer is providing and that is the new filesystems. As I mentioned in the section on filesystems, the `/dev/boot` filesystem was introduced to not only prevent the kernel from existing above the 1024 cylinder boundary, but also because the system cannot boot from the new filesystem types. Therefore, an upgrade installation means that you cannot use any of the new filesystems as your root filesystem.

Personally, I am not bothered by this. Although I have had good experience when doing upgrades, I am *not* an upgrade fan. Personally, I feel that doing a fresh install is safer, particularly when the system has one or more supplements installed. Although I have never had problems, safe is safe. However, you may not have that option. There might be time or other constraints that "encourage" you to do an upgrade.

One aspect of your system that I am sure you will want to keep track of is your users. ODT provides the `ap` (account profile) command which allows you to save account information for every user listed in `/etc/passwd`. For details on this, see the *OpenServer Handbook* or the `ap(ADM)` man-page. However, there is much more information about your system that you may want to save. The *OpenServer Handbook* contains a list of files that may have been changed from their defaults. Keep in mind that the heading "Files likely to be configured" is not entirely accurate (you don't configure `/etc/wmtp`).

If you are doing an install and have third party drivers, then the install is smart enough to keep from creating additional problems. Although the upgrade installation does not remove any drivers or device nodes, it does put an "N" in the `/etc/conf/sdevice.d` files of the drivers that it doesn't recognize. This way any relinks of the kernel during the installation *should* go smoothly. Later, you can change the Ns to Ys and try to relink. Since the drivers and device nodes are still there, the relink has a good chance of being successful.

The upgrade to OpenServer also preserves other aspects of your system such as printers, network settings, and additional filesystems. However, even if you do "need" to do a fresh install, the system is smart enough to pull many configuration settings directly from the old system. These are provided as default values as you go through the install.

## Doing the Install

When it finally comes time to do the install, the first step is gathering all the documentation together. This includes not only all of the SCO doc but all the handbooks (pamphlets?) that came with your hardware. The next thing to get is a notebook. Here you record all the details about your system configuration. Since you haven't installed anything, yet, now is a good time to start writing things down. This is the perfect opportunity to write down manufacturer, model, and settings of all the hardware. This is a valuable set of information if you run into problems, either during the install or later. You should also write down the vendor support number if it's available. Here, again, having everything in one place will save you time later.

Next is the checklist that we talked about earlier. Having a completed installation checklist has a couple of benefits. First, it can be a real time saver during the installation. You don't have to keep bouncing around between the doc and hardware or scratching your head thinking about what a good value for each entry would be. You've made all the decisions before and now you just fill in the blanks. You are therefore less likely to input mistakes or guess at what you should answer. In addition, this "forces" you to plan out the upgrade before you start.

When you boot from the floppy during the installation, one of the first things you need to consider are Boot-Time Loadable Drivers (BTLD). These are drivers for hardware that is not supported by SCO on the release you are currently installing, however the vendor provides the appropriate drivers which are then linked into the kernel at boot time. These are not necessarily drivers for hardware that you install after the OS is finished, but rather for hardware that you need during the installation. A good example would be the host adapter that your root hard disk is installed on. However, the mechanism used to install BTLDs is not just restricted to the installation. You can install a BTLD at any time. These are just drivers that are loaded at boot time, not just install time. For more details, see the section on BTLDs.

When the kernel has finished loading and the root filesystem is uncompressed, the Installation Query Manager (IQM) is started. Although the IQM in OpenServer is conceptually the same as that for ODT, the new one is much more extensive in terms of both what areas are asked as well as the depth of information you can provide. Once you finish answering the questions, the IQM does the rest of the work.

One thing that really impressed me was the ability of the system to recognize my hardware. For example, when asking about my network configuration it asked if it should scan for a network card. When I said "yes," the system came up with the NE2000 card that mine was (supposed to be) compatible with. Later, after I had finished the install and wanted to restore my data, I absent-mindedly started a `cpio` without first running `mkdev tape` to add to the tape drive. No problem. The tape started and the data was restored since the system had recognized and configured my tape drive for me during the install. (I was told by an SCO engineer that by default a tape is configured at SCSI ID whether the tape drive exists or not.)

One of the very first questions asked is the type of keyboard you have. This issue is not as apparent to Americans as it is to people of other countries. Aside from the languages that have different characters than in American English, there are differences in the layout of the keyboard between English speaking countries.

The next step in the installation is the serialization. In OpenServer you no longer have to input your serial number and activation key. Instead you have a license number and license code. In some cases (with certain upgrades), there is license data provided that must also be input during the installation. This is useful information to have when you need to call support, particularly if you don't already have a support contract.

The type of installation you are going to do is an important decision. In ODT, you are given three choices: fresh, overwrite, and upgrade. In a fresh install, you consider your system as untouched and overwrite everything on the hard disk. If you chose the overwrite option, the partition and filesystem information is left intact. Only the root filesystem is overwritten, and user filesystems are untouched. In an upgrade, the old files are moved out of the way, but everything else is left as it was.

In order to save time, many system administrators chose the upgrade option. Although this upgrade functionality has improved considerably since previous releases, it can't catch everything. There are many hardware and software products that become unuseable after an upgrade and must be reinstalled. In the end, the administrator spends more time cleaning up from the upgrade than was saved by not doing a fresh install.

The alternative is doing an overwrite. This essentially removes all third party drivers and other products installed on the root filesystem as this is completely overwritten. However, it is somewhat faster than a fresh install. The problem is that there is no overwrite option for OpenServer. You either upgrade or do a fresh install.

Personally, I'm not bothered by this. When I do an installation it is always a fresh install. Experience has taught me that the best way to avoid problems is not to let them happen. By doing a fresh install, I am much more aware of the effects each action has on my system. It may take longer initially. However, I am saved grief in the long run.

When you do a fresh install, you must ask some key questions. First how should the disk be partitioned? If you have only one operating system, then using the entire disk for SCO is reasonable. If not, you need to consider how much will be used for each. The installation procedure of both ODT and OpenServer asks you how big you want different partitions to be. Despite that fact, there is still the question of, "how big?"

One thing to consider is what other software is going to be installed. Some database applications require an entire partition for its own purposes. Others may require their own filesystem. I've talked with customers who, after installing the OS discovered that they did not leave the necessary room for their application. They frantically call to support asking for some way to change the partition and filesystems without having to reinstall. The answer is no. Therefore know what your application expects before you start installing the operating system.

The next thing to consider is what other operating systems you are going to install. Although you can create the partitions for other operating systems during the SCO installation, it is much better to install them first and then SCO. You can get away with installing DOS after SCO, however if you are going to install OS/2, Windows NT, or Windows 95, these should be installed first. The reason is that they write the partition table differently than SCO or DOS making the SCO partition inaccessible.

If you are planning to install DOS, you will still be limited to the 32MB partition size if you are still running MS-DOS 3.3. Don't use any version of MS-DOS 4.x. This doesn't work well with SCO partitions. If you have anything after MS-DOS 5.0, then the partition size can be anything greater than 3Mb. Keep in mind that if you plan to use DOS DoubleSpace or some other disk compression software, the compressed partition will not be accessible by SCO utilties such as `doscp`, nor will you be able to mount the DOS filesystem. Also pay attention to which partition is active. I have talked with many customers who have overwritten one or the other partitions. Both DOS and SCO install to the active partition. If you install one and then install the other without first making the other partition active, you end up overwriting the first operating system.

Since DOS can be installed after SCO, some people do. Even if you do remember to switch the active partition prior to installing DOS, some people forget about this later. They are used to booting systems with both DOS and SCO and seeing the SCO `Boot:` prompt. When the system boots directly into DOS, they have a heart attack and end up calling SCO Support. The way to correct this problem is to simply use DOS's `fdisk` to change the active partition to the UNIX partition.

Also keep in mind that when the SCO installation routines create the partitions, that's all they are doing. They are not formatting the partition. You must use native DOS programs to do that. Even the `dosformat` command will not format a DOS partition. This partitioning is done by the `fdisk` command, although you don't actually see it doing its work.

When considering the partition size, you need to also consider the swap and filesystem sizes as well. The size of your swap space needs to be considered carefully. The absolute minimum size is slightly more than the amount of RAM you have. The reason is that if the system should panic, it will dump all of the memory to your swap device. If you do not have a large enough swap space, then you do not get a valid dump image and it makes tracking down the cause of the crash more difficult. The extra amount is needed to write crash data if the system panics. By increasing it by a megabyte you don't lose too much space.

I've seen references that say swap should be one-and-a-half to two times the amount of RAM. Personally, I think this is too much, without a good reason. The swap space should be considered a safety net, not an integral part of your memory system. If you are swapping then performance will suffer. If you think you will need the extra swap space, then consider buying more RAM. That way, you are less likely to swap in the first place.

However, you need to consider growth. If you expect to be increasing your RAM in the future, you should consider that when setting how much space you are going to use for swap. RAM just slides into your system. Increasing swap may require reinstalling the operating system. So, how much do you assign to swap? Good question. My suggestion is twice as much as RAM. The "good reason" I mentioned above is that it is easier to do it now and waste the space than to reinstall later. Another good reason is when you have more than one user running graphical applications. In this case, then even setting swap to two times RAM is reasonable. If you have all the space taken up on the primary hard disk, you can add a hard disk and use the `swap` command to add additional swap space.

You also need to keep in mind that swapping takes up system resources. The time to access the hard disk is hundreds of times slower than the time to access RAM. Therefore, if speed is an important consideration, you should think about having enough RAM so you don't swap.

At this point you also want to consider additional filesystems. With OpenServer, things are complicated already. The first question is how big you want your boot filesystem to be (`/dev/boot`). This holds a few files and a couple of copies of the kernel. Therefore, it doesn't need to be too big. However, you need to consider how much the kernels can grow. If you have a 3Mb kernel, then 5Mb for `/dev/boot` is not enough. However, making it 50Mb is going overboard to the other extreme. Personally, I think 10–15 gives you room for a larger kernel, but also gives you room to grow. However, you need to consider that there will probably be at least three kernels here.

The next question is whether you should make additional filesystems. If your application requires a filesystem to itself (usually a raw division), then you definitely need to create it. What about a /u or /home filesystem for your users? There are advantages to having one as well as advantages to not having one.

If you have one, it is easier to come up with a backup schedule if you don't want to do a full back-up of the system every night. For example, you could back up the whole system once a week, and the /u filesystem with the data every night. In addition, most of the hard disk activity is on the root filesystem. If your data is there and there is a head crash, you can lose data. By moving your data to another part of the disk, you decrease the likelihood of data loss.

The disadvantage of a separate filesystem is that system accounts such as root or sys have their home directories in /usr. If you put other users in /u or /home, the home directories are in two different places. This may not be too big a problem if the system accounts rarely, if ever, log in. The other problem is that creation of the filesystem does not mean that it gets mounted automatically (at least not in ODT). As a result customers end up calling to SCO Support saying that half their disk is missing. They had created the filesystem, but didn't run mkdev fs to have it get mounted. Although it is mentioned in the ODT doc that you need to do this, finding it requires that you either know the problem or read the doc cover to cover. OpenServer corrected the problem by asking if you want to create the appropriate entries to automatically mount the filesystem.

The other problem is that the default is to create user home directories in /usr. Therefore you need to change the HOME_DIR variable in /etc/default/authsh on ODT and in /etc/default/accounts on OpenServer. Personally, I think it's a good idea to have data on a separate filesystem and keep the root filesystem as static as possible. This makes backup schedules easier and there is less chance of corruption as the root filesystem is usually the busiest and therefore has a greater potential for corruption.

During the installation it is the divvy program that divides the partition into divisions and then calls mkfs to create the filesystems on those divisions. Although there are eight entries in the division table, the last one (division 7) is reserved and is used to reference the entire partition. If you have a large enough disk, division 6 might be reserved as well. This is the scratch device that is used by fsck.

The filesystems created on the root hard disk are dependent on which OS you are installing. On ODT, the first division (division 0) is for the root filesystem. However, on OpenServer, the first filesystem is /dev/boot which contains the file necessary to boot. The root filesystem is then on the third division. In both cases, the swap division is in division 1. Additional filesystems are created after the systems filesystems.

If you choose block by block control over the filesystems, you can change the starting and ending blocks and therefore the sizes of the filesystems and get around any defaults enforced by the system. Here you can also name the filesystems anything you want. However, I would not change the name of any of the system filesystems. You can also add a filesystem here. If so, you need to ensure that you create it as well. This will run `mkfs` to create the superblock and inode table. Note that the maximum filesystem size that you can create is 1TB for both DTFS and HTFS, and 2GB for other filesystems.

Some of you might see this statement as being incorrect. The SCO doc says that the HTFS can only be 512Gb. The word I got from an SCO engineer is that this is incorrect. Both can handle 1TB.

Another question concerns what type of disk scan to select. If you have an SCSI disk, this step is skipped as it is expected that the SCSI disk will be doing the bad tracking itself. The system will create the bad track table, however, it will not prompt you to scan the disk. If it does a scan, tracks are read from the disk and rewritten. The value that is read is compared to the value that is written. This is done several times to ensure the integrity of the data. If you have an SCSI disk, you can scan it later using the `scsibadblk` utility. (If you have ODT, think about getting the new `badtrk` from SCO support.) If it is a non-SCSI disk you use the `badtrk` utility.

You have two characteristics to choose from. First, you are given the choice between a Thorough and a Quick scan. As one would guess, a thorough scan takes longer than a quick scan—several times longer. However, it is more reliable since the data is read and written more often.

You also choose between a destructive and nondestructive scan. A nondestructive scan reads the data first and then writes back whatever was there originally. A destructive scan writes a known pattern of bytes on the disk first and then reads it. This is obviously destructive because whatever was on that track is overwritten by this pattern. This is more reliable because you always know what the data is supposed to be. Assume the track is not "bad" just "flaky"; that is, only sometimes it is read incorrectly. With a nondestructive scan, you could have read in corrupt data if you write it back and read it again. You don't know what is correct.

The moral? If there is any question about the integrity of the hard disk, then do a thorough, destructive scan. I say it three times: Destructive means destructive. Destructive means destructive. Destructive means destructive. I have had a number of calls from customers who did a thorough, destructive scan of the complete hard disk, only to find the data on the second filesystem (which they had hoped to preserve across the installation) was gone. Their interpretation of destructive was anything from, "destroying the bad tracks" to ,"I'm not a techie. How should I know?"

If `badtrk` finds a problem in the first few tracks of the partition, you are returned to `fdisk`, so you can repartition the disk around these bad spots. If you repeatedly get bad tracks at the beginning of the disk or all of the tracks appear to be bad, then the hard disk geometry is probably wrong. You will have to restart the installation and ensure that the system has the correct hard disk parameters.

When `badtrk` finishes, you are prompted for the number of entries to put in the `badtrk` table. Always put in as many as are recommended, if not more. If sometime in the future your disk develops problems and you need a lot of entries in the table, it can get filled up. Once it's full, there is nothing to do with additional bad tracks. The only solution is to reinstall. To calculate the amount of space lost, multiply the number of entries in the `badtrk` table by the sectors per track, then by 512 bytes per sector. (Think back to our discussion of the layout of the hard disk.)

What components of the product you install is also something to consider. Obviously the easiest thing is just to install everything. That way it's there if you need it. If you have a space problem, then installing everything is not always a good idea. Limited space is one reason why SCO came up with the Desktop product and why the DTFS was implemented. However, if you have ODT or are still cramped for space you might need to consider leaving out some packages.

If you are running NFS, a common package to remove is the man-pages and other on-line documentation. You can then use NFS (see the section on configuring your networking) to mount the doc from a remote machine. By having this on a central machine you not only save space, but it is also easier to include your own, local documentation since you don't have to worry about updating all your machines. Changes made on the "documentation server" are immediately available to everyone. Take a look at the section on automount in the Network chapter for ideas on that.

Whenever I have to do a floppy installation, I often leave out the documentation to save time. Once I am up and running, I can add the doc at my leisure. I will often bring the system up into multi-user mode and configure users or printers while I am installing the doc. Depending on the system and time constraints, I may even leave off packages like X or TCP. However, this is really only an issue with floppies. If I have a CD-ROM or tape install, it's easier to install everything and then later remove the pieces I don't want.

One aspect of the OpenServer installation that I am very grateful for is asking me whether I want `scologin` enabled by default or not. I don't. Although it is easy enough to disable it (`scologin disable`), I was annoyed at someone thinking that they knew better and that I would "naturally" want it enabled. I want the choice of starting X when I go into multi-user mode or not. (Interestingly enough, I almost always go into X. Old habits are hard to break.)

If the machine you are installing is going to be on a network, then the network configuration is also something to consider before you install. There are entries in the installation checklist for the configuration information, such as IP address, netmask, and broadcast. Like the other entries, when the checklist is filled out in advance, it saves you time when doing the install.

One very important thing you need to be aware of is that the OpenServer installation does not prompt you to install the release supplement like it does in ODT. You must, instead, go through the Software Manager to install new software. This is very important as the Release Supplement contains last corrections to known problems (in English: bug fixes). One thing to keep in mind is that when you add the release supplement in OpenServer, you select "Add Patch" and *not* "Add New Software."

If somewhere during the installation you run into a snag and have to restart the installation, you need to be careful. For example, you may get halfway through the installation and realize you did not leave any room for a /u filesystem. So, you need to restart. The problem, depending on how far you've gotten, is that if you power off and reboot from the installation floppy, the system will recognize that it has already reached a particular point and continue on from there. In order to get the system to restart the install from the beginning, you need to enter "restart" at the `Boot:` prompt.

## Boot-Time Loadable Drivers

As their name implies Boot-Time Loadable Drivers (BTLDs) are drivers that are loaded at boot-time. This provides a very effective means of adding drivers to the system that are not contained within the normal distribution. In most cases, BTLDs come from third party vendors and are used to support devices that you need to install from, such as SCSI host adapters. (If you don't need it to install the OS, why not wait until later to install that driver?) Despite this generality, BTLDs can be loaded any time you boot.

The desire to install a BTLD is indicated on the boot line by the `link=pkg` argument to the `boot` program, where `pkg` is the name of the package containing the driver to be installed. For example, I have a Wonder Works host adapter. The package name is "wwha". The boot string would look like this:

```
Boot: link=wwha
```

After the kernel has loaded (but before it starts to execute) the /link program is run. This prompts me to insert the floppy disk containing the BTLD I specified. Next I may be prompted to input values to configure that hardware, such as base address, DMA channel, and interrupt vector. I input values that conflict with existing hardware, `link` will scream at me and give me instructions on what I can do to correct the problem.

If you have multiple BTLDs that you wish to load, you can specify them all at the Boot: prompt. The system will then prompt you for each driver, in turn. For example, if you have the wwha and fyha, the bootstrings would look like this:

```
Boot: link="wwha fyha"
```

Note that you need to include all the drivers between the double quotes. You can also specify the `link` command on its own, in which case you will prompt for the names of the package(s) that should be linked.

One common misconception is that once you have added the driver at boot time, then the driver is part of your system for keeps. Well, it is until the next time you relink your kernel. The problem is that the driver is linked into the kernel that is being loaded, but is not made part of your link kit. The next time you reboot, the driver is gone. To get the driver into the link kit and into all subsequent kernels, you need to run the `installpkg` utility. Here you are prompted to insert the disk containing the BTLD. At this point, all subsequent relinks will include the new driver.

On the other hand, the installation of both ODT and OpenServer *should* prompt you to reinsert the BTLD disk to add it to the link kit. If so, it becomes part of the system for good. However, if you are not prompted, you will need to run `installpkg`.

## After Installation

When you finally get through the installation, the work is not over. OpenServer comes with a very complicated scheme to cut down on software piracy. This is a series of annoying messages that "encourage" you to register. Although the functionality is not obstructed when you don't register, you get a message on your screen every time you boot up and log in, indicating that unregistered software is installed on the system.

Software registration is accomplished in two steps. First you need to fill out the registration card with all the "necessary" information (including the product serial number) and send it to one of the registration centers. A short time later you will receive a registration code that turns off all those annoying messages. This is accomplished in the second step though the License Manager.

There are a couple of things to note here. Every SCO product that you install needs to be both licensed and registered. It's possible to install a product and not license it. This is useful if you wish one machine to be an installation server so you can install software across the network. However, you need to license the software before it will run. It is therefore possible to have several products installed on the license server, none of which work since none of them are licensed.

While you are waiting to get back your registration information, you can do something that can save you a lot of hassles later. You can make your first complete backup of the system. While you're at it, you can make a boot-root floppy set, just in case.

## Solving Problems with Licensing and Registration

The two most common problems that occur when licensing products is with incorrect licensing information. Isn't that one problem? Well, sort of. In ODT this information is the serial number and activation key. In OpenServer this is the license number, license code, and license data. The first problem is having the wrong information for the software you are trying to install. For example, if you are trying to install the Enterprise System then the licensing information for the Host System will not work. Although this is more common in larger installations with multiple systems, it does happen.

The next issue is the process of typing in the licensing information. Many people forget that UNIX is case sensitive. This applies to both the commands and the licensing information. If both upper and lowercase letters are used, I hope it would be obvious that case is important. However, many customers will call into support insisting that the licensing information is incorrect. Turning off the Caps Lock key or pressing the shift key at the correct moment usually solves the problem.

There is one issue with the Certificate of License and Authenticity (COLA) that can cause you problems. The dot-matrix printer that is used to print the COLA makes the lower case q's (the letter right before 'r') look like g's (the letter right before 'h'). If you have both on the COLA, then this is not a problem. However, if you only have the q's (like I did), you may get a message saying you have invalid activation information. Just remember that the g's are curled a little to the left and the q's are not. In the meantime, the printer was replaced, so this should only be a problem with older registration cards.

Another problem occurs when upgrading from stand-alone UNIX to the Enterprise version of OpenServer. Not only are you changing releases, you are changing the scope of your product. As a result, you end up getting two sets of license information. One brings you from your old product to the Host version (the closest in scope) and the second brings you from the Host version to the Enterprise version. The problem is that the Installation Query Manager (IQM, this is the installation program itself) will accept the license information from the Enterprise version without you ever using the information for the Host version. If this happens, the only solution is to start over. Therefore, it is important that you use the Host version information first and then upgrade to the Enterprise version. If you don't, the installation appears to go fine, but when you reboot you get

```
LOGIN: Upgrade license missing
Overriding system login limit on tty01 only,
to allow emergency system maintenance.
```

But that's not all. If you license the Host version and then upgrade to the Enterprise version without having *registered* the Host version, you end up with another message and another problem. Fortunately, all that happens is that you continue to get the message that says your software is unregistered, even though you have registered the Enterprise version.

This is slightly easier to correct. You will first need to remove the Enterprise *license.* This is done in maintenance mode through the License Manager. You now will see the Host system in the License Manager. Next, register the Host system using the License Manager. You can now license and register the Enterprise system.

One change to SCO's upgrade policy that changed with OpenServer is the introduction of the Software Enhancement Service (SES). This is actually a bundle of several products and services that SCO used to provide separately. As of this writing, the only way you can get an update to a product (that is, getting the product at a reduced rate) is through SES. Prices are based on your current platform, so you should see SCO for details.

In principle, you can consider SES a kind of subscription service, that like other subscriptions, you pay for annually. Not only does it include the reduced cost upgrades, but also free Maintenance Supplements as well as the Support Software Library which contains the entire Information Tools Database (IT scripts) as well as many of the more current Extended Functionality Supplements and Support Level Supplements.

# CHAPTER
# 12

- Installing and Configuring Network Software

- UUCP

- TCP/IP

- NFS

- MMDF

# Configuring
# the Network

You may have noticed that this is the first chapter that is specifically intended to help you configure something. Up to this point, I have tried to avoid the issue of configuration because that's not the focus of this book. I want you to be able to understand the complexities of each issue, so that you can figure out how to do the configuration on your own. Also, that's what the manuals are there for. Despite what some people want to believe, the SCO manuals are well written. They contain what you need to configure your system. Even if you don't know what you are doing.

So, why do we have a chapter on configuring your network? Well, it was necessary. The number of network sites is now well over a million and it is growing every day. Unless your office consists of a single server and a couple of terminals, you probably have some kind of network connection. Even if you do have a small site, the excitement of the Internet is something that you just can't miss out on. In order to get involved, you have to connect to the Internet.

There is also the issue that configuring a network is not an easy thing, especially for the uninitiated. You may understand the principles, but unless you have configured it before, you will probably be flipping through the manuals once or twice. Also, there are enough files out there that you may just make a typo or two.

In this chapter, we're going to cover some of the basics of configuring network connections. While we do it, we'll be talking about some of the more common places that mistakes are made. If you know what other people do to make things go wrong, you are less likely to make those same mistakes.

## Installing and Configuring Network Software

One key issue when configuring your network is the issue of user access. If everyone will be connecting to other machines using `telnet` or `ftp`, then all you need to worry about is ensuring that they have an account with that machine. However, when you want to allow access through the remote commands, where a login is not always desirable, then you need to think of something else. This is where the concept of user equivalence comes in.

As its name implies, user equivalence is a mechanism whereby users on two separate machines can be considered the same user. If configured, commands can be issued on a remote machine, without having the user log in. This equivalence is based on the user's name, not the UID.

User equivalence can be established in two ways. You can establish a system-wide equivalence by creating the file `/etc/hosts.equiv`. This file simply contains a list of remote hosts to which user equivalence has been established. Every user will be considered equivalent to his local counterpart so a password will not be required. Keep in mind, however that user equivalence is only one way. The existence of your machine in my `/etc/hosts.equiv` file means you can connect to me. It does not me I can connect to you.

Unless you are in a very trusting environment, creating entries in a `/etc/hosts.equiv` file may not be a good idea. This opens up one machine to *everyone* on the other. On the other hand, setting up user equivalence in this fashion, does not allow root access.

The second way of establishing user equivalence is on a user-to-user basis. By creating the file `$HOME/.rhosts`, you can allow specific accounts from specific machines access to this user. For example, my user (`jimmo`) on scoburg has a `.rhosts` file on my home directory. It contains four lines:

```
siemau jimmo
vesta jimmo
vesta tisha
vesta root
```

Here the user jimmo on the machines siemau and vesta are equivalent to the local user jimmo. That means if I am logged in on siemau as jimmo I can issue a remote command to scoburg. With the root and tisha accounts on vesta it is a little different. When you use a remote command, the default is to assume you are the same user on the remote side. If you aren't you need to use the option `-l` `<user_name>`, where `<user_name>` is the user of the remote machine. For example, if I were on vesta, as either tisha or root, and wanted to run the date on scoburg as jimmo, the command would be:

```
rcmd scoburg -l jimmo date
```

On scoburg the `.rhosts` file in jimmo's home directory is checked for the user tisha. Since tisha is listed, the command is successful.

## UUCP

Despite its appearance to the uninitiated, UUCP is fairly straightforward to configure. As I talked about previously, there are three primary files when dealing with UUCP connections. All three reside in `/usr/lib/uucp` and are simply text files that are edited to configure UUCP. Whether you use a text editor yourself or use `uuinstall` (the UUCP Manager in OpenServer simply calls `.uuinstall`) all that is getting done is editing these files. Since it is these files that are getting edited, I will forgo a discussion of any of the configuration tools. Once you know how to configure it by hand, then using the configuration tools is easy.

In a nutshell, we can say that the `Systems` file says which machines you know about, how to call them, and when it is the right time to contact them; the `Devices` files says what ports to use, at what speeds, and how the device is connected to your system. The `Permissions` file says who can get what file and from whom. In addition to configuring these files, there are a few hardware considerations before you can get UUCP to work.

One of the first things you need is a site to call. Granted most of you already knew that, but I figured it had to be said. Next, you need a serial line/port. If all the serial ports on you machine are taken up, you cannot connect to the remote machine. Now, it may sound like I am being silly, but trust me the question will come up. While in SCO Support, I talked with a customer who could not get his modem to work. He tried several combinations of speeds, parity, and other settings, but it wouldn't even dial out. Finally he called SCO Support and got me. Turns out that he had a terminal on tty1a and was trying to get the modem working on tty1A. (If this means nothing to you, look back on our discussion of major and minor numbers.)

Note that you don't have to have a modem to get a UUCP connection. If you have two machines side by side and no other means of communicating other than serial cables or SNEAKER-net, then UUCP is a viable alternative. For details on SNEAKER-net see the chapter on networking basics.

For right now, let's assume that there is a modem between the machines. Later we'll get into connecting two machines without a modem. Start by logging in as root and changing directories to `/usr/lib/uucp`. First, we'll edit the `Systems` file. As I mentioned a moment ago this is used to determine which sites are known to you and how to contact them. However, before you start editing, I suggest you gather the information about this connection. Let's make a list, using the fields in the `Systems` file entry as a base. Let's take the line that's used for SCO's bulletin board, sosco, which looks like this:

```
sosco Any ACU 300-2400 14084253502 -\r\d-ogin:-\K\d-ogin:-\K\d-ogin: uusls
```

The format of each line is

```
site_name times_to_call device-type connection_speeds phone_no chat-script
```

First, we have a `site_name`. This is what you want to call the machine when using UUCP. This does *not* have to be the same as its TCP/IP name or any other name you previously gave it. Although it does make life simpler, you can call it whatever you like. The only consideration is that you may run into problems with machine names longer than eight characters, so I suggest you keep them shorter.

The next issue to consider is the time to call. In many situations, you will want to set it up to call at any time, in which case this field will be `Any`. However, the site might be far enough away to be long distance. If the information you transfer is not urgent, then allowing connections only between 6PM–8AM is cheaper. One company I know uses UUCP to transfer the daily accounts from their point-of-sale system from the branch offices to the main office. To ensure this is done after all transactions have been completed, they only allow communication from the main to the branch offices *after midnight*. This would require a `Never` in the branch offices and something like 0001–0800 in the main office.

I am aware of cases where connections are allowed only once a week. This too can be configured in the `times_to_call` field. Using the two letter abbreviations for the days of the week, you can come up with any combination you like, for example,

```
MoWeFr1230-1345
```

would allow you to call the remote machine only on Monday, Wednesday, and Friday between 12:30 and 1:45 PM. The abbreviations for the days of the week are Mo,Tu,We,Th,Fr,Sa,Su, plus Wk for every weekday (Mo–Fr). You can also use Wk in conjunction with both times and weekend days. For example, if we wanted to allow calling only between 8PM and 8AM on weekdays, but all day Saturday and Sunday the entry would look like this:

```
Wk2000-0800,SaSu
```

Be careful when you have times that span across midnight. Despite appearances, UUCP interprets the day and time as two separate entries. As a result, you might not get what you expect with the entry

```
Wk2000-0800
```

This appears to mean Mo–Fr, 8PM–8AM, which it does, sort of. What happens on Friday? When we hit midnight on Friday, it is no longer a weekday, but rather Saturday, therefore the system will not be contacted after midnight on Friday. The reverse goes for Sunday after midnight. It is now Monday, a weekday between 8PM–8AM. Therefore, the call will be made.

You can also specify the minimum time to wait before trying the call again, should it fail. This is separated from the calling times with a semicolon and is expressed in minutes. For example, to wait 5 minutes before trying a failed call in the above example, we would write it like this:

```
Wk2000-0800;5
```

Normally, UUCP uses what is called "exponential backoff." This means that the time between when UUCP is able to retry after successive failures increase exponentially. By using this retry field, UUCP will wait that amount of time before you are allowed to retry, instead of using the exponential backoff. Keep in mind, that usually UUCP will make one retry immediately after a failed attempt. This is a retry from our point of view, but not for UUCP.

If the call fails the second time, there must be some mechanism to retry as UUCP will not normally do it on its own. Instead you must either have polling set up (which we talk about later) or start `uucico` by hand (`uutry`). If the retry time has not been reached, you get an error message. (To correct it, remove the status file for that system in `/usr/spool/uucp/.Status`.) However, the system will not allow you to retry if the retry time has not yet been reached.

The next thing to look for is the kind of device you want to connect through (the `device_type` field). The two most common are ACU (Automatic Call Unit) and Direct (a direct connection). There are others, including TCP, however, they are not commonly used so we will have to forgo discussing them. The device type is not really a predefined, carved in stone device, but rather an alias. It points to a particular entry (or group of entries) in the `Devices` file. Therefore, if you have several modems with varying speeds, you could define an alias for each one. This way you contact the remote side with a modem that has the same speed as the remote site.

The next entry is the speed (or baud rate) to use when connecting to the remote site. Keep in mind that these are discrete values. That is, although we specified a range of 300–2400, there is no such thing as a baud rate of 734. When trying to connect, UUCP will try the fastest speed first and only try the slower speeds if it cannot connect. Also note that the speed does not have to be a range. For example, it makes sense to limit calls to a single speed if you don't want to waste the call if it cannot be made at the fastest available speed. Note that not all dialers or modems can handle every speed.

At first glance, it doesn't look like there is much to say about a phone number. Well, a phone number by itself is just a phone number. However, in this context you can use phone numbers is association with what are called "tokens." Just as a bus token is used to represent the money you paid for your fair, phone number tokens represent phone numbers; or at least, parts of them. In the spirit of self-documentation, I might want a way to indicate where I am calling. For example, I have 100 sites thoughout the country and don't want to have to remember every area code. A solution would be to use tokens to indicate the area. I might create an entry in the phone number field that looks like this:

```
SantaCruz4253502
```

From this I immediately know I am calling to Santa Cruz. The translation is made from the file `/usr/lib/uucp/Dialcodes`, where each entry in the file has the format

```
Dialarea    Dialcode
```

So the entry for this example would look like this:

```
SantaCruz    1408
```

Therefore, when the call is actually made, it is interpreted as 14084253502. I can also use the special character equal sign (=) to for a secondary dial tone or the hyphen (-) to pause for a second. For example, if I needed to dial nine to get an outside line, I could have made an entry line this:

```
SantaCruz    9=1408
```

We now get to perhaps the most intimidating part of the `Systems` file: the chat script. As its name implies, this is a script to direct how the calling machine is supposed to "chat" with the remote machine. The chat script is composed of a sequence of characters that are expected from the remote machine and what should be sent in response. This is often referred to as Expect-Send pairs. Usually, if expected characters are not sent, then there is an Expect-Send subpair. Each value is separated by a dash. To clear this up, let's look at the above example:

```
 -\r\d-ogin:-\K\d-ogin:-\K\d-ogin: uusls
```

Here we have four Expect-Send pairs:

```
\r\d ogin
-\K\d ogin
-\K\d ogin
uusls
```

Here we don't expect anything before we send a carriage return (\r) followed by a delay of 1 second (\d). We then expect the characters. We ignore the first character for a couple of reasons. First, it may not have come through and if we were expecting `login:` then the missing `l` would cause it not to match. Second, some sites might have a login prompt that says "Login:" instead of "login:". That would fail to match as well. If it failed to match, (for either of these reasons, or it may not have gotten sent within the 10 second timeout) we go to the next subpair. This time we send a BREAK (\K) and the 1 second delay. This would have the force for the remote side to cycle through the speeds if the port on the remote side was configured to do so. If no match, we go to the third, Expect-Send pair. If this doesn't match, then the entire connection fails.

If we do match, then we skip the remaining and send the last field, `uusls`. This is the login name, for the account we want to use to log in. Here, there is no password. However, for accounts where passwords are expected, there would be another Expect-Send pair; for example,

```
ssword: RegnadKcin
```

Here we also ignore the first character. If we see `ssword`, we send `RegnadKcin`. The reason that there are no Expect-Send subpairs here is that once we get the login: part, we can pretty much be sure that the `ssword` will come across correctly.

One thing that always annoyed me is that chat scripts often require a lot of effort to get them to work correctly. You might have to try several different sequences before you get it right. If you are calling a site that others have successfully called, then talking with the administrator of that site might give you some ideas of what to try.

You can also try the `cu` command to connect to the other site. With both `cu` and `uucp`, you can turn on debugging with -x9 and watch the connection progress. Even though you don't have a normal account, you can try to log in using the UUCP account and password. If you get in that way, then you should be able to get in with UUCP, provided UUCP is configured correctly. Later on I will go through a UUCP session with -x9 debugging turned on.

Next comes the `Devices` file. Which entry in `Devices` is accessed is determined by the device-type entry in the `Systems` file. In the example from the Systems file where we referenced an ACU line, the entry might look like this:

```
ACU tty2A - 2400-9600 hayes2400
```

The general format of the line is

```
device-type tty-device dialerline speed dialer <token dialer token...>
```

Here again we see the reference to the ACU device. It is this line that the device-type field in the Systems file is pointing to. If you had multiple ACU lines here and one was busy, UUCP would try the next one. The tty-device entry is the serial port that you want to call out on. Note that we are referring to the modem control device (big A) since this is a modem connection. With a direct connection (more on that in a moment), we would use the nonmodem control port (little A). For more on the difference, see the section on major and minor numbers and the serial(HW) man-page

The dialer line should be a dash. Just leave it a dash. It's used to indicate the separate Devices line used by an 801-type calling device. To discuss the specifics of an "801-type calling device" is beyond the scope of this book. So, with that in mind, you can safely leave it as a dash.

Next is the speed. In this case, we provide a range (2400–9600). If this could handle multiple speeds, but we only want to use one, we could enter a single speed. If you try to make a connection (with cu, for example) and specify a speed other than specified, the system will reply that there are no devices available. This also applies to specifying speeds outside the range.

For example, say we want to connect to a machine at 2400, but the speed specified here was 9600. We issue a cu command, specifying that speed, like this:

```
cu -s2400 5558672
```

We would end up with a message like this:

```
Connect failed: NO DEVICES AVAILABLE
```

This means what it says, that there are no devices available. If they were all being used, we'd get this message as well. However, here it doesn't mean that someone is using the port, but rather there are no devices *at all* that match that speed. Of course, the same thing would apply if you had ten modems, nine with 9600 and one with 2400 and the one with 2400, just happened to be busy at the time.

The last field might actually consist of multiple fields. Normally, this is only one, like in our case, and represents the dialer (more in a moment). You might have a network where a modem is connected to a switch. You must first connect to the switch and then to the modem. The example of Devices given in the SCO doc looks like this:

```
ACU tty14 - 1200 develcon vent ventel
```

Here we have the dialer-token pair "develcon vent" and a dialer ventel. The develcon entry points to a line in the /usr/lib/uucp/Dialers file which is used to access the switch. The vent field is a flag (token) which is passed to the develcon switch, telling it what devices to connect. Finally, we get to the ventel dialer, which may also be a line in Dialers.

The `Dialers` file is perhaps the simplest way of connecting a modem. It neither expects nor allows many of the options possible with the dialer binary programs. So, just what is a dialer? Well, it's just as its name implies, it dials the modem. There are several provided with your system, which also reside in `/usr/lib/uucp`. These are binary programs that access your modem, configure it according to what you have defined, and dial the number you want.

Instead of having a separate dialer, the entries in Dialers use a simple program internal to UUCP. Since UUCP is getting all of its configuration information from the Dialers file, the entries often come in pairs. The first one is used to prepare the modem for dialing out and the other is used to reinitialize the modem after the call completes. One of the more common entries is that for a Hayes Smartmodem 2400. BY default, the two entries look like this:

```
hayes2400 =,-,      "" ATQ0E0T&D2&C1S0=0X4S2=043\r\c OK\r ATDT\T\r\c Speed
&hayes2400 =,-,     "" +++\dATQ0H OK\r ATE0&D2&C1X4S2=128 OK\r ATS0=1Q1\r
```

The general format is

```
dialer-name translation-table expect-send-pairs
```

The dialer name is anything we want to give it, although both names must be the same, with the terminating (reinitialization) entry beginning with an ampersand (&). This is a one-to-one mapping with whatever dialer you use in the `Devices` file. That is, you can create a new dialer with a new initialization string as long as you use the same name in the `Devices` file.

The translation table is used to translate the the dialtone/pulse codes used for pauses (== and -) into those appropriate for the particular device. In the above example, both types of pauses are translated to the comma, which is all the Hayes 2400 modem understands.

At the end of the line are sets of expects and sends, very similar to the chat script in the `System` file. Keep in mind that what is "sent" is not necessarily the exact characters the modem received. It might be better to think of the send strings as information given to the dialer to tell it what to send. In both lines, above, we have a set of double-quotes ("") with nothing inside. This simply means that UUCP should expect nothing before it sends the first set of characters. In this case, what we are sending is a series of Hayes (AT) commands, followed by a carriage return (\r) without a new-line (\c). It then expects to see "OK" followed by a carriage return. This "OK" tells the dialer that everything went well and it was able to understand the command(s) just sent.

We next send the mode the AT command ATDT, which means to be ready to dial the number following. Instead of a telephone number, here we have a \T which is used to represent the telephone number. What is actually sent to the modem as a phone number is what appears in the Systems file. If that number contains tokens, then those are translated first, before the number is sent to the modem. Following the command to dial the phone number, we once again have the carriage return with no new-line. Table 12–1 contains a list of some of the escape characters used in the Dialers file.

If we decide we want some of the advanced features, then we are probably going to choose one of the existing binary dialers. These come in two flavors. The first has the format dialXYZ; where XYZ will give you some indication of what kind of modem it accesses. For example, the dialHA24 is used to access a Hayes 2400 modem and the dialMUL dialer is used to access a Multitech modem. Each one of these is paired with a .c file, which, as you might have guessed, is the source code for that dialer. If you have access to a C compiler for your SCO system then you can modify the dialers.

The problem is that not everyone has access to a C compiler. Plus, just having a compiler does not mean that you have created a modem dialer before. Unless

**Table 12–1**  Dialers File Escape Sequences

| Commands | Function |
|---|---|
| \p | pause (ca. 1/2 second delay) |
| \d | delay (2 seconds) |
| \D | phone number/token |
| \T | phone number with Dialcodes and character translation |
| \N | null byte |
| \K | BREAK |
| \E | turn on echo checking (for slow devices) |
| \e | turn off echo checking |
| \r | carriage return |
| \c | no new-line |
| \n | new-line |
| \nnn | send octal number nnnn |

you are fairly familiar with how dialers interact with the modem, modifying one of the `.c` files is not easy.

Realizing the need to be able to configure modems, SCO introduced a new set of dialers. These have the format `atdialXYZ`; here again, XYZ gives you some indication of what kind of dialer you are dealing with. The difference is that instead of being separate files, the `atdialers`, as they are called, are actually links to one another. Rather than having their configuration information hardcoded like the dialXYZ files, the `atdialers` get their configuration information from ASCII files that are easily edited.

In ODT, these files reside in `/etc/default` with the same name as the `atdial` file. For example, the `atdialHAY` dialer would read its configuration information from `/etc/default/atdialHAY`. In OpenServer, they have the same format and behavior, but now reside in `/usr/lib/uucp/etc`.

In essence, the information in the `atdial` configuration files is the same information that you provided when you modified the dialers yourself. Instead of having to recompile the binary, you only need to modify the configuration file. This is also a shell script that prompts you for the values you want to assign to each of the configuration strings: `/usr/lib/uucp/make.dialer`. This has the advantage that it not only writes the necessary information into the configuration file, it also links the base dialer (`/usr/lib/uucp/atdial`) to the name you specified. I feel that using `make.dialer` is more awkward, and it's easier to make a copy of an existing file then do the link yourself. Unless you have one of the other modem brands listed, in most cases using the Hayes configuration file (`atdialHAY`) and changing it works well.

When configuring the strings, there is one thing I need to point out that is often a point of confusion; that is, the AT commands themselves. The confusion lies in the name itself. Because they are referred to as AT commands, often people see each commands as an AT followed by the code for the specific function. This is true, however, the AT is *not* required before *every* command. Actually the AT is required only before the first command in each line. The function of the AT is to tell the modem that commands follow. It does not serve as a delimiter to the commands. (Note: If you are communicating with the modem interactively, it is more than likely that there is one command per line and each *must* be preceeded with the AT) Let's take an example of the setup strings from the `atdialUSR` file:

```
MDM_SETUP=AT&FX4Q0&D2&C1&B1S0=1S2=043&W
```

If the AT was required before every command, then this would be seen as a single, very long command. Instead, since the AT is only needed to get the modem's attention, we have 9 seperate commands: `&F`, `X4`, `Q0`, `&D2`, `&C1`, `&B1`, `S0=1`, `S2=043`, and `&W`.

Figuring that out isn't as straightforward as it first seems. There are several things to keep in mind. First, the ampersand (&) indicates an "advanced" command; one that may not be on your modem. Knowing this, I can say that the previous command ends at the character just before the ampersand. Therefore, I can break this command into smaller tokens and have smaller chunks to deal with. This could look like this:

```
&FX4Q0 &D2 &C1 &B1S0=1S2=043 &W
```

The next thing to keep in mind is that none of the AT commands consist soley of, or start with, a number; therefore, &D2 and &C1 cannot be broken down any further. I also know that modems (normally) have memory (called registers) that can be read from or written to. These are the 'S' registers. Since they contain values and are not functions, I have to assign them a value. Also, these are the only ones that can take on values, so I can work from the equal sign using the general format

```
S#=<value>
```

where # is the S-register number and <value> is the value I am assigning. This gives me

```
&FX4Q0 &D2 &C1 &B1 S0=1 S2=043 &W
```

So, we're almost there. All that's left is the very beginning of the command. One thing I can use is that the AT commands are almost exclusively single letters or single letters followed by a number. The exceptions are the S-registers, but those are easy to distinguish. I can take a guess and break the strings down to

```
&F X4 Q0 &D2 &C1 &B1 S0=1 S2=043 &W
```

Now, to make sure that I broke this down correctly, I should verify that there is a command like each one of my tokens. I hope your modem manual has a list of the AT commands that are applicable to your modem. More common ones are listed in Table 12–2.

To understand the behavior of the AT commands, there are some underlying concepts that we need to address first. Modems operate in four modes and how they react to signals will be different. When you first turn on a modem, it is in *idle mode*. It sits there waiting for you to tell it what to do and will remain in idle mode until it is told to change.

The first state it normally changes to is command mode. This is the state it moves into after you poke it in the ribs with "AT" to tell it to wake up and get ready for a command. While in command mode, the modem waits until it sees a carriage return before it will interpret the command. This is why a single line in the configuration file is considered one command, but in interactive mode you need the AT before each command.

**Table 12–2**   Common AT/Hayes Commands

| AT Command | Function |
|---|---|
| &C1 | Raise CDC on carrier detect |
| &D2 | Modem goes off hook and returns to command mode when DTR drops |
| &F | Reset to factory defaults |
| &W | Write S-registers to memory |
| E0 | Do not echo commands |
| E1 | Echo commands |
| Q0 | Do not display result messages |
| Q1 | Display result messages |
| S0= | Number of rings until autoanswer. |
| S2= | ASCII character used to exit data mode |

When one modem has contacted another and a carrier signal has been initiated, the modem enters *data mode*. Once the modem is in data mode, it will remain there until something happens to pull it out. The most common thing to happen is that the modem is simply told to leave data mode. This is when it receives the exit sequnce ("+++"). This also happens when one (or both) computer loses the DTR signal saying that the computer is no longer attached to the modem. Another instance is when the carrier is lost.

If you connect directly to the mode (perhaps using cu) you can enter commands interactively. This is called interactive mode. This is often useful in testing the modem as you can see immediately how it reacts to each command you give it. This is done by using the keyword dir in place of the phone number or system name. For example, to connect directly to a modem attached to tty1a the command would look like this:

```
cu -l tty1a dir
```

There are two things to note here. First, we need to specify the line we want to go out on; in this case tty1a. Second, we need to specify the nonmodem control port. This seems a little counter-intuitive since we are trying to connect to a modem. However, as I mentioned before, the significance of the modem control device is that it reacts to carrier-detect and is not necessarily connected to a modem.

One file we haven't talked about yet isn't necessarily required to get a UUCP connection. This is the Permissions file, which, as we talked about earlier, controls what machines have access to what directories and what programs they can execute on our machine. Like the other UUCP files, you are provided with a

`Permissions` file. This contains an entry that allows anyone with the correct password access. It looks like this:

```
MACHINE=samplesite LOGNAME=uucp \
    COMMANDS=rmail:rnews:uucp \
    READ=/usr/spool/uucppublic:/usr/tmp \
    WRITE=/usr/spool/uucppublic:/usr/tmp \
    SENDFILES=yes REQUEST=no
```

Although this looks like several lines, it is actually one logical line. As in many files, we can separate one logical line into several physical lines by placing a backslash at the end of each physical line. Therefore, we need to talk about fields rather than lines.

The first field, `MACHINE=`, is used to identify a machine that *we* are calling. This is matched with whatever entry we use in the `Systems` file. If there is no direct match then we use the `samplesite` machine entry. Here comes the first big security question. Since any site you call will be able to access your system through this entry, is this really what you want? Although the access they have is limited (and we'll get to that in a moment) it is an issue to consider.

The `LOGNAME` field is used when a machine calls *us*. This is the name of the UUCP account used to log in to our system, hence the name. The usual practice is to create a UUCP account for a machine whose name is similar to the machine name. For example, the machine siemau might get a `LOGNAME` of uusiemau. It is also often the case that there is a `MACHINE-LOGNAME` pair for each machine. In this way you can manage each machine individually, regardless of whether you call it or it calls you. However, you do not have to do it like this.

Note that there must me an account for UUCP users to log in under. It is advisable to create a separate account and not use the account uucp, which is the UUCP administrative user. Because you are creating a UUCP account, there is no "real" user logging in and therefore you need to have a different log in shell. For UUCP users this will be `/usr/lib/uucp/uucico`. For more details on creating accounts see the section on users and security or the `System Administrators Guide`.

Rather than having to list out specific machine or account names, we can set either of these variables to OTHER. This will then match any instance that is not explicitly matched by something else.

For example, you may wish to limit access to machines that call you by having a single account. The entry could look like this:

```
LOGNAME=uucp \      COMMANDS=rmail:rnews:uucp \
   READ=/usr/spool/uucppublic:/usr/tmp \
   WRITE=/usr/spool/uucppublic:/usr/tmp \
   SENDFILES=yes REQUEST=no
```

This is identical to the previous example, except that there is no `MACHINE` field. This says that anyone logging into your system as the UUCP user uucp has the access privileges listed. Then, to limit access to machines we call, we create a separate `MACHINE` entry that looks like this (leaving the last three lines unchanged):

```
MACHINE=samplesite \              .
   COMMANDS=rmail \
```

Here we made a slight change. Instead of allowing the machine you are calling access to the commands `rmail`, `rnews`, and `uucp`, we simply allow it access to `rmail`. That means it can send you mail messages, but cannot use the `rnews` or `uucp` binaries on your machines (for example, using `uux`). On the other hand, since you are doing the calling, you know what each machine is, so you might want to open up the access a little more. You can increase the number of commands the machine you are calling can use. In fact, if you wanted you could let the machines you call have access to anything on your system by using an entry like this:

```
MACHINE=samplesite COMMANDS=ALL \
```

This means that any machine that you call will be able to run any command locally. Well, sort of. At first this looks like a huge security hole. Some malicious user could set up a `uux` job that uses `fdisk` to delete your partitions. Fortunately, `uux` jobs are executed as the user uucp (`/usr/bin/uux` is owned by uucp and is a SUID program). Therefore, even though you give every machine permission to run any command on your machine, it can only run those commands that the user uucp can.

Another way to use the MACHINE entry is to list multiple machines; for example,

```
MACHINE=siemau:scoburg:vesta LOGNAME=uucp \
```

In this example, the permissions that follow are valid for the machines siemau, scoburg, and vesta, as well as when user uucp logs in. Keep in mind that this does not mean that the three machines must use the name uucp to log in or that only these three machines can use the `LOGNAME` uucp. It only means that the permissions for the three machines is the same as that for the user uucp. Potentially, we could have another entry for the user uusiemau that had more permissions than this one. If we called siemau, then `MACHINE=siemau` would apply. However, if siemau called us with the `LOGNAME uusiemau`, then this would apply, instead.

A less-known, and therefore less used field is MYNAME. This tells the remote site what your name is. When you call a remote site (or it calls you), it has to know what machine name you are; otherwise, it cannot transfer files to you correctly. Keep in mind that transfer of files is done by site name and not by the LOGNAME or MACHINE name. Usually, the site name matches the entry in Systems which matches the MACHINE entry in Permissions.

A problem arises when trying to contact a machine that has the same name as you or when you have the same name as some other machine known to the one you are calling. Hopefully, this won't happen if you are calling a machine within your domain. However, if you are calling some machine outside of your domain, this is a possibility. UUCP was developed without the understanding of Internet domains. Therefore, it sees only the machine name. To prevent problems, you can use the MYNAME (field? variable?). If you do so, then when a connection is made, the remote side will think that your machine name is something different. For example, if I had it set like this

```
MACHINE=vesta MYNAME=hilltop \
```

every time I would call vesta, it would think that my machine's name was hill-top.

Okay, we limit access to machines we call via the MACHINE field. We limited access to machines that call us via the LOGNAME field. What programs each has access to on our machine is controlled by the COMMAND field. Where that can be done, is controlled by the fields in the next three lines:

```
READ=/usr/spool/uucppublic:/usr/tmp \
```

```
WRITE=/usr/spool/uucppublic:/usr/tmp \
```

```
SENDFILES=yes REQUEST=no
```

The READ and WRITE fields are as one would expect. They limit what directories the remote machines can read from and write to. Actually, this is not completely true. It is more accurate to say that this limits the root directory of where the remote machine can read or write. In this example, if there was a subdirectory /usr/spool/uucppublic/data, the remote machine would have access to it. By using just the slash, as in

```
WRITE=/
```

you allow the remote system to write in anywhere starting from the root directory. This looks like another security hole, but again, like the COMMAND field, access permissions on directories is limited by what the user uucp can do. Therefore, the above example *does not* give either the machine or the account permission to write into the root directory.

We can also limit access by specifying what directories that cannot be read from or written to. For example, we might want to give a remote site READ access to /, but to keep them from getting the password or group files, we tell UUCP not to allow them to read /etc. This is done with the NOREAD variable. The counterpart to this is NOWRITE, which limits where a machine can write. Put together with READ and WRITE, it might look something like this:

```
READ=/

WRITE=/usr/spool/uucppublic;/usr/tmp

NOREAD=/etc NOWRITE=/etc
```

We further restrict access to files by using the SENDFILES and REQUEST variables. These limit whether the remote machine can send us files or request files from us, respectively. SENDFILES can also be set to 'call'. If defined so, the only time the the local machine will send files is when it has called the other site.

It is doubtful that we will ever call a machine named 'samplesite', although this is actually an alias to mean any machine. So, whenever we call a site that is not specially listed in the permissions file, the default machine 'samplesite' is used.

There are two other variables that can be used to increase security: CALLBACK and VALIDATE. The CALLBACK variable indicates that transactions cannot be initiated by the remote side by calling you. You have to be the one to call the remote side. When CALLBACK=yes, then the requests are denied when the remote machine calls you, the call is stopped, and your side calls back. This adds more security since you have a way of matching the LOGNAME to the MACHINE name. The LOGNAME calls you, and CALLBACK=yes. You call the other site and now the MACHINE variable permissions take effect. Like having two sides setting the callback times to Never, both sides setting CALLBACK=yes means that transactions can never take place. (You can't get much more secure than that.)

The VALIDATE variable is used as a very simplistic authentication mechanism in conjunction with the COMMANDS variable. The VALIDATE variable is set to a list of machines that are tied to a specific LOGNAME. You can then set up a UUCP account with a special password for your trusted machines. An entry might look like this:

```
LOGNAME: goodguys VALIDATE: siemau:scoburg:vesta
```

Keep in mind that anyone who gets this goodguys password can set MYNAME to one of these and easily masquerade as one of the goodguys.

If you are going to be regularly transferring files then you probably want to automate that process. You might have a site that is your mail server. However, they want you to pay for the call, so they have the time to call you set to Never in the

Systems file. Therefore, you have to go get the files yourself. You could set up a crontab that runs uutry at regular intervals. However, there are some mechanisms already built in.

As one might guess, the mechanism used to process UUCP requests at regular intervals is cron. By default there is a cron file for the uucp user, which already does most of what we would want. This is the file /usr/spool/cron/crontabs/uucp, which probably looks like this:

```
39,9 * * * * /usr/lib/uucp/uudemon.hour > /dev/null

10 * * * * /usr/lib/uucp/uudemon.poll > /dev/null

45 23 * * * ulimit 5000; /usr/lib/uucp/uudemon.clean > /dev/null

48 10,14 * * 1-5 /usr/lib/uucp/uudemon.admin > /dev/nullA
```

(For details of what each field is, see the crontab(C) man-page)

The first entry runs /usr/lib/uucp/uudemon.hour once every half hour. This has always bothered me since the command is called uudemon.HOUR. However, every hour, the script runs and starts two other scripts, /usr/lib/uucp/uusched and /usr/lib/uucp/uuxqt whose job it is to check the uucp spool directories looking for work.

The second line runs the /usr/lib/uucp/uudemon.poll script once an hour. The first thing you need to do is to change it to uudemon.poll2. The reason is that uudemon.poll is much older and kludgey. It works by setting up a dummy control file (C. file in /usr/spool/uucp/<sitename>). Instead, uudemon.poll2 calls uucico directly. Another difference is that uudemon.poll gets its polling information from /usr/lib/uucp/Poll while uudemon.poll2 gets it from either Poll.day or Poll.hour, which you need to create yourself.

Which of the configuration files is used depends on whether you start uudemon.poll with the -d option or not. If you leave it off, Poll.hour will read Poll.day. Both have the same basic format as follows:

```
nodename <tab> hour1 hour2 hour3 ....
```

Entries can be followed by a w to indicate that a call should be made only if there is work for the remote site. If the w is not there, a call will be made regardless. This is useful if you want to regularly check your mail server. An example might look like this:

```
mailserver.siemau.com 8w 9 10 11 12 13 14 15 16 17 18 19w
```

Here we have it set to poll between 8AM and 7PM, but the first and last hours are only done if there is work waiting for the remote site. One common question is, "Does this mean you can only poll once an hour?" No, it doesn't. Inside of `uudemon.poll2` a variable (NOW) is set to the current hour. If this matches one of the entries in `Poll.hour`, then `uucico` is started. Therefore, you could have the cronjob run once every twenty minutes and as long as `uudemon.poll2` starts within the specified hour the call will be made.

The `Poll.day` file is similar, however instead of having hours, it lists days of the week with 0 being Sunday and 6 being Friday. The w also means only call if there is work for the remote side.

New to OpenServer is the `/usr/lib/uucp/Configuration` file. With this file you can configure details of the connection that were previously impossible. For example, UUCP exchanges packets of a set size. Prior to OpenServer, there was no way of changing this. Now you can with the `Configuration` file.

Another aspect of the packet exchange is the number of packets sent before UUCP waits for acknowledgement. This is called the *window*. In ODT, the window size was three packets. With the `Configuration` file you can adjust the window to suit your needs. If you have a reliable connection, there is nothing that would prevent you from increasing this value to limit the time spent acknowledging the packets and spending more time sending them. This increases your throughput.

The `Configuration` file allows you to make both site-specific and device-specific definitions. Both have the same format with the first line defining whether this is a device or site definition. The general format is

```
KEYWORD name
    PROTOCOL STRINGS protocol_list
    USE PROTOCOL protocol1
          WITH parameter = value
          WITH parameter = value
    USE PROTOCOL protocol2
          WITH parameter = value
          WITH parameter = value
    USE PROTOCOL protocoln
          WITH parameter = value
          WITH parameter = value
```

KEYWORD can either be SYSTEM for a system definition or DEVICE for a device definition. The name is the specific site name from `Systems` or device type from `Devices`. The `protocol_list` is a list of protocols that are supported by that site or device. If you wish to have different parameters defined for each of the specified protocols, there needs to be an entry for each parameter that is different than the default.

For example, to configure a site-specific definition, the entry might look like this:

```
SYSTEM siemau
    PROTOCOL STRING Gg
        USE PROTOCOL G
                WITH window = 5
                WITH packet_size = 1024
        USE PROTOCOL g
                WITH window = 7
```

Here we have configured UUCP so that it can communicate with *siemau* using either the G or g protocol. If we use the G protocol, the window is 5 packets and each packet is 1024 bytes. If we use the g protocol, the window is 7 packets, but each is the default size of 64 bytes.

Note that this does not force the use of one packet or enable. Both sides must support the specific values for this to work correctly. See the `Configuration(F)` man-page for more details.

Also new to OpenServer is the script `/usr/lib/uucp/remote.unknown`. This script is executed when a site attempts to login whose name is not listed in the `Systems` file. This logs the conversations and prevents the remote side from logging in. If you want to allow unknown hosts to connect, simply change the permissions on `/usr/lib/uucp/remote.unknown` to 000.

## TCP/IP

### *Configuring SLIP*

As we talked about in the first part of the book, the basic concept under SLIP is the idea of a link. The `slattach` command is used to create the SLIP link. Once the link is created, the connections can be made to the remote site, just like any other network connect, such as Ethernet or PPP. New to OpenServer is the ability to connect via a tty device, as you did in ODT, or also to a UUCP site name. This make administration significantly easier. In ODT you needed to define the IP address for each side as you were creating the link. New in OpenServer is the ability to create dynamic incoming and outgoing links as well.

When the SLIP link is created, you have a new network interface that behaves the same as with other types of connections. Although there is a one-to-one relationship between the two sides of the link, (as these are passed to `slattach` as parameters), you still have "normal" network functionality. This includes multiple applications communicating on both ends of the connection.

Before SLIP will work, the SLIP STREAMS stack must have been installed and linked into the kernel. This is not done by default when SLIP is installed.

Also new to OpenServer is the idea of packet filtering. Like PPP, packet filtering with SLIP allows you to let packets through the interface based on IP addresses, packet type, and other criteria. The filter file is `/etc/pppfilter`, and as one might guess is the same file that's used by PPP. We get to packet filtering shortly.

With a dedicated link, the SLIP connection is the only thing that uses the line. Either side may initiate the link, however nothing else ever uses the line. Dynamic links are where the line can be shared. In this case, either UUCP or PPP could use the line if it happened to be free at the moment. A dynamic incoming line is simply one with a shared line that was initiated by the remote host. A dynamic outgoing line is one where the local host initiates the call.

Although you could have a dedicated line for connections across modems, it is more appropriate for leased lines and other cases where you have a permanent connection. As with the other kinds of links, dedicated links are configured with the Network Configuration Manager. To add your first slip connection, select the Add new WAN connection under the Hardware menu. Here you have the choice of adding either PPP or slip. If one is already installed, you are only given the choice of adding the other. To add new connections after the first one, you needed to select Modify Hardware Configuration from the Hardware menu then select Add.

You are then prompted to add a protocol to the SLIP connection. Here, your only choice is TCP/IP, so you create the chain TCP/IP→SLIP. When you get to the screen to select the type of connection you want, you may get confused. The SCO Doc (and I) talk about dedicated, dynamic incoming, and dynamic outgoing links. However, when you get to the window where you add the protocol to the SLIP driver, you are given the choice of Incoming Link, Outgoing Link, and Manual Link. These are your dynamic incoming link, dynamic outgoing link and dedicated link, respectively.

With a dynamic incoming link, you configure the port to accept a login by enabling it, thereby getting `getty` to run. Because you actually go through a login similar to that for a UUCP connection, this type of link requires that you configure a login account on the local machine. On the remote machine, a system name must be configured in the UUCP `Systems` file and in the chat script that logs you in. In addition, a dynamic outgoing link must be configured on the remote side. In essence these two links work together. You can't use one type without configuring the other.

When you are configuring the incoming link, the Network Configuration Manager will create the SLIP account for you. You are prompted for the account name and the name of the script to use when the account logs in. Like with UUCP accounts, the SLIP account gets a special login script instead of the standard login shell. It is this script that runs `slattach` to create the link. Keep in mind that the Network Configuration Manager does not create the script, you must do that by hand and the Network Configuration Manager puts the correct entry in `/etc/passwd`.

As we mentioned, the reverse of the dynamic incoming link is the dynamic outgoing link. When you get through the menus to the point where you are inputting the IP addresses and names there is something to watch out for. If you select a specific tty line, then the UUCP system name is grayed out. If you select "none" for the tty device, then you can enter a name in the UUCP system name field. This makes sense because if you are specifying a line, then it is not dynamic. If you want to use the UUCP name and therefore have a dynamic connection, then you would select a specific tty device. However, if you want to limit the SLIP system name to a particular device, you can do so in the `Systems` file. Instead of using an ACU device, define an SLACU device that has an entry in `Devices` and this points to a **single** tty device.

Like incoming links, the Network Configuration Manager will only configure the connection so far. You will need to edit `/etc/tcp` by hand to add the `slattach` line

```
slattach -d device_name uucp_name
```

where the `-d` indicates that this is a dynamic line, the `device name` is the tty device the connection should be made on, and `uucp_name` is the name of the remote host as it appears in the UUCP `Systems` file. If you leave the `-d` off, the system will try to configure the line as dedicated. You can also add other options to the `slattach` line in `/etc/tcp` such as turning on header compression, or changing the maximum transmission unit. Although there is nothing requiring you to put the the `slattach` line in `/etc/tcp`, it is a logical place as that's where most of the the TCP/IP related programs are started.

When I said that SLIP did packet filtering like PPP, I wasn`t entirely accurate. PPP allows you to filter packets that are used to activate or keep up the connection, however you can only filter "pass" packets with SLIP. What this means is that you can use criteria such as packet type, destination, and packet length as you filter criteria, but not simply those that are used to keep the link up. Like PPP, the filter can be defined for each link separately. This can be useful if you wish to limit access on slower lines, but faster ones can be more open.

Because dynamic links use the UUCP facilities, you can use UUCP to test the connection. For example, you might want to try to connect to the remote side using cu. If you can successfully connect using cu and the remote side accepts the login and password, a failed SLIP connection probably lies in an incorrect configuration of the SLIP half of the link. Note that if you log in to a SLIP account, you are not given a normal login shell, but rather the script where the slattach is started. However, if you connect in this fashion you have narrowed down areas for potential problems. For more details on this, see the section on configuring UUCP.

If you have multiple network interfaces on your system, you may wish to configure it so that packets can be routed over the SLIP link. If so, you will need to establish this as a SLIP gateway. This is one of the options presented to you in the Network Configuration Manager.

If you configure a dedicated link, then a line will be created in /etc/tcp that will establish the link when the system boots up. Remember that /etc/tcp is linked to /etc/rc2.d/S??tcp, so any changes to /etc/tcp effect /etc/rc2.d/S??tcp. If I wanted to make a SLIP connection between siemau and scoburg, the slattach line, might look like this:

```
/etc/slattach /dev/tty1a 194.113.147.47 194.113.147.26\
255.255.255.240 38400
```

Like many configuration files, the logical line can be spread across two physical lines if you escape the end-of-line with the backslash. The syntax is

```
slattach device source_ip destination_ip net_mask baud_rate
```

Note that we did not put the slattach in the background as indicated in the SCO Doc. Per SCO Support, this is a bug in the doc. You want SLIP to be running in the foreground on that port. Here, also, you see that we have hardcoded the line with the tty device and the baud rate.

When you configure the dynamic incoming link, the procedure is basically the same as for a dynamic outgoing link. Two differences is that you need to provide a logname for the SLIP account and then create the login script. The account name is governed by the same limitation as a "normal" account.

The login script is different from the line in /etc/tcp:

```
/etc/slattach /dev/tty1a 132.147.118.6 132.147.246.12 255.255.0.0 38400
```

Here we see that the port is hardcoded to /dev/tty1a and the IP addresses of the source and destination machines are hardcoded as well. This bothers me. If you have a dynamic incoming line, you may have several lines the people can dial with for a SLIP link. This mechanism implies one incoming line per telephone number. The number for this machine is specified in the Systems file and hooks up to a specific number and therefore a specific modem and therefore a specific tty line. However, some companies (including SCO) have single numbers from the outside that are hooked to a set of other phone numbers. If one is busy, the system will search for a free line. When you get one of these systems, there is no guarantee that you get the same tty device every time. However, hardcoding it like this forces you to.

### Packet Filtering

If you want packet filtering enabled you have to do two things. First create the /etc/pppfilter file. If you have already configured packet filtering for PPP, then this file *should* already exist (Otherwise, packet filtering will not work for PPP). If you do not specifically use filtering, then all packets are passed. If the file does exist, then you can simply add entries to it. If you want, you can use existing entries you've defined for PPP links. On the `slattach` line, you use the `-p` option to point to the line in /etc/pppfilter that you want to use. For example, if I did not want to allow connections like ntp, ftp, or timed, I could block them like this:

```
slip1 pass    !port ntp and !port ftp and !port timed
```

The general format is

```
tag filter_type filter_criteria
```

This example has the tag slip1. Therefore, I would reference it on the `slattach` command line as `-p slip1`. The `filter_type` is pass. Remember you can only filter the packets to passthrough; not the packets that bring up or keep up the link. Finally, we have the filter criteria. In this example, we are saying not to pass (because of the !) the packets going to or coming from the ntp, ftp, or time port.

At this point I am going to have to pass you to the `packetfilter(SFF)` manpage. There are literally dozens of different filter criteria that you can use, including destination address, length of the packet, and even specific combinations of these criteria as the `packetfilter` syntax can also use Boolean variables.

You can also use the Network Configuration Manager to set the packet filter tag entry for outgoing SLIP links. Since tag is a just a pointer to a line in a file, there is nothing wrong with multiple SLIP links sharing the same tag line. For that matter you could have sixty-four lines, mixed SLIP, and PPP all using a single tag.

Any changes you make to the filter file will not go into effect until the link is reconnected. In fact, any changes you make to the link are not valid until you bring up the link. Therefore, if you want the changes to take effect, you must bring down the link with `ifconfig` and then back up. Note that if you have a connection to the remote site, `ifconfig` does not stop it, it just brings the link down. Therefore, you might still be running up long distance charges.

Changes can be made in two ways. You can make changes by running the Network Configuration Manager. Select the TCP/IP line under SLIP. Next, select Modify Protocol Configuration in the Protocol menu. You can run `slconf` to make changes as well. I would select the latter since the Network Configuration Manager just runs `slconf`. If you change the name of the host to connect to an outgoing link, make sure that you change the UUCP files if necessary.

### *PPP*

Like the other network protocols, you must add the PPP protocol stack before configuring any PPP links. This is accomplished in ODT 3.0 with the `netconfig` utility or Network Configuration Manager if you are running OpenServer. IN ODT 3.0, this process is called adding a chain. In both instances, the PPP protocol stack is being added to the kernel, so you must relink and reboot before you can establish a link.

If you are running ODT 3.0, PPP is configured using the `netconfig` utility and the Network Configuration Manager if you have OpenServer. Because PPP in ODT 3.0 is limited in the configuration options, there isn't much to the `netconfig` configuration other than specifying the port name, the IP addresses, and the PPP account name. However, the Network Configuration Manager allows you to configure packet filtering, authentication, timeout values, link and communications parameters, as well as what type of PPP connection this should be.

Once you have configured the PPP stack using the Network Configuration Manager, you can use the `pppconf` utility to add, modify, or remove the various PPP configuration options. Although `pppconf` is actually called from the Network Configuration Manager, you save a little time by calling it yourself.

When you configure a link using the Network Manager, two changes are made. First, the necessary changes are made to `/etc/ppphosts`. Second, entries are added to `/etc/hosts` to reflect the new machines on the network.

PPP configuration is essentially the same as for SLIP. In both cases, `netconfig` is used in ODT and the Network Configuration Manager is used in OpenServer. The concept is also the same in both operating systems. Like SLIP, PPP is the network interface driver on which TCP/IP sits. A chain is necessary to create the network interface, and here you would be creating the chain `sco_tcp→ppp`. Like all the other types of network interfaces, once you use the appropriate configuration tool, the chain is then written to `/usr/lib/netconfig/chains`.

A link configuration is necessary for every link, which is based on (at a minimum) an entry in the `/etc/ppphosts` file. This is one of the reasons why you simply can't add chains to `/usr/lib/netconfig/chains` and expect things to work. By running `netconfig` or the Network Configuration Manager (`pppconf`) you add the appropriate entries to `/etc/ppphosts`. Yes, potentially you could make the changes here, however, why bother? This process works and, therefore, you run a greater risk of messing things up by making changes.

One thing I need to point out is that the `ppphosts` file is completely different in the two releases. You cannot copy the file from ODT to OpenServer and expect it to work. Let's take a quick look at each file to see what they look like. In ODT, the `ppphosts` look like this:

```
132.144.147.75  5  - siemau 10 3
132.144.147.75  5  - vesta 10 3
```

where the fields are

```
destination inactivity_timeout tty dest_uucp_name ACK_timeout max_retries
```

Although `netconfig` puts the destination IP address here, this can be the name of the system, provided there is a means to resolve the host name such as `/etc/hosts` or DNS. The inactivity timeout is the amount of time to wait with no activity on the line, before the link is broken. If you are using a direct connection and not the UUCP facilities, then the `tty` field is the name of the device used for the direct connect. The `ACK_timeout`, is the time to wait for a PPP acknowledgment. This is optional and defaults to 10 seconds. The `max_retries` is the number of times the system will retry each PPP protocol request. This, too, is optional and defaults to 3.

So, what does the file look like in OpenServer? Let's take a look:

```
siemau:scoburg staticdev=/dev/tty2a speed=19200 mask=255.255.255.0
name=jmohr
vesta:ppp-scoburg uucp=vesta retry=5 mask=255.255.255.0
*nppp local=ppvesta remote=scoburg
```

Immediately you can see these are significantly different. In the OpenServer file, you have many different options, since there are several different kinds of links that you can establish. In every case, however, the definition of the machine names is the same. In general, the syntax is

```
remote_addr:local_addr
```

The first line is a dedicated line. It lists the tty device (`staticdev`), the connection speed (`speed`), the netmask (`mask`), and the name of the system used when authentication is enabled. In the second line we have a dynamic outgoing line.

Since we are using a dynamic outgoing line, we are using the UUCP facilities, therefore the name of the machine as it shows up in the `Systems` file is here defined with `uucp=`. The `retry=` option is the number of times the systems should try to call the remote hosts before it fails. Then, once again we have the netmask.

If you have a dynamic incoming connection, then it is completely different as you see in the third line. The first entry is the name of the account that the remote side will use to log in. Note that the name *must* be preceded with the asterisk (*) to indicate that this is the account name and not a machine name. The local machine name is defined by `local=` and the remote machine name is defined by `remote=`.

One very important thing to keep in mind is that the remote machine name be resolvable by the local machine *without* using this link. That is, either you use `/etc/hosts` or the name server is on *this* side of the PPP link. Otherwise you have a Catch-22. That is, in order to resolve the name, you have to bring up the link. However, to bring up the link, you have to resolve the name.

Note that all of these values were placed into `/etc/ppphosts` by the `pppconf` command (or through Network Configuration Manager). If we make other configuration changes such as enabling, filtering, or authentication, then the appropriate values would be placed in here as well. For more information, see the `ppphosts`(SFF) man-page or the `/etc/ppphosts` file itself.

As I mentioned, before, in the SCO implementation in OpenServer, there are four different kinds of links that you can configure: dedicated, dynamic outgoing, dynamic incoming, and manual outgoing.

If you have a dedicated serial line to the remote host, then a dedicated link may be advisable. Dedicated serial lines usually refer to such things as serial cables connecting two machines directly or leased telephone lines. This does have some limitation in that dynamic allocation of IP addresses is not allowed and the serial line must be connected to a single remote host.

If the serial line is not static, then a dynamic incoming link configuration might be more applicable. This is what you would need if you wanted to share the same serial line with PPP and UUCP, or when the connection requires a "getty-type" login. The IP addresses can be specified by either the local or remote host.

If the local machine needs to initiate the connection and the local machine also assigns the IP address, you might want to use what is referred to as a "dynamic outgoing, transparent bringup link". This type of link is used over dynamically acquired (maybe shared) serial lines.

If the remote hosts must be the one to assign the IP addresses, then a "dynamic outgoing, manual bringup link" is probably what you will configure. Here, too, the serial line is one that is dynamically acquired.

Because PPP operates over serial lines and therefore can be accessed via modems, it has a connection to the outside world that doesn't exist with other network media. As a result, an extra layer of security may be necessary. This is the concept of PPP authentication. Like UUCP authentication, PPP authentication is not a requirement. It is at the discretion of the administrator. If enabled, a hosts will require that the other host correctly identifies itself. In essence, this is the same as a password and login of "real" users. The default is that no authentication is required.

As I mentioned earlier, SCO PPP provides two methods of authentication (aside for the authentication provided by the login), Password Authentication Protocol (PAP) and Challenge-Handshake Authentication Protocol (CHAP). If enabled, the authentication parameters must be included in the entry in /etc/ppphosts. The auth= parameter enables authentication and sets it to either PAP or CHAP depending on what you set it to. Remember that the remote side must support this kind of authentication as well. By default, PPP waits one minute for the remote side to authenticate itself, however, this can be changed using the authtmout= parameter, which specifies the timeout in minutes.

During the authentication the authenticating host must be able to identify the other hosts. "Generic" authentication is also possible if there is default entry in /etc/pppauth. If not, the configuration entry in /etc/ppphosts must contain the hosts id. This is done with the name= variable. This is matched to an entry in /etc/pppauth which contains a name= entry and a password= entry.

If PAP is used, pppd requests that the remote host sends the corresponding name and password. These are checked against the entries in /etc/pppauth. If authentication is required by the remote host, then the local pppd sends the name and password. In both cases, if there is no match, then connection is refused. Keep in mind that the name and password are *not* encrypted in any way. Therefore authentication provides very minimal security.

If you are using CHAP, pppd sends a CHAP request packet to the remote host, which contains the local host name and a random string generated by the local host. The remote host then computes a "result," using the request packet ID, the random string, and the password. The remote machine then sends the result back to the local machine, which then generates a result based on the same values. If the two results match, then connection is allowed. If the remote side has CHAP authentication enabled, the process is the same, except that the remote side sends the first packet. Since the authentication is done with the calculated result, CHAP is more secure than PAP.

SCO PPP also allows packet filtering. This controls the behavior of PPP depending upon what kind of packet is being sent. For example, PPP can be configured to behave one way if someone wants to make a telnet connection and some other way if they want to connect using `ftp`. This we see in Figure 12–1.

As I mentioned before, a PPP connection is not always up. Attempts to connect with the remote side push `pppd` a little to go out and make the connection. PPP packet filtering is a way to say that if the outbound packet is `ftp`, for example, then not to reinitiate the connection. This can also be used to limit the access to the link in general. For example, even if the link is up, packet filtering can be used to eliminate all `ftp` packets. Since it is these packets that let PPP know that the link is being used, packet filtering can also be used to limit what kinds of packets make the link think it is in use.

This last functionality may not seem too important. Let's consider a dynamic link that is made through a modem. When the connection is initiated, `pppd` must first get the modem to call out, the remote host must answer, and the two sides must negotiate a moment or two until the link is established. If the link is not used within the timeout period, the link is dropped.

Imagine you have an impatient employee who doesn't like to have to wait until the link is re-established. Since multiple connections are possible across a PPP link, he or she just might have a ping to the remote system running in the background. This keeps the link up and there is no time lost re-establishing the connection as the connection is always there.

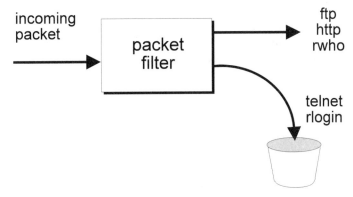

**Figure 12–1**   Packet filtering.

Now imagine what happens if the remote site happens to be somewhere other than the local calling area. It doesn't have to be out of state, just somewhere where you are charged by the minute. What happens if this impatient employee goes on vacation for two weeks and forgets to turn off the ping?

Packets can be filtered at several different levels. The first level is the protocol type, such as tcp, udp, or icmp. You can also make the restriction more specific by preventing connection on specific ports. For example, we could configure it so that tcp packets were allowed in general, but we could deny access to connections on port 23, thus disabling `telnet` across that link. We could restrict access to or from certain IP addresses. For example, if we didn't want our employees downloading megabytes worth of games from archive sites, we could filter out all packets to or from the IP address of that archive.

As with other aspects of PPP, filtering is accomplished on a per-link basis. Therefore, I might allow `telnet` from one site, but disallow it from another. Both SLIP and PPP use the same filter configuration file (`/etc/pppfilter`). See the section on packet filtering for more details.

It is possible to allow your existing UUCP configuration to do most of the work in establishing a PPP link. This requires UUCP connectivity to be established first between the two sites, which may not always be possible. However, testing UUCP first is a good way of testing the physical connection, since the configuration is somewhat the same.

When you bring up a dynamic outgoing PPP, `pppd` requests a UUCP link to the remote host. Like normal UUCP connections, communication characteristics such as baud rate, parity, and flow control are established. Keep in mind that the UUCP configuration is doing this and not PPP. Once the UUCP connection has been established, UUCP passes the tty device name to PPP which then takes over the link.

In order to configure this feature you need to include the `uucp=` variable in `/etc/ppphosts`. The value of the `uucp=` variable is the name of the host you are connecting and must match the name of the host as it is defined in `/usr/lib/uucp/Systems`,

If you are configuring a dynamic link, there are a couple of things to consider. First, note that you can configure a link on an IP-address to IP-address basis, as well as Hostname-to-hostname. If you specify both names and IP address, then the host name will take precedence and an entry is added to `/etc/hosts` that matches up the host name to the IP address. If you specify an IP address, then the remote system must agree to use it. If this hasn't been agreed upon before hand, the connection will be refused.

Although all these changes are carried out by the Network Configuration Manager, all that is really being done is making changes to `/etc/ppphosts`. Therefore, if you were so inclined, you could make the changes yourself. However, I would recommend that you use the tools provided as it's easier and you are less prone to mistakes. On the other hand, there is no problem with copying this file between machines.

On incoming calls, the first barrier the calling system has to get past is the login procedure. Like UUCP, a special account needs to be set up where the login shell is `/usr/lib/ppp/ppp` and not something like `/bin/ksh`. Again, this is similar to UUCP. When you configure PPP with either ODT 3.0 or OpenServer, a PPP user account is set up. In OpenServer you are asked if you want to do this and are even given the choice of what user ID number you want. However, in ODT the account is simply created for you.

When assigning names, you must be sure that the name doesn't match any other interface. For example, if you have an Ethernet card on your machine and it is associated with the name scoburg, then a good choice of name for the host on the PPP connection might be ppp-scoburg. It is close enough that users will (hopefully) know it is the same machine (plus the ppp in front makes it clear what interface it is going over). However, it is a different name, so there will be no conflicts. Again, if you enter both an IP address and a name, the name takes precedence, is written to `/etc/ppphosts`, and the name and IP address are written to `/etc/hosts`.

Leave the name field for the local machine blank if you want the remote system to assign the host name. You must also set the negotiation option to 'yes', which is done by clicking the advanced options button.

If you want the remote side to assign the address too, leave the address field blank as well. If you put an IP address here, the other host must accept this value. Otherwise the link won't be established.

If the local machine is to establish the remote name and IP address, this can be done through an IP address pool. An IP address pool is a set of IP addresses that are set aside for such dynamic connections. To enable this feature, enter the name of an IP address pool instead of a host name. Leave this field blank if you want the remote system to assign a host name. Also, set one of the advanced options for IP address negotiation to 'yes'.

An additional piece of information that you need to include when configuring a dedicated line is what serial port you are going to use. This shows up in `ppphosts` as the `staticdev` parameter. Although you are probably going to be using a modem, you should use a line that does not support modem control.

If you have multiple network interfaces in your system and want to be able to route packets through the PPP connection, you need to establish the PPP interface as a gateway. If not already done, this will turn on ipforwarding and ipsendredirects within the kernel. If you enable this, you need to relink the kernel and reboot. This does not have any influence on the ppphosts file.

### Configuring the Domain Name System (DNS)

I discussed DNS as being a means of centrally administering the file necessary for node name to IP-address translation. Although the relationship of the files is pretty straight-forward, they are rather initimidating to the uninitiated (myself included).

So, what do the DNS configuration files look like? Well, since the first file that *named* looks at is /etc/named.boot, that seems like a good place to start. Let's assume we wanted to set up a primary name server. We might have a file that looks like this:

```
;
; Boot file for Primary Master Name Server
;


;
; type     domain                 source file or host
;

directory  /etc/named.d
primary    siemau.com                    siemau.forward
primary    147.142.199.in-addr.arpa    siemau.rev
primary    0.0.127.in-addr.arpa    named.local
cache      .                       root.cache
```

Lines beginning with a semicolon are considered comments and blank lines are ignored. The first line with configuration information is

```
directory  /etc/named.d
```

This tells *named* that if no path is specified, it should look for the other configuration files in the specified directory; in this case, /etc/named.d. Note that this is the default directory used in OpenServer. ODT used the default directory /usr/lib/named. However, since the named.boot file is read when named starts up, you could change it to anything you want.

The first primary line says that we are the primary name server for the domain siemau.com. This says that the information to resolve forward requests are found in the file siemau.forward. Okay, so what are forward requests? Well, "forward requests" is my term. I use it for two reasons. First, the file containing the information, often ends with `.forward`. Second, I think the primary function of a name server is to translate names to IP addresses. Therefore, this is going forward. Translating IP addresses to names is going in reverse.

Note that you will often see that the forward mapping file is referred to as `named.hosts` or `domain_name.host` and the reverse mapping as `named.rev` or `domain_name.rev`. I like to call one `.forward` and one `.rev` so I know by looking at them what their function is. It doesn't matter what you call them as long as there are pointed to in `named.boot`.

In order to be the primary server we must say that we are. This is accomplished through the Start of Authority (SOA) record, which says we are the start of authority for the given domain. That is, when trying to find the answer to a query, the buck stops here. We have all the right answers when it comes to this domain. The SOA record is required and might look like this:

```
siemau.com.     IN  SOA  siemau.siemau.com. jimmo.siemau.com. (
          8675309 ; Serial
          10800   ; Refresh
          1800    ; Retry
          3600000  ; Expire
          259200 ) ; Minimum
```

The fields in the first line are: domain, data class, type of record, primary name server, responsible individual. The data class will always be IN for Internet. Often you will see root or postmaster as the person responsible for this domain. Here, I picked myself. Note that the format is `jimmo.siemau.com` and not `jimmo@siemau.com` as one might expect.

The `Serial` number is a way for secondary servers to keep track of the validity of their information. If the secondary has a serial number that is lower than on the primary, it knows that the information is outdated. It will then pull over an updated copy.

The `Refresh` is how often (in seconds) the secondary servers should check the primary for updated information. In every implementation I have ever seen, this value is set to 10800 seconds, or three hours. You can change it if your site requires it.

The `Retry` is how often (in seconds) the secondary server should retry to contact the primary. This value of 3600 seconds (one hour) is also something I have seen in almost every case. Again, change it as you need it.

The `Expire` time is how long the secondary will try before it gives up and declares the data it has as invalid. This is based on the attitude that no data is better than old data. Here we have 1000 hours or almost 42 days.

The `Minimum` is the value that other resource records should use as their time-to-live, if no other value is defined for them. The time-to-live is how long a given piece of information is considered valid.

At the end of each of these records you see a semicolon. This is used in DNS database files as the start of a comment. Any text from the semicolon to the end of the line is considered part of the comment. You will also see that many lines have semicolons as their first character. In these cases, the whole line is a comment.

Note also there is a dot after each `.com` entry. This indicates the end of the name. Remember I mentioned that the trailing dot indicates the root domain? In these cases, this dot is required. If you leave it off, the system will assume that it should tack the domain name onto the end. Therefore, you might end up with the domain name twice. This behavior can actually come in handy and we'll get to it shortly.

The SOA record is just one resource record that you find in DNS database files. There are several others that we will get through during the course of this discussion. Resource records have this general format:

```
name {ttl} data-class record-type record-specific-data
```

The `name` is simply something we are looking for. For example, we might have a machine name and we are looking for the IP address. If we have the machine name, this is our value. On the far right is `the record-specific-data` or the IP address. The `ttl` value is the time-to-live. This is an optional value since we already defined a minimum in the SOA record. We could have also defined a `ttl` value for this SOA record, if we had wanted. The `data-class` can be one of several values. However, the IN for Internet class is commonly used, therefore that is the only one we'll use here. The `record-type` tells us what kind of resource record we have. For example, SOA is one record type.

After the SOA record there is usually an entry saying which machines are name servers, such as,

```
siemau.com.   IN   NS   siemau.siemau.com.
```

The value we have is `siemau.com`. For this record type, this value is the domain name. The domain is the same for the SOA record, since we are defining this machine to be the name server as well. The data-class, again, is IN for Internet. Since we are defining which machine is the name server, the record type is `NS`, for name server. Lastly, we get the FQDN of the machine (`siemau.siemau.com.`). Note that in both cases we had the dot at the end of each name.

One thing that I should point out here is that a good choice for which machine is the nameserver is one that is on multiple networks, that is one that servers use as a gateway. This is a good choice since it already has to know about multiple networks to be the gateway. It is said to be *well-connected*. This saves managing one machine as the gateway and the other as the nameserver.

Next, we have the name to address mappings. Let's assume that I only have two other machines in my network. The entries for all my machines might look like this:

```
siemau.siemau.com.     IN     A     199.142.147.1
vesta.siemau.com.      IN     A     199.142.147.2
scoburg.siemau.com.    IN     A     199.142.147.3
```

The general format is

```
machine-name     data-type     record-type     IP-address
```

Note that despite the fact that `siemau` is our name server, we still need to include it here. Otherwise there would be no way to translate its name to an address. The new piece of information here is the `A` record-type. This simply says that this specific record is making the translation from machine name to IP-address. Each entry is referred to as an address record or address resource record. Note again the trailing dot (.).

We also need a mapping for the node "localhost." This is a special name for the local machine and is accessed using a special driver called the "loopback driver." Rather than accessing the card, the loopback driver knows that this is the local machine and does not need to go out to the network card. Certain functions on the system take advantage of the capabilities of this driver:

```
localhost     IN   A   127.0.0.1
```

One thing I need to point out is the dot (.) at the end of each FQDN. This says that the name stops here. Remember that the dot is used to indicate the root domain. By putting the dot here, this says that we have reached the root domain, so we won't go any further.

Leaving the dot off can be a mistake or an intention. In these examples it would be a mistake. In fact, in the time I was doing tech support at SCO, leaving off the dot was (perhaps) the most common mistake made when configuring the name server. However, we can leave it off intentionally in certain circumstances and have it be correct. We can use abbreviations (shortened forms) to indicate the machine name. For example, we could have written the first entry like this:

```
siemau          IN     A     199.142.147.1
```

Because we already defined what the domain name is in the `named.boot` file, the system knows what to append. Therefore, we can try to contact either `siemau` or `siemau.siemau.com` and the name server will translate that correctly to 199.142.147.95.

We now need to make the translations from IP address to name. As I mentioned before, these are reverse translations. The data for these translations is in the file `siemau.rev` as indicated by the line from `named.boot`:

```
primary    147.142.199.in-addr.arpa siemau.rev
```

In general, the format of the entry is similar to that of the forward entries. For our three examples they would look like this:

```
1.147.142.199.in-addr.arpa.      IN     PTR     siemau.siemau.com.
2.147.142.199.in-addr.arpa.      IN     PTR     vesta.siemau.com.
3.147.142.199.in-addr.arpa.      IN     PTR     scoburg.siemau.com.
```

There are a couple of new things here. Notice the record type. Here we have PTR for pointer records. These point to the machine name. The next is the `in-addr.arpa` after the IP address. To understand we need to take a step back.

Assume we wanted to make the translation from machine name to IP address and we had no idea where that machine was. As I mentioned, there are name servers for all of the top-level domains that are aware of the name servers for all of the lower domains. For the .com domain, one such machine is kava.nisc.sri.com. So, if we had wanted to find the machine `vesta.siemau.com`, we could ask the name server that was responsible for the `.com domain` (`kava.nisc.sri.com`). Since kava knows about the siemau domain, and knows that `siemau.siemau.com` is the name server for that domain it tells you to go ask siemau yourself.

Now, let's go the other way. Question: Is the domain with the first octet of the IP address 199 a .com, .edu, or .gov domain? How can you tell? The answer is that there is no way to tell. IP addresses are not arranged by the type of organization. We can guess that the network 199 is probably a class C network (since it is over 192), but it can just as easily be .com a .edu or anything else. So rather than trying to find the name server for every single domain and asking, "Are you the right one?", a quicker way had to be developed.

The solution was to create a portion of the Internet name space that used the addresses as a name. This portion is considered a separate domain and is referred to as the in-addr.arpa domain. The names of both machines and subdomains within the in-addr.arpa domain are simply the IP addresses. There are 256 subdomains of the in-addr.arpa domain, 256 subdomains of each of those domains and so on.

If you look, the names listed in the in-addr.arpa domain have the IP addresses, reversed. This is keeping with the idea that in the names, the more specific names are on the left and get more general as you move to the right. It also makes things easier to manage since we can say that the 147.142.199.in-addr.arpa domain is administered by one organization. (This is because 199.142.147 is a separate Class C network).

Note also that there is a dot at the end of the reverse address. Here, too, this tells the name server where the end is. Since we already said what the in-addr.arpa domain was in the `named.boot` file. We can make a short cut by listing only the host portion, just like we did with the FQDN. The entry for siemau would then look like this:

```
1     IN     PTR      siemau.siemau.com.
```

Note that here we have the dot a the end of the FQDN, but it wasn't at the end of the IP address in the address (A) record. This is because the dot comes at the end of a domain name. In in-addr.arpa notation, the IP address is part of a name, it just happens to look like an IP address, albeit a reversed one. Think of it this way, a period comes at the end of a sentence, which is a bunch of words. If you have a set of numbers, there is no period.

If we had a class B network, we could also make use of these abbreviations. For example, if siemau had an address of 159.144.147.1, its pointer (PTR) record could have been written like this:

```
1.147    IN     PTR      siemau.siemau.com.
```

This reminds me of the second most common error I see in Support and that is using the abbreviations for the reverse address, but not reversing them! That is, in this example above, writing it as:

```
147.1    IN     PTR      siemau.siemau.com.
```

Don't do that! A reverse domain has the IP address portion of the name reversed as well. No matter what part you include.

By writing the IP address reversed like this, we are essentially creating a new domain. The root domain, is still dot (.). However, this time there is just the single top-level domain in-addr.arpa. This notation is often referred to as the *reverse domain*. Because we are defining a new domain in the `siemau.rev` file, we need a new Start of Authority record. We could copy the SOA record from the `siemau.forward` file, however the domain is wrong. The domain is now `147.144.199.in-addr.arpa`. So, all we need to do is replace the old domain name with the new one and the entry would be identical. The first line would then look like this:

```
147.144.199.in-addr.arpa.   IN   SOA   siemau.siemau.com jimmo.siemau.com (
```

We can now duplicate the remainder of the SOA record from the `siemau.rev` file. One thing I do to help keep things straight is to think of the NS record as part of the SOA record. In reality, they are separate records. However, if you think of them together, you won't forget and leave off the NS record. Since we are defining a new domain, we also need the NS record for this new domain. Its NS record would look like this:

```
147.144.199.in-addr.arpa.    IN    NS    siemau.siemau.com.
```

However, I don't like the idea of two SOA records. There is the chance that I may update the database files, but forget to update one of the SOA record with the new serial number. To eliminate that problem, there is a directive that you can give to the name server to include another file while it's reading the information. This is the $INCLUDE directive. To include a single SOA record, we create a file, perhaps siemau.soa, and use the $INCLUDE directive in both the siemau.forward and siemau.rev files. The line would look like this:

```
$INCLUDE siemau.soa
```

Since we already defined the directory in the named.boot file, there is no need for a path here. However, we have a problem. The SOA record in siemau.forward is for a different domain (siemau.dom) than in siemau.rev (147.144.199.in-addr.arpa). We can take advantage of a magic character: @. This will be read as the domain name, provided the domain name is the same as the origin (the origin is the machine that this data is on).

Let's create a single SOA file (i.e., siemau.soa) and make it identical to the others with the exception of the domain name. Instead, we replace it with the "@." Next we remove the SOA records from the siemau.forward and siemau.rev file and replace it with the $INCLUDE directive above. When the name server reads the siemau.forward file, it gets to the $INCLUDE directive and sees that it needs to include the siemau.soa file. When it gets to the "@," the system translates it as siemau.com. Next, when the system reads the siemau.rev file, it sees the same directive, includes the same file, however, this time the "@" is interpreted as 147.144.199.in-addr.arpa.

There are still two lines in the named.boot file that we haven't covered. The first sets up the servers as primary for the "local" domain. This is a special domain that refers to this host only. Remember from our discussion of IP address that the IP addresses for the local host is 127.0.0.1. The network that this host is on is 127.0.0. We always need to be the primary name server for this domain, therefore we have the line in our named.boot:

```
primary    0.0.127.in-addr.arpa    named.local
```

The named.local file could contain just two lines:

```
$INCLUDE named.soa    1    IN    PTR localhost.
```

Note that here, too, we are including the `named.soa` file. When the system reads `named.local`, it includes `named.soa`, and the "@" is translated to 0.0.127.in-addr.arpa as it should.

The last line tells us to read the `cache` file:

```
cache    .                    root.cache
```

The `root.cache` file is the list of the root domain name servers. This file is provided by SCO and is as up-to-date as possible. Unless you are personally aware of any changes, then I suggest leaving this file alone. You can obtain the most current list of root name servers using anonymous ftp from the machine ftp.rs.internic.net. The file is `domain/named.root`.

Let's assume we want vesta to be the secondary name server for this domain. We would then create a `named.boot` file on vesta, that might look like this:

```
directory   /etc/named.d
secondary   siemau.com             199.142.147.1   siemau.forward
secondary   147.142.199.in-addr.arpa  199.142.147.1   siemau.rev
primary     0.0.127.in-addr.arpa                    named.local
cache       .                                       root.cache
```

If we look carefully, we see that the only difference is that for the forward and reverse files, we change "primary" to secondary. Note that vesta is still the primary for the domain 0.0.127.in-addr.arpa (the local domain). The contents of the files are theoretically the same. This is where the concept of the serial number comes in. When the secondary loads its file, it compares the serial number to what it reads from the primary. Note also that the IP address, 199.142.147.1, is the address of the *primary* server. In our case this is the machine siemau.

If we want a caching only server, the named.boot file is a little simpler:

```
directory             /etc/named.d
primary               0.0.127.in-addr.arpa   named.local
cache                 .                      root.cache
```

We still specify the directory and the `root.cache` file. However, we are now the primary for just a single machine, ourselves.

In any of the example named.boot files we could have included a line that simply said:

```
slave
```

That would be a name server, regardless of what of type, that forwards all requests that it cannot satisfy to a list of predetermined forwarders. If this server does not have the answer, it will not interact with any other server, except for those listed as forwarders. Therefore, any time you have a slave server, you must also have a list of forwarders. The entry for the forwarders might look like this:

```
forwarders  199.145.146.1 199.145.148.1
```

The last kind of server is called a remote server in the SCO DOC. Its configuration is the simplest. You need to create a file called `/etc/resolv.conf` and include a line defining the domain and then a list of the name servers or *resolvers* since they resolve your queries. If we had siemau as the primary for this domain and vesta as the secondary, our file might look like this:

```
domain siemau.com
nameserver 199.144.147.1
nameserver 199.144.147.2
```

Note that if this file doesn't exist, your system will expect to get its information from the `/etc/hosts` file. Therefore, you can say that on the client side that if `/etc/resolv.conf` doesn't exist, you are not using DNS.

If you have a larger network with many different departments, you might have already decided to have multiple name servers. As I mentioned, it is a good idea to have your name servers also be the gateway as they are well-connected. This also applies to the gateway you have to the Internet. To make life simpler for you, trying to reach the outside world, and the people, trying to get in, it is a good idea to have the Internet gateway also be the primary nameserver for your entire domain.

If your organization is large, then having the Internet gateway a name server for your entire organization would be difficult to manage. Since you already decided to break your network down by department, then each department should have its own nameserver. One thing you could do is set up the domain nameserver as a secondary for the subdomains. This is easy to set up (as we described above) and saves you from having to maintain a list of every machine within your organization.

What if you have a lot of traffic to and from the Internet? It's possible that your domain name server will get overburdened. Not only does it have to route packets and handle name service queries from both sides of the gateway, it also has to handle name queries from one subnet looking for a machine in the other. For example, assume the machine in the cash.finance.siemau.com wants to contact buyer.sales.siemau.com (two subdomains). The machine cash asks its name server how to get to the buyer, which doesn't know. However, that name server knows about the name server for siemau.com. So it goes and asks how to get to the buyer. If the domain name server is secondary for all the subdomains, it stores copies of the data for all those subdomains. So the domain nameserver needs extra memory and spends time resolving the query. We can save both memory and time by making the domain name server a stub server for the subdomains rather than a secondary. The stub entries in `named.boot` might look like this:

```
stub    finance.siemau.COM    159.144.146.1    finance.stub
stub    sales.siemau.COM      159.144.147.1    sales.stub
```

In order for us to know about the other nameserver, we have to have both NS and SOA records. They look the same as they would on the subdomain nameservers.

When the finance nameserver fails to resolve the query for the sales domain, it asks the domain nameserver which simply passes the buck to the nameserver at IP address 159.144.147.1 (the sales nameserver). This saves time over both having to ask the sales nameserver itself or looking it up in its own database. (Well, it saves time from the perspective of the domain nameserver and not from the perspective of the client.)

There are still several record types that I haven't mentioned. One of them is machine aliasing. For example, you might have a machine that acts as your ftp server, your mail server, and your World Wide Web server. Rather than requiring everyone accessing this machine to know that vesta.siemau.com is the server for all three of these functions, you can create an alias to make things easier. This is done by the CNAME (canonical name) record. Example entries would look like this:

```
ftp              IN       CNAME       vesta
mailserv         IN       CNAME       vesta
www              IN       CNAME       vesta
```

Any reference to these three machines is translated to mean the machine vesta. Keep in mind that if you use such an alias, this should be the only reference in your name server database. You should not have PTR records that point from an IP address to one of these aliases, instead use its canonical (real) name, vesta.

We can also use the name server database to store information about the machine itself. This is done through the HINFO (host information) resource record. We could have the entry for our machine, siemau, that looks like this:

```
siemau     IN       A  199.142.147.14
           N        HINFO  Pentium OpenServer
```

The record-specific data on the right is composed of two strings. The first is the Hardware and the second is the Operating System. The strings may contain spaces or tabs, but you need to include them within quotes or the system will see them as separate strings. "Technically" these two strings should be "machine name" and "system name" and match one of the strings in RFC 1340, but this requirement is not enforced. There is also the problem that many newer machines won't be on the list.

One thing that seems to be missing is the machine name from the HINFO record. Well, this is another shortcut. By leaving the name field out of any record, it defaults to the same value as the previous entry. Here, the previous entry is the A record for siemau. Therefore, the name field of the HINFO record is also siemau.

We can also use the name server to manage certain aspects of our users. For example, you can have mail systems (such as MMDF) read the name server information to determine what machine a particular user gets his or her mail on. This is done with the MB (mailbox) resource record. An example, might look like this:

```
jimmo        IN       MB          siemau.siemau.com.
```

In this domain, mail for the user jimmo should be sent to the machine siemau.siemau.com. Note that this only works if you have unique users within the domain. In addition, there must only be one MB record for each user.

You can make things easier by specifying a single machine as the mail server. This is done with an MX (mail exchanger) resource record. The MX record can also be expanded to include subdomains. For example, the name server for the siemau.com domain has MX records for all the subdomains under it. The resource-specific information contains the presence, which is a numerical value used to determine the order in which mail is sent to different machines. The preference should be 0 unless you have multiple mail servers within the domain.

Let's assume that this is a large company and we have given each department its own domain (regardless of whether they have different IP subnets). We then decide that mail sent to any one in a subdomain goes to the mail server for that subdomain, but any mail to the parent domain, goes to a different server. Some entries might look like this:

```
siemau.com.               IN   MX   0   siemau.siemau.com.
finance.siemau.com.       IN   MX   0   cash.finance.siemau.com.
sales.siemau.com.         IN   MX   0   buyer.sales.siemau.com.
                          IN   MX   1   cash.finance.siemau.com.
market.siemau.com.        IN   MX   0   editdmon.market.siemau.com.
images.market.siemau.com. IN   MX   0   images.market.siemau.com.
```

In this example, mail sent just to a user in the domain siemau.com will go to siemau.siemau.com. Mail sent to either of the other three domains (finance, sales, and market) will be send to a machine in that respective domain. Note that there are two MX records listed for the sales.siemau.com domain. One has a preference of 0 and the other a preference of 1. Since the preference for buyer.sales.siemau.com (0) is lower than for cash.finance.siemau.com (1), the mail program will first try buyer. If buyer can't be reached it will try cash. Keep in mind that the numbers only indicate what order to check. We could have given one a preference of 45 and the other a preference of 66 and they would still have been checked in the same order.

Let's assume that we feel mail to the sales department is so important that we want it to try still another machine before it gives up. We could have a third MX record for `salessiemau.com` that looks like this:

```
IN          MX 2    siemau.siemau.com.
```

In this case, `buyer` will be checked and if the mail message cannot be delivered, `cash` is checked. If `cash` cannot be reached, `siemau` is checked. If we changed the preference of siemau to 1, like the preference for cash, one of them will be chosen at random. This can be used if you want to spread the load across multiple machines.

There are a few other resource record types that we haven't discussed. They are not as commonly used as the others, so we will have to forgo talking about them. If you would like to learn more, check the SCO documentation or the book, *DNS and BIND* by Paul Albitz and Cricket Liu from O'Reilly and Associates.

As I mentioned earlier, you can use the `$INCLUDE` directive to include a file containing the SOA record. However, you can use the `$INCLUDE` directive to include any file. This is very useful if your files have grown to unmanageable sizes and you need to break them apart. Assume your network contains 200 machines. There are A, PTR, and possibly MX records for each machine. You could create three separate files for each of these. ( Normally, A and PTR are in separate files already.) You could then use the `$INCLUDE` directive to include the MX records in one of the other files.

### Debugging the Name Server

Sorry, you're going to have to do it. Unless you are a flawless typist and have every step written down exactly, one day you are going to forget something. As a result, the name server won't function the way you expect. Hopefully, your mistake will be something simple (like forgetting a dot) and you can quickly make the change.

The problem is what to do after you've made the change. Remember, *named* reads the configuration information when it starts. To get *named* to reread the configuration file, you could stop and restart TCP. However, this would not be taken too kindly by the users who have their connection suddenly drop. The solution is to poke *named* in the ribs and tell it go reread the files. This is done by sending the *named* process a hang-up signal with "`kill -1 <pid>`", where `<pid>` is the PID of `named`. To find the PID, either `grep` through `ps -e` or look in `/etc/named.pid`. This also has the side effect of having secondary name servers check the serial numbers, which can be used to force updates.

If you want to have named dump its current database and cache you can send named an interrupt signal SIGINT (kill -2). This dumps the database into /usr/tmp/named_dump.db. Sending named SIGUSR1 (kill -16) you can turn on debugging, the output which is sent to /usr/tmp/named.run. Subsequent SIGUSR1 signals sent to named will increase the debugging a level. Sending it SIGUSR2 (kill -17) turns off debugging completely.

You can also get named to trace all incoming queries, which is sent to /usr/adm/syslog. This is done by sending SIGWINCH (kill -20). Be careful with this, however. Even on smaller networks, the amount of information logged in syslog can be fairly substantial. If you forget to turn it of, you can fill up your root file system. To turn of tracing, send SIGWINCH again. Note that all of these options can be enabled from the start-up script in /etc/rc2.d.

Perhaps the most useful debugging tools is nslookup (name server lookup). The nslookup command can be used either interactively or noninteractively to obtain information from different servers. Depending on how it's set, you can input an IP address and get a name back or input the name and get the IP address back. If you are using the name server, either as a server or a client, nslookup can be used to gather information.

To start it interactively, simply type nslookup at the command line. You are then brought into the nslookup "shell," where you can issue commands and set the options needed to get the information you need. By using 'set all' you can view the current options. By default, nslookup will return the IP address of the input machine name (A forward query). For example, if we ran nslookup on vesta, nslookup would respond with something like this:

```
Default Server: siemau.siemau.com
Address: 199.142.147.1

>
```

This tells us what the default server is and shows that it is ready for the first command by displaying the > prompt.

Let's say we wanted to see what information the name server has when we run nslookup on siemau. We type in scoburg and press return. This gives us,

```
> siemau

Server:   localhost
Address:  127.0.0.1

Name:     siemau.siemau.com
Address:  199.142.147.1
```

This is what we expect. Note that in the first case, the default server was siemau. However, when we run it on the name server itself, the server is localhost.

One question that comes to my mind is whether it translates the IP address back to the host name correctly. Let's see. When we type in the IP address, we get

```
> 199.142.147.3
Server:   localhost
Address:  127.0.0.1

Name:     vesta.siemau.com
Address:  199.142.147.3
```

We can list all the available information for a domain with the ls command. The general syntax is

```
ls [ option ] domain
```

where domain is the name of the domain we would like the information about. If we want we can redirect the output to a file, we can use either type of output redirection (> or >>). If we want to see it on the screen, we get

```
>set all
Default Server:  localhost
Address:  127.0.0.1

Set options:
 nodebug      defname      search       recurse
 nod2         novc         noignoretc   port=53
 querytype=A  class=IN     timeout=5    retry=4
 root=ns.internic.net.
 domain=siemau.com
 srchlist=siemau.com
```

If I want to see everything there is about a domain. I use the ls command. Keep in mind that by itself, the system will think it is a machine name and try to resolve it. However, followed by the domain name we get,

```
> ls siemau.com
[localhost]
 siemau.com.    server = siemau.siemau.com

 siemau          199.142.147.1
 scoburg         199.142.147.2
 localhost       127.0.0.1
 vesta           199.142.147.3
```

However, this does not tell us anything about the mail exchanger or canonical names that we may have defined. To get everything, we use the -d option like this:

```
> ls -d siemau.com
[localhost]
siemau.com. SOA siemau.siemau.com jimmo.siemau.com. (60001 1080 0
1800 3600000 86400)
  siemau.com.    NS              siemau.siemau.com
  siemau.com.    MX        0     vesta.siemau.com
  jimmo          MB              siemau.siemau.com
  siemau         A               199.142.147.1
  scoburg        A               199.142.147.2
  siemau         HINFO           Pentium OpenServer
  localhost      A               127.0.0.1
  www            CNAME           vesta.siemau.com
  mailserv       CNAME           vesta.siemau.com
  ftp            CNAME           vesta.siemau.com
  vesta          A               199.142.147.3
```

As we can see, this gives us everything including mail boxes, HINFO lines, canonical names, the SOA records, and all of the address records. Note that there is only one MB record here. In reality, I probably would have had MB records for all the users on this system. If this network had been even a little larger, then this output would probably be too much to view. Therefore you can use other options to limit what you see. For example, the `-t` option is used to specify a type of query. If we wanted to look for all the mail exchangers, we could use the command `ls -t MX siemau.com`, which gives us,

```
siemau.com.            0   vesta.siemau.com
```

which give us the domain, the preference of the mail exchanger, and the name of the mail exchanger; which is all the information in the MX record.

We can also tell `nslookup` that we want to look for particular kinds of records. Say I want to look for the MX record for a particular machine. I could set the query type to MX and look for that machine, like this:

```
> set type=MX
> siemau.siemau.com
Server: localhost
Address: 127.0.0.1

siemau.siemau.com.siemau.com preference = 0, mail exchanger =
vesta.siemau.com
siemau.siemau.com internet address = 199.142.147.3
```

Okay. This says that the mail exchanger for siemau is vesta. Are you sure? What `nslookup` is actually telling us is that vesta.siemau.com is the mail exchanger for siemau.siemau.com.siemau.com. Why? Because we didn't put the dot at the end of the domain name. Like other aspects of the nameserver, `nslookup` tacked the domain name onto the end of siemau.siemau.com to give us siemau.

siemau.com.siemau.com. If I just use a machine name, the domain name is tacked on as well, but it comes out differently:

```
> siemau
Server: localhost
Address: 127.0.0.1

siemau.siemau.com preference = 0, mail exchanger = siemau.siemau.com
siemau.siemau.com internet address = 199.142.147.1
```

The `nslookup` program also has a configuration file that can come in handy. This is the .nslookuprc file in your home directory. Like the .exrc file for `vi`, the .nslookuprc is read every time you start `nslookup`. The format is also like .exrc, with one entry per line. Assuming I wanted to set the query time to PTR records and set the time out to 5 seconds, I could have these two lines in my .nslookuprc file, like this:

```
set querytype=ptr
set timeout=5
```

This would be the same as starting `nslookup` from the command line like this:

```
nslookup -query=ptr -timeout=5
```

Setting parameters is not the only thing that you can do from the command line. In fact, most anything you can do from inside of `nslookup`, you can do from the command. I could expand the above command to give me

```
nslookup -query=ptr -timeout=5 199.142.147.3

Server: localhost
Address: 127.0.0.1

Name:   vesta.siemau.com
Address: 199.142.147.3
```

So what is this all good for? The most important thing is tracking down problems you might be experiencing. For example, if a particular machine cannot be reached, `nslookup` might show you that there is no A record for that machine. Perhaps mail to a particular machine never ends up where it should. Checking the MX record for that machine will indicate where it is going.

Unfortunately, I cannot list every problem that could arise and what `nslookup` would show. However, with the understanding that you've gained in the last couple of sections of how DNS and `nslookup` work, the best way to proceed is to look at what `nslookup` is telling you. Based on the way you think DNS is configured, try to determine whether `nslookup` records are correct. This may sound like an oversimplification. However, isn't problem solving really knowing what should happen and what would cause it to happen differently?

### Routing

Just because you know the IP address of a particular machine, does not mean you know how to get there. If the machine you are trying to reach is on the same network as yours, then there is normally no problem. If not, then you need to know what path, or route, to take to get to that machine.

Routes are added to and removed from the system using the `route` command. The general syntax is

```
route <option> command destination gateway metric
```

The options include `-f` to flush all entries in the *routing tables*. The two commands used are `add` and `delete`. The `destination` is the IP address of the machine or network you want to reach. You can also use tokens for the network name by including entries in the `/etc/networks` file. This is an ASCII file containing two columns. The first is the name of the network and the second column is the network address. You can then use that name in the `route` command.

The `gateway` is the IP address of the interface to which the packets need to be addressed. Keep in mind that the system must already know how to get to the gateway for this to work.

The `metric` is a value that normally indicates the number of intermediate machines (hops). The system uses this value in determining the shortest route to a particular machine.

For example, let's assume we have an entry in `/etc/networks` like this:

```
sco  132.147
```

Let's also assume that the machine we need to use to access this route has an IP address of 199.142.147.1. We could then run the `route` command like this:

```
route add sco 199.142.147.1 0
```

This says that any packet destinated for the sco network (as defined in `/etc/networks`) should go to the IP address 199.142.174.1 with a metric of 0. Normally, 0 is used when the IP address you specifiy is directly connected to your machine.

If you have a single machine that serves as your gateway to the rest of the world, you can specify `default` instead of a specific address or network as your destination. In the example above, if we wanted to use the same machine for all networks instead of just `sco`, the command would look like this:

```
route add default 199.142.147.1 0
```

In OpenServer, routes are create automatically when you use the Network Configuration Manager. When you add or remove a network interface the system makes a note of what networks you are directly connected to. This information is used to create an entry in the routing tables. This way, your machine always knows about what networks it is directly connected to.

As you move about the network, dynamic entries are created by the routing protocol that you use (most commonly `routed`). The routing protocol communicates with its counterpart on other machines and adds entries to the routing tables automatically.

When it starts, `routed` looks for the file `/etc/gateways`, which contains a list of gateways. (What else?) The general format for this file is

```
<net|host> name gateway metric type
```

The first field specifies whether the gateway is to a specific machine or network. The `name` field is the name of the destination host or network. This can either be an IP address or a token. If using a token, then the host name must be located in `/etc/hosts` or can be determined through DNS. If through DNS, `routed` must be started after `named`. If a network, the name must be in `/etc/networks`.

The `gateway` field is the name or address of the gateway that is to be used. The `metric` is the same as for routes and indicates the number of hops. The type can be either passive, active, or external. A passive gateway is one that is not expected to exchange routing information. Active gateways will exchange information and usually have `routed` running on them. External gateways are ones that are managed by another system, but alternate routes should not be installed.

## NFS

As I have mentioned on numerous occassions, many functions in ODT that were only possible from the command line or by editing files yourself are possible through the "managers" of SCO Admin. One of them is the Filesystem Manager, which allows you to add local filesystems (like you could in ODT with `mdkev fs`), but now you can add remote filesystems as well.

As I mentioned in the section on NFS in the first half of the book, there are two basic terms when talking about NFS filesystems: exporting and importing. The machine with the filesystem that is to be made available (the server) will "export" these filesystems to others. The machines that mount these remote filesystems (the clients) "import" the filesystems.

There are four ways you can mount a remote filesystem. The first is automatically mounting it when the system boots up. This usually requires running the Filesystem Manager in OpenServer or editing `/etc/default/filesys`. The `/etc/default/filesys` file contains not only the mount information for local filesystems, but for remote filesystems as well. For more details on this, see the chapter on filesystems or check out the `filesys(F)` man-page. (NOTE: I don't consider adding a line in some rc script that does a mount command to be automatically mounting the filesystem.)

If the remote mount is a one-time deal, the system administrator can also mount it by hand. Potentially, the administrator could create an entry in /etc/default/filesys that does not mount the filesystem at boot time, but rather is mounted later on. In either event, the system administrator would use the mount command. If necessary, the system administrator can also allow users to mount remote filesystems.

A client machine can also be configured to mount remote filesystems on an "as-needed" basis, rather than whenever the system boots up. This is through the mechanism of the automount program. We'll get into a lot of details about how automount works later on.

The syntax for using the mount command to mount remote filesystems is basically the same as for local filesystems. The difference being that you specify the remote host along with the exported path. For example, if I want to mount the man-pages from scoburg, I could do it like this:

```
mount -f NFS [-o options] scoburg:/usr/man /usr/man
```

Here I told the mount command that I was mounting a filesystem of type NFS and that the filesystem was on the machine scoburg under the name /usr/man. I then told it to mount it onto the local /usr/man directory. There are a couple of things to note here. First, I don't have to mount the filesystem on the same place that it is exported from. I could have just as easily exported it to /usr/doc or /usr/local/man. If I want I can include other options like "normal filesystems" such as read only.

There are a couple of options to mount that are specific to NFS filesystems, so we should take a look at them. The first is the soft option, this tells the mount command to return an error if the server does not respond within a specific time-out. If we want the system to go onto other things rather than wait for the mount to complete, we can use the bg (for background) option. If we don't specify the soft option, then the mount attempt is considered hard and the system will try indefinitely. By setting the intr option, you can kill the attempt to mount the filesystem. Also new to OpenServer is the tcp option. This allows you to use TCP as the protocol instead of UDP. Note that both sides have to be configured to use TCP.

If you are a server, the primary configuration file is /etc/exports. This is a list of the directories that the server is making available for mounting along with who can mount them and what permissions they have. In addition, the server needs a way to find the clients address, therefore mounting will fail if the name cannot be resolved either by DNS or /etc/hosts. Likewise, the clients depend on name resolution to access the server.

As we discussed briefly in the first part of the book, remotely mounted filesystems present a unique set of problems when dealing with user access rights. Because it can have adverse effects on your system, it is necessary to have both user and group ID unique across the entire network. If you don't, access to files and directories can be limited, or you may end up giving someone access to a file that shouldn't. Although you could create each user on every system, or copy the `passwd` files, the most effective method is using NIS.

Normally, NFS is started automatically when the system goes into run-level 2 (multi-user mode) when init executes the `/etc/rc2.d/S89nfs` script. This should be linked to `/etc/nfs`, which allows the root user to stop or start NFS as needed. This would be done simply as `nfs stop` or `nfs` start. Note that since NFS is started and stopped through an `rc` script, moving to run-levels 0, 1, or 6 will stop NFS.

### Configuring lockd

From our discussion on NFS at the beginning of the book, we know that the `lockd` daemon is responsible for maintaining file locks on NFS filesystems. When a process accesses a file that has a lock on it, the request is refused (blocked). Generally, such locks exist a relatively short time before they are removed. By default, `lockd` will wait five seconds before attempting to retry. You can change the length `lockd` waits by using the `-b` flag and specifying the wait time in seconds. For example, to specify a wait time of ten seconds, it would look like this:

```
/etc/lockd -b 10
```

Note that `lockd` should be started by the NFS startup script. Therefore, I would recommend that if you want to change the time-out, you change the `lockd` entry in `/etc/rc2.d/S89nfs`.

When a system has crashed and comes back up, there is a short period in which no lock requests are processed. This is to ensure the integrity of the locks and to ensure that the correct process can reclaim the lost locks. By default, the system waits forty seconds before any new lock requests are processed. This too can be altered, in this case it is done with the `-g` flag. Editing the entry in `/etc/rc2.d/S89nfs` I could change the grace period to sixty seconds like this:

```
/etc/lockd -g 60
```

By default, there are two `lockd` daemons running, one for TCP and the other for UDP. If you have a busy system, you can increase this number by using the `-t` option to increase the number of TCP `lockds` or `-u` to ease the number of UDP lockds; for example,

```
/etc/lockd -t 2 -u 3
```

This allocates two `lockd` daemons for TCP and three for UDP. With no flag, the specified number of *UDP* lock daemons will be allocated; for example,

`/etc/lockd 3`

will allocate three `lockd` daemons for UDP.

### More NFS Mount Options

If you decided to run the Filesystem Manager, the menu options do not indicate clearly what options in `/etc/default/filesys` they refer to. Therefore, let's briefly go through the options so we know what the Filesystem Manager is doing, should we need to edit the `filesys` file.

After filling in the blanks on the first screen, you reach the advanced `mount` options by clicking on the button `Advanced Mount Options`. (Do I hear an echo in here?) The first item is `Mount in background`. If you select "yes" then the `mount` command will wait until the command returns before continuing. A "no" means that the system will start the mount and go onto other business. This is the `bg` option in `/etc/default/filesys`.

The NFS mount type determines whether the mount will be a hard mount, a soft mount or a spongy mount. A spongy mount is one that is hard sometimes and soft at others. If set to hard mount, the system will try indefinitely to complete an operation before it gives up. This operation can be anything such as reading from or writing to the filesystem. It does not just have to be the mount operation. If you specify a hard mount, I suggest that you also enable the interrupt option. That way if you try an operation and it gets stuck, you can break out of it with the interrupt key.

With a soft mount the system will try 'n' times before it reports an error, where 'n' is the number of times to retry as specified in the Filesystem Manager. This can also be specified in the `filesys` file using the `retrans=` option. The default is five times, which equates to `retrans=5`. If you consider a server "unreliable" or the connection slow, soft mounts are a good idea. If you set the mount type to spongy, then the connection behaves like a soft mount on operations like `stat()`, `fsstat()`, `readlink()`, or `readdir()`. In all other cases it behaves like a hard mount.

As we talked about a moment ago, by enabling the keyboard interrupt you can kill NFS operations that have hung while waiting for a response from a hard-mounted filesystem. I have never heard of a logical reason for turning it off, so I would recommend that you never do.

As I mentioned before, permissions are a problem when dealing with NFS mounted filesystems. This is compounded when dealing with SUID and SGID files. The options here are `ignore` and `honor`. If you ignore them, all programs executed on NFS mounted filesystems will be executed as if they have no SUID or SGID bits set. If you set it to honor, the programs will behave like they do on local filesystems. This puts the `suid` option in the mntopts of `/etc/default/filesys`.

The `cache attributes` option is a Boolean variable that determines if file attributes will be cached. By default they are and I recommend you leave it so unless your application requires close synchronization with the server. If you change it to 'no,' performance when accessing the mounted filesystem will be impaired. This is the `noac` option.

The read/write buffer size defines the size of the (what else?) read-write buffers in bytes. Through the Filesystem Manager you size one size which is valid for both the read and write buffers. However, you can change this by editing `/etc/default/filesys` and changing the `rsize` value for the read buffer and the `wsize` value for the write buffer. The only time I would change this from the default of 8k is when you have a slow connection.

The timeout period defines (in seconds) how long each operation should wait before it is considered to have failed. This is the `timeo` option and is set to 300 seconds (5 minutes!) by default. The number of times to retry before reporting an error is valid is only for soft mounts. This is because a hard mount will never give up. The default is five and is defined by the `retrans =` option.

Although you can't specify it in the Filesystem Manager, new to OpenServer is the ability to run NFS across TCP instead of UDP. This is simply done by using the `tcp mount` option. One thing I would like to point out is that if you use the Filesystem Manager and change any one of the advanced options, it will include every one of the options in `/etc/default/filesys`, even the ones that are unchanged.

One thing I need to point out about using the Filesystem Manager is that when you specify the remote host name, you must do so using the fully-qualified domain name. Otherwise, the system won't see it. You can also choose the name from a pull-down list.

As one might guess, you can also use the Filesystem manager to mount and unmount the filesystems, aside from just changing their mount characteristics. You can also use it to administer your `/etc/exports` file by allowing you to add or modify the existing configuration. It also has an option for you to view your existing export configuration. Well, sort of. This is one of those "almosts" that I have grown to expect with OpenServer. When I specify in the `/etc/exports` file that a particular directory can only be accessed by a certain host, the Export

Mode is reported as "read-mostly" and there is no indication of what the limitations are. In addition, changes to the file /etc/exports are reflected immediately in the output of the Filesystem Manager, without first running exportfs. This means the Filesystem Manager does not check the current state of your exported filesystems, but what it *could* be the next time you reboot or run exportfs.

One important function is the ability to define the UID of unknown users. If you are running NIS and all user accounts are distributed to all systems, then you really don't have this problem. If there are cases where a user is unknown then you can specify the anon = option to a particular user ID; potentially to a guest account or someone else who has limited access. This is an extra safety precaution that you can take. Note that the root user is always considered unknown. Therefore if the anon = option is set, the root always gets set to this UID. You can also disable this by setting anon=-1; therefore, unknown users will have no access.

### When Things Go Wrong

There are a couple of tools that can be used to specifically check NFS connections. Because NFS relies on the same mechanism as other programs using TCP/IP, solving NFS problems start with understanding the tools used for TCP/IP. Rather than repeating myself, I suggest you see the section on configuring TCP/IP and the SCO doc.

If you want to see all the programs using RPC on a specific machine, I would run it as:

```
rpcinfo -p <hostname>
```

which might give me something like this:

```
program      vers    proto    port
100000       2       tcp      111     portmapper
100000       2       udp      111     portmapper
100008       1       udp      1184    walld
100002       1       udp      1185    rusersd
100002       2       udp      1185    rusersd
100005       1       udp      1272    mountd
100005       1       tcp      1116    mountd
100003       2       udp      2049    nfs
100003       2       tcp      2049    nfs
150001       1       udp      1273    pcnfsd
150001       2       udp      1273    pcnfsd
150001       1       tcp      1117    pcnfsd
150001       2       tcp      1117    pcnfsd
100024       1       udp      1276    status
100024       1       tcp      1118    status
```

```
100021       1       udp      919      nlockmgr
100021       3       udp      919      nlockmgr
100021       2       tcp      1119     nlockmgr
100021       1       tcp      919      nlockmgr
100021       3       tcp      919      nlockmgr
```

The columns are

```
Program-number    version-number protocol port
```

The program number is the RPC number of that program. You can see what RPC number equates to what program number by looking in `/etc/rpc`. Here we see that all the NFS related daemons are running. If we look carefully, we see that for each program (except `walld` and `rusersd`) there is a copy of the program using both UDP and TCP. If you find that one or more of these is not running then stopping and restarting NFS might work. Otherwise, rebooting should correct the problem. Note that `portmapper`, `mountd`, `nfs`, and `status` are required.

If you want to check if a particular program is running on server, this can also be done with `rpcinfo`. The general syntax for this command is

```
rpcinfo -u <server_name> <program_name>
```

For example, if I wanted to check to see if `lockd` was running on scoburg, I would *not* run it as

```
rpcinfo -u scoburg lockd
```

If I did, I would end up with the message

```
rpcinfo: lockd is unknown service
```

This is because the name of the service in RPC's eyes is `nlockmgr`. Therefore, the correct syntax would be

```
rpcinfo -u scoburg nlockmgr
```

which should give you the response

```
program 100021 version 1 ready and waiting
```

If you don't get this response, then run `rpcinfo -p` to find out what programs are registered.

If you want to find out about what filesystems are being mounted or can be mounted, you can use `showmount`. On the server, `showmount -a` will show you which filesystems have been mounted and by whom. This will be in the form `host:filesystem`. If you want to find out which filesystems are being exported and their permissions, use `showmount -e`. On scoburg system, I get this:

```
export list for scoburg.siemau.com:
```
```
/usr/man (everyone)
/usr/lib (everyone)
/u1      access=siemau
/u2      (everyone)
```

Each of the filesystems listed is accessible from every other system with the ex-pection of `/u1` which is only accesible from siemau.

If a client simply stops responding, it may be because the server is down and you have configured a hard mount. If so, the client may wait indefinitely for the server to come back up. Once it does, the processes can continue as before. If the mount is soft, you will (should) get an error after the number of retries specified (5 by default).

### *Automount*

In order to be able to mount a remote filesystem using automount, you first need to be able to mount it using normal NFS. That is to say that there are no flags that you can set on the remote side (where the filesystem is being ex-ported) that says either to explicitly allow or deny access via automount. The re-mote filesystem simply makes a resource available and you access it with what-ever tool you see fit. Therefore, for the purpose of this discussion, we are going to simply assume that in each case, the remote host has given us permission to access that filesystem. For more details, see the previous section on NFS config-uration.

We mentioned that automount is useful when remote filesystems are infre-quently mounted, such as man-pages or help files. While at SCO, I had auto-mounter configured so I could access the filesystems containing the source code. I could the cd into `/source/ODT3` and would instantly be at the top of the source tree for ODT 3.0.

The basic configuration unit with the automounter is one or more files called "maps." These map the filesystems you want to access to the directory where you want to mount them (the mount points). These map files are fairly easy to configure and can be edited with any text editor. All automount connections are based on references in the master map file. By default this is `/etc/auto.master`, so we will base our discussion on that. However, you can change this by starting automount with `-f <file_name>`, where `<file_name>` is the name of the master map file. This can be done either from the command line or by editing the entry in `/etc/rc2.d/*nfs`.

So, what does a master mount file look like. On my machine, I have two entries and the file looks like this:

```
/- /etc/auto.direct -r
/usr/doc /etc/auto.doc -r
/home/siemau -passwd
```

The general syntax of the file is

```
mount-point map-file mount-options
```

The first line lists /- as the mount point. At first, you might think that I have a directory /-. This would make accessing it quite difficult as many commands would think that the '-' is an option. Well, lucky for us, this is not what is happening. When you specify the mount point like this (/-), automount sees it as being a direct map. It will therefore use the mount point you specify in the map file. Here the map file is /etc/auto.direct. Note that you don't have to name the map file like this. I just gave it the name auto.direct for two reasons. First, the convention is to name the files auto.whatever, with "whatever" usually referring to some characteristic of that mount. Since, this is a direct mount, I named it auto.direct, which is basically the second reason why I named it so: self-documentation.

In the second line, the mount point is an indirect map. Both automount and you can see that immediately because we have a full path name of the mount point. Before I go on, I want to re-address one point. One of the differences between direct and indirect maps is that the directory for indirect maps does not exist anywhere. If you are in the parent directory of the mount point you will not see the mount-point directory. On the other hand, the directory for direct maps does exist (potentially having been created by automount). If it already exists and automount is started, any files in that directory are hidden, just like a "normal" mount.

The map name is the name of the file containing the direct or the indirect map, or the name of the built-in map, if you are using one. In the first line of the above example, the name of the map file is /etc/auto.direct. To insure that automount gets the right file, I recommend that you always refer to the files by their absolute names. In the third line, you see that I am using a built-in map, whereby I am importing the home directories from another machine. Since the path of the mount point must include the system name, we see that the home directories will be mounted from siemau (this is from the -passwd map). Note that because of the built-in map, we do not specify a map file.

At the end of the line are mount options. In the first two cases, I specified the filesystems are read only (-r). Note that this only takes effect if there are no options in the map file that contradict it, as it is the map file that takes precedence. You can use any option that would apply to another NFS filesystem, *except* for the `bg` (background) and `fg` (foreground) options. This is simply because with automount, these options do not apply.

To find out the specifics of the filesystem to be mounted, automount looks in the map file. In general, the format of both indirect and direct map files is the same:

```
mount-point    options remote-host:<path_name>
```

The key difference is the format of the mount point entry. For a direct map, you use the full path name of the mount point. If the directory does not exist, the automount will create it for you. However, you must include a *full path*. For example, my `auto.direct` file looks like this:

```
/usr/direct -rw     siemau:/u1
```

Here I am saying that I want to mount the `/u1` filesystem from the machine `siemau` onto my `/usr/direct` directory. Note the mount option here: `-rw`. In the `auto.master` file I specified that I wanted to mount it read only. However, here I specified read-write, therefore the filesystem will be mounted read-write, as I said that the options in the map file take precedence.

On the other hand, you specify a relative path for the indirect maps. This is the name of the virtual directory underneath the directory specified in `auto.master`. Confused? Let's look at the example on my system:

```
man         -r      siemau:/usr/man
scohelp     -r      siemau:/usr/lib/scohelp
```

As we see, the basic format is the same as for the direct map. The only difference (which is a very important difference) is the absence of full paths for the mount points. If we look back to `auto.master`, we see that the mount point is `/usr/doc`. If I did a cd into, or otherwise accessed the directory, `/usr/doc/man`, then automount would kick in and I would be looking at `/usr/man` on siemau. What automount does is to append the directory listed in the map file to the directory listed in `auto.master`. Here, `man` or `scohelp` are appended onto `/usr/doc`.

If we look in the parent directory (`/usr/doc`) before we mount the filesystem we see that it is *empty*. However, once we cross the mount point there will be the symbolic link that points to directory in `/tmp_mnt`. Remember, too, that automount only mounts filesystems that are being used. Therefore, `siemau:/usr/lib/scohelp` won't be mounted at this point (unless, of course, we already crossed that mount point).

This is where the virtual quality of the mount point comes into play. The directory exists only as the link to `/tmp_mnt` and will disappear from the system if you don't access the mounted filesystem with the time-out (or the system gets rebooted).

In my example `auto.master` file, I have one built-in map: `-passwd`. As I mentioned, this points to a machine containing the home directories that should be mounted. In conjunction with NIS, the `-passwd` built-in map is very useful for allowing users to log into any machine, but still have access to a single home directory.

There are a couple of things to keep in mind when using the `-passwd` map. First, the machine name you specify is the name of the server on which all home directories physically exist. If you are using NIS, this does *not* have to be the same as the NIS server. Second, for the server you need to ensure that all users' home directories (as specified in `/etc/passwd`) are in the directory specified. For example, for each client you need to ensure that the home directory was `/home/siemau/<user_name>`.

If the home directories were scattered across multiple systems, we could create direct maps for each of the users. In the `auto.master` file we could point to, let's say, a file `/etc/auto.user`; for example,

```
/-      /etc/auto.user
```

This would contain the direct mappings for each user's home directory. A few lines might look like this:

```
/u1/jimmo      -rw siemau:/usr/jimmo
/u1/kenton     -rw scoburg:/u/kenton
/u2/yadira     -rw scoburg:/u/yadira
```

There are a couple of things to note. The mount points are not all in the same directory. Both jimmo and kenton have their home directories in `/u1`, while yadira has her's in `/u2`, *even though* her home directory physically resides on scoburg, like Kenton's. The other thing is that we originally made the assumption that we are on the machine siemau. The home directory for jimmo is `/usr/jimmo` on *siemau*. This does not present a problem. There is nothing wrong with mounting a filesystem via NFS from the local machine. It is a little slower since it has to go through all the TCP layers. However, it is easier to administrate since the `auto.user` file can then be distributed to each machine in the network. You could use this same technique for indirect maps as well.

**Grabbing it All.**   Exported file systems are there to be used. There may come a time that you want to access all the filesystems that a machine is making available to you. This is where the `-hosts` built-in map comes in. If you use it, then automount will configure itself to mount all exported filesystems of all known hosts. In this context, "known" is the same as others in that if the host is listed in `/etc/hosts` or can be identified through the name server, then it is known.

Aside from saving you the hassle of listing each filesystem individually, this method allows you to update the list of exported filesystems without having to change all the clients. The disadvantage is that unlike direct or indirect maps, using the `-hosts` built-in map means that you have to use specific mount points.

By convention, the mount point is a subdirectory under `/net`; although you can specify the mount point in `auto.master`. For example, the conventional way would be

```
/net -hosts
```

However, I could write it like this:

```
/auto -hosts
```

Therefore, all mount points would exist under `/auto`. Note that the filesystems are not mounted directly under this mount point, but rather under a subdirectory matching the name of the remote system. Therefore, if I were to have such an entry, there would be subdirectories for scoburg, vesta, *and* siemau. Another difference is that if you want to mount all of the filesystems from a machine, then any time you cross any mount-point, then *every* filesystem gets mounted and with the same mount options.

When you cross the mount point, automount catches this and determines the name of the remote filesystem. This either queries the name server (if it is running) or looks in `/etc/hosts`. Automount then queries the remote mount service to get a list of exported filesystems. The list is then sorted by the length of the pathname to ensure that subdirectories don't get mounted before their parents. With the sorted list, each directory is, in turn, created, and the filesystems are mounted. If the name cannot be resolved, then the filesystems cannot be mounted and therefore whatever command was used to access the mount point will fail.

If you are using a lot of different remote filesystems, you may want to ensure that certain directories do not get mounted. This is accomplished using the `-null` built-in map. This map tells `automount` not to mount any remote filesystems to this mount point. You usually see this when using NIS to distribute maps and one of those maps specifies a directory that you don't want covered. You can include this map either in the `auto.master` file or the direct map file. Why not in the indirect map file? Remember that the directories for indirect maps do not really exist. Therefore, you cannot tell automount to mount a filesystem onto something that isn't there.

**Automount from the Command Line.**    So far, we have been talking about the configuration files as if they were the only way to configure automount. That's not the way it is. Like other types of NFS mounts (or any mount for that matter), automount can be configured from the command line. The only caveat is that the map files must contain the necessary information. In other words, by running automount from the command line, you are bypassing the `auto.master` file. However, all the information that is normally obtained from the master file is gotten from the command line. Let's look at an example:

```
automount /- /etc/auto.data
```

This would be the same as if the `auto.master` file contained the line

```
/- /etc/auto.data
```

Here we have a direct map contained in `/etc/auto.data`. No matter what is contained there, it will be mounted just as if we had referenced the map file in `auto.master`. You can also have multiple references on the command line:

```
automount /- /etc/auto.direct -r /usr/doc /etc/auto.doc -r
/home/siemau -passwd
```

which would be equivalent to the three lines from the example `auto.master` file at the beginning of this chapter.

What happens when you modify one of the maps will depend on which map file you are modifying. The master map is a static entity. It is only read by automount when the automount daemon is started (usually at boot-time). Therefore, you need to restart automount to make any changes in the master file activate.

The SCO doc say that, "Rebooting your machine is the safest way of restarting automount." I would tend to agree. I have tried killing the automount process and restarting it as well as stopping and restarting NFS. Both seem to work a couple of times. However, it seems that once I have used the mount point, automount gets confused and neither of the above techniques work. What usually happens is that I get an error saying that the remote connection was refused, although I can still access the filesystem by hand. However, I have been successful bringing the system into init level 1 and then back up to multi-user mode. This seems to be effective since all mounted filesystems are unmounted and the automount daemon is killed. (Note: If you kill `automount` with -9, the entries in the mount table do not get cleared. Therefore, it is recommended that *if* you do kill automount by hand, you use signal 15, `kill -15`.)

Since indirect maps are only accessed when you cross the mount point, they can be modified at any time and the changes will take effect immediately. Keep in mind that if you add or remove an entry, this is also modifying, therefore changing the map file by adding or removing an entry will also take effect immediately.

Changes to the direct maps sort of fall between the two extremes. Not every change you make will take effect immediately, however, you can make some changes that will. Let's look at it this way: Direct map filesystems are "mounted" when automount starts, although the connection is not established until you cross that mount point. Therefore, any changes you make to the mount point will not take effect until the next time automount is restarted. However, since the connection has not yet been made, changes that affect the connection can be made and are valid the minute you make them. For example, you can change the server that the filesystem is mounted from and the effects will be immediate.

Well, not exactly. If the filesystem is currently mounted, then the entry exists in the mount table. When accessing files across the mount point, automount first checks the mount table to see if the entries are there. If so, that means the filesystem is already mounted and it does not need to do any more work. To force automount to recognize the changes, you can stop and restart NFS. The alternative is to find the PID of the automount process and kill it with signal 15. However, you might experience some of the problems that I mentioned above.

In many regards, remotely mounted filesystems behave the same way as those that are mounted locally. One of the most apparent is the mount point is a flag to the filesystem access routines. They simply say that the subdirectories under the mount point are somewhere else. If you mount a filesystem onto a directory that contains files or directories, these will be "hidden" from you. When the mount point is accessed, the system will start looking elsewhere for the files. For direct maps, this is the name of the parent directory (which is also the mount point). For indirect maps, the "virtual" mount point is the parent directory. In our example, above, any files that existed below /usr/doc would become hidden when automount was started.

What happens if the server containing the man-pages is down? Does this mean that you don't have access to them until the machine is brought up? Well, it all depends on how your system is configured. If you reference only one machine with the man-pages, then yes. If that one machine goes down, then you lose your man-pages. Fortunately, it's possible to get automount to look for an alternate server if the primary one is unreachable. These are referred to as redundant servers and can be specified in either a direct or indirect map. The syntax for redundant servers is basically to list more than one location, for example:

```
/usr/man -r scoburg:/usr/man siemau:/usr/man vesta:/usr/local/man
```

To make it easier to read, we could escape the end of line and write the entry like this:

```
/usr/man -r scoburg:/usr/man \
     siemau:/usr/man \
     vesta:/usr/local/man
```

Note that in the last entry, the path name on the remote machine is different. This is possible since the connection is not made until the mount point is crossed. Therefore, it doesn't matter what it is called until the mount actually takes place.

We can also take a shortcut, since the directories on scoburg and siemau are the same. The resulting entry would look like this:

```
/usr/man -r scoburg,siemau:/usr/man vesta:/local/usr/man
```

This list does not specify any particular order. Just because we list scoburg first, does not necessarily mean it will be the one accessed, even if it is up. The first server that responds that will be connected to. Next, you need to be very careful when using redundant servers. Just because we accessed one server this time, does not mean we will do so the next time. If we update a file on one server, but don't get back to the file for some time, we may find that the change is gone if another server was mounted. However, this only applies for read-write filesystems.

**Syntax Shortcuts.**   There are two metacharacters that can be used when specifing entries in any of the map files. The first is the ampersand (&) and is used as a place holder for the mount point. For example, my `auto.doc` file looks like this:

```
man    -r    jmohr:/usr/man    scohelp    -r    jmohr:/usr/lib/scohelp
```

Since the basename of each directory is the same at each mount point, I could have written the file like this:

```
man        -r    jmohr:/usr/&
scohelp    -r    jmohr:/usr/lib/&
```

When automount tries to mount the filesystem, it automatically translates the place holder. This translation is made every time that automount sees the ampersand. Let's assume we had an indirect map file that looked like this:

```
siemau     siemau:/home/siemau
scoburg    scoburg:/home/scoburg
vesta      vesta:/home/vesta
```

This says to mount the home directories that are being exported from each of these machines. Note that the name of each machine appears three times in each line. The first is the mount point, then again as the system name, as well as the name of the directory under home. We could therefore rewrite the file like this:

```
siemau     &:/home/&
scoburg    &:/home/&
vesta      &:/home/&
```

In both cases on each line, the ampersand is expanded to be the same as the mount point. Since it doesn't matter where in the line the ampersand appears, we could us it in this direct map:

```
/usr/man -r scoburg,siemau:& vesta:/local&
```

or this indirect map:

```
man -r scoburg,siemau:/usr/& vesta:/local/usr/&
```

Let's look at the direct map again. Note that there is no slash after the `/local`. This is because the ampersand replaces the *entire string*. Since the string we use is `/usr/man`, the slash comes with it. In this case, there is nothing wrong with including the slash, we simply end up with `/local//usr/man`. However, this is something you should be aware of.

We can also use an asterisk (*) to indicate "all known servers." If we look at the entries above for exporting the home directories, we see that they all have the same format. We can take advantage of this by rewriting every line as just a single line:

```
*      &:/home/&
```

In this example, the asterisk is first expanded to mean any system. The ampersand is then expanded to mean the `/home/server_name` directory from any server. Once the asterisk is translated, the map file is no longer parsed; for example,

```
/usr/man -r scoburg,siemau:& vesta:/local&   *      &:/home/&
```

is ok. However, reversing the lines like this,

```
    *       &:/home/&
/usr/man -r scoburg,siemau:&
vesta:/local&
```

causes automounter to ignore the `/usr/man` entry.

You might also have cases where you have a large map file or are combining local maps with those propagated with NIS. In that case, you can flag an automount map to include another map file. For example, if we had a map containing both documentation directories and a list of user home directories it would look like this:

```
man     -r   siemau:/usr/man
scohelp  -r  siemau:/usr/lib/scohelp
+/etc/auto.homes
```

When automount reads this map file, it loads in the contents of `/etc/auto.homes` and behaves as if the contents where included in the first file. You could also have additional maps that were included. Each would simply be read in turn.

## MMDF

### Configuring MMDF

There are couple of new features in this version of the Mail package. The first is the Mail Configuration Manager, which is a graphical interface to the mail system. Not only can it do everything the old `mkdev mmdf` script could, but it extends beyond to configure almost every aspect of mail. Two other managers support the Mail Configuration Manager. The Host Administration Manager is used to configure and administer mail hosts and the Aliases Administration Manager is used to administer mail aliases.

Also new to OpenServer is MIME support (conformance). MIME stands for Multipurpose Internet Mail Extensions which is a standard that allows messages to be exchanged which contain graphical, audio, video, multimedia, and other non-text data.

Whether you run the Mail Configuration Manager on OpenServer or `mkdev` `mmdf` on ODT, the information that you need to provide will be the same. Because the `mkdev mmdf` script in ODT allows you to input information only in a particular order, let's run through the script and discuss the information we need to input. As we do, I will talk about where you would need to input this information in the Mail Configuration Manager.

The first thing you see is a description of what will take place during the configuration and some assumptions that are made. Since we want to do the configuration, we should answer yes(y) to the question about whether we want to continue the configuration. The next question is what our fully qualified host name is. In OpenServer this is the box labeled, "Configuring MMDF to use this host name:". In both ODT and OpenServer you are present with a default host name. This is based on other configuration files you may have set up. For example, if you have TCP configured, then this would be your fully qualified domain name, such as siemau.siemau.com. Otherwise the domain defaults to UUCP, such as siemau.uucp. The machine is assigned to the MLNAME variable and the domain name is assigned to MLDOMAIN variable. Unless you have decided to "hide" the machine name (more about that in a moment.)

·Next, you are asked if you want mail to root redirected to a "real" user. In OpenServer this is done by clicking on the button labeled Redirection.... Here you can redirect mail to every system user and not just the three you can in ODT (root, mmdf, postmaster). By filling in the blank with the name of the account or using the list that's provided for you, you select for which account you want the mail redirected. Pressing the Select User(s). button allows you to choose which user(s) will get the mail instead. Click on okay when you are finished setting up the aliases.

In the `mkdev mmdf` script you are then asked questions about which channels you are going to use, based on what the script *sees* as the configuration on your system. If you answer yes to configuring UUCP, you will be asked to supply the host name of the site(s) you want to connect to. You must first have configured these sites in UUCP. At least there must be entries for these sites in the `Systems` file as that's where the `mkdev` script is looking. You are also asked if the host-name for the machine should also be the same for UUCP. Whatever UUCP name you define will be assigned to the UUname variable.

In the configuration manager you have check boxes that allow you to select which networks to configure. It won't be until you click on OK that you are prompted to select the names of the sites you want to contact. When you want to select the site, click on the site name and then the 'Add' button. You will then be prompted for the full qualified name. All this you must do by answering the questions in ODT. In OpenServer, you can select to configure a network without selecting any hosts. Note that what is being configured here is channel programs. To configure individual hosts, use the Host Manager.

In both cases, the system notices whether you are running a name server or not. If you are, MMDF will be automatically configured to use it. Therefore, there will be no need to configure your smtp hosts by hand.

Next, you are asked about configuring mail for a smart host. This is where you configure the baduser and badhosts channels. If you answer yes to either ques-tion you are prompted for the name of that host. Keep in mind, that you must be able to reach that host. The `mkdev` script checks the various channels to make sure. In the Mail configuration manager, this is accomplished by selecting the Forwarding... button. You are given the option of either returning the mail to the sender or forwarding to the "Smart host." If you select Forward, then you must input the name of a smart host. You can also select the host from the list of avail-able hosts. Note: As of this writing it appears that the only hosts you are pre-sented with are via the smtp channel if it is configured.

At this point the `mkdev` script is done. However, there are a couple more options you can configure in the Configuration Manager. For example, there is a button marked "Mailboxes...". This determines whether the users' mailbox should be in `/usr/spool/mail` or their home directory. This would be done in ODT by changing the MMBOXNAME. Although you can edit it by hand to whatever you like, the Configuration Manager only allows you to choose between the `/usr/spool/mail` directory (the default) and the user's home directory. This is done in `mmdftailor` file by first setting the deliver directory (MDLVRDIR). If null, ("") the user's home directory is used. Next, define the name of the mailbox (MMBXNAME). This is the name of the file that your mail will be stored in. This will default to .`mailbox`. If you want, you can also set the protection (permission) on the mail box with the MMBXPROT variable; for example:

MMBXPROT 600

which is the default, means that only the user has read/write permissions on their mailbox.

Here, you can also choose to hide the machine name behind the domain. This option is not as obvious as it is labeled "Select format for mail users address." You are given two choices. One which includes the machine name and one that does not. If you select to include the machine name (the default), the beginning on `mmdftailor` looks like this:

```
MLNAME "siemau"
MLDOMAIN "siemau.com"
```

Here the machine name (MLNAME) is siemau and the domain (MLDOMAIN) is siemau.com. If we decide we want to hide the name, `mmmdftailor` would look like this:

```
MLNAME "siemau"
MLDOMAIN "com"
MLOCMACHINE "siemau"
```

Here the machine name is siemau and the domain is just de. The reason is that the machine name is simply the concatenation of the machine name onto the domain. In the second example, siemau is cat'ted onto de to give us the "machine name" siemau.com. In order to keep track of what the local machine's name really is, we set the MLOCMACHINE variable to the local machine name. Potentially, you could change these to create any domain you wanted.

### *Other Managers*

As with many of the other aspects of your system, there is a Manager to help you configure MMDF. In ODT, this was the `mkdev mmdf` script. Although the script still exists in name on OpenServer, the appearance is significantly different and its functionality has been enhanced. Rather than walking you through either one of these tools, I figured we would talk about them together. Using the information on the structure of MMDF from the first part of the book, we'll talk about what each part of these configuration tools means and what changes take place in the configuration files. Afterwards, I hope you will be able to not only run these utilities yourself, but also edit the files to make the changes, without the need to use the tools.

New to OpenServer is the introduction of several Managers to aid in your mail configuration. These include managers to configure, hosts, aliases, channels, domains, and tables. What is missing here is the Kitchen Sink Manager which is scheduled to be included in the first maintenance supplement.

In order to be able to understand the questions each of these managers is asking, you need to understand the concepts about MMDF that we talked about in the first part of the book. Because of that, I will make the assumption that you already read that section or are somehow familiar with MMDF.

You can use the other configuration managers associated with MMDF to configure things that you need to do by editing the `mmdftailor` file in ODT. One such manager is the Channel Manager, which allows you to change channel-specific parameters. For example, you can select which type of addressing you want on outgoing messages. This is done by clicking the "Addressing..." option button. Should you want addresses in the format @A:B@C, you would select RFC 822-style (the default). If you want addresses in the format B%C@A, you would select RFC 733-style. If the addresses are not to be reformatted, select none. This would be done by editing the ap= entries on the MCHN line in `mmdftailor`. This can be ap=822, ap=733, or ap=same (for no reformatting). This is necessary when contacting machines that can only handle one style of addressing or another.

For example, setting smtp to RFC 733-style address, the line might look like this:

```
MCHN show="SMTP Delivery", name=smtp, que=smtp, tbl=smtpchn,
pgm=smtp, ap=733
```

We also have several deliver options that we can select. For example, we can set the number of minutes to keep retrying to connect to a host before the system considers the connection to have failed. This is set by inputting the value in the time-to-live field in the deliver options or setting ttl in the MCHN entry in `mmdftailor`.

There are several delivery modes that you can select. This is defined in `mmdftailor` with the mod variable Regular (mode=reg) means that the mail is queued, but will not be sent until deliver runs. Background-Only (mod=back) means that this deliver can only be run on this channel as a background process. Passive (mod=psv) means that other sites must pickup from this machine. Immediate (mod=imm) will invoke delivery itself, without waiting for it to run.

The smtp configuration string defines the smtp name and character set to be used. By default for my machine, this is

```
charset=7bit,hostname=siemau.siemau.com
```

The hostname is what you will see in the Received: lines of your mail messages. Because this is required by some smtp implementation, I recommend leaving it. The 7-bit character set is the standard as defined in RFC 821. The problem is international mail that often needs the 8-bit character set to gain access to the characters not available with 7 bits. This shows up in the MCHN entry as

```
confstr="charset=7bit,hostname=siemau.siemau.com.
```

You can also defined logging on a channel-by-channel basis. This is done by selecting the Log File option button. Here you choose the path of the log file or leave the default of `/usr/mmdf/log/chan.log`. You also get a choice of the logging level. This, too, shows up in the MCHN entry as

```
log=/tmp/mmdflog, level=FTR
```

Interestingly enough, here you can Add a new channel if you want. When you select the Add item in the Channel menu, you can define your own channel. Here you are given the choice of what channel program and what tables to use as well as the other configuration options available to the default channels. The channels available are merely the programs residing in `/usr/mmdf/chans`. Copying a program into this directory makes it appear in the list of available channel programs. If you want, you can create a new channel that uses an existing channel program.

The Domain Manager is basically a front end to add entries to the `.dom` files. Here you can add or otherwise modify the domain files. You need to be careful however. When you add or modify a domain, you have a pull down list of the available tables. This also includes the alias files as well. Be careful not to select one of those.

### Mail Aliases

Aliases have changed a fair bit in OpenServer. The whole aliasing scheme has changed and no longer consists of the three aliases: `alias.ali`, `alias.list`, and `alias.user`. Instead, the aliases are grouped according to how they are to be treated and what level of "trust" these aliases have. For example, by default there is only one alias: `alias.n`. Like the aliases files in ODT, this is referenced by an MTBL entry in `mmdftailor`:

```
MTBL show="nobypass aliases", name=alias-n, file=alias.n
```

The `alias.n` files contain aliases for all of the system users such as mmdf, sys, and uucp. Each one is aliased to the user `_mailadmin`, which is in turn aliased to root (at least by default). One thing to note is that in the show entry as well as the `alias.n` file itself, we see that these are no bypass-aliases. This means that you cannot bypass the aliases mechanism. For example, if we look at the first few entries in the `alias.n` file we see

```
postmaster:root
_mailadmin:root
adm:_mailAdmin
asg:_mailAdmin
audit:_mailAdmin
```

If I sent a mail message to `adm`, the alias would kick in and the message would be sent to `_mailAdmin` and the next alias would kick in and it would go to root. If I mailed it to `~adm`, the tilde (~) would *bypass* the aliasing mechanism and send the message to the user adm. Since no one ever logs in as adm, it is probably pointless to send a message to these users. You could also alias root to another in this fashion to ensure that mail messages always get to a "real" user. The .n at the end of the file name indicates that this is a list of no-bypass aliases.

Other characteristics you can apply to aliases is whether or not they are public. That is, can remote sites determine who is a member of this alias? If so, then it is public. Public alias files have a .p on the end. Trusted aliases (those that you *cannot* redirect to a pipe) have a .t on the end. What if you have both public trusted and public no-bypass aliases but they are different lists? Quite simple, each combination gets its own file. For example, it's possible to have the following aliases (among others):

```
alias.n - nobypass
alias.npt - nobypass public trusted
alias.nt - nobypass trusted
alias.pt - public trusted
alias.t - trusted
```

In practice, this works the same way as aliases in ODT. When you mail to a user, MMDF will first check to see if the address is local. If so, it then checks to see if the recipient is an alias by looking through these tables. If a match is found, the alias is expanded and the mail is sent to the user(s) defined in the alias. Otherwise, it is sent to the user it was intended for. (We're assuming here that we aren't using the bypass.)

All of these characteristics can be modified by the Alias Manager. If you want to configure a new alias, select New in the Alias menu. If you want to modify an existing alias, select Modify in the Alias menu or double click on that alias name in the list. Here you can add new members to the alias, remove them, and so on. This is also where you change whether the alias is public or not and whether to allow the address bypass.

If you have a long list of users that you want to make into an alias, you don't have to type them in individually or cut and paste. Instead, you can create a file containing the alias list. This is input in the Name field by using the standard input redirection (<) and the path name of the file. Here I would recommend the full path now so that there is no doubt which file you mean. For example, if we create a list called managers and place it in /usr/mmdf/table, we create an alias. Then the "name" we would give it is </usr//mmdf/table/managers. This name then appears in this format (including the less-than symbol) in both the alias manager and in the file. The advantage of this is that the address is not parsed until mail is sent. You can therefore modify the file any time, without even bothering to tell MMDF.

Because there is a separate file for each of these characteristics, there has to be MTBL entries for each of them in `mmdftailor`. If we had all the aliases that I described above, the MTBL entries would look like this:

```
MTBL show="nobypass aliases", name=alias-n, file=alias.n
MTBL show="trusted aliases", name=alias-t, file=alias.t
MTBL show="nobypass trusted aliases", name=alias-nt, file=alias.nt
MTBL show="nobypass public trusted aliases", name=alias-npt,
          file=alias.npt
MTBL show="public trusted aliases", name=alias-pt, file=alias.pt
```

If you later change your mind, you can go back and change the characteristics so that an alias will end up in another one of these files. If that combination didn't exist, then a new file would be created. Keep in mind that these files are only created, they are never removed. If you change the characteristics of an alias so that there are no more aliases in a particular file, the file remains. It still contains the couple of lines of header, but there are no alias entries in it. In addition, the MTBL entries in `mmdftailor` also remain. Therefore, if you change the alias characteristics, it's a good idea to check the alias files and `mmdftailor` to clean things up.

**Mailing Lists.**   A mailing list is a special kind of alias that is administered by a user, the mailing list, or alias "owner." This is the person who is responsible for adding or modifying users. If mail sent to the mailing list is undeliverable, the mail is sent to the owner and not the originator.

Like other kinds of aliases, mailing lists can be kept in a file. By making that file writeable by the owner he or she can easily change the mailing list. Creating a mailing list is the exact same process as for other types of aliases. You can also change the characteristics using the Alias Administrator. One thing I would like to point out is that despite this new interface, the entries in the alias files for mailing lists are exactly the same as for ODT, with the exception of being in a different file:

```
alias.pt:list42-outbound:</usr/mmdf/tmp/list
alias.pt:list42:list42-outbound@list-processor alias.pt:list42-
request:jimmo
```

### *Problem Solving*

One of my strongest (not fondest) memories of working in SCO Support is MMDF. For the newbie system administrator, MMDF is a valuable package since 1) it's free and 2) it's fairly easy to configure. One of the problems with it is that since it is easy to change things, it is also easy to mess them up. This becomes a serious problem when you have a customer who cannot leave well enough alone.

I dreaded these customers. Since they had a support contract, we were obligated to help them. Regrettably.

One customer in particular made my life miserable; at least as far as supporting MMDF was concerned. Let's call him Mike. Whether that's his real name or not, only the two of us know for sure (plus a couple other people in support who know him as I did). Mike was a system administrator for a small company. The problem was that the company was really too small to have their own administrator. The result was that Mike didn't have much to do. He personified the statement, "Idle hands are the devil's workshop." Boy did he give me a devil of a time.

Mike liked to play. Since he had root access to the system, there were a lot of places he could play that others couldn't. He spent a lot of his time reading the manual or magazines and when he found something interesting he would say, "Boy! I'd like to try that." (At least, that's what I imagine him doing.) The problem was that Mike was not an experienced UNIX administrator. I don't know what kind of background he had, but it wasn't UNIX.

One of those things that he'd go, "Boy!" about was MMDF. When he made a change that he couldn't correct (which happened literally every other week) he'd end up calling SCO Support. Being one of the few people that supported MMDF at the time, I tended to get a lot of his calls. The first couple of times were humorous. After the third time I told him to back up his MMDF configuration files before he started and when he didn't, I started to get annoyed.

The real problem was not that he tried to do things and messed them up. Nor was it that despite repeated instructions to do so he never made backups first. No, the real problem was that Mike just didn't understand. He was the kind of guy who would flip through the manual, find something interesting and then take the example and try to manipulate it to his needs without really understanding what he was doing. As a result, things got messed up and I had to fix them. It is with that, that I dedicate this section to all the Mike's in the world.

If you discover that mail isn't getting delivered, there are several very useful tools to solve the problem. The first one is `/usr/mmdf/bin/checkque` which will, as its name implies, check the MMDF mail queues. This can tell you how many messages are waiting, how long they have been waiting, and in what queues. For each queue there will be several lines, therefore it is a good idea to pipe it through more. So, when I run it on my machine, I get the results shown in Table 12–3.

Hmmm. In my `smtp` queue I have mail waiting. Looking at the time they have been waiting (about a week), I would say that something is wrong here. The first

---

**Table 12–3**   Checkque Output

---

```
/usr/mmdf/bin/checkque
 Sun Sep 10 09:48: 3 queued msgs/512 byte queue directory
                   3 Kbytes in msg dir
   0 msg    0 Kb (local  ) local        :  Local delivery
                       deliver start    :  Sun Sep 3 09:47
                       deliver message  :  Sun Sep 3 09:46
                       deliver end      :  Sun Sep 3 09:46/168 hours
   0 msgs   0 Kb (list   ) list         :  Mailing list processor
                       deliver start    :  Sun Sep 3 09:46
                       deliver message  :  Sun Sep 3 09:46
                       deliver end      :  Sun Sep 3 09:46/168 hours
   3 msgs   1 Kb (smtp   ) smtp         :  SMTP Delivery
                       deliver start    :  Sun Sep 3 09:47
                       No deliver message
 *** OVERDUE ** deliver end             :  Sun Sep 3 09:47/168 hours
 *** WAITING ** First message           :  Sun Sep 3 09:45
   0 msgs   0 Kb (uucp   ) uucp         :  UUCP Delivery
                       deliver start    :  Sun Sep 3 09:34
                       deliver message  :  Sun Sep 3 09:34
                       deliver end      :  Sun Sep 3 09:34/168 hours
```

---

thing I want to check is my `mmdftailor` file. Unless I have sites that I only contact once a week, then 168 hours is much too long without at least a warning that the message could not be delivered. I would then check the MWARNTIME and MFAILTIME to see how many hours they are set for.

At this point, I need to figure out where the messages where going. Fortunately, I can figure that out by looking in the MMDF spool directory, `/usr/spool/mmdf/lock/home`. In this case, I have three messages using the smtp channel, so let's look in `q.smtp`. Doing a long listing I see

```
total 6
-rw-rw-rw-  2 root   sys     81 Sep 3 09:45 msg.aa01203
-rw-rw-rw-  2 root   sys     81 Sep 3 09:46 msg.aa01226
-rw-rw-rw-  2 root   sys     81 Sep 3 09:47 msg.aa01244
```

So, here are the three files. Sure enough, the date is a week ago (assuming today is September 10th). If I look in these files, I can figure out who sent the message and where it is going:

```
810114306m0
root@siemau.siemau.com
- m smtp "scoburg.siemau.com" "root@scoburg.siemau.com"
```

Skipping past the first line (which is a time stamp), I see the sender was root on the local machine. The third line tells me that it is using to `smtp` channel to send to the machine scoburg.siemau.com to the user root@scoberg.siemau.com. This is a fair bit of information. I can then use another tool, `/usr/mmdf/bin/checkaddr`, to see if this is a valid address and what that address is. If I run `/usr/mmdf/bin/checkaddr`, I get

```
root@scoburg.siemau.com: OK
```

Unfortunately, this does not tell me much. Note that there is a common misconception here. Users will see the "OK" and assume that means that the address is right. Without any option, `checkque` simply determines if it can parse the address correctly and knows where to send it. So, instead I need to use the `-w` option to get `checkaddr` to tell me how it parses the address. This time I get

```
root@scoburg.siemau.com: root@scoburg.siemau.com: queueing for
smtp: via 'scoburg.siemau .com': 'root@scoburg.siemau.com' OK
```

This is as I expect. Since the message is being queued correctly, that is for scoburg.siemau.com via the smtp channel, the problem does not appear to be in the address. One possible problem could be that the IP address is incorrect. If I have never sent any mail to this site, then this is a common problem. The quickest way to check is looking in the `smtp.chn` file. If it's wrong, correct it, then run `dbmbuild`.

What if the IP address is correct, then what? Well, we know the address we are sending to is correct. We know that the IP address matches the machine we are sending to. What else could be the problem? If you can't reach that IP address with other tools, then there is no way that MMDF can. Therefore, the first thing to do at this point is to check the physical connection. This can be done with `ping`, `telnet`, or any other such tool. Keep in mind that MMDF is already doing the translation from name to IP address. Therefore, make sure you are checking the connection to the IP address.

If you look in the `q.smtp` directory and it is empty, then the most logical thing is that the message was sent and it is the other guy's fault, right? No. Not always. All this means is that MMDF did not queue the message for the smtp channel. So, where did it go? Well, let's check the address with `checkaddr`. This time we get

```
root@scoberg.siemau.com: root@scoberg.siemau.com: queueing for badhosts:
via 'scoburg.siemau.com': 'root@scoberg.siemau.com' OK
```

Here's the problem. The machine name is actually called scoburg and not scoberg. (This is because Coburg is a castle and not a mountain) We simply made a typo in our mail address. If we run `checkaddr` again. this time on root@scoburg.siemau.com we get

```
root@scoburg.siemau.com: root@scoburg.siemau.com: queueing for smtp: via
'scoburg.siemau.com': 'root@scoburg.siemau.com' OK
```

Now we're cooking.

If you want an easier method to figure out the addresses, you need to take one more step. First look at the appropriate queue file. In this case, let's take `q.smtp/msg.aa01244`. We can look at the full text of the mail message by looking in the msg directory. The file has the same name so the name would be `msg/msg.aa01244`. If we look at that we get

```
From: All around good guy <jimmo@siemau.siemau.com>
X-Mailer: SCO OpenServer Mail Release 5.0
To: kaleth@scoburg.siemau.com
Subject: paq
Date: Sun, 3 Sep 95 9:47:01 METDST
Message-ID: <9509030947.aa01244@siemau.siemau.com>


Qapla'. pltlh. ghltlh vlghltlhta'bogh DalaD'a'

batlh Daqawlu'taH

jim
```

Here we see the complete message to my Klingon friend at scoburg.siemau.com. I can now use `checkaddr -w` to see where this message is supposed to go. (Note: Just because you can read other people's mail doesn't mean you should. This is an administration tool to help user's with mail problems, not a suggestion to stick your nose in where it doesn't belong. Besides do you really think it's safe to be reading a Klingon's mail?)

This same technique can be used on all the other queues to figure out where the messages are supposed to go and how they were addressed. One thing I would like to point out is that if properly configured, the UUCP channel will immediately hand off the message to UUCP. That is, it creates a UUCP job and submits it. The message then leaves MMDF and becomes the responsibility of UUCP. Therefore, just because it is out of the UUCP queue, does not mean it has reached the other site. You need to check the UUCP spool directory first.

Another thing to keep in mind is that configuring the UUCP channel to deliver messages at longer intervals is not a good idea. For example, you could configure MMDF so that the UUCP channel is only delivered once a day. This means that messages through the UUCP channel are handed off to UUCP once a day. If you contact the remote site once a day then it might be *two* days before the message gets delivered. One in the MMDF spool directory and one in the UUCP spool directory. Therefore, you should have sent it immediately to UUCP and let UUCP worry about sending it further.

Another useful tool is `deliver` itself. Let's assume that we just ran `checkque` and got the above output. If we run `deliver` with the `-w` option to watch the delivery (`/usr/mmdf/bin/deliver -w`), we would get

```
[ Checking for Local delivery (local) mail ]
sorting the queue.

[ Checking for Mailing list processor (list) mail ]
sorting the queue.

[ Checking for SMTP Delivery (smtp) mail ]
sorting the queue.
3 messages, 3 to be processed
Message 'msg.aa01203', from 'root@siemau.siemau.com'
Queued: 7 Days, 1 Hours
[ Accessing smtp (SMTP Delivery)]
Channel: smtp
root@scoburg.siemau.com via scoburg.siemau.com: trying...
    connecting to [147.144.142.146]... can't...
destination not available, queuing for retry
Problem address ending: no valid addresses
End of processing for msg.aa01203

Message 'msg.aa01226', from 'root@siemau.siemau.com'
Queued: 7 Days, 1 Hours
root@scoburg.siemau.com via scoburg.siemau.com: dead host
End of processing for msg.aa01226

Message 'msg.aa01244', from 'root@siemau.siemau.com'
Queued: 7 Days, 1 Hours
root@scoburg.siemau.com via scoburg.siemau.com: dead host
End of processing for msg.aa01244

[ Checking for UUCP Delivery (uucp) mail ]
sorting the queue.

[ Checking for Smart-host Routing for hosts (badhosts) mail ]
sorting the queue.

/usr/mmdf/bin/deliver  normal end
```

For the first two queues, local and the list processor, there were no messages. MMDF said it was sorting the queue, but in reality there was nothing to sort. When we get to the smtp queue, we see when it was trying to send the first message. MMDF could not connect to the IP address specified. Therefore, it couldn't send the message. We now can look into why we cannot contact this IP address.

After sitting in the queue for a week, whatever it was I wanted to say is probably invalid. If I wanted to clean up the mail queues, I could remove all the files by hand, but fortunately, I don't have to. MMDF has a utility to do so: `/usr/mmdf/bin/cleanque`. Normally, this is run once a day out of MMDF's crontab. However, you can run it any time to force MMDF to clean up the queues.

Something else you can use to see what's happening are the MMDF log files. They are kept in `/usr/mmdf/log`. The two to look at are `chan.log` and `msg.log`. These log, respectively, channel activity and message activity. How much is written to each file is determined by the values you set for the MCHANLOG and MMSGLOG variables. MCHANLOG determines how much channel logging is done and MMSGLOG determines how much message logging is done (or couldn't you guess?).

There are eight levels of logging from just reporting the fatals errors (FAT) to logging everything, or a full trace (FTR). For most problems, setting both logs to FAT will provide the necessary information. Without knowing the complete syntax of all these components of the logs, you can still gleen a little from them as they are fairly obvious when errors occur. On the other hand, it may be necessary to increase logging. If it comes to that point, then my suggestion is to turn it up all the way to FTR. You will get a lot of information, however, you are sure not to miss anything.

I must warn you, however. If you ever turn on FTR logging, run a few tests, copy the log files somewhere safe, and then *immediately* put it back to FAT. FTR logs *everything*. On a relatively quiet system, I have seen the log files get up to 30Mb in just a few days! It is therefore imperative to watch these files and set logging only as high as necessary. You could also set the size of the logging files through `mmdftailor`. An example would be

```
MCHANLOG level=FTR, size=30
```

This limits the size of the `chan.log` file to thirty 25-block units; that is, 384000 bytes. To find out more about the different logging levels, check out the `mmdf-tailor(F)` and `logs(F)` man-pages.

Whenever you make changes to any of the table files or `mmdftailor`, you need to run `dbmbuild` before the changes take effect. I recommend you use the -n option to `dbmduild`. This takes a little longer, but it recreates the database rather than updating the old one.

# CHAPTER
# 13

- Preparation

- CPU

- RAM

- SCSI Devices

- Hard Disks

- Filesystems

- Floppies

- CD-ROMs

- Tape Drives

- Parallel Ports

- Serial Ports

- Serial Terminals

- Video Cards

- Pseudo-ttys

- Mice

- Miscellaneous mkdv Scripts

# Adding
# Devices

No one really expects your system to remain stagnant. As your company grows, your computer should be able to grow with it. You can add more memory or a new printer with little or no changes to the operating system itself. However, if you need to add something like a hard disk or CD-ROM drive, the operating system needs to be told about these changes. Therefore, you need some mechanism to be able to add new devices. This mechanism is the shell scripts in `/usr/lib/mkdev`, collectively referred to as the mkdev scripts (pronounced make-dev scripts).

Although their appearance has changed between ODT and OpenServer, what they do functionally has changed little. OpenServer provides both a graphical and character based program to configure the hardware. This is the Hardware/Kernel Manager and is functionally the same as the `sysadmsh` in ODT. Despite the outward appearance it is basically the same as the mkdev scripts. In many cases, just like `sysadmsh`, the Hardware/Kernel Manager actually calls the mkdev scripts to configure the hardware. To make life easier, I will be referring to the mkdev scripts throughout this discussion. However, since the scripts are called from `sysadmsh` and the Hardware/Kernel Manager, the information still applies.

One thing I need to point out is that these scripts are not used just to add devices. Originally this was the case, hence the name mkdev. However, as SCO UNIX grew, any addition to the system functionality was made through mkdev scripts. For example, when you run `mkdev fd`, you are not adding a floppy disk to your system, but rather you are giving the choice of creating a boot or root filesystem floppy or one with a UNIX filesystem on it. When you run `mkdev mmdf`, there is no MMDF device to be created; instead, you are configuring MMDF.

However, this is not the only way that devices can get added to the system. Third party drivers can do anything they want. Not that they should, they just can. Even if a driver is installed using custom, there is nothing that guarantees that this mechanism is used.

As with any device you add to your system, I need to remind you to have everything planned out before you start. Know what hardware exists on your machine and what settings each card has. Look at the documentation to see what settings are possible in case you need to change them. If you are adding a new device of a particular type, the odds are you are going to need to make some changes.

On a standard ODT system, there are two dozen different scripts. Talking about each of them in detail would probably take up this whole chapter, if not the whole book. We are going to talk about the scripts in general and then get to some specifics about the more commonly used ones as we address the issues that can crop up.

## Preparation

As I have said before and I will say a hundred times again, before you start to do anything, prepare yourself. Get everything together that will be needed prior to starting. Gather the manuals and diagrams, get your notebook out, and have the settings of all the other cards in front of you. Also, before you start, read both the *Release Notes* and the chapter on installing in the OpenServer Handbook.

Perhaps the most important thing to do before you run any mkdev script is to know how the hardware is really configured. I need to emphasize the word *really*. Many customers have gotten arrogant with me, almost to the point of being angry because they insist that the hardware is set at the "defaults" and I insist that they check anyway.

Unfortunately for me, in most of the cases the devices are set at the default. However, confirming this takes less time then trying to get something installed for a couple of hours and only then finding out that the default isn't set. Therefore, I insist that the customer check before we continue. I did have one customer who made noises like he was checking and "confirmed" the fact that the device was at the default. After almost an hour of trying to get it to work, I asked him to change the settings to something other then the defaults, thinking maybe there was a conflict with some other device. Well, as you guessed, he didn't need to do anything to make things nondefault, they were already there! Lesson learned: *DON'T lie to tech support.*

Another important part of the preparation is to understand what it is you are trying to accomplish. If your modem works, but not correctly, then playing around with `mkdev serial` (which configures the serial port) is not what you want to do. If you are running into trouble getting Merge to work, the problem may lie elsewhere than the `mkdev dos` script (which adds support for DOS filesystems).

One thing I need to point out is that many of these scripts can be used to reconfigure existing devices as well as remove them. Therefore, don't just think of these as scripts to add devices.

There are a few subdirectories in `/usr/lib/mkdev`. Two of them, `oaforms` and `oamenus`, provide the nice menuing capabilities of certain scripts such as `mkdev lp` and `mkdev graphics`. The other subdirectory, `perms`, contains permissions files similar to those in `/etc/perms`. These are accessed when the appropriate devices are added or reconfigured.

The exception is `perms/HDLIST`. This is because of the relatively complex nature of the hard disk minor numbering scheme for the hard disks. We'll get into this in a little more detail when we cover the `mkdev hd` script.

It is a common misunderstanding that the `mkdev` scripts do *not* configure the devices. They configure the device *drivers*. This may appear like a subtle difference, but it is a *very* important one. If you were configuring the device, then you could set the interrupt, DMA, and base address. Instead, you are configuring the software to expect the hardware has a certain configuration. If you run an `mkdev` script and tell it that a device has a certain interrupt, then you must make sure that the hardware is configured the same way.

One of the most important things about installing hardware is knowing what you are doing. Now this may seem like an obvious thing to say, but there is a lot more to installing software than people think.

One of the most common problems I see is that cards are simply snapped into the bus slot with the expectation that whatever settings are made at the factory must be correct. This is true in many, if not most, cases. Unless you have multiple boards of the same type (not necessarily the same manufacturer), you can usually get away with leaving the board at the default. However, what *is* the default?

Unless you are buying your hardware secondhand, there ought to be some kind of documentation or manual that comes with it. For some, like hard disks, this may only be a single sheet. Others, like my host adapter come with booklets of 50 pages or more. These not only give you the default settings, but tell you how to check as well as change the settings.

On ISA cards, settings are changed by either switches or jumpers. Switches, also called DIP switches come in several varieties. Piano switches, look just like piano keys and can be pressed down or popped up. Slide switches move back and forth to adjust the settings. In most cases the switches are labeled in one of three ways:

on-off, 0-1, and closed-open. Do not assume that on, open, or 1 means that a particular functionality is active. Sometimes 'on' means to turn on *disabling* the function. Always check the documentation to be sure.

Jumpers are clips that slide over pairs of metal posts to make an electrical connection. In most cases, the posts are fairly thin (about the size of a sewing needle) and usually come in rows of pin pairs. Since you need both posts to make a connection, it is okay to store unused jumpers by connecting them to just one of the posts. You change the setting by moving the jumper from one pair of pins to another.

The most common things that they configure are base address, IRQ, and DMA. However, they sometimes are used to enable or disable certain functionality. For example, jumpers are often used to determine whether an IDE hard disk is the master or the slave.

The other three bus types, MCA, EISA, and PCI, do not have DIP switches or jumpers. They normally come with some kind of configuration information provided on a diskette. Provided with the machine itself is a configuration program that reads the information from the diskettes and helps to ensure that there are no conflicts. Although hardware settings are configured through these programs, it is still possible in some cases to create conflicts yourself, but the configuration utility will warn you.

Sometimes the configuration utility is provided on a separate floppy. Usually this is a DOS floppy, but is not bootable. Therefore, you will need to first boot off a DOS floppy before you can configure the card. MCA machines have a bootable configuration disk that contain the configuration information for the hardware provided with the machine. If this is the case, then this disk is as important as the SCO UNIX installation media. If this disk gets trashed, then there is no way you will even be able to add another piece of hardware, your kids will hate you, and your co-workers will think you are a geek. On the other hard, you could get a copy from the manufacturer, but that's a hassle. The real problem is that some machines, like the IBM PS/2 series, recognize when you add a new card to the system and won't let you boot until you feed it the configuration disk.

In some cases, the configuration program is part of the hardware (BIOS) or resides in a normally inaccessible part of the hard disk. Check the machine documentation for details.

Knowing what kind of card you have is not only important to configure the card, but unless you know what kind of bus type you have, you may not be able to even stick it in the machine. This is because all of the different cards have a different size or shape. As you would guess, the slots on the motherboard also have different sizes and shapes.

Hopefully, you knew what kind of card to buy before you bought it. However, it is often the case where an administrator will know what kind of slots are on the machine from reading the documentation, but never opened the case up so has no idea what the slots look like. If this is a pure ISA or MCA machine, then this is not a problem as none of the cards for any other bus will fit into one of these slots.

Problems arise when you have mixed bus types. For example, it is very common today to have PCI or VLB included with ISA or EISA. I have also seen MCA machines with PCI slots, as well as both PCI *and* VLB in addition to the primary bus (usually ISA or EISA). If you've gotten confused reading this, imagine what will happen when you try to install one of these cards.

More than likely you are using your SCO machine as a server. Therefore, the computer you bought probably has at least six slots in it. There will be more if you have a tower case or have PCI in addition to the primary bus. Due to their distinct size and shape, it is difficult to get cards into slots where they don't belong. Usually there is some mechanism (notches in the card) that prevent you from sticking them in the wrong slots.

On some motherboards you will find a PCI slot right next to an ISA or EISA slot. By "right next to" I mean that the separation between the PCI slot and the other is much less than between slots of the same type. This is to prevent you from using both slots. Note that the PCI electronics are on the opposite side of the board from ISA and EISA. Therefore, it's impossible to fill one slot and then use the other.

When installing the expansion cards, you need to make sure that the computer is disconnected from all power supplies. The safest thing is to shutdown the system and then pull the plug from the wall socket. That way you ensure that no power is getting to the bus, even if it is turned off. Although the likelihood of you injuring yourself seriously is low, you have a greater chance of frying some component of your motherboard or expansion card.

Another suggestion is to ground yourself before touching any of the electronic components. You can do this by either touching a grounded metal object (other than the computer itself) or wearing a grounding strap. These usually come with a small instruction sheet telling where the best place to connect it is.

When I first started in SCO Support we had a machine that would reboot itself if someone so much as touched it who wasn't grounded. I have also cleared my CMOS a couple of times myself. Therefore, I can speak from experience when I say how important this is.

When you open the case you will see a row of bus card slots, lined up in parallel. Near the outside/back end of the slot, there is a backing plate that is probably attached to the computer frame by a single screw. Since in most cases, there is some connector that sticks out of the slot, this plate will probably have to be removed. In addition, the card will have an attachment similar to the backing plate that is used to hold the card in place. I have seen cards that do not have any external connector, so you could insert them without first removing the backing plate. However, they are not secure since nothing is holding them in place.

This plate has a lip at the top with the hole for the screw. In order to get the orientation right for the screw hole, the card will probably be inserted correctly (provided it is in the right kind of slot). As you are inserting the card into the slot, make sure that it is going in completely perpendicular to the motherboard. That is, make sure that both ends are going into the slot evenly and that the card is not tilted. Be careful not to push too hard, but also keep in mind that the card must "snap" into place. Once the card is seated properly in the slot, you can make the necessary cable connection to the card.

After the cables are connected, your machine can be rebooted. Many people recommend first closing the computer's case before turning on the power switch. Experience has taught me to first reboot the machine and test the card first, before putting the case back on. If, on the other hand, you *know* you have done everything correctly, then go ahead and close things up.

SCO UNIX provides a couple of utilities that can be used to check what you have installed if you are running either EISA or MCA. If you have an EISA system, use the eisa(ADM) utility. The one drawback is that this can only show you what EISA cards you have installed. This is because ISA cards have no way of communicating with the bus the same way EISA can. If you have an MCA machine, you use the slot(ADM) command. Note that both of these commands can only view the configuration and not change it. To change it you need to run the appropriate configuration program.

Avoiding address, interrupt, and DMA conflicts is often difficult. If your system consists solely of non-ISA cards, then it is easy to use the configuration utilities to do the work for you. However, the moment you add an ISA card, then you must look at the card specifically to see how it is configured and to avoid any conflicts yourself.

If you have ISA and PCI cards, you can use the PCI setup program to tell you which interrupts are in use by ISA bus cards. If you don't, then it is possible that there will be interrupt conflicts between the ISA bus card and a PCI bus card, or even two ISA cards.

Unlike DOS, every expansion card that you add to an SCO system requires a driver. Many, such as those for IDE hard disks, are already configured in your system. Even if the driver for a new piece of hardware exists on your system, it may not be linked into your kernel. Therefore, the piece of hardware it controls will be inaccessible.

## CPU

There isn't too much you can say about adding CPUs. There is no mkdev script to run. There are no jumpers to set on the CPU. In some newer machines, there is a lever that pops out the old CPU to allow you to pop in a new one. This is (as far as I have seen) only on 486 machine to allow you to add a Pentium. These are called Zero-Insertion-Force (ZIF) socket, since the lever is used to lock the CPU into place and it requires zero force to insert it.

One thing that needs to be considered is the speed of the CPU. You may want to increase the speed of the CPU by simply buying a faster one. From SCO's perspective this is okay. You plug it in, and it can work with it. However, keep in mind that motherboards are often sold with the same speed as the CPU. This is because they cannot handle faster speeds. Therefore, in many cases you cannot simply replace the CPU with a faster one.

In other cases, the motherboard is of higher quality and can handle even the fastest Pentium. However, if you only had a 50Mhz 486, then you might have to change jumpers to accommodate the slower CPU. Often these changes alter such things as the memory wait states. Here you need to check the motherboard documentation.

## RAM

The day will probably come when you need to expand the RAM on your system. As more users are added, the little RAM you have won't be enough. Once you have decided that you need more RAM, you still have most of your work ahead of you.

In almost all newer machines, RAM comes in the form of SIMM modules. As I mentioned in the chapter on Hardware, these are about the size of a stick of chewing gun, with the chips mounted directly on the cards. These have almost entirely replaced the old RAM that was composed of individual chips.

There are two primary types of SIMMs. The somewhat larger is called a PS/2 SIMM as it was first used on PS/2 machines. This has 72 connectors on it and can be immediately distinguished by the small notch. The other kind is referred to as non-PS/2. This has 30 pins and no notch. There is also a 32-pin SIMM; however, this is uncommon. I have never seen one, but was told of this by someone who works in the chip manufacturing business.

Two important aspects of RAM is the speed and whether or not it has parity. The speed of RAM is measured in nanoseconds(ns). Most RAM today is either 70ns or 60ns, with a few machines still being sold with 80ns. The speed of RAM is a measure of how quickly you can read a particular memory location.

Although it is possible in many cases to mix RAM speeds, I advise against this. First, memory can only be accessed as quickly as the slowest chip. Therefore, you can gain nothing by adding faster RAM, and lose if you add slower RAM. I have also seen machines where mixing speeds actually causes problems. Since the difference between 80ns and 70ns is more than 10%, the delay waiting for the slower (80ns) RAM makes the system think that there is a problem. This usually results in kernel panics.

Another issue is the motherboard design. For example, on my machine, I have two banks of memory with four slots each. Because of the way the memory access logic is designed, I must fill a bank completely, otherwise, nothing in that bank will be recognized. On other machines, you can add single SIMMs. Check the documentation that came with the motherboard.

Another important issue is the fact that SCO UNIX uses only extended not expanded memory. Expanded memory dates back to the early days when the XT bus could only handle up to 1MB of RAM. In order to give programs access to more memory than the computer could handle, some memory board manufacturers came up with the concept of "bank switching." With bank switching, a 64K area between 640K and 1Mb is reserved and then portions above 1Mb are "switched" in to this reserved block as needed.

When the AT bus was developed, it could access more memory. However to make it compatible with older peripherals, the area between 640K to 1MB was left unused. You often see this when SCO UNIX boots. Memory beyond 1MB is known as extended memory.

Some machines have a hardware limitation on the maximum amount of memory that can be installed. Since I use 30-pin SIMMs, the largest available (as of this writing) is 4Mb. Because of this, I max out at 32 MB when I fill all eight of my slots. If you have 72-pin memory, there are larger modules, such as 8, 16, and even 64Mb. Refer to your motherboard manual for details. Currently, OpenServer officially supports up to 512MB of main memory. However, I was told there is a machine at SCO running with 1Gb. I was also told that OpenServer *should* support up to 2Gb.

If you experience repeated panics with parity errors, consider replacing your memory. Because of the way memory is accessed you may have to remove or replace entire banks (like mine). I have also seen cases where mixing memory types and speeds can cause the panics. For example, if you have a machine that "allows" both 4MB and 1MB SIMMs, the demands that SCO puts on the machine may be too much and it will panic. However, running the same configuration with Windows works fine. The panics may also be the result of improperly inserted SIMMs. That is, if the SIMM is loose, it may not make a good contact with the slot. If the machine gets jarred, the contact may be lost.

In some cases you can simply add the memory and the machine will recognize it. However, in some machines you have to set jumpers to enable each bank as you add memory. In other cases, where you have filled up all the slots on the motherboard, you can add a memory expansion card. If this is on a machine like a PS/2, it requires you to tell the system of the memory expansion card using the configuration disk.

## SCSI Devices

If this is the first device you are adding to the host adapter, you need to configure that host adapter into the system. You will then be prompted for such information as IRQ and base addresses. If you have either a PCI or EISA machine, you won't be prompted for these values as these are configured into the CMOS by the appropriate configuration utility and they are then read by the driver at boot time.

If you are adding a second (or anything after that) host adapter you will have to disable the BIOS on it. Remember from our discussion on SCSI in the chapter on hardware, that the system will look for a bootable hard disk. If the BIOS on the second host adapter is enabled, the system may try to boot from this one. If it is the same model host adapter, then it will probably have to change the base address, IRQ, and DMA as well.

Remember that every device on the SCSI bus, including the host adapter itself, is identified by a SCSI ID. SCSI IDs range from 0–7 on standard SCSI and 0–15 on a wide SCSI bus. Regardless of what type, the host adapter is almost exclusively set to ID 7. It is this ID that is used to identify devices on the bus, not their location in relation to the host adapter.

Since there is no real need to have a SCSI host adapter configured unless something is attached, the only "official" way to add a host adapter to the system is to go through the procedures to add one of the attached devices. If the system recognizes that you do not have a configured host adapter, you will be prompted to add one.

If you are adding a device to an existing host adapter, then the driver for that host adapter is already linked into the kernel (at least we hope so). You only need to make the kernel aware of the new device. Each device gets an entry in

`/etc/conf/cf.d/mscsi`. This tells the system what host adapter type the device is attached to, what kind of device it is, which host adapter number it is attached to, the ID, LUN, and bus number for every device on every SCSI bus. The nice thing about the installation is that you don't have to worry about editing the `mscsi` file yourself. All you have to do is supply the correct information and the installation programs will add this for you.

One change that was made in OpenServer was adding an extra column to `mscsi`. This is for SCSI host adapters that provide two channels. The new column in `mscsi` (the sixth one) is for the channel. If the device is on the second channel, this entry will be a 1. If the device is on the first channel or the adapter doesn't support twin-channel, then this entry is 0. If the entry is missing, the system assumes it is 0.

When you run either the Hardware/Kernel Manager or one of the mkdev scripts, the first thing you are asked is the name of the host adapter 'type'. Here you need to put in the internal name of the device driver. The default will be either an Adaptec 154x if this is the first one you are installing or the last host adapter you installed. If you don't know, you can get a list of the available ones either by looking in `/etc/default/scsihas` or entering 'h' when you are asked for the type (it says to do this on the screen).

Next, you are asked for the host adapter number. Since you can only have two of any kind, you are given the choice of either 0 for the first or 1 for the second host adapter. OpenServer also supports twin channel SCSI host adapters. You are, therefore, asked which channel the device is on. If you have a host adapter with only one channel, enter 0 as the channel.

Be careful here. Some host adapters label their channels A and B, rather than 0 and 1. Since both A and 0 come first, these are the same channel. That makes B and 1 the same channel. Although this seems logical unless someone specifically tells you, you are still guessing.

You are next asked the ID of the device. Remember that the ID is not the position on the SCSI bus, but is something that you need to explictly set. Make sure that the ID you are inputting to the mkdev script is correct. Just like base addresses, IRQs, and everything else, this has to match. The problem is that determing the ID is not always easy. Remember from our discussion on SCSI device in the chapter on Hardware. You might have jumpers or switches that can have several different labels. Unless you have used this model of device before, you will probably need to check the doc to be sure (checking the doc is *always* a good idea).

The last question concerns the logical unit number (LUN) of the device. Currently, SCO does not support any device that is set to something other than LUN 0. This is not to say that it won't work. It's simply the fact that all devices that SCO supports directly have embedded controllers so they can only be set to LUN 0.

If the root disk is IDE, EIDE, or ESDI, then you can add another disk of that type or add an SCSI disk (assuming you have an SCSI host adapter). Keep in mind that the number of disks is limited by The `MAX_DISK` dynamic kernel parameter. If set to 0, the maximum number is dynamic.

Some host adapters, like the Adaptec AHA1510 do not have a BIOS. Therefore, you cannot install onto a disk connected to this adapter. This can be used only as a secondary adapter. There are dozens of host adapters supported by SCO, with more being added to each release. Each has certain characteristics that need to be addressed. If there are known problems with a specific host adapter it will be listed in the *Release Notes* or in the *Open Server Handbook*.

## Hard Disks

One of the most commonly used and often messed up scripts is the one that allows you to add hard disks to your system: `mkdev hd`. The reason that the `mkdev` script is so often messed up is that people are not prepared when they start. They do not know the current configuration on their system. As a result, they often guess when running this script. What then happens is that the system fails and dies during the next reboot because it is looking for things that are not there.

Since the `mkdev hd` script is only called after the system itself is installed and you are adding a new disk, there is a better chance that you know what kind of disk you are using. However, this is not always the case. I have talked with customers who are the software consultants and have technicians add the hardware. In some cases they don't even know what kind of hard disk they are installing.

If you have trouble figuring out what kind of hard disk you have, either refer to the documentation that came with the drive, call the vendor, or reread the section at the beginning of the book on hard disks.

It is important to know how your disk is configured. Every drive should come with some kind of documentation. This usually contains information about the default settings of the drive. Don't trust them. Check out the settings yourself to ensure they are correct before you stick the drive in the machine. It is easier to check beforehand than it is after you try to install it.

If it's an IDE drive, then one of the key issues is whether it is the master or slave. If you are adding a second drive to a system that only has one drive, then you are obviously adding the slave. If you already have two drives on the first IDE controller and this is the first one on the second controller, then it is the master.

Another key issue is making sure the cabling is right. In the section on hard disks, I mentioned that the position of the cable is irrelevant for IDE drives; the jumpers determine which drive is which. A problem often crops up when connecting the cable to the drive itself.

Usually there is a small "key" on the connector of the cable which fits into a notch on the drive-side connector. If the key is missing or the drive-side connector is wide enough, it may be possible to fit the connectors together backwards. Fortunately, you don't have to resort to "trial and error" to figure out which is which. On one side of the cable, there will be a colored stripe (usually red). This is line 1 of the 40-line IDE cable. In fact, on almost all ribbon cables, line 1 is marked red.

On the drive side, things are a little more complicated. The IDE cable has 40 parallel lines, but the connectors (both on the cable and on the drive) are in two parallel rows. Usually the connector on the drive is either male (pins) or there is a small "card" sticking out that is similar to an expansion card. These alternate with the odd numbered lines on one side and the even numbered lines on the other.

On the drive near the connector (often on the circuit board itself) will be some small numbers. These tell you which pin is which. Sometimes there will be a 1 and 2 on one end with 39 and 40 on the other. Other times there will be just a 1 and 39. (I have seen cases where there is just a 2 and 40.)

SCSI drives may have jumpers to configure them, but they may also be configured in other ways such as with dials, DIP switches, or piano switches. Like IDE drives, SCSI usually has one set of jumpers. This will be for the SCSI ID of the drive. In some cases there will be up to eight pairs of pins to indicate the SCSI ID. Others have three pins that operate in binary. (For more details on SCSI configuration, see the section on SCSI in the hardware chapter.)

Standard SCSI cables look very similar to the IDE, except that the cable has 50 lines instead of just 40. However, the same issues with the key and slot, as well as the number applies. I can't remember seeing a SCSI device where the key and slot didn't match up correctly.

If you are not sure of how the drive is configured, check the documentation that came with your drive. Most hard disk manufacturers have fax services that will fax you installation information on any drive they have.

The first thing the `mkdev hd` script does is to check your root hard disk. This is important because you cannot have both a SCSI and IDE drive in your system and boot from the SCSI. Therefore, if your system only has SCSI drives and you run this script, you are only given the option to add another SCSI hard disk.

(I talked about the reasons for this in the section on SCSI in the chapter on hardware.)

Well, this is not entirely true. If you are running OpenServer 5.0, then you are given a menu option to add an IDE drive. You can start it and it will go through like it is trying to add the hard disk, but it eventually errors out. To me, this is a bug.

The `mkdev hd` script accesses the functions to determine the hard disk type through two other scripts: `/usr/lib/sh/std_funcs` and `/usr/lib/mkdev/.hdfuncs`. The script `std_funcs` contains several standard functions that provide interfaces for user input and output. This script contains some interesting functions, but unfortunately that is not the topic of this section. I would recommend looking at it because it has some useful functions and uses some interesting tricks of the shell.

The other script, `.hdfuncs`, contains hard disk functions (what else?). This is where most of the actual work gets done when adding a hard disk. Should you be adding a SCSI hard disk, the `.hdfuncs` calls the script `/usr/lib/mkdev/.scsi`.

One of the first things the `mkdev hd` script does is check for the architecture type. Actually this isn't quite true. The system simply asks, "Am I MCA?" If not, it doesn't care if it's ISA or EISA, just that it's not MCA. This is very important as the drivers are very different between MCA and AT architectures; whereas, ISA devices work fine in EISA machines.

Just after this, the system checks for the existence of the link kit. This is a very important step. Without the link kit, none of the necessary drivers are on the system and you won't be able to add anything. The nice thing is that if the system determines that the link kit is not installed, you are asked if you want to install it.

Next we get to see where one of our esoteric devices finally comes of use: `/dev/string/cfg`. The `.hdfuncs` script uses it to find out what the boot hard disk type is. This is because, as I mentioned before, you can't have both SCSI and non-SCSI and boot from the SCSI. If `.hdfuncs` finds that your boot hard disk is SCSI, it will only allow you to add another SCSI. If this is the case, it actually runs the `.scsi` script.

Here you are asked about the host adapter and how the drive is configured. This is where it becomes essential that you know your hardware configuration. The script makes some suggestions about what the values are based on what it can determine, however these are not always the correct values to input.

For example, one of the things it suggests is the prefix of the host adapter you are adding. It firsts checks `/etc/conf/cf.d/mscsi` and uses the last host adapter prefix it finds. This makes sense because if you are adding a SCSI device, then most likely it will be to the same host adapter as the last device added.

If there are no entries in `mscsi`, it looks for a boot device. This is also obtained through `/dev/string/cfg`. This makes sense because in most cases you are adding an SCSI device to an existing host adapter and if there are no entries in `mscsi`, you probably want to add it to the boot host adapter.

This is a place where people run into problems. They simple don't know what to input there. They were given installation instructions for the hardware, but the hardware vendor may not provide instructions for UNIX. In most cases it is safe to take the default. However, be safe! Know what you have. The same also applies to the SCSI ID and LUN. If you don't know, don't guess. If you know you are adding a new host adapter, `.scsi` will prompt you for information about this host adapter to be able to configure it into the kernel.

Once the script decides that your input is a valid device, one of two things will happen. If the hard disk is brand new and the system has never accessed it before, you will have to relink the kernel, reboot, and run `mkdev hd` again before you can access the drive to make the partitions. The reason for this is that the first time you run `mkdev hd`, the kernel is configured to recognize the drive. It is not until you reboot that the system recognizes the drive and is able to access it. Only then can you partition the disk and make filesystems. Remember that the second time you run `mkdev hd`, you *must* use the exact same values.

The second time you run `mkdev hd`, you are brought into `fdisk` to partition the drive. The `fdisk` utility is used to create UNIX partitions. You can define up to four partitions, which can be no larger than 2TB (2 terabytes) or the maximum size of the disk, whichever is smaller. Keep in mind that filesystems are limited to smaller sizes. You may not be able to create a partition that is the full size of the disk, and then create only a single filesystem. Also, if this disk was already used and the partition table is still valid, you could simply quit out of `fdisk` without changing any of the values.

I need to emphasize something here. On ODT, there must be at least one active UNIX partition for `mkdev hd` to work properly. Those of you with a little experience know that if there is only one partition, the system automatically makes it active. So if it's a new drive and you are using the entire disk for UNIX, there is no problem. Also, if you are adding a UNIX partition to a hard disk which already has a DOS partition, this is also no problem, as you can simply make the UNIX partition active.

However, what do you do if the entire disk is used for DOS and you want to be able to access it, let's say, through Merge? Ah, therein lies the rub. The `.hdfuncs` script will not allow you to continue if there is no active UNIX partition. Yes, you can quit out of the mkdev process, however, the system has trapped the interrupt key. If you quit, all the device node information is deleted and you are back to where you started. The solution to this is not really what we're here to talk about. You will either have to edit `mkdev fd` or add the nodes by hand. Fortunately, OpenServer allows you to add a DOS-only disk.

In the `mkdev hd` script, each of the device names must be created as the hard disk is added. There are literally dozens of names that need to get created. For SCSI devices, these names are based on the order drives get installed and not necessarily the order they appear on the bus. Therefore, the devices cannot be created in advance or put in a file like the other devices. These must be created when the script is run.

During this process a "seed" value is calculated, based on which of the remaining minor numbers are calculated. This "seed" value is one of those multiples of 64 that are used for each hard disk. Remember our discussion of major and minor numbers? The first hard disk has major numbers between 0–63, the second between 64–127. The first number in the range (for example, 0, 64, 128, or 192) is the lowest value that the minor number can be for any device on this hard disk. This is the "seed" value and is simply added to the minor number calculated for each device for the hard disks.

If there are already four hard disks on the system, then the seed number will be at least 256. Each is stored in a single byte. Therefore, it is impossible to have a minor number above 255, therefore you can't have more than four hard disks on a system.

Well, several years ago this was true. Four hard disks on a system was considered to be quite a lot. Therefore, it did not bother the "powers-that-be" too much that this limitation existed. As databases grew into the gigabyte range, four hard disks was no longer "a lot." Considering that a SCSI bus could handle six per host adapter, this limitation was becoming a bit annoying. Something had to be done to address this issue. That something was the creation of extended minor numbers.

Well, if you want to find out more about extended minor numbers, read the section on major and minor numbers. If you've already read the section, then you understand what we're taking about.

If the `mkdev hd` script has determined that the seed value is greater than 255, it gets a new major number that is then used for the extended minor numbers.

After completing `fdisk`, `divvy` is called, which is used to create divisions and filesystems on those divisions. By default, one filesystem is created on the active partition that you just made. However, you are asked if you want to make any changes. Even if you don't want to make changes, it's a good idea to say that you do. This way you are brought into an interactive session of divvy and you can see if things look reasonable. I also find it useful to check for typoes that I might have made when inputting the values. In addition, you can name the filesystem that's created. Otherwise you end up with some weird name. You then can exit divvy and the filesystem is created.

You need to be very careful here if this was a disk that you had used before; for example, you updated the OS or had to reinstall after a system crash. Although you are brought into divvy, you don't *have* to change anything. However, there are probably no device nodes for these filesystems, so you will probably at least have to name them. If you want to keep the data, *don't* create the filesystems. Creating the filesystem clears out the inode table, making your data inaccessible.

## Filesystems

Although divvy is used to create the filesystem on the divisions, the mkdev hd process does not actually make the filesystem readily available. You do have the names of the device nodes as well as the name(s) of the filesystem(s). Therefore, every time you boot you could run the mount command by hand to add the filesystem(s). This is obnoxious, but you could do it.

A better alternative would be to have the system mount the filesystem(s) automatically (assuming this is what you wanted). This is done through another mkdev script mkdev fs.

This is one of the scripts where you are not actually "making" any devices. However, you are adding some functionality to your system. During the course of this script you are prompted for the device name of the filesystem (this is the name you input in divvy) and the name of the directory of where you want to mount the filesystem. By convention this is the same as the name of the filesystem, however there is nothing that prevents you from naming it something else.

At this point you see a message that says:

```
Reserving slots in lost+found directory ...
```

Here, the system is creating sixty-two files and removing them. Why? Think back to the discussion of filesystems in Chapter 6.

Next, you are asked for the manner in which the filesystem should be mounted (never, always, or prompt). The convention is to always mount it, which kind of makes sense. Why go through all that trouble to add a filesystem if you never want to access it? If there are conditions at your site where you might not want to mount it, then choose one of the other options.

Finally, you are asked whether users should be able to mount this filesystem. Be careful. If you say, "yes," then every user has the power to do so. Although they may not have access to files underneath the mount point, anyone can still mount it. It is useful if you have a user whose sole function is to do backups, so having the ability to mount filesystems is very useful. However, if the user cannot read the file, it can't be backed-up. If you give them root authority to back everything up, then they don't need to be able to mount the filesystem as a user.

## Floppies

Another commonly used script is `mkdev fd`, for "make device floppy." Again, this is another case where no device is actually created. This script creates floppies that can be used in emergencies to boot your system.

You are prompted to input the type of floppy you want to use as well as whether you want to use either drive 0 or drive 1. If you are creating a filesystem floppy (the next prompt asks what kind of floppy you are creating), then there is no problem in using drive 1. However, if you are creating boot floppy, this must be drive 0. Also, you need to know the kind of floppy drive you have. If you chose the wrong kind (size or density), the script will fail.

After you choose the floppy drive, you are given the choice of what kind of floppy you want to create. A filesystem floppy is essentially empty. It contains the filesystem structure that a filesystem on the hard disk does. However, since it is accessing a smaller space, there are few inodes so the inode table is smaller. Like a newly created filesystem on the hard disk, this one is empty.

The other two types are usually created in pairs and as a pair are often referred to as a boot/root floppy set. A boot floppy is exactly what it sounds like. It contains the necessary information to boot and load the kernel. A root filesystem floppy contains a filesystem as well as the file necessary to get the system going into maintenance mode. In addition, it contains utilities that can be used to recover from a crash and restore your data. To see what files are copied onto the floppy, take a look at `/usr/lib/mkdev/perms/FD`.

It is advisable, recommended, suggested, and desirable, that you create a boot/root floppy set every time you add or delete drivers that will alter the state of either the hard disk or tape drive. These are the most important drivers and devices you have for crash recovery. When your system goes down and you can't access it through the boot/root floppy, then your only alternative is to reinstall.

## CD-ROMs

Just as `mkdev hd` and `mkdev fs` come in pairs, so do `mkdev cdrom` and `mkdev high-sierra`. Just like the first pair, you do not absolutely need to add a `high-sierra` filesystem to be able to access the CD-ROM. If you remember from our discussion on the `/dev` directory, there is such a thing as a cd-tape device. Since you are not actually mounting the device, there is no need to add a filesystem driver for it. Additionally, if you have a UNIX Filesystem CD, then the filesystem driver is already installed.

If you are adding a SCSI CD-ROM, then it must be attached to a supported host adapter to be able to use the configuration utilities. Although you may find a third party driver, you will once again run into the question of who is going to support it.

OpenServer allows a maximum of 255 CD-ROM drivers per system. How many are possible on each host adapter is only limited by the host adapter itself. For example, you can only have seven on a SCSI-1 host adapter, but fifteen on a wide SCSI-2. If this is the first CD-ROM you are installing on the system, you are also prompted to add support for the `high-sierra` filesystem. This is the format that DOS CD-ROMs use, so you must install the `high-sierra` filesystem if you want to access DOS CDs.

Generally, adding floptical drives is the same for any other SCSI device. You need to ensure that there are no conflicts and that the hardware settings match what you tell the system they are. Here, too, you are limited to the number of devices that the SCSI bus supports.

Although there is a wide range of hard disks that are supported in either ODT or Open Server, the combinations that you can add are not that wide. I am not referring to either manufacturers of sizes, but rather the type of hard disk, such as IDE or SCSI. One problem is mixing SCSI and non-SCSI hard disks. Personal preference says not to. It is annoying. You are also limited by the fact that if you have already installed the system on a SCSI disk, then you cannot later add a non-SCSI disk.

The thing to note is that the high-sierra (also known as ISO-9660) is the same type as DOS and Windows use. Therefore, don't think that just because you added DOS functionality to your system, you will be able to access a DOS CD-ROM. The new `Rockridge` filesystem supported in OpenServer is an extension of the `high-sierra` filesystem in that it supports version numbers and long filenames.

There are two nice things about the `mkdev cdrom` script. First, it gives you the option of adding a standard CD-ROM or a cd-tape drive. Therefore, you can save a little space in your kernel by only adding what you need. The second nice thing is that if you are adding a standard CD-ROM, you are asked if you want to add the `high-sierra` filesystem. Now, there is a mkdev script to add to the `high-sierra`, which `mkdev cdrom` calls. However, it's nice to have things done for us, wouldn't you say?

Like hard disks, if you are adding a CD-ROM and there is not already a SCSI device on your system, the kernel will need to be configured for the host adapter. Also, if you are adding it to a second host adapter, you will need to configure that as well.

## Tape Drives

If you are a good little system administrator then you have already bought yourself a tape drive and have configured it into your system. Therefore, I don't need to talk about adding one. On the other hand, there may come a time when the tape drive you have is not sufficient for your needs and you may have to add a new one. As you would guess, the script to do this is `mkdev tape`.

Before you begin to install the tape drive be sure to have read your tape drive hardware manual. This will often contain information about the physical installation of the device as well as configuration. Whenever, I think about installing tape drives, I think of the first SCSI tape drive I had. There were three jumpers to set the SCSI ID. It didn't make sense that you could only set it to ID 0, 1, or 2. Had I read the manual first, I would have known that this was the *binary* representation of the number.

As you expect, the values have to be correct for the device to work. You need to know the type of controller you have, the base address, IRQ, and DMA. Note that for the DMA channel, you only have an option of 3 or 5 when running `mkdev tape`. If the tape drive you are adding has its own controller card, then the base address, IRQ, and DMA channel are configured on ISA machines with jumpers or switches. Non-ISA cards can probably be configured via the configuration utilities.

If you remember our discussion on device nodes, you know there are several different kinds of tape drives. A standard cartridge tape, also referred to as a QIC-02 is about the size of a Betamax video tape. For the younger readers, this is a little smaller than a VHS tape (or twice the size of a music cassette). This kind of tape is installed using the `Cartridge Tape Drive` option. You can either configure this tape drive for autoconfiguration or you can input the parameters yourself.

There are a couple of things that can go wrong when installing a QIC-02 tape drive. The most common is that it simply does not show up at boot. Instead of the standard configuration string, you get a notice that says the tape controller was not found. This is usually the result of the base address configured in the mkdev script not matching the hardware. However, I had one customer who was having a terrible time configuring a QIC-02. He had removed it and reinstalled it several times, with no success. He was sure that the parameters were correct, because he had used the same tape drive in another machine. Normally, there is no problem with switching QIC-02 tape drives from one machine to another, provided you move the controller card and not just the tape drive. Needless to say, the tape drive worked fine when he installed the card. (What he had done was simply move the tape drive over to the new machine and plug power into it.)

As with any piece of hardware, make sure the controller is seated properly. You may also have to try a different slot. Maybe the slot is bad. The first machine that I got when I was in Support that I could install UNIX on was a "hand-me-down." The longer you worked there, the more likely you were to get a newer machine. Conversely, the newbie got the hand-me-downs. The one I got, (datrat, as the previous owner had christened it) was very sensitive. There was only one QIC-02 controller card in the department that worked in my machine. It only worked with one tape drive and in only one slot. Other people could use any combination of drive, card, and slot. Not me. One drive. One card. One slot.

If the drive is recognized at boot, but hangs when you issue `tape` commands, make sure that the DMA and IRQ are correct. Another possible problem is that the controller card is in the slot, but the drive is not connected to the controller. If the tape drive is external, then it probably has to be powered up at boot time to be recognized. An incorrect IRQ can also result in the message

```
Cannot open /dev/rct0
```

The device node may become corrupted. If it's a QIC-02, tape drive, the device node should look like this:

```
crw-rw-rw 1 root root 10, 0 Feb 14 12:00 rct0
```

If not, try removing then reinstalling the tape drive.

The second option is to use a mini cartridge. This option is used to install Irwin tape drives only. The tapes for this kind of drive are about the size of a cigarette pack. The drives are hooked up to the floppy controller. Mini tape drives may use the floppy disk drive controller. Some Irwins will have their own controller. Irwin mini tape drivers differ from others in that they are not configurable and therefore do not require you to enter any parameters when you are installing it. However, you must ensure that the tape drive is set to unit 1.

The third option in `mkdev tape` is for QIC-40/QIC-80 tape drives. The cartridges are the same size as for an Irwin. If you are installing a non-Irwin mini, there are a couple of things to be careful of. First, the installation mkdev script is the QIC-40/80 script, not the mini cartridge. This is for Irwins only. Although the tapes are physically the same, Irwin tape drives require a different driver.

You are prompted to select whether you are installing a QIC-40 or QIC-80 drive. Also you select whether to enable extended length tapes. Not all tape drives support this. Therefore, you must be sure that the drive can support it, before you enable extended length mode.

If either Irwin or QIC-40/80 tape drive is not recognized at boot-up, it displays a message similar to when it can't find a QIC-02. This is due to the standard problems of incorrect configuration.

It is possible to have two floppies and add a QIC-40/80, provided that the tape drive is configurable for *soft select*. On certain tape drives, the unit or drive number can be set by the driver. On Archive and Mountain drives this is called soft select mode. On Wangtek drives this is called Phantom select mode. In each case this is set on the drive, check the hardware doc to see if your drive can handle this. It is a good idea to set it, if you can, as it helps to limit the number of problems.

The fourth option is for a SCSI tape drive. There are five different types of SCSI tape drives you can add: Cartridge, Exabyte, 9-Track, DAT, and Compaq SCSI. On OpenServer there is an Option for generic SCSI tape drives if you are not sure what kind you have. However, being the good little system administrator that you are, you do know, so you don't need to use this option.

As with any SCSI device, you have to be sure of the configuration. You can have multiple SCSI tape drives on the system, provided they have unique SCSI IDs.

With an SCSI tape drive, you may end up with a message indicating there is no controller response. The obvious things to check are the same with any SCSI device, such as proper ID, cabling, and SCSI termination. If you have more than one host adapter, make sure that you specified the correct one. Also, if you have OpenServer, make sure that you have selected the correct bus if your host adapter is twin-channel.

Like cartridge tapes, external SCSI tapes usually have to be turned on when the system boots. If the drive is internal, check to see that the drive initializes when you insert a tape. That is, it will probably make a few "whirring" noises. Also keep in mind that an SCSI tape may appear to boot, even though it is not configured correctly. The initialization routines at boot do not check the hardware, but do print the configuration string. (Remember, this is done with the `printcfg()` routine.) Therefore, you might see that the configuration strings show a device that isn't even on the system, let alone configured correctly.

The one important thing about adding a tape drive is that the boot string can be modified to reflect this. You could rely on the kernel having the correct parameters, or you could pass these parameters to the kernel through the boot string. When adding a tape drive, you are given the chance to modify the bootstring. If improperly typed in, this can cause the system to panic when it's booting. So be careful of what you type in.

The default tape drive accessed by many utilities is `/dev/rct0`. If you install more than one tape drive, the mkdev script will prompt for which drive you want to be the default tape drive. The device node for this will then be linked to `/dev/rct0`. You can do this by hand or through the menu option in the `mkdev tape` script.

## Parallel Ports

In earlier versions of SCO, parallel ports were configured by default on the system. When you installed, you had immediate access to the parallel ports. This was useful as most printers ran off the parallel port. However, things changed. The call load went up. Customers could no longer access their parallel port. This was not surprising as the parallel driver was no longer in the kernel on the N1.

The reason for this is simple: It wasn't needed. Well, it isn't all that simple without understanding the reason why the engineers went through the trouble of removing it. Why fix something that isn't broken or why remove something that isn't bothering anyone?

The same thing applies to the parallel driver. It wasn't needed, that's true, but it was taking up valuable space on the floppy. With all the SCSI drivers in the kernel, there's not much room for anything else. Therefore, some things had to go. One of those things was the parallel driver. As I mentioned, it just wasn't needed during the installation.

This change caused a large number of calls during the first months after the product was shipped. Many hours were spent walking people through the `mkdev parallel` script to add the parallel port. It isn't hard, but for the most part, customers would much rather have someone tell them how to do it rather than read from a book. Besides, finding it in the installation guide isn't all that easy (assuming, of course, you *don't* look in the index or table of contents).

As I said, adding the parallel port is not that difficult. When you run `mkdev parallel` you are given three choices for ports to add. If you are not sure how your parallel port is configured, I would suggest you add all three. When you reboot, the hardware screen will display the one you have and you can then remove the others.

On a new system, it is common to add the parallel port and then immediately add a printer. In many cases the reverse is true: You've added a printer and it won't work because you haven't run `mkdev parallel`.

The `mkdev lp` script is one of the shortest and for good reason: The script itself doesn't do much. Instead it calls `/usr/lib/sysadm/lpsh`. The `lpsh` program is one of the nice looking ones that uses the menus, and so on, in `oamenus` and `oaforms`. You can call this program yourself or even get to it through sysadmsh. Since I talked about adding printers in the section on printers, there really isn't much more I can say here.

## Serial Ports

Similar in function is `mkdev serial`, although as you suspect you use this to add serial ports instead of parallel ports. The real important issue is not to use this script when trying to add intelligent multiport cards such as those from Digiboard or Equinox. Both of these have their own drivers and installation routines. They will modify the kernel appropriately and add the device nodes. The `mkdev serial` script is only to add nonintelligent (also referred to as dumb, for the non-politically correct among us) serial ports.

By default, only the COM1 device is configured into the kernel, *even if* you have a COM2. This can be added later by running `mkdev serial`.

There are many manufacturers of nonintelligent serial cards. These cards do not have any special processor on them and are accessed using the standard `sio` driver. Because of the minor numbering scheme used for serial devices (see the section on the `/dev` directory) you can only add eight nonintelligent serial ports, even though there is an option in `mkdev serial` to add a 16-port card.

Using the `mkdev serial` script, there are only two options for such cards. They represent the standard COM1 and COM2 ports. Depending on the number of ports you want to add, you will be given a number of manufacturers to choose from. Although this does not represent all the ones available on the market, it does cover quite a few. There is a way to add ones if you need to.

Let's first sidestep a minute and take a look at `/etc/conf/sdevice.d/sio`. It looks something like this:

```
sio    Y    53    7    0    3    2f8    2ff    0    0
sio    Y    26    7    0    4    3f8    3ff    0    0
```

In the section on the link kit, I went into details about the files in the `sdevice.d` directory. I said that column three represented the number of "units" of that type that were configured. While this is also true for the `sdevice.d/sio` file, there is a level of indirection we need to address.

If we look at the above example, (which I have not changed from what the system creates by default) we see the two lines that represent COM1 and COM2. It seems rather ridiculous to think that there are 53 COM1 ports and 26 COM2 ports on the system.

In this case, these do not directly represent the number of ports but rather the off-set into an array. This is the sio_sup_brds array in /etc/conf/pack.d/ sio/space.c. If we look at line 54 (remember we start counting a 0) we see the entry for the AT-IBM-COM2 device. Next, if we look at line 27, we see the entry for the AT-IBM-COM1 device. (For details for what each entry means, see the declaration of the board_t structure in <sys/sioconf.h>.)

If you want to add a new board to this list, copy an existing entry and add it to the *bottom* of the array. I want to empathize that this ought to go at the bottom of the list because the entry in sdevice.d/sio is the relative position in the array. Placing an entry before line 27 or line 54 throws things out of whack.

The next time you run mkdev serial, the entry you added will appear as one of the options, provided you've input everything correctly.

The limit of eight serial ports is not because the system does not support it, but rather because there are few entries in pack.d/sio/space.c that support it. The few that exist all micro-channel devices and are only listed for COM2. This is because the minor numbers for COM2 start at 8. If a 16-port board were to be added to COM1, the minor numbers would overlap those for COM2.

One common question that Support gets is why you can't have COM3 or COM4. Well, the official word is that you can't. The reason is that COM1 and COM3 share interrupts and COM2 and COM4 share interrupts and the SCO serial driver cannot support serial devices at the same interrupt. This is generally true on older boards, however, newer ones may allow you to configure both the base address *and* the interrupt.

If we go back to /etc/conf/pack.d/sio/space.c for a moment, we see that there actually are entries for COM3 and COM4. They can be configured like this:

| PORT | IRQ | I/O PORT ADDRESS |
|------|-----|------------------|
| COM3 | 12  | 0x2F0 - 0x2F7 |
| COM3 | 10  | 0x3E8 - 0x3EF |
| COM4 | 11  | 0x2E8 - 0x2EF |

If your card can be configured to one of the configurations above, then you can simply run mkdev serial and select the proper COM port. If not, you can *try* to change the entry in the sio/space.c file to reflect your configuration. However, I cannot guarantee it. I have personal experience with using the three settings above, not with changing the sio/space.c file. However, based on the way the file is put together, it *should* work.

Part of the mkdev script asks you to select a baud rate for the devices attached to this port. This only indicates the default values to be used when creating the entries in /etc/inittab and the files in /etc/conf/init.d. Once completed, the mkdev will add the entries to the Terminal Control Database.

A common problem with serial cards is loss of characters. In certain circumstances, this can be corrected by increasing the NCLIST kernel parameter. If this does not correct the problem, then you may consider getting either an intelligent serial card (one with its own processor) or one with a 16550 UART. This has a multiple character buffer which decreases the number of characters lost.

## Serial Terminals

In general, installing a serial terminal is the same whether it is connected to a standard COM port or an intelligent multiport board. In either case, you obviously have to ensure that the driver for that port is linked into the kernel, otherwise the terminal will not be able to talk to the system.

By default, terminals are set using 9600 baud, 8 data bits, 1 stop bit, no parity, full duplex, and XON/XOFF handshaking. If your terminal cannot handle these settings, then you can either change the line in inittab to reflect the appropriate gettydefs entry, or you can create your own gettydefs entry if none of these fit. See the section on starting your system or the gettydefs(F) man-page.

Pay attention to which pins are which on the terminal. You only need to worry about three: transmit, receive, and signal ground. The serial port will be set up (probably) with pin 2 as transmit, 3 as receive, and 7 as ground if you have a DB25 (25-pin) connector. If you have a DB9 (9-pin) connector pin 2 is receive, 3 is transmit, and pin 5 is ground. Make sure that the cabling is set up so that transmit on one side goes to receive on the other and the two ground pins are connected. In some cases you need a crossed cable, when the pin numbering is the same on both sides (the same number of pins). If pins 2 and 3 are different, then you need a straight through cable.

You need to ensure that there is an entry for the terminal in both /etc/inittab and either /etc/conf/cf.d/init.base or a file in /etc/conf/init.d. If not in inittab, but in either of the other two locations, then potentially the serial port was added to the device driver files, but the kernel was never relinked. Remember from our discussion on the kernel, when you do a relink, part of rebuilding the kernel environment is creating a new inittab file by catting the files in etc/conf/init.d onto the end of /etc/conf/cf.d/init.base. Not relinking would explain why the entry was not in inittab.

On the other hand, if it's not in either of the other files, but is in inittab, then probably someone added it to inittab by hand. This needs to be corrected by putting the entry in one of the other files. Otherwise, the next time you relink, the entry will be gone.

If the entry is correct, you can enable it with the `enable` command. Like this:

```
enable tty1a
```

The `enable` command changes the entry in `inittab` and either of the other locations from `off` to `respawn`. If the terminal is already enabled, you get a message saying so. It is the fact that there is a `respawn` in `inittab` that gives you the login prompt when the system starts and gives you a new one when you log out. For more details, see the section on starting and stopping the system and the `inittab(F)` man-page. When enabled, the corresponding entry might look like this:

```
Se1a:234:respawn:/etc/getty tty1a m
```

If the login prompt doesn't look right (garbage characters) then probably the `gettydefs` entry is incorrect. If you remember from our discussion of starting and stopping the system, this is the last entry on the line; in this case `m`. If the `m` entry in `gettydefs` does not match what the terminal is set for, you get incorrect behavior. See the `gettydefs(F)` man-page for more details.

If you don't see a login on the terminal, it's possible it was sent before the terminal was turned on. Therefore, the terminal cannot display it. If you press ENTER a couple of times an no login prompt appears, maybe it's not really enabled or there is a hardware problem. Disable it and re-enable it. You should also try simply sending the date to the file, with

```
date > /dev/<tty_name>
```

If that still produces nothing, then you may have a hardware problem. If you have enabled the port, you can run

```
ps -t<tty_name>
```

to see if there is a `getty` or `login` running on that port. If not, there may be some serious software problems.

Often the connector on the terminal is female. You can test the terminal if you take a paper clip and put one end in hole two and the other end in hole three. By pressing keys on the keyboard, the data is going out the transmit line (pin 2 or 3, doesn't matter) and comes back in on the other pin. If nothing appears, first make sure that the terminal is turned on (I've had my share of *those* calls). If it is turned on check the brightness (I've had enough of those, as well). If still nothing, the monitor is probably on vacation.

If you suspect the cable or serial port, you can try the terminal on a port that you know is working. Then switch parts one at a time, until you isolate the part that's broken.

## Video Cards

Another script that points elsewhere is `mkdev graphics`. In general, this does the same thing as when you configure the video card through the System→Hardware menu options in `sysadmsh`. In fact, the exact same program is called. This, too, has the same menuing functionality of `lpsh`.

In ODT, your video card and monitor were configured using `mkdev graphics`. As with other mkdev scripts, `mkdev graphics` still exists, but calls the corresponding manager from `scoadmin`. In this case it is the Video Configuration Manager. The `mkdev graphics` script is based on the same functions as the `sysadmsh` so you have the same kind of windowing. The Video Configuration Manager is the same as the other configuration managers.

You will encounter one important difference right away. In ODT you do not "Add" a video adapter, but rather "Update." In OpenServer, there is button "Add Adapter." This is a little confusing since when you get done, you are asked whether you want to *replace* the existing video card. To me this is a bug, or at least a very annoying feature. If I replace the adapter, I am not adding anything. I am either replacing or updating the adapter, but certainly not adding. At any rate, don't be confused when you run into this.

If you select "add adapter", then you are presented with a list of video cards. If you don't have a video card, but rather the video chips are built onto the motherboard, you should look for the chipset you have. If your card or chip set is not there, you should either select one that is closest, or contact SCO or the manufacturer. SCO might have included the driver in the newest copy of the Advanced Hardware Supplement (AHS). If all else fails, try the generic IBM VGA adapter. Although you may not get the resolution you want, selecting this card normally gets you running.

When you finally select one, you may find that your card had "special configuration information." If you select 'yes' to view it, you are brought into SCOHelp, which will give you more details about the card. If there is no additional information or you have finished reading the help file, you need to select the resolution and the monitor configuration. If you just click okay, you are reminded that you haven't configured the card completely and are asked to do so or click cancel.

Interestingly enough, if you have selected (highlighted) the video adapter and then click on Modify instead of Add, you are told that this action will remove the configured card (which is displayed) and that you can cancel on the next screen. The next screen is simply the Add Adapter screen, so you are at the same place.

If you are reconfiguring an existing graphics adapter that uses I/O addresses and a memory mapped window, please be sure to write down your current selections before you choose new ones. When you choose new settings, the current I/O addresses and memory mapped window are not saved. If you reconfigure an adapter, then later choose not to save the configuration, the previous settings for the `grafinfo` file are *not* restored.

When you select the option to modify the monitor, you are given the choice of changing the monitor itself (model, brand, etc), the resolution of the monitor, or adding a resolution. This allows you to have multiple resolutions for the same monitor. There is a list of monitors from which to choose from. Here again, find yours or the one that closely matches. If you don't find one, there are several listed that say, "Other 15-inch," "Other 16-inch," and so on. Find the size you have and select that type.

Next, click on Change Resolution to modify the resolution of your monitor. Here you need to be careful. You might have a video card that supports a higher resolution than the monitor. Remember that any system is only as strong as its weakest link. If you try to push the monitor beyond its limits, you could physically damage it. At best, you might end up with a crazy looking display. Therefore, select the resolution and scan rate that your monitor supports.

Think back to our discussion of video cards. Maybe your card supports a particular resolution "in principle." However, if you do not have enough RAM to support that resolution, then your video card really doesn't support it. Check the card documentation for how much memory is needed for each resolution. Higher resolution on monitors may require setting the monitor to interlaced on noninterlaced mode. Again, check the hardware documentation.

New to OpenServer is the idea of having multiple resolutions. Here you can assign the console multiscreen function keys to different resolutions. The ability to configure the function keys is also new to OpenServer. If you want to use the monitor and resolution you chose for each console multiscreen, select "Assign all function keys." The time you would want to select a different monitor and resolution is when you have a second video card and monitor that have a different resolution. If you are configuring multiple cards and monitors, I suggest that you group the function keys somehow. For example, you could assign F1–F6 to one video card and F7–F12 to the other one.

The Video Configuration Manager does not configure the kernel like other drivers, but instead gets its information from three ASCII files, stored in `/usr/lib/grafinfo`. The `graphinfo` files which contain the information for the graphicsi (video) cards, derives the configuration choices it provides from three sources: `grafinfo` (graphics card information) files, `moninfo` (monitor information) files, function key or device files. The `grafinfo` and `moninfo` files are ASCII text files that are located in subdirectories of the `/usr/lib/grafinfo` directory. These files describe the attributes of the graphics adapters and monitors that are supported by the Graphical Environment.

The `grafinfo` files use the name of the particular adapter they describe and an .xgi extension (for example, wonder.xgi). The `moninfo` files use the name of the particular monitor they describe and a .mon extension (for example, 8514.mon). The function key or device files are text files that are located in the `/usr/lib/vidconf/devices` directory. These files contain the device driver names for all the programmed function keys on the console (<F1> through <F12>) as well as the device driver name for the console. The console driver is used when the system is running in single-user mode.

New to OpenServer are `readme` files for many of the video drivers. In most cases, these can be displayed when running `mkdev graphics`.

## Pseudo-ttys

The scripts `mkdev ptty` and `mkdev streams` usually are associated with either TCP/IP or X Windows. Pseudo-ttys are virtual terminals that do not have any physical counterpart. For example, if you connect to a remote machine via `telnet`, the shell needs to write its output somewhere. That somewhere is the virtual or pseudo-terminal you are using. When installing TCP/IP you are asked how many pseudo-ttys you want installed. If you input a value that later turns out to be too small, you can use the `mkdev ptty` script to add more.

Streams are configured in the system by default when you add either TCP/IP or X Windows, and are a way to add modularity to drivers. Like `mkdev dos`, the `mkdev streams` script is like an on-off switch. Since streams are essential to X Windows and TCP/IP, removing them is not a good idea.

## Mice

Next, we get to `mkdev mouse`. There are several different kinds of mice as you might remember from our discussion on the `/dev` directory. Although not possible in a DOS or Windows environment, it is possible under SCO to have multiple mice configured on your system.

There are three kinds of mice: bus mice, serial mice, and keyboard mice. The most annoying to work with (at least in my mind and from an administrative point-of-view) are bus mice. These have their own cards that are plugged into slots in the machine. In order to configure them correctly, you have to ensure that the jumpers (or switches) match those that you tell the software. There is a problem just in the fact that they require these settings. Most of the ones I have seen do not allow you to set IRQs higher than 9. Since the interrupts below that are already in short supply, taking one away for a bus mouse is annoying. My solution is a serial mouse.

Now a serial mouse does have the disadvantage of taking away a serial port. If you attach a modem to the other serial port, both of them are gone. On the other hand, what else do you need the serial ports for? In order to connect to the system, serial mice will have either a DB9 or a DB25 connector. Some, like my Logitech Trackman have a DB9 on the end of the cable, but provide a DB9 to DB25 adapter.

Another nice thing about serial mice is that you don't have to connect them to a standard COM port. If you have a multiport board (intelligent or not), you can attach the mouse to any port on the multiport board. Be careful, however. You want to be sure that you attach the mouse to the non-modem control port (the lowercase letter, tty1a).

Keyboard mice are connected to a dedicated port at the back of your computer. They will usually have either 6-pin or 9-pin mini-DIN connectors. More and more computer vendors are selling their systems with keyboard mouse plugs built-in. Often, the plug for the console keyboard is the exact same size as the one for the mouse. Needless to say, I got enough calls from customers who were trying to install their OS. They couldn't even boot because of a keyboard error or something similar. (Now, ask yourself one question: "Is this *really* an operating system problem?")

If you think back to the section on starting and stopping the system, the hardware check comes before the system tries to boot. Therefore it hasn't even looked at the installation floppy, so there is nothing the OS could have done to cause the problem. However, the customer, not knowing the phone number for the hardware manufacturer found SCO's quick enough and called us.

Unlike the other mouse types, installing a keyboard mouse without one on your system can cause some problems. It has been known to happen that the keyboard will lock if there is no keyboard mouse port on the machine. If this happens you will need to boot off an old kernel and remove the keyboard mouse driver.

During the installation process of either type of mouse, you are asked the devices to which you want to associate the mouse with. You could associate a mouse on COM1 with /dev/tty01-/dev/tty05 and the mouse on COM2 with /dev/tty06-/dev/tty10. This might be useful if you had two video cards in your system that split the console tty devices between them. There is also an option within the mkdev script to change the association of the mouse. Therefore, you can add a video card later and change the device association.

Keep in mind that if you don't have the mouse configured correctly, you will run into trouble when starting X. Sometimes you just can't log in, so you have to switch screens to get a character login. However, I have seen cases where you cannot even switch multiscreen. Therefore you might want to test the mouse before you use it.

There is a relatively unknown program that not only allows you to test your mouse, but allows you to use it with such things as `sysadmsh` and even `vi`! To start it in `vi` mode, run the command like this:

```
usemouse -t vi -c vi <file_name>
```

I'd recommend choosing a file that already exists to see the behavior. You can also use the mouse with `sysadmsh`. This is one of the other modes that `usemouse` has. This is simply based on one of the configuration files in `/usr/lib/mouse`.

In `vi`, the mouse buttons should result in the follow actions:

- The left button moves the cursor to the beginning of the file.

- The middle button deletes the current character.

- The right button moves the cursor to the end of the file.

To simulate the middle button on a two button mouse, press both buttons at the same time. This is called "chording." You stop the `usemouse` utility simply by typing exit at the shell prompt. This is because `usemouse` starts a subshell when it is invoked.

If this does not produce the correct behavior, go through the normal "sanity checks" of ensuring the cabling is correct, jumper settings match (if applicable), and the card is seated correctly (if it's a bus mouse) and is recognized at boot if it is a bus mouse. Check the serial is recognized if a serial mouse and that the mouse is supported.

In the section on hardware, I mentioned that the resolution of the mouse will determine how much it moves across the screen in proportion to how much you move it across the mouse pad. If you have a keyboard mouse, the resolution can be changed by editing `/etc/conf/pack.d/kbmouse/space.c`. The `kbm_resolution` parameter determines how many "clicks" (or reports or counts) are passed to the mouse driver for every millimeter you move the mouse. The relationship between `kbm_resolution` and the clicks per millimeter for a *high-resolution* mouse are:

| Parameter | Clicks/mm |
|---|---|
| kbm_resolution=0 | 1 |
| kbm_resolution=1 | 3 (default) |
| kbm_resolution=2 | 6 |
| kbm_resolution=3 | 12 |

For a low resolution mouse, the relationship looks like this:

| Parameter | Clicks/mm |
|---|---|
| kbm_resolution=0 | 1 |
| kbm_resolution=1 | 2 |
| kbm_resolution=2 | 4 |
| kbm_resolution=3 | 8 (default) |

If you change this parameter, you must relink the kernel and reboot before the changes will take effect.

A common problem with mice is that they are sometimes slow or "sluggish." That is, they do no appear to move or react as quickly as they should. This can be changed by modifying the kbm_poll, also in /etc/conf/pack.d/kbmouse/space.c. This parameter determines how often the mouse driver will poll the mouse. The greater the value the more often it will poll. If you decrease the value below $0 \times b0$, the system might freeze. A good starting value is $0 \times 400$. Here again, you must relink and reboot for the changes to take place.

## Miscellaneous mkdev Scripts

If you have a Compaq machine, there is one script that would be of special use to you. The mkdev ida script allows you to add an Intelligent Drive Array. This give you the ability to talk to several physical hard disks as one large one.

If you have a Corollary system, the mkdev eccd script allows you to add the memory error checking and correction (ECC) facility. The daemon associated with this device regularly checks memory and is capable of detecting single-bit and double-bit errors. Single-bit errors can be corrected, whereas a double-bit error cause a panic. The ECC facility notifies the system of single-bit errors and decreases the likelihood that they grow into double-bit errors.

Two remaining scripts, mkdev vpixld and mkdev dda, are used if you have VP/ix on your system. If you don't know what VP/ix is don't worry, you don't want to. Since I am not going to be talking about VP/ix at all, we are going to have to leave these alone.

There are two scripts that are linked together: shl and layers. They add shell layers to you system. Shell layers allow you to interact with more than one shell session from a single terminal. This is comparable to repeatedly typing sh to get subshells. The key difference is that with subshells, you can move only in one direction. Once you start a subshell, you do not have ready access to the parent shells. With shell layers, you have access to `all` shells.

One of the simpler scripts is `mkdev dos`. This is really nothing more than an on-off switch. This script is used to either add DOS support or remove it. Once it's added and you reboot, you will be able to mount DOS filesystems and access them like any UNIX filesystem. You do *not* need to have Merge installed to take advantage of this functionality.

Another script that adds functionality without adding devices is `mkdev mmdf`. The `mkdev mmdf` script allows you to configure SCO UNIX's standard mail system MMDF. There are quite a few configuration aspects to cover, which we covered in detail in the section on MMDF.

# CHAPTER 14

# System Monitoring

**M**onitoring your system is more than just watching the amount of free hard disk space or the number of users running a certain application. Many aspects of your system are static over fairly long periods of time, such as the layout of your hard disk. However, such information is as important to really knowing your system as how much free memory there is at any given time.

Both ODT and OpenServer provide a wide range of tools to not only monitor your system as it is running, but to find out how it's configured. In this chapter, we are going to talk about the tools you need and the files you can look in to find out anything about your system that you need. In the next chapter, we are going to take some of these tools and see how they can be used to help us achieve the goal of administering our system.

## Finding out about Your System

One of the challenging aspects of tech support at SCO is OSD, or Operating System Direct. This is a direct line to a support engineer. As a support engineer, the challenge lies in the fact that before you talk to the customer, you have no way of knowing what the problem will be. It can be anything from simple questions that are easily answered by reading the manual to long, drawn-out system crashes.

Late one Monday afternoon I was working the OSD line. Since I was the one who had been idle the longest, my phone rang when the next customer came into the queue. The customer on the other end of the line explained that his computer would no longer boot. For some reason, the system rebooted itself and now it would not boot.

When I asked the customer how far it got and what, if any, error messages were on the screen, he replied, "`panic-srmountfun`." At that point I knew it was going to be a five minute call. A panic with the `srmountfun` message basically means your filesystem is trashed. In almost every case, there is no way to recover from this. On a few occasions, `fsck` can clean things up to be able to mount. Since the customer had already tried that, this was not one of those occasions.

We began discussing the options, which were very limited. He could reinstall the operating system and then the data, or he could send his hard disk to a data recovery service. Since this was a county government office, they had the work of dozens of people on the machine. They had backups from the night before, but all of that days work would be lost.

Since there was no one else waiting in the queue to talk to me I decided to poke around a little longer. Maybe the messages we saw might give an indication of a way to recover. We booted from the emergency boot/root set again and started to look around. The `fdisk` utility reported the partition table as being valid and `divvy` reported the division table as being valid. It looked as if just the inode table was trashed, which was enough.

I was about ready to give up when the customer mentioned that the `divvy` table didn't look right. There were three entries in the table that had starting and ending blocks. This didn't sound right because he only had one filesystem: root.

Since the data was probably already trashed, there was no harm in continuing, so we decided to name the filesystem and try running `fsck` on it. Amazingly enough, `fsck` ran though relatively quickly and reported just a few errors. We mounted the filesystem and holding our breath we did a listing of the directory. Lo and behold *there* was his data. All the files appeared to be intact. Since this was all in a directory named `/data`, he simply assumed that there was no `/u` filesystem, which there wasn't. However, there was a *second* filesystem.

I suggested backing up the data just to be safe. However, since it was an additional filesystem, a reinstallation of the OS could preserve it. Within a couple of hours, he could be up and running again. The lessons learned? Make sure you know the configuration of your system! If at all, possible keep data away from the root filesystem and backup as often as you can afford to. The lesson for me was to have the customer read each entry one-by-one.

Being able to manage and administer your system requires that you know something about how your system is defined and configured. What values have been established for various parameters? What is the base address of your SCSI host adapters? What is the maximum UID that you can have on a system? All of these are questions that will eventually crop up, if they haven't already.

The nice thing is that the system can answer these questions for you, if you know what to ask and where to ask it. In this section we are going to take a look at where the system keeps much of its important configuration information and what you can use to get at it.

As a user, much of the information that you can get will be only useful to satisfy your curiosity. Most of the files that I am going to talk about, you can normally read. However, there are a few of the utilities, such as `fdisk` and `divvy` that you won't be able to run. Therefore, what they have to say will be hidden from you.

If you are an administrator, there are probably many nooks and crannies of the system that you never looked in; many you probably never knew existed. After reading this section, you will hopefully gain some new insights into where information is stored. For the more advanced system administrator, this may only serve as a refresher. Who knows? Maybe the gurus out there will learn a thing or two.

### Hardware and the Kernel

The first place we're going to look is that place that causes the most problems and results in the largest number of calls to SCO Support: hardware.

For those of you who have watched the system boot, you may already be familiar with what SCO calls the "hardware" screen. This gives you a good overview as to what kind of hardware you have on your system and how it is configured. Since many hardware problems are the result of misconfigured hardware, knowing what the system thinks about your hardware configuration is very useful.

Fortunately, we don't need to boot every time we want access to this information. SCO Unix provides a utility called `hwconfig` that shows us our hardware configurations. (At least what the OS thinks is the HW configuration.) On my system, if I run `/etc/hwconfig -hc`, I get this:

```
device    address        vec  dma  comment
======    =======        ==   ===  =======
                         =
fpu       -              13   -    type=80387
serial    0x3f8-0x3ff    4    -    unit=0 type=Standard nports=1
serial    0x2f8-0x2ff    3    -    unit=1 type=Standard nports=1
floppy    0x3f2-0x3f7    6    2    unit=0 type=135ds18
floppy    -              -    -    unit=1 type=96ds15
console   -              -    -    unit=vga type=0 12 screens=68k
parallel  0x378-0x37a    7    -    unit=0
adapter   0x330-0x332    11   5    type=ad ha=0 id=7fts=s
tape      -              -    -    type=S ha=0 id=2 lun=0 ht=ad
disk      -              -    -    type=S ha=0 id=0 lun=0 ht=ad fts=s
Sdsk      -              -    -    cyls=1170 hds=64 secs=32
disk      -              -    -    type=S ha=0 id=6 lun=0 ht=ad fts=s
Sdsk      -              -    -    cyls=518 hds=64 secs=32
cd-rom    -              -    -    type=S ha=0 id=5 lun=0 ht=ad
No obvious conflicts in hardware settings
```

The -h option showed us the output in neat little columns, all will headings over each column (h for headings). Without this option, the same information is there, however, it is not as easy to read. The -c option checked for conflicts of I/O base address, IRQ, and DMA channel (c for conflicts). This will not only catch duplicates, but in the case of the I/O base address, it will tell you if anything is overlapping. For more details about this, check out the hwconfig (ADM) man-page.

From the output you know the base addresses of all devices that have them (the address column), their interrupts (the vec column), the DMA channel (the dma column), and often other pieces of information that can be very useful. For example, under the comment on the first line labeled "floppy", you might see it is unit=0 and the type=135ds18. If this is the way things should be, that's a happy thing.

However, this is not always the case. Customers repeatedly call to SCO Support during installation of the OS with "bad media." This is not because the floppy disk is bad, because the value here is not what the hardware really is. The values for the floppies are read from the CMOS. If they are incorrect, the operating system gets them incorrect. As a result, it may be trying to read a 3.5" floppy as if it were a 5.25". That won't work for long.

There is one "serial" entry for each COM port I have. In this case I have two, labeled unit=0 and unit=1. Each are of type standard (nothing special about them) and each only has one port. If you had a nonintelligent serial board with more than one port, nports= would show you how many ports you have.

One think to keep in mind here is serial mice. I have one on my system, but you couldn't tell that from the output here. At this point, the system has no way to know that a mouse is attached to the serial port.

The "console" entry is referring to both your video card and the way your console is configured. Here we see that I have a VGA card, which is standard (type=0). There are twelve multiscreens set up, with 68k of memory reserved for those screens. From the system's standpoint here, it doesn't matter that I actually have an SVGA as they both use the same driver.

If you have SCSI devices on your system, you will see something like this for your host adapter:

```
adapter    0x330-0x332  11   5   type=ad ha=0 id=7 fts=s
```

In the comments column, the type tells me that it is using the ad device driver, so I know that I have an Adaptec 154x or 174x in standard mode. (This is the same as the corresponding entry in /etc/default/scsihas.) The entries ha=0 id=7 tells me that this is the first (0th) host adapter and it is at ID 7. The entry fts= can mean several things, depending on what's there. The entry `fts=s`, says that I have scatter/gather enabled. Other possible entries are

```
s = scatter/gather
t = tagged commands
d = 32-bit commands
b = commands are buffered
```

The two `disk` entries are for hard disks. Here we see `type=S`, so we know that both of my disks are SCSI. If I had an IDE or ESDI hard disk drive, this would say `type=W`. Since this is SCSI, we also need to know what host adapter the device is attached to (`ha=0`, `ht=ad` ), its ID and LUN (`id=0`, `lun=0`), plus similar characteristics of the host adapter (`fts=s`).

If this were an IDE or ESDI hard disk drive, instead of the SCSI configuration we would have a description of the drive geometry here. In order to be able to show both the SCSI configuration and hard disk geometry, there is an additional entry (`Sdsk`) for each disk. This is where the geometry of each drive is listed. This shows us cylinders, heads, and sectors per track for each drive.

One question that is useful in debugging hardware problems is to know just where the system gets this hardware information. Each of these lines is printed by the device driver. These are the configuration parameters that the drivers have been given. (For those of you who are curious, it is the `printcfg()` routine that is displaying this information. If that means anything to you.)

If you remember from our discussion of the link kit, we know that the kernel is composed of a lot of different files that reside somewhere under `/etc/conf`. It is here where we have stored the configuration information that gets handed off to drivers during a kernel relink.

For our purposes, we only need to be concerned about three subdirectories under `/etc/conf`: `pack.d`, `sdevice.d`, and `cf.d`. Since we went into detail about these in the section on the link kit, I will only review them briefly.

The first directory I want to talk about, `/etc/conf/cf.d`, is the central configuration directory. Here you can find default configuration information, which drivers are being linked into the kernel, the current value of kernel tunable parameters, and so on.

When the system is installed, the defaults for the parameters that the kernel needs are kept in the file `/etc/conf/cf.d/mtune`. As I mentioned before, this is the master tuning file. It is a simple text file, consisting of four columns. The first is the parameter name, followed by the default value, the minimum, and lastly the maximum. Any value that has not changed is set to the default here (the second column).

If any kernel parameters have a value other than a default, the parameter name is placed in `stune` along with the new value. This is the system tuning file. Although changes can be made to `stune` by hand, it is "safest" to use the configuration tool provided with the OS you have. If you have ODT 3.0, then this tool is `sysadmsh`, if you have OpenServer this is the Kernel/Hardware Manager. Both start up the utility `/etc/conf/cf.d/configure`, which you could start yourself, if you wanted.

When the kernel is rebuilt, each parameter is first assigned the value defined in `mtune` and then any value in `stune` overwrites that default. If you want to figure out what each of these parameters mean, take a look at the Chapter entitled "Kernel Parameter Reference" in the *System Administrator's Guide* if you have ODT 3.0 and Appendix B ("Configuring Kernel Parameters") of the *Performance Guide,* if you have OpenServer.

Also in `/etc/conf/cf.d` is the master device configuration file: `mdevice`. As we know, this tells us all the devices that *can* be configured on the system, as well as specific characteristics about that device. This, however, does not tell us what devices are currently configured, just what devices `could` be configured.

The `mdevice` file provides a couple of pieces of information that may come in handy. One of them is the device major number. The block major number is column 5 and the character major is column 6. This is useful when trying to determine what device nodes are associated with what device driver. If the name of the device node is chosen well, then it is easy to figure out what kind of device it is. Otherwise, you have to guess.

For example, it's fairly obvious that the device `/dev/tty1a` has something to do with a `tty` device. What about `/dev/ptmx`? Well, it has a major number of 40. Looking in `mdevice`, I see that this is the clone device driver. Therefore, I know it has something to do with streams (see the discussion of the `/dev` directory). The `mdevice` file also contains the DMA channel the device uses (column 9), which is useful to know when trying to track down hardware conflicts.

What devices are actually configured can be found in the `/etc/conf/cf.d/sdevice` file. This file is generated during the kernel relink by concatenating all the files in `/etc/conf/sdevice.d`. The first column of each entry in `sdevice` matches the first column in `mdevice` We can then make the connection, if we need to, from the device node to the corresponding entry in `sdevice` (major number → `mdevice` → `sdevice`).

As we mentioned in the section on the link kit, we know that the `sdevice.d` files contain (among other things) the IRQ and base address. This is useful when hardware problems arise. We also find in these files a very useful piece of information: whether the device driver will be included at all. If there is a 'Y' in the second column, then this driver will be included. If there is an 'N', this device will be left out.

Although it is not a common occurrence, it has happened that a device could no longer be accessed after a kernel relink. The reason being that there was an 'N' in the second column. More often than not, this is the result of an overzealous system administrator who wants to reduce the size of his kernel by pulling out "unnecessary" drivers. However, on occasion I have seen a third party device driver remove scripts and forget to put things back the way they were.

In this `/etc/conf/cf.d` is also the SCSI configuration file, `mscsi`. This tells us what SCSI devices the administrator wants to configure on the system. This is a place where errors regularly occur. What can often occur is an administrator will be unsure of his SCSI configuration and will try several different ones until he gets it right.

This "shotgun" method of system administration rarely works. You may get the device working, but you can forget adding anything else in the future. This is especially true for SCSI hard disk. Only those devices that are actually configured on the system should be in `mscsi`.

Let's think back to the hardware screen. If you have SCSI devices on your system, they will be listed here and may be configured exactly as you see it on the screen. Just like other kinds of devices, SCSI devices may be configured incorrectly and still show up during boot.

However, you may have installed an SCSI device that does not appear in the hardware screen or there may be one there that you didn't configure. The place to look is the `mscsi` file. If the device is there, then the odds are either that the entry was input incorrectly, or it was not configured the way you expected. More information can be found in the `mscsi (F)` man-page.

A thing to note is that some SCSI devices (like hard disks) do not show up until after they have been accessed the first time; usually when the filesystems on them are mounted. Therefore, if you have mutliple hard disks, the second and subsequent ones will not show up until the filesystems are mounted. This is usually when you go into multi-user mode. In addition, until you go into multi-user mode, the output of `hwconfig` may be invalid. Therefore, you might not see every device at boot.

The reason for this is that the `printcfg()` routine may not get called during system boot-up. The device driver may not do anything special in the initialization routine (where `printcfg()` is normally called) so it simply prints the configuration string. On the other hand, it may wait to call `printcfg()` until the device is first accessed, as in the case of hard disks.

We next jump to another directory at the same level as `cf.d`: `/etc/conf/pack.d`. We know that the `pack.d` directory contains a subdirectory for each device that can be configured essentially matching what is in `mdevice`. In the subdirectory is the device driver itself (`Driver.o`) as well as a configuration file, `space.c`. (Some directories contain files called `stubs.c`. These only contain things like function declarations, but no configuration information.)

The `space.c` files can contain a wealth of information about the way your hardware is configured. Much of the information requires knowledge of how the specific driver functions. However, skimming through these files can give you some interesting insights into what your system can do.

As a warning, don't go playing with the values in these files unless you know what you're doing. You have the potential to really mess things up.

Despite the fact that they're object code, which makes reading them difficult, the `Driver.o` files often provide some useful information. Let's assume that your system is panicking and you cannot figure out what's causing it. By running `crash` on the dump image and entering the command `panic`, you will get a stack trace that tells you the function the kernel was in when it panicked. If the function is not obvious from the name, you can use either the `strings` or `nm` command to search through the `Driver.o` files to find that function. If the panic is always in the same function, this usually indicates a problem with the hardware or something else related to the driver. (We'll talk more about this technique later in the section on problem solving.)

Another directory at the same level as `pack.d` and `sdevice.d` is `init.d`. The files in this directory are concatenated onto the end of the file `/etc/conf/cf.d/init.base` to form your `/etc/inittab` file. This serves a couple of functions. First, many of the processes that are started as the system boots up are started out of `/etc/inittab`. These you find in `init.base`. Second, this is where the initial terminal configuration information is kept. For the console terminal devices this is also found in `init.base`. However, for terminals on the COM port or multiport boards the configuration information is found in the files in `/etc/conf/init.d`. See the chapter on starting and stopping your system for more details.

On a default system, you should have at least the file `/etc/conf/init.d/sio`. This contains the default configuration for the standard serial ports (`tty1a` and `tty2a`). When intelligent multiport boards are added, there will probably be an extra file in this directory. If you are running OpenServer, then you will also find the file `scohttp`, which controls the SCO httpd daemon, `/etc/scohttpd`.

### Terminals

Since we were just talking about terminals, let's take a look at some other information that relates to terminals.

I mentioned that the `init.base` file and the files in `/etc/conf/init.d` established the default configuration for terminals. To a great extent this is true, however, there is a little something extra that needs to be addressed. Whereas the `/etc/conf/cf.d/init.base` and `/etc/conf/init.d/*` files tell us about the default configuration (such as what process should be started on the port and at what run levels), it is the `/etc/gettydefs` file that tells the default behavior of the terminals. (Rather then mentioning both the `/etc/conf/cf.d/init.base` and `/etc/conf/init.d/*` files, I'll just talk about `/etc/inittab`, which is functionally the same thing.)

Each line in `/etc/inittab` that refers to a terminal device, points to an entry in the `/etc/gettydefs` file. The entry for `/dev/tty1a` might look like this:

```
Se1a:234:respawn:/etc/getty tty1a m
```

From our discussion of the `/etc/inittab` file in the chapter on starting and stopping the system, we see that this entry starts the `/etc/getty` command. Two arguments are passed to `getty`: the terminal it should run on (`tty1a`) and the `gettydefs` entry that should be used (`m`). The `/etc/gettydefs` file defines such characteristics as the default speed, parity, and the number of data bits. For example, the `m` entry which the `inittab` entry above points to, might look like this:

```
m # B9600 HUPCL # B9600 CS8 SANE HUPCL TAB3 ECHOE IXANY #\r\nlogin: # m
```

The fields are

```
label # initial_flags # final_flags #login_prompt # next_label
```

The `label` entry is what is being pointed to in the `inittab` file. The `initial_flags` are the default serial line characteristics that are set, unless a terminal type is passed to `getty`. Normally, the only characteristic that needs to be passed is the speed, however, we also set HUPCL (hang up on last close).

The `final_flags` are set just prior to `getty` executing `login`. Here again, we set the speed and HUPCL. However, we also set the terminal to SANE, which is actually several characteristics. (Look at the `gettydefs`(F) man-page for more details.) We also set TAB3, which turns tabs into spaces, ECHOE which echoes the erase character as a backspace-space-backspace combination, and lastly IXANY which allows any character to restart output if stopped by the XOFF character.

In many cases after you log in, you are prompted to input the type of terminal you are working on. This appears like this:

```
TERM = (ansi)
```

This prompt is a result of two things. First, the system checks the file `/etc/ttytype`. This file consists of two columns. The first is the terminal type, followed by the tty name (e.g., `tty02`, `tty1a`). If your tty device is listed here, then the system knows (or thinks) that you are logging in using a specific terminal type *on that port*. This is port dependent and not user dependent.

If your terminal is not listed here, then you are prompted to input it. This is the result of the `tset` line in either your `.profile` or `.login`. Check out the `tset(C)` man-page for more details.

This is a useful mechanism if you have a lot of serial terminals that are always connected to the same port (say, on a multiport board). That way the users don't have to be bothered with typing in their terminal type. In addition, you as the system administrator don't have to worry about users calling up saying their terminal doesn't work when they input the wrong terminal type.

### Hard Disks and Filesystems

A common problem that causes longer calls to support is the layout of the hard disk. Many administrators are not even aware of the number of partitions and filesystems they have. This is not always their fault, as they often inherit the system without any information on how it's configured.

The first aspect of configuration is the geometry. This is such information as the cylinders, heads, and sectors per track. In most cases, the geometry of the hard disk is reported to you on the hardware screen when the system boots. You can also run the `dkinit` program by hand.

To find how your hard disk (or hard disks) is laid out, there are several useful programs. The first is `fdisk`, which is normally used to partition the disk. Using the -p option, you can get `fdisk` to just print out the partition table. This tells you which partitions are on the disk, their starting and ending tracks, the type of partition, and which one is active. The output is not necessarily intuitive, so let's take a quick look at it. On my system, I get output like this:

```
1 9600 41535 31936 UNIX Active
2 1 9599 9599 DOS (32) Inactive
3 41536 74815 33280 UNIX Inactive
```

Each line represents a single partition. The fields are

```
partition_no. start_track end_track size type status
```

Here we have three partitions with the first UNIX partition being active. Note that although the DOS partition is physically the first partition, it shows up as the second partition in the `fdisk` table. In addition, it accurately recognized the fact that it is a 32-bit DOS partition.

If we look carefully and compare the ending blocks with the starting blocks of the next physical partition, we see that, in this case, there are no gaps. Small gaps (just a few tracks) are nothing to have a heart attack over as you are only losing a couple of kilobytes. However, larger gaps indicate that the whole hard disk was not partitioned and you are losing space.

If you have multiple hard disks on your system, `hwconfig` may show you this. What happens if it doesn't? Maybe it's a SCSI hard disk that's never mounted, so it doesn't print out the configuration information. How can you figure out if you have more than one hard disk? You could take a look in `/dev` for any `hd` device. If you look back on the section on major and minor numbers, you can figure out what hard disks have devices assigned. However, it's possible that the hard disk existed at one time, but doesn't anymore. Maybe the previous administrator liked the "shotgun" approach to system administration and tried to configure every possible combination. The device nodes might be there, but without a physical device associated with them. Therefore, you need a way to figure exactly what devices are physically on the system.

No worries! The `fdisk` utility will tell you. If you try to print out the partition table for all the possible hard disks, the worst that can happen is that you will get an error message saying it can't open the device. To do this, run these four commands:

```
fdisk -p -f /dev/rhd00
fdisk -p -f /dev/rhd10
fdisk -p -f /dev/rhd20
fdisk -p -f /dev/rhd30
```

Once you get a response that `fdisk` can't open a device, then you know you've probably found your last hard disk. If you actually do have more than four hard disks, you need to try the same `fdisk` command on the other hard disk devices. If you never do get the message that it cannot open the device, then there are probably physical devices associated with every device node.

To find out what filesystems or divisions are on your disks, you can use the `mount` command. However, this only tells you which ones are currently mounted. This is useful on a running system to determine if a directory is part of one filesystem or another. Although the `df` command (more on that later) will tell you what filesystems are mounted, it doesn't tell you what options were used, such as whether the filesystem is read-only or not. On a few occasions I have had customers call in reporting filesystem problems because they could write to them, only to find out they were mounted as read-only.

What if you suspect there are more filesystems then are mounted? Unfortunately, finding out what filesystems are on your system is not as easy as figuring out what partitions are there. When you run `mkdev fs` or the Filesystem Manager on OpenServer, an entry for each filesystem is placed in `/etc/default/filesys`. If you find more here than you see with `mount`, then they are either not getting mounted properly or the entry is missing the options necessary to mount them automatically. Check the `filesys(F)` man-page for more details.

Sometimes there are filesystems on your disk, without an entry in `/etc/default/filesys`. This happens often when people are not paying attention during the install and specify a `/u` filesystem. When they don't run `mkdev fs` they find half of their disk missing, and they end up calling SCO Support. Fortunately, SCO recognized the problems that this caused and it no longer occurs in OpenServer. Instead you are prompted to add the filesystem.

The easiest ones to find are those that you see simply by running `divvy -P`. This defaults to the partition with your root filesystem on it. For example, if I run it on my system I get

```
0           0              14999
1           15000          39999
2           40000          429941
3           429942         469941
4           469942         509941
6           509942         509951
7           0              510975
```

Each line represents a single division, with the fields in each entry being the division number, the starting block, and the ending block. Note that the block sizes in `divvy` are 1K and not 512 bytes like other utilities. From this output, I see I have five divisions (0–4), plus recover (6), and the whole disk (7). (Think back to our discussion of filesystems.) Since this is the root partition, I know that one of these is probably the swap space. (I know it is division 1.)

If I looked in `/etc/default/filesys` and saw fewer entries than I saw here (taking in swap, recover, and the whole disk), then I would know something is not as it appears. One shortcoming is that this output does not give me the names of divisions. This is because the `-P` option is just reading the entries in the division table and displaying them.

So, where are the names coming from? From the device nodes. When `divvy` is run interactively, you see a table similar to the above output, but with the name of the device included. `divvy` finds that first block device (alphabetically) in `/dev` that has the correct major and minor number. If I created a new block device node with a major number of 1 and a minor number of 41, instead of seeing `swap` as the name of the division, I would see `jim`. This is because `/dev/jim` shows up alphabetically before `/dev/swap`.

We can also pass a device node as an argument to `divvy`. If this is the name of a filesystem, `divvy` will figure out what partition it is on and display the appropriate division table. For example, `divvy -P /dev/root` would give me the exact same output as above.

If we wanted, we could also specify the character device for that partition. If I ran `divvy -P /dev/rhd01`, the output would again be the same. To get all the divisions, you will need to run `divvy` for *all* of the Unix partitions that you found with `fdisk`. We could run `divvy` on all the filesystem names. This would show us all the divisions including any that were not yet given names. However, this won't help us on disks where a filesystem spans an entire partition. The nice thing is that the output of `fdisk` will help us.

We can see from the example above for `fdisk` that to go through the hard disks, we increase the first number in the device name by one. To go through the partitions, we increase the second number by one. However, we don't have to go though each possible partition number to get the results we want. The output of `fdisk` gave us the partition numbers already.

Let's examine the above `fdisk` output:

```
1 9600 41535 31936 UNIX Active
2 1 9599 9599 DOS (32) Inactive
3 41536 74815 33280 UNIX Inactive
```

From this output, I know to run `divvy` on `/dev/hd01`, `/dev/hd02`, and `/dev/hd03`. If this were the second hard disk, I would change the devices accordingly. For example, the `divvy` command to show the first partition would be

```
divvy -P /dev/rhd11
```

You could write a quick shell script that explicitly runs through each value. However, I feel that checking everything yourself gives you a better understanding of how your system in configured. Keep in mind that a division with no filesystem on it may not be wrong. There are applications (such as some databases) that require either a raw partition (no divisions) or a raw division (no filesystem).

### System Defaults

A lot of default information can be found in the `/etc/default` directory. This directory contains a wealth of information about the default state of your system. I guess that's why the directory is called `/etc/default`, huh? If you have just upgraded to OpenServer or are otherwise familiar with ODT 3.0, then I highly recommend looking at this directory right now. You heard me, take a look. There are quite a few changes between the two releases. Because of the significance of this directory, knowing about the differences is an important part of administering your system.

The most obvious change is that virtually all of the files are symbolic links to the "real" files living in `/var/opt/K/SCO/Unix/5.0.0Cd/etc/default`. You will find that there are new files that didn't exist in previous releases as well as files that are no longer used. Note that `5.0.0Cd` is the release number and may, therefore, be different.

Most of the files have man-pages associated with them or are related to programs that have them. For more details, take a look at the `default(F)` man-page. It has a list of other man-pages related to these files.

Going through each file and discussing each entry would not be an effective use of our time. Each of the files either has a man-page specifically for it, or there is a program associated with the file that has a man-page. Instead, I am going to talk about some of the changes as well as address some of the more significant files.

Have you ever wondered why when you simply press Enter at the `Boot:` prompt you get `hd(40)unix`? If so, check out the variable `DEFBOOTSTR` in `/etc/default/boot`. The `/boot` program reads the `DEFBOOTSTR` (default boot string) variable from `/etc/default/boot` and when you press Enter without any other input, the default boot string is echoed. It is the `DEFBOOTSTR` variable that defines the default boot behavior, hence the name. (See the section on starting the system for more details.)

If we wanted, we could change the default boot string to something else. In fact, that's what I did on my system. Instead of `hd(40)unix`, in my `/etc/default/boot` file it looks like this:

`DEFBOOTSTR=hd(40)dos`

Therefore, any time I get to the `Boot:` prompt and simply press `Enter`, I am brought into DOS. The reason I did that was for my son. Since I have loads of educational programs for him on my DOS partition, I wanted a way for him to get to DOS easily. All he needs to do is press Enter at the right place and he gets to where he needs to be. Now he's a little older and understands that DOS is different than UNIX and could type in DOS himself. I leave it in for historical reasons.

So, how do I get to UNIX? Well, one way would be to type in the old `DEFBOOTSTR` by hand ( `hd(40)unix` ). Rather than doing that, I use a trick called *boot aliasing*. We talked about this in some detail in the section on starting and stopping the system.

In the `/etc/default/boot` file you will also find out whether the system automatically boots (AUTOBOOT) or not. If there is no TIMEOUT value, the system automatically boots after sixty seconds. Otherwise, the system boots after the number of seconds defined in the TIMEOUT variable. Sometimes the overzealous administrator will want to set TIMEOUT to 0, so the system autoboots immediately after reaching the `Boot:` prompt. This is *not* a good thing. You want to give yourself at least a couple of seconds, in case you are having problems and need to boot into maintenance mode; otherwise you will automatically go into multi-user mode.

One change to this file in OpenServer is the addition of the `BOOTMNT` variable. This determines how to mount the `/dev/boot` filesystem. If set to read-only(RO), then you can't simply copy files onto this filesystem. However, certain system utilities need to be able to write to this filesystem no matter what.

The `/etc/default/passwd` file contains the default settings for using passwords. This include such things as the minimum allowable length of the password, how often you can change it, and how complex the password has to be. Many of the values are dependent on what level of security you have. Therefore, in order to maintain consistency, I wouldn't recommend making changes unless you change the security level to match.

If you have ODT 3.0, then use the file `/etc/default/authsh` to determine basic aspects of the user's environment, such as their home directory, shell, group, and so on. If you are running OpenServer, this file still exists, but the file `/etc/default/accounts` is used instead. Although the format of the new file is easier to read, the old name has significance since it is the `/tcb/bin/authsh` utility that actually does the work when a user account is created.

### Permissions Files

Another subdirectory of `/etc`, `/etc/perms`, contains more useful information about your system. The files within the `/etc/perms` directory are related to what products and packages are installed on your system. This is useful for finding out where a particular file is without having to do a search of your entire system. For this, input:

```
grep <file_name> /etc/perms/* | more
```

where `<file_name>` is whatever I am looking for. After using this several times, I put it into a shell script. If you are running OpenServer, then the `/etc/perms/*` may exist, but their content is not the same. Basically, OpenServer no longer uses the files in `/etc/perms`, but they are kept for backwards compatibility; therefore this command may not work.

Although the contents of the files do not directly tell you what is currently installed, you can find out what programs are/should be available, plus what their permissions, owner, and group ought to be. (NOTE: You don't need to correct permission's problems by hand. You can use the `fixperm` or `fixmog` utilities.)

Although not quite as verbose or easy to read, OpenServer does have file lists, similar to those in `/etc/perms/`. These are the file lists located within the SSO. You find these in several locations throughout the system. Normally these will be in a subdirectory called .softmgmt under the `/var/opt` directory. For example, the file lists for the operating system portion of OpenServer are found in `/var/opt/K/SCO/Unix/5.0.0Cd/.softmgmt`, whereas those for TCP are found in `/var/opt/K/SCO/tcp/2.0.0Cd/.softmgmt`. The nice thing about ODT was that all this information was concentrated in about a dozen files. OpenServer has it spread over a couple of hundred!

You can use the `swconfig` program to list products as well as packages that are currently installed. In most cases, custom will also tell you if a particular package is partially installed or not at all, as well as indicate programs that have been re-moved. This is usually the case with bundled products such as ODT or the ODT Development System. If you have ODT 3.0 and are curious about what has been installed on your system, check out the file `/usr/lib/custom/history`. Unfortu-nately, this no longer exists in OpenServer. The closest is `/var/opt/K/SCO/Unix/5.0.0Cd/custom/custom.log`, but this is rather difficult to read.

On both ODT 3.0 and OpenServer you'll find the file `/etc/auth/system/files`. This contains a list of files and permissions from the perspective of the TCB and not necessarily related to what is installed. In many cases, individual files are not mentioned as it is expected that every file in a specific directory has the same permissions. Some files may not appear here.

You can enter a one-liner like the one above to look through the OpenServer con-figuration files:

```
egrep <file_name> {,/var}/opt/K/SCO/*/*/.softmgmt/*.fl
```

Using `egrep` is necessary here because of the syntax we are using to look through both the `/opt` and the `/var/opt` directories.

### User Files

The `/etc` directory contains the all-important `passwd` file. This gives important information about what users are configured on the system, what their user ID number is, what their default group is, where their home directory is, and even what shell they use by default.

The default group is actually a group ID number rather than a name. However, it's easy to match up the group ID with the group name by looking at

/etc/group. This also gives you a list of users, broken down into what groups they belong to. Note that "groups" is plural.

Another aspect of information about users is what privileges they have on the system. As we talked about in the section on security, what users have a particular privilege can be found in the files in /etc/auth/subsystem. These are referred to the subsystem authorizations. Privileges listed on a per user basis are found in /tcb/files/auth/?, where ? is the first letter of the user's account name, such as r for root or u for uucp. The default values for these files are kept in /etc/auth/system/default.

### Network Files

If you are running TCP/IP, there are a couple of places to look for information about your system. First, check out the file /etc/resolv.conf. If you don't find it and you know you are running TCP/IP, don't worry! The fact that it is missing, tells you that you are not running a nameserver in your network. (A nameserver is a machine that contains data on how to communicate with other machines in a network.) If it is not there, you can find a list of machines that your machine knows about and can contact by name, look at /etc/hosts. If you are running a nameserver, this information is kept on the nameserver itself.

The content of the /etc/hosts file is the IP address of a system followed by its fully qualified name and then any aliases you might want to use. A common alias is simply to use the node name, leaving off the domain name. Each line in the /etc/resolv.conf file contains one of a couple different types of entries. The two most common are the domain entry, which is set to the local domain name, and the nameserver, which is followed by the IP address of the name "resolver". See the section on TCP/IP for more information on both of these files.

It's possible that your machine is the nameserver itself. To find this out look at the file /etc/named.boot. If this exists, then you are probably a nameserver. The /etc/named.boot file will tell you the directory where the nameserver database information is kept. For information about the meaning of these entries, check out the named(ADMN) man-page as well as the section on TCP/IP.

Another place to look is the TCP startup script in /etc/rc2.d. Often static routes are added there. If these static routes use tokens from either /etc/networks or /etc/gateways that are incorrect, then the routes will be incorrect. By using the -f option to the route command you can flush all of the entries and start over.

Although not as often corrupted or otherwise goofed up, there are a couple of other files that require a quick peek. If you think back to our telephone switchboard analogy for TCP, we can think of the /etc/services file as the phonebook that the operator uses to match up names to phone numbers. Rather than names and phone numbers, /etc/services matches up the service requested to the appropriate port. To determine the characteristics of the connection, inetd uses /etc/inetd.conf. This contains such information as whether to wait for the first process to be finished before allowing new connections.

A common place for confusion, incorrect entries, and the inevitable calls to Support deals with user equivalence. As we talked about in the section on TCP/IP, when user equivalence is set up between machines many remote commands can be executed without the user having to produce a password. One of the more common misconceptions is the universality of the /etc/hosts.equiv file. While this file determines with what other machine user equivalence should be established, the one user it does not apply to is root. To me this makes sense. While is does cause administrators who are not aware of this to be annoyed, it is nothing compared to the problems if it was to allow root and this is not what you expected.

In order to allow root access, you need to create a .rhosts file in roots home directory (usually /) containing the same information as /etc/hosts.equiv, but only applying to the root account. The most common mistake made with this file is with the permission. If the permission is such that any other user other than root (as the owner of the file) can read it, the user equivalence mechanism will fail. Looking in /etc/hosts.equiv and $HOME/.rhosts tells you want remote users have access to what user accounts.

In the section on networking, I introduced the concepts of a "chain." This is the link between network interface and the various network protocols. Which links are configured is kept in /usr/lib/lli/chains. This is simply a list of the various chains, with the upper layer on the left side and the lower layer on the right side.

If you are running NFS, there are two places to check for NFS mounted filesystems. To check for remote filesystems take a look at /etc/default/filesys. This is default location to list all mounted filesystems, not just local ones. If you are the one exporting filesystems or directories, the place to look is /etc/exports.

### Other Files

Next we get to a very foreboding and seldom frequented portion of your system: /usr/include. If you are a programmer, you know what's in here. If not, you probably thought that this directory was only for programmers. Well, sort of.

There are really only three times when you need to be concerned with this directory: first, if you *are* a programmer; second, if you're relinking the kernel. Do you remember all the `space.c` files in `/etc/conf/pack.d`? Well, they all refer to include files somewhere in `/usr/include`.

The parent directory, `/usr/include`, basically contains the include files that are consistent across Unix dialects. There are some useful things in here, such as the maximum value that an unsigned integer can take on. This is 4294967295 and you can find it in `/usr/include/limits.h`. There are some less useful things such as pi divided by 4 out to 20 decimal places. This is defined in the `/usr/include/math.h` as 0.78539816339744830962.

The third reason to be concerned is if you are just curious about your system. Even if you have just a basic knowledge of C, poking around in these files can reveal some interesting things about your system.

## What the System is Doing Now

At any given moment, there could be dozens, if not hundreds, of different things happening on your system. Each requires system resources, which may not be sufficient for every system to have an equal share. As a result, resources must be shared. As different processes interact and go about their business, which resource a process has and the amount of that resource that it is allocated will vary. As a result, performance of different processes will vary as well. Sometimes, the overall performance reaches a point that becomes unsatisfactory.

Users may experience slow response times and so decide to buy a faster CPU. I have seen many instances where this was the case, and afterwards the poor administrator is once again under pressure because the situation hasn't changed. Users still have slow response times. Sometimes the users tell the administrator to increase the speed on their terminal. Obviously 9600 isn't fast enough when they are doing large queries in the database, so a faster terminal will speed up the query, right?

Unfortunately, things are not that simple. Perhaps you, as the system administrator, understand that increasing the baud rate on the terminal or the CPU speed won't do much to speed up large database queries, but you have a hard time convincing users of that. On the other hand, you might be like many administrators who are "unlucky" enough to have worked with a computer before, so you are thrown into the position, as often is the case. What many of us take as "common knowledge," you have never experienced before.

The simplest solution is to hire a consultant who is familiar with your situation (hardware, software, usage) to evaluate your system and make changes. However, computer consultants are like lawyers. They may charge enormous fees, talk in unfamiliar terms, and in the end you still haven't gained anything.

Now, not all computer consultants or lawyers are like that. It's simply a matter of not understanding what they are telling you. If you do not require that they speak in terms that you understand, you can end up getting taken to the cleaners.

If you feel you need a consultant, then do two things. Like any other product, you need to shop around. Keep in mind that the best one to get is not necessarily the cheapest, just as the best one is not necessarily the most expensive. The second key aspect is to know enough about your system to understand what the consultant is saying—at least, conceptually.

In this section, we are going to combine many of the topics and issues we discussed previously to find out exactly what our system is doing at this moment. By knowing what the system is doing, you are in a better position to judge if it is doing what you expect, plus you can make decisions as to what could/should be changed. This also has a side benefit of helping you should you need to call a consultant.

So, where do we start? Well, rather than defining a particular scenario and saying what we should do if this happened, let's talk about the programs and utilities in terms of what they tell us. Many useful programs are listed in Table 14–1.

### Users

It's often useful to know just how many users are logged onto your system. As I mentioned before, each process requires resources to run. The more users logged on to your system, the more processes are using your resources. In many cases, just seeing how many users are logged in rings bells and turns on lights in your head to say that something is not right.

The easy way to figure out how many users are logged in is with the who command. Without any options who simply gives you a list of what users are logged in, plus the terminal they are logged into and the time they logged in. If you use the -q option (for quick), you get just a list of who is logged on, plus the user count. For example:

```
root    root    root    jimmo
# users=4
```

For every user logged in, there is at least one process. If the user first gets to a shell and starts their application that way, they probably have two processes. If you are running OpenServer, each time a user logs in, the login process is still there, so you need to add any extra processes for this. This brings up the total number of processes to three times the number of users. Granted the shell is sleeping, waiting for the application to finish. The log in process is sleeping since

*(text continues on page 659)*

**Table 14–1**    Configuration Files and Where to Find More Information

| File | Purpose | Where to Find More Information |
| --- | --- | --- |
| **User and Security Files** | | |
| /etc/auth/subsystems | Manipulation routines for subsystem database | subsystems(S) |
| /etc/auth/system/authorize | Subsystem authorization file | authorize(F) |
| /etc/auth/system/default | System default database file | default(F) |
| /etc/auth/system/devassign | Device assignment database file | devassign(F) |
| /etc/auth/system/files | File control database | files(F) |
| /etc/auth/system/ttys | Terminal control database file | ttys(F) |
| /etc/group | User group information | group(F), chmod(C) |
| /etc/passwd | User account information | password(F), chmod(C) |
| **Kernel Files** | | |
| /etc/conf/cf.d/init.base | Base for /etc/inittab | inittab(F) |
| /etc/conf/cf.d/mdevice | Device driver module description file | mdevice(F) |
| /etc/conf/cf.d/mevent | Master event file | event(FP) |
| /etc/conf/cf.d/mfsys | Configuration file for filesystem types | mfsys(FP) |
| /etc/conf/cf.d/mscsi | SCSI peripheral device configuration file | mscsi(F) |
| /etc/conf/cf.d/mtune | Master kernel tunable parameter file | mtune(F) |
| /etc/conf/cf.d/sdevice | Local device configuration file | sdevice(F) |
| /etc/conf/cf.d/sevent | System event file | event(FP) |
| /etc/conf/cf.d/sfsys | Local filesystem type file | sfsys(FP) |
| /etc/conf/cf.d/stune | Local tunable parameter file | stune(F) |
| /etc/conf/mfsys.d | Master filesystem configuration file | mfsys(FP) |
| /etc/conf/node.d | Device node configuration files | idmknod(ADM) |
| /etc/conf/pack.d | Device drivers and configuration files | mdevice(F), sdevice(F) |
| /etc/conf/sdevice.d | Device configuration files | mdevice(F), sdevice(F) |
| /etc/conf/sfsys.d | Local filesystem configuration files | sfsys(FP) |
| **Networking Files** | | |
| /etc/auto.master | Default master automount file | automount(NADM) |
| /etc/bootptab | Internet Bootstrap Protocol server database | bootptab(SFF) |
| /etc/exports | Directories to export to NFS clients | exports(NF) |
| /etc/gateways | List of gateways | routed(ADM) |
| /etc/hosts | Hostname to IP address mapping file | hosts(SFF) |
| /etc/hosts.equiv | Lists of trusted hosts and remote users | hosts.equiv(SFF), rhosts(SFF) |
| /etc/inetd.conf | Configuration file for inetd | inetd.conf(SFF) |
| /etc/named.boot | Default initialization file for *named* | named.boot(SFF) |
| /etc/networks | Known networks | networks(SFF) |
| /etc/pppauth | Point-to-point authentication database | pppauth(SFF) |

*(continued)*

**Table 14–1**   Continued

| File | Purpose | Where to Find More Information |
|------|---------|-------------------------------|
| **Networking Files (*cont.*)** | | |
| /etc/pppfilter | PPP packet filtering configuration file | packetfilter(SFF) |
| /etc/ppppool | IP address pool file for PPP network interfaces | ppppool(SFF) |
| /etc/ppphosts | Point-to-point link configuration file | ppphosts(SFF) |
| /usr/lib/named or /etc/named.d | Configuration files for *named* | named(ADMN) |
| /usr/lib/uucp/Configuration | Protocol configuration file for UUCP | uucp(C), Configuration(F) |
| /usr/lib/uucp/Devices | Configured UUCP devices | uucp(C), Devices(F) |
| /usr/lib/uucp/Permissions | UUCP authorization file | uucp(C), Permissions(F) |
| /usr/lib/uucp/Systems | Remote UUCP systems | uucp(C), Systems(F) |
| **X Windows Files** | | |
| $HOME/.mwmrc | MWM configuration file | mwm(XC), X(X) |
| $HOME/.pmwmrc | PMWMconfiguration file | mwm(C), X(X) |
| $HOME/Main.dt | X-Desktop configuration file | dxt3(XC) |
| $HOME/Personal.dt | X-Desktop configuration file | dxt3(XC) |
| /usr/lib/X11/system.mwmrc | System default MWM configuration file | mwm(XC), X(X) |
| /usr/lib/X11/system.pmwmrc | System default PMWM configuration file | mwm(XC), X(X) |
| /usr/lib/X11/app-defaults | Application-specific defaults | X(X) |
| $HOME/.Xdefaults-hostname | Host-specific defaults | X(X) |
| **System Default Files** | | |
| /etc/default | System default database file | default(F) |
| /etc/default/archive | Archive devices | archive(F) |
| /etc/default/authsh /etc/default/accounts | Account creation parameters | authsh(ADM) |
| /etc/default/backup | XENIX backup devices | xbackup(ADM) |
| /etc/default/boot | System boot options | boot(F) |
| /etc/default/cc | Read by /bin/cc | cc(CP) |
| /etc/default/cleantmp | Interval/location for tmp file cleanup | cleantmp(ADM) |
| /etc/default/cron | Cron configuration file | cron(C) |
| /etc/default/device.tab | Device table for package utilities | pkgadd(ADM) |
| /etc/default/dumpdir | XENIX archive device | xdumpdir(ADM) |
| /etc/default/filesys | Fileysystem mount table | filesys(F) |
| /etc/default/format | Floppy disk format device and verification | format(C) |

**Table 14–1**   Continued

| File | Purpose | Where to Find More Information |
|---|---|---|
| | **System Default Files (*cont.*)** | |
| /etc/default/goodpw | Password checking options | goodpw(ADM) |
| /etc/default/idleout | Interval for closing idle logins | idleout(ADM) |
| /etc/default/issue | System default banner | issue(F) |
| /etc/default/lang | System locales | locale(M) |
| /etc/default/lock | Logout interval for locks on serial terminals | lock(C) |
| /etc/default/login | System login parameters | login(M) |
| /etc/default/lpd | Print service options | lpadmin(ADM) |
| /etc/default/man | Man-page configuration file | man(C) |
| /etc/default/mapchan | Character device mapping | mapchan(M) |
| /etc/default/mapkey | Monitor screen mapping | mapkey(M) |
| /etc/default/merge | SCO Merge | |
| /etc/default/mnt | Remote filesystem types | mnt(C) |
| /etc/default/msdos | DOS command configuration file | doscmd(C) |
| /etc/default/passwd | Password parameters | passwd(C) |
| /etc/default/purge | Files to be purged | purge(C) |
| /etc/default/pwr | Power management configuration file | pwrd(ADM) |
| /etc/default/restore | XENIX restore device | xrestore(ADM) |
| /etc/default/scsihas | SCSI host adapter driver names | scsi(HW) |
| /etc/default/slot | MCA adapter configuration data | slot(C) |
| /etc/default/su | Root command parameters | su(C), asroot(ADM) |
| /etc/default/tape | Default tape device | tape(C) |
| /etc/default/tar | Archive devices | tar(C) |
| /etc/default/whois | Parameter is used by the whois service | whois(TC) |
| | **Miscellaneous Files** | |
| /etc/checklist | List of file systems processed by fsck | checklist(F) |
| /etc/dktab | Virtual disk configuration file | dktab(F) |
| /etc/inittab | Configuration file for init | inittab(F), init.base(F) |
| /etc/rc* | System startup scripts | rc0(ADM), rc2(ADM) |
| /etc/ttytype | Terminal type to tty device mapping file | ttytype(F) |

it is only used to monitor the total number of log ins. However, they are still taking up system resources.

Although I rarely use `who` with any option, except `-q`, it does have several other options that I have used on occasion. One is the `-b` option, which tells you when the system was last rebooted. Another, is the `-r` option, which tells you what run-level you are in, is used by both /etc/rc2 and /etc/rc3.

If you use the -u option, the last field in each line is the PID of that user's shell. This is a good starting point if you find that problems are limited to a specific user, or group of users. You can then use this PID to search through the output of the ps command to find out what else the user is doing.

### Processes

The ps command gives you a process status. Without any options, it gives you the process status for the terminal you are running the command on. That is, if you are logged in several times, ps will only show you the processes on that terminal and none of the others. For example, I have four sessions logged in on the system console, when I switch to one and run ps:

```
PID     TTY     TIME        CMD
625     ttyp0   00:00:03    ksh
991     ttyp0   00:00:00    ps
```

This only shows those processes running on the terminal where I started the ps (in this case ttyp0). Note that if you are running ODT 3.0 then the output is slightly different.

If I am not on that terminal, but still want to see what is running there, I can use the -t option. A nice aspect of the behavior of the -t is that you don't have to specify the full device name, or even the 'tty' portion. It suffices just to give the tty number. For example, to get the same output as above I could enter (no matter where I was):

```
ps -tp0
```

Keep in mind that if I was on a pseudo terminal, the terminal number also includes the p. If I have console or serial terminal, then the p isn't used as it is not part of the tty name. For example, if I wanted to check processes on tty04, I would enter:

```
ps -t04
```

Note also that you do *not* specify the /dev/ portion of the device name, even if you specify the tty portion. For example, this works as follows:

```
ps -tttyp0
```

or

```
ps -t ttyp0
```

but this doesn't

```
ps -t /dev/ttyp0
```

If we are curious as to what a particular user is running, we can use the -u option. This will tell us every process that is owned by that user.

Although running ps like this does show who is running what, it tells us little about the behavior of the process itself. In the section on processes, I showed you the -l option, which shows you much more information. If I add the -l (long) option, I might obtain output that looks like this:

```
F    S  UID   PID   PPID C   PRI  NI  ADDR      SZ   WCHAN     TTY     TIME      CMD
20   S  0     608   607  3   75   24  fb11b9e8  132  f01ebf4c  ttyp0   00:00:02  ksh
20   O  0     1221  608  20  37   28  fb11cb60  184  -         ttyp0   00:00:00  ps
```

When problems arise, one column that I use quite often is the TIME column. This tells me the total time that this process has been running. Note that the time for ksh is only 2 seconds although I actually logged in on this terminal several hours before I issued the command. The reason is that the shell spends most of its time either waiting for you to input something or waiting for the command that you entered to finish. Nothing out of the ordinary here.

Unless I knew specifically on what terminal the problem, existed, I would probably have to show every process in order to get something of value. This would be done with the -e option (for everything). The problem I have is that I have to look at every single line to see what the total time is. So, to make my life easier I can pipe it to sort. My sort field will be field 13 (TIME), so I use the -k 13 option. Since I want to see the list in reverse order (largest value first), I also use the -r option. Since I probably only want the first few entries, piping it through head would not be a bad idea. So, the command would look like this:

```
ps -el | sort -r -k 13 | head -5
```

On my system I get this:

```
F  S UID    PID  PPID C  PRI NI  ADDR      SZ    WCHAN     TTY    TIME      CMD
20 S 12709  654  627  0  76  24  fb11bdf0  8588  f0213424  ?      01:22:25  wabiprog
20 S 0      620  619  3  76  0   fb11b738  2692  f0213424  tty01  00:12:31  Xsco
20 S 12709  655  654  0  76  24  fb11c0a0  1012  f0213424  ?      00:00:49  wabifs
20 S 0      624  623  1  76  24  fb11bb40  928   f0213424  tty01  00:00:29  scoterm
```

At the very top of the list we see wabiprog. This is the process that essentially is Wabi. Since I have been typing a lot of this text with Microsoft Word for Windows running under Wabi, it is not surprising that I have such a large value for the time. Every time I press a key, every time I scroll, and every time I click on, a menu is counted towards the total time of wabiprog. If you are running a database application, or something similar, it is probable that you have at least one process with this high a TIME.

Figuring out what is a reasonable value is not always easy. The most effective method I have found is to monitor these values while the system is behaving "correctly". You then have a rough estimate of the amount of time particular processes need, and you can quickly see when something is out of the ordinary.

Something else that I use regularly is the PID-PPID pair. If I come across a process that doesn't look right, I can follow the PID to PPID chain until I find a process with a PPID of 1. Since process 1 is `init`, I know that this process is the starting point. Knowing this is often useful when I end up having to kill a process. Sometimes, the process is in an unkillable state. This happens in two cases. First, the process may be making the transition to becoming defunct, in which case I can ignore it. It may also be stuck in some part of the code in kernel mode. In which case, it won't hear my kill signal. In such cases, I have found it useful to kill one of its ancestors (such as a shell). The hung process is inherited by `init` and will eventually disappear. However, in the meantime, the user can get back to work. Afterwards comes the task of figuring out what the problem was.

In the section on processes, I mentioned the `crash` program. This is a very useful tool to monitor your system. Unlike other monitoring programs, `crash` does not have a pretty graphics interface, so it appears rather unfriendly at first. In fact, it is a quite unfriendly program and doesn't take too kindly to people poking around who don't know what they're doing. Not that you can do any damage, it's just that many of the error messages tell you nothing other than you did something wrong.

Start it up simply as `crash` and this is what you see:

```
dumpfile = /dev/mem, namelist = /unix, outfile = stdout
>
```

The dump file is where the crash program is getting its information. The default location is `/dev/mem`, which is the device used to access memory. Since we want to take a look at the memory on a running system, this is a logical place. If, on the other hand, the system panicked and there was a dump image on the swap device (`/dev/swap`), you could use that as your dumpfile. From the command line, we specify the dump file with the -d option.

The namelist is basically a table that converts machine names to their human readable equivalent. We use the `/unix` program, since that's normally what is used to load the kernel and `crash` needs that file as a reference point. If you have relinked (created a new kernel) then the kernel in memory does not match what is on the hard disk in `/unix`. Therefore, you would need to specify the one you booted with (normally `/unix.old`). This is done from the command line with the -n option. Because we are reading these files (`/dev/mem` or `/dev/swap` and `/unix`) the user running `crash` needs to have read permission. Since most users *don't* have permission to read either, `crash` is usually run by root.

In our case, we want to immediately see the results of our input. Therefore, we want the output to go to stdout. This is our `outfile`. If we wanted we could tell crash to output everything to a file for late examination. The file we want to write to is specified from the command line with the `-w` option. If we do specify an output file, we will still see our prompt ( >), but all output is send to the `outfile`.

The first thing we need is a process to look at, so we need to take a look at the process table to find one that looks interesting. To see the process table, input either `proc` or p. Possibly you have more than a screenful of information. To send this through more, use an exclamation mark instead of a pipe symbol. Note that unlike pipes from the shell, the exclamation mark must be preceded by a space, as in

```
proc ! more
```

or

```
proc !more
```

We now get a list of all the processes on the system sorted by their slot in the process table. In my case, I took a look at the `ksh` process we used above. I found it in slot sixty-six, so I reran the command as `proc 66`, so all I got was the header and the one entry, which looked like this:

```
              PROC TABLE SIZE = 83
SLOT   ST    PID    PPID    PGRP    UID    PRI    CPU    EVENT          NAME    FLAGS
66     s     1107   1106    1107    0      75     0      spt_tty+0x68   ksh     load
```

The entries in this output are: slot in the process table, run state, process ID, parent process ID, process group, user ID, priority of the processes, event it is waiting on, the name of the command, and flags. The list of possible flags can be found in `<sys/proc.h>`. Most of these fields are the same as we saw in the ps output.

One difference is the EVENT column. However, the difference is in name only since this is the wait channel for that process. This makes sense since we wait on events. However, here it is in a slightly different format (`spt_tty+0x68`). This is telling us that the wait channel is at an offset of 0x68 from the start of the `spt_tty` function. The nm function of `crash` will translate a symbol (name) into an address, like this:

```
nm spt_tty
```

This gives me

```
spt_tty  0xf01ebee4  .bss
```

which is the function name, the address in the kernel, and what segment it is in. We see here that the `spt_tty` function is at address 0xf01ebee4. Adding the

0x68 to it, we get `0xf01ebf4c`. If we look back at the `ps` output, this is in the same place.

Now this is a round about way of finding out the same WCHAN value, but we found out something more valuable than the actual wait channel. We found the name of the function, in this case `spt_tty()`. Right off the bat, I can tell that it has *something* to do with a terminal because of the tty portion of the name. Since I am familiar with the system, I know that the spt driver is used for pseudo-ttys. Since I had the `ksh` running on a pseudo-tty, this convinces me that the event being waited on had *something* to do with a terminal.

Unfortunately, for those of you running ODT 3.0 things are a little more complicated. You don't get the nice little symbol name in the `event` column. No worries, there is just another step you need to add. Whereas `nm` translates from the symbol to the address, `ds` translates from the address to the *closest* symbol it can find, *prior* to the address you gave it. So with ODT, you input the hex value you get in the event column and you will get a symbol name back.

Okay, so what good is this information? Well, in this case the primary value is educational and satisfying our curiosity. You might have a process that is asleep and can't seem to wake up (somewhat like me on Monday morning). This is a way of determining what the process is waiting on. For example, we might have just used `ps` to show that one process has a large value in the TIME column. We then check that process using `crash` and discover that it is waiting on the `database_query()` function (which I just made up). You therefore know it is waiting on something having to do with the database (probably).

It is also possible to use `crash` to find out how much memory you have available. There are several variables you can read to find out exactly what you are looking for. To do this you need to use the `od` function of `crash` which will give you the value of the kernel variable you input. For example, to get the current amount of free memory, the command would be

```
> od -d freemem
```

This might give you

```
f0114c1c: 0000000740
```

The first number is the location (address) of the freemem variable in the kernel. The second value is the decimal value (because of the `-d`) of the number of free pages. This is the same value as you would get by running `sar -r`.

To find the amount of swappable memory, look at the `availsmem` variable and at the `availsrmem` variable for nonswappable (resident) memory.

What other information can you get through `crash`? You can find the open files in a process. This is accomplished by first looking at that uarea of the process with either the u or user command. The top part of my ksh process would look like this:

```
PER PROCESS USER AREA FOR PROCESS 66
USER ID's:  uid: 0, gid: 3, real uid: 0, real gid: 3
     supplementary gids: 3 0 1
PROCESS TIMES:      user: 62, sys: 252, child user: 1785, child
sys: 2300
PROCESS MISC:
     command: ksh, psargs: ksh
     proc: P#66, cntrl tty: 58,1
     start: Wed Jun 7 12:25:14 1995
     mem: 0xfdd5, type: exec su-user
     proc/text lock: none
     current directory: I#538
OPEN FILES AND POFILE FLAGS:
     [ 0]: F#305   r  [ 1]: F#305   w [ 2]: F#305    w
     [ 3]: F#214   r w [ 5]: F#305     [31]: F#263 c r w
FILE I/O:
     u_base: 0x806f7ac, file offset: 135349, bytes: 256
     segment: data, cmask: 0022, ulimit: 2097151
     file mode(s): read
```

Although I don't have the space to go over each entry, you can see many of the same entries that we had in both the ps output and the proc listing. One additional entry is the one labeled OPEN FILES AND POFILE FLAGS. By using the values here we can track down what files are being currently used by that process. Since this section is on process, let's wait a minute and talk about that in the section on files and filesystem.

### Files and Filesystems

Knowing how much space is left on your filesystems is another thing you should monitor. I have seen many instances where the root filesystem gets so close to 100% full that nothing more can get done. Since the root filesystem is where unnamed pipes are created by default, many processes die terrible deaths if they cannot create a pipe. If the system does get that full, it can prevent further logins (as each login writes to log files). If root is not already logged in to remove some files, then you will have problems.

The solution is to monitor your filesystems to ensure that none of them get too full, especially the root filesystem. A rule of thumb, whose origin is lost somewhere in UNIX mythology is that you should make sure that there is at least 15% free on your root filesystem. Although 15% on a 200MB hard disk is one-tenth the amount of free space as 15% on 2Gb drive, it is a value that is easy to monitor. If you think of 10–15Mb as a danger sign, you should be safe. However, you need to be aware of how much the system can change and how fast. If the system *could* change 15Mb in a matter of hours, then 15Mb may be too small a margin.

Use df to find out how much free space is on each mounted filesystem. Without any option, the output of df is one filesystem per line, showing how many blocks and how many inodes are free. While this is interesting, I am really more concerned with percentages. Very few administrators know how long it takes to use up 1000 blocks, however most understand the significance if those 1000 blocks mean that the filesystem is 95% full.

Since I am less concerned with how many inodes, the option I used most with df is -v which shows the data block usage. On my system I get something like this;

| Mount Dir | Filesystem | blocks | used | free | %used |
|-----------|------------|--------|------|------|-------|
| / | /dev/root | 779884 | 745434 | 34450 | 96% |
| /stand | /dev/boot | 30000 | 16634 | 13366 | 56% |
| /u1 | /dev/u1 | 80000 | 39312 | 40688 | 50% |
| /u2 | /dev/u2 | 80000 | 64680 | 15320 | 81% |
| /odtroot | /dev/odtroot | 400002 | 382100 | 17902 | 96% |
| /usr/dos/c | /dev/dsk/0sC | 306840 | 284952 | 21888 | 93% |
| /usr/dos/d | /dev/dsk/1sD | 511440 | 482024 | 29416 | 95% |
| /usr/dos/e | /dev/dsk/1sE | 521672 | 468056 | 53616 | 90% |
| /usr/dos/g | /dev/dsk/2sC | 820784 | 128 | 820656 | 1% |
| /odtroot/u | /dev/data2 | 628888 | 173580 | 455308 | 28% |

We see that my root filesystem is getting dangerously full. Although I have about 17Mb free (these are 512-byte blocks) and most of my data is kept on either the /u1 or /u2 filesystem, I need to be aware of the situation. Note however, that the /u2 filesystem is only 81% used but it has less than half the free space as the root filesystem. Since this is where my data is, I am much more concerned with it being at 81% than I am with root being at 95%. Note that I can also monitor free space on my DOS partitions.

The utility dfspace is a shell script that gets its information from df and shows the data in an easier to interpret format. It also shows you what's available in megabytes as well as percentages. Although this is a verbose output, I like df better in that it is easier to read. I can also more easily build a shell script around it to monitor usage automatically.

The shortcoming with df is that is tells you about the entire hard disk and can't really point to where the problems are. A full filesystem can be cause by one of two things. First, there are a few large files. This often happens when log files are not cleaned out regularly. One prime example in the MMDF channel log file (/usr/mmdf/log/chan.log). I have had this file reach to over 30 MB in just a few hours! In this case the solution is to monitor these files and clean them out as often as necessary.

A full filesystem is caused when you have a lot of little files. This is similar to ants at a picnic. Individually they are not very large. However, hundreds swarming across your hotdog is not very appetizing. If the files are scattered all over your system, then you will have a hard time figuring out where they are. However, if they are scattered across the system, then the odds are that no one program created them, so they are all probably wanted (if not needed). Therefore, you simply need a bigger disk.

If, on the other hand, the files are concentrated in one directory, it is more likely that a single program is the cause. As with the large log files, a common culprit is MMDF. Now, I don't want to sound like I am opposed to MMDF, in fact I like it. The issue is that if there is a configuration problem in MMDF, mail will get backed up. If it then has trouble sending a message to the originator to say that it just had trouble sending mail, then this gets backed up as well. On busy systems, this can grow to thousands of messages. This isn't the fault of MMDF, but the person who configured it. Just as it's not the fault of the water company when you get a large bill after leaving your tap running during your vacation.

To detect either case, you can use a combination of two commands. First is `find`, which is used to find files. Next is `du` which is used to determine disk usage. Without any options, `du` gives you the disk usage for every file that you specify. If you don't specify any, it gives you the disk usage for every file from your current directory on down.

Note that this usage is in blocks. Even if a block contains a single byte, that block is used and is no longer available for any other file. However, if you look at a long listing of a file you see the size in bytes. A one-byte file still takes up one data block. The size indicated in a long directory listing will usually be less than what you get if you multiply the number of blocks by the size of the block (512 bytes).

To get the sum of a directory without seeing the individual files, use the `-s` option. To look for directories that are exceptionally large, we can find all the directories and use `du -s`. We also need to be sure that we don't count multiple links more than once, so we include the `-u` option as well. We then sort the output as numerical values and in reverse order (`-nr`) to see the larger directories first; like this:

```
find / -type d -exec du -us {} \; | sort -nr > /tmp/fileusage
```

I do the redirection into the file `/tmp/fileusage` for two reasons. First, I have a copy of the output that I can use later if I need to. Second, this command is going to take a *very* long time. Since I started in /, the first directory found is /. Therefore, the disk usage for the entire system (including mounted filesystem) will be caluclated. Only after it has calculated the disk usage for the entire system does it go on to the individual directories.

We can avoid this problem in a couple of ways. First, by using -print instead of -exec in the find and then piping it first to grep -v. This strips out the / and we can then pipe that output to xargs. This way we avoid the root directory.

This is not very pretty, especially if I were going to be using the command again. I would much rather create a list of directories and use this as an argument to du. That way we can filter out those directories that we don't need to check or only include those that we do want to check. For example, we already know that /usr/mmdf/logs might contain a very large file. This would be a good directory to monitor. Another is the MMDF spool directory (/usr/spool/mmdf/lock/home). If you can find out the directories that your applications use, this would also be a good directory to include.

On occasion, it's nice to figure out what files a process has open. Maybe the process is hung and you want some details before you decide to kill it. In this instance, we can use crash. In the case, I took a look at the vi session I used to write this text. The entry looked like this:

```
PROC TABLE SIZE = 100
SLOT   ST   PID   PPID   PGRP   UID   PRI   CPU   EVENT      NAME   FLAGS
14     s    264   176    264    0     28    0     f0093e84   vi     load
```

Since this process is taking up slot 14, I want to look at the uarea of the process in slot 14. To look at the uarea input either user or just u—we input u 14. This also takes more than a screen, so we need to pipe it through more, as well. Near the top is the entry for open files. Mine looks like this:

```
OPEN FILES AND POFILE FLAGS:
[ 0]: F#25   r   [ 1]: F#25     w [ 2]: F#25     w
[ 3]: F#32       [ 4]: F#23   r w [ 5]: F#47     w
```

These are my file descriptors. The numbers inside the square brackets are the descriptor numbers. The F# numbers are the slots in the file table taken up by those descriptors. Following, are the access rights I have to the descriptor (r-read, w-write). Notice that for file descriptors 0, 1, and 2 the slot in the file table is the same. Do you remember what file descriptors 0, 1, and 2 are? Stdin, stdout, and stderr. Since I have not done any file redirection, these are the same. This shows me that all three point to the same place. In addition to the big three, there are three other files I have open.

To find out what entries these are in the inode table, we first look in the file table. As you might have guessed we need to give the slot number in the file table. If we want to see what slot 25 is, for example, we would input either f 25 or file 25. (This is the file number of my stdin, stdout, and stderr.) The output would look like this:

```
FILE TABLE SIZE = 200
SLOT   RCNT   I/FL   OFFSET FLAGS
25     6      I178   13b3c  read write
```

Here we have the slot number, the reference count, the inode table slot number, the offset, and the read/write flags.

Next, we need to look at the inode table, which is basically the same process. We input either `inode 178` or `i 178` and this gives us the following:

```
INODE TABLE SIZE = 300
SLOT  MAJ/MIN FS   INUMB RCNT  LINK UID  GID SIZE MODE     MNT M/ST RCVD FLAGS
178   1,40    2    130   1     1    0    15  0    c--600   0   S    0    -
```

In this case, the column we are looking for is the `INUMB` entry. This gives us the actual inode number, here 130. When I look at the `MAJ/MIN` column this tells me the major and minor number of the filesystem that this file is on; in this case `1,40`, which I (we?) know to be the root filesystem on ODT 3.0. If I had run this on OpenServer, this entry would probably be `1,42`. Since we now have the *real* inode number we can find what file this is associated with.

To find the file, I have a few choices. There are two commands that can be used: `ncheck` and `find -inum`. If I had no idea where the file was, either of these could work. However, experience has told me that very low inode numbers (< 200) are usually in the `/dev` directory since numbers this low are usually created earlier in the install process. Also, since I know that these are files referred to by `stdin`, `stdout`, and `stderr`, I know that these are probably `tty` devices. So, I only need to look in the `/dev` directory. In this case, `find` would be a better choice since `ncheck` searches entire filesystems and `find` can be told to look in specific directories. So I would run

```
find /dev -inum 130 -exec l -i {} \;
```

This gives me

```
130 crw------  1 root   terminal  0, 0 May 06 12:01 /dev/tty01
```

If you haven't already figured it out, the kernel doesn't use that last step (the conversion from inode to file name). We must figure out the name of the file. Instead, the kernel takes the inode number and the offset into the `fstypesw` table (the `FS` entry in the inode information; in our case 2 for an `EAFS`) to be able to access the file itself.

By following this procedure for any of the file descriptors listed, we can find out every file a process has open. For example, file number 32 in the example uarea above turns out to be `/usr/bin/vi`, which makes sense since `vi` has to be open for me to use it.

### Checking Kernel Parameters

There are three programs that can be used to check the current state of your kernel parameters: `crash`, `configure`, and `sysdef`. When you run `crash`, many of the kernel parameters can be viewed using the `var` function. This is more than a screenful, so you will need to pipe it through something. Although `configure` is used to configure kernel parameters, using the `-x` option to `configure` will give you a list of all the configurable kernel parameters as well as their current values. Despite what the man-page says about listing *all* the kernel tunable parameters, `sysdef` is missing some that are reported by `configure`. Because of this, I find `configure` more informative.

### The System Activity Reporter and Performance Tuning

SCO UNIX performance tuning is often thought of as a black art. I've talked with many customers who call in to SCO Support expecting that we will say a few magic words, wave our wizard's wand and, abracadabra, their system will be running better. This is often compounded by the fact that support engineers don't have the time to go into long, detailed explanations. Instead they quickly look over output from various system utilities and for example, tell the customer to increase kernel parameter X. Miraculously the system instantly runs better. From the customers standpoint, this is "magic."

Well, not really. Some customers do express their frustrations at not being able to improve the situation themselves. This is not because they aren't smart enough, but is the same reason that many people bring their cars to a mechanic for a tune-up. By comparison to replacing the block, a tune-up is a relatively simple procedure. However, many people don't have the skills to be able to do it themselves.

This applies to system tuning as well. Since many customers do not have the skills, they turn to the mechanic to do it for them. When I was about 18, I had a couple of friends who were real car enthusiasts. When their cars suddenly started making a strange sound, I can still remember them saying that the franistan had come loose from the rastulator. Well, at least that's what it sounded like to me at the time. The reason I couldn't figure out what they were saying was that I didn't have the training or experience. However, they did have the experience and could tell just by listening. This is the same as many system administrators, who don't have the training or experience to tune an SCO UNIX system. However, you can.

Although a book like this cannot provide the experience, it can provide some of the training. Keeping with the car analogy, we've talked about the transmissions, the breaks, the drive shaft, the electrical system, and even the principles of the internal combustion engineer. With that knowledge we can now understand why it is necessary to have clean spark plugs or the proper mixture of air and gasoline.

With a car's engine we often get a "feeling" for its proper behavior. When it starts to misbehave, we know something is wrong, even though we may not know how to fix. The same applies, in principle to an SCO system. Many garages can afford the high tech equipment that you plug your car into to find out what the car is doing. From that, it is a simple step for the mechanic to determine the proper course of action. What we need for an SCO UNIX system is a tool that does the same thing. That tool is the system activity reporter—`sar`.

The system activity reporter is a very useful tool to see what your system is doing. It can provide information about a wide range of aspects of your system such as memory usage, number or processes, and even paging activity. By default the system gathers information about your system every 20 minutes during a normal work day (8 AM – 5 PM) and once an hour the rest of the time (on the hour, 20, and 40 minutes after the hour). This is done by the `/usr/lib/sa/sa1` program through the sys user's crontab. Information is stored in the `/usr/adm/sa` directory. The files are of the form `sadd` where `dd` is the day of the month.

On OpenServer, turning off the data collection is fairly easy. There is the `sar_enable` utility that you use to toggle it on and off. See the `sar_enable(ADM)` man-page for more details.

This information in the `sadd` files is processed once a day by the `/usr/lib/sa/sa2` program through root's crontab. This information is also stored in `/usr/adm/sa`. The files here have the form `sardd` where `dd` is the day of the month. Unlike the `sadd` files, the `sardd` files are ASCII and can therefore be read without any problems. They are kept for one month (until the next day of the month with that number), so you have a limited record of system activity. The `sadd` files, on the other hand are in a format that `sar` understands and are read when you run `sar`.

There are so many options to `sar` that uppercase letters had to be used as well. Because of the large number of different options, it would be difficult to talk about all of them. Since they are all listed in the `sar(ADM)` man-page and since many of them would require extensive explanation, we are only going to talk about those options that are most commonly used. The general syntax for `sar` is

```
sar <options> frequency repetitions
```

where `frequency` is how many seconds between readings and `repetitions` is how many readings. Therefore, running

```
sar 5 10
```

would run `sar` with the default options and give a reading once every 5 seconds for 10 seconds. If you leave off the last number (`repetitions`) `sar` waits the number of seconds specified and reports once. It's not recommended that you run sar at intervals less than 5 seconds since the fact that sar is running may have an influence on the output being generated.

If you don't specify a time interval, sar shows you the activity for the current day. If you want to read the activity for some other day, you specify the file you want read (and therefore the day) with the -f option. You can also specify the time of the day you want by using the -s option for the start time and the -e option for the ending time. For example, if I want to find out about system activity in the afternoon on the 26th of the month, the command might look something like this:

```
sar -s12 -e17 -f/usr/adm/sa/sa26
```

If the day I ran this was the 14th, let's say, then this would show me the data for the 26th of the previous month. Keep in mind that the information is gathered by cron every 20 minutes, during "business hours" and once an hour other times. It's possible that the cron job doesn't actually get started until, let's say, 17:00:03. In that case, the above command would not report that entry. If we really wanted that entry, we could use the fact that the start and end times can be specified down to the second. Therefore, I could have used this command:

```
sar -s12 -e17:00:03 -f/usr/adm/sa/sa26
```

Much of the information sar provides is in the form of a percent. In this case, you will see a percent sign (%) in the column heading. If the value reported is units per second, the information is displayed with a trailing /s. The default behavior of sar (that is, with no options specified) is the same as the -u option which shows the cpu usage. We would then see the statistics for today. We could also leave off the reporting criteria (the -u) and just specify the time. For example, we could run it once a second for 5 seconds, like this:

```
sar 1 5
```

This might give us something like this:

```
13:03:13     %usr      %sys      %wio      %idle
13:03:14     5         4         0         92
13:03:15     0         2         0         97
13:03:16     0         2         0         97
13:03:17     0         2         0         97
13:03:18     0         2         0         97


Average      2         2         0         96
```

Since I am the only user on my system, idle times this high are not unexpected. If you add up the entries in each column you'll notice that the sum doesn't always add up to 100%. Sometimes it's a little over (like the first entry) and sometimes it's under (like entries 2-5). This is due to the manner in which `sar` does the calculation and is to be expected (rounding and averaging).

The two columns that need to be monitored more often are `%wio` and `%idle`. The `%wio` column shows what percentage of the time the system is waiting for I/O. The SCO manuals say that if this value is constantly over 15%, then there is an I/O bottleneck, and I agree. (Did you expect that I wouldn't?) The operative word here is "constantly." If you run into cases when the `%wio` shoots up above 15% and then back down, this is normal. For example, when you are doing your daily backups, the `%wio` will probably get a lot higher than at other times. However, if you run `sar` over an extended period (several minutes) and see that most values for `%wio` are under 15% then you're doing well.

The `%usr` and `%sys` columns tell you the percentage of time spent running user and system code, respectively. It is difficult to say what values here are valid or not. This is dependent on your application.

Another very useful option is `-r`, which shows memory usage. A 3-second interval might look like this:

```
13:23:18 freemem freeswp
13:23:19   243   45968
13:23:20   243   45968
13:23:21   243   45968


Average   243   45968
```

The `freemem` column shows how much free physical memory we have. This is in 4K pages. Therefore, I have just under 1Mb of RAM available. The `freeswap` column, as you might have guessed, tells us how much swap we have. This is in 512 byte blocks. Therefore, I have just under 23 Mb of swap. In this case, nothing changed as I am the only one of the system. However, a good example of changing values is if you were to start `sar-r` on one console multiscreen and then change to another screen and start-up X. Things change dramatically.

Personally, the amount of swap I have free makes me think. When I installed the system I configured it with 25Mb of swap. Since I have already used some of my swap space, I will want to monitor this. A little swapping can be tolerated, especially if you can't afford the RAM. Too much swapping can lead to severe slowdowns in the system. This is because every time the system swaps, it has to access the disk, which is slow in comparison to accessing memory. I therefore want to monitor this value as well as both the `%wio` and `%idle` value when I run `sar -u`. If I am using a lot of my swap space and spending a lot of time waiting for

I/O with almost no idle time, then the system is doing a lot of "busy" work and not getting much real work done. Since the *system* has to do the swapping, you also see increases in sio% when you have to swap.

If you have a large %wio value, then things get more complicated if you have multiple hard disks. This is because the %wio value is combined from all the disks. In order to see activity on all drives, you need to use the -d option. We can compare what is being reported for each driver in terms of the percentage of the time the device was busy (%busy) and the number of reads and writes per seconds (r+w/s). If there is a wide gap you might want to consider spreading your data across multiple drives to even the load. If you are running OpenServer, this might be the perfect opportunity to consider something like disk striping. For example, when I ran sar -d for three seconds on my system, I got this.

| 13:50:01 | device | %busy | avque | r+w/s | blks/s | avwait | avserv |
|----------|--------|-------|-------|-------|--------|--------|--------|
| 13:50:02 | Sdsk-0 | 4.50 | 1.00 | 1.80 | 30.63 | 0.00 | 25.00 |
|          | Sdsk-1 | 0.90 | 1.00 | 0.90 | 28.83 | 0.00 | 10.00 |
|          | Sdsk-2 | 0.90 | 1.00 | 0.90 | 28.83 | 0.00 | 10.00 |
| 13:50:03 | Sdsk-1 | 0.97 | 1.00 | 0.97 | 31.07 | 0.00 | 10.00 |
|          | Sdsk-2 | 0.97 | 1.00 | 0.97 | 31.07 | 0.00 | 10.00 |
| 13:50:04 | Sdsk-0 | 0.98 | 1.00 | 0.98 | 31.37 | 0.00 | 10.00 |
|          | Sdsk-1 | 0.98 | 1.00 | 0.98 | 31.37 | 0.00 | 10.00 |
|          | Sdsk-2 | 0.98 | 1.00 | 0.98 | 31.37 | 0.00 | 10.00 |
| Average  | Sdsk-0 | 1.90 | 1.00 | 0.95 | 20.89 | 0.00 | 20.00 |
|          | Sdsk-1 | 0.95 | 1.00 | 0.95 | 30.38 | 0.00 | 10.00 |
|          | Sdsk-2 | 0.95 | 1.00 | 0.95 | 30.38 | 0.00 | 10.00 |

If we look at the %busy (the percentage of the time the disk was servicing requests), we see that at 13:50:02, my first disk was five times more active than the others. If this were consistent throughout the day, then it would tell me that this disk is being overburdened. Since the first disk is where all my applications and other programs are kept (it contains the root filesystem), it is not surprising that this has a higher value. Since the proportion evens out over time, I am not concerned.

Note that the intervals here are less than the 5 seconds I suggested earlier. Since sar is already in memory when this is being read, more than likely the system does not need to read the disk because of sar. However, to be sure that you are getting as accurate a reading as possible, it is a good idea to eliminate sar as much as possible.

When accessing a file, every program does so with that file's name. As we talked about in the section on kernel internals, the name is converted to the inode number by the `namei()` function. The first time a file is opened, `namei()` goes through all the gyrations we talked about before to find the inode number. Once it finds the inode numbers, it caches the name and inode in a structure called (what else?) the `namei` cache. The next time a file is accessed, the system looks in the `namei` cache. If the filename is there, all is well. If not, `namei()` will have to look elsewhere. If the directory is in the `buffer` cache, then no disk access is necessary. `Namei()` can read the inode from the directory. However, this is still not as fast as getting it from the `namei` cache as there is still a delay caused by looking in the `buffer` cache.

The number of times that an entry *is* found in any cache is referred to as a cache hit. The number of `namei` cache hits can be monitored using the -n option. Although showing the same information, the output in OpenServer is different from that in ODT 3.0. This is because OpenServer actually maintains two types of `namei` caches. The first is used to hold the name-to-inode mappings for `AFS`, `EAFS`, and `HTFS` filesystems. The other is for `DTFS` filesystems. On a busy system 5 seconds of `sar -n` run might look like this:

| 14:23:11 | H_hits | Hmisses | (%Hhit) | D_hits | Dmisses | (%Dhit) |
|----------|--------|---------|---------|--------|---------|---------|
| 14:23:14 | 4 | 1 | ( 80%) | 9 | 41 | ( 18%) |
| 14:23:15 | 1 | 1 | ( 50%) | 5 | 29 | ( 14%) |
| 14:23:16 | 2 | 0 | (100%) | 12 | 57 | ( 17%) |
| 14:23:17 | 4 | 6 | ( 40%) | 1 | 7 | ( 12%) |
| 14:23:18 | 1 | 2 | ( 33%) | 0 | 0 | ( 0%) |
| Average | 2 | 2 | ( 54%) | 5 | 26 | ( 16%) |

If these values were to continue like this, I might want to consider increasing the size of my `namei` caches. On the average, the `DTFS` finds the name of the file in the cache only 16% of the time. This means that 85% percent of the time it looks for an inode number it must, at least, look in the buffer cache. Unless a lot of different files are being accessed in the same directory, then a lot of `namei` cache misses probably also means that the directory is not in the `buffer` cache.

The size of the `namei` cache is determined by the S5CACHEENTS kernel parameter in ODT and the HTCACHEENTS and DTCACHENTS kernel parameters in OpenServer, where HTCACHEENTS is for `AFS`, `EAFS`, and `HTFS` filesystems and DTCACHEENTS is for `DTFS` filesystems. Note that names longer than 14 characters are not cached.

Keep in mind that the number of entries in the cache is not the only factor in the speed of access. The cache is an unsorted list. In order to find a particular entry, we would have to search through the entire list. Well, we would if it weren't for something called a *hash queue*. Simply put a hash queue in a list of entries grouped together. Let's assume we have twenty-six such hash queues, one for each letter of the alphabet. Entries are placed in the queue that corresponds to the first letter of the filename. As a result, fewer entries need to be searched to find the right one.

The average length of the hash queue is simply the number of entries in the cache divided by the number of queues. If the hash queues were based on letters of the alphabet, then each queue would be 1/26th the size of the name cache. The rule of thumb is to have the length of each hash queue to be less than or equal to four. In other words, whenever you change the size of the cache you should change the number of hash queues accordingly. Since the size of the table may be dynamic in OpenServer, this ratio may not apply. The kernel parameters for the hash queues are S5HASHQS in ODT 3.0 and HTHASHQS and DTHASHQS in OpenServer.

Although we've sped up the translation from file name to inode, we haven't yet read the hard disk to get our data. As we talked about in the section on filesystems, the inode contains the locations of where the data resides on the hard disk. We cannot keep every inode for every filesystem in memory all the time, so like other aspects of the system, we only keep what is currently needed. It is therefore possible that we may have found the inode quickly through the `namei` cache, but the inode is not in memory so we have to access the disk to read it. If we increased the size of the inode table in memory we would speed things up even further.

First we need to see if this is even necessary. Remember, you should never try to fix something that's not broken. To see the activity in the inode table, we use the `-v` option to `sar`. Running for three seconds, gave me this:

```
16:02:45 proc-sz  ov inod-sz  ov file-sz  ov lock-sz
16:02:46 101/ 154  0 332/ 819  0 302/ 682  0  29/ 128
16:02:47 101/ 154  0 332/ 819  0 302/ 682  0  29/ 128
16:02:48 102/ 154  0 333/ 819  0 304/ 682  0  29/ 128
```

This output shows us the size of the process table (`proc-sz`), inode table (`inod-sz`), file table (`file-sz`), and the record lock table (`lock-sz`). The first three also report how many times the table overflowed between the samplings (`ov`). In each case, the two numbers represent the current value followed by the size of the table. If you are running OpenServer and have not set a maximum table size, this instead shows the maximum that the table has grown to.

If you have OpenServer, then life is easier. With OpenServer the size of the kernel inode table is dynamic. However, you can set the maximum size with the MAX_INODE parameter. On the other hand, if you still have ODT 3.0, then the size of the kernel inode table is determined at relink time by the NINODE parameter. The kernel parameter for the size of the hash queue in both cases is NHINODE.

Here again, we would have to search through every entry except for the existence of the inode hash queues. Like those for the `namei` cache, these decrease the amount of time needed to find the appropriate entry and should maintain the 1:4 relationship with the cache size and the number of hash queues.

As with other types of I/O, terminal I/O can present a serious bottle neck. If it gets too bad, then usually the best solution is getting an intelligent multiport board that takes some of the load off the system. In the meantime, you can take a look to see if there is anything you can do to help relieve the situation. The key aspect of serial I/O that causes problems are `clists`. Both incoming/outgoing characters are placed into a `clist`. When you run out of them, characters get lost.

Using the `-g` option to sar, you can monitor how many times you run out of clists each second. Although decreasing the baud rate of the terminal will help to eliminate `clist` overflows, you normally don't win friends this way. The solution is to increase the number of `clists`.

The next issue we're going to talk is a two-edged sword. This is the size of your `buffer` cache. When you boot your system, you see the size of your `buffer` cache when the system displays `I/O bufs=`. This is determined by the NBUF kernel parameter. If set to 0, then the system allocates space based on the total amount of memory you have. Otherwise, the system will allocate the number of 1K buffers that NBUF is set to.

Let's take the case where you notice that a great deal of time is being spent writing to and reading from the disk (maybe using the `%wio` column of `sar -u`). You conclude that by increasing the size of the `buffer` cache, you could decrease the need to go to the disk so often. In principle, this is a valid conclusion. If you are generally accessing the same data all the time, then increasing the same of the `buffer` cache increases how much of that data is kept in memory. On the other hand, if you are constantly updating and changing different pieces of data, then having a larger `buffer` cache may do you no good. In fact, it may be counter productive, if you are not careful. If you increase the size of the `buffer` cache too much, then there is less memory for processes and you spend more time paging or even swapping.

To monitor the activity in the `buffer` cache, you use the `-b` option to `sar`. You will monitor the percentage of cache hits when reading (`%rcache`) and the percentage of cache hits when writing (`%wcache`). If you think back to the section on the CPU, I mentioned that the system spends about 80% of its time executing 20% of the code. This means that there is a lot of repetition. If you have to go back to the disk every time you need the same portion of code, you are wasting time. Therefore, if you have a low %rcache value, then you might want to think about increasing the size of your buffer cache.

What's low? Well, being consistently above 90% is not unexpected. If you have a lot of users, all using the same application, then they are going to be using the same code. If on the other hand, you have a lot of different applications, then the value will be lower. However, if it averages below 80% I would seriously consider increasing the size of the buffer cache.

There are a couple of things to point out. First, applications typically do more reading than writing, so potentially the %wcache value is of less importance. Therefore, if you increase your buffer cache and the %wcache value doesn't change much, although %rcache does, don't worry about it. Compare the number of kilobytes written per second to the number of kilobytes read (lwrit/s and lread/s, respectively). If the number of reads is substantially higher than writes, then you probably won't get much better write performance out of increasing the buffer cache.

The next issue is the law of diminishing returns. The only time I see either read or write percentages at 100% is when I am the only one on the system and all I am doing is running different options to sar. The sar code is already in memory. Therefore, there is no need to read the buffer cache at all. Zero hits out of zero requests is still a 100% hit rate. (We're optimists here) So, if you get your %rcache up to 98% (which is completely possible) then be happy. Don't give yourself an ulcer trying to squeeze out that last 2%. You probably won't get it anyway.

Another common problem is when the system runs out of regions. If you think back to the discussion on kernel internals, you'll remember that each process has at least three regions: text, data, and stack. If so configured, processes can also have a fourth region: shared data. Unless you are getting close to maxing out the number of processes, then shared memory is not usually a problem. However, you do run into problems when you have either a lot of processes using shared memory or are close to filling up your process table.

This problem occurs when you have not defined enough regions in your kernel. If you have OpenServer, the number of regions grows dynamically, unless you set it with the MAX_REGION parameter. In ODT this is the NREGION parameter. Any time you are using shared memory, you need to account for this when determining the ratio of processes to regions.

We can use sar -v (mentioned above) to monitor the number of processes used (proc-sz). However, we have to return to our old friend crash. The region function inside of crash shows you the current state of the region table. By counting the number of lines (minus the header) we find out how many entries are in the region table. Just like we can pipe the output to more, we can pipe it to any other program. So, to get a count of the number of lines, the command would be

```
region ! wc -l
```

Since this also counts the lines in the header, we need to subtract 4 to give us the number of slots in ODT, but only subtract 2 with OpenServer. Once we've figured out the number of regions being used, we need to compare this to the number of processes.

The key here is to make two checks. The first check is immediately after going into multi-user mode and preferably before any third party applications have started. The first check is to get a base value from which to make later determinations as to what is expected or not. Once users start running the applications, make another check to see what the regions and processes are doing.

SCO also provides another useful monitoring tool: vmstat. Although this does not provide the scope of options available with sar, it does provide a quick overview as well as some of the information available with sar. Like sar, vmstat can be told to run over a period of time. For example, vmstat 1 100 would show output once a second for 100 seconds. I find this a useful tool for monitoring system statistics while some other known event is occurring. For example, if I want to monitor behavior while I run a large application, vmstat would give me a good overview.

You can configure your kernel with tunesh. When you run this, you are asked a set of questions (such as number of serial terminals, network connection, and so on). Based on your answers to these questions and information it determines itself, tunesh adjusts several kernel parameters to best fit the kernel to the system. Although this is not always perfect, it does provide a certain amount of tuning and is valuable to the novice administrator. See the tunesh(AMD) man-page for details.

Unfortunately, there is much more to kernel tuning than this. Entire books have been written about the subject. SCO provides a performance guide that covers many more issues than we have space for. However, I wanted to cover the tuning issues that cause the most problems and are easiest to address.

Refer to *The SCO Performance Tuning Handbook* by Gina Miscovich and David Simons, published by Prentice Hall. Although this was written before the release of OpenServer, it is still applicable when you take into account the dynamic parameters. Not only does this provide some great tuning tips, it provides more insights into the inner working of the kernel.

Although it does not address SCO, another useful book is *System Performance Tuning* by Mike Loukides, published by O'Reilly and Associates. This provides an excellent overview of the concepts involved.

## Getting It All at Once

The basis for the following script was provided to me by Tom Melvin. There were a couple of sections that referred specifically to third party software installed on his system that I didn't include. However, checking versions of installed software would be a good addition. I also removed the entire section that checked the UUCP configuration, as well as a section that did some benchmarking. While this is all useful information, my intention is not to provide you with the complete monitoring tool, but to provide you with some ideas. Note that this script takes for granted that most everything is at the default (file names and locations).

Other things that this script is missing is information on your automount filesystem if you are using it, and your NIS maps. Another enhancement could include the contents of stune to show any changed kernel parameters. If you have a network, you could have this script run out of cron on each machine and then copy it to a central administration machine. You could also include a section that tested connectivity within the network. Other enhancements could include command line (or menu) options that only check certain aspects of the configuration. You could also add some checks by sar to determine system performance.

```
:
# Script to poke around on the system

# In this case I do not use any of the functions in std_funcs. However
# I always include out of habit. If I ever decide to expand the script
# to be more interactive, I don't have to worry about it not finding
# functions. Watch the dot in front of the file name.
. /usr/lib/sh/std_funcs

# Although I may not use then until much later, I always like to
# define my variables at the top of the script.
SYSTEM='uname'
CONFIG_DIR=/usr/local/lib
CONFIG_FILE=${CONFIG_DIR}/cnf.${SYSTEM}
LINE_BREAK="---------------------------------------------"

# This uses the fact that everything inside of the brackets is one
#expression. If it evaluates to false, (that is /usr/local/lib does exist)
# then the second half with the mkdir won't run.

[ ! -d /usr/local/lib ] && mkdir -p $CONFIG_DIR
```

```
# Send all standard out to the configuration file. Any echoes or cat's all
# go to stdout. This exec has redirected stdout to the config file.
# Messages are explicitly sent to /dev/tty
exec > $CONFIG_FILE
is_root()
{
# Is the user sufficiently powerful ( root )
case 'id' in
  *root*) ;;  # root
  "") ;;       # single user
  *)           # someone else
echo "This program must be run by the superuser (root) " >/dev/tty

      exit 1
      ;;
esac
}
sys_conf()
{
echo "SYSTEM CONFIGURATION  On: 'date' \c"
echo "\nO.S. Configuration: \n 'uname -X '"
if [ -s "/usr/bin/uptime" ]
then
      echo "\nSystem stats\n"
      uptime
fi
}
# Note that this shows you only currently mounted filesystems. I added
# the extra line to check the number of inodes used as it can become an
# issue
disk_usage()
{
echo "Checking disk usage" >/dev/tty
echo $LINE_BREAK
echo "Disk usage:"
df -v
df -i
}
hardware_conf()
{
echo "Checking installed hardware" >/dev/tty
echo $LINE_BREAK
echo "Installed hardware:"
```

```
hwconfig -h 2>/dev/null
}
memory()
{
echo $LINE_BREAK
echo "Memory installed"
grep 'mem:' /usr/adm/messages | tail -1
}
software_conf()
{
echo "Checking installed software" >/dev/tty
echo $LINE_BREAK
echo "Installed software: \n"
swconfig 2>/dev/null
}
# This doesn't take into account having more than 2 drives drive_settings()
{
echo "Drive settings" >/dev/tty
echo $LINE_BREAK
echo "Drive settings"
dparam /dev/rhd00 2>/dev/null
dparam /dev/rhd10 2>/dev/null
}
# This doesn't take into account having more than 2 drives. If the drive or
# partition does not exist, errors are simply sent to /dev/null. There two
loops. The
# outer one first prints the partition table and then calls the inner loop.
The inner
# loop runs divvy on all 4 possible parititions.
{
for disk in 0 1
do
fdisk -p -f /dev/rhd${disk}0 >/tmp/ckconfig.$$ 2>/dev/null
if [ $? -eq 0 ]; then
        echo "--------------------"
        echo "Partitions on disk $disk"
        cat /tmp/ckconfig.$$
  for partition in 1 2 3 4
  do
    divvy -P /dev/hd${disk}${partition} >/tmp/ckconfig.$$ 2>/dev/null
    if [ $? -eq 0 ]; then
              echo "----------"
              echo "Divisions on partition $partition of disk $disk"
              cat /tmp/ckconfig.$$
```

```
    fi
  done
fi
done
}
enabled_ttys()
{
echo "Determining enabled terminal ports" >/dev/tty
echo $LINE_BREAK
echo "Active Terminal ports"
grep "respawn" /etc/inittab
}
printers()
{
echo "Checking printer set-up" >/dev/tty
echo $LINE_BREAK
echo "\nPrinter setup"
lpstat -t
echo "\n"
for fle in 'lc /usr/spool/lp/admins/lp/interfaces/*'
do
    xyz='basename $fle'
    echo "Printer - $xyz \c"
    grep "#!" $fle | sed 's/#!//'
    grep "^stty" $fle
    echo "\n"
done
}
filesystems()
{
echo $LINE_BREAK
echo "\n/etc/default/filesys"
cat /etc/default/filesys 2>/dev/null
echo $LINE_BREAK
echo "\nCurrently Mounted filesystem"
mount
}
root_cron()
{
echo "Cron settings for root" >/dev/tty
echo $LINE_BREAK
echo "\nCron settings for root :"
crontab -l
}
```

```
invalid_dev()
{
echo "Invalid device files" >/dev/tty
echo $LINE_BREAK
echo "Files in /dev"
find /dev -type f -exec l {} \;
}

# This is not necessarily the best way to check for this information.
# We are making a lot of assumptions here.
check_net()
{
echo $LINE_BREAK
NAMED='ps -ef | grep -v grep | grep named'
if [ -n "$NAMED" ]
then
    echo "You are (probably) a nameserver"
    return
else
if [ -f /etc/resolv.conf ] then
      echo "You are (probably) a nameserver client"
      return
fi

echo "You are not using the nameserver."
echo "Contents of Hosts file:"
cat /etc/hosts
fi
}

show_messages()
{
echo $LINE_BREAK
echo "\nMessages file\n"
tail -30 /usr/adm/messages
}

echo "This script will have a look around your system to see how it is \
configured." >/dev/tty
echo "Information will be stored in the file $CONFIG_FILE" >/dev/tty

is_root
sys_conf
drive_settings
disk_usage
hardware_conf
memory
software_conf
enabled_ttys
```

```
printers
filesystems
root_cron
invalid_dev
check_net
show_messages

echo "\nFinished" >/dev/tty
```

# CHAPTER
# 15

- Preparation

- Checking the Sanity of Your System

- Problem Solving

- Crash Recovery

- Odds and Ends

# Problem Solving

Using the title "Problem Solving" for this chapter was a conscious decision. I intentionally avoided calling it "Troubleshooting" for several reasons. First, troubleshooting has always seemed to me to be the process by which we look for the causes of problems. Although that seems like a noble task, so often finding the cause of the problem doesn't necessarily mean finding the means to correct or understand the problem.

The next reason is that so often I find books where the troubleshooting section is just a list of problems and canned solutions. I find this comparable to the sign, "In case of fire, break glass." When you break the glass an alarm goes off and the fire department comes and puts out your fire. The cause of the fire may never be known to you.

The troubleshooting sections that I find most annoying list out 100 problems and 100 solutions, but I usually have problem 101. Often I can find something that is similar to my situation and with enough digging through the manuals and poking and prodding of the system I eventually come up with the answer. Even if the answer is spelled out, it's usually a list of steps to follow to correct the problem. There are no details about what caused the problem in the first place or what the listed steps are actually doing.

In this chapter, I am not going to give you list of known problems and their solutions. The SCO documentation does that for you. I am not going to try to give you details of the system that you would need to find the solution yourself. Hopefully, I did that in the first part of the book. What I am going to do here is to talk about the techniques and tricks that I've learned over the years to track down the cause of problems. Also, we'll talk about what you can do to find out where the answer is, if you don't have the answer yourself.

## Preparation

Problem solving starts before you have even installed your system. Since a detailed knowledge of your system is important in figuring out what's causing problems, you need to keep track of your system from the very beginning. One of the most effective problem solving tools costs about $2 and can be found in grocery stores, gas stations, and office supply stores. Interestingly enough, I can't remember ever seeing it in a store that specializes in either computer hardware or software. What I am talking about is a notebook. Although a bound one will do the job, I find a loose leaf one more effective since you can add pages more easily as your system develops.

Include in the notebook all the configuration information from your system, the make and model of all your hardware, and every change that you make to your system. This will be a running record of your system, so the information should include the date and time as well as the person making the entry. Every time you make a change, from adding new software to changing kernel parameters, you should record it in your log.

Don't be terse with comments like, "Changed kernel parameter and relinked." This should be detailed like, "Changed DTHASHQS from 100 to 200. Relinked successful." Although it seems like busy work, I also believe things like adding users and making backups should be logged. If messages appear on your system, these too should be recorded with details of the circumstance. The installation guide contains an "installation checklist." I recommend completing this before you install and keep a copy of this in your log book.

Something else that's very important to include in the notebook is problems that you have encountered and what steps were necessary to correct that problem. One support engineer at SCO told me he calls this his "solutions notebook."

While you are assembling your system, write down everything you can about the hardware components. If you have access to the invoice, a copy of this can be useful for keeping track of the components. If you have any control over it, get your reseller to include details about the make and model of all the components. I have seen enough cases where the invoice or delivery slip contains generic terms like 486 CPU, cartridge tape drive and 500MB hard disk. Often this doesn't even tell you if the hard disk is SCSI, IDE or what.

Next, write down all the settings of all the cards and other hardware in your machine. The jumpers or switches on hardware are almost universally labeled. This may be something as simple as J3, but as detailed as IRQ. SCO installs at the defaults on a wide range of cards and generally they are few conflicts unless you have multiple cards of the same type. However, the world is not perfect and you may have a combination of hardware that neither I nor SCO has ever seen. Therefore, knowing what *all* the settings are can become an important issue.

One suggestion is to write this information on gummed labled or cards that you can attach to the machine. This way you have the information right in front of you every time you are working on the machine.

Many companies have a "fax back" service, where you can call a number and have them fax you documentation of their products. For most hardware, this is rarely more than a page or two. However for something like the settings on a hard disk, this is enough. This has a couple of benefits. First, you have the phone number for the manufacturer of each of your hardware components. The time to go hunting for it is not when your system has crashed. Next, you have (fairly) complete documentation for your hardware. Lastly, by collecting the information on your hardware you know what you have. I can't count the number of times I have talked with customers who don't know what kind of hard disk (let alone the settings) they have.

Another great place to get technical information is the World Wide Web. I recently bought a SCSI hard disk that did not have any documentation. A couple of years ago that might have bothered me. However, when I got home I quickly connected to the Web site of the driver manufacturer and got the full drive specs as well as a diagram of where the jumpers are. If you are not sure of the company name, take a guess like I did. I tried www.conner.com and it worked the first time.

When it is time to install the operating system, the first step is read the release notes and installation guide. I am not suggesting reading them cover to cover, but look through the table of contents completely to ensure there is no mention of potential conflicts with your host adapter or the particular way your video card needs to be configured. The extra hour you spend doing that will save you several hours later, when you can't figure out why your system doesn't reboot when you finish the install. Oh, did I mention that you should read the release notes and installation guide? You should. They're very important.

As you are actually doing the installation, the process of documenting your system continues. Depending on what type of installation you choose, you may or may not have the opportunity to see many of the programs in action. If you choose an automatic installation, then many of the programs are run without your interaction, so you never have a chance to see and therefore document the information.

The information you need to document is the same kinds of things we talked about in the section on finding out how your system was configured. Document the hard disk geometry (`dkinit`), partitions (`fdisk`), divisions and filesystems (`divvy`), the hardware settings (`hwconfig`), and the kernel parameters (`mtune` and `stune`). The output to all of these commands can be sent to a file, which can be printed out and stuck in the notebook.

I don't know how many times I have said it and how many articles it has appeared in (both mine and from others), but some people just don't want to listen. They often treat their computer system like a new toy at Christmas. They first want to get everything installed that is visible to the outside world such as terminals and printers. In this age of net-in-a-box, often that extends to getting their system on the Internet as soon as possible.

Although being able to download the synopsis of the next Deep Space Nine episode is an honorable goal for some, Chief O'Brien is not going to come to your rescue when your system crashes. (I think even he would have trouble with the antiquated computer systems of today.)

Once you have finished installing the operating system, the very first device you need to get installed and configured correctly is your tape drive. If you don't have a tape drive, buy one! Stop reading right now and go out and buy one. It has been estimated that a down computer system costs a company, on the average, $5000.00 an hour. You can certainly convince your boss that a tape drive costing one-tenth as much is a good investment.

One of the first crash calls I got while I was in SCO Support was from the system administrator at a major airline. After about 20 minutes, it became clear that the situation was hopeless. I had discussed the issue with one of the more senior engineers who determined that the best course of action was to reinstall the OS and restore the data from backups.

I can still remember their system administrator saying, "What backups? There are no backups."

"Why not?" I asked.

"We don't have a tape drive."

"Why not?"

"My boss said it was too expensive."

At that point the only solution was data recovery service.

"You don't understand," he said, "there is over $1,000,000 worth of flight information on that machine."

"Not any more."

What is that lost data worth to you? Even before I started writing this book, I bought a tape drive for my home machine. For me it's not really a question of data, but rather time. I don't have that much data on my system. Most of it can fit on a half-dozen floppies. This includes all the configuration files that I have changed since my system was installed. However, if my system crashed, the time I save restoring everything from tape as compared to *reinstalling* from floppies, is worth the money I spent.

The first thing to do once the tape drive is installed is to test it. The fact that it appears at boot says nothing about its functionality. It may appear to work fine, all the commands behave correctly, and it even looks as if it is writing to the tape. However, it is not until the system goes down and the data is needed that you realize you cannot read the tape.

I suggest first trying the tape drive by backing up a small subdirectory such as `/etc/default`. There are enough files to give the tape drive a quick workout, but you don't have to wait for hours for it to finish. Once you have verified that the basic utilities work (like `tar` or `cpio`), then try backing up the entire system. If you don't have some third party backup software, I recommended that you use `cpio`. Although `tar` can backup up most of your system, it cannot backup device nodes. Don't use something like `dump`, as this simply makes an image of your filesystem and getting back individual files is next to impossible.

I personally use a "super-tar" product on my system. These are from third party vendors that not only provide a very usable interface, they often do bit-level verification and provide complex inclusion and exclusion mechanisms. The discussion of which one of these super-tar products to use is almost religious. Like religion, it's a matter of personal preference. I use Cactus' Lone-Tar because I have a good relationship with the company president, Jeff Hyman, who pops up regularly in the SCO Forum on CompuServe. Lone-Tar makes backups easy to make and easy to restore. A working demo of Lone-Tar (as well as other super-tar products) is available from the SCO libraries on CompuServe.

After you are sure that the tape drive works correctly, then you should create a boot/root floppy. A boot/root floppy is a pair of floppies that you use to boot your system. The first floppy contains the necessary files to boot and root floppy contains the root filesystem.

Creating a boot/root floppy can be done by either using `mkdev fd` or `sysadmsh` on ODT or the Floppy Filesystem Manager on OpenServer. Here you want to create both a boot and a root floppy. The primary reason for making this just after you install the tape drive and before anything else, is simply a matter of space. If you have installed too much, the kernel will not be able to fit on the floppy. Once you've made the boot/root floppy set, test it. Also test the tape drive from the floppy. Although not that common, I have seen cases where the major and minor number on the floppy for the tape drive was incorrect.

Now that you are sure that your tape drive and your boot/root floppy set work, you can begin installing the rest of your software and hardware. My preference is to completely install the rest of the software first. This includes other SCO products. There is less to go wrong with the software (at least little that keeps the system from booting) and you can, therefore, install several products in succession. When installing hardware, you should install and test each component before you go on to the next one.

I think it is a good idea to make a copy of your link kit before you make any changes to your hardware configuration. That way you can quickly restore the entire directory and you don't have to worry about restoring from tape. There is a good example of how to copy an entire directory tree on the `cpio(C)` man-page. Use that example to copy the entire `/etc/conf` subdirectory. I suggest using a name that is clearer than `/etc/conf.bak`. Six months after you create it, you have no idea how old it is or whether the contents are still valid. If you name it something like `/etc/conf.06AUG95`, then it is obvious when it was created.

Now, make the changes and test the new kernel. After you are sure that the new kernel works correctly, then make a new copy of the link kit and make more changes. Although this is a slow process, it does limit the potential for problems, plus if you do run into problems, you can easily back out of it by restoring the backup of the link kit.

As you are making the changes, remember to record all the hardware and software settings for anything you install. Although you can quickly restore the previous copy of the link kit if something goes wrong, writing down the changes can be helpful if you need to call to tech support.

Once the system is configured the way you want, make a backup of the entire installed system. It is a good idea to make this back up on a tape other than the one you used for just the base operating system. I like to have the base operating system on a separate tape in case I want to do some major revisions to my software and hardware configuration. That way, if something major goes wrong, I don't have to pull out pieces, hoping that I didn't forget something. I have a known starting point that I can build from.

At this point you should come up with a backup schedule. The *System Administrator's Guide* provides you with some guidelines on this. Keep in mind that these are "guidelines." The information provided there is not a list of unchangeable rules. You should backup as often as necessary. If you can only afford to lose one day's worth of work, then backing up every night is fine. Some people backup once during lunch and once at the end of the day. More often than twice a day may be too great a load on the system. If you feel like you have to do it more often, you might want to consider disk mirroring or some other level of RAID. See the section on filesystems for a discussion of the SCO implementation.

The type of backup you do is dependent on several factors. If it takes ten tapes to do a backup, then doing a full backup of the system (that is, backing up *everything*) every night is difficult to swallow (you might consider getting a larger tape drive). In a case where a full backup every night is not possible. There are two alternatives.

You can use incremental backups. These start with a master, which is a backup of the entire system. Then the next backup only records the things that have changed since the last incremental. This can be expanded to several levels. Each level backs up everything that has changed since the last backup of that or the next lower level.

For example, level 2 backs up everything since the last level 1 or the last level 0 (whichever is more recent). You might do a level 0 once a month (which is a *full* backup of everything), then a level 1 every Wednesday and Friday, and level 2 every other day of the week. Therefore, on Monday, the level 2 will backup everything that has changed since the level 1 on Friday. The level 2 on Tuesday will backup everything since the level 2 on Monday. Then on Wednesday, the level 1 backs up everything since the level 1 on the previous Friday.

At the end of the month, you do a level 0 which backs up everything. Let's assume this is on a Tuesday. This would normally be a level 2. The level 1 on Wednesday, backs up everything since the level 0 (the day before) and not since the level 1 on the previous Friday.

A somewhat simpler scheme uses differential backups. Here, there is also a master. However, subsequent backups will record *everything* that has changed (is different) from the master. If you do a master once a week and differentials once a day, then something that gets changed on the day after the master is recorded on every subsequent backup.

A modified version of the differential backup does a complete, level 0 backup on Friday. Then on each of the other days, a level 1 is done. Therefore, the backup Monday–Thursday will backup everything since the day before. This is easier to maintain, but you may have to go through five tapes.

The third type is the most simple, this is where you do a master backup every day and forget about increments and differences. This is the method I prefer since you save time when you have to restore your system. With either of the other methods, you will probably need to go through at least two tapes to recover your data, unless the crash occurs on the day after the last master. If you do a full backup every night, then there is only one backup to load. If the backup fits on a single tape (or at most two), then I highly recommend doing a full backup every night. Remember that the key issue is getting your people back to work as soon as possible. The average $5000 per hour you stand to lose is much more than the cost of a large (8Gb) tape drive.

This brings up another issue and that is rotating tapes. If you are making either incremental or differential backups, then you *must* have multiple tapes. It is illogical to make a master, the make an incremental on the same tape. There is no way to get the information from the master.

If you make a master backup on the same tape every night, you can run into serious problems, as well. What if the system crashes in the middle of the backup and trashes the tape? Your system is gone and so is the data. Also if you discover after a couple of days that the information in a particular file is garbage and the master is only one day old, then it is worthless for getting the data back. Therefore, if you do full backups every night, use at least five tapes, one for each day of the week. If you run seven days a week, then seven tapes is a good idea.

Although most people get this far in thinking about tapes, many forget about the physical safety of the tapes. If your computer room catches fire and the tapes melt, then the most efficient backup scheme is worthless. Some companies have fireproof safes that they keep the tapes in. In smaller operations, the system administrator can bring the tape home from the night before. This is normally only effective when you do masters every night. If you have a lot of tapes, you might consider companies that provide off-site storage facilities.

## Checking the Sanity of Your System

Have you ever tried to do something only to find that it didn't behave the way you expected it to? You read the manual and typed in the example character for character only to find it doesn't work right. Your first assumption is that the manual is wrong, but rather than calling in a bug to SCO Support, you try the command on another machine and to your amazement, it behaves exactly as you expect. The only logical reason is that your machine has gone insane.

Well, at least that's the attitude I have had on numerous occasions. Although this personification of the system helps relieve stress sometimes, it does little to get to the root of the problem. If you want, you could check every single file on your system (or at least the ones related to your problem) and ensure that permissions are correct, the size is right, and all the support files are there. Although this works in many cases, often it is not easy to figure out what programs and files are involved.

Fortunately help is on the way. SCO provides several useful tools to not only check the sanity of your system, but to return it to normal. The first set of tools we already talked about. These are the monitoring tools such as ps, crash, sar, and vmstat. Although these programs cannot correct your problems, they can indicate where problems lie.

If the problem is the result of a corrupt file (either the contents are corrupt or the permissions are wrong), the system monitoring tools cannot help much. However, there are several tools that specifically address different aspects of your system.

For starters, let's take the issue of incorrect permissions. Under both ODT and OpenServer, there are two options: fixperm and fixmog. The advantage that fixperm has is that it can not only tell you about permissions problems, but it can also tell you the install status of the different packages as well as create missing device nodes and directories. On the other hand, fixmog is fast since it is designed to fix security related problems. Therefore, discrepancies in files such as vi are ignored.

Fixperm uses what are referred to as *permissions lists*. These are represented by the files in /etc/perms. In general, each file represents a single product. If you have TCP/IP, for example, the files contained in the run-time TCP/IP product would be found in /etc/perms/tcprt. If you had the development system for TCP/IP, this would be represented by the file /etc/perms/tcpds. The exception is the operating system itself.

As I mentioned in an early chapter, each product can be broken down into packages. These packages appear in different sections of the permissions lists. Each file within that package is shown on a separate line, like this:

```
RTS     f644     root/sys     1     ./etc/gettydefs     B02
```

The fields are: package (here RTS for run-time system), type of file and mode (here f for regular file, and permission 644), user/group (root/sys), links (1), path (./etc/perms), and volume (B02). Note that the volume was originally designed to tell you what floppy disks this file was on. However, if you have a tape or CD-ROM installation, then everything is on one volume.

If you are a new administrator, you may not know what kind of media you installed on. To find this out, look in /etc/perms/bundle/odtps and find the "mediatype" entry.

If we have a file with more than one link (for example `/usr/bin/mail`), rather than individual entries for each link, there is a single entry like the one we have and then the name of each additional link is listed. So, the entry for `/usr/bin/mail` would look like this:

```
MAIL     sx711     bin/bin 3       ./usr/bin/mail      X02
                                   ./usr/bin/mailx     X02
                                   ./bin/mail          X02
```

As it's making its checks, `fixperm` sees that `/usr/bin/mail` has two more links and can immediately check them. Since they are links, they have the same file and have the same permissions, owner, and group, etc., `fixperm` only needs to ensure that they all exist and check the permissions on one of them. If it corrects the permissions on one of them, it fixes them for all. For more details on the different `perms` files, options, and so on, see the `fixperm(ADM)`, `custom(ADM)`, and `perms(F)` man-pages.

Like `fixperm`, `fixmog` has its own database of information. This is the file `/etc/auth/system/files`, which represents the File Control Database. (See the section on security for more information.) Here we have the same basic information as in the permissions list. However we are not concerned with packages, volumes, or even links. All we are concerned with is access permissions, owner, group, and what type of file it is. In addition to `fixmog`, you can also use `cps`. This works on a single file and not on the entire File Control Database as `fixmog` does.

One major problem that both `fixperm` and `fixmog` have is that they only check for the existence of the file, as well as file attributes such as permissions and owner, but neither the size or checksum of the file. This is a major issue when files become corrupt. The permissions may be correct and even the size might match, however if the file is corrupt, then the checksum is most likely going to be wrong.

SCO provides a utility to compute a checksum on a file, called `sum`. It provides three ways of determining the sum. The first is with no options at all, which reports a 16-bit sum. The next way uses the `-r` option, which again provides a 16-bit checksum, but uses an older method to compute the sum. In my opinion, this method is more reliable since the byte order is important as well. Without the `-r`, a file containing the word "housecat" would have the same checksum if you changed that single word to "cathouse." Although both words have the exact same bytes, they are in a different order and give a (slightly) different meaning.

Because of the importance of the file's checksum, I created a shell script while I was in SCO Support that was run on a freshly installed system. As it ran, it would store in a database all the information provided in the permissions lists, plus the size of the file (from an `ls -l` listing), the type of file (using the `file` command), and the checksum (using `sum -r`). If I was on the phone with a customer and things didn't appear right, I could do a quick grep of that file name and get the necessary information. If they didn't match, then I knew something was out of whack.

Unfortunately for the customer, much of the information that my script and database provided was something that they didn't have access to. Now, each system administrator could write a similar script and call up that information. However, most administrators do not consider this issue until it's too late. OpenServer corrected much of that problem with the introduction of the Software Manager.

Not only can the Software Manager check for the existence of files, but it can also verify the checksum of the files. Many things can be corrected automatically, but some require that you explicitly request the Software Manger to make the corrections. For example, let's assume that a fat-fingered system administrator removed `/usr/bin/mail`. The software manager would tell you that the file was missing, but would not automatically restore the link until you told it to fix the discrepancies.

If the file that we, as users, access is missing or corrupt (such as `/usr/bin/mail`), then this method works fine. However, if the file contained within the SSO is missing or corrupt, then the situation is more serious. This is the same situation you would have in ODT without the Software Manager. You need the installation media. Although it's nice to have the Software Manager tell you you can't fix it and the user must do it by hand, as of this writing there is nothing that I can find that tells you what to do when something is missing. At least none directly available from the Software Manager.

ODT was nice in that the same program that told you what file (or files) was missing also allowed you to reinstall that missing file. Some might be saying that the Software Manager tells you what's missing and also lets you reinstall, so it does the same thing, right? Unfortunately not. Although substantially more powerful in many regards than `custom` and `fixperm` in ODT, OpenServer's Software Manager has broken some of the basic functionality. The primary example is reinstallation of a single file. This also extends to groups of files, even those that are completely unrelated, which were both possible in ODT.

A solution would be to reinstall the public portions of a particular SSO/product. That way you replace the binaries without touching the data files. Unfortunately, that avenue has been blocked. You can no longer reinstall a package, like you could in ODT. Further, you cannot select from the list of packages on the system (within an SSO) to say you want to install that package new (after you have removed it). Instead you must first read the installation media to get a list of software to install. If you have another machine in the network with OpenServer, you can do a network install of that package, which is a bit faster.

However, this doesn't really mean that the only way to get back single files is to reinstall the package. Fortuantely, the SCO engineers are not that viscious. They provided for us the `customextract` utility, whose purpose it is is to extact files from an "SSO distribution source." What this means is that it can pull individuals files from tape, CD, or whatever you used to install. The basic, and most commonly used, sytnax is

```
customextracty -m<device> <SSO_path_name>
```

where `<device>` is the device where the media resides and `<SSO_path_name>` is the path name within the SSO, *not* the path we are used to seeing. For example, to restore `/usr/bin/vi` from a CD, the command might look like this:

```
customextract -m /dev/rcdt0 /opt/K/SCO/Unix/5.0.0a/usr/bin/vi
```

Note that the files are restored based on your current working directory. Therefore, you might want to consider first changing directories to `/`. If you want to extract the files first and copy them into their proper location by hand, you can change directories into `/tmp`. In addition, you can specify a list of files to extract using the `-f` option followed by the name of the file containing the list.

You can also use `custom` in OpenServer to verify your software as well as correct certain problems. These are the same kinds of problems that can be corrected using the Software Manager. To be able to use this functionality, you have to be familiar with the way SSOs are put together. If you are still having trouble, we talked about SSOs in the section on SCO basics.

An example of using `custom` os OpenServer to verify and correct the Run-Time System (RTS) might look like this:

```
custom -v SCO:Unix:RTS -x
```

This says I want to verify (-v) the RTS package of the UNIX product from the manufacturer SCO. The package name can be found in the SSO in the directory `/var/opt/K/<vendor>/<product>/<release>/.softmgt` in the files with the `.fl` ending. For example, the file that the above command is reading is `/var/opt/K/SCO/Unix/5.0.0Cd/.softmgmt/RTS.fl`. These have a slightly different format than the old perms list, but are fairly straightforward to read. See the `custom(ADM)` man-page for more details.

Also new to OpenServer is the `customquery` command. This is a very useful tool for not only finding out what is installed, but also the versions. The basic syntax is

```
customquery function options
```

where the functions include `ListComponents`, `ListPackages`, `ListFiles`, and `ListDescriptions`. See the `customquery(ADM)` man-page for more details.

As we have just seen, there is a way to correct problems when commands, utilities, and other applications are corrupt. If a data file is corrupt, that's a different story entirely. In most cases, it is impossible for the operating system to know what is valid data and what is not. Therefore, it cannot be expected to be able to correct such data corruption.

If you do have corruption in an applications data file, you need to turn to the application vendor for possible means of correcting the problem. Well, what if that vendor is SCO? If there was some corruption in a data file used by an SCO program, they would be the ones who would know how to correct it. In many cases, this is impossible. There is no way the system could correct problems, let's say, in the nameserver data files. There is a certain format the files need to follow, but the nameserver relies on human intervention to ensure that these files are created correctly. Since there is nothing to compare these files to (no reality check), there is little that can be done to correct the problem.

Fortunately, in the case of the TCB, there is such a reality check. This is the `authck` utility. Not only does it understand the formats of the different files and identify problems, it can also correct many of them. So important is the consistency of the TCB, that the system runs `authck` every time you boot. This is done by the shell script `/etc/authckrc`, which is started by `init` from `/etc/inittab`.

The `authck` utility needs to be run either by root, or some other user with the `auth` subsystem privilege. Note also that the `chown` kernel privilege is also necessary if you want to make the changes that `authck` discovers. There are options to check each of the primary TCB databases. The `-p` option checks the Protected Password Database, the `-s` checks the Protected Subsystem Database, and the `-t` checks the Terminal Control Database.

If you plan on checking more than one database at a time, I recommend either using the applicable options together (for example, `-ps` ) or using the `-a` option to check all databases. This is a lot quicker than checking each database individually as the databases do not need to be reloaded every time. If you want you can have `authck` automatically correct problems it finds by using the `-y` option, or by using the -n option you can tell it to correct nothing. Also useful is the -v option. This outputs all the problems that authck finds, whether you tell it to correct them or not.

We now get to the "sanity checker" that perhaps most people are familiar with: fsck, the filesystem checker. Anyone who has lived through a system crash or had the system get shutdown improperly has seen fsck. One unfamiliar aspect of fsck is the fact that it is actually several programs, one for each of the different filesystems. This is done because of the complexities of analyzing and correcting problems on each filesystem. As a result of these complexities, very little of the code can be shared. What can be shared is found within the /etc/fsck program.

When it runs, fsck determines what type of filesystem you want to check, and runs the appropriate command. The "real" fsck command as well as many other commands are found in /etc/fscmd.d, where each of the subdirectories is named for the filesystem type that the commands are used on. Here you find a whole set of commands that are used to access and manipulate a filesystem.

If you look, you will see that there are subdirectories for, among others, ISO-9660 and ROCKRIDGE filesystems. Some of you may know that these are filesystems found on CD-ROMs. CD-ROMs are read-only filesystems. What's the point of running fsck on a filesystem that is read-only? Even if it was corrupt, there is no way to correct things. What purpose does it serve to have fsck even look at these filesystems?

Well, there is no point. That is the point. There is no fsck program for these filesystems. If you looked in /etc/fscmd.d/ISO9660 you would not see an fsck program. In fact, there are only two programs here: fstyp and mount. These are actually links to the same files for the other CD-ROM filesystem: (Rockridge).

Regardless of what kind of filesystem you are checking, fsck is a very complex program because the structure it is cleaning and trying to correct is very complex. Depending on the filesystem type you are checking, fsck goes through up to eight different phases. For HTFS, EAFS, AFS, and S51K filesystems the phases are the same, but for DTFS filesystems, they are different. Therefore, we are going to first talk about the phases for HTFS, EAFS, AFS, and S51K.

 Phase 0 is new to OpenServer. It is during this phase that the intent log is replayed if intent logging has been enabled. Unless you specify a full check, outstanding transactions are completed and the filesystem is marked as clean. Since the filesystem is clean at this point, there is no need to check further, and fsck exits.

In phase 1 of a full check, `fsck` checks the inode table. Part of what is done is comparing the size of the file to the number of blocks allocated on the hard disk. In addition, `fsck` checks to ensure that the number of links to this file is not zero. This could possibly mean that someone had removed the file and the system did not have time to update the inode table before the system went down. Here, too, `fsck` checks the sanity of the disk blocks. If one of the data blocks pointed to in the inode is outside of the boundaries of the filesystem, then fsck knows that something is wrong. The result is that `fsck` removes the incorrect information, which means that the file is removed.

Another key aspect of phase 1 is searching for duplicate blocks. This is where more than one inode point to the same data block on the hard disk. Don't think that this is what a link is. A link is a file name that points to the same inode. Here we have multiple inodes that point to the same data. This is not supposed to happen. Once the situation is corrected, `fsck` checks again to see if there are more duplicate blocks. This is phase 1b.

Phase 2 is used to clean up what was found in phase 1. For example, if we find there are files with duplicate blocks, `fsck` has no choice but to remove both files. This is accomplished in phase 2. Here, too, `fsck` cleans up directory entries that either point to inodes that are empty or ones that are nonexistent. Nonexistent inodes occur when the inode is larger than the maximum possible on the filesystem or when it is negative. You have only as many inodes as were allocated when the filesystem was created.

In phase 3, file connectivity is checked. For example, let's say an inode exists and points to valid data but there is no directory entry on the system for it. This is referred to as an *unreferenced file*. It is placed in the `/lost+found` directory. This is normally in the root directory of the filesystem. It is then given a new name, which is simply its inode number.

This phase brings up a few interesting issues. First, if it is a directory that has no entry in some other (parent) directory, it too will be placed in `lost+found`. Now there is a subdirectory of `/lost+found` with its name being the inode of that subdirectory. However, the contents of the directory "file" are intact. Therefore, the filename inode pairs in this directory are intact. You can `cd` into that directory and see all the file names as if nothing had ever happened. I have seen it where `/bin` (or was it `/usr/bin`?) ended up in `/lost+found`. All that had to be done was to rename it `/bin` (or `/usr/bin`) and things were back to normal.

Next, there can only be a maximum number of unreferenced files found on your system. Remember that each directory is simply a file in a specific format.

All that is done during this phase of `fsck` is that the directory file is being filled with the names of the "lost" files. As I mentioned in the section on filesystems, the size of the `lost+found` directory does not change during `fsck`. Therefore, you run into problems if a lot of unreferenced files are encountered. See the section on filesystems for more details.

If the unreferenced file is empty, there is no logic in placing it in `lost+found`. Therefore, when `fsck` encounters an unreferenced, zero-length file it will prompt you to clear the inode (unless you used the `-y` option, in which case it is cleared automatically). This can be very upsetting to some administrators because often this phase reports a large number of unreferenced, zero-length files. No worries. These are usually only unnamed pipes that have been created on the filesystem. (The HPPS does this all in memory and avoids this issue.)

In phase 4, `fsck` checks the link count of files. For example, if there are only two files that reference a particular inode, but the link count in that inode is 3, then `fsck` needs to correct it.

During phase 5, `fsck` examines the free-block list to resolve any missing or un-allocated blocks. Once all inconsistencies have been corrected, `fsck` rebuilds the free list, in phase 6.

As I mentioned before, `fsck` checks and repairs a DTFS on its own. Because of the nature of the filesystem, there are only four phases. In phase 1, `fsck` reads the inode bitmap and initializes the block bitmap. In phase 2, the inodes are "validated." Part of this process is to ensure that the B-tree structure of each file is maintained, so that the tree remains balanced.

In phase 3, `fsck` rebuilds the directory structure. Remember from our discussion on filesystems I mentioned that the inode of each file contains a pointer to the parent directory. Using this, `fsck` can easily rebuild the directory structure and there is no need for a `lost+found` directory since files are not lost. If the inode is trashed, then the disk blocks exist without an inode. In that case, there is no way to rebuild them into the original file and the blocks can simply be returned to the free list and the block bitmap is updated. In phase 4, the superblock is updated.

You may find yourself cleaning a filesystem so large that all the necessary tables cannot fit into memory. As a result, `fsck` requires a *scratch* file to store the tables. This can be a real file on some other filesystem or you define a separate filesystem just for scratch. If you know that the filesystem is too large, then you can specify the scratch file on the command line with the `-t` option. If you don't, `fsck` will recognize the need for a scratch file and prompt you. If you don't have a special scratch device you can simply used `/dev/swap`.

# Problem Solving

System problems fall into several categories. The first catetory is difficult to describe and even more difficult to track down. For lack of a better word, I am going to use the word "glitch." These are problems that occur infrequently and in circumstances that are not easily repeated. These can be caused by anything from users with fat fingers to power fluctuations that change the contents of memory.

Next are special circumstances in software that are detected by the CPU while in the process of executing a command. We discussed these briefly in the section on kernel internals. These are traps, faults, and exceptions. Many of these events are normal parts of system operation and are, therefore, expected. This includes such things as page faults. Other events like following an invalid pointer are unexpected and will usually cause the process to terminate.

## *Kernel Panics*

What if it is the kernel that causes either a trap, fault, or exception? As I mentioned in the section on kernel internals, there are only a few cases when the kernel is allowed to do this. If this is not one of those cases, the situation is deemed so serious that the kernel must stop the system immediately to prevent any further damage. This is a panic.

When the system panics, it uses its last dying breath to run a special routine that prints the contents of the internal registers onto the console and dumps the contents of RAM onto the swap device. At the end, it will call the kernel function `haltsys()` which stops the system.

Despite the way it sounds, if your system is going to go down, this is the best way to do it. When the system panics in this manner, there is a record of what happened. First, there is the dump image on the swap device. Second, there is the register dump on the console screen. Both of these are *essential* pieces of information when your system goes down.

If the power goes out on the system, then it is not really a system problem in the sense that it was caused by an outside influence; similar to someone pulling the plug or flipping the circuit breaker (which my father-in-law did to me once). Although this kind of problem can be remedied with a UPS, the first time the system goes down before the UPS is installed can make you question the stability of your system. There is no record of what happened and unless you know the cause was a power outage, it could have been anything.

Another annoying situation is when the system just "hangs." That is, it stops completely and does not react to any input. This could be the result of a bad hard disk controller, bad RAM, an improperly written or corrupt device driver. Since there is no record of what was happening, trying to figure out what went wrong is extremely difficult, especially if it is very sporadic.

Since a system panic is really the only time we can easily track down the problem, I am going to start there. The first thing to think about is the fact that as the system is going down it does two things: writes the registers to the console screen and writes a memory image to the dump device. The fact that it does so as it's dying makes me think that this is something important—it is.

The first thing to look at is the instruction pointer. This is actually composed of two registers: the CS (code segment) and EIP (instruction pointer) registers. This is the instruction that the kernel was executing at the time of the panic. By comparing the EIP of several different panics, you can make some assumptions about the problem. For example, if the EIP is consistent across several different panics, this indicates that there is a software problem. The assumption is made because the system was executing the same piece of code every time it panics. This *usually* indicates a software problem.

On the other hand, if the EIP consistently changes, then this indicates that probably no one piece of code is the problem and it is therefore a hardware problem. This could be bad RAM or something else. Keep in mind, however, that a hardware problem could cause repeated EIP values, so this is not a hard coded rule.

If your system was able to successfully write the dump image to the swap device, then things may be a little simpler. If so, you can examine the dump image and find out the name of the function the system was in when it panicked. This is a lot more useful than just an EIP, because the function name can point to something more specific. Say for example the system panicked inside of the Sdskintr() routine, I know that this has to do with the Sdsk (SCSI hard disk) driver. Therefore, I might consider a hardware problem with the SCSI hard disk.

When the system boots after a panic, it recognizes that there is a dump image on the dump device, provided the dump device is /dev/swap. At that time you have the option of saving the image, removing it, or simply leaving it alone. If you leave it alone, it remains on the dump device until you decide to remove it. Note that the first time you swap, the image gets trashed.

When you do boot, you need to go into single user mode (to ensure you don't start swapping). Once there, run crash -d /dev/swap (assuming /dev/swap is the dump device). When you reach the prompt (>), simply type in panic. This will give you a stack trace of the last few system calls executed before the crash.

The top one will be the one the system was running when it crashed. If it is not obvious from the name of the function, you can look through the Driver.o files in /etc/conf/cf.d using either nm or strings to find out which driver the function is in.

Why do I specifically tell you to look in the device driver files? Well, since 99% if the time the cause of the panic is a corrupt or poorly written device driver, this is a good place to start.

One system panic does not necessarily tell you what the problem was. If you run crash and the panic command says that there is something wrong with the Srom driver, you cannot assume there is something wrong with your CD-ROM drive (assuming you knew what the Srom driver was). It could just as easily be a bad sport of RAM that was not detected as having a parity error. If you have multiple panics that seem to point to the same thing, but you cannot figure out exactly what the cause is, should run crash -d <dumpdevice> -o <file> to save the output and run the following functions inside of crash:

- panic - prints the panic information
- trace - prints a kernel stack track
- user - prints uarea of the active process when the system panicked
- proc - prints the process table when the system panicked.

Whoever is providing you with your support should be able to make some sense of it.

The problem with this approach is that the kernel is generally loaded in the same way all the time. That is, unless you change someting, it will occupy the same area of memory. Therefore, it's possible that bad RAM makes it look like there is a bad driver. The way to verify this is to change where the kernel is loaded in physical. You can do this by either re-arranging the order of your memory chips or using the mem= option to boot to limit what memory is accessed.

Keep in mind that this technique probably may not tell you what SIMM is bad, only indicate that you may have a bad one. The only surefire test is to swap out the memory. If the problem goes away with new RAM and returns with the old RAM, you have a bad SIMM.

### Kernel Messages

If you are unfortunate to have the system hang or even reboot itself, then there is no dump image to look at and no EIPs to compare. The first place to look is the system log file, /usr/adm/messages. Even if the system did panic, there may be some information there to indicate what went wrong. This is often in the form of a kernel message.

Kernel messages fall into five categories and usually have the format

`category: name: routine message`

The `category` can be one of the following, in increasing order of severity: `CONFIG`, `NOTICE`, `WARNING`, `FATAL`, and `PANIC`.

Although not always present, the `name` represents the device driver or subsystem name having problems. If it is a device driver, you will probably see the major and minor numbers of the offending devices. This makes tracking down the problem a lot easier. The `routine` portion is also not always present and usually is not as obvious as the major and minor number. However, you can still attempt to track down the device by looking through the `Driver.o` files.

A CONFIG message normally indicates that the value of one of the kernel tunable parameters has been exceeded. This will be followed by the kernel parameter in question and the value that was exceeded. The remedy is to either increase the parameter or limit access to that resource. For example, if you are running ODT or OpenServer with a maximum value for the size of the process table, you might get a message that says you have exceeded that limit. To correct this, either increase the size of the table (NPROC on ODT or MAX_PROC on OpenServer) or limit the number of users so you don't run out of processes. On the other hand, if the problem is caused by some run-away process, rebooting the system might correct the problem. See the section on monitoring system activity for more details.

A `NOTICE` is somewhat more urgent that a `CONFIG` message. This indicates that a situation has occurred that should be monitored. For example, running out of space or inodes on a filesystem would generate a `NOTICE`. Normally, this is not associated with any kernel parameter so a relink and reboot is not necessary. An example of this would be

`NOTICE: Srom: Not ready on SCSI CD-ROM 0 dev 51/0 (ha=0 id=5 lun=0)`

If for some reason, my CD-ROM is not ready, this might indicate a hardware problem. However, in my case this came from the fact that I automatically mounted a CD-ROM during boot up and this time there was no CD in the drive. But, these can also indicate a more serious problem. For example,

`NOTICE: Sdsk: Unrecoverable error reading SCSI disk 0 dev 1/0 (ha=0 id=0 lun=0)`
`block=123808`

When I ran `scsibadblk` (used to check bad blocks on a SCSI device) this block came up as bad. I was personally upset at treating a bad block as something comparable to not having a CD in the drive. In my opinion this error requires a higher level message, like a warning.

`WARNING`s may require immediate attention. The keyword is "may." It's possible that the warning could be something harmless like this:

`WARNING: floppy: Disk is write protected in fd0 dev 2/60`

On the other hand it could be something dramatic:

`WARNING: floppy: Read error on dev 2/60, block=20 cmd=0x03 status=0x01`

which indicates a problem that might make me lose data. To me, a write protected floppy is at the same level as not having a CD in the drive. Being able to determine the severity of the problem from these messages is not always simple.

`FATAL` errors are not happy things. These can be the result of hardware problems such as

`FATAL: Parity error in the motherboard memory`

This means you need to replace some of your RAM. However, this kind of message can be the result on fat fingers. Consider this example:

`FATAL: Bad bootstring syntax - kernel.auito`

Look carefully. There is an extra 'i' in "autio." This was the result of my wanting to go right into multi-user mode by typing `unix.auto` at the `Boot:` prompt. Because `/boot` didn't know what to do with my typo, I got this message. Normally, `FATAL` messages usually appear before the system panics. Therefore it is a good idea to keep track of these messages. This is also a case where the `FATAL` message is immediately followed by

`PANIC: Illegal bootstring, cannot continue`

Some things are just so picky.

Lastly, we find our old friend `PANIC`. When it gets to this stage, things are too severe to continue. It is rare that software is the cause, but do not discount it completely. Corrupt software can cause panics as can drivers that were designed for a different release of the operating system. If you have just installed some new hardware that requires a relink and reboot, and your system panics, this is a good sign that there is a hardware problem. Check the release of the driver to make sure it is supported. If it is, swap out the hardware.

If the kernel is in the process of panicking and something else occurs that would normally cause a panic, then a double panic occurs. Although this sounds a bit more serious, they may have the same cause. Therefore, treat a double panic as you would a single panic.

### *Getting to the Heart of It*

Okay, so we know what types of problems can occur. How do we correct them? If you have a contract with a consultant, this might be part of that contract. Sometimes the consultants are not even aware of what is in their own contracts. I have talked to customers who have had consultants charge them for maintenance or repair of hardware, insisting that it was an extra service. However, the customer would whip out the contract and show them that the service was included.

If you are not fortunate to have such an expensive contract, then you will obviously have to do the detective work yourself. If the printer catches fire, then it is pretty obvious where the problem is. However, if the printer just stops working, figuring out what is wrong is often difficult. Well, I like to think of problem solving the way Sherlock Holmes described it in *The Seven Percent Solution* (and maybe other places):

"Eliminate the impossible and whatever is left over, no matter how improbable, must be the truth."

Although this sounds like a basic enough statement, it is often difficult to know where to begin eliminating things. In simple cases, we can begin by eliminating almost everything. For example, suppose we were having system hangs every time we used the tape drive. It would be safe at this point to eliminate everything but the tape drive. So, the next big question is whether it is a hardware problem or not.

Potentially that portion of the kernel containing the tape driver was corrupt. If this is the case, simply relinking the kernel would be enough to correct the problem. Therefore, when you relink, you link in a new copy of the driver. If that is not sufficient, then restoring the driver from the distribution media is the next step. However, based on your situation, checking the hardware might be easier, depending on your access to the media.

If this tape drive requires its own controller and you have access to another controller or tape drive, you can swap components to see if the behavior changes. However, just like you don't want to install multiple pieces of hardware at the same time, you don't want to swap multiple pieces. If you do and the problem goes away, was it the controller or the tape drive? If you swap out the tape drive and the problem goes away that would indicate that the problem was in the tape drive. However, does the first controller work with a different tape drive? You may have two problems at once.

If you don't have access to other equipment that you can swap, then there is little that you can do other than verifying that it is not a software problem. I have had at least one case while in SCO Support where a customer would call in insisting that our driver was broken because he couldn't access the tape drive. Since the tape drive worked under DOS and the tape drive was listed as supported, either the doc was wrong or something else was. Relinking the kernel and replacing the driver had no effect. We checked the hardware settings to make sure there were no conflicts, but everything looked fine.

Well, we had been testing it using `tar` the whole time, since `tar` is quick and easy when you are trying to do tests. When we ran a quick test using `cpio`, the tape drive worked like a champ. When we tried outputting `tar` to a file, it failed as well. Once we replaced the `tar` binary, everything worked correctly.

If the software behaves correctly, then there is the potential for conflicts. This only occurs when adding something to the system. If you have been running for some time and suddenly the tape drive stops working, then it is unlikely that there are conflicts; unless, of course, you just added some other piece of hardware. If problems arise after adding hardware, remove it from the kernel and see if the problem goes away. If they don't go away, remove the hardware physically from the system.

Another issue that people often forget is cabling. I have done it myself where I had a new piece of hardware and after relink and reboot, something else didn't work. After removing it again, the other piece still didn't work. What happened? When I added the hardware, I loosened the cable on the other piece. Needless to say, pushing the cable back in fixed my problems.

I have also seen cases where the cable itself is bad. One support engineer reported a case to me where just pin 8 was bad. Depending on what was being done, the cable might work. Needless to say, this problem was not easy to track down.

Potentially the connector on the cable is bad. If you have something like SCSI, where you can change the order on the SCSI cable without much hassle this is a good test. If you switch hardware and the problem moves from one device to the other, this could indicate one of two things. Either the termination is messed up or the connector is bad.

If you do have a hardware problem it is often the result of a conflict. If your system has been running for a while and you just added something, then it is fairly obvious what is conflicting. If you have trouble installing, then it is not always clear. In such cases, the best thing is to remove everything from your system that is not needed for the install. In other words, strip your machine to the "bare bones" and see how far you get. Then add one piece at a time, once the problem occurs, you know you have the right piece.

When trying to track down a problem yourself, remain calm. Keep in mind that if the hardware or software is as buggy as you now think it is, the company would be out of business. It's probably one small point in the doc that you skipped over (if you even read the doc) or there is something else in the system conflicting with it. Getting upset does nothing for you. In fact, (speaking from experience) getting upset can cause you to miss some of the details that you're looking for.

As you are trying to track down the problem yourself, examine the problem carefully. Can you tell if there is a pattern to when/where the problem occurs? Is the problem related to a particular piece of hardware? Is it related to a particular software package? Is it related to the load that is on the system? Is it related to the length of time the system has been up? Even if you can't tell what the pattern means, the support rep has one or more pieces of information to help in tracking down the problem. Did you just add a new piece of hardware or SW? Does removing it correct the problem? Did you check to see if there are any HW conflicts such as base address, interrupt vectors, and DMA channels?

I have talked to customers who were having trouble with one particular command. They insist that it does not work correctly and therefore there is a bug in either the software or the doc. Since they were reporting a bug, we allowed them to speak with a support engineer even though they did not have a valid support contract. They keep saying that the doc was useless because the SW did not work the way it was described in the manual. After pulling some teeth, I discovered that the doc the customer used was for a product that was several years old. In fact, there had been three releases since then. They were using the latest software, but the doc was from the older release. No wonder the doc didn't match the software.

## Crash Recovery

It may happen that the system crash you just experienced, no longer allows you to boot your system. What then? The easiest solution (at least easiest in terms of figuring out what to do) is reinstalling. If you have a recent backup and your tape drive is fairly fast, this is a valid alternative, provided there is no hardware problem causing the crash.

In an article I wrote for SCO's DiSCOver magazine, I compared a system crash to an earthquake. The people that did well after the 1989 earthquake in Santa Cruz were the ones that were most prepared. The people that do well after a system crash are also the one that are best prepared. Like an earthquake, the first few minutes after a system crash are crucial. The steps you take can make the difference between a quick, easy recovery and a forced re-install.

In previous sections we talked about the different kinds of problems that can happen on your system, so there is no need to go over them again here. Instead we will concentrate on the steps to take after you reboot your system and find that something is wrong. It's possible, that when you reboot, all is well and it will be another six months before that exact same set of circumstances occurs. On the other hand, your screen may be full of messages as it tries to brings itself up again.

Because of the urgent nature of system crashes and the potential loss of income, I decided that this was one troubleshooting topic I would hold your hand on. There is a set of common problems that occur after a system crashes that need to be addressed. Although the cause of a the crash can be a wide range of different events, the results of the crash is small by comparison. With this in mind, and the importance of getting your system running again, this is one place where I am going to forget what I said about giving you cookbook answers to specific questions.

Let's first talk about those cases where we can no longer boot at all. You need to think back to our discussion of starting and stopping the system and consider the steps the system goes through when booting. I talked about them in details before, so I will only review them here as necessary to describe the problems.

As I mentioned, when you power on a computer, the first thing that happens is the Power-On Self-Test, or POST. If something is amiss during the POST, you will usually hear a series of beeps. Hopefully, there will be some indication on your monitor of what the problem is. It can be anything from incorrect entries in your CMOS to bad RAM. If not, maybe the hardware documentation says something about what the beeps mean.

When finished with the POST, the computer executes code that looks for a device from which it can boot. On an ODT or OpenServer system, this boot device will more than likely be the hard disk. The built-in code finds the active partition on the hard disk and begins to execute the code at the beginning of the disk. What happens if the computer cannot find a drive to boot from is dependent on your hardware. Often there will be a message indicating that there is no bootable floppy in drive A. It is also possible that the system simply hangs.

If you have a hard disk installed and it *should* contain valid data, then potentially your masterboot block is corrupt. If you created the boot/root floppy set like I told you, then you can use `fdisk` from it to recreate the partition table using the values from your notebook. Load the system from your boot/root floppy set and run `fdisk`.

With the floppy in the drive you boot your system. When you get to the `Boot:` prompt, you simply press Enter. After loading the kernel it prompts you to insert the root filesystem floppy. You do that and press Enter. A short time later, you are brought to # prompt, from where you can begin to issue commands.

When you run `fdisk`, what you will probably see is an empty table. Because you made a copy of your partition table in your notebook like I told you to do, you simply fill in the values exactly the way they were before. Be sure that you make the partition active that was previously so. Otherwise, you won't be able to boot or you could still boot but you would corrupt your filesystem. When you exit `fdisk`, it will write out a copy of the master boot block to the beginning of the disk. When you reboot, things will be back to normal.

(I've talked to at least one customer who literally laughed at me when I told him to do this. He insisted that it wouldn't work and that I didn't know what I was talking about. Fortunately for me, each time I suggested it, it did work. However, I *have* worked on machines where it didn't work. With a success rate well over 50%, it's obviously worth a try.)

If you did not follow my friendly advice and write down the `fdisk` parameters, all is not lost. When you installed a copy of you SCO system it made a copy of the masterboot block and stored it as `/etc/masterboot`. When you create a boot/root floppy set, this file is copied onto the root floppy. By using `dd`, which is also on your root floppy, you can rewrite the masterboot block. The command would be

```
/bin/dd bs=376 count=1 if=/etc/masterboot of=/dev/rhd00
```

This means that `dd` will copy one 376-byte block from `/etc/masterboot` to `/dev/rhd00`, which is your boot hard disk. Be careful when you type this. If you mistype the size and make it 736 or type `count=10` you'll need to get out your installation media and start over.

One thing that I would like to point out is that the `/etc/masterboot` file is not updated. If you still have root on your hard disk and later add partitions, you could change the `if` and `of` entries in the above command, which will update the `/etc/masterboot` file to reflect your current masterboot block. If you have written down the configuration, then this is not a problem. You can have a corrupt or outdated `/etc/masterboot` and it won't matter. You always use `fdisk` and input the values by hand.

Some of you might be thinking that once the system is installed, the partition table isn't going to change. Well, if you have used the entire partition for UNIX, this is probably true. However, if you are like me and have multiple operating systems, the issue is not so simple. Once, I had two DOS partitions and a single ODT 3.0 partition on my first drive. When OpenServer arrived I did not want to remove ODT. I reconfigured my DOS partitions so that the first was smaller and I moved everything in the second partition onto a new drive. I then installed OpenServer on the leftover space. From OpenServer's perspective, `/etc/masterboot` is still valid. However, from ODT's perspective it is not.

If the hardware sees that you have a hard disk, but cannot find a valid, active partition, you may see the message

```
NO OS
```

This message is the result of either a corrupt masterboot block, or it is the result of a corrupt `boot0`. If caused by a corrupt masterboot block, you can boot from the boot/root floppy and recreate it as I described above. If the driver parameters are wrong, you end up looking at some other part of the disk from where you should and get this message. If you have an SCSI hard disk, then it is unlikely that this message is the cause of the problem.

The first thing to check is the hard disk parameters (assuming you don't have an SCSI hard disk). To see what the current parameters are, type

```
dkinit 0 0
```

which indicates the first drive on the first controller. You then have a menu from which you select option 1 to display the current disk parameters. If these parameters match your hard disk, then all is well. Leave them alone. If they don't match you can modify them with the correct values. How do you know what the correct values are? These are one of those things that I told you to write down in your notebook.

You may find that the partition table was valid. If so, the problem was more like the result of either a corrupt `boot0` or `boot1`. Unfortunately there is no magic command you can run to replace it like the masterboot block. However, there are also copies of them on the system, so you can use `dd` to copy them onto the hard disk, like this:

```
/bin/dd if=/etc/hdboot0 of=/dev/hd0a
/bin/dd if=/etc/hdboot1 of=/dev/hd0a bs=1k seek=1
```

If you think back to the section where we discussed the hard disk layout, you'll remember that boot0 is a relatively small section on the hard disk. You see that the size of `/etc/hdboot0` is less than 1K. When we use `dd` to write it out to the hard disk, `dd` only writes as many bytes as are in the file. Next, we have boot1.

This is a little larger, but starts 1K from the beginning of the partition. That's why we need to seek in 1 block. Here we set the block size to 1K (bs=1k). If you made a mistake and put in a block size of 2, then dd would seek in 2K before starting to write and you would end up overwriting something.

At this point, the system is trying to load and run the first real program: /boot. If you are running ODT, then this is in the root directory of your root filesystem, and on OpenServer this is in the root directory of the /dev/boot filesystem. Let's just call these both the "boot" filesystem. Since the two operating systems use the same files to boot and just their name is different, calling each the boot filesystem makes life easier.

If boot1 runs into trouble loading /boot, there are several things that could cause this. The easiest to correct is if the division table has become corrupt. If you run divvy from your boot/root floppy set and see an empty table, like the fdisk table, you can simply input the values from your notebook. (Are you beginning to understand why this notebook is so important?) Unfortunately, a copy of the division table is not something that is kept. If your division table is messed up and you didn't write down the values, you're hosed.

One thing is very important when inputting the value into the division table and that is *don't* create the filesystem. Only put in the values for the starting and ending block. You don't even have to name them. (Remember the name comes from the device node.) If you create them, a *new* filesystem will be created. This means that all the data will be lost. Well, not entirely. You see, all that is done is that the inode table gets recreated. It's not like the disk is formatted. This is similar to a quick format under DOS where the FAT is overwritten. The data is still there, but there are no pointers to the data.

I accidentally did this on my own system with no backups. Since this was the second hard disk and there was only one filesystem, things were easier. The data was only text files and the disk was relatively unfragmented, so I used a series of dd commands to write 1Mb files onto my other partition. I could then look through these files and decide if there was anything of value in them. It took several hours, but I estimate I had a recovery rate of at least 95%. Not bad, but I wouldn't recommend trying it yourself.

If /boot is not there or otherwise can't be loaded you end up with a message like this:

```
boot not found
Cannot open
Stage 1 boot failure: error loading hd(40)/boot
```

Since you need /boot to boot off the floppy, then this is a logical place to get it from. The first thing you need to do is to boot from the boot/root floppies, of course. Since you are actually copying files and not dd'ing the contents onto the hard disk, you have to first mount the boot filesystem. If the boot filesystem went down dirty, then the mount will fail since you need to clean it first. More than likely `/dev/boot` on OpenServer is clean since `/dev/boot` is normally mounted read-only. Even if it was clean, there is no harm in cleaning it again. Therefore, before I mount the boot filesystem, I always run `fsck`.

If there were a lot of pipes open when the system went down, there will be a lot of unreferenced files. Therefore, you might find yourself pressing `y` to the prompt to clear all these unreferenced, zero-length files. Instead, you could start `fsck` with the `-y` option to have it assume "yes" to each prompt. The question is, "Do you feel lucky?"

Actually it isn't that bad. If the file contains data, it ends up in `/lost+found`. If it doesn't contain data, it gets trashed. Why do you want a lot of zero-length files taking up vital directory entries in `lost+found`?

My suggestion is that you mount the boot filesystem like this if you are running ODT:

`/etc/mount /dev/root /mnt`

and like this, if you are running OpenServer:

`/etc/mount /dev/boot /mnt`

Now you can copy `/boot` like any other program:

`/bin/cp /boot /mnt`

Now is a good time to check and see if there is a kernel on the boot hard disk. It doesn't have to be the most recent one (probably called `unix`), but anything in the root directory of the boot filesystem. (`unix.old`, `unix.orig`, `unix.N1`). If so, you can copy that to `/mnt/unix`. Once you get past `/boot` and can load your kernel, you are on the hard disk and have a lot more options in terms of how to proceed.

If you discover that your root filesystem is too corrupt to mount and `fsck` fails, you can try to mount the filesystems as read-only and dump the filesystem to tape. If this works, you, at least, have access to your files.

One thing I didn't mention is that we don't have to copy many of these things from the floppy to the hard disk. He can take advantage of some of the book magic I talked about in the section on starting and stopping your system. Assume that just the masterboot block is corrupt, so we can't boot from the hard disk. If we can get to the `Boot:` prompt from the floppy, then we can access the kernel and the root filesystem on the hard disk. For example, if we had OpenServer, at the `Boot:` prompt, we could type in:

```
hd(40)unix swap=hd(41) dump=hd(41) root=hd(42)
```

In each case, it uses the hard disk (hd) driver; first getting the hard disk off of minor 40, using minor 41 for the dump and swap devices, then using minor 42 for the root filesystem. Notice that this takes into account the different filesystems that /unix is on versus the root filesystem. For ODT the same command would look like this:

```
hd(40)unix swap=hd(41) dump=hd(41) root=hd(40)
```

If for some reason, there was no kernel in the boot filesystem, you could change the location that Boot: gets the kernel. Hopefully, the one on the floppy works, so you could use that instead. Here the command might look like this for OpenServer:

```
fd(64)unix swap=hd(41) dump=hd(41) root=hd(42)
```

This takes the kernel from the floppy device (fd) with a minor number of 64, which is /dev/fd0.

If we wanted to extend this, we could take advantage of boot aliasing and modify /etc/default/boot on the floppy. We could create an alias that took the kernel and root filesystem from the hard disk. It might look like this:

```
HDUNIXROOT=hd(40)unix swap=hd(41) dump=hd(41) root=hd(42)
```

Therefore, when we boot off the boot floppy and get to the Boot: prompt, we just type in hdunixroot and it executes that bootstring.

If you have a system crash the "safest" thing is to reinstall. However, "safe" doesn't always mean best. If the crash was caused by a unique set of hardware and software circumstances that won't occur for another six months, then re-installing probably won't fix the problem. Even if you have the CD-ROM distribution, re-installing means several hours of down time. If you have the company president or a hoard of angry users breathing down your neck, this is not a realistic option. You need to get the computer up and running as soon as possible. You need to determine the problem, find a solution and get everyone else back to work.

If you try to boot from the hard disk and get either of these messages:

```
stage 1 boot failure not a directory

PANIC srmountfun- Error 6 mounting rootdev (1/40)
```

or any PANIC with srmountfun, then the best thing is probably to restore from backups. These messages are essentially saying that the system does not recognize the root filesystem. If that's the case, you cannot continue. Out of the dozens of crashes I've had to work users through, only once was this corrected by going through all of the steps I described above.

If you have good, current, reliable backups of your programs and data, then the most reliable method of crash recovery is to restore from backup. If not, there are many professional data recovery services, which stand a good to excellent chance of recovering your data. They are relatively expensive and the turn-around time may be a week or longer. If it is imperative that you recover your data, this is your best chance.

A common problem is that the system appears to hang when it reaches the prompt to press CTRL-D to continue or enter root password for maintenance mode. Neither CTRL-D nor the root password seem to work. Pressing ENTER would normally just repeat that message. However, that too appears not to work. This problems occurs often after the system crashes, as well as when it is shutdown improperly,

The cause of this problem is a corrupt (not missing) /etc/ioctl.syscon file. This controls I/O for the device /dev/syscon, which is what is accepting input at this moment. To correct the problem, you remove the file. When the system reboots, it sees the file is missing and recreates it. Fortunately, you don't have to boot from the floppy to remove it. The issue here is that the file is corrupt and not behaving correctly. Instead of pressing the Enter key, you press CTRL-J. Everything else should work correctly. So, if you wanted to go into multi-user mode, pressing CTRL-D then CTRL-J starts you on your way to multi-user mode. If you enter the root password followed by the CTRL-J, this will bring you into maintenance mode.

Both the *SCO OpenServer Handbook* and ODT 3.0 *System Administrator's Guide* contains steps for recovery from additional boot problems. They also include many of the problems we discussed here, but I felt that the importance of the issue as well as the frequency of these problems warranted repeating the information.

## Odds and Ends

Experience has taught me that sooner or later you will get to a problem that you cannot solve. No matter how many changes you make to the configuration files and no matter how many times you reboot, the problem just won't go away. If the problem is the result of a bug, then SCO Support will help you, even without a support contract. There are often patches available that fix many known problems. These are called Support Level Supplements, or SLSs. SLSs are available for download via UUCP, ftp, and SCO's Web Server.

In addition to SLSs, there are Enhanced Features Supplements, or EFSs. These are not patches or bug fixes, but rather ehnancements to the system. As a result,

**Table 15-1**    Files Used in Problem Solving

/bin/pstat - Reports system information

/bin/who - Lists who is on the system

/bin/whodo - Determines what process each user is running

/etc/badtrk - Checks for bad spots on your hard disk

/etc/crash - Examines the running kernel

/etc/custom - Displays information about install packages (also used to
    install and remove software)

/etc/dfspace - Calculates available disk space on all mounted filesystems (front end to df)

/etc/divvy - Creates and administers divisions

/etc/fdisk - Creates and administers disk partitions

/etc/fixperm - Corrects and reports on file permissions and ownership

/etc/fixmog - Corrects and reports on file permissions and ownership

/etc/fsck - Checks and cleans filesystems

/etc/fuser - Indicates which users are using particular files and filesystems

/etc/hwconfig - Displays hardware configuration information

/etc/ifconfig - Configures network interface parameters

/etc/ps - Reports information on all processes

/tcb/bin/authck - Examines and corrects system security files

/tcb/bin/integrity - Examines and corrects system files against security database

/usr/adm/hwconfig - Hardware configuration log file

/usr/adm/lastlog - Log-file for each user's last login

/usr/bin/cpio - Creates archives of files

/usr/bin/last - Indicates last logins of users and teletypes

/usr/bin/llistat - Administers network interfaces

/usr/bin/lpstat - Prints information about status of print service

/usr/bin/netstat - Administers network interfaces

/usr/bin/sar - System activity report

/usr/bin/swconfig - Reports on software changes to the system

/usr/bin/tar - Creates archives of files

/usr/bin/w - Reports who is on the system and what they are doing

/usr/lib/acct/lastlogin - Keeps record of date user last logged in

/usr/spool/lp/pstatus - Printer status information

See also the list of configuration files in Chapter 16, p. 720.

many are not available free of change. Depending on where the EFS comes from and what features it includes, you may have to pay for more than just the media costs, but also royalties or "development" costs.

SCO also provides free access to their Information Tools (IT) scripts via the SCO Web Server. This is a set of thousands of articles covering everything from a description of virtual memory to details on how to get multiple SCO operating systems on the same *partition* to instruction on how to overcome bugs and other problems.

Available on CD is the SCO Support Services Library. This contains the IT scripts as well as character-based and X-based search and viewing programs. Along with the IT scripts are many of the SLSs *and* EFS. This is available through a yearly subscription from SCO. Although the price might seem a bit much at first. It is well worth the money considering the time saved by having the information and supplements immediately available. For more tips on getting help, I suggest you read the next chapter. See Table 15–1 for a list of some of the more common tools used in system monitoring and trouble shooting.

# CHAPTER
# 16

- Calling Support
- Consultants
- Other Sources

# Getting Help

**I**f you're like me, you think a manual is for cowards. Any good computer hacker should not be afraid to open up the box and start feeding in disks without regard for the consequences. You tear open the box, yank out the floppies, pop the first one in the drive and startup the Software Manager and happily go through the thankless task of installing the software. After everything has been installed and your desktop icons have been created, you double-click on the icon and start you new multimedia Web Viewer. But wait! It doesn't work right. No matter how much you point and click and click again, nothing happens. In frustration, you get on the phone and frantically dial the 800 number in back of the manual (the first time you opened it).

When you finally get through to support after waiting for two hours (it was actually only 5 minutes), you lash out at the poor tech support representative who was unlucky enough to get your call. You spend more time ranting about poorly written software than you spent on hold. When you finally get done insulting this person's ancestry, he calmly points out that on page 2 in the manual where it describes the installation procedure it says that in order to get the Web to work correctly, you have to have a network installed. Since you decided not to install TCP/IP when you first loaded the system, there is no way for the Web viewer to work. You're embarrassed and the whole situation is not a happy thing.

The obvious solution is to read the manual before, during, and after the installation. This tends to limit the embarrassing calls to tech support, but the world is not perfect and eventually something will go wrong. Programs are (still) written by human beings who can make mistakes, which we users call bugs. Perhaps the QA technician who was checking your SCSI host adapter sneezed at the very moment the monitor program reported an incorrect voltage. Maybe they never tested that one, and a rare set of circumstances causes the program to freeze on your machine. The end result is that you've read the manual, checked and rechecked the hardware, and it still does not behave the way it is supposed to. You can't solve the problem yourself, so you need help.

## Calling Support

The most commonly known source of help is the company's tech support department. Tech support is like any system. You put garbage in and you're likely to get garbage out. Calling in, demanding immediate results or blaming the support rep for the problem will probably get you one of two things. Either you are told that it's either a hardware problem if you've called a software company, a software problem if you've called a hardware company, or they say there is "something" else on the machine conflicting with their product, but it's your job to figure it out. You may get an answer that, yes, that board is bad and you can return it to the place of purchase to get a refund or exchange. In other words, they blow you off.

If the board was bad, getting a replacement solves the problem. If however, there is a conflict, you will probably spend even more time trying to track it down. If the problem is caused by some program problem (conflicts or whatever), reinstalling may not fix the problem.

Rather than spending hours trying to track down the conflict or swapping out boards, you decide to call tech support. The question is "which one?" If there is only one program or one board, it's pretty obvious which one to call. If the problem starts immediately after you add a board or software package, the odds are that this has something to do with the problem. If, however, the problem starts after you've been running for a while, tracking down the offender is not that easy. That's why you're going to call tech support. So grab that phone and start dialing.

Stop! Put that phone down! You're not ready to call, yet. There's something you need to do first. In fact, there are several things you need to do before you call.

Calling tech support is not as easy as picking up the phone and dialing. Many people who are having trouble with their system tend to think that it is. In many cases, this is true. The problem is basic enough that the tech support rep can answer it within a few minutes. However, if it's not, lack of preparation can turn a two minute call into a two hour call.

Preparation for calling tech support begins long before that first phone call. In fact, preparation actually begins before you install anything on your system. I mean anything. Before you install your first program, before you make the change to `.profile` to change your prompt, even before you install the operating system.

In previous chapters, we talked about purchasing a notebook and detailing your system configuration. This kind of information is especially important when you need to call a hardware vendor to help track down a conflict. You may never use most of this information. However when you do need it, you save yourself a great deal of time by having it in front of you.

By knowing what product and what release you have before you call, you save yourself time when you do call. First you don't have to hunt through notes or manuals while the clock is ticking on your phone bill. Even if you can't find the release, don't guess or say "the latest". Although you can get the release number from the installation media, this may not be exactly what was used to install. The best source is to run `uname -X`. This tells you exactly what release the system is currently running.

If you guess, then the support technical might have to guess too. This is important because fixes are almost always release specific. If you say "the latest" and it isn't and the "bug" you have was corrected in the latest release, the analyst is not going to give you the fix, because he thinks you already have it. This wastes his time, wastes your time and in the end you don't get the correct solution.

Should it be necessary to contact SCO Support, at the very minimum you should have the following information:

- Operating System(s) and versions

- Machine type: XT, AT, PS/2

- Make and model of all hardware (rarely is just the brand sufficient)

- Controller make, model, and type

- Symptoms of problem: Noises, messages, previous problems

- An *exact* description of the error message you receive and the context in which you receive it

- Drive organization: partition sizes, special drivers

- Special devices/drivers such as disk array hardware and software

- What was the machine doing when the problem occurred?

- What was the sequence of events that preceded the problem?

- Has this problem occurred more than once? How often?

- Did you install any third party device drivers or additional hardware recently?

- What was the last thing that you changed?
- When did you change it?
- Is this a production machine and are you down now?

The last question is essential to getting you the service you need. If you are not clear to support about the urgency of the situation, you may end up waiting for the available support analyst or you might get the "try this and call back later answer." By explaining the urgency to everyone you contact, you are more likely to get your answer quicker.

On the other hand, tech support (at least at SCO) is based on an honor system. SCO Support will believe you when you call in and say your system is down. Many of the customer service people are not in a position to judge the severity of the problem; however, the support analyst is. Saying that your company is down because you can't figure out the syntax for a shell script is unfair to other people who have problems that are really more severe than yours.

Once you have all the details about the problem you are now ready to call, right? Well, not yet. Before you actually start dialing, you need to make every effort to track down the problem yourself. The first reason is pretty obvious. If you find it yourself, then there is no need to call tech support.

If you can't find it and have tried everything you can think of, you can save a great deal of time by telling the support rep what you tried. The support rep does not have to go through all the basic stuff again and can concentrate on more detailed issues.

Many vendors, including SCO, have bulletin boards containing answers to commonly asked questions. There is even a WWW page for the SCO bulletin board to make access even easier. Unless your system won't boot at all, this is usually a good place to look before you call support. Again it's an issue of time. It is generally much easier to get through to a bulletin board than to a support engineer. You may have to spend a little time becoming familiar with the particular interface that this company uses. However, once you have learned your way around, not only can you find answers to your questions, but you often find treasures such as additional programs that are not part of the base distribution. Even if you don't find the solution, knowing that you did look on the bulletin board saves the support engineer a step. In addition, accessing a web page or a bulletin board can keep you up-to-date on patch releases.

I mentioned that some companies have fax-back services. Often times answers to common questions are available. Another source is newsgroups or on-line services like CompuServe. Even if you don't get the solution to your problem, you may get some of the suggestions that the tech support rep would give you. Since you already know that something doesn't work, you have saved yourself the problem of getting a "try this and call back answer."

From the tech support perspective this is very helpful. First, there is the matter of saving time. If it takes twenty minutes just to get through the basic "sanity" checks, then that is twenty minutes that could have been used servicing someone else. Why do you care if someone else gets help instead of you? Well, if you happen to be the one waiting to talk to the support rep, you want him or her to be done with the other customer as soon as possible to be able to get to you quicker. The bottom line is that the quicker the rep helps one customer, the quicker it is for everyone.

Make sure the hardware is supported before you call to SCO Support. If not, getting effective support is difficult at best. They may have to guess at what the problem is and possibly give you erroneous information. In many cases you will either be referred to the hardware vendor and simply told they can't help you. Not that they won't try. The issue is usually that they don't have any information about that product, so the best they can do is advise you from knowledge they have about similar products. If the product you want to use deviates from the norm, then generic information is of little value.

If a piece of equipment is not officially supported, the support rep may never have seen this before and may be unaware of quirks that this machine has. A printer may claim to be HP LaserJet compatible, but the interface script may send commands to the printer that the clone does not have. Many people will insist that this is a problem with the operating system. SCO never claimed the hardware was going to work. So, if the hardware vendor claims it is 100% compatible, it is up to them to prove it.

On the other hand, because of the nature of the job, support analysts have encountered hardware that is not officially supported. If they try to get it to work and they succeed, then they are in a position to try it the next time. If they have successfully installed something similar, then many of the same concepts and issues apply.

This same thing applies to software. Make sure the software is supported by the OS. It may be that the particular release of the application is only supported on the newer version of the OS. In that case, neither the OS vendor nor the application vendor will be able to help. They know that it will not work. I remember one call into Support where the customer was having trouble with a version of SCO's Professional Spreadsheet Product that has been discontinued for over two years. To make things more interesting they were trying to get it to work on Interactive's UNIX, not SCO.

Try to determine if it is really an operating system problem and not specific to just one application. If you call SCO Support with a problem in WordPerfect, make sure the problem also occurs outside of WordPerfect. For example, if you can print from the command line, but can't print from WordPerfect, it's not an operating system problem. However, if the OS, SCOMail, and WordPerfect all have trouble printing, then it is probably not an issue with WordPerfect. The reverse is also true. It would be much better to call SCO support with such a problem than to call WordPerfect. Maybe you are only using WordPerfect, but the problem is with operating system and not just WordPerfect.

If the problem is software and deals with configuration, make sure that all of the associated files are configured correctly. Don't expect tech support to check your spelling. I had one customer who had problems configuring his mail system. He spent several minutes ranting about how the manuals were wrong because he followed them *exactly* and it still didn't work. Well, all the files were setup correctly except for the fact that he had made something plural although the manual showed is as being singular.

Even after you have gathered all the information about your system and software, looked for conflicts, and tried to track down the problem yourself, you are still not quite ready to call. Preparing for the call itself is another part of getting the answer you need.

One of the first questions you need to ask yourself is, "Why am I calling tech support?" What do you expect? What kind of answer are you looking for? In most cases, the people answering the phones are not the people who wrote the code. Many have spent hours digging through it, looking for answers or may have created an SLS or two. However, this is not the same as writing the SCSI hard disk driver. Therefore, they may not be in a position to tell you why the program behaves in a certain way, only how to correct it

If you are contacting the support reps via fax, email, or any other "written" media, be sure that there are no typos. When relating error messages, always make sure that you have written the text *exactly* as it appears. I have dealt with customers who have asked for help and the error message they report is half of one release and half of another. The change required is different depending on the release you are running. This is also import to know when calling. Telling the support rep that the message was "something like" may not do any good. If there are several possible errors, all with similar content, the exact phrasing of the message is important.

This is also a problem with two systems when one is having the problem and the other is not. It is not uncommon for a customer to describe the machines as "basically the same." This kind of description has little value when trying to track down a problem. I get annoyed at people who use the term when trying to describe a problem. I don't want the basics of the problem, I want the details. Often customers will use it as a filler word. That is, they say "basically," but still go into a lot of detail.

Many customers insist that the two systems are identical. If they were identical, then both would be behaving the same way. The fact that one works and the other doesn't indicates that the machines are not identical. By trying to determine where the machines differ, you narrow down the problem to the point where tracking down the problem is much easier. You may even find the problem yourself, thus avoiding the call to support.

Once you get tech support on the phone, don't have them read the manual to you. This is a waste of time for both you and the support rep, especially if you are paying for it. Keep in mind that although there may be no charge for the support itself, you may be calling a toll number. If this is during the normal business day (which it probably is), the call could still cost $20–$30. However, this is also dependent on your support contract. Many SCO customers will pay tens of thousands of dollars a year for support so that the can have the manual read to them. They don't have the time to go searching for the answer, therefore they pay someone else (SCO Support) to do it for them. If you want a premium service, you have to pay a premium price.

If you do read the manual and it still does not behave the way you expect or you are having problems relating the doc to the software, ensure that the doc matches the SW. A customer was having trouble changing his system name under Unix 324.0. He said the doc was bad because the SW did not work the way it was described in the manual. It turned out the doc he was using was for 3.2.2. not 324! No wonder the doc did not match the software.

If you don't know the answer to the question, tell the support rep, "I don't know." Do not make up an answer. Above all, don't lie outright. I had a customer who was having problems running some commands on his system. They were behaving in a manner I had never seen before, even on older releases. In order to track down the problem I had him check the release his was on. None of the normal tools and files were there. After poking around a while, I discovered that although this was a version of Unix, it was not SCO. When confronted with this, the customer's response was that their contract for the other operating system had run out.

I once had a customer that was trying to do remote printing. He first said he had two copies of the "latest" version of ODT. I had him run `swconfig` and found out that the TCP/IP release was not the latest. As it turns out it was not ODT either, just the OS and TCP/IP. We then wanted to check out the other side. Well, it wasn't the latest either. In fact, it was not even UNIX at all but OS/2. So, I put the customer on hold to see if anyone knew about OS/2 connectivity. When I got back on, the customer was talking to his dealer (it was a conference call), the customer asked, "Why do they need to know the release anyway?"

Getting information from some customers is like pulling teeth. They won't give it up without a fight. In order to get the right answer you must tell the analyst everything. Sometimes it may be too much, but it is much better to get too much than not enough.

When talking to support, have everything in front of you. Have your notebook open, the system running if possible, and be ready to run any command the support rep asks you. If you have a hardware problem, try to have everything else out of the machine that is not absolutely necessary to the issue. It is also helpful to try to reinstall the software prior to calling. Reinstalling is often useful and several companies seem to use this method as their primary solution to any problem. If you have done it in advance of calling and the problem still persists, the tech support rep won't get off with that easy answer. I am not professing this as the standard way of approaching things, however if you believe reinstalling would correct the problem and you have the opportunity, doing so either solves the problem or forces support to come up with a different solution.

Another common complaint is customers calling in and simply saying that a particular program doesn't work right. Although this may be true, it doesn't give much information to the technician. Depending on its complexity, a program may generate hundreds of different error messages, all of which have a different cause and solution. Regardless of what the cause really is, it is almost impossible for the technician to be able to determine the cause of the problem simply by hearing you say that the program doesn't work.

A much more effective and successful method would be to simply state what program you were trying to use, then describe the way it behaved and how you expect that it should behave. You don't even need to comment on it not working right. By describing the behavior, the technician will be able to determine one of three things. Either you have misunderstood the functionality of the program, you are using it incorrectly, or there really is a bug in the program.

People calling into tech support often have the attitude that they are the only customer in the world with a problem. Many have the attitude that all other work by the entire company (or at least tech support) needs to stop until their problem is resolved. Most tech support organizations are on schedules. Some have phone shifts scattered throughout the day, and can only work on "research" problems during specific times of the day. Other organizations have special groups of people whose responsibility it is to do such research. In any event, if the problem requires special hardware or a search through the source code, you may have to wait several hours or even days for your solution. For the individual this may be rather annoying, but it does work out better for everyone in the long run.

The idea that the analyst needs to stop what he or she is doing and work on one customer's problem becomes a major issue when problems are caused by unique circumstances. The software or hardware company may not have that exact combination of hardware available. Although the combination ought to work, it is difficult to guarantee there will be no problems. As a result, the support rep may have to wait until they are not working on the phone to gather that combination of hardware. It may also happen that the rep may need to pass the problem to someone else who is responsible for problems of this type. As a result, the answer may not come for several hours, days, weeks, or even *months* depending on the priority level of the contract.

In addition to the priority of the contract, there is also the urgency of the problem. If you have a situation where data is disappearing from your hard disk, you will be given a higher priority than your contract would imply.

While I was working in SCO Support, I talked with many other support reps. Often a customer would have a support contract with their vendor and the vendor would have the contract with us. The vendor would call us if they could not solve the problem. I had a chance to ask many of them some of the more common problems.

There are several common complaints among tech support reps. Although it may seem like an obvious thing, many people are not in front of their machine when they call. It's possible that the solution is easy enough that the support rep can help even without you at the machine. However, I talked to a customer who had printer problems and wanted me to help him fix things while he was driving down the freeway talking on his car phone.

Another very common issue that support reps brings up is customers who come off thinking they know more than tech support. When they are given suggestions their response is usually, "That won't work." Maybe not. However, the behavior exhibited by the failure often does give an indication of where the problem lies. If you are going to take the time to call support, you must be willing to try everything that is suggested. You have to be receptive to the suggestion of the support rep and willing to work with them. If necessary, be willing to start the problem from scratch and go over the "basics." The customers that get the best response from support are usually the ones who remain calm and are willing to try whatever is suggested.

People have called computer manufacturers to be told how to install batteries in laptops. When the support rep explains how to do this and that the directions are on the first page of the manual, one person replied angrily, "I just paid $2,000 for this damn thing, and I'm not going to read a book."

At first glance this response sounds reasonable. A computer is a substantial investment and costs a fair bit of money. Why shouldn't tech support tell you how to do something? Think about a car. A car costs more. So, after spending $20,000 for a new car, you're not going to read the book to figure out how to start it? Imagine what the car dealer would say if you called in, asking how to start the car.

The computer industry is the only one that goes to this level when supporting its products. Sometimes customers are very naive; at least they are naive when it comes to computers. In attempting to solve a customer's problem it is often essential that the rep know what release of the operating system they are using.

Some customers are missing some basic knowledge about computers. One customer was having trouble when we needed to know the release. Although he could boot, he was having trouble typing in basic commands like `uname`. We told him to type `uname` then press return and it responded `dave: command not found` (you name).

We then asked him to get the N1 floppy and read us the release number off the floppy. He couldn't find it. Not the floppy, the release number. So after ten minutes of frustration, we decided to have him photocopy the floppy and fax it to us.

"Wow!" he said. "You can get information from the floppy that way?"

"Sure," we said. "No problem." (What's so hard about reading a label?)

A few minutes later a fax arrived from this customer. It consisted of a single sheet of paper with a large black ring in the center of it. We immediately called him back and asked him what the fax was.

"It's the floppy," he said. "I'm still amazed that you can get information from the floppy like that. I must tell you, I had a heck of a time getting the floppy out of the case. After trying to get it out of that little hole, I had to take a pair of scissors to it." (The case was actually the plastic jacket).

Many of us laugh at this because this is "common knowledge" in the computer industry. However, computers are the only piece of equipment where the consumer is not expected to have common knowledge. If you drive a car, you are expected to know not to fill it up with diesel when it takes normal gasoline. However, trying to load a DOS program onto an UNIX system is not unexpected.

One customer I had was having trouble installing a network card. The documentation was of little help to him because it was using a lot of "techno-babble" that most "normal" people couldn't understand. The customer could not answer the basic questions about how his hardware was configured. He insisted that it was our responsibility to know that because we wrote the operating system and he's not a computer person. Well, I say, it's like having a car that won't start. You call the car dealership and tell them it won't start. The service department asks you what model you have. You say that they should know that. They then ask if you have the key in the ignition. You say that you are not a "car person" and don't know this technical stuff.

In the past few years, many software vendors have gone from giving away their support to charging for it. This ranges anywhere from $25 a call for application software to $300 for operating systems like Unix. As more and more computers are being bought by people who have never used one, the number of calls to support organizations have gone up considerably. People treat computers differently than any other piece of equipment. Rather than reading the manual themselves, they prefer to call support.

Would you ever call a car manufacturer to ask how to open the trunk? Would you ever call a refrigerator manufacturer to ask how to increase the temperature in the freezer? Computer tech support phones are often flooded with calls at this level, especially if their support is free or free for a specific warranty period.

The only way for a company to recover the cost of the support is to either include it with the cost of the product or to charge extra for it. The bottom line is that there is no such thing as a free lunch, nor is there free tech support. If you aren't paying for the call itself, the company will have to recover the cost by increasing the sales price of the product. The result is still money out of your pocket. In order to make the situation fair for everyone involved, companies are charging those people who use the tech support system.

I remember watching a television program a couple of years ago on airplane accidents and how safe planes really are. The technology exists today to decrease the number of accidents to almost zero. Improvement to both airplane operations, air traffic control, and positioning could virtually eliminate accidents. However, this would result in increasing the cost of airline tickets by a factor of 10! People won't pay that much for safety. The risk is too low.

The same thing applies to software. It is possible to write code that is bug free. The professor who taught my software engineering class insisted that with the right kind of planning and testing, all bugs could be eliminated. The question is,

"At what cost?" Are you willing to pay ten times as much for SCO OpenServer just to make it bug free? Another support rep at SCO put it like this: "How can you ask us to hold up the entire product for an unknown length of time, to fix a single problem which affects few users, and is not fatal? Would you expect Ford to ship their next year's model of Escort three months late because they found out that the placement of the passenger door lock was inconvenient for people taller than 6'9"?" As ridiculous as this seems, calls reporting bugs are often at this level.

SCO, like many other software vendors realize that bugs will occur. SCO even goes to the extent of documenting some of the known ones in the release notes (another good reason for reading it). In addition, because of the production issues involved, SCO (as well as many other vendors) will consider a product "ready" months before it ships. Only fatal bugs will cause the product not to ship. Known bugs are still included and maintenance supplements are already in the works by the time the first box goes out the door. To me this is acceptable behavior compared to other companies that call their bug-fixes "updates."

After years of tech support, I am convinced that the idea that the customer is always right was not coined by some businessman trying to install a customer service attitude in his employees. It must have been an irate user of some product who didn't bother to read the manual, tried to use the product in some unique way, or just generally messed things up. When this user couldn't figure out how to use whatever he bought, he decided it was the fault of the vendor and called support.

You, as the customer, are not always right. Granted it is the responsibility of the company to ensure you are satisfied. This job usually falls on the shoulders of tech support, as they are usually the only human contact customers have with hardware and software vendors. However, by expecting tech support to pull you out of every hole you dig yourself into or by acting like a "know-it-all," you run the risk of not getting your question answered. Isn't that the reason for calling support in the first place?

You may have noticed that throughout the discussion on support, I didn't mention the different levels of support that are offered by SCO. This is difficult at best. SCO Support policies change as the demand and customer requirements change. To be safe and find out the latest prices and policies, it is best that you call SCO directly.

## Consultants

You may find yourself in a position where you cannot continue to try and solve problems over the phone. You need someone to come to your office to look at the problem first hand. This is where the computer consultant comes in. Sometimes consultants are called in to evaluate and analyze the current situations and make recommendations and sometimes even implement these recommendations.

Computer consultants are like lawyers. They often charge outrageous fees (several hundred dollars an hour) and rely on the fact that you know little or nothing about the subject. They have a service that you need and they want you to pay as much as you are willing to pay. Fortunately, all you need to do to see if a lawyer is qualified is to look on his wall. If the diploma is from Joe's Law School and Barber College, you'll probably go somewhere else. However, there are few laws governing who can act as a computer consultant. Therefore, you need to be extra careful in choosing a consultant.

I had one consultant call for a customer of his who was having trouble with a SCSI tape drive. The consultant almost got upset when I started talking about the technical issues involved such as termination and proper cabling. You see, he had a master's degree in electrical engineering and was, therefore, fully aware of the technical issues at hand. I asked him how much RAM his system had. He responded, "Do you mean memory? Well, there is, uh, 32, uh, what do you call them, megabytes." (No, I'm not making this up.)

Another time a customer was having a similar problem getting a network card working. Again it was the issue that the customer did not have the basic computer knowledge to know about base addresses and interrupts. The difference between thin-net and twisted pair was foreign to him. He had worked for many years on mainframes and had never had to deal with this level of problem. After over half-an-hour of *trying* to help him, it became apparent that this was really beyond the call of tech support. I suggested he hire himself a consultant. In the long run, that would ensure he got the attention and service he needed. There was a long pause, and then he said, "I *am* the consultant."

One of my favorite stories is about a consultant in Texas who was trying to do long-distance hardware trouble shooting for a site in Alaska. Despite the fact that they had a modem connection, it is often quite difficult to check hardware settings and cabling through a modem.

My auto mechanic has a PC running a DOS application written specifically for automobile workshops. Aside from the fact that the consultant had them start Windows and then click on an icon to start this *DOS* application, it does its job (it's the only thing the machine is used for). Recently my mechanic discovered that he was running out of hard disk space. The consultant told him he needed a larger drive. So, the consultant came in and put in a larger hard drive and things looked better. Since it was not part of their contract, the consultant charged for two hours labor to replace the drive, plus 10% more than the average market price for the hard disk. Now, so far, this seems like an acceptable practice. However, the consultant took the smaller drive with him, although he charged full price for the larger drive. It wasn't defective, just too small.

These stories represent four basic problems with computer consultants. First, you don't have to study computer science or even a related field to open shop as a computer consultant. Although electrical engineering is a related field and the person may know about the computer at the transistor level, this is comparable to saying that a chemist who knows what goes on at the molecular level inside an internal combustion engine is competent enough to fix your brakes.

The next issue is that although a consultant has worked with computers for years, they may know little about PCs or operating systems. I have seen consultants assume that all computer systems are the same. They worked for years on Windows so they are qualified to install and support UNIX, right?

Consultants must make house calls. They have to be willing to come to your site and check the situation themselves. You cannot be expected to shut down operations to bring a computer to their office, nor should you tolerate them trying to do remote support (for example, across a modem).

Lastly, if you do need to hire a consultant, make sure you know what you are paying for. When you do decide on a consultant, make sure that you know *specifically* what services are being provided and what obligations the consultant has. These services include not only hardware and software, but what work they are going to provide. For example, if they need to replace a defective hard disk, the cost of the disk is included, but the time to replace it may not.

The best solution is to ask your friends and other companies. If you have a good relationship with another company of similar size and product, maybe they can recommend a consultant to you. Another source is the Internet and on-line services like CompuServe. Ask people there what they have experienced. Also, contact SCO. They provide a list of authorize resellers and consultants based on region of the country. This way you get one that is from your area and knows SCO.

## Other Sources

Although, as I said, there is no such thing as a free lunch, you can get pretty close sometimes. For about less than a $30 start-up fee and about $10–$20 a month, you can get support that is comparable to SCO Support. The only problem is that it might be several hours (rarely longer) before you get an answer. I am talking here about the SCOFORUM on CompuServe.

The September 1995 issue of *SCO World* magazine included an article on the CompuServe SCOFORUM. It was written by Jean-Pierre Radley, one of the system operators (sysops) for the SCO Forum. Rather than repeating the contents of the article or the CompuServe literature, I would simply like to say it is well worth the money.

The topics range from basic shell programming issues to kernel internals and beyond. You will find people who have been working with SCO products for years and who can provide valuable insight into the various SCO products. There are many professional writers who pop up, such as John Esak, who is a columnist for *SCO World* magazine. I, too, am a regular contributor.

Despite the delays that are caused by the very nature of this media, responses are fairly quick. Unless your system has crashed and you are losing thousands of dollars an hour, this is an excellent source of information. If you have email and fax support with SCO, you probably end up getting your answers faster through CompuServe.

CompuServe customer service can be reached at 800–848–8990 or 614–529–1340. In addition, there are offices all over the world. The CompuServe starter-kit that is available through many computer software sources contains a list of phone numbers.

Another valuable source is the USENET newsgroups. In order to gain access, however, you need a news feed; that is, some other site that will provide you with the newsgroups. Because USENET uses "store and forward," turn around time, can be days, depending on where you get your feed. CompuServe, on the other hand, stores all of its messages in a central location. The minute your message is posted, it is available for everyone.

Throughout this book I made references to several other works that I feel will be helpful if you want to learn more about a particular subject. Aside from books, there are many magazines that provide useful information. Although more geared toward DOS and Windows, *BYTE* magazine often provides good technical articles about both new and existing technologies.

In addition, there are several generic UNIX magazines, such as *SysAdmin* magazine, that cover topics of interest on all UNIX systems. Even non-UNIX magazines like *Windows* magazine often brings me hardware and compatibility related issues. There is, of course, *SCO World* magazine, which provides technical information as well as SCO related news.

One magazine that is beginning to make its mark in the SCO marketplace is *Inside SCO UNIX Systems* published by The Cobb Group. For those who are not familiar with them, The Cobb Group publishes dozens of technical magazines covering a wide range of topics.

I think the biggest difference between *SCO World* and *Inside SCO UNIX Systems* is like the difference between commercial TV and public television. Commericial television is paid for by advertisements. As a viewer, the fee you pay is nominal if you have cable or free if you use your antenna. It is similar with *SCO World*.

Public television is paid for by the viewers. Although the yearly pledge you make to your local PBS station is comparable to your fees for cable, you are only paying for one channel. With *Inside SCO UNIX Systems* the situation is similar. There are no adds, not even small ones. The publication of the magazine is paid for *exclusively* by subscription fees. I like not having my programs interrrupted by commericals, that's why I was a member of a PBS station when I was living in California. I also like to be able to read articles without commerical breaks.

Please don't get me wrong. I subscribe to *SCO World*, as well. Just as I watch commerical TV. Both PBS and commercial TV have their place, just as *SCO World* and *Inside SCO UNIX Systems* each have their place.

For subscriptions, *SCO World* can be reached at 800–879–3358 or 303–604–1464. You can also use their email address, which is circ@scoworld.com. *Inside SCO UNIX Systems* can be reached at 800–223–8720 or 502–493–3232. Or for information and subscriptions, their email address is inside_sco@merlin.cobb.ziff.com.

Another information source is the Internet. Unfortunately it's hard to be more specific. There are thousands of resources out there for every conceivable topic. Most major computer companies have a Web site. Often all you need to do is add www to the company name to get access to the Web page. I have done this in getting to Intel (www.intel.com), Conner (www.conner.com), and even CNN (www.cnn.com). Here you can get product information as well as press releases. Many of these have links to other sites so it's easy to bounce from site to site.

# Glossary

This glossary contains a list of commonly used terms and expressions. Note the boldface words or phrases within the definitions. An understanding of these highlighted terms and the glossary terms will give you a strong base knowledge of the necessary terminology.

**absolute mode**—Changing file permissions using the 3-digit octal numbers, instead of the letters.

**absolute pathname**—A pathname for a file or directory beginning at the root directory and including the leading slash (/).

**accelerator keys**—Keystrokes that select menu options of functions without explicitly pressing the button or selecting the menu.

**access control**—see **security**.

**account**—The environment that a user accesses in order to log into the system.

**active partition**—The **partition** from which the hardware will try to boot.

**active window**—The window currently accepting input.

**ACU —Automatic Call Unit**. The term used in UUCP files to refer to a modem.

**address**—1) A memory location. 2) The user and machine name used to send an electronic mail message.

**ADF—Adapter Description File**. File provided with **MCA** devices on the **options disk** which contains configuration information for that device

**administrator**—The person who manages your computer system or network.

**AFS—Acer Fast Filesystem**. Older filesystem used on SCO systems that increases preformance by grouping files into 16K clusters.

**AHS—Adavanced Hardware Supplement**. A supplement provided by SCO that includes drivers to newer hardware.

**alias**—A name that is more commonly used or is easier to remember that represents something else. If your shell supports aliases, an alias can be a command that represents another command. In mail, this is an address that represents another address.

**alias tracks**—Tracks that are used to store data contained in bad tracks.

**anchors**—Hypertext links. An anchor or hypertext link is a link from one document to another

**ANSI**—American National Standards Institute.

**anti-caching**—Occurs when adding more memory makes the machine run slower. Sometimes, the CPU cannot cache eveything, so it caches nothing, thereby making the whole system run slower.

**APM**—Advanced Power Management.

**application**—A computer program that performs a particular task, such as word processing or managing a database.

**arbitration**—Process to determine which device has access to a particular resource, such as the system bus.

**argument**—See **command argument.**

**ARP**—Address Resolution Protocol.

**ASCII**—American Standard Code for Information Interchange. This is only the 128 character set and does not contain non-English characters.

**AT command set**—See **Hayes command set.**

**attribute**—See **permissions**.

**authorization**—Ability to access a particular system function.

**auto answer**—Setting your modem to automatically pick up when an incoming call is received.

**automounter**—The process that automatically mounts an NFS filesystem when a file or directory under the mount point is accessed.

**awk**—A programming language on many UNIX systems.

**background process**—A process that does not require interaction with the user to run. While a background process runs, the user can continue using other programs or commands.

**back-slash**—Slash that goes from the upper left to lower right (\). Also called a descending slash. Used to "escape" the special meaning of certain characters.

**back-ticks**—Similar to an apostrophe except that it slants from upper right to lower left. Used to "hold" the output of a command.

**backup**—A copy of files, directories, or filesystems, normally used as protection against accidental deletion, but also used to maintain a copy of an object in a known state.

**bad track**—A track on the hard disk that can no longer be read from or written to properly. Bad tracks are listed in a **bad track table** which points to good **alias tracks**.

**badhosts channel**—A mail channel through which all mail addressed to unrecognized machines is sent. The machine to which the mail is sent is a **smart host**.

**baduser channel**—A mail channel through which all mail addressed to unrecognized machines is sent. The machine to which the mail is sent is a **smart host**.

**bandwidth**—Refers to the maximum I/O throughput of a system. Although this normally refers to communications channels such as Ethernet or serial lines, it is often used to refer to any system.

**base address**—The setting used to access expansion cards.

**basename**—The file name component of a path. This can also refer to the "primary" portion of a file name. For example, the base name of the file *program.c* could be thought of as *program*. This is also the name of the command used to extract the basename. Compare this to directory name or **dirname**.

**baud**—One change in the electrical state of a signal.

**baud rate**—The number of electrical state changes per second.

**bdflush**—The buffer flushing daemon, which writes the contents of dirty buffers from the buffer cache to disk.

**binary**—The numerical system of counting with only two digits: 0 and 1. Also called **base 2**.

**binding**—The process of joining two components. Networking programs are often bound to a port, or key presses in the X Windows systems are bound to a specific function.

**BIOS—Basis Input/Output Services**. Special chip set on the computer that is used to access the hardware. SCO mainly uses this during boot-up and shutdown, although operating systems such as DOS use it as the primary means of accessing the hardware. The term BIOS is used for both the chip itself and the routines contained within the chip.

**bit**—A binary digit; either a 0 or a 1.

**bitmap**—A representation such as a picture or table that is stored as a series of 0s and 1s. Each character represents a single dot in the image or a particular value in the table.

**block device**—A hardware device that is accessed with buffering within the operating system. Although such a device can be read by an application a character at a time, input and output is buffered within the system's **buffer cache.** Compare this to a **character device.**

**blocking I/O**—I/O where the process is forced to wait until the operation is complete. Also known as synchronous I/O.

**boot**—The process by which the computer is powered on and goes through the necessary stops to load and start the operating system. This also refers to the program in the root directory that loads and starts the operating system.

**boot device**—The device (usually a floppy or a hard disk) from which the system is booted.

**bootstring**—The string passed to the **boot** program that it uses to determine what operating system to load and execute as well as how to do so.

**bottleneck**—When demand for a particular resource is beyond the capacity of that resource or beyond the ability of the operating system to provide that resource.

**bps—bits-per-second**.

**bridge**—A computer or other network device used to connect two networks. Bridges are often considered to connect similar systems, such as two Ethernet networks. Compare this to a **gateway**.

**bss**—Uninitialized data. An acronym for block started by symbol. (Often called blank static storage.)

**BTLD—Boot-Time Loadable Driver**. A **device driver** that is added to the operating system as it is booted. Unless such a driver is added permanently to the system or added the next time the system boots, it will not be available again.

**buffer**—An area of computer memory or the hardware that is used to temporarily store information.

**buffer cache**—The system buffer that stores the most recently accessed blocks. Note this is only used when accessing block devices.

**bus**—A set of lines (such as wires or leads) used to transfer data or control information. See also **expansion bus**.

**bus arbitration**—The process of deciding which device has control of the bus.

**bus mastering devices**—Also **bus masters**. Devices which are capable of taking control of the system bus.

**byte**—Eight **bits**.

**cache memory**—Also called just **cache**. High-speed memory usually placed between a CPU and main memory. Cache memory holds recently accessed memory as it is more likely that this memory will be accessed again. See also **level-one (L1) cache** and **level-two (L2) cache**.

**carriage return**—The keyboard key usually labeled <Return> or <Enter>. When your are typing at the command line, sending a carriage return indicates to the system that you are ready for the system to process the command. The term comes from the days when pressing the carriage return actually returned the carriage of the typewriter to its starting position.

**carrier**—Signal that is used as a reference point from which frequency changes are measured. These frequency changes are the actual data.

**CCITT**—**Comite Consultatif International Telegraphique et Telephonique**.

**CD-ROM**—A read-only optical storage media that uses the same technology as music CDs.

**Centronics connector**—Official name of the printer side of a parallel cable connection.

**CGA**—**Color graphics adapter**. Old video card.

**chain**—Term used to describe the connection between different layers in a network.

**channel**—The program used to phsyically transfer mail.

**character device**—A hardware device that is accessed with no buffering within the operating system. Although such a device can be read by an application in blocks, input and out is *not* buffered within the system's **buffer cache**. Compare this to a **block device**.

**CHARM**—Character **MOSAIC**.

**chat script**—Set of Expect-Reply pairs used by UUCP to log into a remote system.

**checkpointing**—The process by which specific filesystems have data and control structures written regularly to the disk.

**checksum**—A value that is calculated based on the bytes within a file. Some checksums are dependent on the order of the bytes within a file, whereas others are not. Two files with *identical* content must have the same checksum.

**child process**—The process created when one process (the **parent**) calls the fork() system call.

**class**—1) A group of printers, normally all of the same type that behave from the users' perspective as a single printer. 2) Description given to computer networks depending on what portion of their **IP address** is the network and which is the host.

**clean**—The state of a data object when it has not had its contents altered. "Dirty" buffers or pages can be marked clean when the data is written to disk. Filesystems are marked as clean when the control structures are written to the disk.

**client**—A process or machine that is using a particular resource that is provided by a **server**. In X Windows, a client is usually an application that creates a display on the screen. In a network, a client is a machine that accesses a remote filesystem or other resource.

**client-server model**—A model in which some components act as servers, providing resources or services and other components are clients that use those resources or services.

**clock tick**—The term used for an interrupt received at regular intervals from the programmable interrupt timer or clock. Clock ticks are signals to the kernel to allow it to initiate actions that need to be taken at regular intervals.

**CMOS**—**Complementary Metal-Oxide Semiconductor**. Technically any chip that uses the CMOS technology, but more commonly used to refer to a special chip that retains the basic configuration information about your machine.

**COFF**—**Common Object File Format**. One of the executable program formats used by SCO.

**COLA**—**Certificate of License and Authenticity**.

**COM port**—Common term for a serial port. Although this is actually the DOS term, it is used often. The term comes from "communications port."

**command**—A set of words or characters that is interpreted by the operating system as a request for action on the part of the system.

**command alias**—An alternative name for a command. See also **alias**.

**command argument**—Subsequent information passed to a command. This normally refers to information (such as the name of a file) that needs to be acted upon. Normally arguments that change a command's behavior are called flags or options.

**command flags**—See **command options**.

**command line**—A place on your screen where you input commands. The command line is usually indicated by a **prompt**. Also refers to the string of characters that form your command.

**command line interpreter**—The program that accepts your command line and reacts to it. See also **shell**.

**command options**—Arguments passed to a command that change its behavior.

**compile**—The process of taking the **source code** for a program and converting it into machine readable instructions.

**concatenated disk**—A logical disk composed of parts of multiple physical disks.

**contention**—When two devices or processes request a system resource at the same time. For example, when two devices want to use the **bus** at the same time.

**context**—The set of data, including the CPU register values and **uarea** that describe the state of a process.

**context switch**—The process the system goes through to change from one process being the current/active one to another.

**control character**—A character that has an ASCII value less than 32. These are often created by pressing the <Ctrl> key and another key. Programs can also generate control characters. These get their name from the fact that they are often used to control certain functions of an application.

**control key**—The key marked CTRL on most keyboards. This is used to modify the value sent by another key that is pressed at the same time.

**CPU—Central Processing Unit** . The primary chip or processor in a computer. The CPU is what reads and executes the machine's instructions and makes the computer go.

**cpu privilege level**—The level of access a process has while running. This essentially determines what memory and hardware can be accessed.

**crash**—An abnormal shutdown of the computer. Often this exhibits itself as the system "freezing," but it can also be that the system reboots itself or **panics**.

**cross-over cable**—A serial cable in which the transmit pin on one end of the cable goes to the receive pin on the other end and vice-versa.

**current working directory**—The directory that the system accesses when no paths are given. The current directory can also be specified as . or ./ depending on the context. This directory is taken as the starting point for all relative pathnames.

**cursor**—The symbolic indicator of where input is being taken. This is usually in the form of a box, underline, I-shaped character, or other shape that may or may not be blinking.

**cylinder**—The set of all **tracks** on a harddisk that are equadistant from the center of the disk.

**DAC**—1) **Digital to Analog Converter**. Chip (usually) on a video card that converts the digital signals from the operating system to analog signals that the monitor uses. 2) **Discretionary Access Control**.

**daemon**—A process that performs a service for the system. Normally, daemon processes are in the **background** and are waiting for something to occur that they must react to.

**DAT**—**Digital Audio Tape**. A form of backup (tape) media.

**data mode**—The mode a modem is in when it is transferring data.

**DCE**—**Data Communication Equipment**.

**decimal**—The numerical system of counting with ten digits:0123456789. Also called **base 10**.

**decode**—To convert data from an encoded format into a form that is readable by the appropriate process (human, program, etc.). See also **encode.**

**default**—The standard configuration or values for a program, field, or any other aspect of the system.

**default boot string**—The bootstring that is executed when you press return at the `Boot:`. This is the defined in `/etc/default/boot` by the entry `defbootstr`.

**defunct process**—A process that has made the `exit()` system call. This process does not use any system resources (including memory) except that it takes up a slot in the process table.

**descriptor**—Pointers to specific memory locations that are used by the kernel. These are stored in **descriptor tables**.

**device**—Any peripheral hardware attached to the system. These are accessed by **device drivers** through **device nodes**.

**device driver**—A set of routines internal to the kernel that performs I/O with a peripheral device. Although it is normally a user's process that wishes to access that peripheral device, it is the kernel that is actually doing the work.

**device nodes**—Special files that are the entry points into the **device drivers**. Also referred to as **device files**.

**digitalus enormus**—The technical term for making mistakes while typing. This translates as "fat fingers."

**DIN connector**—Deutsche Industrie Norm connector. Small 9-pin connector used to attach peripheral device such as mice and keyboards.

**DIPP**—**Dual In-line Pin Package**. Usually refers to memory chips that are connected via two rows of parallel pins.

**directory**—A file in a particular format that is read by the system as an inode and filename pair. The files contained within a directory can also be other directories.

**directory name**—Also referred to simply as **directory**. This is the name of the directory path used to access a file. The directory component can be accessed with the `dirname` command.

**dirty**—The state of a buffer or memory page that has had its contents changed.

**discretionary access control**—Security of a system where access is determined by the system administrator (at his or her discrention) and not forced by the system.

**disk mirroring**—The process by which the entire contents of a hard disk are duplicated on another disk.

**disk pieces**—The components of a **virtual disk**.

**disk striping**—The process by which parts of a logical or **virtual disk** is spread across multiple physical disks. This differs from a **concatenated disk** in that disks are not seen as being read in sequence, but rather in parallel. The portion of the virtual disk that resides on a physical disk is referred to a **stripe**.

**diskette**—Also called a **floppy disk** or **floppy**. A thin, flexible data disk within a protective jacket. Data is stored on the floppy and accessed through the **media access hole**.

**division**—A portion of a hard disk **partition** that may or may not contain a **file system**. The start location of each division is stored at the begining of the partition in the **division table** or **divvy table**.

**DLPI**—**Data Link Provider Interface**. A standard by which networking protocols access networking hardware.

**DMA**—**Direct Memory Access**. The means by which devices can access memory directly without the intervention of the **CPU**. DMA is controlled by the **DMA controller**.

**DNS** —**Domain Name System**. Also called Domain Name Service and Domain Name Server. The system by which information about a computer network is stored on specific machines rather than spread out on every machine. Information is obtained by making a **query** which is then **resolved** by the **domain name-server** or nameserver.

**domain**—A set of machines on a network that are controlled by a single administrative authority. The **domain name** is the name by which the domain is known.

**DOS**—A sort of operating system. Although the term refers to several different operating systems, it is most commonly associated with Microsoft's DOS, **MS-DOS**.

**dot file**—A UNIX file that has a period (dot) as its first character. With the exception of the root users, dot files are normally not visible. Because they are only visible with specific options to certain commands, they are often equated to DOS "hidden files."

**dotted-decimal notation**—The notation used to indicate **IP addresses** as decimal numbers.

**double-quotes (")**—Used to partially remove the special significance of certain characters. Characters such as the **$, single-quotes(')** and **back-ticks (`)** retain their special significance.

**DPI—Dots-Per-Inch**.

**DRAM**—Dynamic Random Access Memory. Must be refreshed regularly with electric signals. Compare this to **SRAM**.

**Driver.o**—The machine readable version of a device driver. The Driver.o files are **linked** into the kernel to provide access to the **devices.**

**DTE—Data Terminal Equipment**.

**DTFS— Desk Top File System**. SCO's compression filesystem.

**dtnode**—An inode from a DTFS.

**Dual In-Line Pin Package**—See **DIPP**.

**dump device**—The device that the system will write to (if it can) when the system **panics**.

**Dynamic Link Libraries (DLLs)**—Libraries of functions that are linked into the program as needed (at **run-time**) and not when the program is compiled.

**EAFS—Extended Acer Fast Filesystem**.

**ECC—Error Checking and Correcting**.

**edge-triggered interrupts**—**Interrupts** that are activated by the rising edge of the signal. That is when the signal is making the transition from low to high. Compare this to **level-triggered interrupts**.

**EFS**—Extended Functionality Supplement. Supplement supplied by SCO that provides functionality not included in the standard product. Compare this to **SLS**.

**EGA**—**Enhanced Graphics Adapter**. Another old video adpater.

**EIDE**—**Enhanced Integrated Digital Electronics**. A newer device interface. Most often used in hard disks and can overcome size limitations of **IDE** drives.

**EIP**—**Extended Instruction Pointer**. The register containing the memory location that the CPU is currently executing.

**EISA**—**Extended Industry Standard Architecture**. Enhanced version of the **ISA**. Developed by a consortium of companies providing advantages over ISA.

**ELF**—**Executable and Linking Format**. A new executable program format used by SCO.

**encapsulation**—The process by which one data format is enclosed inside of another. This technique is used in networking to pass data between the various layers.

**encode**—Converting data from one form to another. The newer form is generally more easily handled than the original. For example, 8-bit data converted to 7-bit data to send via mail is encoded.

**encrypt**—Encode something so that it is no longer readable by humans or other processes.

**encrypted password**—The user's password that is stored in encoded form in the /etc/shadow and the Protected Password Database.

**end user**—See **user**.

**environment**—The settings and values that control the way you work on the system. These include the shell you use, your home and current directories, and your user and groups IDs. There are also a set of variables called **environment variables** that contain many of these settings and values.

**environment variable**—Variables that modify the behavior of your login shell as well as other programs.

**error message**—A message indicating a problem. This can be something as simple as when input incorrect syntax to a command or something more significant like a needed file is missing. Usually the message indicates the nature of the problem.

**escape character**—Decimal 27, octal 033, and hexidecimal 1b. Character used in many cases as a flag indicating the following sequence of characters has special meaning.

**escape key**—The key which is marked ESC on most keyboards. This key is used to generate an escape character that is often used to remove the special significance of certain other characters.

**escape sequences**—A sequence of characters preceeded by an **escape character**. This usually changes the behavior of something. For example, escape sequences to printers might turn on bold printing.

**escaping characters**—The process by which you remove the special significance of characters. This is often accomplished by preceeding the special character by a **back-slash**.

**ESDI—Enhanced Small Device Interface**. An older hard disk interface.

**Ethernet**—A local area network standard developed by the Xerox corporation.

**event**—An occurrence on the system. For the kernel this might be that a device is ready to provide requested data. For X Windows this can be keystrokes, mouse movement, or resizing windows.

**exception**—An unexpected event.

**exception handlers**—Special functions within the kernel that are used to deal with expections.

**executable file**—A file containing a program or a set of commands. In order to be executable, these files must also have the execute **permission bit** set.

**exitcode**—The value returned by a process as it is completing.

**expanded memory**—In DOS-based computers a means of getting around the 640K base memory problem. With this technique, blocks of 64k are shuffled in and out of "accessible" memory.

**expansion bus**—The **bus** in a computer into which **expansion cards** are inserted.

**expansion card**—A card inserted into the **expansion bus** that expands the functionality of the system such as a hard disk controller or a serial port.

**export**—The process by which a filesystem or directory is made available to be remotely **mounted**.

**extended memory**—Additional memory above 1Mb. This memory is not switched in as with **expanded memory** but is treated as a single, linear unit.

**extended minor numbers**—A technique used to allow the system to have more devices that are permitted by the single byte available for minor numbers. Normally extended minor numbers are only used for hard disks.

**fault**—An **exception** that occurs before the instruction is executed (for example, **page faults**).

**field separator**—A special character used to delimit fields within a file or input.

**file**—A named collection of information stored on a hard disk, floppy, or other media. Although a file is normally considered to contain data or executable instructions, hardware in UNIX is accessed through files. These do not have any size and therefore contain no data, their mere existence is what contains the information.

**file creation mask**—See **umask**.

**file descriptor**—A number associated with an open file. This is used to refer to files during I/O operations.

**file permissions**—The access permissions on a specific file.

**file table**—A table internal to the kernel that maintains the relationship between the **file descriptors** and the physical file on the hard disk.

**filesystem**—A hierarchical organization of directories and files.

**first level cache**—The cache contained with the **CPU**.

**flags**—See **command options**.

**flow control**—The process by which data transfer is regulated so that it does not arrive too quickly for the receiving process.

**foreground**—A process is said to be in the foreground when it is interacting with the user.

**fork**—The process and system call by which new processes are created.

**format**—The process by which a disk is prepared for use.

**forward slash**—Slash that goes from the upper right to lower left (/). Also called an ascending slash. Used as the path separator.

**FQDN**—**Fully Qualified Domain Name**. Machine name containing both the host name and the domain name. This name is used to *uniquely* indentify a computer.

**fragmentation**—When parts of a file are spread out across different parts of a hard disk. Although the term is also used to refer to memory, accessing memory from different locations does not alter the process. However, when reading a file, being forced to go to different locations, the physical movement of the hard disk components slow down the access.

**freelist**—A linked list of unallocated (free) data structures.

**ftp**—A file transfer program that allows you to copy files to and from a remote computer in a network.

**full path**—See **absolute pathname**.

**gateway**—A computer or other network device that is used to connect one system to another. Gateways are often considered as connecting dissimilar systems such as one network running TPC/IP and the other running NetWare.

**Gb**—See gigabyte.

**GDT**—**Global Descriptor Table**.

**GID**—**Group ID**.

**gigabyte**—$2^{30}$ bytes. Often thought of (erroneously) as one billion bytes.

**group**—A set of users. These users are listed under a group name within the /etc/group file. The group name is associated with a **GROUP ID (GID)**. Each file on the system has a group associated with it. This is indicated by the GID of the file.

**GUI**—**Graphical User Interface**. A graphic oriented interface such as X Windows.

**hard link**—A file with a different full path name but the same inode number. Compare this to a **symbolic link**.

**hardware flow control**—Controlling the flow of data across a serial cable by using line signals rather than control characters.

**hardware-mediated bus**—A bus to which the access is determined by special hardware and not software.

**Hayes command set**—Standard set of modem commands.

**header**—Information included at the beginning (head) of transmitted data. A header will indentify the information being sent and may contain other information. For example, a mail header would contain the recipient whereas an IP header contains the source and destination **IP addresses**.

**hexadecimal**—The numerical system of counting with sixteen digits: 023456789ABCDEF. Also called **base 16**.

**hit ratio**—The ratio of times that information was available to the number of times it was requested. For example, if data is requested from **cache memory** and is available, this is a **cache hit**. If the data is not available, this is a **cache miss**.

**home directory**—The directory defined by your $HOME environment variable. This is normally the same directory you end up in after you log into the system.

**hops**—The number of connections that need to be made to reach a destination. For example, if you want to go from machine A to machine B, but first need to go to machine C, this is two hops (A->C then C->B).

**host**—Any computer. Normally used when the computer is on a network.

**host adapter**—An expansion card that serves as the interface between the system's **expansion bus** and an **SCSI** bus. This is often (erroneously) called an **SCSI** controller.

**hostname**—The system name or machine name.

**HPPS**—**High-Performance Pipe System**. System used in SCO OpenServer where pipes are stored in memory and not on the hard disk.

**htepi_daemon**—The kernel daemon that manages filesystem control structures.

**HTFS**—**High-Throughput File System**. One of SCO's new filesystems.

**HTML**—**HyperText Markup Language**. Text formatting language used in WWW documents.

**HTTP**—**HyperText Transfer Protocol**. Protocol used to transfer WWW documents.

**I/O**—Abbreviation for input/output. This refers to the transfer of data to and from peripheral devices.

**ICMP**—**Internet Control Message Protocol**.

**icon**—A graphical representation of something.

**IDE**—**Integrated Drive Electronics**. Common hard disk interface.

**IDT**—**Interrupt Descriptor Table**. Table containing pointers to the interrupt handling routines.

**init**—The process "spawner" that is created at system start-up.

**inode**—Index or Information Node. This is a structure containing the basic information about a file such as owner, type, access permissions, and pointers to the actual data on the disk. Inodes are stored in the filesystem **inode table** and are referenced through **inode numbers.** See also **file**.

**intent logging**—Process by which pending filesystem transactions are logged. If the system goes down unexpectedly, such transactions can be completed or ignored depending on the state they were in.

**interrupt**—A signal from a hardware device indicating the devices wants "attention." This can include things like an indicator that requested data is available or an error has occurred.

**interrupt handler**—Special routines within the kernel that handle interrupts.

**Interrupt Service Routine**—See **interrupt handler**.

**IP**—**Internet Protocol**. Standard by which packets of information are sent to the appropriate location within a network.

**IP address**—Unique address within a network that uses the **Internet Protocol**.

**IQM**—**Installation Query Manager**. SCO's installation program.

**IRQ**—**Interrupt vector**. The hardware setting indicating on what line a device will generate an interrupt.

**ISA**—**Industry Standard Architecture**.

**ISDN**—**Integrated Services Digital Network**.

**ISO**—**International Standards Organization**.

**ISR**—**Interrupt Service Routine**. See **interrupt handler**.

**ITU**—**International Telecommunications Union**.

**K or Kb**—See **kilobyte**.

**kernel**—The primary part of the operating system. This manages all system functions such as memory, task scheduling, and how devices are accessed.

**kernel mode**—See **system mode**.

**kernel parameter**—A value defined that controls the configuration of the kernel.

**kilobyte**—$2^{10}$ bytes.

**LAN**—**Local Area Network**.

**LDT**—**Local descriptor table**.

**level-one (L1) cache**—Cache memory within the CPU.

**level-triggered interrupts**—Interrupts that are indicated by the eletrical signal being level, but at the state opposite from what it normally is.

**level-two (L2) cache**—Cache memory external to, but directly accessed by the CPU.

**library call**—A call to a library function. **Library functions** are collections of **system calls**.

**link**—1) **Hard link**. 2) **Soft link**. 3) The processes of combining all the drivers and other kernel components to create a new copy of the kernel.

**link count**—The number of file names that point to a particular set of data.

**link kit**—The name used to refer to the collection of tools and files used to create a copy of the kernel.

**LLI—Link Layer Interface.** Older method used on SCO systems to interface network protocols with network device drivers.

**locale**—The set of values that indicate your location such as language, keyboard type, etc.

**local host**—The special name given to the machine you are currently working on.

**locality principle**—Principle that the computer instructions which are executed are generally within the same area of memory (**spatial locality**) and that the same instructions are likely to be executed again (**temporal locality**).

**logging**—See **transaction intent logging**.

**logical block addressing**—The means by which blocks on the hard disk are accessed based on a logical address and not the absolute address on the hard disk. The logical address is what is presented to the operating system by the hard disk controller.

**login**—The process of gaining access to the system. Here you enter your login name (**logname**) and **password**.

**login group**—The **GID** that you are assigned by default.

**logname**—The name you use to gain access to the system.

**logout**—The process of disconnecting yourself from the system.

**LUN—Logical Unit Number.** Number used to identify a device controller by a single **SCSI host adapter**. Compare this to **SCSI ID**.

**MAC address—Media Access Control address**. The unique identifier given to a network interface card (**NIC**).

**magic number**—A number at the beginning of a file used to indicate what type of file it is.

**maintenance mode**—See **system maintenance mode**.

**major number**—A number indicating which **device driver** should be used to access a particular device. See also **minor number**.

**man-page**—A reference page containing useful information about a specific topic.

**mask**—A series of bits that "cover up" existing settings. For example, the **umask** masks out file permissions and the **netmask** masks out network addresses.

**maskable interrupts**—Interrupts that can be "ignored."

**masterboot block**—The first block of your hard disk (or floppy) containing information necessary to find the **active partition** and boot your operating system.

**Mb**—See **megabyte**.

**MBR**—**Master Boot Record**. See **masterboot block**.

**MCA**—**Micro-Channel Architecture**. A computer bus architecture developed by IBM. It provides many advantages over the **ISA** architecture.

**megabyte**—$2^{20}$ bytes.

**metacharacter**—A special character that is replaced by character strings by the shell.

**MIME**—**Multipurpose Internet Mail Extensions**. A standard for mail exchange, which supports graphical, audio, video, and other binary data.

**minor number**—A number serving as a flag to a **device driver**. See also **major number**.

**mirroring**—See **disk mirroring**.

**MMDF**—**Multichannel Memorandum Distribution Facility**. One of the two SCO **MTAs**.

**MO drives**—**Magneto-Optical drives**. A storage media that uses both magnetical properties and lasers to store data.

**modem control port**—A serial port that reacts to the carrier signal.

**modem**—**Modulator/Demodulator**. An electronic device attached to your computer that converts digital signal from the computer to analog signals (modulation) to be transmitted across telephone cable. When receiving the analog signals, a modem converts them back into digital signals (demodulation).

**mount**—The process by which **filesystems** are made available.

**mount point**—The directory through which the mounted **filesystem** is accessed.

**mount table**—The table containing all of the mounted **filesystems**.

**mouse**—A pointing device used to move a pointer on the screen.

**MTA**—**Mail Transfer Agent**. The collection of programs used to transfer mail from one system to another. SCO systems provide two MTAs: **MMDF** and **sendmail**.

**MTU**—**Maximum Transmission Unit**. Maximum size of a transmitted piece of data.

**MUA**—**Mail User Agent**. The program that you use to interface into the mail system, including reading and composing mail.

**multitasking**—The process by which a computer system is able to maintain multiple programs (tasks) in memory and to switch fast enough to appear as if all programs are being run simultaneously.

**multi-user**—The process by which a computer system is able to maintain multiple programs (tasks) in memory and to ensure that they do not interfere with each other. Normally each task is associated with a specific user.

**multi-user mode**—The run state of the system in which access is allowed on terminals other than the system console.

**multiprocessor system**—A computer system with more than one CPU.

**multiscreen**—One of the twelve console "terminals."

**mwm**—**Motif window manager**. A program that controls window configuration and behavior and creates window frames.

**name server**—A program running on a network that provides a centralized database of information on the names and **IP Addresses** of machines on that network.

**namecache**—A data structure within the kernel that stores the most recently accessed translations of pathnames to inode numbers.

**netmask**—A binary mask used to mask out the network portion on an **IP address**.

**network**—A group of computers that are linked together.

**NFS**—**Network Filesystem**. The set of programs and the protocol used to make filesystems and directories available across a network.

**nice value**—A weighting factor that is used to calculate the **priority** of a process.

**NIS**—**Network Information System**. System by which files and user information can be automatically spread across a network.

**NMI**—**Non-Maskable Interrupt**. An interrupt that cannot be ignored.

**octal**—The numerical system of counting with eight digits: 01234567. Also called **base 8**.

**ODT**—A common abbreviation for SCO's Open Desktop.

**OMF**—**Intel Object Module Format**. One of the executable program formats used by SCO.

**operating system**—A group of programs and functions that provide basic functionality on a computer. This software manages access to a system's hardware and other resources.

**options disk**—A disk provided with MCA devices that contains an **ADF** for that device.

**OSD**—**Operating System Direct**. A support service provided by SCO.

**owner**—1) The user who created a file or directory. 2) The user that started a process.

**package**—A collection of related programs that perform a common function. Packages are parts of **products**.

**packet**—A unit of data being sent across a serial line or network.

**page**—A 4KB block of memory. The primary unit of memory.

**page directory**—A structure in memory that the kernel uses to access **page tables**.

**page fault**—A hardware event that occurs when a process tries to access a virtual address that is not in physical memory.

**page table**—A structure in memory that the kernel uses to access **pages**.

**panic**—The process the kernel goes through when an unexpected event occurs that it cannot deal with.

**parallel**—The process by which data is sent, bytes at a time. Compare this to **serial.**

**parent directory**—The directory which contains the directory you are referring to. For example, if you refer to the `/etc/default` directory, then the parent directory is `/etc`. If your current directory is `/usr/jimmo`, then the parent directory is `/usr`.

**parent process** —The process that executed a `fork()` system call to create a new **child process.**

**parity**—An error detection mechanism in which the number of bits is counted and an extra bit is added to make the total number of bits set even for **even parity** or odd for **odd parity**.

**parity bit**—The extra bit used for parity.

**partition**—A section of a hard disk, which can be the entire hard disk. The starting location and size of each partition is stored in a **partition table**.

**password**—A string of characters that you use to confirm your identity when you log in. An encrypted version of this is stored in the TCB and `/etc/shadow`, which then compares to your input when attempting to login.

**path**—1) The set of directories that are needed to reach a specific file. Also referred to as the **pathname**. 2) The list of directories through which the shell searches to find the commands you type.

**PCI**—1) **Peripheral Component Interconnect**. One of the newer bus types. 2) **PC-Interface**. Product provided by SCO that allows PCs access to an SCO system.

**PCL**—**Printer Control Language**.

**peer**—Another computer at the same "level" as yours. You can provide services to them and they to you. Computers in this situation use a **peer-to-peer** model. Compare this to a **client-server model**.

**permissions**—The settings associated with each file or directory that determine who can access the file and directory and what types of access is permitted. Also called properties or attributes.

**physical memory**—RAM.

**PIC**—**Programmable Interrupt Controller**. Chip on the motherboard that manages hardware interrupts.

**PID**—**Process ID**. Unique identifier for a process. This is simply the slot number of the process in the **process table**.

**pipe**—A way of joining commands on the command line where the output of the first command provides the input for the next. The term also refers to the symbol used to create the pipe: |.

**PMWM**—**Panning Motif Window Manager**.

**polling**—The process by which a device driver queries devices for a response rather than waiting for the device to generate an interrupt.

**POST**—**Power-On Self-Test**. Self-test that the computer goes through when you first turn it on.

**PPID**—**Parent Process ID**.

**PPP**—**Point-to-Point Protocol**. Networking protocol used across serial lines.

**pre-initialized data**—Variables and other structures within a program that have their value set *before* the program is run.

**pre-emption**—What occurs when a process that was running on a CPU is replaced by a process with a higher priority.

**print queue**—A queue (waiting line) in which print requests are stored awaiting to be sent to the printer.

**print spooler**—The term used to describe the files and programs used to manage files to be printed.

**printer class**—Multiple printers that are treated as one destination in order to spread the load more equally.

**printer interface scripts**—Shell scripts that actually send the file to the printer.

**priority**—The value that the scheduler calculates to determine which process should next run on the CPU. This is calculated from its **nice value** and its recent CPU usage.

**privileges**—See **subsystem authorizations**.

**process**—An instance of a program that is being executed. Each process has a unique **PID,** which is entered in the kernel's **process table.**

**process table**—A data structure within the kernel that stores information about all the current processes.

**prompt**—One or more characters or symbols that identify that the system is ready to accept a command.

**protected mode**—A CPU mode in which mechanisms are implemented to allow or deny access to particular areas of memory. In other words, memory is *protected.*

**protected subsystems**—Certain actions within the system that are controlled by **system privileges.**

**protocol**—A set of rules and procedures used to establish and maintain communication. That can be between hardware or software.

**protocol stack**—A set or protocols which appears to be stacked as one protocol hands off information to another.

**protocol suite**—A collection of related **protocols.**

**pseudo-terminal**—Also called a **pseudo-tty**. A device driver that allows one process to communicate with another as if it were a physical terminal.

**queue**—A list. A waiting line.

**quoting**—The mechanism that is used to control the substitution of special characters. See **single-quotes, double-quotes,** and **back-ticks.**

**RAID**—**Redundant Array of Inexpensive Disks**. Combining multiple disks to improve reliablility or performance.

**RAM**—Random access or main memory.

**raw device**—See **character device**.

**redirection**—The process by which one of the three base file descriptors (stdin, stout, and stderr) reference something other than the default.

**region**—An area of memory grouped by function. For example, text, data, and stack.

**region descriptor**—A descriptor pointing to a **region**.

**region table**—A structure within the kernel pointing to the currently active regions.

**regular expression**—A notation for matching sequences of characters without having to specify all possible combinations. Regular expressions are composed of literal characters as well as **metacharacters**.

**relative path**—A pathname that shows a **path** in relation to the current **working directory**.

**relink**—The process by which a new **kernel** is generated.

**remote host**—A computer in a network other than the one that you originally logged in to.

**RFC**—**Request for Comments**. A specific document that relates to networking standards and activity.

**ROM**—**Read-Only Memory**.

**root**—1) The top directory of a UNIX filesystem, represented as a slash (/). Also called the **root directory**. 2) The login name of the superuser.

**root filesystem**—The file system onto which all the other filesystem are mounted and which usually contains most of the system files.

**route**—A path to a particular computer. The set of other computers need to reach that destiantion.

**router**—A device used to redirect network connections to the proper machine.

**RPC**—**Remote Procedure Call**. A **system call** that is executed on a remote machine.

**RTS/CTS flow control**—A form of flow control using the two signals **Request-To-Send** and **Clear-To-Send**.

**run-level**—Also called **run-state**. An abstract term that is used to determine which process should be run or started.

**scatter-gather**—The process by which request for data from a hard disk that are spread out across the disk (scattered) are ordered into a more efficient list (gather) to minimize the total access time.

**sched**—The system swapper daemon. This deamon determines which process gets to run.

**SCO**—**The Santa Cruz Operation**.

**SCSI**—**Small Computer System Interface**. An expansion bus that is controlled by a **host adapter** and supports several different device types.

**second level cache**—See **L1 Cache**.

**security**—The mechanisms and policies used to prevent unauthorized access to system resources.

**sector**—The smallest administrative unit on a hard disk. It contains 512 bytes of data.

**sed**—Stream editor. A stream/file manipulation program. The term is also used to refer to the language used to program the *sed* program.

**segment**—See **Region**.

**serial**—The process by which data is sent one bit at a time. Compare this to **parallel**.

**serial ports**—A device port that supports serial communication.

**SES—Software Enhancement Service**. A service provided by SCO giving up-grades and updates at a reduced cost as well as the **Software Support Library**.

**shared data region**—A data region that can be accessed by multiple processes.

**shared libraries**—Sets of common library routines that are not part of a pro-gram, but exist as separate files on the disk and can be accessed by different processes.

**shell**—The program that controls the user interaction to the operating system.

**shell escape**—A command or character you type from inside an interactive pro-gram to escape to the shell.

**shell script**—A text file containing written UNIX commands, shell built-in com-mands and shell programming syntax. Shell scripts must be made executable by setting the execute permission bit.

**shell variable**—A variable associated with a shell script.

**signal**—A flag sent to a process indicating a certain event has occured.

**SIMM—Single In-Line Memory Module**.

**single-quotes (')**—Quotes that remove the special significance of all other charac-ters. See **double-quotes** and **back-ticks**.

**single-user mode**—See **system maintenance mode.**

**SLIP—Serial Line Internet Protocol**. A networking procotol used on serial lines.

**SLS—Support Level Supplement**. Supplement provided by SCO free of charge that usually includes patches or updates.

**smart host**—A computer that has more complete information about the mail net-work. This includes both information on users and other machines.

**SMTP—Simple Mail Transfer Protocol**. A mail transfer protocol used over TCP/IP and the Internet.

**SNEAKER-Net**—A old method of transferring data between two machines using sneakers.

**SNMP—Simple Network Management Protocol**. A protocol used to manager information within a network.

**SOA—Start of Authority**. A record with **DNS** used to determine which machine is the authoritative soruce of information.

**soft link**—See **symbolic link.**

**Software Enhancement Service**—See **SES**.

**software flow control**—Flow control using the XON and XOFF characters. Compare this to **hardware flow control**.

**software interrupts**—Interrupts generated by software and not hardware.

**sosco**—The name of the machine with SCO's bulletin board.

**space.c**—A file within the **link kit** containing device driver configuration information.

**SPL—Software Priority Level**.

**spooler**—Although referring to any process that routes requests to a file or memory for later processing, this term is normally used for the print spooler.

**SRAM**—Static RAM.

**SSL—Software Support Library**. A CD containing SCO's Information Tools, SLSs, and EFSs.

**SSO—Software Storage Object**. The primary way of storing files and packages in OpenServer.

**stack**—A list of temporary data used by a process when making function calls.

**stack region**—The area of a process' virtual memory that contains its stack.

**standard error**—The place where a process usually writes error messages by default to the screen. Also called stderr.

**standard input**—The place where a process usually takes its input, by default, to the keyboard. Also called stdin.

**standard output**—The place where a process usually writes its output, by default, to the screen. Also called stdout.

**start bit**—The bit indicating the begining of a byte being transmitted.

**stop bit(s)**—The bit(s) indicating the end of a byte being transmitted.

**streams**—A mechanism for implementing a layered interface between applications and a device driver. Most often used to implement network protocol stacks and X Windows.

**stripe width**—The number of physical drives in a striped disk. See **disk striping**.

**striped array**—See **disk striping**.

**subshell**—A shell that was started by another process.

**subsystem authorizations**—Access to specific, but varied, parts of the system, such as printing, backups, and memory.

**subdirectory**—A directory residing within another directory.

**subdomain**—A name that describes a smaller organization unit within a domain. An example would be the SCO subdomain within the COM domain.

**subnet**—A logical portion of a network.

**SUID—SET USER ID.** The premissions bit that enables the process to run under a different user ID.

**superblock**—An area at the beginning of a filesystem containing information about that filesystem.

**superuser**—The user who has the special privileges needed to administer and maintain the system. The superuser logs in as root.

**SVGA—Super VGA.** A newer video standard.

**swap device**—An area on the disk reserved for swapping out portions of processes, if the physical memory available becomes too small.

**swapping**—The action taken by the operating system (the swapper daemon) when the system is short of physical memory. The changeable portion (data) of a process is moved from physical memory to the **swap device.**

**symbolic link**—A file that contains the path to another file or directory. Since this is just a path, symbolic links can cross mount points. Depending on the length of the path specified and the filesystem, symbolic links can also be stored within a file's **inode**.

**symbolic mode**—Changing file permissions using keyletters to specify the set of permissions to change and how to change them. Compare this to **absolute mode**.

**system call**—A low-level system function. Compare this to a **library call**.

**system maintenance mode**—The **run-level** in which access is only allowed through the system console. Used for maintenance, hence the name.

**system mode**—The state of a CPU where the kernel needs to ensure that it has privileged access to data and physical devices. Also called kernel mode.

**Tb**—See **terabyte**.

**TCB—Trusted Computing Base**. The file used to control and manage C2 security on an SCO system.

**TCP—Transmission Control Protocol**. A reliable protocol that is used to transmit data from one process to another across a network.

**terabyte**—$2^{40}$ bytes.

**terminal**—Video display unit with a keyboard and a monitor.

**terminating resistors**—Resistors at the end of a thin-wire network connect or **SCSI** bus that absorb the signals and prevent them from bouncing back, potentially interfering with other signals.

**text**—The executable machine portion of a program. That is, the part of a program containing the instructions that a CPU can interpret and act on.

**text file**—A file containing text.

**text region**—Also called **text segment**.

**thrashing**—When the system spends all of its time **swapping** and not performing any real work.

**throughput**—The amount of work that a part of the system can process in a specified time. This can be anything from the number of bytes sent to the number of jobs completed.

**time slice**—The maximum amount of time a process can run without being preempted.

**TLB—Translation Lookaside Buffer**. Buffer within the CPU that contains pointers to pages.

**toggle**—To switch between any two conditions. For example, to toggle from OFF to ON.

**track**—The set of sectors on a hard disk at the same distance from the center and on the same surface.

**transaction intent logging**—A new feature in OpenServer and one of the functions of the htepi_daemon. This is the process by which the the intention to change filesystem control data is written to a log file on disk.

**transport layer**—The layer of a network protocol stack responsible for getting the data from one machine to another.

**trap**—An exception that is processed immedaitely after executing the instruction that generates the exception.

**TSS—Task State Segment**. Contains the contents of all registers when a process is context switched out.

**type**—The category that describes whether the file is a regular file, a directory, or other type of file.

**uarea**—The area of a process (user area) that contains the *private* data about the process that only the kernel may access. Also called ublock.

**UART**—**Universal Asynchronous Receiver-Transmitter.**

**ublock**—See **uarea**.

**UDP**—**User Datagram Protocol**. An unreliable protocol that is used to transmit data from one process to another across a network.

**UID**—**User ID.**

**umask**—A mask that controls the permissions assigned to new files as they are created.

**UNIX**—An operating system originally developed at Bell Laboratories. The version developed by SCO is the topic of this book.

**UPS**—**Uninterrupted Power Supply.**

**URL**—**Uniform Resource Locator**. A "network extension" to the standard file-name concept. This allows access to files and directories on remote machines, to which you may not have a constant connection, such as NFS. URLs can also point to resources on the local machine and provide a means of transporting the base files without having to change paths.

**user account**—1) The enviroment under which a user gains access to the system. This includes the **logname, shell, home directory,** etc. 2) The records and other information a UNIX system keeps for each user on the system.

**user equivalence**—The process by which accounts on two system are considered equal and authentication is no longer required for certain network operations.

**user mode**—The state of a CPU when it is executing the code for a user program that is accessing its own data space.

**user name**—See **logname**.

**utilities**—Any command that performs more than just a simple function. An example would be *fdisk* as you can use it to create, delete, and make partitions active.

**UUCP**—**Unix-to-Unix Copy**. A set of programs and protocols used to transfer files across serial lines, as well as perform remote execution of commands.

**variable**—An object known to a proces that stores a particular value. Shell variables are known to a particular shell process and enviroment variables (generally) are known to all of a particular user's processes.

**VDM**—**Virtual Disk Manager.**

**version number**—The number associated with a particular version of a file.

**versioning**—The ability to store multiple copies of the "same" file on the system.

**VESA**—**Video Electronics Standards Association**.

**VGA**—**Video Graphics Array**.

**vhand**—The system name for the **page stealing daemon**.

**virtual address**—An **address** that exists within the **virtual memory** space of a process.

**virtual disk**—A disk composed of pieces of several physical disks.

**virtual memory**—A method of being able to access more memory than is physically available on your system. This combines physical RAM with the **swap space** as well as taking advantage of the fact that the entire program is not accessed at once and does not need to all be in memory.

**VLB**—**Video Electronics Standards Association Local Bus**.

**Wabi**—**Windows Application Binary Interface**.

**wait channel**—The addresss of an event on which a particular process is waiting.

**WCHAN**—See **wait channel**.

**well-connected host**—A host that is connected to many machines or networks.

**whitespace**—A space, tab, or carriage return.

**wildcard**—Any character (such as ? or *) that is substituted with another character or a group of characters. See also **metacharacter**.

**write policy**—How cache memory writes its contents to main memory.

**Write-Back**—The **write policy** when cache memory is written to main memory at regular intervals.

**Write-Dirty**—The write policy when cache memory is written to main memory only when it has been changed.

**Write-Through**—The **write policy** when cache memory is written to at the same time as main memory.

**WWW**—**World Wide Web**. A collection of machines on the **Internet** that contain **documents.** These documents contain hypertext links to other documents which may or may not be on the same machine.

**X**—See **X Windows System**.

**X client**—A process that communicates with an X server to request that it display information on a screen or to receive input events from the keyboard or a pointing device such as a mouse.

**X server**—The software that controls the screen, keyboard, and pointing device under X.

**X Window System**—A windowing system based on the client-server model.

**XON/XOFF flow control**—Flow control using the XON (Ctrl-Q) and XOFF (Ctrl-S) character. Also called software flow control.

**ZIF**—**Zero Insertion Force**. A special socket with a lever that locks the chip (normally the CPU) with no force required.

**zombie process**—An entry in the process table that corresponds to a process that no longer exists. This is used to hold the **exitcode** of that process.

# Suggested Reading

This is a list of books that I think you will find to be helpful and enjoyable. Many of these I have used as sources for this book and may have mentioned them in the text. This is not a bibliography, but as the heading says, "suggested reading." The list is intended as a starting place to look for more information on the subjects we discussed.

## SCO Specific

The SCO Documentation!

CUTLER, ELLIE, *SCO UNIX in a Nutshell*, Sebastapol, CA: O'Reilly & Associates, 1994.

*This is a quick reference guide that is based on ODT 3.0. It's more than just a command reference as it covers some of the basics on using and administering an SCO system. I was one of the technical editors for this one.*

KETTLE, PETER and STEVE STATLER, *Writing Device Drivers for SCO UNIX*, Cambridge, England: Addison-Wesley, 1993.

*Okay, so you're not a device driver programmer. Neither am I. This is a great book for getting into the guts of SCO device drivers to learn how they interact with the rest of the system.*

MISCOVICH, GINA and DAVID SIMONS, *The SCO Performance Tuning Handbook*, Englewood Cliffs, NJ: Prentice Hall, 1994.

*This covers system performance tuning as well as the internals of the kernel that you need to understand to tune the system and what that tuning is doing.*

VANN, KEITH, *Essential SCO System Administration*, Englewood Cliffs, NJ: Prentice Hall , 1995.

*This is a quick reference that focuses on the process of administering a system rather than the commands you use.*

## UNIX General

RUSSEL, CHARLIE and SHARON CRAWFORD, *Voodoo UNIX*, Chapel Hill, NC: Ventana Press,1992.

*My first reaction to this book was that it was another one of those ". . . for dummies" books. Although the book is written for beginner UNIX users, I recommend it highly.*

CURRY, DAVID A., *Using C on the UNIX System*, Sebastapol, CA: O'Reilly & Associates, 1998.

*If you want to learn more about programming on a UNIX system, this is a good starting point.*

DOUGHERTY, DALE, *sed & awk*, Sebastapol, CA: O'Reilly & Associates, 1990.

*You can learn a lot of tricks about both sed and awk from this one.*

KERNIGHAN, BRIAN W. and ROB PIKE, *The UNIX Programming Environment.* Englewood Cliffs, NJ: Prentice Hall, 1990.

*A more in-depth coverage of programming under UNIX.*

KOCHAN, STEPHEN G. and PATRICK H. WOOD, *UNIX Shell Programming*, Carmel, IN: Hayden Book Co., 1985.

*A very good tutorial if you want to learn more about shell programming.*

LAMB, LINDA, *Learning the vi Editor*, Sebastapol, CA: O'Reilly & Associates, 1990.

*Another place to learn a lot of tricks.*

ROSENBLATT, BILL, *Learning the Korn Shell*, Sebastapol, CA: O'Reilly & Associates, 1993.

*Everyone should learn the Korn Shell and this is a good place to start.*

## Operating Systems

BACH, MAURICE, *The Design of the UNIX Operating System*, Englewood Cliffs, NJ: Prentice Hall, 1986.

*This is THE book about UNIX internals. It may seen out of date, but it addresses the foundations of UNIX and is an invaluable tool. This is not for the beginner. You need to have some understanding of the principles to get the most out of this one.*

MIKES, STEVEN, *UNIX for MS-DOS Programmers,* Reading, MA: Addison-Wesley, 1989.

*If you are coming from the DOS world then this is a good place to go. Don't be scared off by the implication that this is for programmers. It presents a good comparison/contrast between the two.*

SILBERSACHATZ, ABRAHAM, JAMES L. PETERSEN, and PETER B. GALVIN, *Operating System Concepts, 3rd Edition*, Reading, MA: Addison-Wesley, 1991.

*Good intro to operating systems. A lot of historical stuff that may no longer apply. However, it is filled with a lot of background information.*

TANENBAUM, ANDREW S., *Modern Operating Systems,* Englewood Cliffs, NJ: Prentice Hall, 1992.

*Another good intro to operating systems. It also covers in detail some real OSs like UNIX and DOS.*

## System Administration

DOUD, KEVIN, *High Performance Computing,* Sebastapol, CA: O'Reilly & Associates, 1993.

*This has some excellent coverage of the concepts involved with system performance and tuning.*

FIELDER, DAVID and BRUCE H. HUNTER, revised by BEN SMITH, *UNIX System V, Release 4 Administration, 2nd Edition* Carmel, IN: Hayden Book Co., 1991.

FRISCH, AELEEN, *Essential System Administration,* Sebastapol, CA: O'Reilly & Associates, 1991.

*The concepts are easily applied to SCO systems.*

LOUKIDES, MIKE, *System Performance Tuning,* Sebastapol, CA: O'Reilly & Associates, 1991.

*Goes into the concepts as well as the practical side of system tuning. There is quite a bit of stuff here that's applicable to SCO.*

NEMETH, EVI, GARTH SNYDER, and SCOTT SEEBASS, *UNIX System Administration Handbook,* Englewood Cliffs, NJ: Prentice Hall, 1989.

*This is a friendly approach and contains a lot of information.*

PEEK, JERRY, TIM O'REILLY, and MIKE LOUKIDES, *UNIX Power Tools,* Sebastapol, CA: O'Reilly & Associates, 1993.

*This book comes with a CD and is loaded with goodies to use on your system.*

STRANG, JOHN, LINDA MUI, and TIM O'REILLY, *Termcap and Terminfo*, Sebastapol, CA: O'Reilly & Associates, 1991.

*If you have a lot of different terminals or have application problems, then this is a good source.*

## Security

GARFINKEL, SIMSON and GENE SPAFFORD, *Practical UNIX Security*, Sebastapol, CA: O'Reilly & Associates, 1991.

*The concepts are applicable to every system.*

RUSSELL, DEBORAH and G.T. GANGEMI, Sr., *Computer Security Basics*, Sebastapol, CA: O'Reilly & Associates, 1991.

*Not just for administrators, this presents some valid information for anyone using any kind of computer.*

WOOD, PATRICK H. and STEPHEN G. KOCHAN, *UNIX System Security*, Carmel, IN: Hayden Book Co., 1985.

*A good approach and loaded with information.*

## Networking

ALBITZ, PAUL and CRICKET LIU, *DNS and BIND*, Sebastapol, CA: O'Reilly & Associates, 1992.

*If you are setting up a nameserver of any size, this is the book to have. However, you need to have some TCP/IP background to understand it.*

BANKS, MICHAEL A., *The Modem Reference*, New York: Brady Books, 1991.

*Although this goes into a lot about on-line services and other things you can do with a modem, it does go into details about the technical aspects of modems.*

CHESWICK, WILLIAM R. and STEVEN M. BELLOVIN, *Firewalls and Internet Security*, Reading, MA: Addison-Wesley, 1994.

*This is a very friendly and often humorous approach to network security. In some places it even reads like a spy novel. The first computer book I felt I could read in bed.*

COMER, DOUGLAS E., *Internetworking with TCP/IP, Volume 1: Principle, Protocols and Architecture*, Englewood Cliffs, NJ: Prentice Hall, 1991.

*Hard core stuff. Descriptions are quick and to the point. Not for the faint of heart, but very much worth it if you want to get into details about the TCP/IP protocol suite. A good reference.*

HUNT, CRAIG, *TCP/IP Network Administration*, Sebastapol, CA: O'Reilly & Associates, 1992.

*Great intro to TCP/IP. Very informative (like all the O'Reilly books) and enjoyable. This was what I used as my introduction to TCP/IP. I was even a reviewer for it!*

Krol, Ed, *The Whole Internet,* Sebastapol, CA: O'Reilly & Associates, 1992.
*One of the first books to tell you what's out there on the Internet. Loaded with goodies.*

O'Reilly, Tim and Grace Todino, *Managing UUCP and Usenet,* Sebastapol, CA: O'Reilly & Associates, 1990.
*Goes into a lot of details on setting up and administering UUCP and Usenet. Frequently recommended while I was in SCO support for those wanting to get more out of UUCP.*

Stern, Hal, *Managing NFS and NIS,* Sebastapol, CA: O'Reilly & Associates, 1991.
*A must if you want to go beyond the basics of NFS and NIS. There are a lot of neat tricks to both that I learned from this book. A lot was later added to the SCO doc.*

Stevens, W. Richard, *TCP/IP Illustrated, Volume 1: The Protocols,* Reading, MA: Addison-Wesley, 1994.
*This is another hard core TCP/IP book, but is a little more friendly than the Comer book. This would be a good textbook (it includes exercises at the end of each chapter). However, not optimal as a "quick reference."*

Stevens, W. Richard, *UNIX Network Programming,* Englewood Cliffs, NJ: Prentice Hall, 1990.
*This is a good book to learn about both programming and networking in a UNIX environment. I would really recommend knowing a little about both before you jump into this one.*

Tanenbaum, Andrew S., *Computer Networks, 2nd Edition,* Englewood Cliffs, NJ: Prentice Hall, 1989.
*This covers loads of different aspects of networking. In comparison to other books, there isn't much that is directly related to SCO. However, I like Tanenbaum's style and you learn a lot.*

Todino, Grace and Dale Dougherty, *Using UUCP and Usenet,* Sebastapol, CA: O'Reilly & Associates, 1991.
*A good one for going beyond the basics.*

## X Windows

Mui, Linda and Eric Pearce, *X Window System Administrator's Guide,* Sebastapol, CA: O'Reilly & Associates, 1992.
*A little more for the administrator as it goes into administration issues like security, font servers, etc.*

BURGARD MICHAEL and MIKE MOORE, *The X.Desktop Cookbook*, Englewood Cliffs, NJ: Prentice Hall, 1992.

*A great introduction to the X Desktop provided by SCO. Mike Moore had a column in SCO World magazine and Michael Burgard is the editor of SCO World.*

QUERCIA VALERIE and TIM O'REILLY, *X Window System User's Guide*, Sebastapol, CA: O'Reilly & Associates, 1990.

*Good introduction to what X is all about. It is loaded with information on how to configure X to your tastes.*

## Hardware

HEATH, CHET and WINN L. ROSCH, *The Micro Channel Architecture Handbook,* Indianapolis, IN: Brady Books, 1990.

*Chet Heath was the primary engineer for MCA at IBM. Combining his expertise with Win Rosch's writing ability makes for an enjoyable book.*

*Intel Pentium Microprocessor Data Book, Intel Corporation, 1994.*

*Intel486 DX Microprocessor Data Book, Intel Corporation, 1992.*

*Both of these require some hardware or operating system background to get much from them. There is a lot that is not applicable to SCO, but you can also learn a lot about what the CPU does to help out the OS.*

MUELLER, SCOTT, *QUE's Guide to Data Recovery*, Carmel, IN: QUE Corporation, 1991.

*This has some great information on the physical characteristics of floppies and hard disks.*

ROSCH, WINN L., *The Winn L. Rosch Hardware Bible, 3rd Edition* Indianapolis, IN: Brady Books, 1994.

*This contains over 1000 pages of information. Although there is a lot that is not necessarily useful (do you still have a CGA card in your machine?), this is an invaluable reference. I had the first edition and got the third edition when it came out. I will buy the next one.*

STANLEY, TOM and DON ANDERSON, *ISA System Architecture*, Mindshare Press, 1993.

STANLEY, TOM and DON ANDERSON, *PCI System Architecture*, Mindshare Press, 1994.

STANLEY, TOM, *80486 System Architecture*, Mindshare Press, 1994.

STANLEY, TOM, *EISA System Architecture*, Mindshare Press, 1993.

*These four are part of the PC System Architecture Series. They give a much more friendly approach than the Intel data books. Well-written and very understandable.*

TANENBAUM, ANDREW S., *Structured Computer Organization, 3rd Edition*, Englewood Cliffs, NJ: Prentice Hall, 1990.

*Tanenbaum covers a lot of the hardware concepts that you may be missing. This was used as the textbook for my intro to computer hardware course at the university. I still go back to it as a reference.*

WORAM, JOHN, *The PC Configuration Handbook*, New York: Bantam Books, 1990.

*Another basic PC hardware book. A good approach and easy to read.*

# Index